An Introduction to Transnational Criminal Law

Second Edition

NEIL BOISTER

University of Canterbury

OXFORD

UNIVERSITY PRESS

OXFORD
UNIVERSITY PRESS

Great Clarendon Street, Oxford, OX2 6DP,
United Kingdom

Oxford University Press is a department of the University of Oxford.
It furthers the University's objective of excellence in research, scholarship,
and education by publishing worldwide. Oxford is a registered trade mark of
Oxford University Press in the UK and in certain other countries

© N. Boister 2018

The moral rights of the author have been asserted

First Edition published in 2012
Second Edition published in 2018

Impression: 1

Published in the United States of America by Oxford University Press
198 Madison Avenue, New York, NY 10016, United States of America

British Library Cataloguing in Publication Data
Data available

Library of Congress Control Number: 2017958195

ISBN 978-0-19-879599-5 (hbk.)
ISBN 978-0-19-879608-4 (pbk.)

Printed and bound by
CPI Group (UK) Ltd, Croydon, CR0 4YY

Preface

The six years since the publication of the first edition of this book have seen some significant changes in the development of transnational criminal law. At a substantive level, there has been a perceptible shift in global attention from core transnational crimes such as drug trafficking, corruption, and organized crime to a range of ever more demanding concerns such as cybercrime and migrant smuggling, as priorities in the inter-state system of crime control change. At a procedural level, the emphasis remains on making cooperation between states in the exchange of information, things, and sometimes people more efficient and therefore simpler. While members of the transnational law enforcement community appear to be content to go along with the necessity of international criminal cooperation with an ever-broadening scope of states, there are some signs of a domestic political backlash against the acquiescence to the 'long-arm' jurisdiction that this entails. Finally, when it comes to the shape of transnational criminal law itself, the swing away from reliance on treaty-based agreement to structure relations between states in the suppression of cross-border crime, to greater reliance on a combination of soft law and direct legislating through the UN Security Council, appears to be becoming entrenched.

This book explores these changes and others in a general examination of the nature and main features of transnational criminal law. Part I examines the nature of transnational crime and introduces the concept of transnational criminal law. Part II examines the substantive offences. Part III examines the allied procedures which make cooperation in regard to these offences possible. Part IV looks at the institutions that perform different functions within the system and the implementation of the system, and makes some remarks about how the future development of the system might be structured using a system of general principles to achieve better protection for those subject to it—potentially any one of us.

Acknowledgements

My grateful thanks to Dan Coulson who assisted with research, and to the support of the University of Waikato and Canterbury for the time to revise the work. I am also grateful to all those who I have either taught or spoken to over the last six years about issues in transnational criminal law, and in particular Roger Clark (Rutgers), Robert Currie (Dalhousie), and Florian Jessberger (Hamburg) for their comments and criticism. I would also like to thank the staff at OUP for their exemplary professionalism. And finally, I must thank my long-suffering family, Wendy, Eve, and Mimi, for putting up with my absences during this period in pursuit of a better understanding of transnational criminal law.

Contents

II. CRIMES

IV. INSTITUTIONS, IMPLEMENTATION, AND DEVELOPMENT

Table of International Cases

EUROPEAN COURT OF HUMAN RIGHTS (ECTHR)

EUROPEAN COURT OF JUSTICE

INTERNATIONAL ARBITRAL DECISION

INTERNATIONAL COURT OF JUSTICE

INTERNATIONAL CRIMINAL TRIBUNAL FOR
THE FORMER YUGOSLAVIA

PERMANENT COURT OF ARBITRATION

PERMANENT COURT OF INTERNATIONAL JUSTICE

SPECIAL TRIBUNAL FOR THE LEBANON

UN HUMAN RIGHTS COMMISSION

Table of National Cases

ISRAEL

ITALY

JAMAICA

KENYA

LEBANON

LESOTHO

NETHERLANDS

UNITED STATES OF AMERICA

Table of Legislation

Table of Treaties and Other International Instruments (In Chronological Order)

List of Abbreviations

AML	Anti-Money Laundering
APG	Asia/Pacific Group on Money Laundering
ASEAN	Association of South East Asian Nations
AU	African Union
BeNeLux	Belgium Netherlands Luxembourg
BSA	Bank Secrecy Act
CCAMLR	Commission for the Conservation of Antarctic Living Marine Resources
CCE	Continuing Criminal Enterprise
CCPCJ	(UN) Commission on Crime Prevention and Criminal Justice
CDD	Customer Due Diligence
CEPOL	European Police College
CFT	Countering the Finance of Terrorism
CFATF	Caribbean Financial Action Task Force
CIA Offences	Confidentiality, Integrity, and Availability Offences
CICAD	Inter-American Drug Abuse Control Commission.
CITES	Convention on International Trade in Endangered Species of Wild Fauna and Flora
CLPRC	Criminal Law of the People's Republic of China
CND	(UN) Commission of Narcotic Drugs
CoE	Council of Europe
COP	Conference of the Parties
COSP	Conference of States Parties
DEA	Drug Enforcement Administration
EAG	Eurasian Group (on money laundering)
ECOSOC	UN Economic and Social Council
ECOWAS	Economic Community of West African States
EITI	Extractive Industries Transparency Initiative
ESAAMLG	Eastern and Southern Africa Anti-Money Laundering Group
EU	European Union
Eurojust	European Prosecutors Office
Europol	European Police Agency
FAO	(UN) Food and Agriculture Organization
FATF	Financial Action Task Force
FCPA	Foreign Corrupt Practices Act
FIU	Financial Intelligence Unit
Frontex	European Border Security Office
FSRBs	FATF Style Regional Anti-money Laundering Bodies
G8	Group of Eight Industrialized Nations
GA	General Assembly
GABAC	Central African Group on Money Laundering
GAFISUD	The Financial Action Task Force on Money Laundering in South America
GIABA	Inter Governmental Action Group against Money Laundering in West Africa

GIFCS	Group of International Finance Centre Supervisors
GIFT	Global Initiative to Fight Human Trafficking
GPAT	Global Programme against Trafficking
GRECO	Group of States against Corruption
GRETA	Council of Europe's Group of Experts on Action against Trafficking in Human Beings
IAIS	International Association of Insurance Supervisors
ICAO	International Civil Aviation Organization
ICCPR	International Covenant for Civil and Political Rights
ICJ	International Court of Justice
ICRG	International Cooperation Review Group
IGO	Inter-governmental Organization
IMO	International Maritime Organization
IMoLIN	International Monetary Laundering Information Network
INCB	International Narcotics Control Board
Interpol	International Police Organization
IOM	International Organization of Migration
IOSCO	International Organization of Securities Commissions
ISPAC	International Scientific and Professional Advisory Council
IUU	Illegal, Unregulated, and Unreported (Fishing)
JCLEC	Jakarta Centre for Law Enforcement Cooperation
KYC	Know Your Customer
Legat	Legal Attaché
MARPOL	International Convention for the Prevention of Pollution from Ships
MENAFATF	Middle East and North Africa Financial Action Task Force
MLCA	Money Laundering Control Act
MONEYVAL	The Council of Europe Committee of Experts on the Evaluation of Anti-Money Laundering Measures and the Financing of Terrorism
NGO	Nongovernmental Organization
OAS	Organization of American States
OCG	Organized Criminal Group
OECD	Organisation for Economic Co-operation and Development
OFCs	Offshore Financial Centres
OGBS	Offshore Group of Banking Supervisors
OLAF	European Anti-Fraud Office
OSCE	Organization for Security and Cooperation in Europe
PCIJ	Permanent Court of International Justice
RFMOs	Regional Fishing Management Organizations
RICO	Racketeer Influenced and Corrupt Organizations Act
SAARC	South Asian Association for Regional Cooperation
SALW	Small Arms and Light Weapons
SAR	Suspicious Activity Reporting
SC	Security Council
SFO	Serious Fraud Office
STR	Suspicious Transaction Reporting
SUA Convention	Convention for the Suppression of Unlawful Acts against the Safety of Maritime Navigation and the Protocol for the Suppression of Unlawful Acts against the Safety of Fixed Platforms on the Continental Shelf

TI	Transparency International
TIP	Trafficking in Persons
UNESCO	UN Educational, Scientific and Cultural Organization
UNCAC	UN Convention against Corruption
UNCLOS	UN Convention on the Law of the Sea
UNICRI	UN Interregional Crime and Justice Research Institute
UNIDROIT	International Institute for the Unification of Private Law
UNODC	UN Office on Drugs and Crime
UNODCCP	UN Office for Drug Control and Crime Prevention (forerunner of UNODC)
UNTOC	UN Convention against Transnational Organized Crime
UN GIFT	UN Global Initiative to Fight Human Trafficking
WCO	World Customs Organization

PART I

INTRODUCTION

If crime crosses all borders, so must law enforcement.

> Former UN Secretary-General Kofi Annan upon the signing
> of the UN Convention against Transnational Organized Crime,
> Palermo, 12 December 2000

1

What is Transnational Crime?

1.1 Introduction

A state's borders represent the geographical boundaries of its enforcement jurisdiction, yet borders neither prevent criminals from exiting nor entering states. Criminals cross borders in a range of ways, walking, riding, driving, sailing, and flying across them, and tunnelling under them.[1] They cross at regulated and unregulated points of entry, or they dispatch or transmit things across them—every kind of contraband, humans, body parts, digital information, messages, money, things of value. They appear to work in a borderless world, whilst the authorities that pursue them are constrained by borders. But they rely on these geo-political boundaries for advantage. Borders create markets with different prices for illicit goods, which the criminals exploit. Borders also provide impunity from the criminal jurisdiction of states seeking to arrest and prosecute these criminals. For criminals engaging in trans-national crime in the unembellished sense of cross-border crime, borders are part of their business.

As transnational crime has increased, increasing efforts have been made to bridge the gaps between the criminal laws of different states. This book is an introduction to the law designed to suppress transnational crime—transnational criminal law. Transnational criminal law is constitutive of transnational crime—nameless activities only become transnational crimes once they have been described, identified as a threat, and criminalized. This chapter takes a look at the distinctive features of cross-border activities and the kinds of harm they cause. It then charts the policy process for the development of special international legal measures to suppress these activities as transnational crimes. This analysis is cross-disciplinary in nature, embracing criminology, international relations theory, security studies, and other disciplines.

1.2 The Nature of Transnational Crime

1.2.1 The meaning of 'transnational crime'

In 1971 the international relations theorists Keohane and Nye argued that transnational relations—the movement of money, physical objects, people, or other tangible and intangible items across state boundaries when at least one of the actors involved in the movement is non-governmental—was becoming as significant as inter-state relations in international relations.[2] The term 'transnational crime' was first used at

---

[1] P Williams, 'Organizing Transnational Crime: Networks, Markets and Hierarchies' in P Williams and D Vlassis (eds), *Combating Transnational Crime: Concepts, Activities and Responses* (London, Portland: Frank Cass, 2001), 57, 61 et seq.

[2] R Keohane and J Nye, *Transnational Relations and World Politics* (Cambridge, MA: Harvard University Press, 1971), xii.

the Fifth UN Congress on Crime Prevention and the Treatment of Offenders in 1975 by the UN Crime Prevention and Criminal Justice Branch 'in order to identify certain criminal phenomena transcending international borders, transgressing the laws of several states or having an impact on another country'.[3] The Fourth UN Survey of Crime Trends and Operations of Criminal Justice Systems made in 1976 defined transnational crimes as 'offences whose inception, perpetration and/or direct or indirect effects involved more than one country'.[4] This tendency towards broad definition is reflected in article 3(2) of the 2000 UN Convention against Transnational Organized Crime (UNTOC).[5] An offence is 'transnational' if it satisfies one of a number of alternative conditions:

(a) it is committed in more than one State;

(b) it is committed in one State but a substantial part of its preparation, planning, direction, or control takes place in another State;

(c) it is committed in one State but involves an organized criminal group that engages in criminal activities in more than one State; or

(d) it is committed in one State but has substantial effects in another State.

Transnational crime has been criticized as over-inclusive.[6] One problem is that it contains different types of crime including organized, white-collar, and political crime. Indeed, cross-border activity can potentially include most forms of currently recognized criminal activity.

Transnational crime can also be criticized for being under-inclusive. In the 1970s the UN took a broader view of transnational crime, including within it both trafficking offences like narcotics trafficking and corruption, but also harmful (but not necessarily strictly criminal) cross-border economic exploitation by powerful trading partners.[7] A further criticism is that 'transnational' implies cross-border activity when in fact not all crimes understood to fall within this category actually cross borders.[8] Trans-boundary drug supply, for example, is dependent on national production. The counter argument is that purely local criminal activity may be a legitimate concern of other states because it supports or creates conditions conducive to transnational criminality and criminal activity in those states. These criticisms suggest that transnational crime is perhaps better understood as a precondition for a transnational normative response than as a concept for understanding the different types of crimes

[3] GOW Mueller, 'Transnational Crime: Definitions and Concepts' in P Williams and D Vlassis (eds), *Combating Transnational Crime: Concept, Activities, Responses* (London, Portland: Frank Cass, 2001), 13.

[4] United Nations, *Fourth UN Survey of Crime Trends and Operations of Criminal Justice Systems* UN Doc A/CONF.169/15/Add.1 (1995).

[5] United Nations Convention against Transnational Organized Crime, New York, 15 November 2000, 2225 UNTS 209, in force 29 September 2003.

[6] D Friedrichs, 'Transnational Crime and Global Criminology: Definitional, Typological and Contextual Conundrums' 34(2) *Social Justice* (2007) 4, 5.

[7] 'Changes in Forms and Dimensions of Criminality—Transnational and National', Fifth UN Congress on the Prevention of Crime and the Treatment of Offenders, Toronto, Canada, 1–12 September 1975, UN Doc A/CONF.56/3, 4.

[8] C Fijnaut, 'Transnational Crime and the Role of the United Nations' 8 *European Journal of Crime, Criminal Law and Criminal Justice* (2000) 119, 120.

it includes. The threshold at which purely intra-national conduct is sufficiently serious to justify foreign interest may vary widely depending on the type of crime, the sensitivity of the interested state to that crime, and the acceptance of that interest by the state in which it occurs.

A more profound criticism of the concept of transnational crime considers it a construct of the law itself, rather than an empirical reality (and by extension each of the sub-categories examined in the chapters in this book, from piracy to counterfeiting of medicines).[9] In this view transnational criminal law makes transnational crime in order to transform otherwise unregulated conduct into an object of governance. Transnational crime is thus a contested concept, or as Sheptycki puts it 'an object of study [that] has not been a disinterestedly academic matter of purely scientific inquiry'.[10]

1.2.2 Characteristics and causes of transnational crime

The institutionalization of responses to transnational crime at the intergovernmental level has led to the development of a bureaucratic criminology that attempts to serve the interests of states both at the national and international level while trying to maintain theoretical integrity in analysis of transnational crime.[11] Nonetheless, realist criminological analyses are most influential in the law-making process. They identify a loosely defined range of characteristics and causes, currently considered typical of illicit markets.

Private crime

Transnational crimes are commonly characterized as private or non-governmental crimes,[12] that is crimes, usually of a transactional nature, committed by non-state actors, either individually or in groups, for unofficial ends. These individuals may be private natural persons, or juridical persons such as companies, or they may be officials acting in their private capacity, or government organizations such as the police acting unlawfully.[13] Importantly, however, transnational crimes are not (at least not usually) sanctioned by a state. It follows that the threat they present is usually asymmetric unless it grows to such proportions that it challenges state authority.

Economic crime

Most transnational criminal activity is considered to be driven by desire for personal economic gain. Put simply, transnational criminals take advantage of the production

---

[9] See J Sheptycki, 'Transnational Crime: An Interdisciplinary Perspective' in N Boister and RJ Currie (eds), *The Routledge Handbook of Transnational Criminal Law* (Abingdon: Routledge, 2015), 41, 52.

[10] ibid, 56.

[11] SM Redo, *Blue Criminology: The Power of United Nations Ideas to Counter Crime Globally* (Helsinki: HEUNI, 2012), 49, and authors cited there.

[12] See MC Bassiouni, 'An Appraisal of the Growth and Developing Trends of International Criminal Law' 45 *Revue Internationale De Droit Penal* (1974) 405, 421.

[13] See, eg, M De Flem, 'International Police Cooperation in North America' in DJ Koenig and DK Das (eds), *International Police Cooperation: A World Perspective* (Lanham, MD: Lexington, 2001), 81.

of cheap goods or services in one state and move them across borders to another state where there is strong demand and the goods or services can be sold or hired out at a profit. This illicit arbitrage may take any of a myriad forms ranging from small-scale smuggling to transnational activities of great complexity and value. It includes white-collar crime in the sense of financially motivated cross-border transactions by individuals of a relatively high social status, but it is a much broader concept. There is nothing characteristic about the kind of person nor the products involved. They could be anyone smuggling anything amenable to trafficking across a border: cigarettes, cars, drugs, radioactive waste, stolen works of art, women for prostitution, firearms, information. The differences in the nature of the 'goods' involved lead to markets that are differently organized, demanding a nuanced approach if these markets are to be properly understood, and suggesting different legal responses may be necessary.[14] Transnational criminal flows are essentially cross-border chains of supply—the mechanisms for the illicit trade itself—composed of producers, wholesalers, distributors, transporters, exporters, and importers and retailers that exist for each illicit product or service. Sometimes supply chains are used only for one product or service, sometimes for multiple purposes. The main difference with licit economic activity is that these activities are prohibited in respect of the particular product or service in one or other or both states. The key to responding to chains of illicit supply is to understand the incentives and disincentives that operate at each stage of the chain.[15]

Economic disparities between states are among the main causes of transnational crime because they strengthen demand for illegal products and services across borders.[16] Poverty or relative poverty is the main 'push' factor in source or producer states, but political conflict, culture, and opportunity also play a role. Low wages mean that illicit products and services are cheap to produce or secure. Various facilitative factors make cross-border supply possible including the availability of transport and corruption. 'Pull' factors in destination or consumer states include the demand for products and services. The absence of appropriate law and/or enforcement in a particular state may push or pull by facilitating production, supply, or consumption. Some states may seek to attract crime because of the benefit from taxation of financial activity (eg bank secrecy jurisdictions) while others may try to repel it because of the cost to victims (eg the US and drug use).[17] A range of domestic policies can influence the growth of transnational crime including economic protectionism, fiscal austerity, privatization, public procurement, promotion of domestic industries, domestic prohibition of commodities like drugs, and the imposition of quotas on

---

[14] P van Duyn and M van Dijck, 'Assessing Organised Crime: the Sad State of an Impossible Art' in F Bovenkerk and M Levi (eds), *The Organised Crime Economy: Essays in Honour of Alan Block* (New York: Springer, 2007), 101, 121.

[15] M Tonry, 'Transnational Organized Crime—Prospects for Success of the UN Convention' in H-J Albrecht and C Fijnaut (eds), *The Containment of Transnational Organized Crime* (Freiburg: Iuscrim, 2002), 253, 264–65.

[16] N Passas, 'Globalization and Transnational Crime: Effects of Criminogenic Asymmetries' in P Williams and D Vlassis (eds), *Combating Transnational Crime: Concepts, Activities and Responses* (London, Portland: Frank Cass, 2001), 22, 23.

[17] T Broude and D Teichman, 'Outsourcing and Insourcing Crime: The Political Economy of Globalized Criminal Activity' 62(3) *Vanderbilt Law Review* (2009) 795, 810 et seq.

immigration. Strategies and tactics in enforcement of these laws shape illicit markets, conditioning the steps taken by traffickers to avoid apprehension including the use of corruption.[18] And while one set of factors may explain the rise in incidence of a transnational crime, an unrelated set of factors may explain its spread. For example, the collapse of the Colombian drug cartels gave Mexican criminals the opportunity to switch from the transit to the production of illicit drugs, and the failure of local policing, corruption, and poverty in Mexico explain the spread of this involvement, although the instigation of a war on drugs by President Felipe Calderón in 2006 is blamed for the recent upsurge in drug-related violence.[19] Criminal markets are also spread through displacement; they react to suppression by relocating their activities or switching to other less visible crimes.

Although these illegal markets often have close relationships with legal markets by, for example, using the banking system to launder profits, illegal and legal markets are not identical in form.[20] Government regulation of cross-border transport of licit goods usually requires permission to import/export and the payment of duty of some kind, but for illicit goods, corruption, secrecy, and intimidation are the options, and the costs involved in avoiding apprehension have to be built into the market prices of illicit goods. Moreover, legal markets rely on contract and solve disputes through a variety of legal means. Illegal markets must rely on personal relationships, ethnic, and other group loyalties, although violence may be used to 'enforce' contracts as well as to gain market share.

Political crime

Not all transnational criminals pursue economic advantage. Some transnational criminals seek political advantage through violence or the threat of violence. Violence may be used for instrumental or ideological purposes. Transnational terrorists, for example, may hatch a plot in one state and execute it in another. Though shocking, violence is an incidental feature of their activity, as their main aim is to influence either official or public opinion to achieve their own political goals.

Organized crime

Although organization is not a necessary condition of transnational crime—cross-border smuggling by one person would suffice—transnational crime is heavily associated with organized crime. The concept of organized crime is, however, not settled and remains highly controversial.[21] The difficulty is what is meant by 'organized': it may mean a range of things from hierarchical organizations to individuals in the loosest of

---

[18] P Andreas, 'Illicit Globalization: Myths, Misconceptions, and Historical Lessons' 126(3) *Political Science Quarterly* (2011) 403, 411.

[19] F Gonzalez, 'Mexico's Drug War Gets Brutal' 108 *Current History* (2009) 72.

[20] P Arlacchi, 'The Dynamics of Illegal Markets' in P Williams and D Vlassis (eds), *Combating Transnational Crime: Concepts, Activities and Responses* (London, Portland: Frank Cass, 2001), 7.

[21] See generally, M Levi, 'The Organization of Serious Crime for Gain' in M Maguire, R Morgan, and R Reiner (eds), *The Oxford Handbook of Criminology*, 5th edn (Oxford: OUP, 2012), 595.

relations, a range so broad as to render the term almost meaningless. The *organizing* of transnational crime is perhaps a more productive focus.[22]

Globalized crime

An economic model of crime suggests that it is rational for criminals to go where they can to do business and to spread out into unregulated areas. In antiquity, when formal boundaries were weak, it was relatively easy for criminal activity to cross borders. The 'harder' borders (border controls, passports) characterized by the rise of the nation states of the post-Westphalian era made cross-border crime more difficult and tended to offset improvements in transport and communication mechanisms. It is believed today that the conclusion of the Cold War led to ideal conditions for transnational crime to flourish because legal controls became weaker as transport became cheap, frequent, rapid, and easy to access, communication became international and mobile, and financial transactions instantaneous and unregulated.[23] The conclusion of free trade agreements reduced or removed the legal barriers to trade. As market control of the legal economy grew and state control withered it became easier for criminals to move goods, persons, and money. In what he calls the 'dark side of globalization', Levitsky claims that transnational criminals responded more rapidly in exploiting these new market opportunities than states did in shutting the markets down.[24]

Others recommend caution when equating the apparent boom in transnational crime on globalization.[25] Political events such as the breakdown of the Soviet bloc have also contributed, as have insufficiently regulated markets in the finance sector or over-regulated markets in the labour and agricultural sectors.[26] Moreover, some question whether transnational crime is a novel phenomenon, pointing out that cross-border trade of an illegal kind is a long-standing practice predating the current phase of globalization and many modern economies are rooted in contraband capitalism.[27] Technological developments have always impacted on the spread of crime, triggering calls for a legal response. In 1934 Kuhn commented:

> Modern civilization and the relative shrinking in the size of the planet on which we live have given impetus to the principle that the efficient administration of criminal justice is a matter of importance not only to a single community or state but to civilized society as a whole.[28]

[22] See AA Block and WJ Chambliss, *Organizing Crime* (New York: Elsevier, 1981).
[23] JH Mittelman and R Johnston, 'The Globalization of Organized Crime, the Courtesan State and the Corruption of Civil Society' 5 *Global Governance* (1999) 103, 108 et seq.
[24] M Levitsky, 'Transnational Criminal Networks and International Security' 30 *Syracuse Journal of International Law and Commerce* (2003) 227; M Levitsky, 'The Dark Side of Globalization' 5 *International Studies Review* (2003) 253.
[25] D Nelken, 'The Globalization of Crime and Justice' 50 *Current Legal Problems* (1997) 251, 260 et seq.
[26] M Glenny, *McMafia* (New York: Knopf, 2008), 345.
[27] Andreas, above n 18, 403, 406, 415; P Andreas, *Smuggler Nation: How Illicit Trade Made America* (New York: OUP, 2013), 2.
[28] AK Kuhn, 'International Cooperation in the Suppression of Crime' 28(3) *American Journal of International Law* (1934) 541, 544.

Whether or not there is a strong relationship between globalization and the upsurge in transnational crime, it should always be borne in mind that states are not always in an antagonistic relationship with these dark forces of globalization. Frequently they are in symbiosis: states have been compliant in sanctions busting, money laundering, transfer of nuclear technology, weapons trafficking, counterfeiting, drug trafficking, among other things.[29] A strict division between transnational crime and other forms of transnational harmful activity carried out by politicians, business, and even law enforcement organizations ignores the fact that in many cases the latter frequently act in partnership with the alleged transnational criminals. Moreover, global business activities can be much more harmful than transnational crime. It has been pointed out that in the 1970s transnational crime was conceived of by UN officials as the abuse of power by transnational corporations in developing states, until in the mid-1980s it was 'bleached' from the UN's agenda as a more narrowly defined crime control emerged as the principal concern.[30]

Localized crime

Prioritizing the global aspects of transnational crime also ignores its local aspects. As Hobbs, puts it: 'The notion of ... "transnationality" needs to be reconsidered in the light of empirical research, which indicates that ever mutating interlocking networks of locally-based serious criminality typifies the current situation.'[31] All transnational processes have domestic roots.[32] Transnational criminals are both global and local, able to operate across borders but based locally.[33] Hobbs coined the neologism 'glocalization' to describe the locally embedded nature of transnational crime.

1.2.3 Categorizing transnational crimes

Transnational crimes are usually categorized by the harm they cause. Transnational crimes harm a range of different private and public interests including security, human rights, social interests, religious beliefs, and morality.[34] The most obvious harm is to individuals and to the fabric of societies in which they live. Drug use, for example, has negative effects on individual users and on the society in which those users live. The degree to which society respects the choices of the individuals being harmed when there is no clear harm to others presents a significant difficulty in deciding whether criminalization is the appropriate response. Moreover, one person's harm is usually to

---

[29] Andreas, above n 18, 417.

[30] P van Duyne and MDH Nelemans, 'Transnation Organized Crime: Thinking in and Out of Plato's Cave' in F Alum and S Gilmour, *Routledge Handbook of Transnational Organized Crime* (Abingdon: Routledge, 2011), 36, 37–40, citing the final Reports of the UN Crime Congresses in Toronto (1975) and Caracas (1980).

[31] R Hobbs, 'Going Down the Glocal: The Local Context of Organised Crime' 37(4) *The Howard Journal of Criminal Justice* (1998) 407, 419.

[32] JS Nye, 'Soft Power' 80 *Foreign Policy* (1990) 153, 163 et seq.

[33] M Naím, *Illicit: How Smugglers, Traffickers, and Copycats are Hijacking the Global Economy* (New York: Anchor Books, 2006), 34.

[34] See P Williams and D Vlassis, 'Introduction and Overview' in P Williams and D Vlassis (eds), *Combating Transnational Crime: Concepts, Activities and Responses* (London, Portland: Frank Cass, 2001), 1.

another's benefit. While the consumption of copyright-violating movies downloaded from the Internet harms the intellectual property of their creators and producers, for consumers they are a source of satisfaction. At a larger scale, it has been argued that the narcotics economy had significant benefits in drug-producing regions in Latin America.[35] This relativism is intrinsic to the identification of harm at the transnational level because different value systems prevail in different states, and frequently those who are being 'harmed' live in other states.

At a broader economic level, transnational crime causes harm by compromising financial and commercial institutions, making economic management difficult and eroding tax bases. It can slow economic development in poorer states by, for instance, forcing the diversion of scarce resources to combat crime. Yet it does not always have a negative impact and can produce significant profits in underdeveloped areas through, for example, the use of forced labour in agricultural production.

Transnational crime can also undermine the internal sovereignty of states by providing an alternative system of authority. It can provide order and security in social spaces where the state's authority is negligible or absent. It can undermine public institutions through, for example, the corruption of the police force. It can openly challenge the state's authority, particularly when that authority is re-asserted. A recent example is the 2010 violence in Kingston, Jamaica, precipitated by the attempt to capture wanted drug trafficker Christopher 'Dudus' Coke in order to extradite him to the US.[36] Potentially more dangerous situations emerge when transnational criminals and the state enter into a symbiotic relationship. Regional or local state capture is most common. In 2014 in Iguala, Mexico, for example, forty-three college students protesting at the influence of organized crime disappeared after being arrested by local police with the cooperation of the corrupt local mayor. They had been turned over to a Mexican crime group, Guerroros Unidos.[37] Naím coined the term 'mafia states' to describe what he argues is a novel phenomenon: the situation where instead of using criminals for their purposes, governments fuse with criminal organizations, presenting a political rather than merely a law and order problem to other states.[38] The break-away borderland of Moldova, Transnistria, is considered an example of such a 'criminal state'.[39] Others respond, however, that this fusion is nothing new and the threat exaggerated.[40] Nonetheless, it serves as additional grist for the categorization of foreign organized crime as a national security issue.[41]

---

[35] D Corva, 'Neoliberal Globalization and the War on Drugs: Transnationalizing Illiberal Governance in the Americas' in 27 *Political Geography* (2008) 176, 186 and authors cited there.

[36] A Klein, 'Peculiar and Perplexed—The Complexity of Ganja Cultivation in the English Speaking Caribbean' in T Decorte, G Potter, and M Bouchard (eds), *World Wide Weed: Global Trends in Cannabis Cultivation and its Control* (Farnham: Ashgate, 2010), 23, 29.

[37] JS Beittel, *Mexico: Organized Crime and Drug Trafficking Organizations* (US Congressional Research Service Report R41576, 2015), 7.

[38] M Naím, 'Mafia States: Organized Crime Takes Office' 91 *Foreign Affairs* (2012) 100, 101–02.

[39] M Spinner, *Civil War and Ethnic Conflict in Post-Soviet Moldova—The Cases of Gaugazia and Transnistria Compared* (Munich: Grin Verlag, 2003), 24.

[40] P Andreas, 'Measuring the Mafia-State Menace: Are Government-Backed Gangs a Grave New Threat?' 91 *Foreign Affairs* (2012) 167, 170.

[41] See US President Clinton's Presidential Decision Directive 42, 1995, which assigned transnational organized crime as a threat to US security.

Transnational crimes can also be categorized using an orthodox criminal law tax-onomy based on the values protected in the sense of individual human rights or interests. Harms against personal interests might include slavery, harms against property inter-ests piracy, harms against social interests drug trafficking, harms against the state ter-rorism, and so forth. The likelihood of considerable overlap in these categories suggests that a more useful division might be made between essentially violent crimes directed at humans' bodily integrity, such as terrorism, and essentially non-violent crimes based on contraband, such as drug trafficking, in order to justify a more severe deterrent response. Nevertheless, even this demarcation has its difficulties—human trafficking being a case in point of commercial exploitation through violence. Finally categorization may also be made in terms of violations of individual or collective morality. Offences such as slave trading are the product in part of collective moral condemnation. It is difficult, however, to construct degrees of such condemnation at a transnational level in order to differ-entiate levels of suppression, the diverse moral positions on drug trafficking at a global level being a case in point. Perhaps even more troubling are the obvious cases of select-ive morality used, for example, to control the transnational mobility of certain kinds of individuals—migrants and sex workers—through offences of migrant smuggling and human trafficking—but not others.[42] Finally, we should always be wary of the possibil-ity that interest-based agendas such as control of the high seas will evolve into normative arguments such as condemnation of drug trafficking on the high seas with a potential for transformation into law.

Using categorization to tailor a response is made more difficult by the fact that trans-national activities affect different states at different levels of intensity. Moreover, these activities only become 'crimes' in the legal sense through legal suppression—the use of legal authority to prohibit as criminal offences certain activities and to use executive power to enforce these prohibitions and punish these offences. In addition, the legal sup-pression of transnational activities creates illicit markets and as a result can itself harm consumers through unreliable product quality, incidental violence, and corruption. Finally, it is not always clear which links in chains of illicit supply are responsible for most harm (and are thus most deserving of the attention of the law)—the producers, suppliers, or consumers. Given the variable nature of these activities and their impact, how is a glo-bal consensus for criminalization generated?

1.3 Assessing and Responding to Transnational Crime

1.3.1 Global cooperation: an unavoidable response to a global threat?

It is claimed that transnational crime will be among the defining security threats of this century.[43] It is a threat said to arise out of the global spread of powerful criminal networks, which take advantage of weak law enforcement in many states. It is argued

---

[42] B Bowling and J Sheptycki, 'Global Policing and Transnational Rule with Law' 6(1) *Transnational Legal Theory* (2015) 141, 162.

[43] L Shelley, 'Unravelling the New Criminal Nexus' 6(1) *Georgetown Journal of International Affairs* (2005) 5. See also S Strange, *The Retreat of the State: The Diffusion of Power in the World Economy* (New York: CUP, 1996), 121.

that transnational crime can only be suppressed by the cooperation of states and that the failure of states to do so provides an opportunity to transnational criminals to use the barriers of sovereignty to protect themselves and to operate with impunity. However, other commentators warn against reflexively accepting this logic.[44]

What evidence supports the identification of specific threats and who is making that assessment? These are not always questions of concern to the officials and diplomats who operate the system; many consider the problems self-evident and unworthy of analysis.[45] Van Duyne and Nelemans comment caustically: 'At UN policy-making level proper substantiation appears to be a mere detail if unanimity can be attained by formulating strings of emotive words.'[46] International civil servants are, however, often asked to make policy forecasts by their political masters in areas where they have no expertise and no or very poor data exists.

Criminalization of transnational activity that is the result of unaddressed social, economic, and political pressures, is a suspect tool for its effective suppression. Moreover, both the size and novelty of different transnational threats are commonly overblown. Current efforts to analyse the global spread of crime have been criticized as justifying legal action because law enforcement have a direct interest in playing up the scale of the problem.[47] Sterner critics argue that transnational crime is being constructed as a global threat in order to increase the coercive power of states.[48] As Chapter 2 of this book illustrates, responding to transnational crime is a form of international relations that reorders global political power and is at least in part an end in itself.

1.3.2 The scale of transnational crime

Although we do not know the true scale of transnational crime, the scale of offending is the main driver of criminalization. Policy documents are replete with frighteningly large figures representing the incidence of particular transnational crimes and the amounts of money made by those engaging in them. There has, however, been little thorough research in regard to the incidence of transnational crime.[49] The figures are not always reliable, and the transnational context allows them to be amplified by policy-makers seeking to raise concern. The danger is that facts worthy of a response are created by this repetition and amplification.[50] An example of this is the way in which a self-acknowledged speculative estimate by two researchers that there were 1,420 cases of human trafficking in the UK in 1998 blew out first to an estimated 4,000 cases in a

---

[44] Nelken, above n 25, 252.

[45] M Pieth, 'The Harmonization of Law against Economic Crime' 1(4) *European Journal of Law Reform* (1999) 527.

[46] P van Duyne and MDH Nelemans, above n 30, 36, 39.

[47] P van Duyn and M van Dijck, 'Assessing Organised Crime: the Sad State of an Impossible Art' in F Bovenkerk and M Levi (eds), *The Organised Crime Economy: Essays in Honour of Alan Block* (New York: Springer, 2007), 101, 104–06, 110.

[48] J McCulloch, 'Transnational Crime as a Productive Fiction' 34(2) *Social Justice* (2007) 19.

[49] See generally R Barberet, 'Measuring and Researching Transnational Crime' in PL Reichel and J Albanese (eds), *Handbook of Transnational Crime and Justice*, Second edn (Thousand Oaks, CA: Sage, 2014), 47.

[50] See M Levi, M Innes, P Reuter, and V Rajeev, *The Economic, Financial and Social Impacts of Organised Crime in the EU* (Brussels: EU DG for Internal Policies, 2013), 63.

UK Home Office report in 2003, and then to a Labour MP's estimate that there were 25,000 sex slaves working in the UK in 2007; all of which started with actual data of seventy-one cases.[51] The unavailability of crime statistics in many states and their notorious unreliability when available, justifies scepticism about many of the global figures based on these national statistics. Moreover, it is uncertain what percentage of all crime is transnational and thus how concerned we should be about it compared to purely national crime. The UN Office on Drugs and Crime (UNODC), the main administrative organ in the UN's criminal justice system, is making an effort to be more precise in this regard. For example, in 2002 it estimated that there were 185 million users of illegal drugs worldwide.[52] In 2015 it more circumspectly estimated that 246 million people used drugs but within a range of 162 million to 329 million, which points to the underlying problem of precision.[53] The UNODC responded to criticisms that there was no overall threat assessment in regard to transnational crime with publication in 2010 of *The Globalization of Crime: A Transnational Organized Crime Threat Assessment*.[54] In spite of this the critics are still unconvinced, stressing that evaluations of this kind do not withstand careful analysis.[55] The UNODC appears to be responding by producing regional and thematic threat assessments.[56] The methodology for data gathering remains problematic. For one thing, comparative data gathering is extremely difficult: the response to the UN Crime Trends Surveys is, for example, low and mainly from developed states, making evidence-based policy-making at a global level difficult.[57] Only substantially improved national level data collection can provide an unassailable rationalization for action at the international level. Finally, quantifying the problem is only one step towards understanding it. Tonry believes that the only rational way to respond is to make a better effort to understand the activities in question, to 'develop rich narrative and econometric models of transnational markets in which goods move, identifying both push and pull factors that facilitate their movement'.[58]

1.3.3 Threat identification, the formation of a transnational interest, and pathways to the development of a policy response

There is no clear international system to identify and respond to transnational criminal threats and nor is it clear what weight of evidence of a threat is necessary to tip the scale towards suppression. The history of transnational criminalization indicates that

---

[51] See N Davies, 'Prostitution and trafficking—the anatomy of a moral panic' *The Guardian*, 20 October 2009, <http://www.guardian.co.uk/uk/2009/oct/20/trafficking-numbers-women-exaggerated> last visited 18 April 2016.

[52] UN Office for Drug Control and Crime Prevention (UNODCCP), *Global Illicit Drug Trends 2002* (New York: UN, 2002), UN Sales No. E.02.XI.9 (2002), 213.

[53] UNODC, *World Drug Report 2015* (New York: UN, 2015), 1.

[54] UN Publication Sales No. E.10.IV.6.   [55] Andreas, above n 18, 403, 408.

[56] See UNODC, 'Transnational organized crime threat assessments' available at <https://www.unodc.org/unodc/en/data-and-analysis/TOC-threat-assessments.html> last visited 17 May 2017.

[57] A Alvazzi del Fratte, 'Statistical Analysis and the United Nations Crime Trends Surveys as Capacity Building' in Redo, above n 11, 163, 165.

[58] M Tonry, above n 15, 253 at 267.

while in regard to some crimes it requires exposure of considerable evidence, sometimes little more than a single headline-grabbing incident is sufficient. The hijacking of the cruise ship *Achille Lauro* in 1985, for example, led to the adoption of the Conventions for the Suppression of Unlawful Acts at Sea discussed in Chapter 3.[59]

The development of a transnational interest in suppression of the activity is the key to international action. Such interests are common. Latin American states, for example, have a valid interest in the control of firearms in the US because of the flow of these weapons across their borders and consequent rise in violent crime.[60] The development of a transnational interest does not always, however, lead to a coherent position among affected states. In the 2015 migration crisis into Europe, for example, the European Union (EU) argued that central European states were unable to control their borders while they responded that the problem lay with Germany for issuing an open invitation to migrants.[61]

Many different actors with their own motivations may try to use this transnational interest—well-grounded in evidence or not—to trigger what ultimately becomes a legal response. Non-governmental organizations (NGOs) have been active in highlighting criminal threats and developing responses at least as far as back as the nineteenth century when the British Anti-Slavery Society agitated for the suppression of slavery. It played a significant role in the passage of the Slave Trade Act of 1807, which made slave trading illegal throughout the British Empire. It was followed by Royal Naval action to interdict the trade in the next half century. Finally, it culminated in the abolition of slavery itself, first in Great Britain and then elsewhere. Modern analogues of the Anti-Slavery Society include international NGOs such as Transparency International, which played a key role in the development of the corruption conventions discussed in Chapter 9.

States have the most significant formal role in identifying and responding to transnational crime through international cooperation. Commonly a law-enforcement agency will raise the alarm at the national level, but any agency with a relevant mandate may do so. Threats may also be identified by legislators through the proposal of new legislation. Pressure within a state will sometimes reach a sufficient threshold to transform into pressure from that state on others to cooperate in suppression. For example, the recent elaboration of a Protocol on the Illicit Trade in Tobacco Products originated in pressure from the EU's customs fraud unit, OLAF.[62]

Private individuals and public officials have always played a prominent role in identifying and responding to transnational criminal threats. A good example is Harry Anslinger, who joined the US Federal Bureau of Narcotics from the Bureau of

---

[59] On 7 October 1985, eg, the BBC reported that 'Gunmen Hijack Italian Cruise Liner'—see <http://news.bbc.co.uk/onthisday/hi/dates/stories/october/7/newsid_2518000/2518697.stm> last visited 17 May 2017.

[60] See M Krantz, 'Walking Firearms to Gunrunners: ATF's Flawed Operation in a Flawed System' 103 *Journal of Criminal Law and Criminology* (2013) 585, 587.

[61] I Traynor, 'Refugee Crisis: east and west split as leaders resent Germany for waiving rules' *The Guardian*, 5 September 2015, <http://www.theguardian.com/world/2015/sep/05/migration-crisis-europe-leaders-blame-brussels-hungary-germany> last visited 6 April 2016.

[62] See N Boister, 'Recent Progress in the Development of a Protocol on the Illicit Trade in Tobacco Products' 5 *Asian Journal of WTO and International Health Law Policy* (2010) 53.

(Alcohol) Prohibition as its first Commissioner of Narcotics in 1930 and held the office until 1962. As the US representative at a number of international drug control conferences and on the UN Commission on Narcotic Drugs (CND) from its establishment until 1970, he embarked on a personal crusade which linked domestic US drug policy to foreign drug policy and saw the threat to the US as primarily external in origin.[63] His efforts resulted inter alia in establishing total drug prohibition after the Second World War, and the identification of cannabis as a major threat at the national and international levels.[64] Officials such as investigators, prosecutors, and judges that link up in transnational law enforcement networks with officials from other states can be highly influential in steering the response to transnational crime when they share a global understanding of the problem.[65]

The battles about if, and if so how, to respond to particular threats are fought out in various international institutions, including the UN's criminal justice organizations discussed in greater detail in Chapter 21.[66] There is no single pathway within the UN system for identifying emerging transnational threats; Redo wryly notes 'the meandering way in which such ideas surface at the global level'.[67] Various organs have a mandate to explore criminalization. The quinquennial UN Crime Congress serves as a talking shop to explore new concerns. The CND makes policy in regard to drug offences, the Commission on Crime Prevention and Criminal Justice (CCPCJ) makes policy in regard to other crimes of concern, and the conferences of the states parties (or COPs) to the various crime-suppression conventions make policy in regard to the specific crimes that fall within their mandates. The process may begin with a state calling attention to a threat by, for example, a resolution of the CCPCJ. With sufficient support that resolution could become a resolution of the UN Economic and Social Council (ECOSOC) and finally receive General Assembly endorsement calling on the Secretary-General to initiate the treaty development process. Alternatively, a COP might be asked by a state party to consider passing a resolution urging further steps against a particular form of conduct that falls within the COP's mandate. To study emerging threats the UN relies inter alia on the International Scientific and Professional Advisory Council (ISPAC), an umbrella organization bringing together NGOs and the professional and scientific community, and the United Nations Interregional Crime and Justice Research Institute (UNICRI). The UNODC also plays a key policy-making role. As the secretariat to the CCPCJ, CND, and the various COPs, its principal function is to administer the policy they develop, but it contributes to that policy development because it shapes and leads much of the work of these bodies. Other inter-governmental organizations (IGOs) with a strong role in transnational criminal policy and law making include the Organisation for Economic Co-operation

[63] WO Walker III, *Opium and Foreign Policy: The Anglo American Search for Order in Asia 1912–1954* (Chapel Hill, NC: The University of North Carolina Press, 1991), 57.

[64] See J McWilliams, *The Protectors: Anslinger and the Federal Bureau of Narcotics (1930–1962)* (Newark, DE: University of Delaware Press, 1990).

[65] J Sheptycki, 'Law Enforcement, Justice and Democracy in the Transnational Arena: Reflections on the War on Drugs' 24 *International Journal of the Sociology of Law* (1996) 61.

[66] See RS Clark, *The United Nations Crime Prevention and Criminal Justice Program* (Philadelphia, PA: University of Pennsylvania Press, 1994), 58 et seq.

[67] Redo, above n 11, 132.

and Development, G8, G20, EU, Council of Europe, Association of Southeast Asian Nations, International Maritime Organization, World Customs Organization, etc. The list is growing. Even the UN Security Council has begun to play a role in the identification of and response to transnational criminal activities such as terrorism that threaten international security.

1.3.4 The nature of the policy-making process

When NGOs, individuals, states, and IGOs engage in policy-making to suppress emerging transnational crimes they act as transnational norm entrepreneurs, developing rules to protect a range of economic, political, moral, and emotional interests.[68] In many instances, a general sense of social unease and anxiety creates the fertile ground for developing a response. The transnational moral entrepreneur focuses public attention on the perceived threat and links it to those societal anxieties. Their ability to point to a few examples of behaviour provides supporting evidence for the recommendation of legal action.[69] Moral proselytism, for example, underlies the development of laws such as slavery and drug prohibition. Norm entrepreneurs mobilize support for a particular norm beyond national boundaries in jurisdictions where the particular activity may still be regarded as legitimate. They seek to redefine the activity as an evil. The proselytizers agitate actively for the suppression and criminalization of the activity by all states and the formation of an international convention. While a transnational interest motivates and aids the norm entrepreneur, it is the transnational hook—'it affects all of us'—which serves to rally interest in other states. Their targets are the political elites that control the legal systems of potential partners in action. Their ultimate goal is law reform in those states. Slowly what Nadelmann terms a 'global prohibition regime' emerges—the activity becomes the subject of criminal laws and police action throughout much of the world, and international institutions and conventions emerge to play a coordinating role. The success of a prohibition regime will depend on a complex array of factors, not least of which is a proper understanding of the problem addressed. A weak understanding of the problem may lead to the adoption of inappropriate strategies, laws, and institutions that fail to achieve their goals, as well as a variety of consequential social ills including over-criminalization and law enforcement overreach.

---

[68] See E Nadelmann, 'Global Prohibition Regimes: The Evolution of Norms in International Society' 44 *International Organization* (1990) 479, 481.
[69] Sheptycki, above n 9, 44.

2

What is Transnational Criminal Law?

2.1 Introduction

In the 1970s, the UN's Crime Prevention and Criminal Justice Branch developed a concept of transnational crime as the 'criminal activities extending into and violating the laws of several countries'.[1] The Director of the Branch and author of this concept Gerhard Mueller noted: 'The media, and indeed, many criminologists, think of any form of criminality, which transcends even a single international frontier as "international crime". That is far from accurate.'[2]

In a working paper delivered to the Fifth UN Crime Congress in Geneva in 1975 the Branch argued that 'a trend from national to transnational and finally international action is clearly discernible' in the suppression of crime.[3] This transnational action relies implicitly on Jessup's definition of transnational law as 'all law which regulates actions or events that transcend national frontiers',[4] but limits it to action against transnational crime. Transnational criminal law thus describes the law that suppresses crime that transcends national frontiers;[5] it can be defined as 'the indirect suppression by international law through domestic penal law of criminal activities that have actual or potential trans-boundary effects'.[6]

States have long been interested in suppressing crime that occurs in or emanates from other states. The difficulty has been in deciding precisely what degree of international cooperation is required to take effective action. In 1931 the League of Nations Fifth Committee produced a lengthy report for the League Assembly on 'the possible intensification of the war upon crime through international cooperation'.[7] It revealed some confusion about how to achieve this goal. For the League Assembly the goal

---

[1] F Adler, GOW Mueller, and WS Laufer, *Criminal Justice* (New York: McGraw Hill, 1994), 567.

[2] GOW Mueller, 'Transnational Crime: An Experience in Uncertainties' in S Einstein and M Amir (eds), *Organized Crime: Uncertainties and Dilemmas* (Chicago: Office of International Criminal Justice, University of Illinois, 1999), 3.

[3] Working paper by the Secretariat, 'Changes in Forms and dimensions of Criminality—Transnational and National', Fifth UN Congress on the Prevention of Crime and the Treatment of Offenders, Toronto, Canada, 1–12 September 1975, UN Doc A/CONF.56/3, 5–6.

[4] P Jessup, *Transnational Law* (New Haven: Yale UP, 1956), 2.

[5] See R Cryer, 'The Doctrinal Foundations of International Criminalization' in MC Bassiouni (ed), *1 International Criminal Law: Sources, Subjects and Contents*, 3rd edn (Dordrecht: Nijhoff, 2008), 108; R Cryer, H Friman, D Robinson, and E Wilmshurst, *An Introduction to International Criminal Law and Procedure*, 3rd edn (Cambridge: CUP, 2014), 5; RJ Currie, *International and Transnational Criminal Law*, 2nd edn (Toronto: Irwin, 2014) generally; C Kreβ, 'International Criminal Law' in R Wolfrum (ed), *Max Planck Encyclopedia of Public International Law: online edition* (2009 update), para 6.

[6] N Boister, 'Transnational Criminal Law?' 14 *European Journal of International Law* (2003) 953.

[7] League of Nations, *Gradual Unification of Criminal Laws and Cooperation of States in the Prevention of and Suppression of Crime*, Official Series of the League of Nations Publications, No. 7 (Geneva: League of Nations, 1933).

appeared to be 'achieving a gradual unification of criminal law and the cooperation of states in the prevention and suppression of crime'.[8] It recommended 'standardization' of certain criminal laws and procedures necessary for the suppression of internationally significant offences. Britain's response was illustrative of more pragmatic concerns. It thought standardization could only be achieved in regard to specific topics such as the traffic in woman and drugs because here there was some hope of unanimity. It did not, however, consider unification of criminal laws the goal; rather the goal was to address the problem of policing crime through prosecution and punishment.[9] Kuhn commented at the time:

> The crux of the problem is that the divergences of law and procedure be fully recognized and yet that the administration of criminal police and criminal justice be coordinated throughout the world by a full exchange of information, by active cooperation in apprehending criminals, and in a logical and just division among the various countries of their sovereign jurisdiction to punish for crime.[10]

International society still struggles to settle clearly whether the means to the goal of suppression of transnational crime is substantive standardization of national criminal laws or a more utilitarian procedural cooperation of dissimilar systems. This uncertainty has led to some indeterminacy about the nature of transnational criminal law.

2.2 Transnational Criminal Law as a Legal System

2.2.1 Transnational criminal law distinguished from transnational criminal procedure

Transnational criminal law consists of (a) horizontal international obligations between states to criminalize and cooperate, and (b) the vertical application of criminal law and procedures by those states to individuals in order to meet these international obligations. This transversal arrangement exists in respect of some crimes, such as hijacking, and not in regard to others, such as theft. If a thief crosses a border into another state and their extradition is requested, then the offence becomes an inter-state—some might say transnational—legal problem. But just because theft is an offence from Kiribati to Kazakhstan does not mean that states are under an international obligation to adopt theft as an offence or to extradite the thief. A treaty obligation to criminalize theft would illustrate that a transnational interest had manifested a degree of coordinated concern about the offence.[11] Theft is left to national law because there is insufficient transnational interest in national coordination of substantive criminalization or specific allied procedural cooperation. This is because in its general form it is so commonly criminalized in national law and many instances are so trivial or parochial. Only specific forms of theft such as theft of cultural property discussed in Chapter 14 are of transnational interest. The transnational enforcement of a national

[8] Cited in AK Kuhn, 'International Cooperation in the Suppression of Crime' 28(3) *American Journal of International Law* (1934) 541, 542.
[9] ibid, 543.   [10] ibid.
[11] See the US Court for Appeals in *Flores v Southern Peru Copper Corp* 343 F.3d 140 (2nd Cir 2003).

crime that is not the product of such an international obligation through, for example, a bilateral extradition treaty, is, however, more accurately described as transnational criminal procedure than transnational criminal law because of the absence of any reciprocal obligation to criminalize.[12]

2.2.2 The inter-state dimension

The history of most transnational crimes suggests that their development has been driven by the desire to extend national interest across borders. The reciprocal cooperation of other states is required because of the limitations sovereignty imposes on the validity and effectiveness of criminal law outside a state's territory. A state acting alone cannot succeed in suppressing serious threats from non-state actors beyond its borders, so states cooperate out of mutual interest, as a matter of international necessity.[13] As the Supreme Court of Canada put it in *Libman v Queen*,[14] '[i]n a shrinking world, we are all our brother's keepers'. But Nye notes that in international relations '[c]ontrary to some rhetorical flourishes, interdependence does not mean harmony. Rather, it often means unevenly balanced mutual dependence.'[15]

The adoption of an international instrument to provide for a mutual obligation to criminalize conduct provides evidence of a legal inter-sovereign relationship, and distinguishes transnational criminal law from international relations. States usually rely on a crime control treaty or 'suppression convention' to multilateralize this transnational interest. From early beginnings such as Britain's bilateral anti-slave-trading treaties in the early nineteenth century,[16] through early multilateral treaties like the 1929 Anti-Counterfeiting Convention,[17] to the large framework conventions of the late twentieth century such as the 1988 Drug Trafficking Convention[18] and more recent emphasis on regional treaties, the suppression conventions have been the main vehicle for state coordination against transnational crime. They provide for a tortious or delictual treaty obligation on states parties to criminalize specified activities in their national law and to engage in international cooperation in regard to these activities. Article 20 of the 1794 Jay Treaty between Britain and the US[19] is a very early example:

> The Contracting Parties shall not only refuse to receive any Pirates into any of their Ports, Havens or Towns, or permit any of their Inhabitants to receive, protect,

---

[12] Currie calls them 'transnational crimes of domestic concern', which he distinguishes from 'transnational crimes of international concern' falling under transnational criminal law. Currie, above n 5, 19–20.

[13] E Creegan, 'A Permanent Hybrid Court for Terrorism' 26 *American University International Law Review* (2011) 237, 246–51.

[14] [1985] 2 SCR 178, 214.   [15] JS Nye, 'Soft Power' 80 *Foreign Policy* (1990) 153, 158.

[16] See, eg, the bilateral treaties with France of 1831 and 1833.

[17] The International Convention for the Suppression of Counterfeiting of Currency, 20 April 1929, 112 LNTS 371, in force 22 February 1931.

[18] United Nations Convention against Illicit Traffic in Narcotic Drugs and Psychotropic Substances, 20 December 1988, 1582 UNTS 95, in force 11 November 1990.

[19] Treaty of Amity, Commerce and Navigation between Great Britain and the United States, signed at London, 19 November 1794, 52 CTS 243. See RS Clark, 'Some Aspects of the Concept of International Criminal Law: Suppression Conventions, Jurisdiction, Submarine Cables and the Lotus' 22 *Criminal Law Forum* (2011) 519, 523.

harbour, conceal or assist them in any manner, but will bring to consign punishment all such Inhabitants as shall be guilty of such acts or offences.

It sets a model for all such treaties, requiring the contracting parties to criminalize the specified behaviours, establish their jurisdiction, and enforce it.

Suppression conventions generate a downward cascade of norms which impacts heavily on domestic criminal law. Some states directly transpose these norms into their national law, others translate their essence.[20] The traffic is not all one way; the relationship between the vertical and horizontal elements is recursive in the sense that adaptations in national law can feed back into alterations of the international template and on to other national laws.

There are multiple reasons why some harmful activities generate sufficient transnational interest leading to calls for international cooperation: the level of societal anxiety, media interest, strategic concerns, morality, security, and so forth. The legitimate boundaries of this transnational interest are not clear, and depend on the influence of interested states and willingness of others to go along. The sum of these cosmopolitan concerns is much 'thicker' in regard to some offences than others; currently, for example, there is more concern about terrorism than environmental crime. This imbalance is unsurprising because certain states and groups of states have a greater capacity to project self-interest than others. The history of transnational criminal law reveals that many of the suppression conventions are rooted in the crime control policies of powerful Western states battling to block criminal flows originating in developing states. In particular, Britain—the nineteenth-century 'global policeman'—and the US—the twentieth-century global policeman—have driven the development of transnational criminal law in directions that suited them. An 1817 Anti-Slavery Convention between Great Britain and Portugal is an expression of the overweaning transnational interest of a more powerful state, and of how that interest is to be achieved through normative harmonization with the laws of the powerful state.[21] Article III reads

His Most Faithful Majesty engages, within the space of two months of the ratifications of the Present Convention, to promulgate in His Capital, and in other parts of his dominions, as soon as possible, a Law, which shall prescribe the punishment of any of His Subjects who may in the future participate in the illicit traffic of Slaves ... and *engages to assimilate, as much as possible*, the Legislation of Portugal in this respect, to that of Great Britain.

State sponsors of new transnational crimes usually turn to their own law to provide a model. The 'forerunner' legislation for the Organisation for Economic Co-operation and Development (OECD) Anti-Bribery Convention,[22] for example, is the US Foreign Corrupt Practices Act.[23] Regional political bodies can act as normative entrepreneurs, hawking their regional models for transplantation. For example, the Council

---

[20] C Nowak, 'The Internationalization of Polish Criminal Law: How Polish Law Changed Under the Influence of Globalization' 59 *Crime, Law and Social Change* (2013) 139, 144.

[21] Additional Convention between Great Britain and Portugal for the Prevention of the Slave Trade, signed at London, 28 July 1817, 67 CTS 373.

[22] Convention on Combating Bribery of Foreign Public Officials in Transnational Business Transactions, 17 December 1998, 37 ILM 1 (1998), in force 5 March 2002.

[23] 15 US § 78dd-1 et seq; see Chapter 8 below.

of Europe Cybercrime Convention[24] was effectively cloned with strong European support in the Economic Community of West African States (ECOWAS) Directive on Fighting Cybercrime.[25] Self-interest can also be cajoled into paternalistic global moralism by individual norm entrepreneurs. For example, when the many colonial powers attending a conference on the control of opium held in 1925 in Geneva failed to limit the production of opium to the chagrin of the US, one of the architects of the global drug control system, the Episcopal Bishop to the Philippines Charles Brent appealed to them: 'Is it just for an International Conference of such weight and solemnity as this to deal with the ten percent of the subject which affects Europe and America, leaving almost untouched the other ninety percent which affects Asia?'[26]

This normative activity produces what Nadelmann calls 'global prohibition regimes'—international regimes prohibiting piracy, slavery, drugs, and so forth established for pragmatic purposes such as the elimination of safe havens, but which also serve to enforce the contingent, parochial morality of their authors.[27] That the goals of these regimes can shift over time is nicely illustrated by this quote from the pirate William Kidd's indictment in 1701. He was charged because he did

> pyratically and feloniously set upon, board, break, and enter a certain ship called the
> *Quedagh Merchant* and pyratically and feloniously assault the mariners of said ship,
> and put them in corporeal fear of their lives, and did pyratically and feloniously steal,
> take, and carry away the said ship, with ... seventy chests of opium ...[28]

As new regimes are added expanding the subjects of regulation, transnational criminal law expands. The different prohibition regimes emerge and evolve through different phases of interstate order, exhibiting looser and tighter degrees of coordination, depending on the international context at the time. Their development, however, is governed by the dominant political perceptions that they are necessary to respond to the problem of crime control.[29]

The construction of these prohibition regimes does not necessarily require formal treaty obligations.[30] The binding resolutions of international organizations such as the Security Council have been used to build prohibition regimes in regard to terrorism.[31] It is uncertain whether counterterrorism is a special case or whether this

---

[24] Budapest, 23 November 2001, ETS No 185, in force 1 July 2004.

[25] Directive C/DIR. 1/08/11 on Fighting Cyber Crime Within ECOWAS. See N Dalla Guarda, 'Governing the Ungovernable: International Relations, Transnational Cybercrime Law, and the Post-Westphalian Regulatory State' 6(1) *Transnational Legal Theory* (2015) 211, 227, 237.

[26] Pennsylvania State University, Special Collections, Historical Collections and Labor Archive, Harry Anslinger Papers, Box 9, File 59, Opium (1924–1945), in an undated document entitled 'An Appeal to my Colleagues', p 13.

[27] E Nadelmann, 'Global Prohibition Regimes: The Evolution of Norms in International Society' 44 *International Organisation* (1990) 479.

[28] *The Tryal of Captain William Kidd for Murder and Piracy, Upon Six Several Indictments* (London, 1701), 322.

[29] Supporting Garland's general observation in this regard—see D Garland, *The Culture of Control: Crime and Social Order in Contemporary Society* (Chicago: University of Chicago Press, 2001), 102.

[30] CC Murphy, 'Transnational Counter-terrorism Law: Law, Power and Legitimacy in the "Wars on Terror"' 6(1) *Transnational Legal Theory* (2015) 31, 33.

[31] See Chapter 7.

'supreme' executive law-making will be used to suppress other transnational crimes in the future. A more commonly used normative source is soft law. The conferences of states parties to suppression conventions and the UN's functional commissions like the Commission on Narcotic Drugs can and do adopt resolutions, which do have domestic legal effects. The virtues of soft law are that it is faster to make, easier to adapt to changing patterns of transnational criminality, and in many states can be implemented directly by national executives without domestic legislation. Perhaps the 'hardest' soft laws are the recommendations of the Financial Action Task Force (FATF),[32] which provides the governing standards on anti-money laundering (AML) and counter-terrorist financing (CTF). They have proved powerful instruments in fleshing out the AML and CTF regimes because they have allowed a small group of powerful states to achieve a consensus and then implement these norms more broadly through economic pressure. There is, however, a clear tension between using treaties to formalize cooperation in the suppression of transnational crime, and the turn to novel forms of softer power by those states most interested in suppression—the dominant powers in the OECD and the G7/G8. As Rose puts it, the formation of the FATF was a 'pivot away' from the UN's approach to suppression.[33] She points out that the UN in its treaty making is 'trapped' in meeting general concerns in a way that less representative organizations like the FATF are not.[34] It is true that treaties capture a response to transnational crime that is by definition outdated by the time it is adopted and implemented. More intriguingly, the decisions of these international organizations and those of international banking organizations,[35] transnational corporations,[36] non-governmental organizations (NGOs),[37] and transnational law enforcement agencies[38] can appear disconnected from state authority and consent[39] and suggest the emergence of a separate transnational criminal law-making space.[40]

Although transnational criminal law does require a horizontal element, it appears that this can be constituted by a treaty, a custom, a resolution, soft law, any form of

---

[32] The FATF Recommendations: International Standards on Combating Money Laundering and the Financing of Terrorism and Proliferation, 16 February 2012, updated October 2016. See generally KS Blazejewski, 'The FATF and its Institutional Partners: Improving the Effectiveness and Accountability of Transgovernmental Networks' 22 *Temple International and Comparative Law Journal* (2008) 1.

[33] C Rose, *International Anti-Corruption Norms: Their Creation and Influence on Domestic Legal Systems* (Oxford: OUP, 2015), 2.

[34] ibid, at 12.

[35] See, eg, Basel Committee on Banking Supervision (BCBS), International Association of Insurance Supervisors (IAIS), and International Organisation of Securities Commissions (IOSCO).

[36] See, eg, the anti-tobacco smuggling agreements signed between major tobacco products manufacturers and the European Anti-Fraud Office (OLAF), available at <https://ec.europa.eu/anti-fraud/investigations/eu-revenue/cigarette_smuggling_en> last visited 17 July 2017.

[37] See, eg, Transparency International's work as the UNCAC Coalition Secretariat—see <http://www.transparency.org/whatwedo/activity/our_work_on_conventions> last visited 16 June 2016.

[38] The US Drug Enforcement Agency is just one of many significant national agencies operating at a transnational level—see EA Nadelmann, *Cops Across Borders: The Internationalization of U.S. Criminal Law Enforcement* (University Park, PA: Pennsylvania State University Press, 1993), 189 et seq.

[39] U Sieber, 'Legal Order in a Global World—The Development of a Fragmented System of National, International and Private Norms' in A von Bogdandy and R Wolfrum (eds), 14 *Max Planck Yearbook of United Nations Law* (2010), 1, 17.

[40] See C Scott, ' "Transnational Law" as Proto-Concept: Three Conceptions' 10 *German Law Journal* (2009) 859, 873–75; HH Koh, 'Transnational Legal Process' 75 *Nebraska Law Review* (1996) 181, 199.

international arrangement making for coordination of approach among states and for legal acts at a domestic level. Different kinds of international instrument can be used for different purposes, depending on levels of domestic resistance to change. It should be noted, however, that the suppression conventions provide a penal anchor for much of this transnational governance, even when it takes on a more administrative or regulatory form. The vertical dimension of transnational criminal law can also be deepened to include all forms of coercive power operative in the transnational space including regulatory offences, labour laws, immigration laws, property laws, even states' enforcement of contract, corporate, and banking laws.[41] This more sociologically complete picture has the advantage of capturing the full range of activities against transnational crime, penal and non-penal, in both the international and vertical dimensions of suppression of transnational crime. It risks doctrinal coherence,[42] but doctrinal incoherence is common in criminal justice systems that embrace administrative control of crime. The view of transnational criminal law being described here does, however, subordinate all these elements to state interest[43] mainly because powerful states still control the regulatory agenda.[44]

2.2.3 Transnational crimes and penalties

The obligation to criminalize in these international instruments (whether a clear treaty obligation or in a 'softer' form) ultimately serves two purposes: (i) to suppress the targeted activities domestically; and (ii) to enable inter-state cooperation in this suppression by ensuring double criminality (ie ensuring the same crime exists in both states). The suppression conventions leave the right to criminalize—the *ius puniendi*—with the state. Thus the 'crimes' in the conventions are not 'crimes' at all. In order to protect sovereignty over criminal justice, the suppression conventions are not generally designed to be self-executing. The treaty provisions are 'incomplete' in that the international norms they set out are not fully defined. References in provisions like article 1 of the Hague Hijacking Convention (discussed in Chapter 7) to the 'unlawful' commission of offences confirms, somewhat circularly, that the convention itself does not criminalize that action, but that national law does, and any exemptions are for national law. It is left to national criminal law to complete them by giving them penal authority within domestic conceptions of legality. The suppression conventions thus oblige parties to adopt a base line of criminalization and punishment and they cannot adopt narrower offences or more lenient punishments without being in breach of their treaty obligations; this does not prevent them from adopting offences with a broader scope or more severe punishments. The suppression conventions leave parties a very broad discretionary margin of appreciation as how precisely to implement their

---

[41] P Kotiswaran and N Palmer, 'Rethinking the "International Law of Crime": Provocations from Transnational Legal Studies' 6(1) *Transnational Legal Theory* (2015) 55, 77–80.
[42] Murphy, above n 30, 39–42.   [43] Kotiswaran and Palmer, above n 41, 70 et seq.
[44] See generally D Drezner, *All Politics is Global: Explaining International Regulatory Regimes* (Princeton, NJ: Princeton UP, 2007). This is revealed, eg, in the donation by states of funds for earmarked special projects rather than into the general purpose funding of the United Nations Office on Drugs and Crime (UNODC), which allows donor parties to dictate the direction of UNODC activity.

criminalization provisions through incorporation of standard provisions such as article 11(6) of the UN Convention against Transnational Organized Crime:[45]

> Nothing contained in this Convention shall affect the principle that the description of offences established in accordance with this Convention and of the applicable legal defences or other legal principles controlling the lawfulness of conduct is reserved to the domestic law of the State Party and that such offences shall be prosecuted and punished in accordance with that law.

The legislative context in which transnational criminal laws are applied thus determines their meaning in a particular state,[46] and as Wise notes, the 'application of criminal law involves any number of local peculiarities'.[47] For dualist and weakly monist states which require domestic criminalization, further legislation enacting the offence produces the crime. Even if the international obligation is applied directly into national law the resulting criminal laws derive their normative authority from the state that applies them, not from international law. In terms of article 8(2) of Portugal's Constitution, for example, treaties are self-executing except for provision for criminalization; they must be concretized by adoption in domestic law. Article 9 of the Criminal Law of the People's Republic of China (CLPRC), in further example, provides that the CLPRC shall be applicable to all crimes which are stipulated in international treaties concluded or acceded to by China. It is article 9 which makes the provisions they contain crimes in Chinese law.

The form of the national norm is, however, shaped by international obligation, although the degree differs from norm to norm and state to state. Paradoxically, where the criminalization provision in a suppression convention is entirely novel it will tend to be followed very closely by national legislative drafters.[48] But where offences exist prior to the development of the suppression convention, parties to the treaties will tend to adapt and thus dilute the substance of the treaty obligations into existing statutory schemes.[49]

The high cost of developing suppression conventions suggests that states would only bother to use them to criminalize cross-border activity if that activity was serious. However, much of transnational criminal law involves systems not of crimes *malum in se* (evil in themselves) but of crimes *mala prohibita*—regulatory offences involving exchanges of goods and services which usually do not harm those involved in the exchange but where wrongfulness derives from violation of a rule laid down for policy reasons by states.[50] Only in crimes like human trafficking and terrorism is violence intrinsic to the 'production' of the services. It is not usually the intrinsic nature of the activity but rather the inability to control transnational criminal markets that provoke

---

[45] 15 November 2000, 2225 UNTS 209, in force 29 September 2003.
[46] Kotiswaran and Palmer, above n 41, 86.
[47] EM Wise, 'International Crimes and Domestic Criminal Law' 38 *DePaul Law Review* (1989) 923, 938.
[48] See, eg, Niue's Terrorism Suppression and Transnational Crimes Act 2006, which picks up many convention definitions almost verbatim.
[49] See the examples of organized crime legislative provisions surveyed by A Schloenhardt, *Palermo in the Pacific: Organised Crime Offences in the Asia Pacific Region* (Leiden: Martinus Nijhoff Publishers, 2009), 354–56.
[50] JD Michels, 'Keeping Dealers off the Docket: The Perils of Prosecuting Serious Drug-Related Offences at the International Criminal Court' 21(3) *Florida Journal of International Law* (2009) 449, 452.

international cooperation. Logically then these offences depend on a stipulation of what is lawful as opposed to unlawful behaviour in regard to a particular good or service. Two broad forms of prohibition system can be distinguished. In absolute prohibition systems the scope of lawful behaviour is usually very narrowly prescribed by the relevant suppression conventions. For example, the drug conventions do not prohibit drugs—they spell out that only supply and use of drugs for 'medical and scientific purposes' is lawful, and they expressly prohibit all other forms of behaviour.[51] In derivative prohibition systems the scope of lawful behaviour is broad and variable, and the treaty will not spell it out. For example, the Protocol to Eliminate the Illicit Trade in Tobacco Products[52] does not spell out all forms of lawful behaviour, but it does spell out the situations in which otherwise lawful behaviour becomes unlawful, such as the non-payment of income duty on the importation of tobacco.[53]

The suppression conventions usually define the (i) material/conduct/*actus reus* elements and (ii) mental/fault/*mens rea* elements of these crimes. A product of lowest common denominator inter-state agreement, these definitions may only set a standard designed to produce the degree of correspondence between national definitions of crimes sufficient to enable international cooperation.

The kinds of conduct criminalized vary widely from suppression of actions that use violence and are heavily invasive of human rights such as hijacking to others more regulatory in nature such as import of contraband of various kinds. The different conventions describe in great detail a bewildering array of forms of conduct (eg 'trafficking' in persons involves inter alia the 'recruitment' of persons), circumstances (eg piracy must take place 'on the high seas'), states of affairs (eg drug 'possession'), and causation (eg unlawful acts against civil aviation include inter alia the causing of damage to an aircraft rendering it 'incapable of flight'). There is only very limited provision for liability for omissions in situations such as the corruption offence of failure to perform an official function, although this is likely to increase as conventions set out more complex regulatory frameworks in areas such as the environment. Only a very few offences include a specific transnational element among their conduct elements. An example is article 3 of the 2010 Arab Convention on Combating Information Technology Offences, which include both cross-border conduct and effects.[54] Most transnational crimes are defined without a transnational element. An offence such as money laundering, for example, can encompass conduct that crosses borders as well as conduct that does not. The omission is deliberate; the conventions are designed to suppress intra-state as well as inter-state offences because of the tendency of the former to lead to the latter. Transnational criminal law therefore includes behaviour that (i) actually crosses borders; (ii) has substantial effects in other states; and (iii) local crime that has only the most tenuous potential extraterritorial impact but which is of transnational interest whether for moral[55] or other more prudential reasons.

---

[51] See, eg, article 4(1)(c) of the 1961 Single Convention on Narcotic Drugs, 30 March 1961, 520 UNTS 151, in force 13 December 1964.

[52] 12 November 2012, not yet in force.   [53] Article 14.

[54] 21 December 2010, not yet in force.   [55] Nadelmann, above n 27, 525.

Mens rea standards are normally only set in more recent treaties, and then in a subjective form because of the need for states to meet legality obligations. This usually means they require intention if the objective element takes the form of an action (eg intention to supply drugs), and knowledge if there is a circumstantial element involved (eg knowledge that funds are going to be used for terrorist financing, knowledge that the person assaulted has an internationally protected status, knowledge that the material stolen is nuclear). The conventions thus usually require criminalization of 'intentional' commission of the offence; this does not preclude a party of its own accord broadening the scope of the offence by relying on principles to increase the scope of the offence like *dolus eventualis*, recklessness, or negligence. A trend towards risk-based preventive criminalization is clearly indicated by heavy reliance on ulterior intentions or knowledge in terrorism offences (eg the purposive element in hostage-taking of compelling a government to do or abstain from doing an act), usually in order to restrict liability but also to anchor liability where the conduct itself is fairly innocuous. Negligence is seldom stipulated as a form of fault, although many of the later conventions expressly permit the use of inference to establish this subjective element.

In an effort to extend criminal liability 'up' the chain of involvement, most of the suppression conventions provide specifically for complicity for secondary participation (aiding and abetting, accomplice liability) and in more recent treaties for common purpose/joint enterprise liability as well as inchoate forms of liability such as criminalize 'association or conspiracy' and 'attempts'. The conventions never define these provisions, leaving it to the parties which may rely on the general provisions in their domestic criminal law to cover these obligations. However, the introduction of 'alien' doctrines may require fundamental change of domestic principles of participation and obligations of this kind are commonly subject to chapeaus that make their application dependant on compatibility with the basic legal or constitutional concepts of the parties. Again, in spite of the alien nature of the notion to many states' legal systems, an increasing number of suppression conventions oblige parties to provide for the criminal liability of legal persons because of the involvement of companies in transnational crime, although they do not prescribe what theory of liability should be followed.

The suppression conventions make no provision for defences in the sense of justifications or excuses, but they do, on occasion, remove defences. The anti-terrorism conventions have, for example, progressively removed any defence based on political, ideological, racial, ethnic, or religious considerations if the accused possessed an intention to terrorize.

The suppression conventions say very little about penalties, because of massive variation in value systems and punishments schemes among states. The little that can be gleaned from the suppression conventions in regard to punishment includes:

(a) the agreement in the early suppression conventions to the application of severe penalties to these offences;

(b) provisions in later treaties to apply severe penalties proportional to the gravity of the offences; and

(c) provisions in regard to selected crimes to apply certain aggravating factors, such as the involvement of an organized criminal group.

Transnational criminal law provides no further guidance on severity, proportionality, or aggravation—these remain national legal variables (both in legislation and in the sentences handed down by judicial organs).

These substantive crimes and penalties in transnational criminal law are discussed in detail in Part II of this book. The chapters roughly follow the historical development of the substantive transnational crimes in order to illustrate the evolution of transnational interest and the modes adopted to suppress transnational crime. The analysis proceeds by first identifying the nature of the activity suppressed, in order to get some idea of why these offences were created and how they are likely to be applied. The bulk of each chapter provides a technical legal analysis broken down into the material and mental elements of a crime required for a conviction and the principles to be applied to punishment or sentencing. Note is made of any provisions for different forms of complicity (perpetrators, accomplices) and inchoate offences (attempts, conspiracy, incitement).

2.2.4 Provisions for procedural cooperation

The legal regimes created by these suppression conventions also provide for procedures for international cooperation in order to pursue alleged offenders. The substantive provisions are linked to this allied procedural regime because such cooperation is impossible on a global scale without some standardization of criminalization; states will not cooperate in regard to conduct they do not regard as criminal.

In order to take effective steps against transnational crime, national law must first establish jurisdiction and then enforce it. If, for example, someone engages in conduct in State A which causes harm in State B, prosecution in State B will depend on whether it establishes extraterritorial jurisdiction over the particular offence, whether State A will give it information on the suspect's location and legal assistance in the gathering of evidence, and ultimately whether State B can extradite the alleged offender. Only then can the duties of procedural cooperation between states meet the Grotian maxim, 'dedere, judicare, punire' (deliver, adjudicate, punish).[56]

States rely on provisions in the suppression conventions to permit the establishment of extraterritorial jurisdiction, although these jurisdictional provisions stand somewhat apart from the other provisions of transnational criminal procedure because of their dual substantive and procedural nature. In the suppression conventions (i) obligatory jurisdiction is still primarily territorial with some limited extensions of the doctrine, but (ii) permissive jurisdiction is much broader and includes controversial principles such as the 'potential effects' doctrine and the rapidly expanding (in scope) protective principle. In practice this does not result in a globally harmonized system of jurisdiction over transnational crime but rather (i) a minimum standard adhered to by most, and (ii) a maximum standard adhered to by a few. In situations of concurrent

---

[56] *De Jure Belli Ac Pacis*, (1758) Chapter 31, Section 76.

jurisdiction, although there is no extant principle, there is clearly support for the view that the state with the greatest centre of gravity in regard to the crime should take precedence.

The provisions in the suppression conventions designed to enable the enforcement of jurisdiction permit the procedural interaction of national criminal justice systems. The development of transnational criminal law has seen progressively more extensive provisions for transnational procedural cooperation, to facilitate the sharing of information between law enforcement agencies, to gather evidence abroad, to retrieve assets, and to extradite alleged offenders. These procedural provisions overlap with the much larger system of international criminal cooperation that has been developed to deal with serious crime. The conventions largely ignore the criminal trial itself, which they leave to the state concerned.

The specific concern in regard to law enforcement cooperation is to make sure articulation between different systems is possible through, for example, provisions for information storage and exchange. Limited provision is also made for operational cooperation such as in regard to joint investigation teams. Again, a minimum/maximum dualism appears to be emerging: many states will accept operational cooperation at home; few engage in it abroad but are permitted by the others to do so.

More formal legal assistance involves a request from one state to another for the latter to exercise its enforcement jurisdiction on the former's behalf. The suppression conventions reinforce the general trend to less formality, to greater speed, and to more forms of assistance at ever earlier stages in the investigation, to counterbalance the fact that the requested state can only be asked to exercise the powers that it can exercise in its own right. The suppression conventions have also been used to expand the scope of asset recovery and provide for mutual assistance in this regard on the basis of the rationale that the state has the right to relieve anyone of an asset tainted by any crime.

Finally, the suppression conventions have been used to reform extradition law in two ways. First, there has been a strong effort to expand the numbers of extraditable offences. This has been achieved by relying on the modifying influence of the suppression conventions to shift from enumerative to evaluative thresholds, and by moving from exclusively bilateral/regional-treaty-based extradition to extradition on the basis of national law or even the suppression conventions themselves. Second, there has been a major effort to remove the barriers to extradition. States have agreed to reduce even further what remains of a substantive inquiry into the criminal laws of the requesting state, to scrap inquiry into the evidence that the requesting state has to support trial, to abandon any possible exceptions that they might take to the process, and to remove any political influence over the process.

Effective cooperation does not require states to apply the criminal laws of other states in their own jurisdictions, it requires states to apply their own laws to assist other states. Law enforcement cooperation is still governed by the general principle that the law of the receiving/requested state is paramount. These different forms of international cooperation do not involve a choice of law problem of the kind endemic to conflict of laws. To apply the criminal laws of another sovereign would be to negate the sovereignty that criminal law expresses.[57] They involve rather a question of which state shall get the chance to apply its laws.[58]

The different forms of procedural cooperation in transnational criminal law are examined in Part III of this book. This part is organized thematically rather than by specific crime, with selective examples from different suppression conventions. It deals first with rules for establishing jurisdiction, and then with the three modes of cooperation in regard to enforcing jurisdiction over transnational crime: international law enforcement cooperation (including law enforcement on the high seas and through the anti-money laundering regime), formal legal assistance in gathering of evidence (including in regard to asset recovery), and extradition. These chapters explore the framework for enforcement activity provided by the suppression conventions; they are not a comprehensive account of international law enforcement cooperation, something beyond the scope of this book.

As noted above, many of the newer measures adopted in the suppression of transnational crime are of an administrative nature. Often they involve preventive and regulatory measures, such as the risk assessment tools used in the anti-money laundering regime, or the passport control measures used to combat people smuggling. Considerations of space militate against a full treatment of these measures here; instead the book treats these measures as elements of the procedural enforcement regime covered in Part III, dealing with them on a selective basis.

2.2.5 Subjects and objects of transnational criminal law

Identifying the subjects of transnational criminal law depends on which part of the bifurcated system we are talking about. States are the subjects of the treaty obligations that serve as the framework for the system. Those obligations generate responsibility to other states. If, for example, a party to the 1988 Drug Trafficking Convention does not legislate drug trafficking offences into their law, or deliberately chooses not to apply them, that party may be in breach of its obligations under the treaty to the other parties and state responsibility may follow. On those rare occasions when parties to a suppression convention engage directly or indirectly in the perpetration of transnational crimes the legal consequences are two-fold: the individuals involved commit criminal offences while the state breaches its treaty obligations opening it to state responsibility. Actions of this kind may also serve to establish one or more of the elements of a core international crime. State-sponsored drug trafficking within another state may, for example, constitute evidence of the crime of aggression.[59]

Persons, whether natural or juridical, that actually commit the crimes, are the objects, not the subjects, of the obligations in the suppression conventions. Crawford and Olleson note pithily that pirates '[do] not acquire international legal personality

---

[57] MD Dubber, 'Criminal Law in Comparative Context' 56 *Journal of Legal Education* (2006) 433, 434.

[58] *Ze'ev Rosenstein v Israel* Appeal judgment, Crim A 4596/05, para 43; ILDC 159 (IL 2005), 30 November 2005.

[59] See, eg, N Boister, 'Punishing Japan's "Opium War-making" in China: The Relationship between Transnational Crime and Aggression at the Tokyo Tribunal' in Y Tanaka, T McCormack, and G Simpson (eds), *Beyond Victor's Justice? The Tokyo War Crimes Trial Revisited* (Leiden and Boston: Nijhoff, 2011), 323.

by being hanged at the yardarm'.[60] Individuals do, however, enjoy national personality under the national criminal laws enacted as a result of those treaty obligations (although juridical persons represent a particular challenge in this regard). The treatment of the individual as an object reflects the top-down approach pursued by states to the problem of transnational crime. It has been criticized for ignoring the procedural and due process concerns of individual defendants facing this normative onslaught.[61] Some of these concerns arise because of the incoherence of the system; it is a patchwork of laws made of overlapping national criminal jurisdictions.[62] In a system where states retain their independent authority to enforce their jurisdiction, yet are urged to cooperate, defendants may find themselves subject to multiplications of penal power in a transnational space where they may have very little in the way of positive legal protections.

2.2.6 Distinguishing transnational criminal law from international criminal law *stricto sensu*

Transnational criminal law is a part of international criminal law in a broad sense of criminal law with an international legal dimension. However, it is distinguishable from the core international criminal law. The core international crimes in articles 5–8 of the Rome Statute[63]—genocide, war crimes, crimes against humanity, and aggression—involve a direct customary international law-based obligation on individuals regardless of the position in national law.[64] A transnational crime may find its original normative source in international law, but the suppression conventions do not make provision for direct criminalization in international law; the actual criminal prohibition on individuals is entirely national. In principle, a custom could create an indirect transnational crime, and a treaty, a direct international crime, so it is not the source but rather the nature of the obligation which distinguishes them. It follows that adjudicative jurisdiction over transnational crimes is exclusively national; there is no international criminal jurisdiction such as that over the core international crimes.

The 'supranational character of international criminal law'[65] flows from its naissance in the international community. Article 5 of the Rome Statute limits the International Criminal Court's jurisdiction 'to the most serious crimes of concern to the international community as a whole'. States have chosen not to cede their sovereign criminal jurisdiction over transnational crime to some larger international jurisdictional unit; they seek rather to accommodate their systems, over which they still

---

[60] J Crawford and S Olleson, 'The Nature and Forms of International Responsibility' in MD Evans (ed), *International Law*, 3rd edn (Oxford: OUP, 2010), 441, 445.

[61] S Gless, 'Bird's-Eye View and Worm's Eye View: Towards a Defendant-Based Approach in Transnational Criminal Law' 6(1) *Transnational Legal Theory* (2015) 117, 119 et seq.

[62] ibid, 127.

[63] Rome Statute of the International Criminal Court, 17 July 1998, 2187 UNTS 90, in force 1 July 2002.

[64] Article 25(2).

[65] *Maktouf and Damjanovic v Bosnia and Herzegovina*, Application nos 2312/08 and 34179/08, Grand Chamber, ECtHR, 18 July 2013, para 46.

retain sovereignty, with other states' systems. The suppression conventions establish transnational crime control regimes that encompass principles, norms, rules, and procedures around which the ideals and expectations of the participating states converge, but stop well short of uniting because the commission of these crimes is neither subject to universal opprobrium nor threatens the security of the international community.[66] Although their suppression does require cooperation and a certain erosion of sovereignty, international solidarity is much weaker. Suppression of transnational crime does not require (and nor would states welcome) the density of institutionalization that the core international crimes require in the form of an international criminal tribunal.

This was something understood by early writers. Trainin, for example, saw the suppression conventions solely as vehicles for mutual assistance in the struggle against crime.[67] In 1950, Pella distinguished 'international crimes', which he said involve the 'irregular exercise of its sovereignty by a state' and consist 'of acts against the peace and security of mankind', from 'so-called international crimes, such as piracy, slave trade, traffic in women and children, drug traffic', which unlike the former 'did not prejudice international relations'.[68] The former required an international jurisdiction, the latter could be left to national jurisdiction as '[a]ll civilized states are interested in the repression of such offenses and there is no reason to suppose that national courts are not objective in dealing with them'.[69] More recently, Fletcher considered these treaty-based crimes too parochial to deserve the status of core international crime.[70] Courts agree. In *Pushpanathan v Canada*[71] the Canadian Supreme Court held there was no indication that drug trafficking on any scale was contrary to the purposes of the UN or that its prohibition protected core human rights. A transnational crime may, however, increase in scale and systematicity to the point where it does threaten international peace and security or shock the conscience of mankind, thus becoming a core international crime.[72] State support for the introduction of individual criminal liability for this crime in international law would be a clear indicator of this change of status.

International and transnational criminal law do, nevertheless, share many (although not all) tools of a procedural kind because they confront similar problems of investigating and apprehending fugitive offenders.[73] Moreover, both systems are

---

[66] See principle 3 of the 'Report of the UNWCC summarising the elements of Crimes Against Humanity in Eight Principles' in UNWCC, *History of the United Nations War Crimes Commission* (London: HMSO, 1948).

[67] AN Trainin, *Hitlerite Responsibility Under Criminal Law* (London: Hutchinson, nd), 28–29.

[68] VV Pella, 'Towards an International Criminal Court' 44 *American Journal of International Law* (1950) 37, 54.

[69] ibid, 56.

[70] G Fletcher, 'Parochial versus Universal Criminal Law' 3 *Journal of International Justice* (2005) 20, 23.

[71] 1 SCR 98, ILDC 182 (CA 1998), paras 64, 69, 72.   [72] Cryer, above n 5, 125–26.

[73] F Mégret, 'The "Elephant in the Room" in Debates about Universal Jurisdiction: Diasporas, Duties of Hospitality, and the Constitution of the Political' 6(1) *Transnational Legal Theory* (2015) 89, 91, 116; M Reed-Hurtado, 'International Criminal Law's Incongruity in Colombia: Why Core Crime Prosecution in National Jurisdictions Should be Included in Analyses of Transnational Criminal Law?' 6(1) *Transnational Legal Theory* (2015) 174, 175.

fractured and have issues with implementation and legitimacy.[74] Critics who point
this out take issue with the idealized account that the neat dichotomy between international and transnational criminal law presupposes, and argue that transnational
criminal law should be placed back into the broader context of all international law
relating to crime.[75] In German doctrine *Internationales Strafrecht* is an umbrella
term containing all of the doctrinal categories which involve international aspects
of criminal law and criminal aspects of international law.[76] Adopting this kind of
taxonomy may help to expose similar social and political realities, and allow useful
comparisons between protection of rights and application of general principles in
the core international criminal law and their neglect in transnational criminal law. It
would, however, obscure the different levels of intensity of international cooperation
that international and transnational criminal law entail. The idealized account of
international criminal law held by its exponents at the beginning of the twenty-first
century tended to submerge transnational criminal law and its peculiar social and
political character including the heavy sovereign interests that shape it, to the detri-
ment of a better understanding of its character.[77] Transnational criminal law provides
a methodological lens[78] of sufficiently sharp focus to avoid the supranational con-
notations associated with 'international criminal law' and reveal the 'transnational
interest' obscured by more ambiguous labels like 'crimes of international concern'.[79]

2.2.7 Transnational criminal law as a system of laws

Transnational criminal law is not a coherent legal order with a hierarchy or rules and
an ultimate arbiter on the meaning of those rules.[80] There is no single point of origin for these transnational criminal laws; there are multiple points of origin. These
points of origin may be the unilateral domestic actions of states, or agreements
based on treaties or other more informal relations between states, or perhaps even
arise out of the actions of transnational actors. The system is plural—the order dispersed in nature. All of these rules are, however, specifically created to deal with transnational criminal matters.[81] That functional goal has, as this book illustrates, led to
the adoption of rules with similar forms. While the variation of practice among states

---

[74] Kotiswaran and Palmer, above n 41, 57–69.   [75] ibid, 55.
[76] Including Völkerstrafrecht (international criminal law in a strict sense), Europäisches
Strafrecht (European Criminal Law), Strafanwendungsrecht (criminal jurisdiction), internationale
Zusammenarbeit in Strafsachen (international cooperation in criminal matters), and, increasingly,
Transnationales Strafrecht (treaty originating criminal law dealing with crimes of a transnational character). See Kreβ, above n 5, para 6.
[77] See MC Bassiouni, 'The Sources and Content of International Criminal Law: A Theoretical Framework'
in MC Bassiouni (ed), 1 *International Criminal Law*, 2nd edn (Ardsley on Hudson: Transnational,
1998), 1, 46.
[78] P Zumbansen, 'Defining the Space of Transnational Law: Legal Theory, Global Governance and
Legal Pluralism' 21 *Transnational Law & Contemporary Problems* (2012) 305, 307.
[79] The term used by MC Bassiouni, 'An Appraisal of the Growth and Developing Trends of International
Criminal Law' in J Dugard and C Van den Wyngaert (eds), *International Criminal Law and Procedure*
(Aldershot: Dartmouth, 1996), 85.
[80] Murphy, above n 30, 41.
[81] S Gless and JAE Vervaele, 'Editorial: Law Should Govern: Aspiring General Principles for
Transnational Criminal Justice' 9 *Utrecht Law Review* (2013) 1.

undermines any claim to global codification, the substance of elements of crimes and rules of procedure are now becoming standardized at the international level, and at the national level there are indications of a slow convergence of domestic laws—they are conformal in nature. Normative correspondence exists across the various prohibition regimes that make up transnational criminal law. The process of development of new treaties frequently borrows innovations already adopted in older treaties concerned with different crimes, because of their supposed effectiveness and acceptability. For example, the provision in article 3(c) of the Terrorist Bombings Convention which obliges states parties to extend criminal liability for terrorist bombing based on a version of the common purpose or joint criminal enterprise doctrine, has found its way into many other anti-terrorist treaties including for example, article 4(5)(c) of the 2004 Protocol to the South Asian Association for Regional Co-operation (SAARC) Regional Convention on the Prevention of Terrorism,[82] but now applied to all terrorist offences. This kind of normative borrowing arguably increases the normative integration of transnational criminal law, although it leaves intact the plurality of sources of authority—international, regional, national—that enforce these norms. It is too loose to describe transnational criminal law as a non-hierarchical field of norms of similar content, type, and purpose.[83] Transnational criminal law is more accurately described as non-hierarchical order of formally equal national centres of legal authority based on reciprocity, equality, and sovereign consent,[84] which are interlinked, coexist, and overlap,[85] and uses norms of similar form to coordinate suppression of transnational crime. A domestic criminal lawyer dealing with the local impact of a transnational crime will only be concerned with that part of their national system that is transnational in origin and purpose. But the perpetration of a transnational crime has multifarious normative impacts; it reveals that the alleged transnational criminals are members of multiple normative communities.[86] Only a view which takes account of the inter-relationship of the rules of all those communities gets the full picture.

2.3 The System's Goals and Values

2.3.1 Effective suppression

The primary goal of transnational criminal law is effective suppression of transnational crime. Article 2(1) of the 1988 Drug Trafficking Convention, for example, provides that the purpose of the convention 'is to promote cooperation among the parties so that they may address more effectively the various aspects of the illicit traffic in narcotic drugs and psychotropic substances having an international dimension'. However, there are a number of factors that militate against the effectiveness of

---

[82] Additional Protocol to the South Asian Association for Regional Co-operation (SAARC) Regional Convention on Suppression of Terrorism, 6 January 2004; in force 12 January 2006.
[83] See Scott, above n 40, 868–72; a similar point is made by Gless and Vervaele, above n 81, 4.
[84] See RA Falk, 'International Jurisdiction: Horizontal and Vertical Conceptions of Legal Order' 32 *Temple Law Quarterly* (1959) 295.
[85] PS Berman, *Global Legal Pluralism: A Jurisprudence of Law Beyond Borders* (Cambridge: CUP, 2012), 25.
[86] ibid, 11.

international cooperation. Not all states are always equally committed to the effective suppression of every transnational crime. At the same time that Britain was working to suppress slavery, for example, it was engaged in the opium trade into China.[87] Moreover, pursuit of legal suppression at an international level does not always translate into practical suppression at a national level, and it is easy to overstate the coercive power of the suppression conventions, which is why in areas such as anti-money laundering and anti-terrorism there has been increasing resort to more easily mobilized norms in soft law and to Security Council resolutions.

2.3.2 Supply interdiction

Transnational criminal law can be conceived of as a system of trade barriers. The domestic consumption of goods, illicit in national law, that originate in other jurisdictions, drives resort to transnational criminal law. In most part it expresses a policy of supply interdiction, the idea that the interdiction and prosecution of chains of supply originating abroad are the only way to dry up local markets by increasing the price of these goods thus reducing demand. The human trafficking regime discussed in Chapter 4 is, for example, concerned largely with prosecuting human traffickers and not the individual users of sexual services. Only utter social pariahs, like possessors of child pornography, find that demand receives equally harsh treatment. This fails to take proper account of the responsibility of domestic consumption as a driver of supply.

Transnational criminal law has historically been preoccupied with the suppression of supply from developing states rather than demand in developed states. But this balance of interests is changing as demand for illicit products grows across the world. At the 2015 UN Commission on Crime Prevention and Criminal Justice (UNCCPCJ), for example the Turkish delegate said that '[t]he priority should be to stop terrorist fighters at their point of origin'.[88] The implication was that the duty of suppression was on the Western states which supplied these fighters and not on Turkey, the transit state to Syria and Iraq. Moreover, developed states can also be subject to intense international pressure to suppress transnational activity, as occurred when the United Kingdom (UK) was pressured to adopt the Bribery Act 2010 in response to an increasingly hostile attitude from the OECD's Working Group on Bribery.[89]

2.3.3 Security

Concern with supply interdiction is easily transformed into concern with transnational crime as an issue of general security, and in particular that transnational organized crime can threaten a state's internal sovereignty, both political and economic and by extension threaten international order. There is ample evidence of growth of that concern[90] and of

---

[87] P Andreas, 'Illicit Globalization: Myths, Misconceptions, and Historical Lessons' 126(3) *Political Science Quarterly* (2011) 403, 414.
[88] UNCCPCJ, Wednesday 20 May 2015 (notes on file with the author).
[89] Rose, above n 33, 29.
[90] A Dupont, 'Transnational Crime, Drugs and Security in Asia' 39(3) *Asian Survey* (1999) 433.

the growth in the security establishment's interest in developing different prohibition regimes in transnational criminal law to combat transnational organized crime.[91] In 2012 the President of the UN Security Council, supported by the Council, articulated a concern not just about terrorism (where it has engaged in regular action) but about all cross-border trafficking as a threat to international peace and security, and implicitly questioned whether the existing approach relying largely on the suppression conventions, was sufficient to provide an adequate response.[92]

2.3.4 Preservation of sovereignty

Ironically, while the sovereign interests of states are the main drivers of transnational criminal law, national sovereignty and non-interference in internal affairs present the most significant barriers to the development of transnational criminal law. States are primarily concerned with the establishment and enforcement of their own criminal jurisdiction and the limitation of the criminal jurisdiction of other states. The suppression conventions express these contradictory concerns. Article 2(2) of the 1988 Drug Trafficking Convention, for example, provides that '[t]he Parties shall carry out their obligations under this Convention in a manner consistent with the principles of sovereign equality and territorial integrity of States and that of non-intervention in the domestic affairs of other States'.

Sovereignty may shield criminal justice incapacity. States with strong external but weak internal sovereignty cannot manage the transnational criminal activity that emanates from within their boundaries. However, their sovereignty forces other states affected by this crime to pressure them for ever greater levels of cooperation and to provide technical assistance to facilitate this cooperation. Although this cooperation is couched in the language of reciprocity, developed states in particular have had, and continue to have, an inordinate amount of influence on transnational criminal law. In contrast, developing states struggle to defend themselves from the overreach of more powerful states keen on exporting their domestic criminal law. Vlassis notes:

> Dominant amongst the concerns remains safeguarding sovereignty, which is for many smaller developing countries and countries with economies in transition (or emerging democracies) the last bastion of national integrity and identity. Criminal justice matters are at the core of sovereignty concerns, being perceived as essentially domestic in nature, touching as they are on institutions ranging from national constitutions to legal regimes and systems.[93]

Sovereignty may also shield unwillingness. States may have political differences that make it difficult for them to cooperate. The US, for example, regularly refused to extradite Irish Republican Army members to the UK because it considered them political offenders.

---

[91] A Edwards and P Gill, 'The Politics of "Transnational Organized Crime": Discourse, Reflexivity and the Narration of "Threat"' 4(2) *The British Journal of Politics and International Relations* (2002) 245.

[92] PRST/2012/16, Presidential Statement by US Ambassador Susan Rice, 25 April 2012.

[93] D Vlassis, 'The United Nations Convention Against Transnational Organized Crime and Its Protocols: A New Era in International Cooperation' in *The Changing Face of International Criminal Law* (Vancouver, BC: International Centre for Criminal Law Reform and Criminal Justice, 2002) 75, 76.

Sovereignty, however, always implies difference. Working within civil, common law, mixed, and other legal traditions, states have different constitutional arrangements, unrecognizable administrative arrangements, unfamiliar procedures, distinct grammars of criminal law, all spelled out in their own national languages. Effective international cooperation often requires the surrender of long-held rules or procedures of national criminal law and the introduction of entirely novel ones, and states are deeply resistant to these changes during the negotiation and implementation of the suppression conventions.

2.3.5 Legitimacy

Transnational criminal law can be criticized from the perspective of normative legitimacy,[94] because of limited participation, transparency, and accountability in its development and implementation. Designed by technical legal experts, the public has very little knowledge and little say in the process. It is easy to point fingers at organizations like the FATF but treaty-based bodies such as the UN Convention against Corruption's Implementation Review Group are notably less transparent than the FATF.[95] Domestic lawmakers who transform these international norms into criminal laws may be as ignorant as the general public. The absence of democratic legitimacy has been specifically criticized because of criminal law's importance as a tool of social control, an expression of a community's culture and history, in the hands of elected leaders.[96] However, this criticism only bites in regard to those states that embrace democracy. Many undemocratic states are willing partners in transnational criminal law, which raises the further question of whether and if so to what extent democratic states should cooperate with them.

The conclusion of a treaty injects an element of global legitimacy into the suppression of transnational crime because of the nominal equality of the negotiating parties, opportunities for debate and dissent,[97] and the fact that the parties consent to these international obligations. In consenting, however, states act for their own contingent reasons, which may have little to do with pursuit of normative legitimacy. Moreover, in this process there is a tendency for some states to be active 'law-givers' while the majority are passive 'law-takers'.[98] A number of inducements contribute to this normative transfer: the prestige of the law-givers, shared legal traditions, accessibility of their laws,[99] promises of technical assistance, the potential increase in the penal power

---

[94] On normative legitimacy see A Buchanan, 'The Legitimacy of International Law' in S Besson and J Tasioulas (eds), *The Philosophy of International Law* (Oxford: OUP, 2010), 79.

[95] Rose, above n 33, 41.

[96] T Weigend, 'Strafrecht durch internationale Verinbarungen—Verlust an nationaler Strafrechtskultur?' 105 *Zeitschrift für die gesamte Strafrechtswissenschaft* (1993) 774, 789.

[97] ME Beare, 'Shifting Boundaries—between States, Enforcement Agencies, and Priorities' in HG Albrecht and C Fijnaut (eds), *The Containment of Transnational Organized Crime* (Freiburg: Iuscrim, 2002), 171, 185.

[98] See S Silbey, '1886 Presidential Address: "Let Them Eat Cake": Globalization, Postmodern Colonialism, and the Possibilities of Justice' 31 *Law and Society Review* (1997) 207, 221.

[99] Conditions for transferability isolated by A Watson, 'Legal Change: Sources of Law and Legal Culture' in 131 *University of Pennsylvania Law Review* (1982) 1121, 1147.

of the law-takers, political pressure, perception of domestic threats, and concern for the rule of law.[100] Criminalization in the name of universal values has served as a transparent disguise for instrumentalism based on domestic criminal law models.[101] Britain used the abolition of the slave trade to legitimize policing the high seas.[102] Suppression of drug trafficking has long served the US as a similar normative justification. Referring to the policy of drug prohibition in 1951 US Drug Commissioner and representative on the UN Commission on Narcotic Drugs, Harry Anslinger, said: 'If the World were at peace the US with its prestige and dollars could whip the rest of the world into line through international agreements.'[103] More recently, the US's expansion of interest in regard to transnational crime generally has resulted in macro-level transplantation of American models through international law into the national laws of many different states. [104] This transnational interventionism[105] is particularly troublesome when the policies in question are being laundered in developing states, a subtle form of neo-colonialism.[106] McCulloch comments:

> Under the pretext of criminal justice agendas, transnational crime has allowed the penetration of concerns and interests of strong states into the sovereign domain of weaker states. These agendas are internationalized in asymmetrical ways that reflect the interests of the stronger states, but are packaged in ways that suggest more neutral and universal concerns over morally repugnant or socially damaging behaviors, such as terrorism, people smuggling, sex trafficking, organized crime, money laundering, and drug trafficking.[107]

Support for intervention usually emanates from groups within a state; the state is simply the vehicle for its expression. For example, pharmaceutical companies played a role in the development of the drug control system,[108] while Western NGOs continue to play a significant role in fostering treaty development in their respective areas of concern. Transnational criminal law thus reflects a multiplicity of domestic concerns; it is their legal expression in relations with other states that gives an illusion of a uniform position on the problem.

---

[100] See P Lloyd, B Simmons, and B Stewart, 'Combating Transnational Crime: The Role of Learning and Norm Diffusion in the Current Rule of Law Wave' in M Zürn, A Nollkaemper, and R Peerenboom (eds), *Rule of Law Dynamics: In an Era of International and Transnational Governance*, 1st edn (Cambridge: CUP, 2012), 164, 165.

[101] See generally P Andreas and E Nadelmann, *Policing the Globe: Criminalization and Crime Control in International Relations* (New York: OUP, 2006), 17, 105.

[102] M Mazower, *Governing the Word: The History of an Idea* (London: Allen Lane, 2012), 395–96.

[103] Pennsylvania State University, Special Collections, Historical Collections and Labor Archive, Harry Anslinger Papers, Box 5, File 11, Scrapbooks, as quoted in the 'New York World Telegraph', 7 August 1951.

[104] M Delmas-Marty, *Ordering Pluralism: A Conceptual Framework for Understanding the Transnational Legal World* trans by Naomi Norberg (Oxford and Portland: Hart, 2009), 107 citing her own work, *Les Forces imaginantes du droit (I): Le Relatif et l'Universel* (Paris: Seuil, 2004).

[105] A term used by D Corva, 'Neoliberal Globalization and the War on Drugs: Transnationalizing Illiberal Governance in the Americas' 27 *Political Geography* (2008) 176, 184.

[106] Kotiswaran and Palmer, above n 41, 85.

[107] J McCulloch, 'Transnational Crime as a Productive Fiction' 34(2) *Social Justice* (2007) 19, 27.

[108] J Lilja, S Salek, A Alvarez, and D Hamilton, *Pharmaceutical Systems: Global Perspectives* (Chichester: Wiley and Sons, 2008), 13.

Opportunities for debate are also rare during the operationalization of these agreements.[109] Transnational law enforcement networks[110] composed of national officials playing both an international and transnational role, assist both in the design of the international obligation at the macro-level and its fleshing out at the meso and micro levels. It is these lower level contacts where the bulk of the actual 'technology transfer' of policy, model laws, practical know-how, administrative arrangements, and institutions takes place, all part of the Western *mission civilisatrice*.[111] The agents of this transfer are largely unaccountable whether they work for sponsoring states, intergovernmental organizations, NGOs, or receiving states. When implemented these changes may be held up by weak domestic legal capacity, unenthusiastic local political elites, basic incompatibilities of values and criminal laws, and the national margin of appreciation permitted by the suppression conventions which differs from regime to regime. If taken up, they may overburden the creaking criminal justice infrastructure of developing states.

As noted above, more recently powerful Western states have tried to escape the limitations of the multilateral suppression conventions by developing systems of soft law even less respectful of state consent, like the FATF standards. They have been working in the European Union, the Council of Europe, the G8, and other organizations to develop these alternative normative pathways so as to avoid having to reach consensus; other states may join in but only on Western terms and their membership is vetted.[112] These new pathways provide tougher more enforceable standards but their legitimacy is even more questionable.

Legitimacy is, however, a key ingredient in the effective implementation of transnational criminal law. Cotterrell notes that from a Weberian perspective the main problem of transnational criminalization is whether there is adequate political authority to engage in this activity, while from a Durkheimian perspective the issue is whether there is adequate cultural authority to do so.[113] Thus while for Weber the formal authority of states to agree to and enact crimes would be enough, for Durkheim these crimes should be regarded by citizens in different states as constituting a serious threat to the moral security of their societies if they are to be effective. However, the common rationalization of transnational criminal law reform—our purposes are the same so our legal differences are irrelevant—does not create a community. Nor does the rhetorical reference in UN documents to a mythic international community. Nor do rhetorical tropes such as the claim that pirates are enemies of all mankind, when piracy is actually based on the convergent economic interests of states in keeping transnational

[109] Beare, above n 97, 185.
[110] On transnational networks see A-M Slaughter, *A New World Order* (Princeton, NJ: Princeton UP, 2004), 231.
[111] See D Dolowitz and D Marsh, 'Who Learns From Whom? A Review of the Policy Transfer Literature' 44 *Political Studies* (1996) 343, 344.
[112] U Sieber, 'The Forces Behind the Harmonisation of Criminal Law' in M Delmas-Marty, M Pieth, and U Sieber (eds), *Les Chemins de l'harmonisation penale* (Paris: Société de Législation Comparée, 2008), 385, 412.
[113] R Cotterrell, 'The Concept of Crime and Transnational Networks of Community' in V Mitsilegas, P Alldridge, and L Cheliotis (eds), *Globalisation, Criminal Law and Criminal Justice* (London: Hart, 2015), 7, 10 et seq.

trade open. Cotterrell concludes: 'Like all transnational law, transnational criminal law has to find secure grounding in populations that can culturally 'own' this law. To ignore that requirement is to risk stretching the politico-legal authority of regulation beyond the point where its success can be assumed.'[114]

The problem is how to make transnational criminal law more accountable to the communities in which it is applied. It has been suggested that it would be sounder to pursue the harmonization of responses to transnational crime based on a set of principles rather than on more specific provisions, thus leaving intact a mosaic of systems dealing with similar problems.[115] This 'lighter' touch requires a more adaptable regulatory concept such as functional equivalence, mutual recognition, or graded compatibility, one that preserves national flexibility sufficient to adjust to international obligations.[116] This regulatory concept could be part of a framework of general concepts or governing principles that guide the development of principles more specific to particular crimes. One such general principle might be an outcomes-based principle which would test each new transnational criminal policy to ensure a measurable equal benefit for all. Another might be a precautionary principle: a willingness to question criminalization and procedural cooperation as a response to certain practices. It also seems essential to make legality and respect for human rights governing principles.

2.3.6 Legality

The principle of legality (*nullum crimen sine lege*—no crime without law),[117] implies that legislation must define clearly offences and the penalties they attract, placing the individual in a position where they know or are reasonably able to discover which acts or omissions will make them criminally liable.[118] There is no clear framework of legality principles applied consistently in transnational criminal law because transnational criminal law entails a multiplicity of domestic legal systems in loose array. This raises questions about the procedural legitimacy of transnational criminal law. The principle of fair warning demands—particularly if the crime is relatively obscure—that the offender should be warned in advance of the transgressive potential of their conduct. Obligations in cooperating states to enact the same offence meet the requirements of legality because this enables fair warning. If a state unilaterally establishes extraterritorial criminal jurisdiction to suppress the activities of individuals located in another state without similar laws being enacted in that state, legality demands that mistake or ignorance of the law should be an excuse.[119] If that state is party to a suppression convention criminalizing the conduct it cannot rely on the existence of the treaty to establish a reasonable basis for fair warning. The principle of certainty requires that a state suppressing a particular transnational crime—say money laundering—proscribe

---

[114] ibid, 22.   [115] Delmas-Marty, above n 104, 14, 17 et seq.

[116] ibid, 159, 161 citing JF Coste and M Delmas-Marty, *Le Genre humain* (Paris: Seuil, 1998), 135.

[117] Article 11(2) of the Universal Declaration of Human Rights, GA Res 2174 (III), UN Doc A/810, 71, 10 December 1948; see K Gallant, *The Principle of Legality in International and Comparative Criminal Law* (Cambridge: CUP, 2008), 11 et seq.

[118] *Bacelar de Souza Machada v Portugal*, [2000] ECHR 233, para 145.

[119] S Gless, 'General Principles of Transnational Criminal Law', Paper given at a Joint Conference of the ICCLR and ISRCL, 8 August 2011, Ottawa.

the conduct with precision, in order to give clear warning of this proscription. What is not clear is, if the offender is in State A, but commits a crime in State B, whether both states must proscribe the conduct in the same way or in a similar way in order to meet the dictates of legality. In order to respect legality, states that seek closer cooperation in the suppression of transnational crime must also respect fair labelling, individuality of guilt, and the prohibition on retroactive application of crimes.

2.3.7 Human rights

Certain transnational offences harm individuals directly and put their individual rights in danger while others endanger collectively held rights like public health. The duty on states to protect individual victims from transnational crime is not usually explicitly recognized in the suppression conventions. An exception is article 33 of the Convention on the Rights of the Child,[120] which obliges parties to take all appropriate measures to protect children from illicit use of narcotics and prevent their being used in illicit production and trafficking. Provisions in some suppression conventions also put states under an explicit obligation to help those already victimized by transnational crime.[121]

The enforcement of transnational criminal law threatens human rights in various ways. Drug laws may threaten the property rights of innocent farmers caught up in drug eradication operations involving the use of herbicides. Innocent bank account holders may find their privacy violated by banks adhering to AML regulations. Trafficked persons may be subject to detention as illegal aliens rather than treated as the victims of crime. Fugitives may be denied the right to be informed of an extradition request, the right to be heard, and the right to legal representation. Unfair trial may follow. Legal assistance in evidence gathering may not be available for exculpatory purposes. Cruel and inhuman punishment may be imposed, including the death penalty. Although the goal must be to balance the suppression of crime and the respect for human rights,[122] that balance is currently heavily skewed in favour of suppression. The 1988 Drug Trafficking Convention, for example 'is deliberately draconian in character'[123] and has, as we shall see in Chapter 6, spawned even more draconian national laws. The suppression conventions themselves pay only scant regard to the protection of the human rights of those affected by their enforcement. Article 11(3) of the UN Convention against Transnational Organized Crime,[124] for example, obliges parties to have 'due regard to the rights of the defence' but only in the context of the obligation 'to seek to ensure that conditions imposed in connection with decisions to release

---

[120] 20 November 1989, 1577 UNTS 3.

[121] See the examples in N Boister, 'Human Rights Protection in the Suppression Conventions' 2 *Human Rights Law Review* (2002) 199.

[122] J Dugard and C Van den Wyngaert, 'Reconciling Extradition with Human Rights' 92 *American Journal of International Law* (1998) 187.

[123] *Commentary on the United Nations Convention Against Illicit Traffic in Narcotic Drugs and Psychotropic Substances, 1988* (New York: UN, 1998) UN Doc. E/CN.7/590; UN Publication Sales No.E.98.XI.5, 144.

[124] United Nations Convention against Transnational Organized Crime, New York, 15 November 2000, 2225 UNTS 209, in force 29 September 2003.

pending trial or appeal take into consideration the need to ensure the presence of the defendant at subsequent criminal proceedings'.

In place of specific protections contained in the conventions, the system relies on the existing human rights obligations of states. The obligation to provide 'fair treatment' in article 17 of the International Convention for the Suppression of the Financing of Terrorism, for example, refers to applicable protections in domestic and international law.[125] In practice, this means that the level of human rights protection available to a perpetrator or victim of transnational crime will be that generally available in the particular state in which they find themselves. This will depend on: whether that state is a party to a relevant human rights treaty (and in particular, to a regional human rights treaty with rights of individual petition); whether that state accepts that older human rights treaty obligations trump its application of a newer obligation under a suppression convention (some states may find it difficult to accept that human rights constitute a superior normative order, particularly if they are heavily engaged in the effective suppression of crime);[126] whether that state has made adequate provision for the protection of human rights in its national law; and whether, if that state is requested by another to cooperate, it is prepared to enquire into potential human rights violations in the requesting state.

The suppression of transnational crime and international human rights protections are out of alignment.[127] To achieve the correct balance, the individual defendant will have to be seen not as an object but as a rights holder. This can be done, it has been argued, by ensuring a global *nemo bis in idem* rule, rules for the coordination of enforcement of jurisdiction, and the provision of a functional equivalent to constitutional protections for citizens to aliens accused of transnational crimes guaranteeing them the rights to a fair trial.[128]

2.4 Conclusion

A range of different approaches have been adopted by states to overcome the difficulties of cooperating in the suppression of transnational crime. In 1990 Heymann argued that states adopted more formal legal relations with less compatible states and more informal relations with more compatible states.[129] He suggested that when states have strong legal and political differences they tend to adopt an 'international law' approach characterized by precise treaty obligations which respect sovereignty but which sacrifice effectiveness. Where states have better relations and trust each other they tend to adopt a 'prosecutorial' approach characterized by more informal

---

[125] New York, 9 December, 1999, 2178 UNTS 197, in force 10 April 2002.

[126] See R Currie, 'Human Rights and International Mutual Legal Assistance: Resolving the Tension' 11 *Criminal Law Forum* (2000) 167.

[127] RJ Currie, 'The Protection of Human Rights in the Suppression of Transnational Crime' in N Boister and RJ Currie (eds), *The Routledge Handbook of Transnational Criminal Law* (Abingdon: Routledge, 2015), 27.

[128] Gless, above n 61, 130–34.

[129] PB Heymann, 'Two Models of National Attitudes toward International Co-operation in Law Enforcement' 31 *Harvard International Law Journal* (1990) 99, 102.

reciprocal relations where effectiveness is a priority and sovereignty and formality are less important. This dichotomy reflects the classic distinction between restrictive and permissive models in international relations.[130] It echoes Kuhn's point made in the Introduction to this chapter about whether suppression of transnational crime is best achieved through a standardization of national approaches or a less restrictive more goal-directed procedural (and more recently administrative) cooperation against transnational crime. The indeterminacy in the nature of transnational criminal law arises out of the simultaneous use of a range of these strategies in different prohibition regimes. In the suppression of transnational crime, penal power has been jealously guarded by the state. But the international framing of that power, and the function of suppressing similar activities in different places, has created a perceptible system of transnational criminal law.

---

[130] See GA Raymond, 'Problems and Prospects in the Study of International Norms' 41 *Mershon International Studies Review* (1997) 205, 229.

PART II
CRIMES

3

Piracy and Maritime Safety Offences

3.1 Introduction

The crime of piracy is designed to ensure maintenance of the freedom of the high seas[1] and suppress criminal activity that interferes with it. This chapter argues that piracy is the first historical example of a transnational crime. It discusses the history of the crime and then examines the elements of the modern forms of piracy and of the maritime security offences developed under the auspices of the International Maritime Organization (IMO), exposing how the shortcomings of the former led to the development of the latter. The recent resurgence of piracy in international waters makes this discussion of significant practical importance.

3.2 The Nature of Piracy

The piracy of commercial shipping is an ancient practice, common when other forms of coastal economic activity are not as lucrative. The absence of official sanction distinguishes it from privateering, which is directed against a state's enemies during wartime.[2] The upsurge in piracy in the waters off Somalia in the last decade has drawn a lot of attention to the nature and shortcomings of the crime. The IMO listed 489 incidents of piracy and armed robbery against ships in 2010.[3] Said to be a response to massive illegal fishing and dumping of waste in Somali waters,[4] piracy quickly entrenched itself as what the United Nations Office on Drugs and Crime (UNODC) called transnational organized crime.[5] Heavily armed pirates operated from shore or from previously captured 'mother-ships' in small high-speed skiffs, taking both vessels and crew and holding them for large ransoms. The impact on shipping was high and the cost in ransoms paid, insurance costs, re-routing of ships, security equipment, naval forces, prosecutions, anti-piracy organizations and costs to regional

---

[1] Article 87 of the United Nations Convention on the Law of the Sea, Montego Bay, 10 December 1982, 1833 UNTS 3, in force 16 November 1994.

[2] The Paris Declaration Respecting Maritime Law in 1856 abolished all forms of privateering.

[3] IMO, *Reports of Acts of Piracy and Armed Robbery against Ships: Annual Report 2010*, MSC.4/Circ.169 1 April 2011, para 5.

[4] T Dagne, 'Somalia: Prospects for Lasting Peace' 20(2) *Mediterranean Quarterly* (2009) 95, 106. While the UN Secretary-General suggests there is little to substantiate this claim (Report of the Secretary-General Pursuant to Security Council Resolution 2020 (2011) UN Doc. S/2012/783, 22 October 2012, paras 64 et seq), the Contact Group on Piracy off the Coast of Somalia (CGPCS) called for Somalia to declare an exclusive economic zone (EEZ) in order to promote 'effective governance' of the waters off Somalia. CGPCS, 13th Plenary Session, Communique, 11 December 2012.

[5] UNODC, *Awash with Money—Organized Crime and Its Financial Links to Somalia*, 25 May 2011, available at <http://www.unodc.org/unodc/en/frontpage/2011/May/awash-with-money---organized-crime-and-its-financial-links-to-somali-piracy.html?ref=fs1> last visited 11 August 2016.

economies was estimated in 2010 at between \$7 billion and \$12 billion per annum.[6] Recent steps against piracy have, however, had a suppressing effect and there has been a sharp decline in Somali piracy since 2012. The International Maritime Bureau (IMB) Piracy Reporting Centre notes there were 190 incidents globally in 2015, a significant drop from the 439 reported in 2011.[7] Although attention has shifted back to more traditional areas of concern including the coast of West Africa and South-East Asia, Somalia is still considered a potential threat if the law enforcement effort falters.

3.3 Piracy: International or Transnational Crime?

Piracy is a crime of universal jurisdiction on the high seas. Gardner considers that 'the point of defining the crime of piracy under international law is, in many respects, to define and therefore circumscribe the extent to which states may exercise universal jurisdiction over the citizens and ships of other countries'.[8] This jurisdictional function has led to divergent views on the legal nature of piracy. The orthodox view that it is an offence under customary international law was set out by the Permanent Court of International Justice in the *Lotus Case*:

> As the scene of the pirate's operations is the high seas, which it is not the right or duty of any nation to police, he is denied the protection of the flag which he may carry, and is treated as an outlaw, as the enemy of mankind—*hostis humani generis*—whom any nation may in the interest of all capture and punish.[9]

The narrower view is that piracy is defined but not criminalized in international law, and that it is only a special jurisdiction permitting states to take enforcement action on the high seas against vessels flying the flags of or registered in other states (in an exception to exclusive flag state jurisdiction on the high seas) because of the threat to the particular state (ie they act only in their own interests). Support for this view can be found in the origins of piracy in the extension of sovereignty over the sea through the instrumentality of naval power.[10] In *Rex v Dawson and others*,[11] for example, the Court held that '[t]he king of England hath not only an empire and sovereignty over the British seas, but also an undoubted jurisdiction and power, in concurrency with other princes and states, for the punishment of all piracies and robberies at sea'.

The authors of the 1932 Harvard Research in International Law, Draft Convention on Piracy with Comments,[12] argued that as there was neither an international agency to capture pirates nor international tribunal to punish them, piracy was not an international crime but an 'extraordinary jurisdiction in every state to seize and to prosecute

[6] Oceans Beyond Piracy, *The Economic Costs of Piracy*, <http://www.saveourseafarers.com/assets/files/The_Economic_Cost_of_Piracy_Summary.pdf> last visited 11 May 2016.
[7] International Maritime Bureau's Piracy Reporting Centre, <https://www.icc-ccs.org/piracy-reporting-centre/piracynewsafigures> last visited 11 May 2016.
[8] M Gardner, 'Piracy Prosecutions in Domestic Courts' (2012) 10 *Journal of International Criminal Justice* 797, 808 citing Harvard Research Draft Piracy, 757, 782.
[9] (1927) PCIJ Reports Series A No.10, para 236.
[10] AP Rubin, *The Law of Piracy*, 2nd edn (Irvington on Hudson: Transnational, 1997), 41–42.
[11] 13 *State Trials* (1696), 451, 455.
[12] 26 *Supplement to the American Journal of International Law* (1932), 739, 756.

and punish persons and to seize and dispose of property'.[13] The lack of enthusiasm among states for the inclusion of piracy within the jurisdiction of the International Criminal Court (ICC) supports this view; piracy was excluded from the International Law Commission (ILC) Draft Statute for the ICC because the preponderance of views was that it was no longer considered a sufficiently international crime.[14]

Piracy is arguably a prototype transnational crime designed to respond to threats to the commercial interests of states that occur on the high seas, an area beyond the territorial jurisdiction of every state. It is a transnational crime for three reasons. First, the pirates commonly cross from the jurisdiction of the flag state of the vessel they are in into the jurisdiction of the flag state of the vessel that they are pirating—so the criminal activity is trans-national. Second, because the activity of suppression of the pirates commonly crosses from the jurisdiction of the flag state of the policing vessel into the jurisdiction of the flag state of the pirate's vessel. Finally, because enforcement is pursued by individual countries and not by the international community as a whole acting *eo nomine*.

3.4 The Definition of the Crime of Piracy

From the 1600s persons who engaged in robbery or an act of private violence on the high seas were generally considered *hostis humanis generis*. The definition of piracy, however, varied in state practice. In the seventeenth century English law defined piracy as 'sea-robbery' requiring a violent dispossession committed with *animus furandi*, an intention to rob a vessel on the high seas or in territorial waters.[15] While in the nineteenth century the US Supreme Court had defined piracy as robbery on the high seas,[16] the Federal Statute of 1909[17] simply referred to piracy 'as defined by the law of nations'. Variation of definition led the Harvard Research to conclude in the 1920s that 'piracy under the law of nations and piracy under municipal law are entirely different subject matters' and to lament the absence of a settled definition in customary international law.[18] In 1934 the Privy Council in *In re Piracy Jure Gentium*[19] expanded the definition of piracy in custom to include attempts to commit piracy.

Piracy was finally given a definition, now considered to reflect customary international law,[20] in article 15 of the 1958 High Seas Convention,[21] which was replicated in article 101 of the 1982 UN Convention on the Law of the Sea (UNCLOS):[22]

---

[13] See Rubin, above n 10, 341.

[14] ILC, *Report of the International Law Commission on the Work of its Forty-Sixth Session*, Report no A/49/10 (1994), 68.

[15] *Rex v Dawson*, above n 11.

[16] *United States v Furlong* (*United States v Pirates*) 18 US (5 Wheat) 184 (1820); *United States v Smith*, 18 US (5 Wheat) 153 (1820).

[17] 18 USC § 1651.

[18] Harvard Research in International Law, 'Draft Convention on Piracy', 26 *Supplement to the American Journal of International Law* (1932) 739, 749, 763.

[19] [1934] AC 586, 600.

[20] D Guilfoyle, 'The Legal Challenges in Fighting Piracy' in B van Ginkel and FP van der Putten (eds), *The International Response to Somali Piracy: Challenges and Opportunities* (Leiden: Martinus Nijhoff, 2010), 127, 128.

[21] Convention on the High Seas, Geneva, 29 April 1958, 450 UNTS 11, in force 30 September 1962.

[22] Montego Bay, 10 December 1982, 1833 UNTS 3, in force 16 November 1994.

Piracy consists of any of the following acts:

(a) Any illegal acts of violence or detention, or any act of depredation, committed for private ends by the crew or the passengers of a private ship or private aircraft, and directed:
  (i) on the high seas against another ship or aircraft, or against persons or property on board such ships and aircraft;
  (ii) against a ship, aircraft, persons or property in a place outside the jurisdiction of any state;
(b) Any act of voluntary participation in the operation of a ship or an aircraft with knowledge of facts making it a pirate ship or aircraft.
(c) Any act of inciting or of intentionally facilitating an act described in paras (a) or (b).

The UNCLOS definition has been used in a number of international instruments.[23]

3.5 The Elements of the Crime of Piracy

3.5.1 Violence, detention, or depredation

Article 101(1)'s definition includes '[a]ny illegal acts of violence or detention, or any act of depredation'. These acts must be intentional. National case law holds that intentional acts constitute piracy even if they are rapidly repelled.[24] The acts must be 'illegal' in the sense they have been criminalized by the state taking jurisdiction and cannot be justified for example through self-defence or some other justified conduct under domestic law or the laws of war. Piracy's conduct element is thus broader than acts committed *animo furandi*. The idea of piracy as sea-robbery persists, however. Charges of piracy laid by the US (a non-party to United Nations Convention on the Law of the Sea (UNCLOS)) against six Somalis who attacked a US Naval vessel were dismissed, for example, because following the definition of piracy in early US case law (rather than in customary law which was considered too vague to serve as a basis for criminal liability) they did not rob, board, or take control of the ship.[25] In contrast, five Somalis were convicted of piracy for an attack on a US Naval vessel they thought was a merchant vessel, and the court placed explicit reliance on article 101's more expansive definition which does not require the intention to rob.[26] The latter analysis was ruled correct on appeal,[27] and is to be preferred because piracy is more than just a property crime and involves threats or violence. Moreover the definition in article 101

---

[23] Eg, the Djibouti Code of Conduct—The Code of Conduct Concerning the Repression of Piracy and Armed Robbery against Ships in the Western Indian Ocean and the Gulf of Aden, IMO Council Doc C 102/14, Annex (2009) 29 January 2009, available at <http://www.imo.org/OurWork/Security/PIU/Documents/DCoC%20English.pdf> last visited 12 August 2016.

[24] *Republic of Seychelles v Dahir* [2010] SCSC (26 July 2010).

[25] *United States v Said* 757 F Supp 2d 554 (ED Va 2010), relying on *United States v Smith* 18 US 153 (1820).

[26] *United States v Hasan* 747 F Supp 2d 554 (ED Va 2010); see also the Kenyan decision *Republic v Hassan Mohamud Ahmed*, Criminal Case No 434 of 2006, 155 (Chief Magistrates Court, 1 November 2006).

[27] *United States v Dire* 680 F 3d 446 (4th Cir 2012), 469.

is sufficiently precise and is capable of evolving to function as a more effective instrument against piracy.[28]

Article 101(1)'s definition nevertheless has limitations. It does not expressly include inchoate offences such as attempts, important in practice because pirates are usually/ideally apprehended on their way to commit piracy and not during or after the act. Under article 101(2), however, piracy includes voluntary participation in a pirate vessel—a vessel used for or intended for use in piracy or which is under the control of pirates—with knowledge of the facts that make it a pirate vessel. This can be used to suppress actions of a preparatory nature once pirates are at sea, although not the earlier processes of gathering material support for the piratical action. Article 101(3) extends piracy to any act of inciting or facilitating such a pirate act, which arguably includes financing or organizing piracy. In convicting a Somali go-between who negotiated the release of hostages but took a cut, the court in *United States v Ali*[29] held that 'facilitating' was equivalent to aiding and abetting (although not conspiracy), and that a 'facilitative act need not occur on the high seas so long as the predicate offence has'.

3.5.2 The limitation to acts for private ends

Under the customary definition of piracy, an attack carried out by the armed forces of a state or an unrecognized belligerent power on vessels of a state with which they are at war is not piracy. Early commentators disagreed on the breadth of this exception: Gentili believed all depredations on the sea illegal unless authorized by a sovereign, while Grotius's view was that only those who had banded together to commit crime implicitly for their own gain were pirates.[30] Article 101(1) broadens this exception, restricting piracy to attacks made for 'private ends', following a formula introduced by the League of Nations and Harvard Research without any basis in previous state practice.[31] However, the breadth of this exception is still in dispute.

One issue is whether private ends excludes political purposes. States tend to be wary of accepting the label of politically motivated conduct as piracy. For example, when the Portuguese-registered passenger ship *Santa Maria* was seized in 1961 by Portuguese dissidents, although Portugal's Government called it piracy and asked for help in their pursuit,[32] no government agreed with the classification or offered help. In the *Achille Lauro* incident an Italian-registered cruise liner was taken by force by members of the Popular Liberation Front of Palestine, who then executed a Jewish-American hostage.[33] The hijackers made their way to Egypt but were captured fleeing

---

[28] SB Richard, '*United States v Dire*: Somali Pirates, and the Fourth Circuit's Choice to Apply an Evolving "Law of Nations" to the Problem' 36 *Boston College International and Comparative Law Review* (2014) 76, 89.

[29] 718 F3d 929 (DC Cir 2013), 933, 937, 941.

[30] DM Johnston, *The Historical Foundations of World Order: The Tower and the Arena* (Leiden: Nijhoff, 2008) 401.

[31] See D Guilfoyle, *Shipping Interdiction and the Law of the Sea* (Cambridge: CUP, 2009), 32 et seq.

[32] See BH Dubner, 'On the Definition of the Crime of Sea Piracy Revisited: Customary vs. Treaty Law and the Jurisdictional Implications Thereof' 42 *Journal of Maritime Law and Commerce* (2011) 71, 146.

[33] See N Ronzitti, 'The Law of the Sea and the Use of Force against Terrorist Activities' in N Ronzitti (ed), *Maritime Terrorism and International Law* (Dordrecht: Nijhoff, 1990), 1.

Egypt after their plane was forced down by US warplanes in Sicily and finally prosecuted by Italy, which had flag state jurisdiction. Although they did not represent
a state, their claim to be fighting for Palestinian self-determination was enough to
ensure that the accused were not convicted of piracy but of 'kidnapping for terrorist
ends that caused the death of a person'. Although not piracy but an internal hijacking,
this example further illustrates the political wariness of labelling politically motivated actions piracy. Political violence at sea of this kind is more prudently dealt with
through the Convention on the Suppression of Unlawful Acts against the Safety of
Maritime Navigation or SUA Convention (discussed further below).[34]

An emerging challenge is whether the actions of environmental activists can be
labelled piracy. In 1986 the Belgian Court of Cassation decided that Greenpeace activists who boarded and damaged ships involved in dumping waste at sea were acting for
private ends.[35] More recently a US Court called members of the Sea Shepherd organization pirates for boarding whaling vessels in an attempt to impede them.[36] This view
has been criticized on the argument that they were acting in the interests of the public
as a whole.[37]

Some commentators argue that private ends are not limited to those for personal
gain only, taking the view that it is undesirable to permit the collateral motives or
purposes of an offender to control the subject matter of state jurisdiction.[38] Yet this
narrower interpretation has support from the IMO's legal committee[39] and in state
practice.[40] The narrower interpretation also supports the view that piracy is a transnational crime and that pirates are not the enemies of all mankind but of commercial
interests.

3.5.3 The 'two ship' requirement

Article 101(a)(i) also requires that the illegal conduct be 'directed' 'against another ship
or aircraft, or against persons or property on board such ships and aircraft' ('private
ship' includes any seagoing vessel including military vessels that are no longer in the
control of the state). This implies that the conduct must originate from another ship
and that criminal acts by the crew or mutiny against the captain do not fall within the
scope of piracy. Acts of mutiny or other forms of internal seizure such as the *Achille
Lauro* thus fall outside of the scope of piracy, but do fall within the jurisdiction of the
flag state in regard to other applicable crimes.[41]

---

[34] In *Dahir* above n 24, at paras 37 and 47, the Seychelles Supreme Court refused to entertain a charge
of terrorism and piracy as alternatives reasoning that the private ends requirement precluded the charge
of terrorism.

[35] *Castle John and Nederlandse Stichting Sirius v NV Mabeco and NV Parfin* 77 ILR 537 (1986).

[36] *Institute of Cetacean Research v Sea Shepherd Conservation Society* 725 F3d 940 (9th Cir 2013).

[37] W Magnuson, 'Marine Conservation Campaigners as Pirates: The Consequences of Sea Shepherd'
44 *Environmental Law* (2014), 924.

[38] See Guilfoyle, above n 31, 32.

[39] IMO Legal Committee, *Piracy: Uniform and Consistent Application of the Provisions of International
Conventions Relating to Piracy*, Leg 98/8, 18 February 2011, para 9.

[40] See Magnuson above n 37, 949 et seq.   [41] Article 94 of UNCLOS.

3.5.4 The limitation to the high seas

Article 101(a) of UNCLOS limits piratical acts to those taking place (i) on the high seas or (ii) in other places outside the jurisdiction of any state. An act equivalent to piracy that occurs within the territorial waters of a state is armed robbery at sea. The shrinking extent of the high seas (through the extension of territorial seas from three to twelve nautical miles[42] and the application of straight baselines) thus diminishes the scope of piracy (although nothing in article 56 which lists coastal state's rights in EEZ's impacts on the scope and thus the enforcement of piracy[43]). Piracy cannot (now) be committed, for example, in the Malacca Straits because they fall entirely within the jurisdiction of the littoral states, Malaysia, Indonesia, and Singapore.[44] Where territorial waters are indeterminate, such as Somalia's contested claim to a 200-nautical-mile territorial, the zone of criminality is indeterminate (although in Somalia's case states simply assume the 12 nautical mile rule applies and behave accordingly). The highly problematic jurisdictional limitation[45] means that states cannot use UNCLOS as a basis for enforcement action against pirates within the territorial waters of other states, a problem that became acute in Somalia because it had no capacity to enforce its domestic law. In an extraordinary and expressly non-precedential measure, the UN Security Council adopted a number of resolutions that in effect extended the offence of piracy into Somalia's territorial waters thus permitting naval forces operating against pirates to operate in those waters to interdict pirates.[46] The IMO has responded more prosaically by classifying acts of piracy in territorial waters as 'armed robbery against ships', and defining the latter in very similar terms to piracy but without the jurisdictional limitation.[47] In principle, piracy can occur within that part of the contiguous zone of twenty-four nautical miles (where coastal states have jurisdiction in customs, fiscal, sanitary, and immigration matters)[48] and of the EEZs (resource/environmental purposes) of 200 nautical miles[49] beyond the territorial limit. Even though there is a debate as to whether these areas are part of the high seas or a *sui generis* zone, either way the coastal state does not have special rights over piracy in these areas.[50]

3.5.5 The key weakness of the UNCLOS definition

The key weakness of article 101 is that it is definitional only. It rests on the assumption that piracy is a crime in customary international law and there is no need for an explicit treaty obligation to criminalize piracy in national law. Self-execution of the definition has not been entirely successful. Some national legislation refers to the definition of piracy in the

---

[42] Article 3 of UNCLOS.   [43] *Dahir* above n 24 at para 57.

[44] R Beckman, 'Combating Piracy and Armed Robbery against Ships in Southeast Asia: The Way Forward' 33 *Ocean Development and International Law* (2002) 317, 328.

[45] See D Doby, 'Piracy Jure Gentium: The Jurisdictional Conflict of the High Seas and Territorial Waters' 41 *Journal of Maritime Law and Commerce* (2010) 561, 568.

[46] It began with SC Res 1816, S/Res/1816 (2 June 2008), para 3; the scheme was renewed in SC Res 2246, S/Res/2246 (20 November 2015), para 14 until November 2016.

[47] Para 2(2) of the IMO's Code of Practice for the Investigation of Armed Robbery against Ships, IMO Res A1025 (26), A 26/Res 1025, 18 January 2010.

[48] Article 33 of UNCLOS.   [49] Articles 55–57 of UNCLOS.

[50] Article 58(2) of UNCLOS.

law of nations thus implicitly relying on article 101 to give it meaning,[51] some makes this connection explicit,[52] some uses the same wording,[53] some includes attempts and party liability,[54] and some retains sea-robbery.[55] In 2015 the UN Security Council called 'upon all states to criminalize piracy under their domestic law'.[56] However, although couched in highly coercive language the absence of direct reference to Chapter VII authority suggests that the Security Council is not yet legislating in this area.

3.6 The Maritime Safety Offences

The *Achille Lauro* incident exposed the shortcomings of the crime of piracy in suppressing the full range of threats to safety at sea. Alternative terrorism offences such as hostage-taking or hijacking appeared to provide a less complicated alternative model. States responded by developing the 1988 SUA Convention[57] under the auspices of the IMO. The SUA Convention offences are spelled out in article 3(1):

Any person commits an offence if that person unlawfully and intentionally:
(a) seizes or exercises control over a ship by force or threat thereof or any other form of intimidation; or
(b) performs an act of violence against a person on board a ship if that act is likely to endanger the safe navigation of that ship; or
(c) destroys a ship or causes damage to a ship or to its cargo which is likely to endanger the safe navigation of that ship; or
(d) places or causes to be placed on a ship, by any means whatsoever, a device or substance which is likely to destroy that ship, or cause damage to that ship or its cargo which endangers or is likely to endanger the safe navigation of that ship; or
(e) destroys or seriously damages maritime navigational facilities or seriously interferes with their operation, if any such act is likely to endanger the safe navigation of a ship; or
(f) communicates information which he knows to be false, thereby endangering the safe navigation of a ship; or
(g) injures or kills any person, in connection with the commission or the attempted commission of any of the offences set forth in subparagraphs (a) to (f).

Article 3 obliges parties to enact a list of serious offences directed at suppressing actions that endanger the safety of navigation.[58] The high threshold of these

---

[51] See, eg, section 74 of the Canadian Criminal Code 1985.
[52] See, eg, section 26(1) of the United Kingdom (UK)'s Merchant Shipping and Maritime Security Act 1997.
[53] See, eg, section 51 of Australia's Crimes Act 1914 (Cth).
[54] See, eg, section 24 of South Africa's Defence Act 2002.
[55] See, eg, article 215 of the Greek Code on Public Maritime Law (Law 187/1973).
[56] SC Res 2246, S/Res/2246 (2015), para 19.
[57] IMO Convention for the Suppression of Unlawful Acts against the Safety of Maritime Navigation and the Protocol for the Suppression of Unlawful Acts against the Safety of Fixed Platforms on the Continental Shelf, Rome, 10 March 1988, 1678 UNTS 201, in force 1 March 1992. See S Davidson, 'International Law and the Suppression of Maritime Violence' in R Burchill, N White, and J Morris (eds), *International Conflict and Security Law* (Cambridge: CUP, 2009), 265.
[58] See, eg, Part II of the UK's Aviation and Maritime Security Act 1990.

offences ensures that there is still a place for piracy. Thus, for example, force used to rob the ship's captain of the money in a ship's safe may be piracy, but would not usually amount to a SUA offence because it does not offer a threat to the safety of navigation (unless, eg, the captain halted the vessel in the middle of a major shipping lane during the course of the robbery). The focus on violence also leaves a role for piracy that only involves 'depredation' or taking of property. Conversely, an act of violence committed during the course of the taking of a ship could be both piracy and an article 3(1)(a) offence. The most notable gap addressed by the SUA Convention is the criminalization under domestic law of attempts to commit and abetting the commission of article 3(1) offences in article 3(2)(a) and (b). The latter provides for criminalization under national law of secondary participants such as financiers and those in support roles on mother ships and ashore. Article 3(2)(c) also obliges parties to make it an offence to threaten to commit an article 3(1) offence 'if that threat is likely to endanger the safe navigation of the ship in question'.

The article 3 offences are in other respects broader than piracy because the motives of the accused are irrelevant and there is no 'two ship' requirement. There is, however, some limitation on where these offences can occur. In terms of article 4 the SUA Convention does not apply when the offence (i) takes place entirely within a state's territorial waters, (ii) the vessel concerned was not 'scheduled to navigate' out of those waters, and (iii) the alleged offender was found within that state's territory. Thus the SUA Convention does not apply to armed robbery against ships at anchor or in port, or in cases where the ship is navigating from one port to another within the same state's territorial sea. Article 4 imports a transnational element into the definition of the offences, ensuring that the proscribed actions are of concern or potential concern to states other than the territorial state.

A 1988 Protocol provides for offences to suppress actions endangering the safety of offshore platforms.[59] A 2005 Protocol[60] introduced new offences of maritime terrorism, such as using a ship as a means to carry out a terrorist attack, requiring a specific purpose of intimidation of a population or compulsion of a government or inter-governmental organization to do or abstain from doing an act.[61] Offences relating to non-proliferation of weapons of mass destruction were also introduced, as was an offence of transporting by sea someone who had committed an offence under the SUA Convention, Protocol, or any other terrorism convention.[62] These offences illustrate that the SUA Convention and its Protocols expanded well beyond the narrow scope of piracy into the realm of anti-terrorism and nuclear non-proliferation discussed in Chapter 7.

---

[59] Protocol for the Suppression of Unlawful Acts against the Safety of Fixed Platforms Located on the Continental Shelf, 10 March 1988, 1678 UNTS 304, in force 1 March 1992.

[60] The 2005 Protocol to the Convention for the Suppression of Unlawful Acts against the Safety of Maritime Navigation, 14 October 2005, [2005] ATNIF 30, in force 28 July 2010 (the treaties have been consolidated).

[61] Articles 3*bis*, 3*ter*, and 3*quater*.

[62] The full list of terrorism conventions were added as a schedule to the Protocol.

3.7 Punishment of Piracy and SUA Offences

Historically piracy was severely punished, with public flogging, enslavement, brand-ing, and execution all available. UNCLOS does not prescribe a penalty; article 105 leaves it to national courts 'to decide upon the penalties to be imposed'. Article 5 of the SUA Convention follows suit, only obliging parties to adopt 'appropriate penal-ties which take into account the grave nature of these offences'. Yet the retributive and deterrent legacy remains and punishment for piracy in domestic law is severe. Although certain states impose corporal punishment[63] typically states prescribe heavy terms of imprisonment[64] rising to life[65] and in some states death[66] if life is endangered or lost. Heavy sentences have been imposed on Somali pirates. Research from 2011 concluded that the average sentence for piracy was sixteen years, but that there was massive variation globally, depending on national law.[67] Interestingly, this research shows that courts tended not only to focus on individual factors of use of violence and threats in particular cases, but also on issues of general deterrence to threats to free-dom of navigation.[68]

3.8 Problems and Progress off Somalia

Apart from the problems of policing piracy in Somali territorial waters discussed above and in Chapter 17, policing piracy off Somalia has also had problems with the scope of punishable actions, and the rights and duties of states apprehending and try-ing suspects.[69] The Contact Group on Piracy off the Coast of Somalia (CGPCS) estab-lished in 2009[70] exposed a litany of legislative inadequacies in the states trying to suppress piracy off Somalia. Many had not actually criminalized piracy. Spain had struck piracy from its Criminal Code in 1995 because it considered piracy redun-dant; it was reinstated in 2010. The CGPCS was forced to look at the viability of using other crimes such as armed robbery at sea, hijacking, kidnapping, hostage taking, the SUA offences (while Somalia is not a party, its regional neighbours are), and organ-ized crime offences. It also identified other problems. Inchoate offences and secondary participation were inadequately criminalized. There was no agreement on the legal-ity of paying ransoms, or provision for suppression of the flow of paraphernalia such

---

[63] Eg, in terms of section 130B(2) of the Singapore Penal Code.

[64] Article 198 of Argentina's Codigo Penal provides for penalties from three to fifteen years; article 147 of Mexico's Codigo Penal Federal provides for fifteen to thirty years' imprisonment; article 227 of the Criminal Code of the Russian Federation provides for five to ten years' imprisonment, and if firearms were used eight to twelve years, and if lives were lost, ten to fifteen years.

[65] See, eg, section 74(2) of the Canadian Criminal Code, 1985; section 94 of New Zealand's Crimes Act 1961; section 130B of the Singapore Penal Code; and 18 USC § 1651.

[66] See, eg, section 130B(2) of the Singapore Penal Code.

[67] E Kontorovich, 'The Penalties for Piracy', One Earth Foundation, available at <http://oceansbeyondpiracy. org/sites/default/files/attachments/obp_penalties_for_piracy_final.pdf> last visited 16 August 2016.

[68] ibid, at 12.

[69] J Ashley-Roach, 'Countering Piracy off Somalia: International Law and International Institutions' 104 *American Journal of International Law* (2010) 397.

[70] In response to Security Council Resolution 1851; see further Chapter 17.

as weapons, engines, and vessels to the pirates. The CGPCS has played a coordinating role in supporting law reform to plug the substantive gaps in national laws. It has urged all states, for example, 'to ensure that conspiracy to commit piracy is punishable under national law'.[71]

3.9 Conclusion

Piracy has the virtue of carrying universal jurisdiction but is poorly defined and states are not under an obligation to criminalize it. The SUA offences are defined with greater precision but do not enjoy universal jurisdiction. These contrasting characters neatly illustrate the customary and treaty roots of these two offences. Piracy was a pre-Westphalian international crime, but in the Westphalian era that status appears to have eroded as the crime became uncommon and the state-interest model of transnational criminal law became dominant. Today, piracy has arguably lost its status as a core international crime. In 2010 the Ukraine developed a draft comprehensive convention on the suppression of acts of piracy at sea,[72] which drew upon UNCLOS and the SUA Conventions as well as the United Nations Convention against Transnational Organized Crime,[73] but while Ukraine continues to push for international attention to its initiative,[74] the draft convention has yet to garner sufficient support.

---

[71] Fourteenth Plenary Session, UN HQ, 1 May 2013, page 3, available at <http://www.lessonsfrompiracy. net/files/2015/03/Communique_14th_-Plenary.pdf> visited 16 August 2016.

[72] UN Doc A/65/489.　　[73] 15 November 2000, 2225 UNTS 209, in force 29 September 2003.

[74] Statement by the delegation of Ukraine at the UN Security Council open debate on piracy and armed robbery at sea in the Gulf of Guinea, 25 April 2016, <http://ukraineun.org/en/press-center/55-statement-by-the-delegation-of-ukraine-at-the-unsc-open-debate-on-piracy-and-armed-robbery-at-sea-in-the-gulf-of-guinea/> visited 16 August 2016.

4

Slavery and Human Trafficking

4.1 Introduction

The 'discovery' that the commercial trade in human beings still exists has sparked renewed interest in suppression of slave trading and related practices. In 2012 the International Labour Organization (ILO) estimated that 20.9 million people around the globe were victims of modern-day slavery, with 11.7 million (58%) in the Asia Pacific and 3.7 million (18%) in Africa.[1] In 2014 the ILO estimated that US$150 billion was generated annually by forced labour, involving US$99 billion from commercial sexual exploitation and US$51 billion from forced economic exploitation, including domestic work, agriculture, and other economic activities.[2] The 2016 Global Slavery index estimates some 46 million people are in some form of slavery in 167 countries.[3] Specific forms of exploitation have generated their own startling statistics: revelations that human trafficking for the purposes of organ removal was occurring in Kosovo[4] has led to greater attention to this specific problem and it is currently estimated that there are 10,000 organ transplants from trafficked donors per annum.[5] More recently the UN's International Organization for Migration (IOM) has released descriptions of slave markets in Libya.[6]

The apparent size of the problem has justified a massive legislative and institutional response. However, these activities are difficult to assess because they are covert, and different methods have been used to collect data.[7] The majority of cases of trafficking are said to be unreported and unknown.[8] The potential inaccuracy of the evidence has led to questions as to whether it justifies the enormous amount of resources being

---

[1] *ILO Global Estimate of Forced Labour*, 2012, 13, 15, available at <http://www.ilo.org/wcmsp5/groups/public/---ed_norm/---declaration/documents/publication/wcms_182004.pdf> visited 1 April 2017.

[2] ILO, *Profits and Poverty: The Economics of Forced Labour* (Geneva: ILO, 2014), 12, available at <http://www.ilo.org/wcmsp5/groups/public/---ed_norm/---declaration/documents/publication/wcms_243391.pdf> visited 1 April 2017.

[3] *The Global Slavery Index*, at <http://www.globalslaveryindex.org/findings/> visited 1 April 2017.

[4] Dick Marty, Rapporteur to Council of Europe Committee on Legal Affairs and Human Rights, *Inhuman Treatment of People and Illicit Trafficking in Human Organs in Kosovo*, AS/Jur (2010) 46, 12 December 2010.

[5] See N Sheper-Hughes, 'Human Traffic: Exposing the Brutal Organ Trade', *New Internationalist*, 1 May 2014, available at <https://newint.org/features/2014/05/01/organ-trafficking-keynote/> visited 10 April 2017.

[6] IOM, 'IOM Learns of "Slave Market" Conditions Endangering Migrants in North Africa' 11 April 2017, available at <https://www.iom.int/news/iom-learns-slave-market-conditions-endangering-migrants-north-africa> visited 12 April 2017.

[7] See generally DA Feingold, 'Trafficking in Numbers: The Social Construction of Human Trafficking Data' in P Andreas and KM Greenhill (eds), *Sex, Drugs, and Body Counts: The Politics of Numbers in Global Crime and Conflict* (Ithaca, NY: Cornell University Press, 2010), 46.

[8] See AA Aronowitz, 'Overcoming the Challenges to Accurately Measuring the Phenomenon of Human Trafficking' 81(3) *International Review of Penal Law* (2010) 493, 494.

dedicated to combat it.[9] This institutional response turns upon the development of criminalization of different forms of exploitation of humans, a piecemeal and reactive process. This chapter charts the gradual criminalization of slave trading as a trans-national crime. It then examines the evolution of its modern analogue, human traf-ficking, and the development of the container concept, modern slavery, before dealing with the protection of victims.

4.2 Slavery

4.2.1 Enslavement and slave trading

Chattel slavery entails the assertion of legal rights of ownership and/or possession over one human by another, rights that could be alienated by sale or transfer. Slave trading and owning has been practised throughout human history, most infamously in the importation of more than 15 million slaves from Africa into the New World.[10] This excerpt from the US Supreme Court case, *The Amistad*,[11] illustrates the nature of this chain of supply:

> [T]hey were, on or about the 15th of April, 1839, unlawfully kidnapped and forcibly and wrongfully carried on board a certain vessel on the coast of Africa which was unlawfully engaged in the slave trade, and were unlawfully transported in the same vessel to the island of Cuba for the purpose of being there unlawfully sold as slaves.

Chattel slavery as a legal status is no more. More recently, the definition of slavery as an unlawful condition has slowly been expanded upon to include a remarkable variety of forms of coercive human exploitation short of legal ownership where the emphasis is on temporary use value.[12]

4.2.2 Suppression of slavery under international law

The nineteenth century

The conduct described in *The Amistad* was rendered unlawful globally through the intervention of nineteenth-century enlightenment morality. Non-governmental organizations (NGOs) such as the Anti-Slavery Society (formed in 1823 to abolish slav-ery in the British Empire) and the British and Foreign Anti-Slavery Society (formed in 1839 for the global abolition of slavery) combined with the commercial interests of emergent industrial capitalism to suppress slavery. In 1807 Great Britain declared the slave trade unlawful within its empire.[13] The US prohibited the importation of slaves

---

[9] J Goodey, 'Human Trafficking: Sketchy Data and Policy Responses' 8 *Criminology and Criminal Justice* (2008) 421, 434.
[10] MC Bassiouni, 'Enslavement as an International Crime' 23 *New York University Journal of International Law and Politics* (1991), 445, 451.
[11] 40 US 518 (1841).
[12] K Bales, 'Expendable People: Slavery in the Age of Globalization' 53 *Journal of International Affairs* (2000) 461, 462, 466.
[13] Slave Trade Act 1807.

that same year. Attempts to analogize slavery to piracy as a crime against the law of nations, however, failed. In 1817 in *Le Louis*[14] an English court held that slave trading was not a violation of international law and in 1825 in *The Antelope*[15] the US Supreme Court followed suit. The British turned to treaty obligations to suppress the global slave trade.[16] In the Treaty of London (1841)[17] the slave trade was declared tantamount to piracy. The General Act of the Berlin Congo Conference (1885) affirmed that 'trading in slaves is forbidden in conformity with the principles of international law'.[18] Bilateral treaties tended to be more specific. In terms of article 2 of the 1835 Treaty for the Abolition of the Slave Trade between Great Britain and Spain,[19] for example, the Queen of Spain promised to enact 'a penal law, inflicting a severe punishment on all those of Her Catholic Majesty's subjects who shall, under any pretext whatsoever, take any part whatever in the Traffic in Slaves'. Rejecting the notion that these treaties established slave trading as an international crime, Schwarzenberger argues that they established an exceptional jurisdiction over suspected slave-trading ships 'to apply to slave-traders relatively uniform rules of municipal criminal law, prescribed in some cases by international treaties'.[20]

The 1926 Slavery Convention

In the twentieth century stronger multilateral steps were taken, most significantly the adoption of the Slavery Convention by the League of Nations on 25 September 1926.[21] Article 1(1) of the Convention defines slavery as 'the status or condition of a person over whom any or all of the powers attaching to the rights of ownership are exercised'. Article 1(2) includes within slave trading

> all acts involved in the capture, acquisition or disposal of a person with intent to reduce him to slavery; all acts involved in the acquisition of a slave with a view to selling or exchanging him; all acts of disposal by sale or exchange of a slave acquired with a view to being sold or exchanged, and, in general, every act of trade or transport in slaves.

Under article 2 the parties embraced a general obligation to prevent and suppress the slave trade and to bring about the complete abolition of slavery in all its forms. More specifically, article 6 provided that parties whose laws made inadequate 'provision for the punishment of infractions of laws and regulations enacted with a view to giving effect to the purposes of the ... Convention' undertook 'to adopt the necessary measures in order that severe penalties may be imposed in respect of such infractions'.

---

[14] [1817] 2 Dods 210.   [15] 23 US 66 (1825).

[16] See RS Clark, 'Steven Spielberg's *Amistad* and Other Things I Have Thought about in the Past Forty Years: International (Criminal) Law, Conflict of Laws, Insurance and Slavery' 30 *Rutgers Law Journal* (1999) 371, 397 fn78, 399 fn83.

[17] Article I of the Treaty for the Suppression of the African Slave Trade (Treaty of London), London, 20 December 1841, 2 Martens Noveau Recueil General des Traites 392, in force 20 December 1841.

[18] 26 February 1885, Article 9.   [19] 28 June 1835, 85 Consol TS 177 (1835).

[20] G Schwarzenberger, 'The Problem of an International Criminal Law' 3 *Current Legal Problems* (1950) 263, 285.

[21] Geneva, 60 LNTS 253, in force 9 March 1927.

There is no claim here that slavery or slave trading is an international crime; the jurisdiction to prescribe remains firmly with the state.

The core of the concept of slavery as defined in article 1 of the 1926 Slavery Convention is the exercise of a right of legal ownership over the victim which reduces them to an object.[22] The 2008 Australian case of *R v Tang*[23] illustrates the importance of the proof of exercise of the powers of ownership by the accused and the concomitant intention of the accused to reduce the slave to ownership, even though de jure ownership is no longer possible. The complainants were sex workers recruited in Thailand to work in the respondent's licensed brothel in Australia. The respondent had a 70 per cent stake in a syndicate that 'bought' the complainants. In order to pay off their contract debt of AU$45,000 (each), they were required to work six days per week, serving up to 900 customers over a period of four to six months. Their passports and return tickets were retained by the respondent. Tang was convicted under section 270.3(1)(a) of the Australian Criminal Code of five counts of intentionally possessing a slave and five counts of intentionally exercising over a slave a power attaching to the right of ownership, namely use, but the conviction was overturned on appeal. In allowing a further appeal by the prosecution, the High Court of Australia noted in regard to the material element of the offence the importance of the appellant's power to make the victims an object of purchase, their power to use the victim in an unrestricted manner without compensation, and the power to control their movements. Justice Haynes in support of the majority confirmed that '[t]o establish the relevant fault element . . . it was necessary to show that the respondent meant to engage in the conduct, in respect of each complainant, of exercising powers attaching to the right of ownership'.[24] In partial dissent, however, Justice Kirby argued this was 'not simply an "intention" addressed to the "physical elements" concerned with "possession" or the exercise of powers attaching to the "right of ownership".[25] In his view it has also to consist of an intention directed to the underlying entitlement that gives rise to those elements. The question whether the powers exercised over the victim by the accused are of such degree that they cross the threshold into slavery and are not merely harsh employment practice is difficult in itself for courts to answer. Establishing awareness not only of the exercise of these powers but the source of the accused's entitlement, narrows the scope of the offence and makes it difficult to prove, especially when it is putative as there is no de jure entitlement to slave-holding. Unsurprisingly most courts do not insist on it. In the *State v Raikadroka*,[26] for example, the Fiji High Court found the accused guilty of slavery because he had treated teenage girls as 'products' whose earnings from sex work he entirely appropriated for himself. The victims' apparent freedom and their consent was considered irrelevant because the accused had placed them in a state of 'situational coercion' (the lack of anywhere else to go) which the Court equated to use of threats or force. Responding to the argument that the accused had spent lavishly on clothes, food, and entertainment for the victims, the judge commented that 'slaves can live in palaces as well as sordid hovels'. The intention to exploit them

---

[22] *Siliadin v France*, ECtHR, Application no. 73316/01, 26 July 2005, para 122.
[23] [2008] HCA 39; (2008) 237 CLR 1.   [24] ibid, page 58, para 134.
[25] ibid, page 45, para 95.   [26] [2014] FJHC 402.

suggests, however, that they were more open to prosecution for human trafficking (see below).[27] The difficulty in cases like these as pointed out by Justice Kirby in *Tang* is 'not every exploitative employment arrangement will warrant the description of slavery'.[28] Putative ownership and awareness of that ownership is what distinguishes slavery from less serious forms of exploitation.

Post-war measures

Upon formation, the UN came out very firmly against slavery; article 4 of the 1948 Universal Declaration of Human Rights[29] and article 8 of the International Covenant of Civil and Political Rights[30] expressly prohibit slavery and slave trading in all 'their forms', and expressly prohibits servitude. Concerns about the restriction of the scope of the Slavery Convention to chattel slavery led to the adoption in 1956 of the Supplementary Convention on the Abolition of Slavery, the Slave Trade and Institutions and Practices Similar to Slavery.[31] In terms of article 6(1) the states parties agreed to criminalize in their domestic law '[t]he act of enslaving another person or of inducing another person to give himself or a person dependent upon him into slavery, or of attempting these acts, or being accessory thereto, or being a party to a conspiracy to accomplish any such acts', and to punish persons convicted thereof. The more serious offence is in article 3(1) where the parties agreed to criminalize '[t]he act of conveying or attempting to convey slaves from one country to another by whatever means of transport, or of being accessory thereto' where those convicted had to be open 'to very severe penalties'. Enslavement has been included as a species of crime against humanity in article 7(1)(c) of the Rome Statute of the International Criminal Court.[32] However, it must occur within the context of the general requirements of a crime against humanity (ie as part of an attack on a civilian population, widespread, and systematic[33]), thus leaving intact the transnational crime in the slavery conventions to suppress the vast majority of cases that do not meet this threshold.

4.3 Forced Labour and Debt Bondage

Unlike slavery, forced labour/debt bondage is not a question of ownership but of involuntary labour, and thus does not fall within the scope of the central provisions of the 1926 Slavery Convention. The weakness of article 5 of the 1926 Slavery Convention, which only obliged states parties to prevent forced labour from developing into conditions analogous to slavery, led to the adoption in 1930 of the ILO Forced Labour Convention.[34]

---

[27] They were also convicted of domestic trafficking in children.   [28] Above n 23, 37.
[29] 10 December 1948, GA Res 217A(III).
[30] New York, 19 December 1966, 999 UNTS 171, in force 23 March 1976.
[31] 7 September 1956, Geneva, 226 UNTS 3, in force 30 April 1957.
[32] Article 7(1)(g) includes sexual slavery as a crime against humanity.
[33] *Prosecutor v Kunarac, et al* Case No IT-96-23 and IT-96-23/1-A (12 June 2002).
[34] ILO Convention No 29: Convention Concerning Force and Compulsory Labour, 28 June 1930, 39 UNTS 55, in force 1 May 1932.

It defines forced labour in article 2(1) as 'all work or service which is exacted from any person under menace of any penalty and for which the said person has not offered himself voluntarily' and obliges parties in article 25 to criminalize 'the illegal exaction of forced or compulsory labour' and to ensure 'that the penalties imposed by law are really adequate and are strictly enforced'. Steps were taken in the ILO's 1957 Abolition of Forced Labour Convention[35] to require parties to take effective measures to abolish forced labour, while article 1 of the 1956 Supplementary Convention on the Abolition of Slavery obliges parties to abolish debt bondage, defined in article 20(1)(a) as:

> [t]he status or condition arising from a pledge by a debtor of his personal services or those of a person under his control as security for a debt, if the value of those services as reasonably assessed is not applied towards the liquidation of the debt or the length and nature of those services are not respectively limited and defined.

In addition, article 6(2) obliges parties to criminalize inducing someone to place himself in debt bondage.

4.4 'White' Slavery and Trafficking for Prostitution

In the early twentieth century European states adopted a number of treaties to suppress so-called 'white slavery', the procuring of 'white' women for 'immoral purposes abroad'.[36] The exclusive focus on 'white' victims was abandoned in 1949 in the Convention for the Suppression of the Traffic in Persons and of the Exploitation of the Prostitution of Others.[37] These treaties were, nonetheless, noteworthy for introducing the important principle that the consent of the victim is irrelevant where the means used were coercive or fraudulent.[38] Article 1 of the 1949 Convention, for example, obliges the parties to criminalize anyone who 'in order to gratify the passions of another person, has procured, enticed, or led away, even with her consent, a woman or girl under age, for immoral purposes'. Article 2 obliges parties to criminalize those who with the same purpose 'by fraud, or by means of violence, threats, abuse of authority, or any other method of compulsion, procured, enticed, or led away a woman or girl over age'. The shortcomings of the convention included the failure to provide a definition of trafficking and the exclusive focus upon prostitution.

---

[35] ILO Convention No 105: Abolition of Forced Labour Convention, 25 June 1957, 320 UNTS 291, in force 17 January 1959.

[36] International Agreement for the Suppression of the White Slave Traffic, 18 May 1904, 35 Stat 1979, 1 LNTS 83, in force 18 July 1905; International Convention for the Suppression of the White Slave Traffic, Paris, 4 May 1910, 7 Martens Nouveau Recueil (3d) 252, 98 UNTS 101; in force 5 July 1920; International Convention for the Suppression of the Traffic in Women and Children, 30 September 1921, 9 LNTS 415, in force 15 June 1922; International Convention for the Suppression of the Traffic in Women of Full Age, 11 October 1933, 150 LNTS 431, in force 24 August 1934.

[37] New York, 2 December 1949, 96 UNTS 271; in force 25 July 1951.

[38] Article 1 of the 1910 Convention.

4.5 Human Trafficking

4.5.1 The nature of human trafficking

In human trafficking ownership is not the goal; traffickers exploit for profit only certain of the victim's capacities, usually their sexual or labour services. It must involve a human. Thus while a child can be trafficked for the purpose of exploitation in order to make child pornography, and a victim can be trafficked for the purpose of having their organs removed, human trafficking does not include the trafficking in child pornography or trafficking in human organs. Trafficking implies movement on a chain of supply. Coercion or deception is used to move victims from their homes, either intra- or inter-state,[39] to the place of demand. Victims may be easily led by fraud, for example, because of poverty, lack of employment opportunities, conflicts, corruption, and so forth, but then later be subject to coercion when they realize the true nature of the enterprise. The modus operandi of the traffickers ranges from complete deception to partial deception and from extreme forms of violence to more subtle means of subjugation such as threats to inform the authorities.

4.5.2 Criminalization of human trafficking under the Human Trafficking Protocol

Background

When human trafficking was first highlighted as a significant global problem in the 1990s the existing treaties were considered inappropriate. The requirement in both the 1926 Slavery Convention and the 1956 Supplementary Convention that slave trading be carried out with 'an intent to reduce persons to slavery'[40] was difficult to meet when the trafficker's purpose was temporary commercial exploitation, not ownership. Relying on the prohibition of forced labour meant categorizing trafficking for prostitution as trafficking for 'labour' and was directed at the end result, not the process to reach that result. The 1949 Convention for the Suppression of Trafficking in Persons for the Purposes of Prostitution was too limited in scope. Provisions in human rights conventions calling for the suppression of trafficking of women and children[41] did not impose specific obligations to criminalize. Law reform was thus aimed in part at criminalizing exploitative practices in the process of trafficking itself. Reform was undertaken through the adoption, in Palermo in 2000, of the Protocol to Prevent, Suppress and Punish Trafficking in Persons, Especially Women and Children, supplementing the United Nations Convention against Transnational Organized Crime.[42] The Human Trafficking Protocol's aim is to prevent and combat human trafficking and protect

---

[39] LG Potts, 'Global Trafficking in Human Beings: Assessing the Success of the United Nations Protocol to Prevent Trafficking in Persons' 35 *George Washington International Law Review* (2003) 227, 229–31.
[40] Articles 1(2) and 7(c) respectively.
[41] Article 6 of the Convention on the Elimination of all Forms of Discrimination against Women, New York, 3 September 1981, 1249 UNTS 13, in force 3 September 1981; Article 35 of the Convention on the Rights of the Child, New York, 2 September 1990, 1577 UNTS 3, in force 2 September 1990.
[42] 15 November 2000, 2237 UNTS 319, in force 9 September 2003.

trafficking victims.[43] Supplementary to the UN Convention against Transnational Organized Crime (UNTOC),[44] the Protocol originated in a US proposal and its substance echoes the US's '3P' response to human trafficking: prevention, prosecution, and protection.[45]

Criminalization of human trafficking

One of the primary functions of the Human Trafficking Protocol is to establish a separate offence of human trafficking. Article 5(1) obliges parties 'to establish as criminal offences the conduct set forth in article 3 of this Protocol, when committed intentionally'. Article 5(2) further obliges parties to criminalize 'attempting to commit' such an offence, 'participating as an accomplice' in such an offence, and 'organizing or directing other persons to commit' such an offence ('subject to the basic concepts of its legal system', which recognizes that not all legal systems criminalize these activities). Article 5's obligations thus turn on the definition of 'trafficking in persons' in article 3(a), which has three elements.

Action

(i) Firstly, there must be an 'action': 'the recruitment, transportation, transfer, harbouring or receipt of persons'. These actions are links in the chain of supply. They can, however, all be committed by the same person. Theresa Mubang was convicted in the US, for example, of holding a juvenile to a term of involuntary servitude for recruiting, transporting, and exploiting a girl of between ten and twelve years of age from Cameroon.[46] The nature of the actions listed in article 3(a) indicates that the Protocol is a supply control measure. Suppression of demand through criminalization is not a goal of the Protocol, even though demand drives trafficking. In contrast, article 19 of the 2005 Council of Europe Convention on Action against Trafficking in Human Beings[47] shifts the focus of criminalization onto demand, requesting parties to consider criminalizing 'the use of services which are the object of exploitation . . . with the knowledge that the person is a victim'. What it has in mind is not simply the criminalization of payment for sexual services, as in Norway[48] and Sweden,[49] but criminalization of demand with knowledge of victimization.

Although some of these actions imply the movement of the victim, movement is not an element of the offence. None requires the crossing of a border. Thus domestic trafficking offences enacted under article 5(1) should include purely intra-state trafficking. Article 4, however, imposes two conditions for the use of the Protocol (and for

---

[43] Article 2.
[44] See D McClean, *Transnational Organized Crime: A Commentary on the UN Convention and its Protocols* (Oxford: OUP, 2007), 309 et seq.
[45] Potts, above n 39, 239.
[46] See *Mubang v US*, CC No. DKC 03-0539, United States District Court, D. Maryland, 9 August 2011.
[47] CETS No 197, opened for signature 16 May 2005, in force 1 February 2008. See Council of Europe, Treaty Series No 197, *Explanatory Report on the Council of Europe Convention on Action against Trafficking in Human Beings*, 16.V.2005.
[48] Section 202(a) of the Norwegian General Civil Penal Code No 10 of 1902.
[49] Section 6.8 of the Swedish Penal Code 1999.

the UNTOC itself[50]) for international cooperation in regard to the 'prevention, investigation and prosecution' of the article 5 offences and to the 'protection of victims' of
such offences: the offences must be (a) 'transnational in nature' and (b) 'involve an
organised criminal group' (cross-border offences involving structured groups of three
or more acting for economic motives).[51] The Protocol/UNTOC cannot thus be used
as the basis for international cooperation for purely intra-state offences or for transnational offences involving only two persons. In contrast, article 2 of the 2005 Council
of Europe Trafficking Convention specifically excludes the Protocol's transnationality
and organized criminality elements as conditions for international cooperation.

Means

(ii) The actions must be carried out using a particular 'means': the 'threat or use of
force or other forms of coercion, of abduction, of fraud, of deception, of the abuse of
power or of a position of vulnerability or of the giving or receiving of payments or
benefits to achieve the consent of a person having control over another person'. While
the means includes force it also includes control of the victim through deception, such
as where the accused tricks the victim into thinking he is her boyfriend.[52] More recent
regional instruments have expanded the list as different means have been identified.
For example, article 2 of the 2011 EU Directive on Preventing and Combating Human
Trafficking[53] includes 'the exchange or transfer of control over' trafficking victims and
the 'giving or receiving of payments or benefits to achieve the consent of a person having control over another person', which reaches, for example, parents who do not traffic directly but who 'sell' their children.

   Following the principle laid down in earlier 'White Slave' conventions, under the
Human Trafficking Protocol the victim is not forced to prove the absence of consent.
Earlier treaties used the term 'irrespective of consent', which implied the victim had
to provide evidence they did not consent. In contrast, recognizing the role that mis-
representations and half-truths[54] play in the offence but also because many victims are
believed to have some sense of the illegality of what they are getting involved in, the
Protocol in article 3(b) provides that where the particular means spelled out in article 3(a) are used, the consent of a trafficking victim to any of the forms of exploitation
spelled out in article 3(a) 'shall be irrelevant'. Even if a victim initially consented but
is later subjected to one of the means in article 3(a), then their initial consent is irrelevant. If the victim is a child (anyone younger than 18), proof of one of the article 3(a)
means is not essential.[55] Article 3(a) lists a range of different exploitative methods,

---

[50] Article 1(2) of the Protocol states that the provisions of UNTOC apply *mutatis mutandis* to the
protocol unless the Protocol otherwise provides, but article 3(1) of the UNTOC applies the conditions of
transnationality and involvement of an organized criminal group.
   [51] Articles 3(2) and 2 of the UNTOC, discussed in Chapter 8.
   [52] See, eg, the Canadian case *R v Burton* 2016 ONCJ 103.
   [53] Directive 2011/36/EU of the European Parliament and of the Council of 5 April 2011 on preventing
and combating trafficking in human beings and protecting its victims, and replacing Council Framework
Decision 2002/629/JHA, OJ L101/1, 15 April 2011.
   [54] See, eg, *Switzerland v A and B* Final appeal judgment; ILDC 347 (CH 2002), BGE 128 IV 117, 29
April 2002.
   [55] Article 3(c) and (d).

each with a separate meaning. Someone in a position of 'vulnerability', for example, was defined in an Interpretive Note made by the negotiators as referring to 'any situation in which the person involved has no real and acceptable alternative but to submit to the abuse involved'.[56]

Purpose

(iii) The action must be for 'the purpose of exploitation', defined as including 'at a minimum, the exploitation of the prostitution of others or other forms of sexual exploitation, forced labour or services, slavery or practices similar to slavery, servitude or the removal of organs'. All that is required is the presence of this ulterior purpose; not actual exploitation. This ulterior purpose distinguishes slavery from human trafficking: the former involves an intention to reduce to ownership but the latter only an intention to exploit. Trafficking can become slavery if the exploitation illustrates an intention to assert ownership, something that can be inferred from the length of time the victim is exploited, the accused's claims to ownership of the victim, and the absolute nature of their control of the victim.[57] The enumeration of different forms of exploitation gives the offence in the Protocol breadth, and compares positively, for example, to that in the 2005 South Asian Association for Regional Cooperation Convention on Preventing and Combating Trafficking in Women and Children for Prostitution,[58] which defines trafficking in article 1(3) only as 'the moving, selling or buying of women and children for prostitution'. The forms included in the Protocol definition were, however, a compromise; states agreed not to provide further definition of these forms because of the absence of universally agreed criteria on acceptable sex work or labour conditions.[59] The reference to 'prostitution' nevertheless presents difficulties, particularly if prostitution is legal in the state party. The United Nations Office on Drugs and Crime (UNODC) Model Law on Trafficking in Persons attempts a definition with 'the unlawful obtaining of financial or other material benefit from the prostitution of another person'.[60] 'Unlawful' implies that prostitution must be forced in some way, which means that in this particular context victim consent may be relevant. When referring to 'forced labour or services', the Protocol does not stipulate the particular kind of forced labour. In comparison, article 3(c) of the ILO Child Labour Convention[61] includes among the worst forms of child labour 'the use,

---

[56] Report of the Ad Hoc Committee on the Elaboration of a Convention against Transnational Organised Crime on the Work of its First to Eleventh Sessions, Interpretative notes for the official records of the negotiation of the United Nations Conventions against Transnational Organised Crime and the Protocols thereto, 55th Sess., Agenda Item 105, para 63, UN Doc A/55/383/Add. 1.

[57] *Prosecutor v Kunarac* (Trial Judgment) IT-96-23 (22 February 2001), 542; see T Obokata, 'Trafficking of Human Beings as a Crime against Humanity: Some Implications for the International Legal System' 54 *International and Comparative Law Quarterly* (2005) 445, 449.

[58] 5 January 2002, in force 1 December 2005; available at <http://www.saarc-sec.org/userfiles/-conv-traffiking.pdf> last visited 31 January 2012.

[59] Potts, above n 39, 238.

[60] UNODC Model Law on Trafficking in Persons, no date, at 13, available at <https://www.unodc.org/documents/human-trafficking/UNODC_Model_Law_on_Trafficking_in_Persons.pdf> visited 1 April 2017.

[61] ILO Convention No 182 concerning the Prohibition and Immediate Action for the Elimination of the Worst Forms of Child Labour, 17 June 1999, 2133 UNTS 161; in force 19 November 2000.

procuring or offering of a child for illicit activities, in particular for the production and trafficking of drugs as defined in the relevant treaties'. Human trafficking for the purpose of 'removal of organs' was a fortuitous inclusion in the Human Trafficking Protocol because in 2000 the threat was not well understood and legislatures unprepared.[62] Importantly, however, while the trafficking of humans for the purposes of organ removal falls within the scope of the Protocol the trafficking in separate organs themselves do not.[63] The list of forms of exploitation has been expanded upon by parties in their domestic law to respond to particular problems faced by them. Article 188A of the Colombian Penal Code provides, for example, that exploitation includes 'the exploitation of the begging of others, servile matrimony, . . . sexual tourism or other forms of exploitation'.[64]

The scope of the human trafficking offence

Any combination of one or more of the elements of action, means, and exploitative purpose involves trafficking. The breadth of the offence is revealed in *Frudenthal v Israel*,[65] where the Israeli Appeal Court interpreted the crime of human trafficking under section 203(a) of Israel's Penal Law to include the appellant keeping the victims in his flat through threats of violence and by taking their passports and money with the intention of exploiting them for prostitution. Some non-parties to the Protocol have only criminalized aspects of trafficking. Burma's Anti-Trafficking in Persons Law of 2005, for example, prohibits trafficking for sex work but is silent on trafficking for forced labour. Conflation with other crimes such as people smuggling, prostitution, immigration, or labour law violations is also common.[66]

Punishment

There is no provision on penalties in the Protocol; article 11(4) suggests only that parties consider denying or revoking a convicted trafficker's entry visas. However, the UNTOC provisions that criminal sanctions should be proportionate to the gravity of the offence and the gravity of the offence should also be taken into account when considering the options of parole or early release,[67] apply *mutatis mutandis* to the Protocol

---

[62] See, eg, *State v Netcare Kwa-Zulu (Pty) Limited*, Commercial Crime Court of Regional Court of Kwa Zulu Natal Case No 41, 3 September 2010, where a South African hospital pleaded guilty to 102 counts related to charges stemming from having allowed its 'employees and facilities to be used to conduct ... Illegal kidney transplant operations'. The charges related to 109 illegal kidney transplant operations which took place between June 2001 and November 2003 within a scheme whereby Israeli citizens would be brought to the hospital for a kidney transplant with the kidney removed from inter alia Brazilian and Romanian donors at very low cost. Human trafficking charges were unavailable because at that point South Africa was not yet a party to the Human Trafficking Protocol.

[63] See A Schloenhardt and S Garbutt, 'Trafficking in Persons for the Purpose of Organ Removal: International Law and Australian Practice' 36 *Criminal Law Journal* (2012) 145, 147 et seq.

[64] Translation in UNODC, *Toolkit to Combat Trafficking in Persons* (2008), 99.

[65] Appeal Judgment, CA 11196/02; ILDC 364 (IL 2003), 3 August 2003.

[66] It's a common theme of US State Department *Trafficking in Persons Reports*. See the 2016 *Trafficking in Persons Report*, June 2016, 137.

[67] Article 11(1) and (4).

offences. Developing on this foundation the 2005 Council of Europe Convention obliges parties to ensure that penalties imposed on natural persons involve deprivation of liberty which can give rise to extradition, and to include a list of aggravating circumstances including deliberate or grossly negligent endangerment of the life of the victim and the commission of an offence against a child, by a public official in the course of their duties, and in the framework of a criminal organization.[68] Although penalties are light in many states, maximum penalties have increased in some states. In the US, for example, the maximum penalty may be life imprisonment where sex trafficking of a minor is carried out by means of 'force, fraud, or coercion'.[69] The 2011 EU directive sets maximum penalties of at least five years' imprisonment or in specific circumstances ten years' imprisonment.[70]

In specific cases particular considerations apply. The most obvious is the nature of the particular form of exploitation engaged in which may impact on the available penalty. Punishment for organ trafficking is, for example, severe in some countries.[71] The penalty applied usually depends on the degree of involvement. In *R v Makai (Atilla)*[72] the appellant's limited role in a conspiracy to traffic Hungarian women into the UK for sexual exploitation, which involved posting adverts on Hungarian websites inviting girls to contact him and once they did so to pass them on to others who ran brothels, was one of the factors which led on appeal to reduction of his sentence from forty to thirty months' imprisonment. In more egregious cases with more direct involvement, penalties are likely to be higher. In *R v Maka*[73] the English Court of Appeal confirmed two consecutive nine-year sentences on the appellant for his role in handling a 15-year-old Lithuanian girl tricked into coming to the UK by others and then forcibly sold by him on four different occasions, raped repeatedly, and forced to work in brothels. Subsequent to this case, the UK's Modern Slavery Act 2015 increased the penalty to life imprisonment.[74]

The limitations of the human trafficking offence

Many of the limitations of the human trafficking offence flow from the fact that it is a product of the first phase of responses to human trafficking, when between 2000 and 2009[75] trafficking was conflated with sex trafficking at a substantive level and enforcement of the offence was focussed on border control concerns rather than on the harm to the victim.[76] In the second phase from 2009 to 2014, attention shifted to labour trafficking and in particular the considerable number of illegal immigrants brought into host countries by purveyors of cheap labour to meet local demand, and kept in poor living conditions and very poorly treated by unscrupulous middlemen. Dependent

---

[68] Articles 23 and 24.   [69] See, eg, 18 USC § 1591(b)(1).   [70] Article 4(1) and (2).
[71] Eg, under article 1 of Senegal's Act no 2005-06 of 10 May 2005, on the fight against human trafficking and similar practices and the protection of victims, the punishment is 10–30 years.
[72] [2008] 1 Cr App R (S) 73.   [73] [2005] EWCA Crim 3365.   [74] Section 5(1).
[75] P Kotiswaran and N Palmer, 'Rethinking the "International Law of Crime": Provocations from Transnational Legal Studies' 6(1) *Transnational Legal Theory* (2015) 55, 74.
[76] JC Hathaway, 'The Human Rights Quagmire of "Human Trafficking"' 49 *Virginia Journal of International Law* (2008) 1, 46.

upon intentional exploitation, the human trafficking offence was not always able to reach the individuals who used the services of victims, especially commercial enterprises involved in the use of exploited labour 'hired' to them. Difficulties of this kind led to enforcement through civil claims for damages. In the landmark UK decision *Galdikas & others v DJ Houghton Ltd*[77] a company and its directors were held liable for exploiting victims of human trafficking by underpaying them and making them work in shocking conditions. Significant damages can serve as an incentive for companies to do better due diligence on the source of their labour.[78] In the current phase of response from 2014, slavery and forced labour have been incorporated along with human trafficking into the concept of modern slavery.

4.6 Modern Slavery

The concept of modern slavery includes slavery and human trafficking.[79] Its use is advocated by leading activists who argue that 'the means of enslavement, the vehicle by which a person arrives in the state or condition of slavery, while important for understanding the particular nature of the case of slavery, does not determine that state, it is simply the means by which a person arrives under the control of another'.[80] The collective label 'modern slavery' has been criticized because although it is heavily used in the discourse it is not used in any of the legal instruments.[81] It has been pointed out, however, that there is a distinction between human trafficking and enslavement as a crime against humanity and that although they should not be conflated, case law is muddying the waters.[82] A fine line is steered, for example, in *Rantsev v Cyprus and Russia*,[83] where the European Court of Human Rights held that 'trafficking in human beings, by its very nature and aim of exploitation, is based on the exercise of powers attaching to the right of ownership'. The Court shied away from classifying trafficking as modern slavery.

While many states were still playing catch up and enacting the human trafficking offence, a new legislative trend towards associating these offences began with Australia's Crimes Legislation Amendment (Slavery, Slavery-like Conditions and People Trafficking Act) 2013, which in addition to introducing new slavery-like offences such as forced marriage, organ trafficking, and harbouring a victim, expanded the definition of 'exploitation' in human trafficking to cover situations in which the accused 'causes the victim to enter into any of the following conditions: (a) slavery, or a condition similar to slavery; (b) servitude; (c) forced labour; (d) forced marriage;

---

[77] [2016] EWHC 1376 (QB).

[78] Eg, the jury in *David et al v Signal International LLC* (2015) case number 2:08-cv-01220, in the US District Court for the Eastern District of Louisiana, made a US$14 million award of damages in a labour trafficking case, the largest ever.

[79] See A Gallagher, *The International Law of Human Trafficking* (Cambridge: CUP, 2010), 177–91.

[80] J Allain and K Bales, 'Slavery and its Definition' 14 *Global Dialogue* (2012) 1, 6.

[81] N Siller, 'Modern Slavery: Does International Law Distinguish between Slavery, Enslavement and Trafficking' 14(2) *Journal of International Criminal Justice* (2016) 405, 406.

[82] See H Van Der Wilt, 'Trafficking in Human Beings, Enslavement, Crimes against Humanity: Unravelling the Concepts' 13 *Chinese Journal of International Law* (2014) 297, 315.

[83] Application no 25965/04, ECtHR, 7 January 2010, para 281.

(e) debt bondage'.[84] The most significant legislative support for the notion of modern slavery came in Britain, when it enacted the Modern Slavery Act in 2015. The Act consolidates trafficking and slavery offences in one piece of legislation, although it keeps them in separate sections.[85] They share in common the fact that victim consent is explicitly irrelevant to both offences[86] and the *mens rea* requirement has been expanded to the objective test 'knows or ought to know'.[87] Consolidation of this kind allows the application to both kinds of offences of procedural measures such as confiscation of assets,[88] reparation orders,[89] slavery and trafficking prevention orders,[90] and risk orders,[91] overseen by an 'Independent Anti-Slavery Commissioner' responsible for encouraging good practice in the 'prevention, investigation and prosecution of slavery and human trafficking offences'.[92] Other innovations include the requirement that commercial organizations report annually on steps taken to eradicate slavery or human trafficking in their supply chain.[93] The thrust of these provisions is similar in nature to California's Transparency in Supply Chains Act 2010, which requires retailers doing business in California whose annual income exceeds US$100 million to make specific disclosures about the efforts it makes to 'eradicate slavery and human trafficking from its direct supply chain'.[94] The Brazilian Ministry of Labour and Employment's publically accessible 'dirty list' of individuals and companies found using forced labour is a different method of trying to achieve the same ends.[95]

4.7 Protection of Victims

4.7.1 General

The enslaved, trafficked, or victims of other related offences can find themselves in a very vulnerable position. Adequate protections would include provision of immediate protection and support, provision of legal assistance including temporary residency, and safe and voluntary return.[96] The anti-slavery conventions said little about the protections available to victims, and the adequacy of the protections offered by the Human Trafficking Protocol has been the subject of criticism.[97] Although article 2(b) identifies victim protection as one of the aims of the Protocol, the Protocol is primarily focused on law enforcement rather than human rights.[98] This is reflected in the provisions in Part II, aimed at the protection of trafficking victims in the destination state. It fails, for example, to even identify in detail who is a victim, a pre-condition for their protection. In contrast, article 11(2) of the 2011 EU Directive obliges EU member

---

[84] Section 22 inserting s 271.1A of the Criminal Code.
[85] Slavery, servitude, and forced or compulsory labour are dealt with in s 1, human trafficking in s 2.
[86] Section 1(5) and section 2(2) respectively.   [87] Section 1(1) and section 2(4)(b) respectively.
[88] Section 7.   [89] Section 9.   [90] Sections 14 and 15.   [91] Section 23.
[92] Section 41.   [93] Section 54.
[94] A Federal Business Supply Chain Transparency on Trafficking and Slavery Bill 2015 is still before Congress.
[95] Decree no 540 of 2004, suspended in 2014 but reinstated in 2016.
[96] Gallagher, above n 79, 276.
[97] JA Chuang, 'Exploitation Creep and the Unmaking of Human Trafficking Law' 108 *The American Journal of International Law* (2014) 609, 616.
[98] Hathaway, above n 76, 2.

states to take the necessary measures to ensure assistance and support are provided 'as soon as the competent authorities have a reasonable-grounds indication for believing that the person might have been subjected to' trafficking. The Irish High Court in *P v Chief Superintendent of the Garda National Immigration Bureau*[99] held, for example, that a decision by the police that the applicant was not a victim relied on a mechanism to make this decision that was not appropriate inter alia because it could not explain why she was locked inside the building in which she was found with a large-scale cannabis growing operation.

Article 6(1) of the Human Trafficking Protocol protects victims during legal proceedings against their traffickers through, for example, protection of their privacy and identity, but only in 'appropriate cases and to the extent possible under . . . domestic law'. Article 6(3) only requires parties to 'consider' implementing 'measures to provide for the physical, psychological and social recovery' of victims. The Protocol only makes limited provision for victim participation in proceedings, housing, and counselling of victims, and ensuring their safety and compensation, although article 9 obliges parties to take comprehensive measures to protect victims (especially women and children) from re-victimization. One specific difficulty is that the Protocol is a law enforcement instrument and while law enforcers have to rely on victims for evidence against traffickers, they are not well-equipped to respond to or interested in victims' problems, which leaves victims with little incentive to help them (particularly as giving evidence makes them vulnerable to revenge by traffickers).

The UN Human Rights Commissioner tried in 2002 to compensate for the weakness of the Protocol's protections to victims by presenting Recommended Principles and Guidelines on Human Rights and Human Trafficking to the Economic and Social Council (ECOSOC), which place human rights at 'the centre' of efforts to suppress trafficking and protect victims.[100] The UN's Special Rapporteur on Trafficking has also played a constructive role in focusing the attention of states on the victims of trafficking.[101] The Council of Europe Convention provides a minimum framework of assistance to be given to all victims, assistance that cannot be conditional on willingness to assist authorities.[102]

Certain states have responded positively to the plight of victims of trafficking. Nepal has made compensation of trafficking victims a right.[103] South Africa has recognized a right of trafficking victims to access public health care.[104] Australia has provided special protections to vulnerable complainants and special witnesses subject to potential

[99] IEHC 222, 15 April 2015.
[100] *Guidelines on the Handling of Cases of Human Trafficking*, February 2015, cited in *Compendium of Good Practices on the Implementation of the Council of Europe Convention on Action against Trafficking in Human Beings*, Strasbourg, no date, para 1, available at <https://rm.coe.int/CoERMPublicCommonSearchServices/DisplayDCTMContent?documentId=09000016806af624> visited 12 April 2017.
[101] See the discussion in H-J Heintze and C Lülf, 'The UN Protocol to Prevent, Suppress and Punish Trafficking in Persons 2000' in P Hauck and S Peterke (eds), *International Law and Transnational Organized Crime* (Oxford: OUP, 2016), 150, 164.
[102] Article 12.
[103] Article 29 of the Nepalese Constitution 2015 provides for a right for victims to receive compensation.
[104] Section 21 of the Prevention and Combating of Trafficking in Persons Act 2013.

intimidation.[105] The UK's Modern Slavery Act has made it a duty of the Independent Anti-Slavery Commissioner to identify victims of those offences, as well as provision for 'Independent Child Trafficking Advocates' to support suspected child victims of trafficking.[106]

4.7.2 Non-penalization of victims

Most controversially, however, the Protocol leaves the victims open to prosecution themselves for offences committed while being trafficked, and does not give them a right to remain in the state where they are discovered. In practice it is common for trafficking victims to be arrested, convicted, and punished for status offences such as immigration offences, offences consequential to being trafficked like prostitution or illegal labouring, or offences involved in trying to regain their freedom such as potentially assisting in the trafficking of others.[107] In states under Islamic law, for example, prostitution is viewed as adultery, and the trafficked female may be punished for the Shari'ah offence of *zina*.[108] The criminality of the victim makes it possible to charge their traffickers as secondary parties to the victim's offences, but it also serves more cynical functions: justifying deportation or serving as a bargaining chip for information on traffickers. In the Dominican Republic, for example, exemption from criminal liability depends on the victim's ability to 'cooperate' with authorities.[109] The Protocol does not oblige parties to grant victims immunity from criminal liability. This lacunae has led to various calls for a 'principle of non-criminalisation of victims of trafficking in persons' in the sense that they should not be prosecuted for offences committed during the course of their being trafficked or for offences connected to their status as a victim.[110] The principle's rationale is that victims are being persecuted for activities over which they had no control and leaving them open to prosecution fails to recognize that lack of autonomy.[111] More recent instruments oblige parties to enable their prosecutorial authorities not to prosecute. Article 26 of the Council of Europe Convention, for example, obliges each party to 'in accordance with the basic principles of its legal system, provide for the possibility of not imposing penalties on victims for their involvement in unlawful activities ...'. However, just because authorities are entitled to choose not to prosecute does not mean they will not prosecute.

---

[105] Australian Crimes Legislation Amendment (Law Enforcement Integrity, Vulnerable Witness Protection and other Measures Act) 2013.

[106] Section 48.

[107] See A Schloenhardt and R Markey-Towler, 'Non-Criminalisation of Victims of Trafficking in Persons—Principles, Promises and Perspectives' 4(1) *Groningen Journal of International Law* (2016) 10, 13 et seq.

[108] L Smith and M Mattar, 'Creating International Consensus on Combating Trafficking in Persons: US Policy, the Role of the UN, and Global Responses and Challenges' 28 *Fletcher Forum of World Affairs* (2004) 155, 170.

[109] Article 8 of Law 137-03.

[110] See Gallagher, above n 79, 284. See generally RW Piotrowicz and L Sorrentino, 'Human Trafficking and the Emergence of the Non-punishment Principle' 16(4) *Human Rights Law Review* (2016) 669.

[111] See OSCE Office of the Special Representative and Co-coordinator for Combating Trafficking in Human Beings, *Report: Policy and Legislative Recommendations: Towards the Effective Implementation of the Non-Punishment Provision with regard to Victims of Trafficking*, 2013, paras 4 and 5, at <http://www.osce.org/secretariat/101002?download=true> accessed 1 April 2017.

The courts can serve to restrain executive action in this regard. In *R v L and Others (The Children's Commissioner for England and Equality and Human Rights Commission intervening)*[112] the English Court of Criminal Appeal per Lord Judge CJ confirmed that while it was the decision for the prosecutor whether to proceed against a trafficking victim or not the court had a supervisory role to protect the rights of the victim by overseeing the decision of the prosecutor and refusing to countenance any prosecution which failed to acknowledge the victim's subservient situation. Prosecutors can also bind themselves. The Danish Director of Public Prosecutions has issued binding guidelines that oblige prosecutors to waive the indictment of a suspected victim of trafficking provided the alleged offence relates to the trafficking and cannot be characterized as a serious crime. Moreover, the victims will usually have to give evidence of some connection between their illegal activities and their own victimization, normally in one of two different ways.

The more restrictive 'duress model' is illustrated by article 26 of the Council of Europe Convention which obliges each party 'to provide for the possibility of not imposing penalties on victims for their involvement in unlawful activities, *to the extent that they have been compelled to do so*'.[113] Article 8 of the 2011 EU Directive establishes a stronger version of this duress obligation requiring, however, that the duress be the result of commission of trafficking crimes against them:

> Member States shall, in accordance with the basic principles of their legal systems, take the necessary measures to ensure that competent national authorities are entitled not to prosecute or impose penalties on victims of trafficking in human beings for their involvement in criminal activities *which they have been compelled to commit as a direct consequence of being subjected to any of the acts* referred to in Article 2. [114]

Article 4(2) of the ILO Protocol of June 2014, updating ILO Convention 29 on Forced Labour is in almost identical terms.[115] States may rely on the principle of exculpatory necessity found in general criminal law to fulfil these obligations, but the limitations are obvious and the bar high.

The somewhat broader shield provided by the 'causation' model is exemplified by Principle 7 of the UN Office of the High Commissioner for Human Rights Recommended Principles and Guidelines on Human Rights and Trafficking,[116] which enjoins states not to detain, charge, or prosecute trafficked persons 'for their illegal entry into or residence in countries of transit or destination, or for their involvement in unlawful activities to the extent that such involvement is *a direct consequence* of their situation as trafficked persons'. [117] Article 14(7) of the 2015 ASEAN (Association of Southeast Asian Nations) Convention against Trafficking in Persons, Especially Women and Children[118] takes a similar position though it is couched in an even more qualified obligation: 'Each Party shall, subject to its domestic laws, rules, regulations

---

[112] [2013] EWCA Crim 991.   [113] My emphasis.   [114] My emphasis.

[115] Protocol of 2014 to the Forced Labour Convention, 1930, Adoption: Geneva, 103rd ILC session, 11 June 2014; in force 9 November 2016.

[116] UN Doc E/2002//68/Add.1.   [117] My emphasis.

[118] ASEAN Convention against Trafficking in Persons, Especially Women and Children, 21 November 2015, available at <http://www.asean.org/wp-content/uploads/2015/12/ACTIP.pdf> visited 20 April 2017.

and policies, and in appropriate cases, consider not holding victims of trafficking in persons criminally or administratively liable, for unlawful acts committed by them, if such acts are *directly related to the acts of trafficking*.'[119]

Argentina has adopted the causation model in article 5 of its Prevention and Criminalization of Trafficking in Persons and Assistance to Victims of Trafficking Act 2008,[120] which provides that '[v]ictims of trafficking in persons are not punishable for the commission of any crime that is the *direct result* of having been trafficked'. In a more restrictive version of this causation model, article 15 of Georgia's Law on Combating Human Trafficking 2006 lists the offences which victims of human trafficking are exempt from.[121]

The UK's Modern Slavery Act embraces a comprehensive hybrid approach providing that a person will not be guilty of an offence either if they are compelled to do it or if it was a direct consequence of their exploitation (or both), but with two important caveats: (i) that a reasonable person would also have been so compelled or would have done the act as a consequence;[122] and (ii) the defence is not available for a list of serious offences set out in Schedule 4.

4.7.3 Right to remain

Repatriation exposes victims to danger from their former traffickers (especially if they have given police information). Nevertheless, fearing it would be used as a means to illegal immigration, parties to the Human Trafficking Protocol did not agree to the inclusion of a right to remain in the destination state.[123] In terms of article 7(1) they merely promised to 'consider' adopting 'legislative or other appropriate measures that permit victims of trafficking in persons to remain in its territory, temporarily or permanently, in appropriate cases'. In 2002 the US broke new ground in this regard through the provision of the T-Visa, designed specifically to allow victims of 'severe' trafficking to remain in the US if they cannot return to their home countries due to extreme hardship.[124] To qualify the victim must comply except in the case of increased trauma with 'any reasonable request for assistance' in 'investigation or prosecution of acts of trafficking'.[125] Italy has since 1998 provided for a six-month renewable visa to victims without any requirement that they be willing to assist law enforcement; they need only be 'in danger' and willing to engage in a social reintegration programme.[126] Reports suggest, however, that authorities have given preference to those who do collaborate.[127] In 2004 the EU adopted a directive along very similar lines, which also provides for a 'reflection period' to allow victims to recover and escape the influence

---

[119] My emphasis.   [120] Law 26.364.   [121] My emphasis.

[122] Section 45(1)–(3) (compulsion) and (4) (consequence).

[123] Revised draft Protocol to Prevent, Suppress and Punish Trafficking in Persons Especially Women and Children, supplementing the United Nations Convention against Transnational Organised Crime, 11th Sess., Agenda Item 3, at 7, UN Doc A/AC.254/4/Add.3/Rev.7 (2000).

[124] Section 107(b)(1) et seq of Victims of Trafficking and Violence Protection Act of 2000, 114 Stat. 1464, Pub Law 106–386—28 October 2000; 22 USC § 7101.

[125] Section 107(b)(1)(a) and (e).   [126] Article 18, Decreto Legislativo, 25 July 1998, No 286.

[127] US State Department, *Trafficking in Persons Report 2016, Country Narrative: Italy,* available at <https://www.state.gov/j/tip/rls/tiprpt/countries/2016/258790.htm> visited 16 April 2017.

of their traffickers before making an informed decision about whether they should cooperate with authorities.[128] The 2005 Council of Europe Convention follows suit, but also obliges parties to grant victims renewable residence either on humanitarian grounds and/or on the basis of their cooperation with the authorities, as well as addressing issues such as access to information, legal representation, and legal aid.[129] For most states, however, deportation of the victim, potentially in violation of the principle of *non-refoulement* (the prohibition on returning aliens to states where their lives might be at risk), remains a potential outcome. Article 8 of the Human Trafficking Protocol deals with repatriation, the right to return, the safety of and facilitation of return, and as pointed out above article 9 obliges parties to prevent re-victimization, which is most likely to occur on their return.

4.8 Pressure to Implement

The fight against human trafficking has led to an almost continuous process of global law reform under the guidance of various inter-governmental organizations (IGOs) such as the ILO[130] and through regional processes like the Bali Process on People Smuggling, Trafficking in Persons and Related Transnational Crime.[131] Performance in the investigation and prosecution of human trafficking cases was initially poor but appears to be improving. From 2003 to 2008 40 per cent of states with human trafficking laws did not record a single conviction for contravention of these laws.[132] In 2008 the US Trafficking in Persons (TIP) Report estimated that there were 5,212 prosecutions and 2,983 convictions with the identification of 30,961 victims, while by 2015 those numbers had increased to 18,930, 6,609, and 77,823 respectively.[133] Various IGOs have taken steps to improve the response.[134] The Organization for Security and Co-operation in Europe (OSCE) launched the Alliance against Trafficking in Persons aimed at streamlining responses to every aspect of human trafficking. The Council of Europe's Group of Experts on Action against Trafficking in Human Beings (GRETA) has been active in providing policy guidance. The UNODC's Global Programme against Trafficking in Human Beings (GPAT) was set up in 1999 as a focus for best practice guidelines, and in 2007 the UN Global Initiative to Fight Human Trafficking (UN GIFT) was formed to facilitate international cooperation. NGOs have also become increasingly important as sources of information in operational anti-trafficking efforts, and increasingly work hand in hand with IGOs.[135]

---

[128] Article 6 of Council Directive 2004/81/EC of 29 April 2004 on the residence permit issued to third-country nationals who are victims of trafficking in human beings or who have been the subject of an action to facilitate illegal immigration, who cooperate with the competent authorities, OJ L261 6 August 2004.
[129] Articles 13, 14, and 15.
[130] ILO, *Human Trafficking and Forced Labour Exploitation: Guidance for Legislation and Law Enforcement* (Geneva: ILO, 2005), 10.
[131] See Bali Process, <http://www.baliprocess.net> last visited 7 April 2017.
[132] UNODC, *The Globalization of Crime: A Transnational Organized Crime Threat Assessment* (Vienna: UNODC, 2010), 52.
[133] United States Department of State, *Trafficking in Persons Report 2016*, 40.   [134] ibid, 414.
[135] See M Lagon, 'Traits of Transformative Anti-Trafficking Partnerships' 1(1) *Journal of Human Trafficking* (2015) 21–38.

The most direct pressure on states has come from the US, which makes an annual survey of the performance of other parties in implementing the Protocol, ranks each party, and if it considers them as failing, subjects them to sanctions.[136] The TIP report assesses whether each party to the Protocol's anti-trafficking efforts meet 'minimum standards' (with a heavy emphasis on convictions). States are ranked as follows: Tier 1 states are fully compliant; Tier 2 states have made significant efforts to comply; and Tier 3 states have made no efforts to comply. A Tier 2WL (watch list) is reserved for those states not fully compliant where the problem is getting worse. States frequently protest at their rankings, sometimes successfully.[137]

Individuals have also resorted to the courts to force implementation by states. In *Rantsev v Cyprus and Russia*[138] the appellant argued before the European Court of Human Rights that Cyprus and Russia had insufficiently investigated the death of his daughter, and had failed to protect her and to prosecute the traffickers responsible for her death. He alleged inter alia breaches of the right to be free from slavery and forced servitude.[139] The Court recognized that human trafficking fell within this right and that under article 4(a) of the Council of Europe Trafficking Convention these states were under an obligation to investigate allegations of trafficking domestically and to cooperate effectively with other states concerned.

4.9 Conclusion

Whilst the de jure legal status of slavery may have disappeared from the world, the de facto condition of being enslaved in its multifarious forms, sometimes under de jure disguises of legal contracts of employment, remains a major problem. This explains the shift in emphasis from the suppression of slavery to the suppression of slavery-like practices in transnational criminal law. While slavery and human trafficking are primarily human rights violations, it is noteworthy that the emphasis of suppression has been on supply—slave trading and human trafficking—not demand—slaveholding, debt bondage, purchase of sex, and illegal labour. In addition, the incremental but fairly frequent additions of new offences suggest that international society has struggled to fully grasp the nature of the problem and the harm done. New labels such as Modern Slavery have allowed states to take a step back from the problem to try to see and respond to it in its entirety. Responding to the harm without fully realizing and responding to the plight of the victims of the multifarious abuses, nonetheless, remains a problem.

---

[136] In terms of Section 110, Victims Of Trafficking and Violence Protection Act of 2000, 114 Stat. 1464, Pub Law 106–386—28 October 2000.

[137] In 2016 Thailand's angry reaction to its placement in Tier 3 led to an upgrade to Tier 2. See J Szep et al, 'Exclusive: U.S. to upgrade Thailand in annual human trafficking report—sources', *Reuters*, 29 June 2016, available at <http://www.reuters.com/article/us-humantrafficking-thailand-idUSKCN0ZE2NH> accessed 16 April 2017.

[138] [2010] ECHR App No 25965/04 (7 January 2010).

[139] Under article 4 of the European Convention for the Protection of Human Rights and Fundamental Freedoms, Rome, 4 November 1950, ETS No 5, in force 3 September 1953.

5

Migrant Smuggling

5.1 From Refugees to Smuggled Migrants

Individuals fleeing persecution have a legal right to claim refugee status under the Refugees Convention[1] and the right not to be expelled, or returned to the state from which they fled.[2] Providing they present themselves without delay and show good cause for their unauthorized entry into other states to claim this refugee status, they also have immunity from penalization for their unauthorized entry or presence in that state.[3] 'Irregular migration' in the sense of unauthorized crossing of borders even if in pursuit of asylum raises two questions: whether the movement of individuals whose status as refugees is yet to be determined is a lawful form of migratory movement or not; and whether assisting these individuals to cross borders is lawful or not? In regard to the first question, migrants are legally vulnerable because they may break the law of both the state they leave and that in which they arrive by bribing officials and because they have no papers or visas required for entry. However, the main target of international action is not the migrants themselves—the Refugee Convention prohibits the penalizing of refugees for their illegal entry and their presence[4]—but taking steps against those who facilitate the unauthorized movement of migrants from one state to another.

The mass migration of people in the late twentieth and twenty-first centuries fleeing from persecution, armed conflict, and collapsing economies to the relative safety and material security of other states, coupled with ever tighter immigration controls in these destination states, has brought the need for actions against migrant smugglers who facilitate this migration sharply into focus. The convergent interest of various states in the maintenance of their borders has led to a series of legal steps being taken against those who smuggle migrants in what has been aptly termed 'crimmigration', a hybrid of immigration and criminal law used to control suspect populations in the transnational space.[5] Central to this process has been the recharacterization of the refugee as smuggled migrant, which has enabled the relabelling of assisting their flight to asylum as a crime, allowing a shift in focus away from the dilemmas of the migrants to action against the migrant smuggler and the trumping of the Refugees Convention by crime suppression conventions designed to suppress smuggling as a guide to national response.[6] It also permits the characterization of migrant smuggling

---

[1] Article 1(A)(2) of the Convention Relating to the Status of Refugees, 28 July 1951, 189 UNTS 150; in force 22 April 1954. See also, article 7 of the International Covenant on Civil and Political Rights (ICCPR), the right not to be returned to a country where they may be 'subjected to torture or to cruel, inhuman or degrading treatment or punishment'.
[2] Article 32 and 33.   [3] Article 31.   [4] Article 16.
[5] J Stumpf, 'The Crimmigration Crisis: Immigrants, Crime and Sovereign Power' 56(2) *American Studies Law Review* (2006) 367.
[6] S Pickering, 'Transnational Crime and Refugee Protection' 34(2) *Social Justice* (2007) 47, 50–2.

as a security threat which as Gallagher points out serves in turn to 'justify and explain the growing externalization of border controls and the increased militarization of all aspects of border control—from surveillance to deterrence'.[7]

5.2 The Nature of Migrant Smuggling

Migrant smuggling 'is the unauthorized movement of individuals across national borders for the financial or other benefit of the smuggler'.[8] Migrant or people smuggling occurs when migrants, prevented from entering a state because of heavily enforced restrictive immigration policies, turn to smugglers for assistance to gain entry. Perversely, the more effective border controls, the greater the demand for the services of smugglers. States have responded by developing policy and law aimed at deterring migrant smugglers by punishing them. In Australia, for example, the large number of 'suspected irregular entry vessels' (SIEVs), 849 in the period 2008–2014 carrying more than 50,000 people, has been met with prosecution of the crew and sometimes of those who organize these operations.[9]

Unlike human trafficking, the primary motivation of the smugglers is not the exploitation of those smuggled but payment—usually part in advance and part on arrival—for their services. In addition, migrant smuggling, unlike human trafficking, occurs with the consent of the migrants and is not carried out with the purpose of their exploitation. And while human trafficking harms individuals, in migrant smuggling the harm is felt by the destination state, particularly in its control of its borders and management of immigration. The distinction blurs, however, when a migrant is subject to coercive exploitation during the course or at the conclusion of their journey such as being made to 'work' to pay off their debt.[10] If migrants withdraw their consent, they are not necessarily victims of human trafficking because the smugglers may use violence to keep them moving but without the purpose of exploiting them. This places the onus on the migrant who is also a victim of trafficking to establish that they have been trafficked.[11] It has also been pointed out that the notion that migrants choose to be smuggled is misleading because they are often forced through poverty, humanitarian crises, and persecution to migrate under the coercive conditions of smuggling.[12]

---

[7] AT Gallagher, 'Migrant Smuggling' in N Boister and R Currie (eds), *The Routledge Handbook of Transnational Criminal Law* (Abingdon: Routledge, 2015), 187, 188.

[8] ibid, 187.

[9] A Schloenhardt and C Craig, 'Prosecution of People Smugglers in Australia 2011–14' 38 *Sydney Law Review* (2016) 49, 52.

[10] See A Schloenhardt, 'The UN Protocol against the Smuggling of Migrants by Land, Sea and Air 2000' in P Hauck and S Peterke (eds), *International Law and Transnational Organized Crime* (Oxford: OUP, 2016), 169, 176.

[11] A Gallagher, 'Human Rights and the New UN Protocols on Trafficking and Migrant Smuggling: A Preliminary Analysis' 23 *Human Rights Quarterly* (2001) 975, 1001.

[12] T Obokata, 'Smuggling of Human Beings from a Human Rights Perspective: Obligations of Non-State and State Actors under International Human Rights Law' 17 *International Journal of Refugee Law* (2005) 394, 397 et seq.

5.3 Background to the Migrant Smuggling Protocol

Prior to resort to transnational criminal law, an existing web of human rights law, specialist refugee law, laws of the sea, and migration control treaties regulated this area.[13] Concerns about increased flows of illicit migrants led to calls by Italy and Austria for the development of an instrument aimed at coordinating efforts to suppress those who facilitate the flow through the use of the criminal law.[14] Italy proposed a convention to the International Maritime Organization specifically to interdict migrant smuggling at sea but it was the Austrian proposal for a UN General Assembly Convention criminalizing migrant smuggling which ultimately bore legal fruit.[15] The problem identified by supporters of criminalization was the rationale that underpins all criminal law: without criminalization in all countries smugglers were free to operate as they please and were not open to extradition.[16] The problem was taken up during the negotiation of the UN Convention against Transnational Organized Crime (UNTOC) because of the perception that opportunities for financial gain through migrant smuggling were being exploited by organized criminals.[17] In 1999, the UN General Assembly, which had in 1993 resolved that smuggling of aliens was an issue of 'transnational concern' deserving of multilateral response,[18] asked the intergovernmental ad hoc committee established to negotiate the UNTOC to consider further instruments, one being to address specifically, the smuggling of migrants.[19] The end result, the Protocol against the Smuggling of Migrants by Land, Sea and Air, Supplementing the United Nations Convention against Transnational Organized Crime,[20] is the principal legal instrument directed at the suppression of people smuggling. Its stated purpose is to 'prevent and combat the smuggling of migrants', 'while protecting the rights of smuggled migrants'.[21] In order to serve as the anchor point for a range of law enforcement measures,[22] the Migrant Smuggling Protocol requires each party to criminalize three distinct forms of conduct, each built around the definition of 'smuggling of migrants'.

5.4 Crimes

5.4.1 Smuggling migrants

Article 6(1)(a) is the focal offence. It requires criminalization of the key conduct of 'smuggling of migrants', which article 3(a) defines as 'the procurement, in order to

---

[13] See generally A Gallagher and F David, *The International Law of Migrant Smuggling* (Cambridge: CUP, 2014), 23 et seq.

[14] See Schloenhardt, above n 10, 169–73.

[15] IMO Legal Committee, 'Proposed Multilateral Convention to Combat Illegal Migration by Sea', IMO Doc LEG 76/11/1, 1 August 1997; 'Letter dated 16 September 1997 from the Permanent Representative of Austria to the United Nations addressed to the Secretary-General', UN Doc A/52/357, 17 September 1997.

[16] Gallagher, above n 7, 187–88.

[17] 'Measures to Combat Alien Smuggling: Report of the Secretary-General', UN DOC A/49/350, 30 August 1994.

[18] GA Res 48/102 of 8 March 1994, adopted 20 December 1993.

[19] GA Res 53/111, 20 January 1999, adopted 9 December 1998.

[20] 15 November 2000, 2241 UNTS 507; in force 28 January 2004.   [21] Article 2.

[22] Article 4. These cooperation provisions are found in Articles 11, 12, and 15. Articles 7–9 deal with the specific problem of smuggling of migrants by sea.

obtain, directly or indirectly, a financial or other material benefit, of the illegal entry of a person into a State Party of which the person is not a national or a permanent resident'. In terms of article 3(b) 'illegal entry' is defined as 'crossing borders without complying with the necessary requirements for legal entry into the receiving State'. Illegal entry thus implies smuggling into a state.[23] Thus while human trafficking may take place entirely within a state, migrant smuggling must be transnational in this limited sense. This appears to contradict the requirement in article 34(2) of the UNTOC that offences in the Convention and its Protocols must be established in domestic law independently of transnationality. Although the United Nations Office on Drugs and Crime's Legislative Guide to implementing the UNTOC and the Protocols clarifies that '[i]n the case of smuggling of migrants, domestic offences should apply even where transnationality and the involvement of organized criminal groups does not exist or cannot be proved',[24] this general rule does not apply to the illegal entry offence. As the Legislative Guide notes somewhat contradictorily, '[s]muggling, on the other hand, contains a necessary element of transnationality, which requires illegal entry from one country to another'.[25] While the offence depends on illegal entry, parties have expanded the scope of the offence to include individuals on their way to the destination state prior to entry, although how early in their journey this extends to before it becomes mere preparation for the offence is difficult to say.[26]

The requirement that entry must be 'illegal' excludes from the scope of the offence procurement of the entry of nationals or those with rights of residence. The offence was not designed to be used in cases where a valid document is used improperly and the entry was technically legal.[27] In *R v Konsaijan*[28] the New Zealand High Court held that an entry into New Zealand is not 'unauthorized' for the purposes of section 98C of the Crimes Act 1961, which implements the article 6(1)(a) offence, if the migrant enters with a valid visitor's visa even if they intend to work. Some parties have clarified that the scope of the offence in their legislation does include procurement of the illegal entry of individuals who may have a valid claim to asylum. This is the case, for example, in section 228B(2) of Australia's Migration Act 1958, which explains that the offence includes smuggling of non-citizens who do not hold a valid

---

[23] Section 57 of Singapore's Immigration Act 1989, which criminalizes smuggling out of Singapore, thus extends beyond the scope of the Protocol obligation. See *Mohd Hazwan bin Moh Muji v Public Prosecutor* [2012] SGHC 203.

[24] UNODC, *Legislative Guide for the Implementation of the United Nations Convention against Transnational Organised Crime and the Protocols Thereto* (Vienna: UN, 2004), 333.

[25] ibid, 341.

[26] See section 233A of Australia's Migration Act. An earlier version of this section has been authoritatively interpreted as including the smuggling of migrants who have not yet crossed the boundary into Australia—see *R v Ahmad* (2012) 31 NTLR 38, 43–44 [17]. New Zealand avoids this problem by specifically allowing in section 98C of the Crimes Act 1961 for the prosecution of a smuggler who brings a migrant to New Zealand or arranges for them to enter New Zealand even when in fact the migrant did not enter or was not brought to New Zealand.

[27] Legislative Guide, above n 24, 341.

[28] [2012] NZHC 2293. A similar point was made in BGH 4 StR 142/12 (Bundesgerichtshof, 25 September 2012) where the German Court distinguished between migrant smuggling which involves illegal entry and situations where migrant enters lawfully but has no permit to work.

entry visa including those 'seeking protection or asylum (however described), whether or not Australia has, or may have, protection obligations in respect of the non-citizen because the non-citizen is or may be a refugee, or for any other reason'. Schloenhardt and Stacey note:

> Persons brought to Australia with the assistance of migrant smugglers (or 'people smugglers') are generally referred to as unauthorised arrivals or, in reference to s 14 of the *Migration Act 1958* (Cth), as unlawful non-citizens, that is, persons with no valid travel authority to enter into (or remain in) Australia.[29]

It follows that all the prosecution has to show is that the smuggled individuals did not have valid visas for entry into Australia, and implies that Australian immigration law dictates how an individual may exercise their rights to claim refugee status from Australia; if they engage others to facilitate their migration to Australia outside of these channels their rights under international law do not clothe the actions of the individuals who smuggle them in legality.

'Procurement' of illegal entry is a very broad term drafted to cover the full range of migrant smuggling services from leading them across physical land and sea borders to expensive forged visa-based smuggling. The requirement that the accused smuggler's conduct must be intentional, implies a requirement that the smuggler know they are procuring the illegal entry of a migrant into a state. For example, in the Australian case *PJ v The Queen*[30] a Court in Victoria held that the individual concerned must know that the destination was Australia (ie another country to which their passengers had no lawful right of entry). In practice, parties have lowered the threshold. The Netherlands, for example, only requires that the alleged people smuggler 'knows or has serious reason to suspect'[31] while English law only requires that they have knowledge or a 'reasonable cause to believe'.[32]

In addition, the smuggler must procure this illegal entry for the specific purpose of obtaining 'a financial or other material benefit'. The motivations of the smugglers might be pecuniary or non-pecuniary (sexual favours, labour, etc) but the offence excludes humanitarian or familial motivations. It requires an intention to profit, excluding from the scope of the offence the conduct of those NGOs which support migrants for humanitarian reasons or individuals who do so on the basis of close family ties.[33] Individuals who act out of necessity by providing transport, food, medical care, clothing, and temporary accommodation, or by rescuing wrecked migrants, may in fact serve to foster the unauthorized entry of migrants

---

[29] A Schloenhardt and KL Stacey, 'Assistance and Protection of Smuggled Migrants: International Law and Australian Practice' 35 *Sydney Law Review* (2013) 53, 66.

[30] (2012) 36 Victoria 402, 405 [50] interpreting section 233C of the Migration Act.

[31] Article 197a of the Criminal Code.

[32] Section 25 of the Immigration Act 1971. See *Kapoor and Others* [2012] EWCA Crim 435.

[33] UNGA, 'Report of the Ad Hoc Committee on the Elaboration of a Convention against Transnational Organized Crime on the work of its first to eleventh sessions; Addendum: Interpretative notes for the official record (*travaux préparatoires*) of the negotiations for the United Nations Convention against Transnational Organized Crime and the Protocols thereto', UN doc A/55/383/Add.1, 3 November 2000, para 88.

into another state but they do so without the necessary venal intentions. The absence of this profit motive in article 1 of the 2002 EU Directive on Facilitation of Unauthorized Entry, Transit and Residence[34] which requires only intentional assistance, and in some domestic legislation, is considered a fundamental flaw by critics because it permits the prosecution of those who help migrants for entirely altruistic reasons.[35] It contrasts with the Canadian Supreme Court decision in *R v Appulonappa*[36] where the court found Canada's law criminalizing smuggling, section 117 of the Immigration and Refugee Protection Act, to be inconsistent with the Protocol's object of protecting the rights of smuggled migrants by allowing prosecution of those who provide support for humanitarian or familial reasons, was over broad and should be 'read down ... as not applying to persons providing humanitarian aid to asylum-seekers or to asylum-seekers who provide each other mutual aid (including aid to family members)'. The EU Directive does suggest in article 1(2) that member states may decide not to impose sanctions but leaves it to them. Unfortunately, there is nothing in article 5 of the Migrant Smuggling Protocol preventing this more comprehensive criminalization and indeed, article 34(3) of the parent convention, the UNTOC, provides explicit permission to parties to adopt more strict or severe measures. Many states do not require a profit motive as an element of the crime and do prosecute individuals who help migrants for humanitarian reasons.[37] France, for example, only treats a financial motive as an aggravating factor, not as an essential element of the offence.[38] Other states do, however, explicitly require a financial motive. Germany requires an intention to achieve a 'pecuniary advantage'[39] and in Austria convictions for smuggling have been overturned for want of such an intention.[40] Some states have a hybrid approach. There is thus no such requirement in the offence of 'assisting unlawful immigration' in section 25 of the UK's Immigration Act 1971, but the offence of 'helping asylum seekers' in section 25A must be done for 'gain'.

---

[34] Council Directive 2002/90/EC of 28 November 2002 defining the facilitation of unauthorised entry, transit and residence, OJ L 32/17, 12 May 2002. See also Council Framework Decision 2002/946/JHA of 28 November 2002 in the strengthening of the penal framework to prevent the facilitation of unauthorized entry, transit and residence, OJ L 328/1, 5 December 2002.

[35] See Gallagher and David, above n 13, 392 et seq; A Schloenhardt and H Hickson, 'Non-Criminalization of Smuggled Migrants: Rights, Obligations, and Australian Practice under Article 5 of the Protocol against Smuggling of Migrants by Land, Sea, and Air' 25 *International Journal of Refugee Law* (2013) 39, 56, commenting on the Australian offence.

[36] [2015] 3 SCR 754, para 44, 85.

[37] See D Dzananovic, 'European Courts and Citizens Struggle to do "What's Right" Amidst Reactionary Migration Law and Policy', Center for Migration Studies, Radbouts University, available at <http://cmsny.org/publications/dzananovic-eu-courts-and-citizens/> visited 28 April 2017.

[38] *Code de l'Entrée et du Séjour des Étrangers et du Droit d'Asile* (Code on the entry and stay of foreigners and the right of asylum) (CESEDA), Article L622-1.

[39] German Law on the residence, employment and the integration of foreigners in the federal territory, Bundesgesetzblatt Teil I, 2014-12-31, vol. 64, 2439, section 96.

[40] Case 14Os91/12g (OGH, 25 September 2012). This contrasts with the Australian decision in *Ahmadi v The Queen* (2011) 254 FLR 174 where a conviction was confirmed despite the motive being to help the migrants out of religious conviction because of the absence of such a requirement in Australian law.

5.4.2 Document fraud

Article 6(1)(b) makes similar provision for offences involving document fraud. It requires criminalization of (i) producing or (ii) procuring, providing, or possessing a fraudulent travel or identity document. Article 3(c) defines a 'fraudulent travel or identity document' as any travel or identity document:

(i)   That has been falsely made or altered in some material way by anyone other than a person or agency lawfully authorized to make or issue the travel or identity document on behalf of a State; or

(ii) That has been improperly issued or obtained through misrepresentation, corruption or duress or in any other unlawful manner; or

(iii) That is being used by a person other than the rightful holder.

The phrase 'falsely made or altered in some material way' can be interpreted as including not only the making of fake documents but also the modification of genuine documents and the filling in of blank stolen documents. It would include forged documents and authentic documents being used by someone other than the lawful holder.[41] The production of such a document can be achieved, for example, through complete forgery or through alteration of a signature. 'Procuring' a document involves obtaining it, 'providing' involves giving it, and 'possession' must be for the purposes of smuggling migrants, not possession by a smuggled migrant for their own unauthorized entry.[42]

In regard to the mental element of criminal liability, these document offences must also be committed intentionally but with (i) the specific purpose of 'financial or other material benefit' in terms of article 3(a) (which again excludes altruistically motivated actions) and (ii) with the further specific purpose of enabling the smuggling of migrants, so as to avoid too broad an offence.

5.4.3 Enabling a person to remain clandestinely or otherwise illegally

Article 6(1)(c) is aimed at suppressing the actions of those individuals who facilitate the ability of migrants who may enter legally but who remain in the host country clandestinely or otherwise illegally.[43] It requires the criminalization of enabling a person who is not a national or a permanent resident to remain in a state without complying with the necessary requirements for legally remaining in the state. The conduct of enabling itself must occur by the means outlined in article 6(1)(b), that is producing, procuring, providing, or possessing a fraudulent travel or identity document or 'any other illegal means' defined as illegal by domestic law. Again, the offence must be committed intentionally with the purpose of obtaining some 'financial or material benefit', thus excluding altruistically motivated actions.[44]

---

[41] Legislative Guide, above n 24, 343–45.   [42] Interpretative Notes, above n 33, para 93.
[43] Legislative Guide, above n 24, 342–43.   [44] In terms of article 3(a).

5.4.4 Attempts, secondary parties, organizing and directing, corporate liability

Article 6(2) obliges parties to criminalize attempts, accomplice liability, and organizing or directing other persons to engage in article 6(1) offences. This provision expands the scope of criminality considerably reaching individuals who not only try to commit these offences, but who both assist and arrange these offences. Not all states criminalize inchoate offences like attempt, hence the obligation in regard to attempts is subject to the 'basic concepts' of the party's legal system. So too is the obligation under article 6(1)(b)(ii) because of the difficulty associated with being an accomplice to 'possessing' a fraudulent travel or identity document.[45] Domestic offences such as 'facilitation' of migrant smuggling under section 232A of Australia's Migration Act in a sense transform secondary liability into stand-alone offences, which can, for example, apply to a migrant who voluntarily acts as an interpreter between migrant smugglers and other passengers.[46] Finally, while corporate liability is not specifically referred to in article 6, it has been suggested that following the UNTOC provision for corporate criminal liability should also be made for people smuggling offences.[47]

5.4.5 Limitation of international cooperation to transnational migrant smuggling by an organized criminal group

Like the Human Trafficking Protocol, article 4 of the Migrant Smuggling Protocol limits international cooperation in the prevention, investigation, and prosecution of its offences to those which are transnational in nature and involve an organized criminal group. These conditions are not included in the definition of most of the offences (except the transnational aspect in article 6(1)(a)), and it may be that the latter will present a major obstacle to effectively suppressing migrant smuggling where, for example, only the crew of a boat are apprehended and they are less than three in number (thus not qualifying as an organized criminal group in terms of the UNTOC).

5.4.6 Punishment

The only provision which refers directly if partially to punishment in the Protocol is article 6(3), which obliges parties to establish as aggravating, circumstances '(a) that endanger, or are likely to endanger, the lives or safety of the migrants concerned; or (b) that entail inhuman or degrading treatment, including for exploitation, of such migrants'. It applies to all article 6(1) offences except those in article 6(1)(b), that is producing, procuring, providing, or possessing a fraudulent travel or identity document.

These aggravating circumstances are of two kinds. Endangering the lives of or safety of migrants may include, for example, setting to sea in an unseaworthy boat,

---

[45] D McClean, *Transnational Organized Crime: A Commentary on the UN Convention and its Protocols* (Oxford: OUP, 2007), 395.
[46] See *Kadem v The Queen* (2002) 129 A Crim R 304, [2002] WASCA 133, discussed in Schloenhardt and Hickson, above n 35, 58.
[47] See Schloenhardt, above n 10, 181–82.

forced journeys in desert terrain with no water, or smuggling in shipping containers without adequate heating, cooling, food, water, or fresh air. Interestingly, a Greek court decided that the aggravating factor of endangering the lives of the migrants had to be derived causally from the smuggler's conduct itself and could not arise out of his attempts to avoid police interception by driving recklessly (he crashed the car transporting them while attempting to get away).[48] Inhuman or degrading treatment includes a broad range of forms of abuse, which if it is exploitative in nature may overlap with human trafficking. A recent Spanish decision involved, for example, enforced prostitution to pay for the cost of the smuggling.[49]

States can implement this aggravation in two ways—as a separate aggravated offence or as aggravating factors to be taken into consideration on sentence.[50] Australia has adopted the former option, with some domestic tailoring. The punishment for people smuggling under section 233A of Australia's Migration Act is, for example, a maximum of ten years. It can, however, be aggravated to twenty year maximum in two ways: under s 233B where the smuggler subjects the smuggled migrant to 'cruel inhuman or degrading treatment' or their actions give 'rise to a danger of death or serious harm to the victim' and the smuggler is 'reckless' in that regard, or under s 233C by smuggling five or more individuals (it carries a mandatory minimum sentence of five years or eight years for repeat offenders[51]). While the former implements article 6(3) of the Protocol, the latter is driven by Australia's domestic anti-migrant smuggling stance. Severe penalties are imposed. A prominent Iranian people smuggler responsible for sending five unseaworthy vessels to Australia, one of which foundered off Christmas Island with the loss of fifty lives, was, for example, given a fourteen-year sentence under the latter form of aggravation and his appeal against sentence failed.[52]

Finally, article 6(4) of the Protocol does provide that nothing in the Protocol 'shall prevent a state from taking measures against a person whose conduct constitutes an offence under its domestic law', which has been interpreted to include both administrative and criminal sanctions.[53]

5.5 The Protection of Migrants' Human Rights

5.5.1 General

Article 2 of the Protocol provides that one of its purposes is to protect the rights of smuggled migrants, who are vulnerable to life-threatening modes of transport, exploitation, deception, threats and violence from smugglers, dangerous conditions of arrest

---

[48] *Court of First Instance of Thesprotia (in Council)*, Case Reference 16/2008, in a prosecution under article 88(1)(c) of Law 3386/2005, available at <https://www.unodc.org/cld/case-law-doc/migrantsmugglingcrimetype/grc/court_of_first_instance_of_thesprotia_in_council_162008.html?lng=en&tmpl=sherloc> visited 19 April 2017.

[49] *Resolucion 807/2016*, of 27 October 2016, available at <https://www.unodc.org/cld/case-law-doc/migrantsmugglingcrimetype/esp/2016/resolucion_8072016.html?lng=en&tmpl=sherloc> last visited 19 April 2017.

[50] See Schloenhardt, above n 10, 182.   [51] Section 236B.

[52] *Heydarkhani v The Queen* (2014) 240 A Crim R 195, 203, paras 52–53.

[53] Legislative Guide, above n 24, 351.

(particularly at sea), and poor conditions of detention.[54] Some of these protections relate to the protection from others including smugglers and some of these protections relate to restraint of the behaviour of the state from which they leave or their destination state. Most of the provisions protecting rights in the Protocol refer to the parties' existing obligations under other international laws. Of particular importance in this regard is the savings clause in article 19:

> Nothing in this Protocol shall affect the other rights, obligations and responsibilities of States and individuals under international law, including international humanitarian law and international human rights law and, in particular, where applicable, the 1951 Convention and the 1967 Protocol relating to the Status of Refugees and the principle of non-refoulement as contained therein.

This means, for example, that nothing contained in the Protocol affects the principle of *non- refoulement*, even when it operates extra-territorially because the migrant falls under the effective control of the destination state. Thus nothing in the Protocol could justify push-back operations where states send undocumented migrants and asylum seekers intercepted at sea back to the country of departure without processing them or examining the potential human rights abuses they face on return, a policy condemned by the European Court of Human Rights in *Hirsii Jamaa et al v Italy*[55] as inter alia a violation of the prohibition against protection from torture and inhuman or degrading treatment under article 3 of the European Convention on Human Rights.

Crucially, however, the human rights provisions in the Protocol flesh out these general human rights obligations with specific content relevant to the activity of migrant smuggling, which provides a specific framework for action where parties to the Protocol are either not party to the relevant human rights or refugee convention or have not implemented their general human rights and refugee law obligations.

5.5.2 Migrants' immunity from prosecution for Protocol offences

Migrants have in the past been subject to harsh penalties and detention even where they have had legitimate claims to asylum.[56] The offences in the Protocol are, however, aimed at traffickers, not migrants. It follows that in terms of Article 5 migrants shall not be criminally liable 'under this Protocol' for being the 'object of the conduct' set out in article 6. Article 2 of Egypt's Law on Combating Illegal Migration and Smuggling of Migrants, for example, provides that 'smuggled migrants bear no criminal responsibility'.[57] It has been argued that under the Protocol migrants may face criminal prosecution for an offence unrelated to migrant smuggling, such as criminal damage or harming other migrants.[58] The ability to impose liability under some other law is retained through operation of article 6(4), which clarifies that '[n]othing in this

---

[54] For the background on the controversy surrounding introduction of these human rights concerns see Schloenhardt and Stacey above n 29, 56–58.

[55] App No 27765/09, ECtHR 23 February 2012.

[56] See Schloenhardt and Hickson, above n 35, 44.

[57] Law no 82 for 2016.

[58] See McClean, above n 45, 389.

Protocol shall prevent a State Party from taking measures against a person whose conduct constitutes an offence under its domestic law'.

One area of difficulty is whether prosecution by a party of a migrant who themselves engages in facilitation of the smuggling of migrants is in some way a violation of article 5. A migrant who fixes the engine of a boat in which they are a passenger would not necessarily fall foul of an offence that directly transcribed article 5 with its specific intention of material benefit into domestic law, but would definitely fall foul of a people smuggling offence that did not require this direct intention.[59]

The scope of the immunity offered by article 5 is narrower than in the Refugees Convention which gives a broad protection from penalization to asylum seekers,[60] but it is broader in the sense that it is offered to all smuggled migrants and not just to those claiming refugee status, and does not impose any further conditions for immunity such as coming directly from a territory where their life or freedom was threatened or showing good cause for their entry.[61] It has been argued that article 5's protection should be extended through a good faith interpretation of article 5's purposes beyond prohibiting criminalization to prohibiting the application of administrative measures as a disguised form of punishment and deterrent to smugglers.[62] An example of this is the mandatory detention of all 'unlawful non-citizens' under the Australian Migration Act.[63]

5.5.3 Reinforcing existing protections

Article 16(1) of the Migrant Smuggling Protocol obliges parties to take appropriate measures 'to preserve and protect the rights of persons' smuggled, 'in particular, the right to life and the right not to be subjected to torture or other cruel inhuman or degrading treatment of punishment'. Although this provision does not confer any rights on smuggled migrants beyond those already recognized in international human rights or humanitarian law,[64] it would, for example, oblige parties to take positive action in certain situations such as ensuring the rescue of migrants abandoned in the desert by smugglers or wrecked in heavy seas, and to provide them with emergency food, shelter, and medical care, in order to respect the right to life in article 6(1) of the ICCPR.[65]

Article 16(2) obliges parties to ensure the protection of migrants from violence perpetrated by 'individuals or groups', which would include violence perpetrated by the smugglers, vigilantes, and local populations who resent the entry of smugglers or prey on them, or even law enforcement officers. No further guidance is provided as to what this might entail, and parties are left to take 'appropriate' measures.

Article 16(3) provides for an obligation to 'afford appropriate assistance' to 'migrants whose lives or safety are endangered' by reason of being the object of the Protocol

---

[59] As was the situation in the Australian case *SRBBBB and Minister for Immigration and Multicultural and Indigenous Affairs* [2003] AATA 1066, [19] discussed in Schloenhardt and Hickson, above n 35, 50.
[60] Article 31.   [61] See Schloenhardt and Hickson, above n 35, 47.   [62] See ibid, 48 et seq.
[63] In terms of sections 178 and 179 of the Migration Act.
[64] Interpretative notes, above n 30, 20, para 109.
[65] See Schloenhardt and Stacey, above n 29, 59.

crimes, while article 16(4) requires parties to 'take into account the special needs of women and children'. Article 16(5) reinforces the obligation under the Vienna Convention on Consular Relations[66] of informing smuggled persons 'without delay about the provisions concerning notification to and communication with consular officers'. This implies a duty to enable contact between the smuggled migrants and their consular authority. Article 18 obliges parties to accept the safe return of smuggled nationals or those with residence. As noted above, efforts made during the negotiations to ensure that illegal entry into a party would not bar a migrant from claiming asylum bore fruit in article 19, which provides that the Protocol leaves unaltered the obligations of states and the rights of individuals under the Refugees Convention. Implementation of this protection and assistance does not appear to prevent deportation in the case of a failed claim to asylum.[67]

5.5.4 Criticisms of the human rights protections in the Protocol

While the Protocol thus reaffirms the right of refugees not to be returned, and gives smuggled migrants specific protections in the conditions they may face including protection from prosecution, the Protocol offers slimmer specific protection to migrants than the Human Trafficking Protocol offers trafficking victims, mainly because it does not view migrants as victims of this crime but rather objectifies them as contraband like illicit drugs or tobacco.[68] It is not clear to what extent if any this shift in emphasis has encouraged policies like Australia's processing of migrants on offshore detention centres where their rights might be endangered, in what is essentially an exercise in punitive pre-emption of their right to asylum.[69] The Protocol also ignores the rights of the smugglers themselves. A controversial issue in the prosecution of Indonesian smugglers in Australia has been ascertaining their age in order to ensure that those who are actually juveniles are not prosecuted as adults, because of the absence of an accurate biomedical marker.[70]

5.6 Conclusion

The crime of migrant smuggling arises from supply-side concerns and the preoccupations of wealthy states with border and immigration control. Migrants are referred to as the 'objects' of this process. Yet they, like the victims of trafficking, have struggled to escape being tainted by smuggling. The effectiveness of the criminalization of migrant smuggling has also been questioned. Schloenhardt and Craig point out that

[66] 24 April 1963, 596 UNTS 261, in force 19 March 1967.
[67] See articles 25–27 of Egypt's Law on Combating Illegal Migration and Smuggling of Migrants, Law no 82 of 2016, which speaks specifically of facilitating 'safe return'.
[68] See Schloenhardt and Stacey, above n 29, 65, and authors cited there.
[69] See generally L Weber, 'Policing the Virtual Border: Punitive Preemption in Australian Offshore Migration Control' 34(2) *Social Justice* (2007) 108.
[70] Australian Human Rights Council, *An Age of Uncertainty: Inquiry into the Treatment of Individuals Suspected of People Smuggling Offences Who Say That They Are Children* (2012), 48, available at <https://www.humanrights.gov.au/sites/default/files/document/publication/an_age_of_uncertainty.pdf> visited 18 April 2017.

prosecutions in Australia have not deterred individuals from engaging in the business of migrant smuggling.[71] One reason for this is that most of those prosecuted have been the crews of smuggling vessels. Of the 305 people convicted of smuggling in Australia from 1 June 2010–20 October 2014, 294 were crew and only ten organizers (3.3%).[72] Reaching organizers who do not enter the destination state's jurisdiction is not as effective as taking action against smugglers or their vessels because it depends on the vicissitudes of international cooperation. The likely response is, however, ever more severe measures against migrant smuggling rather than addressing its underlying causes.

[71] Schloenhardt and Craig, above n 9, 50.   [72] ibid, 58.

6

Drug Trafficking

6.1 Introduction

In the twentieth century a sophisticated treaty regime, now a centrepiece of transnational criminal law, was developed both to ensure the supply and use of drugs for medical and scientific purposes and to suppress the nonmedicinal supply and use of drugs. The focus of this chapter is on the latter function. The chapter traces the development of the global prohibition of illicit drug supply and use from fairly rudimentary roots to very detailed rules. The rationale of the international illicit drug control system is that effective domestic control of drug abuse is impossible if other states do not (i) control illicit drug production and trafficking in the territories under their control and (ii) coordinate these efforts globally. The criminalization and punishment of illicit drug production, supply, and use is considered crucial to these goals.

6.2 Drugs and Harm

6.2.1 Illicit use and harm

The main purpose of most drug consumption is medicinal—pain relief, relief from anxiety, etc. But humans also consume a broad range of substances—including organics such as heroin, morphine, codeine, cocaine, cannabis, hallucinogenic mushrooms, khat, etc; inorganic substances such as amphetamines, methamphetamines, ecstasy, LSD, etc; plus an ever-expanding list of laboratory-made analogues—for non-medicinal purposes such as stimulation and narcosis. The number of illicit users is high; although statistics about quantity of illicit usage are notoriously unreliable,[1] the UN estimates that 247 million people worldwide used illicit substances in 2015 and there were 187,100 drug-related deaths in 2013.[2] Use and choice of drugs varies at regional and national levels, between age groups, social classes, and ethnic groups. Illicit drug use can cause a range of health problems to users depending on the substance, volume consumed, and method of use, and consequential problems for health and welfare systems. Funding of drug use is considered to be a significant motivating factor in 'drug-related' property crimes such as theft and burglary.

---

[1] See generally FE Thoumi, 'The Numbers Game: Let's All Guess the Size of the Illegal Drug Industry!' 35 *Journal of Drug Issues* (2005) 185.
[2] UNODC, *UN World Drug Report 2016* (Vienna: UNODC, 2016), x, iii.

6.2.2 Illicit supply and harm

The illicit drug supply chain has four links: production of the raw materials, refinement into the usable product, transportation to the market, and wholesale and retail distribution. While use may be widespread, significant production and refinement occurs in limited areas (eg South and Central America for cocaine, Central and South East Asia for opium, and North Africa for cannabis resin) and relatively few states (eg Afghanistan produced almost two-thirds of global opium poppy cultivation in 2015).[3] Illicit drugs transit through many states and are distributed widely. Profits are high. In 2014 it was estimated, for example, that the US market for cocaine, heroin, cannabis, and methamphetamine was worth US$100 billion.[4] Supply is associated with a range of harms: production can distort local agriculture, refinement can have negative environmental impacts, and transportation and distribution are associated with crimes of violence as networks battle to control market share. Finally, all stages are associated with corruption, which can become endemic.

6.2.3 Drug prohibition and harm

Many of the harms associated with supply and use are, however, a product of drug prohibition itself. It creates the illicit market: users are forced to purchase an unregulated product from criminals (often in dangerous places) and to hide dependence from medical authorities. Police resources are directed into drug enforcement and police are exposed to violence and corruption, while they often resort to violence themselves. The UN High Commissioner for Human Rights has identified threats to the right to health, due process, prohibition against torture, life, prohibition against discrimination on race and gender, the rights of children, and indigenous peoples, as a result of domestic practices in the suppression of drugs.[5] Finally, the 'war on drugs', waged primarily by the US, weakens state sovereignty, particularly when it escalates to include foreign military intervention. In the late 1980s, US officials argued that the US could rely on self-defence to counter activities of drug traffickers through intervention in foreign states.[6] In 1988, then US Secretary of State George Schultz said in a speech in Bolivia: 'A person must say "no" to drug abuse or eventually he will say "no" to life. A nation must say "no" to narcotics or eventually it will say "no" to democracy.'[7] Ironically, successful suppression of, for example, the Colombian cocaine cartels has led to their downsizing, global dispersion, and

[3] ibid, xiii.

[4] B Kilmer et al, 'How Big is the US Market for Illegal Drugs?' *Rand Corporation Research Brief*, RB-9770-ONDCP, http://www.rand.org/pubs/research_briefs/RB9770.html.

[5] Study on the impact of the world drug problem on the enjoyment of human rights, UN DOC A/HRC/30/65, 4 September 2015.

[6] Statement of US State Department Legal Advisor AD Sofaer before a Congressional Subcommittee in 1989, quoted in MN Leigh, 'Contemporary Practice of the United States relating to International Law: Territorial Jurisdiction' 84 *American Journal of International Law* (1990) 724, 727.

[7] Quoted in D Corva, 'Neoliberal Globalization and the War on Drugs: Transnationalizing Illiberal Governance in the Americas' 27 *Political Geography* (2008) 176, 184.

the rise of Mexican cartels formerly engaged in illicit drug transit to meet market demand.[8]

6.3 The Institutionalization of Drug Prohibition through International Law

6.3.1 Origins

The origins of international drug prohibition lie in the international rejection of the Indo-Chinese opium trade. The trade flourished when European colonial powers and in particular Britain encouraged opium production in India for supply to China. European prosecution of the 'opium wars' (1839–42 and 1856–60) forced China to legalize the trade in 1858. Negative reaction to the wars and the trade fed support for the anti-opium lobby in Europe and the US. The US, faced with a growing domestic opium problem (exacerbated by its occupation of the Philippines where use was heavy), passed the first federal drug control law, the Opium Exclusion Act, on 9 February 1909. The 1914 Harrison Act,[9] which regulated coca products and opium, was the first to treat drug supply and use for non-therapeutic purposes as a criminal rather than a medical problem. The US threw its weight behind global prohibition. Pressure from the anti-opium lobby led by missionaries to the Far East[10] culminated in the phasing out of the licit Chinese opium trade and the development of a global drug control system (i) to regulate the commercial production and trade in medicinal drugs and (ii) to suppress illicit drugs.

6.3.2 Commercial regulation of medicinal drugs[11]

In 1909, thirteen states, led by the US, joined the Shanghai Opium Commission. The Commission resolved to suppress opium smoking, to limit its use to medical purposes, and to control its export and its harmful derivatives—proposals taken up in the 1912 Hague International Opium Convention.[12] In 1921 the League of Nations set up the Opium Advisory Committee (forerunner of the UN Commission on Narcotic Drugs or CND) to advise it on the control of opium and other dangerous drugs. Further more sophisticated multilateral conventions followed, confining the production, trade, and consumption of drugs to medical and scientific purposes.[13] The Permanent Central Board (the forerunner of the International Narcotics Control Board or INCB) was established to monitor drug production and licensed trade in

---

[8] See R Vogler and S Fouladvand, 'The Convention against the Illicit Traffic in Narcotic Drugs and Psychotropic Substances and the Global War on Drugs' in P Hauck and S Peterke (eds), *International Law and Transnational Organized Crime* (Oxford: OUP, 2016), 107, 109.

[9] Act of 17 December 1914, 38 Stat 785 as amended; 26 USC §§ 4701–33.

[10] See AH Taylor, *American Diplomacy and the Narcotics Traffic, 1900–1939: A Study in International Humanitarian Reform* (Durham, NC: Duke University Press, 1969), 29.

[11] See B Renborg, 'International Control of Narcotics' 22 *Law and Contemporary Problems* (1957) 86.

[12] 23 January 1912, 8 LNTS 187, in force 23 January 1922. On the Shanghai Commission see H Wright, 'The International Opium Commission' 3 *American Journal of International Law* (1909) 648, 823.

[13] See N Boister, *Penal Aspects of the UN Drug Conventions* (The Hague: Kluwer, 2001), 28–41.

order to ensure availability of drugs for licit purposes and to prevent diversion into the illicit market. The most important of these conventions today are the 1961 Single Convention on Narcotic Drugs[14] and its 1972 Protocol,[15] and the 1971 Convention on Psychotropic Substances.[16]

6.3.3 Penal measures

The 1936 Convention for the Suppression of the Illicit Traffic in Dangerous Drugs[17] was the first significant attempt to harmonize drug offences and provide for procedural cooperation against traffickers, but it failed to come into force. The 1961 Convention included limited penal measures (articles 35 and 36), and these measures were elaborated in the 1972 Protocol. The 1971 Psychotropic Convention also made provision for measures for cooperation against the illicit traffic and for criminal sanctions in national law (articles 21 and 22). A growing global traffic in the 1980s led to stiffer penal measures through the adoption in Vienna of the 1988 United Nations Convention against Illicit Traffic in Narcotic Drugs and Psychotropic Substances.[18] It provides the framework for an extensive and largely mandatory legal regime for the suppression of the illicit drug traffic (and serves as a model for treaties suppressing other transnational crimes). In terms of article 2, the purpose of the Convention is to address the international dimension of the illicit traffic. However, article 2 also asserts state sovereignty and territorial inviolability. The latter provision reveals tensions between states where drugs are produced and those where they are consumed about which states bears most responsibility for the problem, and in particular the fears of the former that the latter would use the Convention as an excuse to police drugs within their territories without their consent.

6.3.4 The relationship between licit and illicit supply

The determination of what is licit use and supply in the conventions also determines what is illicit use and supply. Thus the 1961 Convention defines 'illicit traffic' as conduct 'contrary to the provisions' of the Convention[19] and specifically as drug-related conduct for non-medical and non-scientific purposes.[20] In fact, illicit conduct is conduct contrary to the national legislation used to implement the Convention, as it is the parties that criminalize the conduct, not international law. Article 22(1)(a) of the 1971 Convention more correctly obliges parties to criminalize all forms of intentional conduct contrary to the law or regulations adopted by parties in pursuance of the 1971 Convention. Article 22(5) makes it clear that these offences 'shall be defined, prosecuted and punished in conformity with the domestic law of a Party'.

---

[14] New York, 30 March 1961, 520 UNTS 151, in force 13 December 1964.
[15] Protocol Amending the Single Convention on Narcotic Drugs, 1961, Geneva, 25 March 1972, 976 UNTS 3, in force 8 August 1975.
[16] Vienna, 21 February 1971, 1019 UNTS 175, in force 16 August 1976.
[17] Geneva, 26 June 1936, 198 LNTS 300, in force 26 October 1939.
[18] Vienna, 20 December 1988, 1582 UNTS 95, in force 11 November 1990.   [19] Article 1(1)(l).
[20] Article 4(1)(c).

6.3.5 Drug classification

The classification of certain substances as harmful and thus suitable for control is central to international drug control. The general principle is that all substances with recognized dependence-producing properties are subject to international control. Scheduling does not prohibit these drugs; the conventions prohibit certain actions in regard to them. The conventions arrange drugs in schedules corresponding to different levels of control; changes in the level of control are made by rescheduling. Thus under the 1961 Convention, Schedule I drugs (more addictive narcotics such as opium) are subject to greater control than those in Schedule II (less addictive narcotics such as codeine). Inclusion in either schedule by the CND on the recommendation of a World Health Organization Expert Committee in the first instance depends on whether the substance in question is liable to similar abuse to that of substances already in that schedule. Schedule III is limited to preparations not liable to abuse, while Schedule IV contains a selection of Schedule I drugs considered particularly liable to abuse (such as heroin) not offset by therapeutic advantage and thus subject to special control measures. Under the 1988 Drug Trafficking Convention drug precursor substances are arranged in two different tables by the INCB. Most national misuse of drug legislation adopts an analogous classification system used to spell out different levels of regulation. The inclusion or exclusion of certain drugs in specific schedules is to some degree a product of historical factors rather than scientific evidence. It is arguable, for example, that alcohol and tobacco should be scheduled substances.

6.4 Supply Reduction in the Drug Conventions

6.4.1 Suppressing the chain of supply

The penal provisions of the drug conventions are designed to suppress every action in the illicit chain of production and supply. Article 36(1) of the 1961 Convention (as amended by the 1972 Protocol) provides:

> Subject to its constitutional limitations, each Party shall adopt such measures as will ensure that cultivation, production, manufacture, extraction, preparation, possession, offering, offering for sale, distribution, purchase, sale, delivery on any terms whatsoever, brokerage, dispatch, dispatch in transit, transport, importation, and exportation of drugs contrary to the provisions of this Convention, and any other action which in the opinion of such Party may be contrary to the provisions of this Convention, shall be punishable offences when committed intentionally, and that serious offences shall be liable to adequate punishment particularly by imprisonment or other penalties of deprivation of liberty.

Parties are thus required (somewhat ambiguously) to render these different forms of conduct 'as punishable offences', unless their constitutions do not permit them to do so. Supply, deal, or traffic drugs and you will be prosecuted using an offence derived from this provision or its more recent iteration in the 1988 Convention. Article 15 of Afghanistan's Counter-Narcotics Law of 2004 defines drug trafficking, for example, as the 'production, manufacture, distribution, possession, extraction, preparation, processing, offering, sale, delivery, brokerage, dispatch, transportation, importation, exportation, purchase, concealment, or storage' of any scheduled substance. Except notably for possession, which is dealt with separately in article 3(2), article 3(1)(a)(i)– (iv) of the 1988 Convention requires that parties establish the same forms of conduct more explicitly as criminal offences under its domestic law.[21] Both conventions provide that each of the proscribed acts must be 'committed intentionally', [22] although precisely how this is applied will depend on the specific form of conduct involved and how it is interpreted domestically. There must, for example, be a clear intention not just to cultivate but to do so with the intention of supplying a drug if the accused is to be found liable for dealing in (supply of) drugs under South African law.[23] The 1961 Convention also provides that commission of any one of these offences across different states results in the commission of a distinct offence in each state.[24] The following sections discuss each of the different forms of supply-related conduct in greater depth, moving step by step along the supply chain.

6.4.2 Production and refinement

Suppression at source is simplest because production is difficult to hide: cultivated plants are bulky and difficult to conceal, and laboratories require sophisticated equipment and skills. 'Cultivation' includes within its scope the unregulated, illicit, prohibited cultivation of the opium poppy, coca bush, or cannabis plant.[25] 'Production' is the agricultural 'separation of opium, coca leaves, cannabis and cannabis resin from the plants from which they are obtained'.[26] 'Manufacture' 'means all processes, other than production, by which the drugs may be obtained and includes refining as well as the transformation of drugs into other drugs'.[27] 'Extraction' is the physical or chemical means of separating and collecting substances from mixtures.[28] 'Preparation' means mixing for use.[29]

6.4.3 Transportation

The most difficult aspect of supply control is interdiction of the movement of drugs within states and across international borders to market. 'Dispatch' involves the sending of drugs to a specific destination while 'dispatch in transit' involves sending drugs to a destination outside that territory or to one of which the dispatcher or carrier are ignorant. 'Transport' involves the conveying of drugs from one place to another by any mode through any medium. The 'import' and 'export' of drugs is the 'physical transfer of drugs from one State to another State, or from one territory to another

---

[21] In contrast, article 22 of the 1971 Convention simply states that actions contrary to the laws adopted by parties to implement the Convention shall be criminal offences.
[22] Article 36(1) and article 3(1) respectively.   [23] *S v Mbatha* [2012] ZAKZPHC 22.
[24] Article 36(2)(a)(i), inserted by 1972 Protocol.   [25] Article 1(1)(i) of the 1961 Convention.
[26] Article 1(1)(t) of the 1961 Convention.   [27] Article 1(1)(n) of the 1961 Convention.
[28] *Commentary on the United Nations Convention against Illicit Traffic in Narcotic Drugs and Psychotropic Substances, 1988* (New York, 1998, UN Doc. E/CN.7/590; UN Publication Sales No.E.98. XI.5), 54.
[29] Article 1(1)(s) of the 1961 Convention.

territory of the same State'.[30] They have traditionally been regarded as two separate offences even if they involve the movement by the same person of a consignment of drugs from one state to another. *Batkoun*,[31] for example, transported 50 kg of heroin in his car from France to Canada. A charge in Canada of illegal importation of drugs failed, but in France he was convicted of illegal export of drugs. He appealed on the basis that the export and import of the drugs were a single offence and the matter was now *res judicata* because of the Canadian decision. The French Court dismissed his appeal, holding that in article 36(1) 'the terms "importation and exportation of drugs" constitute two separate offences and not simply two different aspects of the same offence'.[32] In the EU, however, such prosecutions are now hit by the prohibition on *ne bis in idem* because they are based on the same set of facts (rather than different legal breaches in different states), even if the amount of drugs involved does not match.[33] Whether other states outside of Europe will follow suit remains to be seen.

6.4.4 Distribution

Wholesale and retail distribution of drugs involves transactions.[34] 'Offering' is undefined but usually involves tendering a drug to a potential consumer for acceptance or refusal. It may involve gifting, whereas 'offering for sale' implies offering for purchase. In 'brokerage' agents negotiate on behalf of buyer or seller to facilitate the transaction. 'Distribution' ensures that drugs move through the chain of supply from producer to consumer, 'purchase' the buying of drugs for resale not use, and 'sale' the disposal of drugs for some consideration. The catch-all 'delivery on any terms whatsoever' ensures the inclusion of any form of delivery including constructive delivery through, for example, the transfer of keys to a storage facility.

6.4.5 Possession and purchase for supply

It is difficult in practice to prove actual illicit supply of drugs, so as a fallback the 1988 Convention obliges parties to criminalize possession or purchase of drugs for the purpose of any of the activities set out above.[35] Domestic courts have interpreted criminal laws of this kind very broadly, including within them, for example, possession of drugs in order to give them back to the owner so that the owner may put them to whatever purpose they have in mind (including supply).[36] Such a purpose may be difficult to prove. Although the conventions are silent in this regard, the UN's Official Commentary on the 1961 Convention suggests that states provide for a 'legal presumption that any quantity exceeding a specified small amount is intended for distribution'.[37] Presumptions of this

---

[30] Article 1(1)(m) of the 1961 Convention.   [31] (1987) 73 ILR 249.   [32] ibid, 251.
[33] *Van Esbroek*, ECJ Case C-436/04, 9 March 2006, European Court Report 2006 I-2333.
[34] *1988 Commentary*, above n 28, 54–55.   [35] Article 3(1)(a)(iii).
[36] *R v Maginnis* [1987] 1 AC 303 (HL) interpreting section 5(3) of the 1971 Misuse of Drugs Act (UK).
[37] *Commentary on the Single Convention on Narcotic Drugs, 1961* (New York, 1973) UN Publication Sales No. E.73.XI.1, 113.

kind[38] are fairly common in post-1961 domestic drug legislation (although states do not set the same threshold quantities). For example, in Malaysia, a possessor 'otherwise than in accordance with' statutory authority inter alia of more than 15 gm of heroin, 1 kg of opium, 200 gm of cannabis, 40 gm of cocaine, or 50 gm of amphetamines is presumed to be trafficking in the drug.[39] In a number of jurisdictions, presumptions of this kind have been subject to successful constitutional challenges on the basis that they breach the presumption of innocence.[40] In contrast, the European Court of Human Rights, recognizing the deterrent goals of such measures, has steadfastly adopted the position that such presumptions are not a denial of justice because the prosecutor still needs to prove possession in a trial that is subject to adequate procedural safeguards.[41] Thailand's Constitutional Court considered a similar presumption in the Drug Act[42] compatible with Thailand's constitutional presumption of innocence, because it was designed, according to the court,

> to enable efficient suppression and control of narcotics and to show accordance with the international narcotics convention to which Thailand is a member. This is because nowadays narcotics are an international concern and pose serious risks against human health and life. Therefore, punishments must be harsher than usual and the punitive measures must be absolute.[43]

The perception that the convention calls for a harsh deterrent function thus shapes derogation of human rights in domestic law.

6.4.6 Support and organization of supply

The 1988 Convention reaches back down the chain of supply, adding two new sets of offences relating to equipment, materials, and precursor substances used in drug production and supply: their manufacture, transport, or distribution,[44] and their possession.[45] These offences must be carried out with specific knowledge of the illicit purpose to which these things are to be put in order to avoid extending their scope to innocent suppliers. National implementation of these new offences has not always been speedy. In 2004, for example, when Fijian authorities discovered a large methamphetamine laboratory near Suva containing tonnes of precursors,[46] they also discovered that

---

[38] Domestic legislation provides for a variety of other kinds of presumptions facilitating prosecution, including, eg, presumptions of possession of drugs within a vehicle in which the accused is a passenger—see for example section 11(2) of Botswana's Habit Forming Drugs Act 1982.

[39] Section 37(d)(a) of the Malaysian Dangerous Drugs Act 234 of 1952.

[40] For example, see _R v Oakes_ [1986] 1 SCR 103 [Canada]; _R v Lambert_ [2001] UKHL 37 [UK]; _R v Sin Yau-ming_ [1992] 1 HKCLR 127 [Hong Kong]; _R v Hansen_ [2007] NZSC 7 [New Zealand]; _S v Bhulwana_ [1995] ZACC 11 [South Africa].

[41] _Salabiaku_ Case ECHR Series A No. 141-A (1988) [France—ECtHR]; _Willcox v UK and Hurford v UK_ [2013] ECHR 292, 8 January 2013.

[42] B.E. 2510 (1967).

[43] Cited by the European Court of Human Rights in _Willcox and Hurford v UK_ [2013] ECHR 292, 8 January 2013, para 41; see also the early Privy Council decision on appeal from Singapore, _Ong Au Chuan v Public Prosecutor_ 1980 UKPC 32.

[44] Article 3(1)(a)(iv).   [45] Article 3(1)(c).

[46] _State v Yuen Yei Ha_ [2005] FJHC 165; HAC0012.2004 (27 July 2005).

although Fiji was party to the 1988 Convention (it acceded on 25 March 1993), Fiji's Dangerous Drugs Act 1938 had not been amended to suppress precursors. Suitable changes were hurriedly drafted and the Illicit Drugs Control Act 2004 was not ready to put before Parliament until the day of the raid.

Although subject to constitutional limitation, the 1961 Convention obliges parties to criminalize secondary participation, inchoate, or uncompleted forms of those offences.[47] It also obliges them to criminalize the conduct of persons engaged in financial operations in connection with all illicit trafficking offences. Conspiracy permits the prosecution of the entire drug trafficking operation rather than just those directly involved with the drugs, while the prosecution of financiers reaches out to those who seldom have any contact with drugs at all, yet who make trafficking possible. The 1988 Convention obliges parties to criminalize the 'organization, management and financing' of the supply offences but without constitutional limitation.[48] Its obligations to criminalize 'public' incitement (through the media),[49] conspiracy, and inchoate forms of article 3(1) offences[50] are, however, still subject to the constitutional limitation, as is criminalization of 'participation in, association or conspiracy to commit, attempts to commit and aiding, abetting, facilitating and counselling the commission of any' article 3(1) offence.[51] The general term 'association' provides an alternative to conspiracy as an option for civil law states that reject conspiracy as too broad a basis for criminalization.

6.4.7 Punishment for supply offences

Article 36(1) of the 1961 Convention provides (i) that all the forms of drug-related conduct enumerated in article 36(1) shall be 'punishable offences' and (ii) 'serious offences shall be liable to adequate punishment particularly by imprisonment or other penalties of deprivation of liberty'. The 1971 Convention also adopts this dual punishment regime. Article 3(4)(a) of the 1988 Convention points to more severe penalties. It requires that parties must ensure that article 3(1) offences are punished by penalties that take into account their 'grave nature', using punishments 'such as' 'imprisonment or other forms of deprivation of liberty', 'pecuniary sanctions', and 'confiscation'. Parties retain, however, the discretion to decide on the appropriate form in the particular case and they are not precluded from using other punishments. The 1988 Convention also provides a non-exhaustive list of aggravating factors[52] which may characterize an article 3(1) offence as 'particularly serious', and which parties must permit their courts to take into account. These include the involvement of an organized criminal group in the offence (a concept defined in the UN Convention against Transnational Organized Crime[53]); the involvement of the offender in other international organized criminal activities; the involvement of the offender in other illegal activities facilitated by the offence; the use of violence or arms by the offender; the holding of public office by the offender; the use of minors; the commission of

---

[47] Article 36(2)(a)(ii) (inserted by the 1972 Protocol).   [48] Article 3(1)(a)(v).
[49] *1988 Commentary*, above n 23, 74.   [50] Article 3(1)(c)(iii) and (iv).
[51] Article 3(1)(c)(iv).   [52] Article 3(5).   [53] See Chapter 8.

the offence in a prison, educational facility, or social service facility; and previous convictions.[54]

In practice, although sentencing differs widely, parties generally punish trafficking offences relatively heavily. Taking into account factors like the volume of the substance involved (on the rudimentary theory that greater quantity means greater profit deserves greater punishment[55]) or its estimated 'street' value,[56] and the harmful potential of the particular class of drugs (revealed by its scheduling), supply is usually punished by periods of imprisonment or fines or a combination of the two. But what is a 'heavy' penalty in one party may not be considered so in another. In *Recognition of a Sentence Imposed by a Thai Court, Constitutional Complaint*,[57] the Czech Constitutional Court refused to alter a fifty-year sentence (later reduced to twenty-nine years) handed down to a drug trafficker in Thailand after the trafficker had been transferred to the Czech Republic under a prisoner transfer treaty (which reserved Thailand's exclusive jurisdiction in regard to guilt and punishment) even though there was a ten-year maximum penalty for the same offence in the Czech Republic. In contrast in *Willcox and Hurford v The United Kingdom*,[58] the European Court of Human Rights found that there was no violation of the European Convention on Human Rights when British authorities continued inter alia to enforce a life sentence (later reduced to twenty-four years) set for trafficking in Thailand after a prisoner transfer to the UK, because the perverse effect of overturning it would be to prevent such transfer.

Resort to the death penalty for drug trafficking is a modern phenomenon, dating in most states to legislation enacted since the adoption of the 1961 Convention.[59] Thirty-three states retain capital punishment for drug trafficking, executing more than one thousand individuals a year.[60] China, for example, employs capital punishment where aggravating factors such as participation of organized crime or significant volumes (more than 1 kg of opium or more than 50 gm of heroin) are present.[61] In Iran, several convictions for possession of less than 5 kg of heroin can be accumulated to take the individual over the 5 kg threshold triggering the death sentence.[62] Although there is no provision for the death penalty in the 1988 Convention, the Convention does not explicitly rule out its use. Human rights bodies have criticized

[54] See, eg, section 13 of Sierra Leone's National Drugs Control Act 2008 which reproduces these grounds in large part.
[55] J Fleetwood, 'Five Kilos: Penalties and Practice in the International Cocaine Trade' 51 *British Journal of Criminology* (2011) 375, 380.
[56] See, eg, the Kenyan Court of Appeal in *Kitsao Ali Kadenge v Republic*, Criminal Appeal No 304 of 2010, where the Court stated 'Punishment in drug trafficking is predicated upon the value of the drugs.'
[57] I US 601/04; ILDC 990 (CZ 2007) 21 February 2007.
[58] [2013] ECHR 292, 8 January 2013.
[59] See generally UN CCPCJ, Capital punishment and implementation of the safeguards guaranteeing protection of the rights of those facing the death penalty: Report of the Secretary-General, UN Doc E/CN.15/2001/10, 29 March 2001.
[60] P Gallahue and R Lines, *The Death Penalty for Drug Offenses: Global Overview 2015* (HRI, 2015), available at <https://www.hri.global/files/2015/10/07/DeathPenaltyDrugs_Report_2015.pdf> last visited 4 December 2017.
[61] Article 347 of the 1997 Revision of the Criminal Law.
[62] Anti-Narcotic Drug Law of 25 October 1988 as amended, articles 6 and 8(6).

executions for drug offences as violations of international law.[63] The UN Office on Drugs and Crime advocates its abolition on the basis that the weight of opinion is that drug offences do not make the threshold of most serious crimes.[64] Somewhat timorously the INCB has advised retentionist states to consider abolishing capital punishment for drug offences.[65] Domestic challenges to the use of the death penalty on human rights grounds have not succeeded. In *Sianturi and ors v Indonesia*[66] the Indonesian Constitutional Court dealt with the constitutionality of death sentences imposed on Indonesian and Australian drug traffickers under Indonesia's Narcotics Law.[67] Noting that this law implemented Indonesia's obligations under the 1988 Drug Trafficking Convention, the court relied on the exception in article 6(2) of the International Covenant on Civil and Political Rights, which implicitly permits the imposition of the death penalty for the 'most serious' crimes as an exception to the right to life. It rejected the opinion of the UN Human Rights Commission that drug offences were not among the 'most serious crimes'. In its view the Indonesian drug trafficking law implementing the death sentence fell within the exception; there was no substantial difference between these drug trafficking offences and 'most serious crimes' such as genocide because they also affected the 'economic, cultural and political foundations of society' and carried 'danger of incalculable gravity'.[68] Apart from the political difficulties in a case such as this when the accused is a foreign national, the Court's reasoning ignores the fact that the core international crimes involve serious harms to individuals committed with state or official sanction, characteristics which underpin the international community's decision to condemn them as crimes under international law. Drug supply offences, on the other hand, are private crimes that do not involve harms of this severity. Moreover, absent the aggravating factors spelled out in the 1988 Convention, the Convention itself does not classify drug trafficking as 'particularly serious'.[69] Unsurprisingly, imposition of the death penalty poses a problem for international cooperation as parties that do not apply the death penalty to trafficking offences may refuse extradition or legal assistance to parties where the penalty is available without assurances it will not be applied.

6.5 Demand Reduction Provisions in the Drug Conventions

6.5.1 Under the 1961 Convention

'Use' of drugs in the sense of personal consumption is not listed in article 36 of the 1961 Convention. Article 36(1) does, however, oblige parties, subject to their constitutional

---

[63] Concluding Observations of the United Nations Human Rights Committee, UN Doc CCPR/CO/84/THA, 8 July 2005, para 14, and Report of the United Nations Human Rights Committee, UN Doc A/50/40, 3 October 1995, para 449.

[64] UNODC, Drug Control, Crime Prevention and Criminal Justice: A Human Rights Perspective. Note by the Executive Director, UN Doc E/CN.7/2010/CRP.6*–E/CN.15/2010/CRP.1*, 3 March 2010, paras 25 and 26.

[65] INCB, *Report for 2015* (UN: New York, 2015) UN Doc E/INCB/2015/1, 6.

[66] Constitutional Review, Nos 2, 3/PUU-V/2007; ILDC 1041 (ID 2007), 23 October 2007.

[67] No 22 of 1997.   [68] ibid, para 3.24.

[69] R Lines, 'A "Most Serious Crime"? The Death Penalty for Drug Offences and International Human Rights Law' 21 *Amicus Journal* (2010) 21, 24.

limitations, to 'adopt such measures as will ensure that ... possession' is a punishable offence when committed intentionally. 'Simple' possession serves as a proxy for use. Although most parties criminalize it, some parties consider that the anti-trafficking thrust of the 1961 Convention means they are not obliged to criminalize possession for use. Article 36(1)(b) (inserted by article 14 of the 1972 Protocol) states that 'when abusers have committed these offences', parties 'may provide ... that abusers shall undergo measures of treatment, education, aftercare, rehabilitation and social re-integration' as alternatives to conviction and punishment or in addition to conviction and punishment, no matter how serious the offence. Thus, although article 36(1) appears to require 'possession' to be a 'punishable offence', parties can avoid this obligation for any of three reasons: (i) if their constitution limits their ability to require possession to be a punishable offence; (ii) they can decide that possession is not a 'serious' offence and that they are thus not required to impose imprisonment as punishment; or (iii) they may retain it as a punishable offence but make it possible for the authorities to choose as an alternative to conviction and punishment in a particular case to order that a possessor undergo treatment, education, aftercare, rehabilitation, and social reintegration. This interpretation has been approved by the Official Commentary on the 1961 Convention which opines that states 'may ... choose not to provide for imprisonment of persons found in such possession, but to impose only minor penalties such as fines or even censure'.[70]

6.5.2 Under the 1988 Convention

In the 1988 Convention, however, stronger measures were taken to criminalize demand, which calls for separate explanation. Pressure from drug producer states on drug consumer states to do something about demand in order to compensate for the pressure placed on them to do something about supply[71] resulted in the adoption of article 3(2), which provides:

> Subject to its constitutional principles and the basic concepts of its legal system, each Party shall adopt such measures as may be necessary to establish as a criminal offence under its domestic law, when committed intentionally, the possession, purchase or cultivation of narcotic drugs or psychotropic substances for personal consumption contrary to the provisions of the 1961 Convention, the 1961 Convention as amended or the 1971 Convention.

Article 3(2) obliges the parties to establish possession, purchase, or cultivation for personal consumption as a criminal offence, when that possession, purchase, or cultivation for personal use is 'contrary to' the provisions of the 1961 and 1971 Conventions. Articles 4 and 33 of the 1961 Convention very generally oblige parties to 'limit' possession to medical and scientific purposes and to 'not permit' possession except under legal authority. The parties to the 1988 Convention, in adopting article 3(2), appear arguably to have agreed subsequently inter se, to a more restrictive interpretation of

[70] *Commentary on the Single Convention on Narcotic Drugs, 1961* (New York, 1973) UN Publication Sales No E.73.XI.1, para 19.
[71] See Boister, above n 13, 123–24.

the obligations of the 1961 Convention, to 'limit' the impermissible possession of drugs by establishing possession for personal use not just as a 'punishable offence' but as a criminal offence. In that sense, article 3(2) is an authoritative interpretation of article 36(1)'s obligation to treat possession as a punishable offence. The more recent practice of parties such as Mexico, which has passed legislation decriminalizing possession,[72] however, contradicts this interpretation (ironically it was Mexico which introduced article 3(2) into the Convention as a counterweight to the general bulk of the provisions being directed at supply). These parties may simply be in breach of article 3(2), and this appears to be why the INCB expressly points out their article 3(2) obligations in its Annual Report for 2009.[73] Article 3(2)'s obligation is, however, subject to domestic constitutional principles and basic concepts of states parties. Taking advantage of this 'get-out', the Argentine Supreme Court has declared criminalization of possession a constitutional breach because it interferes with the right to personal autonomy.[74] The most space for national reform within the constraints of the Convention is provided by exploring what is meant by 'to establish as a criminal offence' in article 3(2). The softening of criminalization can occur through the discretionary use of non-prosecution; diversion; treatment and rehabilitation as an alternative to prosecution; civil, or administrative sanctions; treatment and rehabilitation as an alternative to punishment; or use of non-custodial sentences. Just because breach of the law results in an infringement notice or a 'civil' penalty does not mean that such breach is not per se a criminal offence. Portugal has taken the view that administrative penalties are sufficient; the INCB accepts this practice.[75] Most parties still prosecute possession, however, as a criminal offence and impose punishment, including imprisonment.[76] The enactment of harsh penalties for drug users in many jurisdictions is to some extent contradicted by the reality that these penalties are seldom imposed.[77]

6.6 Treatment and Harm Reduction

The limited non-punitive options built into the system are reinforced by the fact that article 38 of the 1961 Convention provides for obligations to give attention to providing facilities for treatment, care, and rehabilitation of addicts. Article 20 of the 1971 Convention is even stronger in this regard. The conventions do not make direct provision for harm reduction, a strategy that tries to mitigate the negative consequences of drug use (but without requiring abstinence) through measures such as clean needle exchanges to prevent HIV infection from shared needles, prescription of substitute medicines, and drug-consumption rooms.[78] Initially the INCB considered these

---

[72] Narcomenudeo Decree 2009.

[73] *Report of the International Narcotics Control Board for 2009*, UN Doc E/INCB/2009/1, para 408.

[74] 'Arriola' Ruling, Case No A 891 XLVI Supreme Court of Justice, Argentina, 25 August 2009.

[75] *Report of the International Narcotics Control Board for 2004*, UN Doc E/INCB/2004/1, para 538.

[76] Section 220.03 of New York State's Controlled Substances Law makes possession of any controlled substance in any amount a class A misdemeanour subject to a penalty of up to one year's imprisonment.

[77] See D Bewley Taylor et al, *The Incarceration of Drug Offenders: An Overview* (London: The Beckley Foundation Drug Policy Programme March 2009, Report 16), 1.

[78] See UNDCP, *Flexibility of Treaty Provisions as Regards Harm Reduction Approaches*, UN Doc E/INCB/2002/W.13/SS.5, 30 September 2002 (Restricted), para 3.

measures in breach of the conventions but then softened its position to warning of their danger.[79] The UN's 1998 Declaration on the Guiding Principles of Drug Demand Reduction accepts that demand reduction includes 'reducing the adverse consequences of drug abuse'.[80] The drug conventions are sufficiently flexible to permit harm reduction methods. Offences under the conventions such as facilitating or inciting the illicit use of drugs[81] have to be very broadly interpreted to include within their scope the provision of needle exchange or sterile injection rooms[82] because of the difficulty of proving an intention to incite. Particularly apt in regard to harm reduction are the conventions' obligations to provide treatment. In terms of article 36(1)(b) of the 1961 Convention (inserted by article 14 of the 1972 Protocol) parties have the discretion to implement measures such as treatment, education, and rehabilitation as alternatives to conviction and punishment or in addition to conviction and punishment, no matter how serious the offence, when the offender is an abuser. Article 3(4)(c) of the 1988 Convention allows parties 'in appropriate cases of a minor nature' to provide as an alternative to punishment measures such as treatment and aftercare for drug users engaged in article 3(1) drug supply offences. Article 3(4)(d) permits Parties to 'provide either as an alternative to conviction or punishment, or in addition to conviction or punishment' for measures such as education and treatment for the offences in article 3(2). These provisions open the door to employment of a wide variety of programmes including drug counselling, drug education, therapeutic support groups, relapse prevention, clinical maintenance, and overview by relevant health professionals in order to enable the 'social reintegration' of drug users.[83] Compulsory detention for drug treatment has, however, come under withering criticism as a human rights abuse.[84]

6.7 The Enforcement of the International Drug Control System

Although the 1961 Convention[85] permits the use of limited sanctions against non-compliant states this power has never been used. The UN bodies rely instead on diplomatic pressure or publicity. The US also polices the system directly though without an international mandate. In terms of the Foreign Assistance Act the Federal Authorities must report on any country or entity that received assistance from the US and which failed in the last two financial years to meet 'the goals and objectives of the' 1988 Drug Trafficking Convention.[86] These goals are taken to be meeting the obligations in the Convention. To meet this duty the President identifies, for example, a list of 'major

---

[79] See, eg, INCB *Report of the International Narcotics Control Board for 1999*, UN Doc E/INCB/1999/1 (UN Sales No E.00.XI.1) para 176; INCB *Report of the International Narcotics Control Board for 2003*, UN DOC E/INCB/2003/1 (UN Sales No E.04.XI.1), para 226.

[80] GA Res S/20/3 Annex, 10 June 1998.   [81] Article 3(1)(c)(iii) of the 1988 Convention.

[82] See, eg, *Attorney General of Canada et al v PHS Community Services Society et al* [2011] 3 SCR 134.

[83] *1988 Commentary*, above n 28, 88–89.

[84] See Human Rights Watch, *Torture in the Name of Treatment: Human Rights Abuses in Vietnam, China, Cambodia and Lao PDR* (Human Rights Watch, 2012).

[85] Article 14.   [86] Section 489(a)(1)(A), section 490(b); 22 USC § 2151.

drug producing' states, and then designates certain of them as having 'failed demonstrably' to meet their obligations under the conventions. This may lead to de-certification, denying the de-certified state economic aid.[87] The US also uses soft power such as support by the Drug Enforcement Administration for an annual International Drug Enforcement Conference (IDEC) in Support of Strengthening International Relations to share drug-related intelligence and to develop operational strategies.

6.8 Conclusion: Towards Reform?

The international drug control system has tried for a century to balance its two goals: ensuring the supply of drugs for licit purposes, and suppressing the supply of drugs for illicit use. Poor availability of licit drugs in most states suggests questionable success as a commercial regulatory measure; the strategy to extinguish the illicit drug problem has thus far been an enormous normative success in generating a lot of criminal law and enforcement but it has failed to suppress drug use for non-medical and scientific purposes. Whether drug supply and use for non-medicinal purposes would be far more widespread and would constitute a far greater menace to the whole world without international drug prohibition remains speculation. It is clear that the cost of suppression using draconian provisions adopted in 'the spirit of the conventions' is high, and enforcement pays little attention to the stated goal in the preamble of the 1961 Convention that the primary goal is the health and welfare of humankind. Even the CND has been forced to reiterate that when parties carry out their drug convention obligations to criminalize they must respect a

> range of rights, including the right to health, to the protection of the child, to private and family life, to non-discrimination, to the right to life, the right not to be subjected to torture or cruel, inhuman or degrading treatment or punishment, and the right not to be subjected to arbitrary arrest or detention.[88]

There is growing pressure to reform the conventions. A number of states have relied on exclusionary clauses in the conventions to engage in soft defection from their obligations.[89] Bolivia has repudiated the 1961 Single Convention and ratified it with an exception to obligations relating to use and cultivation of the coca plant for traditional purposes, while states within the US are increasingly opting to legalize the market in cannabis, bringing the US into conflict with its international obligations, and in Canada analogous legislation is before Parliament.[90] The Global Commission on Drugs Policy comprising of nineteen world leaders including former UN Secretary-General

[87] US Department of State Bureau for International Narcotics and Law Enforcement Affairs, *International Narcotics Control Strategy Report: Volume I: Drug and Chemical Control*, March 2016 (2016), 2 et seq.
[88] CND, *Drug Control, Crime Prevention and Criminal Justice: A Human Rights Perspective*, 3 March 2010, UN Doc E/CN.7/2010/CRP.6–E/CN.15/2010/CRP.1, 2010, 8.
[89] See the discussion in Vogler and Fouladvand, *above* n 8, 12 et seq.
[90] See N Boister, 'Waltzing on the Vienna Consensus on Drug Control? Tensions in the International System for the Control of Drugs?' 19 *Leiden Journal of International Law* (2016) 389. For Canada see Bill C45, The Cannabis Act.

Kofi Annan has called for the end of criminalization.[91] The UN General Assembly Special Session on drug policy held in 2016 revealed a growing divergence between ardent prohibitionist states and reform-minded states.[92]

---

[91] *War On Drugs: Report of the Global Commission on Drug Policy* (June 2011) available at <http:// www.globalcommissionondrugs.org/Report> last visited 24 November 2016.
[92] D Bewley-Taylor and M Jelsma, 'UNGASS 2016: A Broken or B-r-o-a-d Consensus?' 45 *Drug Policy Briefing* June 2016.

7
Terrorism

7.1 Introduction

In 2016 the French Prime Minister responded to an attack in Nice which killed eighty-four people with the statement that terrorism is now 'part of our daily lives'.[1] The harms caused by acts of terror are immediate and graphic: death, maiming and traumatization of immediate victims, destruction or damage to property, political, economic, and environmental damage. Yet the incidence of terrorism is difficult to measure because of disagreement about the concept itself. Relying on a fairly broad definition of terrorism as 'premeditated, politically motivated violence perpetrated against non-combatant targets by sub-national groups or clandestine agents',[2] the US's Bureau of Counterterrorism and Countering Violent Extremism estimates that there were 11,774 attacks worldwide in 2015.[3]

Legal responses to terrorism have slowly shifted from treating terrorism as a criminal matter subject to conventional law enforcement, to the enactment of special rules which approach terrorism as an emergency situation justifying an emergency response which derogates from normal principles of criminal law and procedure. This evolution can be seen in the content of the impressive range of treaties that have been adopted in regard to terrorism or aspects of terrorism since the 1960s.

This chapter examines the suppression of terrorist activities in these different 'sectoral treaties' dealing with the criminalization of aviation offences, hostage-taking, attacks on UN personnel, nuclear terrorism, maritime security crimes and offences, terrorist bombing, and terrorist financing. It then looks at the prospects for a comprehensive UN Anti-terrorism Convention, before moving to a discussion of the novel and precedent-setting criminal-law-making role of the UN Security Council in taking counter-terrorism measures. Lastly, it assesses the suppression of terrorism's vexed relationship with human rights and efforts to reclassify terrorism as a core international crime, an attempt to try to take the particularist state-interest dimension out of anti-terrorism and replace it with a more general international community interest.

---

[1] 'The New France: Terrorism "part of our daily lives"', *CBS News*, <http://www.cbsnews.com/news/france-terrorism-nice-attack-mohamed-lahouaiej-bouhlel/> last visited 17 May 2017.
[2] 22 USC § 2656f (d)(2).
[3] US Department of State, *Country Reports on Terrorism 2015, Annex of Statistical Information*, available at <https://www.state.gov/j/ct/rls/crt/2015/257526.htm> last visited 2 May 2017.

7.2 Defining Terrorism

Terrorism has been notoriously difficult to define.[4] It appears to consist of actions of
a different quality from 'ordinary' murders, assaults, or damage to property. In order
to avoid reliance on political elements in the definition, terrorism can be conceptu-
alized as a range of distinctive but 'political motive free' acts of violence—hostage-
taking, bombing, hijacking, and so forth—undertaken by non-state actors against
civilian targets. Initially, as we shall see, states followed this path in a slow thematic
development of the law to suppress such actions. One problem with this approach was
whether to include actions that do not involve intentional violence to persons but only
to property.[5] The more serious weakness was that these offences neither describe fully
the perpetrator's conduct or purpose nor address the full extent of the harm done to
their victims. More specific concepts of terrorism have relied on the inclusion of a special intention to inculcate terror in the victim with further specific purposes in mind,
in order to try to embrace otherwise distinct acts of violence within a single offence.
This is not a new approach. The definition of terrorism, for example, in article 1(2) of
the failed 1937 League of Nations Convention for the Prevention and Punishment of
Terrorism[6] includes 'criminal acts directed against a state and intended or calculated
to create a state of terror in the minds of particular persons, or a group of persons
or the general public'. More recently, the United Nations Office on Drugs and Crime
(UNODC)'s Terrorism Prevention Branch added a further specific goal-directed purpose for inculcating this terror when it noted that in terrorism the 'direct targets of
violence are not the main targets', they 'serve as message generators' to 'manipulate
the main target'.[7] The UK's requirement of a specific motive, 'the purpose of advanc-
ing a political, religious, racial, or ideological cause', takes this approach even further.[8]
While former colonies that used violence to achieve self-determination initially found
this more political concept of terrorism difficult to accept,[9] and the question whether
political motives should be part of the definition of terrorism or serve to excuse terrorism has plagued agreement on a general definition of terrorism, supporters of this
approach have promoted it with some success. For example, UN Security Council
Resolution 1566,[10] which recalled in operative paragraph 3

> that criminal acts, including against civilians, committed with the intent to cause
> death or serious bodily injury, or taking of hostages, with the purpose to provoke
> a state of terror in the general public or in a group of persons or particular persons,
> intimidate a population or compel a government or an international organization to
> do or to abstain from doing any act, which constitute offences within the scope of

---

[4] On the problems of definition see generally B Saul, *Defining Terrorism in International Law*
(Oxford: OUP, 2006).
[5] Addressed, eg, by section 1(2)(b) of the UK's Terrorism Act 2000.
[6] 16 November 1937, 19 LNOJ 23 (1938), never in force (only India ratified).
[7] A Schmidt et al, *Political Terrorism* (Amsterdam: Transaction Books, 1988), 5.
[8] Section 1(1)(c) of the Terrorism Act 2000. In *R v Gul* [2013] UKSC 64 the UK Supreme Court held it
requires proof of a specific intent.
[9] See, eg, A Sofaer, 'Terrorism and the Law' 64 *Foreign Affairs* (1986) 901, 904–05.
[10] S/Res1566 (2004).

and as defined in the international conventions and protocols relating to terrorism, are under no circumstances justifiable by considerations of a political, philosophical, ideological, racial, ethnic, religious or other similar nature, and calls upon all States to prevent such acts and, if not prevented, to ensure that such acts are punished by penalties consistent with their grave nature.

A problem is that even very complex definitions of this kind taking into account multiple dimensions of terrorism can never take them all into account because they are hardly ever all present in a particular case or situation.[11] Furthermore, many broadly drawn definitions have been criticized for being too broad, failing to reserve the stigma of terrorism for those offences that truly threaten the social fabric.[12]

It has also proved difficult to control the expansion of this now standard definition. States add elements serving different regional and local purposes. For example, the Organisation of African Unity Convention on Prevention and Combating of Terrorism[13] relies on what might now be termed the general approach of intentional violent action carried out with a further broadly political intention while adding an intention to disrupt public services or to create general insurrection, issues of regional concern.[14] The Shanghai Convention on Combating Terrorism, Separatism and Extremism[15] uses a variant of this 'standard' approach but adds separate definitions for separatism (acts committed in a violent manner intended to violate the territorial integrity of a state) and extremism (seizing or keeping power through the use of violence or changing violently the constitutional regime), issues of concern for its parties.[16] The scope of terrorism also expands in other ways. At a national level, a recent US law defines 'international terrorism' as inter alia acts which 'occur primarily outside the territorial jurisdiction of the US, or transcend national boundaries in terms of the means by which they are accomplished, the persons they appear intended to intimidate or coerce, or the locale in which their perpetrators operate or seek asylum'.[17] Including a specific transnational aspect allows states to take measures directed against this peculiar form of terrorism by both establishing and enforcing extraterritorial jurisdiction. These examples illustrate that despite achieving a modicum of stability, 'terrorism' remains a highly volatile concept.

7.3 Aviation Offences

Hijacking, which involves the taking control of a civil aircraft by force in mid-air or on the ground, was initially difficult to categorize legally. Classification as air piracy under article 101 of United Nations Convention on the Law of the Sea[18] was inadequate because of the necessity of an attack from another plane for private ends inside international airspace, whereas almost all hijackings involve politically driven

---

[11] See G Fletcher, 'The Indefinable Concept of Terrorism' 4 *Journal of International Criminal Justice* (2006) 894, 910.

[12] See T Weigend, 'The Universal Terrorist: The International Community Grappling with a Definition' 4 *Journal of International Criminal Justice* (2006) 912, 928.

[13] 14 July 1999, in force 6 December 2002.   [14] Article 1(3)(a)(ii) and (iii).

[15] 15 June 2001; in force 29 March 2003.   [16] Article 1(1)(2) and (3) respectively.

[17] 18 USC § 2331(1)(c).   [18] See Chapter 3.

passengers taking over aircraft by force in domestic airspace. When the International Civil Aviation Organization undertook law reform it faced the dilemma of avoiding classification of the offence as political in order to circumvent the political offence exception to extradition. This led to a focus on what is done by the hijackers and not their aims.

The 1963 Convention on Offences and Certain Other Acts Committed on Board Aircraft (the Tokyo Convention)[19] did not provide for obligations on parties to enact specific offences but only for a range of enforcement powers for existing offences in national law. It did, however, explicitly exclude actions of a political nature.[20] States responded to the wave of hijackings that occurred in the late 1960s by adopting the 1970 Hague Convention for the Suppression of Unlawful Seizure of Aircraft.[21] Article 1 provides: 'Any person who on board an aircraft in flight: (a) unlawfully, by force or threat thereof, or by any other form of intimidation, seizes, or exercises control of, that aircraft, or attempts to perform any such act, … commits an offence.'

Closely followed in national legislation,[22] the material element of this offence is the unlawful use of force or threats to seize or attempt to seize the control of an aircraft. The offence is in neutral terms; it focuses on force or threats of force without any requirement of a specific intent or even of a general intent, although in national law the latter is likely to be required.[23] The offence can only be committed when the aircraft is 'in flight' (the period between the closing and opening of the doors[24]). It does not apply to aircraft used in military, police, or customs services.[25] One of the features of the convention is that it is limited to transnational crimes—it only applies if the place of take-off or landing is outside the state of registration of the aircraft,[26] although measures for procedural cooperation are not subject to this exclusion.[27] This is a jurisdictional limitation rather than a necessary element of the offence as enacted in national law. Article 1(a) also criminalizes attempts (although not conspiracies) while article 1(b) makes provision for accomplice liability, particularly important if all the perpetrators on board are killed (as happened in 9/11). Finally, article 2 provides that each party undertakes to make the treaty offences 'punishable by severe penalties', an example of an early attempt to add specific sanctions in transnational criminal law, which left parties to decide what 'severe' means in the context of their particular punishment scale.

A spate of bombings on civil aircraft exposed the limitations of the Hague Hijacking Convention and led to complementary development of the Convention for the Suppression of Unlawful Acts against the Safety of Civil Aviation (the Montreal Convention).[28] Article 1(1) provides that any person 'commits an offence' (again these offences have been criminalized in national law) if they perform any one of a range of

---

[19] 14 September 1963; 704 UNTS 219, in force 4 December 1969.   [20] Article II.
[21] 16 December 1970; 860 UNTS 105, in force 14 October 1971.
[22] See, eg, section 3 of New Zealand's Aviation Crimes Act, 1972; section 2(1)(i) of South Africa's Civil Aviation Offences Act 10 of 1972.
[23] In the implausible South African case *S v Hoare* 1982 (4) SALR 865 (N) the majority of accused hijackers were acquitted because they believed the captain of the Air India Boeing they were accused of hijacking had volunteered to fly them to safety from a failed coup in the Seychelles.
[24] Article 3(1).   [25] Article 3(2).   [26] Article 3(3).   [27] Article 3(5).
[28] 23 September 1971; 974 UNTS 177, in force 26 January 1973.

actions that must either be likely to endanger the safety of aircraft or do so. Article 1(1)(a) criminalizes the performance of acts of violence on board an aircraft in flight. The definition of acts of violence is left to the parties. Section 7 of the Civil Aviation Act 1982 (UK), for example, lists murder, attempt, manslaughter, assault, etc. Article 1(1)(b) criminalizes the destruction of an aircraft in flight (such as the destruction of Pan Am Flight 103 over the Scottish town of Lockerbie[29]) or the causing of severe damage of an aircraft. Article 1(1)(c) makes it an offence to 'place or cause to be placed' on board an aircraft a device or substance likely to destroy it. Article 1(1)(d) and (e) relate to direct and indirect interference with the navigation of an aircraft. Unlike the Hague Hijacking Convention, the Montreal Convention insists that these actions be committed with 'intention', but avoids requiring some kind of ulterior intent linked to political activity. The Montreal Convention also provides for accomplice liability[30] and for the application of severe penalties.[31]

The 1988 Protocol for the Suppression of Unlawful Acts of Violence at Airports Serving International Civil Aviation[32] took the principles of the Montreal Convention and applied them to airports.[33] The response to the Lockerbie bombing included the adoption of the 1991 Convention on the Marking of Plastic Explosives for the Purpose of Detection,[34] which sought to enforce the detectable chemical marking of explosives.[35] The latest development in the aviation security sector is the Beijing Convention on the Suppression of Unlawful Acts relating to International Civil Aviation adopted in 2010.[36] A response to 'new threats against civil aviation',[37] article 1 expands the range of offence committed on board aircraft dramatically by inter alia criminalizing 'using an aircraft in service for the purpose of causing death, serious bodily injury, or serious damage to property or the environment',[38] a response to the poor fit of the Montreal Convention with the use in the 9/11 attack of the aircraft itself as a weapon. Article 1 also responds to novel threats posed by, for example, cyberterrorism to aviation safety by criminalizing destruction or damage to air navigation facilities or interference in their operation, if any such act is likely to endanger the safety of an aircraft in flight[39] (pre-flight checking to 24 hours after landing[40]). Spreading the net of criminalization as comprehensively as possible, in addition to criminalizing threats to carry out such activities,[41] the Convention also criminalizes attempts, organization, direction, participation, and assisting someone to evade investigation,[42] as well as conspiring to and participation in a common purpose to commit the offences.[43] All offences must be punished by 'severe penalties'.[44]

[29] Section 2(1)(a) of the UK's Aviation Security Act 1982; see M Scharf, 'Terrorism on Trial: the Lockerbie Criminal Proceedings' 6(2) *ILSA Journal of International and Comparative Law* (2000) 355.

[30] Article 1(2).

[31] Article 3. See, eg, section 2(5) of the UK Aviation Security Act 1982 which provides for life imprisonment.

[32] 24 February 1988; 1589 UNTS 474; in force 6 August 1989.

[33] Article II inserting Article 1 *bis* into the Montreal Convention.

[34] Montreal, 1 March 1991, 2122 UNTS 359, in force 21 June 1998.   [35] Articles II–IV.

[36] 10 September 2010; not yet in force. See R Abeyratne, 'The Beijing Convention of 2010 on the Suppression of Unlawful Acts relating to International Civil Aviation—an Interpretative Study' 4(2) *Journal of Transportation Security* (2011) 131.

[37] Para 3 of the Preamble.   [38] Article 1(f).   [39] Article 1(d).   [40] Article 2(b).

[41] Article 3.   [42] Article 4.   [43] Article 5.   [44] Article 3.

7.4 Crimes against Internationally Protected Persons

The 1973 Convention on the Prevention and Punishment of Crimes against
Internationally Protected Persons, including Diplomatic Agents,[45] was adopted
to respond to the kidnapping and murder of diplomatic agents, a problem that
has not abated as illustrated by the killing of the Russian ambassador to Turkey
on camera in 2016.[46] Article 2 follows the approach of earlier treaties by focusing on specific actions of the perpetrators rather than their ulterior intentions or
motives. It requires parties to criminalize the intentional commission of violent
attacks on internationally protected persons (heads of state, ministers for foreign
affairs, state representatives, or officials entitled to special protection and their
families[47]) and violent attacks on their premises or transport likely to endanger
their persons or liberty, or threats, attempts, or secondary participation in such
attacks.[48] Available penalties must be appropriate taking into account the grave
nature of the crimes.[49]

7.5 Nuclear Terrorism

The 1980 Convention on the Physical Protection of Nuclear Material[50] provides
mainly for the security of nuclear material, but article 7 does require parties to 'make
a punishable offence' each of the following activities in regard to nuclear material: (a)
unlawful handling which causes or is likely to cause death or serious injury or substantially damage property; (b) theft or robbery; (c) embezzlement or fraudulent
obtaining; (d) demanding it by threat or use of force or other form of intimidation;
(e)(i) threats to use it to cause death or serious injury or substantially to damage property. Paragraph (e)(ii) introduced a specific purpose destined to become popular in
later anti-terrorism conventions: it made it an offence to commit theft or robbery of
nuclear material 'in order to compel a natural or legal person, international organization or state to do or to refrain from doing any act'. Heightened anxiety about the
sale of nuclear material to potential terrorists, particularly in the wake of exposure
in 2003 of the AQ Khan Network (the 'father' of the Pakistan nuclear bomb who
allegedly bought and sold nuclear weapons know-how and components for twenty
years[51]), led to the amendment of the Convention in 2005[52] to add to the range of
offences.

---

[45] New York, 14 December 1973, 1035 UNTS 167, in force 20 February 1977.
[46] 'Russian Ambassador to Turkey Shot Dead by Police Officer in Ankara Gallery', *The Guardian
Online*, 21 December 2016, <https://www.theguardian.com/world/2016/dec/19/russian-ambassador-to-
turkey-wounded-in-ankara-shooting-attack> visited 7 January 2017.
[47] Article 1(1).   [48] Article 2(1).   [49] Article 2(2).
[50] 3 March 1980, 1456 UNTS 101, in force 8 February 1987.
[51] See D Albright and C Hinderstein, 'Unravelling the AQ Khan and Future Proliferation Networks' 28
The Washington Quarterly (2005) 111, 112.
[52] The Amendment to the Convention on the Physical Protection of Nuclear Material, 8 July 2005,
attached to IAEA Director's Report, *Nuclear Safety: Measures to Protect Against Nuclear Terrorism*,
GOV/INF/2005/10-GC(49)/INF/6, 6 September 2005.

The 2005 International Convention for the Suppression of Acts of Nuclear Terrorism[53] addressed nuclear terrorism more directly. Article 2(1)(a) requires parties to criminalize possession of radioactive material or possession or making of a device for dispersal of such material or radiation with either the intent to cause death or serious bodily injury or with the intent to cause substantial damage to property or the environment. Article 2(1)(b) requires parties to criminalize use of such material or device or use or damage of a nuclear facility in a manner which releases or risks the release of radioactive material, with similar intentions as in article 2(1)(a) as well as the additional 'intent of compelling a natural or legal person, state or international organization to do or refrain from doing an act'. Article 2(2) requires parties to criminalize threatening to commit such an offence and demanding by threats such material, device, or facility. Much of the rest of the Convention follows the provisions in other conventions (inchoate and participatory liability, appropriate penalties taking into account gravity) but importantly excludes political justification of such offences as a defence.[54]

7.6 Hostage-taking

With the adoption of the 1979 International Convention against the Taking of Hostages,[55] states moved closer to a more general definition of terrorism. Article 1 obliges parties to criminalize the taking of hostages. The offence has two material elements—the seizure or detention of the hostage, and the threat to kill, injure, or continue detention of the hostage. The mental element is an early version of the now standard formula: the accused must detain and threaten the hostage with the specific purpose of compelling a third party (state, inter-governmental organization (IGO), natural or juridical person or group of persons) to do or not do an act. The compulsion on the third party must arise out of the condition that the accused will not release the hostage unless they do as asked. Provision is also made for accomplice and inchoate liability. Article 2 uses the common formula obliging parties to make hostage-taking punishable 'by appropriate penalties which take into account the grave nature of the offences'. Like the Hague Hijacking Convention, article 13 does not introduce a transnational element into the offence but does limit the application of the Convention to transnational hostage-taking (ie either the offence occurs in more than one state, or the hostage or alleged offenders are nationals of more than one state, or the alleged offender is not found in the state where the offence was committed).

7.7 Maritime Safety

The Convention for the Suppression of Unlawful Acts against the Safety of Maritime Navigation discussed in Chapter 3, adapted aviation offences to maritime safety.

---

[53] New York, 13 April 2005, 2445 UNTS 89, in force 7 July 2007.
[54] Article 15.   [55] New York, 17 December 1979, 1316 UNTS 205.

7.8 Terrorist Bombings

The 1997 International Convention for the Suppression of Terrorist Bombings[56] grew out of the General Assembly's 1994 Declaration on Measures to Eliminate International Terrorism, which called for review of the existing conventions.[57] The Convention has a much sharper focus on terrorism. Article 2(1) requires parties to criminalize the unlawful and intentional delivery, placing, discharging, or detonation of an explosive or other legal device 'into or against a place of public use, a State or government facility, a public transportation system or an infrastructure facility'. These actions must be done with either the intent to cause death or serious injury or cause extensive destruction which results in or is likely to result in major economic loss. In addition to provisions on attempts, accomplice liability, and liability for organizing and directing such offences,[58] article 2(3)(c) introduces a novel provision in transnational criminal law that broadens the scope of party liability considerably. It obliges parties to criminalize the conduct of someone who:

> (c) In any other way contributes to the commission of one or more offences as set forth in paragraph 1 or 2 by a group of persons acting with a common purpose; such contribution shall be intentional and either be made with the aim of furthering the general criminal activity or purpose of the group or be made in the knowledge of the intention of the group to commit the offence or offences concerned.

It entails a form of common purpose or joint criminal enterprise liability that provides for complicity in the principal's crime. There must be a group with a common purpose to commit one of the bombing offences. The accused must make an intentional contribution either to further the general purpose or at least have knowledge of that purpose. The level of contribution is unstated; it could include provision of help in any number of ways so long as it is done with knowledge of the common purpose.

The Terrorist Bombings Convention follows earlier anti-terrorism conventions in that it is only directed against transnational crime.[59] It also obliges parties to provide for appropriate penalties that take into account the grave nature of the Convention's offences.[60] Article 5, however, adds a new dimension. It obliges parties to ensure that the Convention's crimes,

> in particular where they are intended or calculated to provoke a state of terror in the general public or in a group of persons or particular persons, are under no circumstances justifiable by considerations of a political, philosophical, ideological, racial, ethnic, religious or other similar nature and are punished by penalties consistent with their grave nature.

---

[56] 15 December 1997, 2149 UNTS 256, in force 23 May 2001.

[57] Declaration on Measures to Eliminate International Terrorism, Annexed to GA Res 49/60 of 9 December 1994; see also the Declaration to Supplement the 1994 Declaration on Measures to Eliminate International Terrorism, annexed to GA Res 51/210 of 17 December 1996 and the 2005 World Summit Outcome, Resolution 60/1.

[58] Article 2(2), 2(3)(a) and (b).   [59] Article 3.   [60] Article 4(b).

This provision is probably the first mention of 'terror' in a treaty since the 1937 Convention, treating the presence in a particular case of an intention to provoke terror as an aggravating factor on sentence. It is also a rare example of a treaty provision that obliges parties to curtail the availability of a defence—in this case again where there is a terrorist intention, to deny any defence based on political, ideological, racial, ethnic or religious, or other similar purposes.

7.9 Terrorist Financing

In an inversion of the logic of the suppression of money laundering (see Chapter 10), in 1999 the International Convention for the Suppression of the Financing of Terrorism[61] was adopted, in order to prevent and counteract the financing of terrorists through groups claiming to have charitable, social, or cultural goals or which engage in 'ordinary' transnational criminal activities such as drug or weapons trafficking. Article 2(1) provides for an independent offence of terrorist financing, rather than an inchoate form of terrorism or secondary participation in terrorism because from a legal point of view these ancillary forms of liability require too close a link to specific acts of terrorism. The policy justification is that financing is itself as serious as the terrorist acts that are financed.[62] Article 2(1) reads:

> Any person commits an offence within the meaning of this Convention if that person by any means, directly or indirectly, unlawfully and wilfully, provides or collects funds with the intention that they should be used or in the knowledge that they are to be used, in full or in part, in order to carry out:
>
> (a) an act which constitutes an offence within the scope of and as defined in one of the treaties listed in the annex [all of the extant counter-terrorism conventions]; or
> (b) any other act intended to cause death or serious bodily injury to a civilian, or to any other person not taking an active part in the hostilities in a situation of armed conflict, when the purpose of such act, by its nature or context, is to intimidate a population, or to compel a government or an international organisation to do or to abstain from doing any act.

The material element of the crime is the 'collection or provision' of funds. This can be done by any means, direct or indirect, but it must be unlawful. 'Funds' do not include only money, they include 'assets of every kind'.[63] The mental element of the crime is more complex. Provision or collection of funds must be wilful but it must occur with either the intention or the knowledge that the funds (in whole or in part)[64] are to be used to carry out one of two different sets of (by implication terrorist) actions. The collection or provision of funds does not thus actually have to result in the commission of a hijacking, etc or of violence (article 2(3)); it need only be intended for or carried out with the knowledge of that purpose. The

---

[61] New York, 9 December, 1999, 2178 UNTS 197, in force 10 April 2002.
[62] Implicit in preambular paras 10 and 11.   [63] Article 1(1).
[64] See FATF, *Guidance on Criminalising Terrorist Financing* (Paris: FATF, October 2016), para 12.

first set of actions incorporates by reference the acts criminalized in existing sectoral conventions—hijacking, hostage-taking, etc. The second set of actions sets out a self-contained definition of a terrorist act. Such an act must be intended to cause death or serious injury to a limited class of persons—civilians and non-combatants. In addition, they must be carried out with an ulterior purpose: intimidation of a population or compulsion of a government or IGO to do or not do something. It is, however, the hijacker who must act intentionally, or killer who must kill intentionally with the ulterior manipulative purpose, not the funder, who only, as noted above, need have knowledge of this outcome. Knowledge does not require approval. Indeed, the money might be specifically earmarked for humanitarian purposes yet the accused would still be liable if they knew that the funds might be used for one of the specified terrorist acts. This breadth raises similar issues to those raised when in response to petition by a non-governmental organization that it should be allowed to provide legal assistance in the US to the PKK and Tamil Tigers, designated Foreign Terrorist Organizations under US law, the US Supreme Court held that such assistance would be unlawful because it did fit the crime of material support to foreign terrorist organizations.[65]

The Convention also requires the criminalization of attempts, participation, and organization of the offences.[66] Following the model in the Terrorist Bombings Convention, article 2(5)(c) requires parties to criminalize an accused's intentional contribution to the commission of any article 2(1) offence by a group acting with a common purpose to commit that offence, where the accused either aims to further the common purpose or acts in the knowledge of the intention of the group to commit the article 2(1) offence.[67] In the Swedish case *Public Prosecutor v A B and F J, Appeal judgment*[68] the Court confirmed on appeal that the accused had violated the Swedish law implementing article 2(5)(c) of the Convention (the *Lag om straff för finansiering av särskilt allvarlig brottslighet i vissa fall*, SFS 2002: 444), by collecting US$115,000 and sending some of the money to an EU scheduled Iraqi terrorist group, Ansar Al-Islam, with the knowledge or the intention that it was for use in terrorism.

The Convention follows the Terrorist Bombings Convention in limiting its application to transnational offences,[69] insisting on adequate punishment taking into account the grave nature of the offence[70] and on measures to ensure that all the Convention's crimes are not justifiable by political or related considerations.[71]

The Terrorist Financing Convention sought to criminalize a range of activities in the financial system in an unprecedented way, drawing upon innovations in earlier anti-terrorism treaties but expanding upon them. Many states considered it flawed and did not ratify it. As we shall see, this reluctance disappeared after 9/11.

---

[65] *Holder et al v Humanitarian Law Project et al* 561 US 1 (2010). Listing as a Foreign Terrorist Organization in the US is a predicate for the crime of material support under 18 USC 2339B and among other administrative penalties restricts access to assets and restricts travel.
[66] Articles 2(4) and 2(5)(a) and (b).   [67] Article 2(5)(c).
[68] Case no B 3687-05; ILDC 280 (SE 2005) 3 October 2005, paras 63–64.   [69] Article 3.
[70] Article 4.   [71] Article 6.

7.10 A Comprehensive Counter-terrorism Convention?

The Ad Hoc Committee that negotiated the Terrorist Bombing and Terrorist Financing Conventions was mandated by the UN General Assembly in Resolution 51/210 to begin work on a draft comprehensive convention on terrorism. Working on a draft submitted by India, by 2002 the Committee had reached broad agreement on twenty-seven articles. It could not, however, agree on provisions dealing with the definition of terrorism, its relation to liberation movements, or on the possible exemptions to the scope of the treaty, in particular the activities of armed forces.[72] By 2005 the Ad Hoc Committee had agreed upon a definition of terrorism which enumerated different forms of serious violence carried out with the now familiar purpose of intimidating a population or compelling a government or an IGO to do or to abstain from doing any act. Agreement still eluded it on the exclusion of the actions of national liberation movements fighting for self-determination, the actions of individuals fighting against occupation, and the killing of civilians during armed conflict (which can currently be justified as collateral damage).[73] In 2006 the General Assembly adopted a UN Global Counter Terrorism Strategy[74] which urged states to reach agreement on a comprehensive convention. There has, however, been little further progress on the draft convention.[75] In 2016 the UN General Assembly Resolution 71/151 recommended to the Sixth Committee that it establish a working group to finalize the process of drafting the convention and to discuss the convening of a diplomatic conference to carry the matter forward.[76] In effect, the draft comprehensive treaty on terrorism is almost fully negotiated but remains in limbo because of conflict over the use of terrorism in the Palestinian situation.

7.11 Regional Counter-terrorism Conventions

Early anti-terrorism conventions at a regional level such as the 1977 European Convention on the Suppression of Terrorism[77] were designed not to criminalize but to facilitate extradition by removing the political offence exception for terrorism offences. The 1987 South Asian Association for Regional Cooperation Regional Convention on Suppression of Terrorism[78] was more in the nature of a criminalizing convention, although it simply rounded up a selection of offences from the existing sectoral conventions and ensured that states from the region criminalized them and

---

[72] Draft Comprehensive Convention against International Terrorism Annex, App II, UN Doc A/59/894, 3 August 2005.

[73] See Saul above n 4, 63.

[74] Annexed to GA Res 60/288 of 20 September 2006. Reaffirmed in GA Res 62/272, 15 December 2008.

[75] The current text has been consolidated by a UN Sixth Committee Working Group, UN Doc A/C.6/65/L.10.

[76] UN Doc A/RES/71/151, 20 December 2016.

[77] Strasbourg, 27 January 1977, 1137 UNTS 93, in force 4 August 1978. It was supplemented by the Protocol amending the European Convention on the Suppression of Terrorism, Strasbourg, 15 May 2003, CETS 190; not yet in force.

[78] 4 November 1987, in force 22 August 1988. An Additional Protocol was signed 6 January 2004 and came into force on 12 January 2006.

engaged in international cooperation in their regard.[79] The Association of Southeast Asian Nations Convention on Counter-terrorism[80] adopted a similar listing international cooperation approach but also emphasized the rehabilitation and social reintegration of the accused.[81] The 2005 European Convention on the Prevention of Terrorism[82] took things further by introducing new offences of *apologie du terrorisme* (indirect incitement to terrorism) in article 5(1), recruitment for terrorism in article 6, and training for terrorism in article 7.

7.12 Suppressing Terrorism through the UN Security Council

The 'war on terror' that enveloped international society in the 1990s resulted in a dramatic increase in military responses to terrorism. It also impacted on criminal law by abandoning the 'take it or leave it' approach to participation and implementation in the sectoral conventions. The UN Security Council became a 'single issue' legislator compelling participation in the global anti-terrorism regime and filling gaps in law revealed by new threats.[83] This new 'legislative' role for the Security Council was first trialled by the US and the UK after the Lockerbie bombing when they turned to it to impose sanctions on Libya as an alternative to action under the 1971 Montreal Convention.[84] According to Resolution 748 adopted unanimously on 31 March 1992, the Security Council was 'convinced that the suppression of acts of international terrorism, including those in which states are directly or indirectly involved, is essential for the maintenance of international peace and security'. The '1267 Committee' was established by Security Council Resolution 1267[85] as a response to Al-Qaeda bombings in East Africa. Its task was to apply smart sanctions such as travel bans and freezing of assets against entities (Taleban) and individuals (Osama Bin Laden) nominated by states. This quasi-criminalization without rights of appeal set the tone for the various 'legislative' resolutions passed by the Security Council in the wake of 9/11.

The Security Council first condemned the attacks in Resolution 1368,[86] considering them to be a threat to international peace and security, then in Resolution 1373[87] declared that the 'acts, methods and practices of terrorism are contrary to the purposes and principles of the United Nations'. It called on all states to become party as soon as possible to the sectoral counter-terrorism conventions and to criminalize terrorist activities.[88] It also used its Chapter VII powers to determine that all UN member states would prevent and suppress the financing of terrorist assets and freeze funds and financial assets. Most significantly for the evolution of transnational criminal law, however, operative paragraph 1(b) obliges all states to 'criminalize the wilful provision or collection, by any means, directly or indirectly, of funds by their nationals or in their territories with the intention that the funds should be used, or in the knowledge

---

[79] See article 1.   [80] 13 January 2007.   [81] Article 11.

[82] 16 May 2005, CETS No 196, in force 1 December 2009.

[83] See P Szasz, 'The Security Council Starts Legislating' 96 *American Journal of International Law* (2002) 901; S Talmon, 'The Security Council as a World Legislature' 99 *American Journal of International Law* (2005) 175.

[84] S/Res/731 (1992) and S/Res/748 (1992).   [85] S/Res/1267 (1999).

[86] S/Res/1368 (2001).   [87] S/Res/1373 (2001).   [88] Paras 1(b) and 3(d).

that they are to be used, to carry out terrorist acts'. Thus the obligation already undertaken by parties to the Terrorism Financing Convention was also imposed on non-
parties, a dramatic step in the enforcement of transnational criminalization through
the Security Council. In a novel provision, paragraph 2(a) specifically requires member states to suppress recruitment of terrorists (which has been taken by the UNODC
to mean criminalization).[89] Finally, the Resolution obliges member states to report
to the Security Council's Counter-Terrorist Committee (CTC) on the steps they had
taken to implement this Resolution.[90]

By this time, the Security Council had the hang of legislating, and began to criminalize with gusto. In Resolution 1566[91] the Security Council drew on the sectoral conventions for a definition of terrorism that includes:

> criminal acts, including against civilians, committed with the intent to cause death
> or serious bodily injury, or taking of hostages, with the purpose to provoke a state
> of terror in the general public or in a group of persons or particular persons, intimi-
> date a population or compel a government or an international organization to do or
> to abstain from doing any act, which constitute offences within the scope of and as
> defined in the international conventions and protocols relating to terrorism.

The Resolution sews the sectoral convention offences into one offence. It also recalls
treaty provisions that such actions were not justifiable on political grounds, and calls
upon member states to punish them with penalties consistent with their grave nature.
It does not, however, impose a transnationality requirement. The Security Council has
continued to criminalize. Resolution 1624[92] requires member states to 'prohibit by law
incitement to commit a terrorist act or acts'.

Although it has been questioned whether the Security Council actually has the
authority to adopt measures affecting individuals,[93] these resolutions have precipitated a frenzy of domestic law-making, much of it introducing domestic criminal laws
with a much broader scope than those contemplated by the conventions or the resolutions. This activity has been supported by organizations like the Financial Action
Task Force (FATF), which responded to 9/11 with the IX Special Recommendations
on Terrorist Financing published in 2001. Recommendation 36 of the 2012 consolidation FATF recommendations[94] recommends that countries take immediate steps to
ratify and fully implement the Terrorist Financing Convention. Recommendation 6
provides that countries should implement targeted financial sanctions regimes providing for the freezing of terrorist funds in compliance with Security Council Resolutions
1267 and 1373. However, from the point of view of the development of transnational
criminal law, it is Recommendation 5 that is of most interest. In order to avoid the
difficulty of having to prove that an alleged terrorist financier intended or knew

---

[89] See UNODC Anti-Terrorism Branch, *Draft Model Legislative Provisions against Terrorism* (Vienna,
February 2009), 26.
[90] Para 6.   [91] S/Res/1566 (2004), para 3.   [92] S/Res/1624 (2005), para 1(a).
[93] A Bianchi, 'Assessing the Effectiveness of the UN Security Council's Anti-Terrorism Measures: The
Quest for Legitimacy and Cohesion' 17(5) *European Journal of International Law* (2006) 881.
[94] FATF Recommendations: International Standards on Combating Money Laundering and the Financing
of Terrorism and Proliferation, 16 February 2012, available at <http://www.fatf-gafi.org/publications/
fatfrecommendations/documents/fatf-recommendations.html> last visited 2 May 2017.

they were financing an act of terrorism as required by article 2(1) of the Terrorism Financing Convention (see above), Recommendation 5 states that 'countries should criminalise ... the financing of terrorist organisations and individual terrorists even in the absence of a link to a specific terrorist act or acts ...'.[95] FATF justifies this expansion of criminalization on the basis that a lot of financing is not used to support specific attacks but rather for broad organizational support.[96] FATF claims that Recommendation 5 is consistent[97] with Security Council Resolution 2253 of 2015,[98] which in a circular fashion 'highlights that FATF Recommendation 5 applies to the financing of terrorist organisation or individual terrorists for any purpose, including but not limited to recruitment, training, travel, even in the absence of a specific link to a terrorist act'.[99]

7.13 Foreign Terrorist Fighters

According to Murphy the Security Council has become 'a key site for the diffusion of transnational counterterrorism law around the world',[100] and this has recently been illustrated by its response to the volume of foreign recruits who flocked to help the Islamic State in its attempts to recreate the Caliphate by violence, which prompted the Security Council to further action in 2014.[101] In Resolution 2170 it required UN member states to 'take national measures to suppress the flow of foreign fighters'.[102] In Resolution 2178[103] it went much further. Paragraph 5 defines these foreign terrorist fighters as 'individuals who travel to a State other than their States of residence or nationality for the purpose of the perpetration, planning, or preparation of, or participation in, terrorist acts, or the providing or receiving of terrorist training, including in connection with armed conflict ...' and obliges states to 'prevent and suppress the recruiting, organizing, transporting or equipping of' foreign terrorist fighters 'and the financing of their travel and of their activities'.[104] Paragraph 6 obliges all states to criminalize foreign fighters, the collection or provision of funds with the intention they be used to finance foreign fighters, and the organization or facilitation of the travel of foreign fighters.[105] The provisions must be effective both in the sense they enable prosecution and punishment 'in a manner duly reflecting the seriousness of the offense'. These provisions for criminalization are classic attempts to interdict the 'supply' of fighters using transnational criminal law because of the obvious difficulties of preventing their 'use', and form the centrepiece of a range of other tailored measures such as obligations to prevent movement,[106] transit,[107] and radicalization,[108] backed by a range of measures for international cooperation.

---

[95] FATF Recommendation 5.
[96] *Guidance on Criminalising Terrorist Financing*, above n 64, para 19.   [97] ibid, para 18.
[98] S/Res/2253 (2015).   [99] Para 17.
[100] CC Murphy, 'Transnational Counter-terrorism Law: Law, Power and Legitimacy in the "Wars on Terror"' 6(1) *Transnational Legal Theory* (2015) 31, 46.
[101] See generally A De Guttry, 'The Role Played by the UN in Countering the Phenomenon of Foreign Terrorist Fighters' in A de Guttry, F Capone, and C Paulussen (eds), *Foreign Fighters under International Law and Beyond* (The Hague: Asser, 2016), 259.
[102] S/Res/2170 (2014), para 8.   [103] S/Res/2178 (2014).   [104] Para 5.
[105] Para 6(1), (2), and (3).   [106] Para 2.   [107] Para 7.   [108] Para 4.

Elements of these Security Council resolutions have trickled down into other international agreements, including the 2015 Additional Protocol to the Council of Europe Convention on the Prevention of Terrorism,[109] which requires criminalization of an expanded range of terrorist acts including 'participating in an association or group for the purposes of terrorism',[110] 'receiving training for terrorism',[111] and 'travelling abroad for the purpose of terrorism'[112] (which adopts the substance of the Security Council's definition of foreign fighters), 'funding travelling abroad for the purpose of terrorism',[113] and 'organising or otherwise facilitating travelling abroad for the purpose of terrorism'.[114]

While some states have relied on existing legislation, many have enacted new criminal laws in response to Resolution 2178's obligations. A number have created the novel offence of 'traveling abroad for a terrorist purpose'[115] while others have expanded extant terrorism provisions to cover a wider range of acts.[116] Peculiar legislative innovations that go further than the requirements of the Security Council have begun to emerge, including Australia's 'declared area offence', which makes it an offence to enter an area declared by the Minister as an area where a terrorist organization operates, where the person knows or should know the area is such declared area.[117] It is not limited by a requirement of a wrongful purpose, although there are humanitarian exceptions available.

Relying on these new offences, states have prosecuted a range of actions from inciting foreign fighters to go to Syria to fight to actually travelling to Syria. In the *Prosecutor v Imane B et al*,[118] for example, a Dutch Court convicted a number of individuals for inter alia inciting and recruitment of others online to take part in an 'armed jihadi struggle'. The Dutch Supreme Court held in *Prosecutor v Omar H*[119] that the offence of participating and cooperating in training for terrorism under article 134a of the Criminal Code was committed by an individual who engaged in online research. In the *Prosecutor v Harun P*[120] a German court convicted the accused under section 129(a) of German Penal Code for travelling to Syria and joining a foreign terrorist group. In *Federal Prosecutor v Hamza B et al*[121] a Belgian court convicted

---

[109] Riga 22 October 2015, CETS 217. See also the EU Draft Directive of the European Parliament and of the Council on Combating Terrorism (2015), Com (2015) 625.

[110] Article 2.   [111] Article 3.   [112] Article 4.   [113] Article 5.   [114] Article 6.

[115] See, eg, article 259a of the Polish Criminal Code introduced in 2016, article 140 of the Belgium Criminal Code, and article 575 of the Spanish Penal Code, both introduced in 2015.

[116] See, eg, Ireland's Criminal Justice (Terrorist Offences) (Amendment) Act 2015, which added offences of recruitment, provocation, and training, and Montenegro which amended its Criminal Code in 2015 to include a new offence in article 449B, 'participation in foreign army formations'.

[117] Section 119.2 of the Criminal Code Act 1995.

[118] District Court in The Hague, 10 December 2015, ECLI:NL:RBDHA:2015:14365, available in English at <https://uitspraken.rechtspraak.nl/inziendocument?id=ECLI:NL:RBDHA:2015:16102> last visited 9 May 2017.

[119] 31 May 2016, ECLI:NL:HR:2016:2120, summary available at <http://www.internationalcrimes database.org/Case/3274> last visited 9 May 2017.

[120] 7 St 7/14 (4), 15 July 2015, Oberlandesgericht München—summary at <http://www.internationalcrimes database.org/Case/3283/Harun-P/> last visited 7 May 2017.

[121] Tribunal de Première Instance Francophone de Bruxelles, 6 November 2015, FD.35.98.212/11, summary available at <http://www.internationalcrimesdatabase.org/Case/3288> last visited 17 November 2017.

a number of accused for participation in a terrorist group under article 140 of the Belgian Criminal Code. At these trials the defence that the accused were fighting for 'an organized armed group' engaged in armed conflict and have lawful combatant status under international humanitarian law is generally dismissed. The Dutch Court in *Imane B*, for example, held that '[p]articipation in the armed struggle in Syria on the side of these jihadi armed groups always entails the commission of terrorist crimes'.[122] These new offences have also withstood constitutional challenge. In *Alqudsi v Commonwealth of Australia*[123] the plaintiff's challenge that the offence of promoting incursions into a foreign state to engage in hostile activity there under section 7(1)(e) of the Crimes (Foreign Incursions and Recruitment) Act 1978 (Cth) was too remotely connected with the section 51 Constitutional power to make laws for the peace order and good government of Australia failed because it was considered a law connected with the external affairs of Australia on the basis that 'the tolerance or acquiescence by a State of actions on its territory for the purpose of supporting foreign incursions' is 'inimical to its relationship with other States generally' and the offence was designed to 'support the principle of the sovereignty and equality of States as well as the principle of non-intervention'.[124] The lesson here is that there is only one way to intervene by force in another state legally—with international sanction.

There have, however, been fewer prosecutions than might have been anticipated not because of absence of appropriate criminal offences but because of the difficulties of collecting evidence and difficulties in proving elements of offences including intent.[125] Some states have responded by amending their rules of evidence. Australia, for example, recently amended its Foreign Evidence Act 1994 to include a new Part 3A relating to admissibility of foreign material and foreign government material in terrorism-related proceedings, which removes the requirement to comply with normal rules of evidence in regard to material from these sources. Many states have also enacted administrative measures relating to the suspension[126] or revocation of passports, citizenship, and nationality in order to prevent movement of freedom fighters. While some are dependent on conviction for acts of terrorism,[127] others are based on administrative discretion.[128]

7.14 The Expanding Scope of Domestic Anticipatory Offences

Steps against foreign terrorist fighters are just part of the rapid expansion of criminalization of all activities connected with terrorism in domestic criminal laws through a range of stand-alone 'anticipatory' offences. Although used heavily against foreign

---

[122] Para 8.11.   [123] [2015] NSWSC 1222.   [124] Para 139.
[125] See Challenges in Prosecutions related to Foreign Terrorist Fighters, UN Security Council Report S/2015/123, para 23, 24.
[126] See, eg, section 22A of the Australian Passports Act 2005 which allows temporary suspension of travel documents (up to 14 days) when it was suspected the person may leave Australia and engage in conduct to prejudice the security of Australia or a foreign country.
[127] See, eg, article 25 of the French Civil Code.
[128] Eg, under section 40(2) of the UK's Nationality Act 1981 the Home Secretary has the power to deprive a British citizen of their nationality if it is 'conducive to the public good', even if the person is rendered stateless, so long as there are reasonable grounds they can obtain another nationality.

fighters,[129] the US offence of provision of 'material support'[130] is the archetype of this expansion. Other states have broken up the conduct involved into multifarious offences. After the London bomb attacks in 2004 the English enacted the offence of 'encouragement of terrorism',[131] which criminalizes statements likely to be understood as glorifying terrorism as encouragement, disseminating terrorism publications, training for terrorism, attendance at a place where training takes place, etc. France has caught this 'legislative fever' and has enacted a broad range of preparatory terrorism offences.[132] While previous legislation had mainly covered *association de malfaiteurs offences* (acts done in association with a terrorist organization), the new offences of research, procurement or production of dangerous objects or substances, surveillance with a view to a terrorist attack, training for armed conflict, visiting websites to procure documents to instigate terrorist acts, and staying in a terrorist camp abroad, apply to individuals acting alone.[133]

The range of anticipatory offences has been expanded in many different national laws to the extent that it can encompass a broad array of different levels of criminality that overlap, leading to confusion as to which crime and what penalty should apply. Sentencing practice in certain states has also become significantly preoccupied with the potential for harm and the ideological challenges presented by Islamist terrorists, rather than with the actual harm they perpetrate; defence arguments relating to proximity and rehabilitation have generally been rejected in favour of condemnation and incapacitation.[134] In the Australian case of *Lodhi v R*[135] the sentencing judge stated that

> the obligation of the Court is to denounce terrorism and voice its strong disapproval of activities such as those contemplated by the offender here. … In my view, the courts must speak firmly and with conviction in matters of this kind. This does not of course mean that general sentencing principles are undervalued or that matters favourable to an offender are to be overlooked. It does mean, however, that in offences of this kind, as I have said, the principles of denunciation and deterrence are to play a substantial role.

In *R v Mohamed Kahar*[136] the Court of Criminal Appeal gave an authoritative guidance on how to approach the maximum of life imprisonment under English law, which it considered the starting point. It made it clear, for example, that pleading that the act of terrorism was in a noble cause such as fighting for the Free Syrian Army in Syria is irrelevant to mitigation,[137] and so was whether the acts were intended to take place abroad rather than in the UK.[138] In its view conduct threatening democracy and state security is uniquely serious, deterrence and incapacitation are paramount, and

---

[129] See, eg, *United States v Nader Salem Elhuzayel, 2016* US Dist LEXIS 104328 (SD Cal 15 August 2016).
[130] 18 USC Section 2339A–C.   [131] Section 1 of the Terrorism Act 2006.
[132] *Loi no* 2014-1353, 13 November 2014, amending the Penal Code.
[133] Article 421-2–6, Penal Code; see V Chalkiadaki, 'The French "War on Terror" in the post-Charlie Hebdo Era' 1 *Eucrim: The European Criminal Law Associations' Forum* [2015] 26, 29.
[134] See A Pyne, 'The Mood and Temper of the Public: *R v Lodhi* and the Principles of Sentencing in the War on Terror' 23 *Current Issues in Criminal Justice* 164.
[135] (2006) 199 FLR 364 at [91]–[92].   [136] 2016 EWCA Crim 568.   [137] Para 13.
[138] Para 18.

rehabilitation is 'unlikely to play a part'.[139] The depth of involvement, length of time, depth of radicalization, and role in indoctrinating others were all aggravating factors,[140] as was the intention to fight British forces.[141] The particular vulnerability of the offender and the extent to which they were groomed were mitigating factors.[142]

7.15 Anti-terrorism and Human Rights

Terrorism threatens the right to life, liberty, and security of the person. So does anti-terrorism, which also threatens the right to a fair trial, rights to property and privacy, and in more extreme cases rights to freedom from torture and cruel or inhuman punishment. Anti-terrorism threatens human rights because it creates special crimes and special procedures for dealing with terrorists, such as the special measures against foreign fighters.[143] The anti-terrorism conventions, which shape those crimes and procedures, provide for limited express protection of human rights. The Terrorist Financing Convention, for example, cautions parties to prosecute or extradite only after an investigation of the facts[144] and guarantees the rights of an accused to communication with and visits by consular representatives.[145] More trenchantly, article 15 of the Inter-American Convention against Terrorism of 2003[146] provides that '[t]he measures carried out by the states parties under this Convention shall take place with full respect for the rule of law, human rights, and fundamental freedoms'. In Resolution 1456 of 2003[147] the Security Council somewhat tardily declared that states must ensure that measures taken in the suppression of terrorism should comply with human rights law. Security Council Resolution 2178 on foreign fighters contains more explicit reference to respecting human rights, noting in paragraph 5 that the obligation to suppress recruitment etc of foreign fighters must be 'consistent with international human rights law, international refugee law, and international humanitarian law'.[148] This notional respect for human rights in anti-terrorism measures has been recognized by the European Court of Human Rights in *Al Jedda v The United Kingdom*[149] when it presumed 'that the Security Council does not intend to impose any obligation on member States to breach fundamental principles of human rights'.

At a domestic level, judicial restraint of executive action based on human rights has been balanced by judicial recognition of legislative and executive discretion in responding to terrorism. In the *Belmarsh* case,[150] for example, the House of Lords ruled that the detention of nine terrorist suspects without charge pursuant to section 23 of the UK's 2001 Anti-Terrorism, Crime and Security Act was in breach of

---

[139] Para 15.   [140] Para 18.   [141] Para 19.   [142] Para 22.

[143] See, eg, L Tayler, ' "Foreign Terrorist Fighter" Law: Human Rights Rollbacks under UN Security Council Resolution 2178' 18 *International Community Law Review* (2016) 455; A Conte, 'States' Prevention and Responses to the Phenomenon of Foreign Fighters against the Backdrop of International Human Rights Obligations' in A de Guttry, F Capone, and C Paulussen (eds), *Foreign Fighters under International Law and Beyond* (The Hague: Asser, 2016), 283.

[144] Art 9(1).   [145] Art 9(3).   [146] 3 June 2002; in force 10 July 2003.

[147] S/Res/1456 (2003).   [148] See also article 11, 17.   [149] App no 27021/08, 7 July 2011.

[150] *A v Secretary of State for the Home Department* [2005] 2 AC 68.

articles 14 and 15 of the European Convention on Human Rights. But in *A v The United Kingdom*,[151] a case involving potential torture of individuals upon their extradition, the European Court of Human Rights noted that national authorities enjoy a wide margin of appreciation in assessing whether a state could derogate from its obligations in response to terrorism, in this case the threat from Al Qaeda.

The impact on human rights of over-criminalization is a particularly difficult problem to confront. The UN Human Rights Council has warned that ambiguity leads to illegitimate restrictions on liberty.[152] The first UN Special Rapporteur on the Promotion and Protection of Human Rights and Fundamental Freedoms while Countering Terrorism, Martin Scheinin, has noted:[153]

> The adoption of overly broad definitions of terrorism therefore carries the potential for deliberate misuse of the term—including as a response to claims and social movements of indigenous peoples—as well as unintended human rights abuses. Failure to restrict counter-terrorism laws and implementing measures to the countering of conduct which is truly terrorist in nature also poses the risk that, where such laws and measures restrict the enjoyment of rights and freedoms, they will offend the principles of necessity and proportionality that govern the permissibility of any restriction on human rights.

The suppression of terrorism poses a major rule of law problem; crimes that are too broadly drawn provide a tool for the suppression of legitimate political activity. Yet, as discussed above, a freedom of speech challenge to US legislation forbidding material support to terrorist organizations even if that support was of a humanitarian nature, failed before the US Supreme Court.[154] It is easier to attack the method of substantiating the offence where there was, for example, a real risk that evidence was obtained for a preparatory offence through torture, than it is to attack the legality of the offence itself, no matter how broadly drawn.[155]

7.16 Terrorism as a Core International Crime?

The counter-terrorism conventions treat terrorism by non-state actors as a transnational crime. Cassese argues, however, that state-sponsored terrorism is an international crime because of the implications for international peace and security.[156] Despite national authority expressly rejecting this view[157] in 2011 the Special Tribunal

---

[151] *A v The United Kingdom* (2009) 49 EHRR 29 at 180.
[152] *Report on the Protection of Human Rights and Fundamental Freedoms while Countering Terrorism*, UN Doc A/HRC/8/13, para 20.
[153] *Report of the Special Rapporteur on the Promotion and Protection of Human Rights and Fundamental Freedoms while Countering Terrorism, Martin Scheinin: Ten Areas of Best Practice in Countering Terrorism*, UN Doc A/HRC/16/51, 22 December 2010, para 27.
[154] *Holder et al v Humanitarian Law Project et al* 561 US 1 (2010).
[155] See, eg, *El Haski v Belgium*, App no 649/08, 25 September 2012.
[156] A Cassese, 'Terrorism is also Disrupting Some Crucial Legal Categories of International Law' 12 *European Journal of International Law* (2001) 993, 994.
[157] *Tel Oren v Libyan Arab Republic* 726 F2d 774, 795 (DC Circ 1984) affirmed in *US v Yousef and others*, 327 F3d 56 (2nd Circ), para 135.

for the Lebanon (per Cassese P)[158] held that there was a definition of terrorism in customary international law and it had three key elements:

> (i) the perpetration of a criminal act (such as murder, kidnapping, hostage-taking, arson, and so on), or threatening such an act; (ii) the intent to spread fear among the population (which would generally entail the creation of public danger) or directly or indirectly coerce a national or international authority to take some action, or to refrain from taking it; (iii) when the act involves a transnational element.

It is doubtful, however, whether the sectoral conventions constitute sufficiently harmonious state practice to establish a universal international community interest in the suppression of terrorism imposing individual criminal responsibility in customary international law.[159] As we have seen they address different problems—aviation offences, maritime security, etc—and the offences themselves have different structures; some enumerate acts of violence in specific circumstances, some add special motives. Interestingly, the judgment uses a 'transnational' element to exclude those offences that are of purely domestic concern.[160] Transnationality by itself is insufficient to transform terrorism into a core international crime. What is missing is support by states in their practice for direct criminalization of terrorism in international laws. The rationale of the Special Tribunal appears to have been to escape the constraints of national implementation of these offences by allowing for the import of much broader customary crimes of terrorism into Lebanon's law; doing so avoids the fundamental nature of transnational criminal law which is that states choose to sign up to the suppression conventions and enact the specific offences. Support for Security Council resolutions may provide better evidence but it too has eschewed criminalization of a general offence of terrorism and expressly followed the indirect system of requiring states to criminalize. It may 'legislate' obligations on states but it has not yet legislated an international crime placing an obligation directly on individuals. Subsequent domestic court decisions have rejected the claim that terrorism is an international crime focussing on the disagreement about the definition of terrorism and the fact that norms established under treaties like the Terrorism Financing Convention were controversial with many declarations and reservations.[161] At a more conceptual level, critics have responded that the offence of terrorism does not belong in the realm of international criminal law because its difficult fit with the goals of the international community suggest it is a response to demands from the public for security and is thus a domestic policy offence used by states as a tool of governance.[162]

---

[158] *Interlocutory Decision on the Applicable Law: Terrorism, Conspiracy, Homicide, Perpetration, Cumulative Charging* (STL-11-01/I) Appeals Chamber, 16 February 2011, para 85.

[159] As held at para 102. For a critique see B Saul, 'Legislating from a Radical Hague: The United Nations Special Tribunal for Lebanon Invents an International Crime of Transnational Terrorism' 24 *Leiden Journal of International Law* (2011) 677.

[160] Para 90.

[161] *Chiquita Brands International Incorporated and ors v Valencia and ors, Decision on motion to dismiss*, 792 F Supp 2d 1301 (SD Fla 2011), para 48 et seq.

[162] M Aksenova, 'Conceptualizing Terrorism: International Offence or Domestic Governance Tool?' 20 *Journal of Conflict and Security Law* (2015) 277, 280.

7.17 Conclusion

The story of the anti-terrorism conventions is one of structured expansion of domestic criminalization. The early conventions initially criminalized specific actions causing direct harm and then expanded their scope to include actions in support of these acts extending as far as the financing of these acts. In order to avoid politicization of the subject, the mental element required was colourless intention. Over time, new conventions began to incorporate more complex specific intentions which sought to distil the difference between these offences and ordinary murder, assaults, damage, etc. They did so by incorporating specific purposes to compel the primary rather than immediate target to do or abstain from doing an act. Counter-terrorism law post 9/11 has seen an expansion of pre-emptive criminalization and administrative sanction based not on evidence of actual harmful wrongdoing but on suspicion of risk.[163] The official response has become more prevention oriented and thus less evidence based.[164] Any scepticism about the necessity of special anti-terrorist laws when existing crimes cover the personal and property harms concerned and existing arrangements for legal assistance make international cooperation possible,[165] is now largely ignored in an effort to enact broadly drawn terrorism offences to which have been added broadly drawn notions of complicity and inchoate offences. While it may be thought that this expansion to ever more tenuous offences might have been accompanied by provisions in the terrorism conventions that required stricter oversight of the decision to investigate and press charges, this is not the case. Progress towards a convention that applies to all forms of terrorism has been bypassed by the Security Council which has pressed on obliging states to enact offences that respond to emerging challenges with ever more varied and specific offences. States have responded by expanding the range of terrorism offences in their legislation. And more activity is likely. In 2014 the UN Security Council, concerned that terrorists benefit from various forms of trafficking, urged states in Resolution 2195 to break the link between terrorism and organized crime.[166] It remains to be seen whether we shall see some new hybrid organized crime/terrorist offences. Terrorism is, however, a shifting puzzle, and more crimes seem likely.

---

[163] CC Murphy, 'Transnational Counter-terrorism Law: Law, Power and Legitimacy in the "Wars on Terror"' 6(1) *Transnational Legal Theory* (2015) 31, 35.

[164] See generally J Waldron, *Torture, Terror, and Trade-Offs* (Oxford: OUP, 2010).

[165] R Higgins, 'The General International Law of Terrorism' in R Higgins and M Flory (eds), *International Law and Terrorism* (London: Routledge, 1997), 28.

[166] S/Res/2195 (2014).

8

Transnational Organized Crime

8.1 Introduction

Transnational organized crime is considered by many to be a modern plague. In 2011 then US President Barak Obama wrote 'criminal networks are not only expanding their operations, but they are also diversifying their activities, resulting in a convergence of transnational threats that has evolved to become more complex, volatile, and destabilizing'.[1] In 2017 President Donald Trump joined the refrain when he introduced a new executive order on transnational organized crime as follows: 'Transnational criminal organizations and subsidiary organizations, including transnational drug cartels, have spread throughout the Nation, threatening the safety of the United States and its citizens.'[2] Official statistics do provide some basis for these opinions. Europol, for example, reported that at least 5,000 internationally operating organized crime groups were active in the EU in 2017, up from 3,600 in 2013. It is a change which may, however, reflect better intelligence and the emergence of smaller groups than an overall increase in organized crime activity.[3]

The legal response at an international level to the threat of transnational organized crime has been plagued by difficulty in deciding on an appropriate target: the 'king pins' involved in diverse forms of transnational crime, the suppression of criminal activities that criminal organizations become involved in, or pursuit of the organizations themselves. This chapter explores the nature of transnational organized crime and the failure of efforts to settle on a definition. It then turns to the substitute adopted at an international level—the notion of an 'organized criminal group', and examines how it serves as the linchpin of a set of offences developed to try to counter transnational organized crime.

8.2 The Nature of Transnational Organized Crime

Organized crime is generally considered to be an endemic problem, but policy-makers and criminologists have struggled to formulate a universally acceptable definition. Testing hypothesized models against sociological reality is difficult because by definition its structures and organizational methods are secret. It seems logically to include systematic crime of any kind—white collar, corporate—yet study of the

---

[1] 'Strategy to Combat Transnational Organized Crime', National Strategic Document, The Office of the President of the United States of America (Washington, 2011).

[2] Section 1, Executive Order, Enforcing Federal Law with respect to Transnational Criminal Organizations and Preventing International Trafficking, 9 February 2017.

[3] Europol, *Serious Organised Crime Threat Assessment 2017: Crime in the age of technology* (Europol, 2017), 14.

phenomenon has been marked by stereotypes modelled on the Sicilian Mafia (the Russian Mafiya, Chechen Mafia, and so forth) that have served to limit the scope of the notion. They reify the view that organized crime is separate from the rest of society, which ignores the fact that in many cases organized criminals carry out their activities within society and are indistinguishable in almost every way from members of that society. The notion of transnational organized crime creates a target that may not exist—a 'folk-devil'—and critics argue that transnational organized crime is merely the emergence of an international 'folk-devil' that obscures alternative explanations.[4]

Models of criminal organizations based on the 'Mafia' model emerged first in the US.[5] In this model the 'Mafia' functions by usurping the role of the state and in particular the state's monopoly on violence; it becomes essentially a monolithic, hierarchical, shadow government. Its persistence is well illustrated in the following description of an enterprise known as the 'Cuban Mafia' or 'Corporation' given in 2009 in the *United States v Acuna*:[6]

> The corporation was run by a godfather (the Padrino), a Vice Chairman, and a Counselor (Consejero), and was operated by groups known as Divisions and Crews, each of which had Lieutenants, Soldiers and Operators. Criminal activity such as gambling, money laundering and enforcement were conducted within geographic areas. 'Enforcers' of the Corporation enforced discipline, intimidation of competition and induced fear of physical and financial injury to members of the Corporation as well as outsiders.

The model of organized crime evolved in the post-war period, to networks of organizations subversive of government, then to separate parasitic criminal groups with diversified functions, and then to criminal cartels run along corporate lines. Organized criminals were identified as engaging in a range of harmful activities—protection rackets, corruption, trafficking in harmful substances, etc—where agreements were enforced by violence. Collective action was considered as concentrating power and thus more harmful. Evidence that criminal groups operate transnationally to exploit market opportunities and escape government interference began to be considered significant in the 1990s[7] and opened the door to recognition of a plurality of organized crime groupings in every state.

The rise of the concept of criminal cartels saw a growing emphasis on the nature of the business they engaged in—hence 'drug' cartels. Commentators introduced the idea of social systems that emerge out of traditional social structures such as

---

[4] M Woodiwiss, 'Transnational Organized Crime: The Strange Career of an American Concept' in ME Beare (ed), *Critical Reflections on Transnational Organized Crime, Money Laundering, and Corruption* (Toronto: University of Toronto Press, 2003), 3, 26; J Sheptycki, 'Against Transnational Organised Crime' also in Beare, 120, 134.

[5] D Cressey, *Theft of a Nation: The Structure of Organized Crime in America* (New York: Harper and Row, 1967); D Cressey, *Criminal Organization: Its Elementary Forms* (New York: Harper and Row, 1972).

[6] 313 FApp'x 283 (11th Circ 2009), 285.

[7] P Williams and EU Savona, 'Problems and Dangers Posed by Organized Transnational Crime in the Various Regions of the World' in P Williams and EU Savona (eds), *The United Nations and Transnational Organized Crime* (London: Frank Cass, 1996), 1, 6.

kinship, friendship, and other social bonds,[8] which made for convenient stereotypes (Colombian drug traffickers, Albanian human traffickers, etc). Theoretical models multiplied, from highly centralized organizations to more loosely structured organizations, to the recent emphasis on models of a more fluid kind, networks of traffickers. They are 'polycriminal' in the sense they respond to constantly shifting markets and changing conditions by being highly adaptable and operating globally.[9] Tonry suggests that their speciality is distribution: 'Those distribution networks are typically not controlled by vertically-integrated organisations that carry out each stage of the distribution but, instead, consist of large numbers of organisations of different size and permanence that perform particular functions for pay in a particular place at a particular time.'[10]

Specialization in a particular product, Naím suggests, is obsolete:

> In fact, the economic and technical possibilities bred by globalization make it easier than ever for traders to combine their cargos or shift from one to another—and less of a competitive advantage to control, end to end, a given product's supply chain. They have mutated accordingly, focusing on the skills instead of the commodities. As the FBI's deputy director, Maureen Baginski, told me, 'The specialization became the network itself, and its ability to procure, transport, and deliver illegal merchandise across countries. What the merchandise was became almost irrelevant.'[11]

These different models of organized crime present a shifting target for legal suppression: hierarchical organizations, commodity specializing organizations, ethnic organizations, non-specialized logistical networks. The criticism that 'organized crime' is not a term that can adequately reflect social reality and is open to political abuse precisely because it is so malleable, appears to bite.[12] Moreover, insisting on a division between organized crime even in this very broad sense and corporations, which, for example, engage in major tax fraud, is problematic. A study for the EU concluded in 2013: 'Our imagery of organised crime in the movies and newspapers retains the dramaturgy of *The Godfather*, *The Sopranos* and possibly *The Wire*. This is helpful as a threat image but unhelpful as a guide to the complexity of the organisation of serious crime and their varied impacts.'[13]

Transnational criminal law has struggled to develop an adequate legal response to this complexity.

---

[8] ibid.

[9] M Naím, *Illicit: How Smugglers, Traffickers, and Copycats are Hijacking the Global Economy* (New York: Anchor Books, 2006), 13, 226 et seq.

[10] M Tonry, 'Transnational Organised Crime—Prospects for Success of the UN Convention' in H-J Albrecht and C Fijnaut (eds), *The Containment of Transnational Organized Crime* (Freiburg: Iuscrim, 2002), 253 at 264–65.

[11] Above n 9, 32.

[12] See, eg, M Levi, 'The Organization of Serious Crime for Gain' in M Maguire, R Morgan, and R Reiner (eds), *The Oxford Handbook of Criminology* (Oxford: OUP, 2012), 595; J Sheptycki, 'Transnational Crime: An Interdisciplinary Perspective' in N Boister and R Currie (eds), *The Routledge Handbook of Transnational Criminal Law* (Abingdon: Routledge, 2015), 41, 42–46.

[13] DG For Internal Policies, *The Economic, Financial & Social Impacts of Organised Crime in the EU* (Brussels: EU, 2013) 47, available at <http://www.europarl.europa.eu/studies> last visited 7 May 2016.

8.3 Early Legislative Steps against Organized Crime

Existing crimes were considered unsuitable to suppress the activities of criminal organizations for two reasons: the problem of participation too remote from the actual perpetration of the offence to be considered criminal under normal principles of criminal participation, and the problem of preparatory actions too unclear to be considered criminal under normal principles of inchoate liability.[14] It was particularly difficult to prove the involvement of the leaders of organizations as either participants in illegal activities in which they seldom participated directly, or in inchoate crimes such as conspiracy because of the difficulty of establishing their agreement to commit a specific offence.

Legislative responses pioneered in the US tended to adopt very broad models of organized crime to try to reach remote participation. The Racketeer Influenced Corrupt Organizations (RICO) Act[15] and Continuing Criminal Enterprises (CCE) Act[16] introduced the legal principle that the participation in a criminal enterprise is a crime in itself. A RICO violation requires the commission of more than one predicate offences, including offences such as gambling, prostitution, drug offences, fraud, extortion, bribery, labour law violations, and even cigarette bootlegging, in a 'pattern of racketeering' activity. It is an offence 'for any person employed by or associated with any enterprise engaged in, or the activities of which affect, interstate or foreign commerce, to conduct or participate, directly or indirectly, in the conduct of such enterprise's affairs through a pattern of racketeering activity or collection of unlawful debt'.[17] A criminal 'enterprise' is defined as any individual, partnership, corporation, association, or other legal entity, or any group of individuals, who though not a legal entity, are associated in fact. These very broad offences attract increased penalties, powers of confiscation, and the possibility of a supplementary civil law suit with treble damages. CCE convictions are directed at drug trafficking in particular. The prosecution must prove: (i) the accused violated one of the substantive drug supply offences; (ii) the accused engaged in a series of federal drug felony violations (three or more); (iii) the series of violations must be conducted with five or more people; (iv) the accused served as organizer, supervisor, or some other type of leader in the operation; and (v) the accused derived substantial income or resources from the criminal operation. A CCE conviction carries a mandatory minimum sentence of twenty years and the CCE authorizes confiscation of illicit gains. Importantly, the RICO and CCE introduced a legal framework—the criminal enterprise—elastic enough in both space and time to allow law enforcement to gather evidence about the complete picture of what the accused was doing rather than just to prove different fragmented crimes.[18]

---

[14] See A Schloenhardt, *Palermo in the Pacific: Organised Crime Offences in the Asia Pacific Region* (Leiden: Martinus Nijhoff Publishers, 2009), 387.

[15] 18 USC §§ 1961–68.

[16] 21 USC § 848. See generally N Abrams, 'The New Ancillary Offenses' 1 *Criminal Law Forum* (1989) 1, 12.

[17] 18 USC § 1962(c).

[18] See E Wise, 'RICO and Its Analogues: Some Comparative Considerations' 27 *Syracuse Journal of International and Commercial Law* (2000) 303, 310.

Statutory measures against organized crime in Europe also proscribe member-ship of criminal organizations but take a narrower approach to the definition of these organizations by attempting to isolate their sociological features. Article 260*ter* of the Swiss Penal Code, for example, refers to 'an organization which keeps its structure and personnel a secret and whose aims are to commit criminal acts of violence or procure financial advantage by criminal means'. Some national laws are even more historically contextual in their derivation. Article 416*bis* of the Italian Penal Code defines 'mafia-type organizations' as follows:

> An association is a mafia-type organisation when its members make use of intimida-tion derived from their association, and the ensuing subjection and 'gagging' in order to commit crimes or to manage either directly or indirectly, or otherwise control, business activities, concessions, authorizations, public markets or public services, or to obtain unfair profits or advantages for themselves or others.

In 1992 article 416*bis* was amended to include the further aim of 'preventing or imped-ing the free exercise of voting rights or procuring votes for oneself or for other persons during elections'.

In summary, these specific national laws on organized crime have dual dimen-sions: they (i) define an entity by what it does (types of crime, continuity of activity) or what it is (organizational features, size) and then (ii) proscribe membership or partici-pation, rather than direct participation in criminal activity. The threshold of partici-pation is set fairly low,[19] which opens these measures to the criticism that in violation of the principle of personal culpability they establish guilt by association. Many indi-viduals are involved with criminal organizations—they feed them, fix their vehicles, house them, take their largesse—but should it be said that they are 'of them' for the purposes of criminal liability?[20]

8.4 Responding to Transnational Organized Crime: The Development of the UN Convention against Transnational Organized Crime (UNTOC)

Despite these shortcomings, these national laws served as models for the international community's response to transnational organized crime. Although transnational organized crime is a compound noun of transnational and organized crime, it was understood initially to mean harmful activities engaged in by transnational corpor-ations in the Third World. Its meaning changed in the 1980s because of increased concern about the spatial dimensions of potential harm that emerge when organ-ized criminals begin to operate across borders.[21] This freedom was exacerbated by globalization as national borders became more porous, finance/telecommunications systems meant global connectivity, and there were fewer trade restrictions. 'Relative

---

[19] Abrams, above n 16, 16.   [20] See Schloenhardt, above n 14, 27–30.
[21] PC Van Duyne and MDH Nelemans, 'Transnational Organized Crime: Thinking in and out of Plato's Cave' in F Allum and S Gilmore (eds), *Routledge Handbook of Organized Crime* (London: Routledge, 2012), 36, 42.

immunity' from law and enforcement enabled organized criminals to use developing states as bases for provision of illicit goods and services to areas where the risks are higher. 'National sanctuaries' occurred where weak government control and convenient physical locations provided a congenial environment for transnational criminal organizations and made them difficult to suppress. Critics of the emphasis on transnationality point out that much organized criminal activity is actually local or 'glocal' (global and local),[22] and even when transnational the actual crossing of the border whether by contraband, criminal, or proceeds is relatively limited in scope, and much of the productive and supply activity is local.[23]

The push for a global multilateral treaty to suppress transnational organized crime grew out of the success of the UN with the negotiation of the 1988 Drug Trafficking Convention (discussed in Chapter 6). The new treaty was developed from within the framework of the UN crime prevention and criminal justice programme proper.[24] Supporters argued that criminal organizations that operate transnationally were beyond the control of any one state and this demanded a coordinated international response. In July 1992 ECOSOC put 'action against national and transnational organized and environmental crime' on the agenda of the UN Congress on the Prevention of Crime and Treatment of Offenders.[25] In December 1992 the General Assembly called for 'global efforts' against 'national and transnational crime'.[26] The major political step was the adoption by the World Ministerial Conference on Organized Transnational Crime in 1994 of the Naples Political Declaration and Global Action Plan against Organized Transnational Crime.[27] It called for more effective international cooperation to fight transnational organized crime and recommended consideration of the development of a treaty. The need for a new convention was not undisputed, however. While developing states were generally in favour of a new treaty in order to help them tackle a problem for which they were totally unprepared, Western states were initially sceptical whether a treaty could be agreed that would adopt a concept of organized crime sufficiently general to cover all forms of organized criminality yet sufficiently specific to address the problem of organized crime effectively.[28] During the treaty negotiation process, however, the situation reversed as Western delegations pushed through models of laws familiar to them, and developing states became sceptical of the burden being imposed by the convention.[29] Poland placed the development of the

---

[22] R Hobbs, 'Going Down the Glocal: The Local Context of Organised Crime' 37(4) *The Howard Journal of Criminal Justice* (1998) 407, 419.

[23] C Fijnaut, 'The UN Convention and the Global Problem of Organized Crime' in H-J Albrecht and C Fijnaut (eds), *The Containment of Transnational Organised Crime: Comments on the UN Convention of December 2000* (Freiburg im Breisgau: Iuscrim, 2002), 57–58.

[24] See A Schloenhardt, 'Transnational Organised Crime' in N Boister and R Currie (eds), *The Routledge Handbook of Transnational Criminal Law* (Abingdon: Routledge, 2015), 409, at 410 for a summary of the UNTOC's development.

[25] ECOSOC Res 1992/24 of 30 July 1992.

[26] UN GA Res 47/87 of 16 December 1992 (UN Doc A/RES/47/87).

[27] UN GA Res 49/159, 23 December 1994.

[28] See the discussion in P Gastrow, 'The Origin of the Convention' in H-J Albrecht and C Fijnaut (eds), *The Containment of Transnational Organised Crime: Comments on the UN Convention of December 2000* (Freiburg im Breisgau: Edition Iuscrim, 2002), 19 at 29.

[29] ibid.

convention on the agenda of the UN General Assembly in 1996 and submitted a draft convention.[30] An open-ended intergovernmental group of experts[31] met in Warsaw in 1998 and produced a preliminary draft text and the process was then taken up by an Ad Hoc Committee[32] open to all states, which elaborated the convention and three draft protocols—in illegal trafficking in migrants, on illicit manufacturing of and trafficking in firearms and ammunition, and on trafficking in women and children. In 2000, a diplomatic conference held in Palermo, Sicily, symbolically the home of the Mafia, finally adopted the United Nations Convention against Transnational Organized Crime (the Palermo Convention or UNTOC).[33] Article 1 of the UNTOC provides that its purpose is to 'promote co-operation to prevent and combat transnational organised crime more effectively'. This is to be achieved through legislative harmonization and more effective suppression while remaining within the bounds of human rights safeguards.[34] The UNTOC contains a series of detailed measures for international procedural cooperation[35] and a number of criminalization provisions, although somewhat paradoxically it does not define organized crime, or its transnational extrapolation, transnational organized crime.

8.5 The Failure to Define Organized Crime in the UNTOC

One of the main problems faced during the negotiation of the UNTOC was finding consensus on a legal definition of organized crime. The Naples Declaration which called for a definition, listed six characteristics of organized crime: (a) group organization to commit crime; (b) hierarchical links of personal relations which permit leaders to control the group; (c) violence, intimidation, and corruption used to earn profits or control territories or markets; (d) laundering of illicit proceeds to further criminal activity and to infiltrate the legitimate economy; (e) the potential for expansion into new activities beyond national borders; and (f) cooperation with other organized transnational groups.[36] The definition in the Polish draft convention also focused on the structural features of criminal organizations such as membership of three or more persons, hierarchical management, profit-making, and the use of violence, intimidation, and corruption, without limitation to any type of organized criminal activity. In discussion it was felt that the definition could focus on the special features of organized criminal groups or on the types of serious criminal activity committed by

---

[30] *Question of the Elaboration of an International Convention against Organized Transnational Crime*, UN Doc A/C.3/51/7, 1 October 1996.

[31] Established by UN GA Res 52/85, 30 January 1998.

[32] Established by UN GA Res 53/111, 20 January 1999.

[33] The United Nations Convention against Transnational Organized Crime, 15 November 2000, 2225 UNTS 209, in force 29 September 2003.

[34] V Militello, 'Participation in an Organised Criminal Group as International Offence' in H-J Albrecht and C Fijnaut (eds), *The Containment of Transnational Organised Crime: Comments on the UN Convention of December 2000* (Freiburg im Breisgau: Iuscrim, 2002), 97, 106.

[35] Articles 16–21 and 27. See N Boister, 'The Cooperation Provisions of the UN Convention against Transnational Organised Crime: A "Toolbox" Rarely Used?' 16 *International Criminal Law Review* (2016) 39.

[36] See D McClean, *Transnational Organized Crime: A Commentary on the UN Convention and Its Protocols* (Oxford: OUP, 2007), 3–4.

organized criminal groups.[37] The Intergovernmental Group of Experts noted in 1998, however, that differences in the legal understanding of organized crime were going to make it difficult to reach a comprehensive definition in a timely manner, while organized crime was continuing to evolve. In contrast, it felt that there was a general understanding of criminal organizations, and it recommended that the convention build on that understanding and focus on action against those groups.[38] The drafters of the UNTOC thus chose to build the convention around the notion of an 'organized criminal group', defined in article 2(a) as: 'a structured group of three or more persons, existing for a period of time and acting in concert with the aim of committing one or more serious crimes or offences established in accordance with this Convention, in order to obtain, directly or indirectly, a financial or other material benefit.'

Many of the elements in article 2(a) were analytical concepts developed by the EU.[39] Article 2(c) defines a 'structured group' as one 'not randomly formed for the immediate commission of an offence'. 'Random' may mean anything from three people who meet by chance and decide to commit an offence to a more planned situation. An interpretative note to the UNTOC suggests that the concept is thus broad enough to include both any arrangement from highly stratified criminal hierarchies of individuals with distinctive roles to much flatter networks of individuals with indeterminate roles.[40] Commentators feel this renders the concept practically meaningless.[41]

'Immediate commission' may exclude offences that occur straight away. The group 'does not need to have formally defined roles for its members, continuity of membership or a developed structure'. However, it does, according to article 2(a), require three or more persons and it does have to exist for a period of time, the precise length being a matter of domestic law although highly dependent on the particular case.

There is no definition of 'acting in concert'. The implication appears to be a common purpose or shared mandate, whether tacit or express. The members of the group must have the 'aim of committing one or more serious crimes or offences established in accordance with the Convention' (note they need only have the aim of committing a serious crime, they need not actually have committed it). This differs from the 'enterprise' model used by the US in RICO, where the emphasis is on the actual criminal activities carried out by the organization because of the requirement of proof of the commission of one or more of the listed predicate offences to establish patterns of racketeering.

---

[37] ibid, 7.

[38] See also Interpretive Notes for the official records (Travaux Préparatoires) of the negotiations of the United Nations Convention against Transnational Organized Crime and the Protocols thereto, UN Doc A/55/383/Add.1, xxii.

[39] 29 December 1998 Joint Action of 21 December 1998 on making it a criminal offence to participate in a criminal organisation in the Member States of the European Union 98/733/JHA OJ L 351/1 (1998). The EU has since adopted the definition in article 2(a)—see EU Council Framework Decision 2008/841/JHA of 24 October 2008 on the fight against organized crime OJ L 300 (2008).

[40] Travaux Préparatoires, above n 38, para 4.

[41] AV Orlova and JW Moore, '"Umbrellas" or "Building Blocks"?: Defining International Terrorism and Transnational Organised Crime in International Law' 27 *Houston Journal of International Law* (2005) 267, 283.

The multilateral measure of seriousness in article 2(b) is whether the state party in question applies a maximum penalty of four years or more deprivation of liberty. Initial suggestions that a list of serious crimes be included were rejected. The treaty sets the standard of seriousness and parties make a choice as to which crimes will meet that standard, thus dictating the material scope of the convention. The UN has suggested the raising of penalties for certain offences to meet the threshold of seriousness[42] and parties have done so unilaterally in regard to others,[43] but the UNTOC does not contain a mechanism to compel parties to do so. There is thus no definition of organized crime in the UNTOC. The Convention is directed, rather, at the involvement of organized criminal groups in serious crime.

Finally the group members' motivation must be 'to obtain, directly or indirectly, a financial or other material benefit', which according to the Travaux Préparatoires can also include non-material benefits such as sexual gratification.[44] The use of 'material' has been relied upon in the Legislative Guide to exclude groups with political or social motives such as terrorist groups, unless they engage in material pursuits to fund their activities.[45]

The model of an organized criminal group (OCG) adopted permits the UNTOC to be used against a diverse range of networks from the ephemeral ranging all the way to the essentialist Mafia-like stereotype that dominate the discourse,[46] and in theory is flexible enough to be used against new manifestations of organized crime as they appear ensuring its continued relevance.[47] Its major shortcomings are that it fails to specifically label and denounce high-end large-scale organizations, while at the same time potentially over-criminalizing low-end small-scale organizations (even three youths engaged in a serious crime would qualify as an OCG).[48] In addition, the material motive means that the concept of OCG does not cover organized crime groups where the main motive for membership is identity, psychological benefit, or social status. Thus it may be useful against trafficking groups that are flexible and profit oriented but it will be less apt against territorial groups whose orientation is territorial and ideological. Finally, if parties do increase penalties for domestic offences past the threshold of seriousness for the simple instrumental reason of engaging the UNTOC they may well overpenalize offences that do not warrant such penalties. This points to a further weakness of the scheme—it does not

---

[42] See Resolution 66/180 of 19 December 2011 relating to trafficking in cultural property.

[43] In 2002, eg, New Zealand became a party to the UNTOC and in 2003 imposed a maximum five-year penalty for making or dealing with objects that infringe copyright in section 131 of the Copyright Act 1962.

[44] Above n 38, para 3.

[45] *Legislative Guide for the Implementation of the United Nations Convention against Transnational Organized Crime and the Protocols thereto* (New York, UN, 2004), para 26, available at <https://www.unodc.org/pdf/crime/legislative_guides/Legislative%20guides_Full%20version.pdf> last visited 7 May 2017.

[46] L Paoli and T Vander Beken, 'Organized Crime: a Contested Concept' in L Paoli (ed), *The Oxford Handbook of Organized Crime* (Oxford: OUP, 2014), 13, 24.

[47] P Arlacchi, 'After the Palermo Convention: New International Prospects in the Fight against Organised Crime' in S Betti (ed), *Symposium: The United Nations Convention against Transnational Organised Crime: requirements for effective implementation* (Turin: UNICRI et al, 2002), 15, 17.

[48] Tonry, above n 10, 253, 261.

provide for global convergence of the elements of offences that organized criminals typically engage in.

8.6 Conditions for the Application of the UNTOC to UNTOC and Protocol Crimes: Transnationality and Involvement of an Organized Criminal Group

Article 3(1) provides that the Convention shall apply to the 'prevention, investigation and prosecution of' two sets of crimes: in terms of article 3(1)(a), to the offences established by articles 5 (participation in an organized criminal group), 6 (money laundering), 8 (corruption), and 23 (obstruction of justice); and in terms of article 3(1)(b), to other serious crime (discussed further below). Article 3(1) requires that in both cases two general conditions must be satisfied—the offence in question must be transnational in nature and involve an OCG. Article 34(2) makes it clear that these two conditions are not required for the criminalization of the convention offences by parties, because imposing these elements would narrow the domestic definitions of these crimes unnecessarily. However, they are required if parties seek to use the UNTOC for international cooperation in regard to these offences. The definition of an OCG is spelled out above. The other condition, 'transnational' is defined broadly in article 3(2) as follows:

2. For the purpose of paragraph 1 of this article, an offence is transnational in nature if:
    (a) It is committed in more than one State;
    (b) It is committed in one State but a substantial part of its preparation, planning, direction or control takes place in another State;
    (c) It is committed in one State but involves an organised criminal group that engages in criminal activities in more than one State; or
    (d) It is committed in one State but has substantial effects in another State.

Every alternative requires that the commission of a serious crime in one state be linked to activity in another/other state(s). Under article 3(2)(a) that activity is the commission of the crime in other states, under article 3(2)(b) it is planned, etc in another state, under article 3(2)(c) it involves an OCG that operates in some fashion in other states, and under article 3(2)(d) it has 'substantial effects' in another state. The latter may include situations where an offence in State X is intended to result in an offence in State Y but is frustrated before it has any impact in State Y (eg transit of drugs on the way to State Y is interdicted in State X).[49] Article 3(2) serves as a jurisdictional trigger providing a legal justification for states' interest in the activities of OCGs occurring extraterritorially, rather than an exhaustive legal definition of the substantive nature of transnational organized crime. This point is reinforced by the fact that, as noted, article 34(2) provides that national laws criminalizing participation in an OCG (article 5), the laundering of criminal proceeds (article 6), corruption (article 8), or

---

[49] See the discussion of the effects principle in Chapter 16.

obstruction of justice (article 23) and the various Protocol offences must be established independently of any transnationality requirement.

The Human Trafficking Protocol,[50] Migrant Smuggling Protocol,[51] and Firearms Protocol[52] deal with specific crimes—human trafficking, migrant smuggling, and small arms trafficking—which are stipulated as serious enough to justify application of the procedural regime within UNTOC. The offences in the Protocols simply add to the list of offences in the UNTOC. Thus, for example, article 1(3) of the Human Trafficking Protocol provides that 'offences established in accordance with the Protocol shall also be regarded as offences established in accordance with the Convention'. In consequence the UNTOC's procedural regime applies in respect of these offences so long as the particular offence meets the further conditions or transnationality and involvement of an organized criminal group under article 3(1)(a).

8.7 Conditions for the Residual Application of the UNTOC to other 'Serious Crimes'

One of the key functions of the UNTOC is to serve in a residual role as the basis for international cooperation in regard to 'serious crime'. Article 3(1)(b) applies the UNTOC to the 'prevention, investigation and prosecution' of '[s]erious crime as defined in article 2'. As noted, article 2(b) defines a 'serious crime' as one which carries a maximum period of deprivation of liberty of at least four years or more in the particular party's national law. Thus if an offence carries a maximum penalty of three years the UNTOC is not available; if it carries a maximum penalty of five years the UNTOC is available. There is no obligation on the parties to enact new penalties; they may leave their penalty scheme unaltered. If they wish specific offences carrying maximum penalties of less than four year to be classed as 'serious' for the purposes of UNTOC application, they must increase the maximum penalties for those offences to four years or more. The use of the four-year-or-more evaluative condition is a crude measure of seriousness. Nevertheless, states have taken up the invitation to legislate accordingly. For example, section 467.1 of Canada's Criminal Code defines serious crime as an indictable offence carrying a penalty of five years or more, and many offences in Canada now carry the five-year maximum penalty.

A difficulty raised by cooperation among parties to the UNTOC in regard to this residual category of offences is whether the offence in question has to meet the UNTOC criterion for 'serious' in both parties. Thus if State A applies a five-year maximum penalty to trafficking in stolen cultural artefacts and State B only applies a three-year

---

[50] Protocol to Prevent, Suppress, Punish Trafficking in Persons, Especially Women and Children, supplementing the United Nations Convention against Transnational Organized Crime, New York, 15 November 2000, 2237 UNTS 319, in force 25 December 2003.

[51] Protocol Against the Smuggling of Migrants by Land, Sea and Air, supplementing the United Nations Convention against Transnational Organized Crime, New York, 15 November 2000, 2241 UNTS 507, in force 28 January 2004.

[52] Protocol against the Illicit Manufacturing of and Trafficking in Firearms, Their Parts and Components and Ammunition, supplementing the United Nations Convention against Transnational Organized Crime, New York, 31 May 2001, 2326 UNTS 208, in force 3 June 2005.

penalty, can State A require cooperation on the basis of UNTOC in the investigation of an alleged trafficker resident in State B? The express terms of article 2(b) of the UNTOC and the principle of reciprocity that underpins all forms of cooperation suggests that State B is only obliged to cooperate if the penalty is at least four years or more in both its law and State A's law, and this approach has been followed in practice.[53]

Moving beyond enumeration to an evaluative standard, article 3(1)(b) presents the potentially broadest ground for application of the UNTOC as a procedural instrument; whether that potential will ever be realized is difficult to say.

8.8 The UNTOC's Double-pronged Strategy against Organized Crime

The measures for criminalization in the UNTOC itself are aimed at the organizational aspects of organized crime, those structural characteristics that make organized crime dangerous because they enable the commission of diverse basic profit-making crimes.[54] These entrepreneurial/organizational/logistical structures are necessary conditions for the commission of basic crimes from human trafficking to running protection rackets. In response the authors of the UNTOC have pursued a double-pronged strategy of prevention[55]—one against the basic crimes (those proscribed in the Protocols and as serious crimes by the parties) and one against the entrepreneurial/logistical/organizational crimes (those proscribed in the UNTOC itself—participation in an OCG, corruption, money laundering, and obstruction of justice). Parties can as noted add to the list of basic crimes by either lifting the punishment of their domestic offences over the four-year punishment threshold for serious crimes or in pursuit of a more universal response supplementing the UNTOC with new protocols, although the latter is a much more difficult proposition. The list of organizational crimes, examined below, is closed, but not comprehensive because it does not include violent crimes directed for instrumental purposes by the OCGs.[56]

8.9 Criminalization of Participation in an Organized Criminal Group

8.9.1 Introduction

One of the main features of the UNTOC is the offence provided for by article 5(1):

1. Each State Party shall adopt such legislative and other measures as may be necessary to establish as criminal offences, when committed intentionally:

---

[53] See *Ortmann et al v United States* [2017] NZHC 189, at para 153.

[54] V Ruggiero, 'Legal Pre-requisites and Socio-economic Structures for a Successful Implementation of the Palermo Convention' in S Betti (ed), *Symposium: The United Nations Convention against Transnational Organised Crime: requirements for effective implementation* (Turin: UNICRI et al, 2002), 149, 150.

[55] M Kilchling, 'Substantive Aspects of the UN Convention against Transnational Organised Crime' in H-J Albrecht and C Fijnaut (eds), *The Containment of Transnational Organised Crime: Comments on the UN Convention of December 2000* (Freiburg im Breisgau: Iuscrim, 2002), 84, 86.

[56] ibid, 87–88.

(a) Either or both of the following as criminal offences distinct from those involving the attempt or completion of the criminal activity:

    (i) Agreeing with one or more other persons to commit a serious crime for a purpose relating directly or indirectly to the obtaining of a financial or other material benefit and, where required by domestic law, involving an act undertaken by one of the participants in furtherance of the agreement or involving an organized criminal group;

    (ii) Conduct by a person who, with knowledge of either the aim and general criminal activity of an organized criminal group or its intention to commit the crimes in question, takes an active part in:

        a. Criminal activities of the organized criminal group;

        b. Other activities of the organized criminal group in the knowledge that his or her participation will contribute to the achievement of the above described criminal aim;

The authors of article 5 had a number of national models which they could draw on: conspiracy (the common law concept of both an inchoate offence and a form of participation in crime), criminal associations (recognized in many civilian criminal legal codes), the racketeering offences (United States), and mafia-type associations (Italian Penal Code). They settled for two options, although states parties can opt for both if they choose. This significant innovation, an aggravated form of participation in the basic offences, requires a party to criminalize either (i) the conspiracy option or (ii) the participation in the organized criminal group option (or both), as offences distinct from other existing completed and inchoate offences involved in the criminal activity. The chapeau in article 5(1)(a) clarifies that whichever option is chosen, the new offence must be 'distinct from those involving the attempt or completion of the criminal activity', clarifying their stand-alone character.

8.9.2 The conspiracy model

The option in article 5(1)(a)(i) requires that the accused must conspire to commit a serious crime which benefits them. The conduct required is agreement. It must involve 'one or more persons'. It must be 'to commit a serious crime', that is a crime penalized by four years or more deprivation of liberty. Commission must be intentional (although agreement and intention can also be inferred)[57] although a specific confining purpose is required: one 'relating directly or indirectly to the obtaining of a financial or other material benefit'. There is also provision for further possible conditions 'where required by the domestic law' of the party either 'involving an act undertaken by one of the participants in furtherance of the agreement, or involving an organised criminal group'. The first of these extra conditions applies because in some parties agreement is insufficient for criminal liability and their law requires a step in the execution of the agreement. Involvement of an organized criminal group avoids such a requirement.

---

[57] Article 5(2).

The conspiracy model fits well with existing common law principles but has a number of practical shortcomings.[58] Not all the individuals implicated may be party to the same agreement; they may simply know of or suspect its existence or they may be party to different agreements which raises the possibility of multiple overlapping agreements rather than a single agreement, and the potential for highly complex and unwieldy prosecutions. Similarly they may not actually have much knowledge of the individual criminal activities the group undertakes. Finally, for those states which insist on proof of an overt act such proof may make it difficult to reach those who play a more organizational oversight role.

8.9.3 The participation model

The difficulty that civil law states have with the criminalization of mere agreement without conduct led to the option to proscribe involvement in an OCG in terms of article 5(1)(a)(ii).[59] Modelled on the French *association de malfaitures*,[60] it requires 'conduct by a person' with a specific mental state: 'knowledge of either the aim and general criminal activity of an organised criminal group or its intention to commit the crimes in question'. The first alternative is more vague and broader, the second more specific and narrower in ambit. The individual has to have 'taken an active part in' either the 'criminal activities of the organised criminal group' or 'other activities of the organised criminal group in the knowledge that his or her participation will contribute to the achievement of the above described criminal aim'. Precisely just how active a part is not made clear; it appears to include engagement in serious crime as well as supportive activities of a non-serious nature.[61] Although active implies advertent conduct, whether the accused must know about the broader nature of the group has been left to national law. The reference to OCG, defined, as noted above, as a structured group of three or more acting in concert with the aim of committing serious crime, ensures that the article 5(1)(a)(ii) offence is also linked to the notion of serious crime as those crimes designated as such by parties through the imposition of a four-year or more maximum penalty, which is at the heart of the UNTOC.[62] But it is also clear that although they may (and thus become liable for both the basic crime and the participation crime) the offender doesn't have to commit these serious crimes themselves in order to be liable for the participation crime.[63] They must, however, intentionally participate and have actual knowledge of the groups' aims and activities or criminal intentions.

The virtue of this alternative is that it allows for a much broader scope of criminalization. As Schloenhardt points out it reaches individuals more remotely connected to specific criminal activity because there does not need to be proof of agreement to commit specific offences. It can be used long before such offences have actually been

---

[58] See Schloenhardt, above n 24, 425.   [59] Wise above n 18, 313 et seq.
[60] Article 450-1 of the French Penal Code.   [61] Legislative Guide, above n 45, para 64.
[62] See RS Clark, 'The United Nations Convention against Transnational Organized Crime' 50 *Wayne Law Review* (2004) 161, 169.
[63] ibid, 172.

committed, and can involve relatively innocuous activities such as provision of transport, food, housing, legal or accounting services, in fact anything done with the relevant knowledge of the group's ultimate intentions.[64] But it does require some active and conscious involvement supportive of the criminal aims of the group and thus does not cast as broad a net as the 'labelling/registration' model such as that used in Japan,[65] which rather than making membership of criminal organizations illegal, labels organizations as proscribed and then criminalizes association with those organizations. Having said that, both of these forms of organizational-based criminality are open to the criticism that they involve collective punishment rather than personal criminality.

8.9.4 Secondary participation

Article 5(1)(b) expands the net of liability by requiring parties to criminalize different forms of secondary participation in the 'commission of a serious crime by an organised criminal group, namely: organising, directing, aiding, abetting, facilitating and counselling'. Organizing and directing reveal that the drafters' intentions here were to reach those individuals who lead an OCG although they may, however, have little direct role in the execution of its plans.[66] The actual level of contribution and accompanying state of mind has been left to domestic law, although someone who aids the commission of a crime by an OCG does not necessarily have to be a member of that OCG.

8.9.5 State practice

Article 5 is an attempt to grapple with the problem of organized criminal activity while respecting distinctive legal traditions, by setting out a list of organizational offences adaptable with minimum effort to different traditions. It extends criminal liability beyond preparatory offences and secondary participation in a novel way difficult for some states to accept, and in spite of efforts to develop model legislation[67] implementation was initially patchy. In Europe, for example, while a 1998 Joint Action[68] adopted a very similar definition of criminal organization and provided for the two options of participation in an OCG or conspiracy, EU member states did not change their existing national conceptions of organized crime resulting in a 'legal patchwork'.[69] Alongside continued resistance, however, some states have begun to engage

---

[64] Schloenhardt, above n 24, 429.

[65] 1991 Law to Prevent Unjust Acts by Organized Crime Group Members (bōtaihō), Law no 77 of 1991.

[66] Legislative Guide, above n 45, para 66.

[67] See, eg, UNODC, *Model Legislative Provisions against Organized Crime* (New York: UN, 2012).

[68] See Joint Action 98/733/JHA, above n 39, article 2(1)(a) and (b). Updated in articles 1 and 2, EU Framework Decision on the Fight against Organized Crime, 2008/841/JHA, above n 39.

[69] Council of the European Union, *Questionnaire on the Criminal Liability of Legal Persons in the Member States of the European Union as regards Organized Crime; Analysis of Replies*, doc 6740/00 LIMITE, CRIMORG 40, Brussels, 9 March 2000.

in enthusiastic remodelling of their law.[70] Singapore, for example, initially relied on its general law of conspiracy requiring only agreement and an intention to pursue the agreement.[71] In response to criticism that it was too broad in comparison to the UNTOC standard because it did not require that the conspiracy have the specific purpose of gaining or obtaining a financial benefit,[72] it has since enacted a new Organised Crime Act 2015 adopting the UNTOC definition of an OCG[73] and making membership of a 'locally linked' OCG an offence.[74] Law-reforming legislatures have tinkered, however, with the UNTOC model in order to adapt it to local circumstances. The New South Wales offence of participation in a criminal organization[75] has been criticized as being both too broad because it does not include the UNTOC requirement of structure and too narrow because the shared objective of material benefit from serious violent crime is more narrowly drawn than the UNTOC specific purpose of financial benefit. Moreover, it criminalizes reckless participation in such a group,[76] which broadens the ambit significantly from that anticipated in the UNTOC. Britain has also taken the participation option and it only requires participation in the criminal activities (activities punishable by seven years or more carried out with a view to obtaining directly or indirectly a gain or benefit) of an OCG with only a reasonable suspicion that they are the activities of the OCG.[77] It might be complained that this textual variation blurs the essence of organized crime but we should recall that the UNTOC does not adopt a definition of organized crime; the approach adopted (i) identifies a few common characteristics of the problem and is (ii) loose enough to cover a range of different manifestations of the problem as it appeared under local conditions. Despite the haphazard implementation there is no doubt that the OCG has entered legal parlance as an elastic basis for criminalization; the real difficulty is that the tendency of the OCG concept to be used as a basis for over-criminalization is exacerbated by domestic loosening of the concept to provide for even broader offences.

8.10 Money Laundering

Somewhat less novel than article 5(1), article 6, entitled 'criminalization of the laundering of the proceeds of crime', requires parties to criminalize an array of money laundering offences (money laundering is discussed in Chapter 10 of this book). At a minimum, parties are obliged to criminalize the laundering of the proceeds of serious offences (ie those carrying a four-or-more-year sentence of deprivation of liberty). The novel step taken in the UNTOC was to expand the range of predicate offences. In terms of article 6(2)(a) states parties agree to 'seek to criminalise laundering of proceeds from

---

[70] See Paoli and Vander Beken, above n 46, 25; F Calderoni, *Organized Crime Legislation in Europe: Harmonization and Approximation of Criminal Law, National Legislations and the EU Framework Decision on the Fight against Organized Crime* (Heidelberg: Springer, 2010), 115 et seq.
[71] Section 120A(1) of its Penal Code.   [72] Schloenhardt, above n 24, 226.
[73] Section 2(1).   [74] Section 5(1).
[75] Section 93S(1) of the New South Wales Crimes Act 1900; introduced into the New South Wales Crimes Act 1900 by the Crimes Legislation Amendment (Gangs) Act 2006; Schloenhardt above n 24, 117–24.
[76] Section 93T(1).   [77] Section 45 of the Serious Crime Act 2015.

the widest range of predicate offences' while more specifically they agree to include as predicate offences all 'serious crime' as defined in article 2 of the UNTOC and the offences established in accordance with articles 5, 8, and 23 of the UNTOC.

8.11 Corruption

Article 8 obliges parties to criminalize corruption. Article 8(1)(a) requires parties to criminalize 'active bribery'—the 'promise, offering or giving to a public official, directly and indirectly, of an undue advantage, for the official himself, or herself, or another person or entity, in order that the official act or refrain from acting in the exercise of his or her official duties'. Article 8(1)(b) requires parties to criminalize 'passive bribery'—'the solicitation or acceptance, by a public official' in the same circumstances for the same purpose. Article 8(2), however, only recommends that transnational bribery—the making of bribes by individuals in one party and the taking of bribes by individuals in another—be criminalized, because transnational bribery was still lawful in many states at the time. Article 8(3) requires criminalization of participation as an accomplice in corruption. These provisions are fairly rudimentary compared to what followed in the UN Convention against Corruption (discussed in Chapter 9).

8.12 Obstruction of Justice

Finally, article 23 requires 'criminalization of the obstruction of justice'. One of the features of organized crime has been its ability to avoid investigation and prosecution by interfering with the administration of justice through (i) bribes and (ii) threats. The purpose of this offence is to ensure parties take steps to suppress obstruction of the application of justice to transnational organized criminals. Article 23(a) requires criminalization of 'the use of physical force, threats or intimidation or the promise, offering or giving an undue advantage'. An undue advantage may be corporeal or incorporeal, pecuniary or non-pecuniary, and includes the promise of an advantage.[78] The action must be intentional but must also be accompanied by a special purpose— 'to induce false testimony or to interfere in the giving of testimony or the production of evidence in proceedings related to offences covered by this Convention'. In this way the obstruction must be linked to the UNTOC offences (participation in an OCG, corruption, money laundering, and obstruction), the offences in the Protocols, and 'serious' crimes under domestic law. 'Proceeding' is intended to embrace all official governmental proceedings, including the pretrial stages of the case.[79] Article 23(b) requires criminalization of the 'the use of physical force, threats or intimidation'. Again it must be intentional and with a special purpose—'to interfere with the exercise of official duties by a justice or law enforcement official in relation to the commission of offences covered by this Convention'. Article 24 supplements this provision by requiring states to provide for the protection of witnesses.

---

[78] *Model Legislative Provisions*, above n 67, 42–43.   [79] Legislative Guide, above n 45, 92.

8.13 Penalties for UNTOC Offences

Following the usual practice in the suppression conventions the UNTOC makes little provision with regard to punishment. Article 11(1) of the UNTOC provides that the parties shall make the commission of its offences 'liable to sanctions that take into account the gravity of that offence', a brevity that reflects the absence of universal agreement on tariffs or on the policy of punishment. Article 26(2) and (3) encourage parties to consider mitigating punishment, indulgence, or immunity for individuals who cooperate with law enforcement action against organized crime. Provisions for recovery of the proceeds of crime under article 12 of the UNTOC serve, however, as a form of condign punishment.

8.14 Criminal Responsibility of Legal Persons

Organized crime frequently involves the activities of legal persons such as corporations. These legal persons may serve to shield organized criminal activity or to serve as an instrument of organized crime. Many states are still struggling to come to terms with the concept of imposing criminal liability on legal persons. Article 10 of the UNTOC takes a direct approach. Article 10(1) provides that subject to their legal principles, parties shall adopt measures that may be necessary to establish the liability of legal persons for participation in serious crimes involving an organized criminal group, for the protocol offences and for offences under articles 5, 6, 8, and 23.[80] Giving way to the fundamental reservations of some states this liability need not, however, be criminal; article 10(2) details that it may be criminal, civil, or administrative. It follows that parties may use civil or administrative penalties against offences by corporations such as active bribery under article 6; nonetheless, large pecuniary penalties may have the required suppressive effect. Article 6(4) obliges parties to ensure that legal persons held liable under article 6 be subject to 'effective, persuasive and dissuasive criminal or non-criminal sanctions'.

8.15 Conclusion

The UNTOC does not provide a unified concept of transnational organized crime. It rather depends on the interplay of the concepts of an OCG, serious crime, *dolus specialis*, and (less so) transnationality in order to overcome the problems of remote participation and incoherent preparatory action to try to suppress transnational organized crime. The definitions of these terms set low thresholds, which makes for broad suppression but not for precise denunciation. The commercial/enterprise and governmental/power functions of organizations like the Mafia,[81] for example, fall within the scope of UNTOC offences but are not particularly well captured by them because they do not subject them to specific denunciation. There have been some suggestions made

---

[80] ibid, 119.
[81] J Dickie, *Cosa Nostra: A History of the Sicilian Mafia* (London: Hodder, 2007), 299–301.

in the EU that it is necessary to return to the drawing board and come up with a standardized definition.[82] The UNTOC's definitions thus illustrate an inability to agree on
what organized crime is and what may be the best way of suppressing it. However, the
concept of organized crime is so contingent and so complex that it may not be amenable to comprehensive definition.

The UNTOC does illustrate, however, a fundamental shift in transnational criminal justice policy away from the criminalization of specific individual acts to criminalization based on some form of relationship to the actions of others, a shift dictated
by the realization that suppression of the latter did not have the desired effect of disa-
bling the structures that make these offences possible, but a shift which has negative implications for traditional notions of criminal responsibility based on individual
conduct and fault.[83] Some states have been very wary of the UNTOC's innovations.
Bolivia, for example, declared that it will first apply its national legislation in force
and then only secondly the definitions in articles 5, 6, 8, and 23 of the UNTOC.[84]
Nevertheless, the UNTOC has proved useful in bypassing the limitations of pursuing
individuals for basic transnational crimes by relying on the OCG as an aggravating
circumstance justifying exceptional measures. The notoriously corrupt Abacha family, for example, was dubbed an OCG in Switzerland in order to enable various legal
steps to be taken against their assets in Switzerland not otherwise available against
individuals.[85] In 2010 President Obama used executive orders to impose sanctions on
named Transnational Criminal Organizations, signalling something of a cross pollination of approaches from terrorism, and a renewed enthusiasm to attack transnational
organized crime through public diplomacy.[86]

When, however, someone is convicted for participating in an OCG based on the
activities of three individuals engaged in smuggling a relatively small number of
untaxed cigarettes, the label OCG seems to express a level of penal denunciation disproportionate to the crime.

Moreover, the policy models used were in the end largely of Western origin, some-
thing that has inevitably impacted negatively on its global implementation.[87] Samuel
Witten, a legal advisor to the State Department, argued for US ratification of the
UNTOC before the Senate as follows: 'The value of these Convention provisions to the
United States is that they oblige other countries that have been slower to adapt to the
threat of transnational organized crime to adopt new laws in harmony with ours.'[88]

---

[82] Parliamentary Committee of Inquiry into Mafia related and Other Criminal Organisations: Report
on the Italian Presidency of the EU and on the Fight Against Mafia Related Crime in Europe and Outside
Europe, Conclusions, Recommendation (i).

[83] Schloenhardt, above n 24, 431.

[84] Declaration of Bolivia, 18 May 2006, text available at UNTS, Status of Treaties, <http://treaties.
un.org/Pages/ViewDetails.aspx?src=TREATY&mtdsg_no=XVIII-12&chapter=18&lang=en> last visited
8 March 2017.

[85] B Ige, 'Abacha and the Bankers: Cracking the Conspiracy' 2(1) *Forum on Crime and Society* (2002)
111, 113.

[86] B Zagaris, 'Obama Executive Order Imposes Sanctions on Transnational Organised Crime Groups'
(2011) 27(10) *International Law Enforcement Reporter* 925–27.

[87] Fijnaut, above n 23, 59.

[88] P Andreas and E Nadelmann, *Policing the Globe: Criminalization and Crime Control in International
Relations* (Oxford: OUP, 2006), 173.

Unsurprisingly there is an impression that the UNTOC's promise has never been fully realized. The 2015 Doha Declaration on Integrating Crime Prevention and Criminal Justice into the wide UN Agenda, for example, calls on states parties 'to implement and make more effective use of' the UNTOC, fifteen years after the UNTOC was adopted.[89]

---

[89] The declaration on integrating crime prevention and criminal justice into the wider United Nations agenda to address social and economic challenges and to promote the rule of law at the national and international levels, and public participation, adopted at the 13th UN Congress on Crime Prevention and Criminal Justice, 12–19 April 2015, Doha; UN Doc A/CONF.222/L.6, 31 March 2015.

9

Corruption

9.1 Introduction

Corruption is in many ways one of the most significant forms of transnational crime both because of the harm it does in its own right, and because the 'greasing of palms' is so important to transnational illicit markets. Deep-rooted corruption is a significant problem in developing states.[1] In *Glenister v President of the Republic of South Africa and Others*[2] the South African Constitutional Court noted: 'Corruption has become a scourge in our country and it poses a real danger to our developing democracy. It undermines the ability of the government to meet its commitment to fight poverty and to deliver on other social and economic rights guaranteed in our Bill of Rights.'

This chapter examines the development of the various corruption offences showing how the emphasis in regard to criminalization of corruption offences expanded from a narrow focus on transnational corruption to a broader focus that included different forms of domestic corruption, and the extension of the scope of criminality through related offences such as trading in influence and unexplained enrichment. It looks at the origins of these offences in domestic law, the development of measures based on regional conventions, and finally at the measures developed under the auspices of the UN and through soft law, before surveying their effectiveness.

9.2 The Nature of Corruption

Taking measures against corruption was hampered at least initially by a failure to agree at a global level on what constitutes corruption and by arguments that corruption is a relativistic concept heavily loaded with a Western normative baggage that does not translate well into other regions of the world.[3] The further economic argument that in some circumstances corruption works to open closed markets also initially clouded responses. The problem of agreeing a general definition has as we shall see simply been avoided by law makers, while arguments about relativity and efficiency have fallen silent in the face of the scale of corruption. The World Bank estimates that businesses and individuals pay an estimated US$1.5 trillion annually in bribes, and this impacts more heavily on poor than high income households (12.6% of

---

[1] See the discussion in TR Snider and W Kidane, 'Combating Corruption through International Law in Africa: A Comparative Analysis' 40 *Cornell International Law Journal* (2007) 691, 692.

[2] [2011] ZACC 6; 2011 (3) SA 347 (CC); 2011 (7) BCLR 651 (CC) (Glenister II), para 57.

[3] See SH Alatas, *The Sociology of Corruption: The Nature, Function, Causes and Prevention of Corruption* (Singapore: D Moore Press, 1968).

annual income to 6.4% in Paraguay, for example).[4] In impoverished states petty corruption is a daily reality and a matter of survival for those who wish to access services. The poor also lose the most from 'grand' corruption by notorious kleptocrats like Nigeria's General Sani Abacha. Transparency International has defined grand corruption as occurring when

> [a] public official or other person deprives a particular social group or substantial part of the population of a State of a fundamental right, or causes the State or any of its people a loss greater than 100 times the annual minimum subsistence income of its people, as a result of bribery, embezzlement or other corruption offence.[5]

Intimately related to bad governance and the capture of the instruments of government for the purposes of personal economic gain by politicians and public officials, corruption goes well beyond traditional gift giving.

Corruption takes many forms, from large bribes paid through agents, to the abuse of influence to sell favours, to making use of authority to commit theft.[6] It can occur entirely within a state or involve bribes paid across borders. The key element is the link between inducement and the misuse of authority (whether public or private) for personal gain of some kind. The conduct is wrongful because the recipients of a bribe make an unfair decision in favour of the person making the bribe; they take account of a reason (personal gain) not among the reasons they are entitled to take into account. The harmful effects of corruption may be immediate (the refusal of a service for want of a bribe) or remote (the impact on the economic and social well-being of a group of people).[7] One of the problems of the remote nature of the harm, however, is that there is often no obvious complainant. Costa Rica has developed a notion of general social damage caused by corruption in article 38 of the Code of Criminal Procedure. Its Criminal Court of Finance explained in the *Finland Case*[8] that: 'the deleterious effect [the particular incident of corruption] has on the national economy, the payment of unlawful commission, financed with funds from the concessional loan granted by the Finnish Government represents a social damage whose holder is the national collectivity as a whole, represented by the Attorney-General of the Republic.'

Corruption deters and undermines trade, investment, and aid, dilutes growth, taxes economic activity, and reduces funding for public services. It can penetrate all levels of government and all kinds of private commerce. It facilitates other forms of transnational criminal activity because it provides a mechanism for transnational criminals to conduct crime without official interference and makes it possible for criminals to secure impunity from the law.

---

[4] World Bank Brief; Combatting Corruption, 11 May 2017, available at <http://www.worldbank.org/en/topic/governance/brief/anti-corruption> last visited 17 May 2017.

[5] Transparency International, 'What is Grand Corruption and how can we stop it?', 21 September 2016, available at <http://www.transparency.org/news/feature/what_is_grand_corruption_and_how_can_we_stop_it> last visited 17 May 2017.

[6] See J Wouters, C Ryngaert, and S Cloots, 'The International Legal Framework against Corruption: Achievements and Challenges' 14 *Melbourne Journal of International Law* (2013) 205, 238 for a list.

[7] See J Horder, 'Bribery as a Form of Criminal Wrongdoing' 127 *The Law Quarterly Review* (2011), 37.

[8] Sentence 370-2009, 10 May 2009.

9.3 Forerunner Legislation

Prior to the development of international efforts to suppress corruption, most states
had domestic anti-corruption laws, usually criminalizing the making and taking of
bribes.[9] The former involved the giving of something of value by the briber in order
to get someone in authority to do or refrain from doing something, the latter the taking of something of value by someone, in return for the misuse of their authority to
the advantage of the briber. Bribery does not require agreement—what is criminalized
are unilateral actions on either side (or both). The terms 'active' and 'passive' bribery
are thus misnomers because those in authority may not only passively take bribes but
actively solicit bribes—'supply-side' and 'demand-side' corruption are more apt.[10] In
order to reach other forms of misuse of public office, over time the scope of domestic bribery offences has been expanded to embrace a range of analogous offences,
such as trading in influence,[11] illicit enrichment, corrupt accounting, and so forth.
These offences remained strictly domestic until the US took unilateral action against
cross-border bribery. In the 1970s the implication of US multinationals in bribery
by the Watergate investigations led to investigations by the Securities and Exchange
Commission (SEC), which revealed that major companies such as Lockheed Martin
had engaged heavily in bribery of public officials in other states in order to get business.[12] Payment of bribes to foreign officials in order to facilitate business was standard practice. Indeed, in many states bribes were tax deductible. French authorities,
for example, permitted the deduction of 'exceptional commercial expenses' until the
enactment on 29 December 1997 of article 39-I of the French Tax Code expressly to
prohibit this deduction.

The US responded by enacting the 1977 Foreign Corrupt Practices Act[13] (FCPA),
the first domestic legislation designed to suppress the bribery of foreign public officials
by individuals or organizations operating from the US. The FCPA sets out a compliance regime (record keeping standards)[14] and civil or criminal penalties in regard to
certain kinds of foreign trades.

The FCPA penalizes the intentional giving of 'anything of value', which could be
anything from cash to paying for a training course, in order to induce a foreign official, defined to include public officials, political parties, candidate of political parties
in foreign states, and even a corporation in which the state owns a minority share, to
misuse their official position to direct their business wrongfully to the person making the bribe or any other. The question of whether a Haitian Telecommunications
company was an instrumentality of the Haitian government and thus bribery of its
officials fell within the FCPA was resolved in the affirmative in the *United States v*

---

[9] See, eg, articles 333 (offering or promising an undue advantage) and 317 (requesting or receiving an
undue advantage) of Brazil's Criminal Code of 1940 (Law No 2848 of 7 December 1940).
[10] P Delaney, 'Transnational Corruption: Regulation across Borders' 47 *Virginia Journal of
International Law* (2007) 413, 422–23.
[11] See, eg, article 432-1.1 of the French Penal Code.
[12] See generally PW Schroth, 'The United States and the International Bribery Conventions' 40
American Journal of Comparative Law (2002) 593, 593–98.
[13] 15 USC §§ 78dd-1, et seq.   [14] 15 USC § 78m(b).

Esquenazi[15] because it was controlled by the government (it had a majority interest, controlled employment in the company, took profits, and would provide support if necessary) and performed a function that the government treated as its own (the government subsidized costs, the company enjoyed a monopoly, and was perceived as performing a public function).

The FCPA was designed to ensure fair competition and so the bribe must be 'to obtain or retain business', not to obtain or retain some non-commercial service. But again, like the phrase 'anything of value', this phrase is interpreted broadly.[16]

The jurisdictional scope of the offence is critical. The FCPA applies to: (i) 'issuers', any company whose shares are traded in the US thus including foreign companies whose shares are traded in the US;[17] (ii) to 'domestic concerns', effectively US companies and individuals;[18] and (iii) to any person who 'while in territory of the United States' corruptly makes use of a means or instrumentality of interstate commerce in order to further any act of bribing a foreign official.[19] Acts within the territory of the US include all acts that cause a result in the US, such as the use of correspondent banking accounts to transfer money for corrupt purposes.[20] It also applies to the officials, directors, employees, agents, even shareholders acting for the company making the bribe. This broad jurisdictional scope made it possible, for example, to use the FCPA to prosecute Siemens AG in 2008 (which paid penalties of US$800 million) because although it is a German company and carried on corrupt activities in many parts of the world, it traded in the US and certain of its subsidiaries had offices in the US.[21] Though broad, this jurisdictional scope did not however reach non-US companies that did not act even in these attenuated ways in the US.

The FCPA also contains three affirmative defences. The first, added in 1988, excludes 'facilitation payments', payments to foreign officials to expedite the performance of 'routine governmental actions', non-discretionary actions such as the issuing of papers, from the FCPA's scope.[22] The second excludes reasonable payments and bona fide expenses.[23] The third excludes payments legal under the foreign official's country's laws.[24]

The enforcement of the FCPA has placed a heavy regulatory burden on companies.[25] Encouraged to do due diligence by the imposition of vicarious criminal liability for the corrupt actions of their employees and agents, the requirement to do due diligence has also been reinforced by heavy reliance by prosecuting authorities on deferred prosecution agreements—an agreement with a defendant company to defer

---

[15] 752 F3d 912 at 925 et seq (11th Circ 2014).

[16] In *US v Kay*, 359 F3d 738 (5th Cir 2004) it included payment to customs officials to reduce customs duties.

[17] 15 USC §§ 78dd-1.   [18] 15 USC §§ 78dd-2.   [19] 15 USC §§ 78dd-3.

[20] NN Wilson, 'Pushing the limits of Jurisdiction over Foreign Actors under the Foreign Corrupt Practices Act' 91 *Washington University Law Review* (2014) 1063, 1070 et seq.

[21] See A Liebold, 'Extraterritorial Application of the FCPA under International Law' 51 *Williamette Law Review* (2015) 225, 242.

[22] 15 USC §§ 78dd-1(b), 78 dd-2(b).

[23] 15 USC §§ 78dd-1(c)(2), 78 dd-2(c)(2), and 78dd-3(c)(2).

[24] 15 USC §§ 78dd-1(c)(1), 78 dd-2(c)(1), and 78dd-3(c)(1).

[25] See generally M Koehler, 'The Facade of FCPA Enforcement' 41(4) *Georgetown Journal of International Law* (2010) 907.

prosecution in consideration of the payment of fines and undertakings to comply with standards. Further incentive for compliance is provided by a whistleblower provision under US SEC regulations which sets out that provision of information leading to a sanction of US$1 million or more means that the whistleblower will receive between 10 and 30 per cent of the penalty for their efforts.[26]

Not surprisingly, US companies were keen to internationalize the FCPA's obligations in treaty form so as to deny any competitive advantage to foreign companies not subject to it.

9.4 The Inter-American Convention against Corruption

The first international instrument adopted, however, a distinctive kind of model, addressing not just transnational but domestic corruption. In 1996 the Organization of American States (OAS) confronted by widespread corruption in the Americas, adopted the Inter-American Convention against Corruption.[27] Expressly linking corruption to drug trafficking, a major concern in the region,[28] the Convention aims to improve the parties' domestic mechanisms for prevention, detection, and eradication of corruption, and to provide for international cooperation in this regard.[29] It adopts a range of measures to achieve this aim including the criminalization of acts of national and transnational corruption, mutual assistance, extraterritorial jurisdiction, extradition, seizure and confiscation of property, conduct standards, and removal of bank secrecy.

The Convention does not define corruption; instead article 6 defines certain domestic 'acts of corruption'. Article 6(1)(a) defines the taking (the direct or indirect solicitation or acceptance) of bribes (defined very broadly as any article of monetary value or other benefit such as a gift, favour promise, or advantage for himself or for another person or entity) by a public official (all those carrying out public functions)[30] in exchange for any 'official' action on their part (any act or omission in the performance of their public functions). Article 6(1)(b) defines the giving of a bribe. Article 6 defines various other offences preparatory to or consequent upon bribery including the performance of 'any act or omission' by a government official in the discharge of their duty 'for the purpose of illicitly obtaining benefits' (the so-called 'breach of duty' offence),[31] the use or concealment of the proceeds,[32] and conspiring to perform and various forms of participation in the main offences.[33] Article 7 requires parties to criminalize the actions defined in article 6 in their national law.

---

[26] 17 CFR section 240.21F-3(a) (2012) made under 17 USC § 78u-7 (2012).
[27] 29 March 1996, 35 ILM 724, in force 6 March 1997.   [28] Preambular para 8.
[29] Article 2.
[30] Article 327 of Brazil's Criminal Code 1940 defines a public official as 'any person who holds a public position, employment or exercises a public function even if temporarily or without pay'.
[31] Article 6(1)(c). This option overlaps with the solicitation under article 6(1)(a) and the US opted out of it because of its potential criminalization of a single act of preparation with the necessary intention—Snider and Kidane, above n 1, 725.
[32] Article 6(1)(d).   [33] Article 6(1)(e).

Following in the footsteps of the FCPA (and the soon to be concluded Organisation for Economic Co-operation and Development (OECD) Anti-Bribery Convention) article 8 introduces a heavily qualified obligation (subject to the constitution and fundamental principles of the party's legal system) to criminalize supply-side corruption of foreign government officials. Again a broader approach is taken however as the bribe can relate to 'any act or omission in the performance' of an official's public function and thus unlike the FCPA is not restricted to business transactions.

The novel offence in article 9, 'inexplicable illicit enrichment', defined as 'a significant increase in the assets of a government official that he cannot reasonably explain in relation to his lawful earnings during the performance of his functions', is designed to operate in those situations where law enforcement agents suspect bribery, but cannot prove it; they need only prove the incommensurate increase in an official's income and the onus shifts to the accused to explain the source of the increase, something which is peculiarly within their own knowledge. But this reversal of the onus and the potential breach of the right to privacy means that this obligation is also subject to the constitution and fundamental principles of the legal system of each party, and while it has been enacted in South American states,[34] Canada and the US have demurred because of its conflict with the presumption of innocence.[35]

9.5 The OECD Anti-bribery Convention

The US pursuit of firmer obligations on its main trading partners stumbled in the UN which failed to come to agreement on a Draft International Agreement on Illicit Payments. They were more fruitful in the OECD with the development of the 1997 Convention on Combating Bribery of Foreign Public Officials in International Business Transactions (the OECD Anti-Bribery Convention).[36] The true international child of the FCPA, the Convention obliges parties to criminalize transnational official bribery and attempts to strengthen international cooperation in the investigation and prosecution of offences. It is particularly important because most of the major multinational companies are domiciled in states parties to the convention, and suppressing transnational supply-side corruption is the main purpose of the OECD Convention. Compliance in the states that 'host' the corruption is irrelevant.[37] This is reflected in its penal provisions. Article 1 obliges parties

> to make it a criminal offence under their law for any person intentionally to offer, promise or give, any undue pecuniary or other advantage, whether directly or through intermediaries, to a foreign public official, for that official or for a third party,

---

[34] See, eg, article 9 of Brazil's Law on Administrative Improbity (Law No 8429 of 2 June 1992).

[35] Senate Resolution Advising and Consenting to the Treaty on Inter-American Convention on Corruption S. REP. No. 106-7809 (2000); Canada's reservation at OAS Department of International Law, Inter-American Treaties, Inter-American convention against Corruption (B-58) Signatories and Ratifications <http://www.oas.org/en/sla/dil/inter_american_treaties_B-58_against_Corruption_signatories.asp> last visited 17 May 2017.

[36] 18 December 1997, 37 ILM 1, in force 15 February 1999.

[37] C Rose, *International Anti-Corruption Norms: Their Creation and Influence on Domestic Legal Systems* (Oxford: OUP, 2015), 60.

in order that the official act or refrain from acting in relation to the performance of official duties, in order to obtain or retain business or other improper advantage in the conduct of international business.

The influence of the FCPA is patent. The offence is limited to giving a bribe; taking a bribe is not an offence under the OECD Convention. It is also limited to bribery of foreign public officials, defined[38] as those who hold legislative, administrative, or judicial offices in or exercise public functions for a foreign country (all levels of government[39]), and including officials or agents of public international organizations. The offence excludes bribery of national public officials and of private individuals/companies of any nationality.

Article 1 requires that the accused make the bribe intentionally, in order (i) to get the official to 'act or refrain from acting in performance of official duties', which includes 'any use' of the official's position, whether doing so is within or outside of their competence,[40] with (ii) the further purpose of obtaining or retaining improper advantage in the conduct of international business. The dual purposes serve to limit the offence and to emphasize the core mischief to which it is directed—bribery of foreign state officials to get business (a transplant from the FCPA). It reflects the business orientation of the OECD, although as a result this offence is more restrictive in scope than that in article 8 of the OAS Convention. The OECD position that article 1(1) does not cover small facilitation payments because they are not made 'to obtain or retain business or other improper advantage',[41] has been criticized for ignoring the consequences of such payments which can alter the competitive position of a business.[42] The OECD's response has been to discourage such payments and tax deductions for them.[43] In practice, attitudes to facilitation payments appear to have toughened and many states have eliminated this exception,[44] although the US has not done so arguing these recommendations amend the treaty thus requiring Senate approval.[45]

Article 1(2) of the Convention broadens the scope of liability by providing for obligations to criminalize 'complicity in, including incitement, aiding or abetting or authorization of' an act of bribery of a foreign public official. 'Authorization', also a transplant from the FCPA,[46] is absent from other corruption suppression conventions, so the FCPA and the OECD Anti-Bribery Convention reach much further 'upstream' than these other conventions.[47] Somewhat more tentatively, article 1(2) also provides that attempt or conspiracy to bribe a foreign public official shall be criminal

---

[38] Article 1(4)(a).   [39] Article 1(4)(b).   [40] Article 1(4)(c).

[41] 'Commentaries on the Convention on Combating Bribery of Foreign Public Officials in International Business Transactions and Related Documents' in OECD, *Convention on Combating Bribery of Foreign Public Officials in International Business Transactions and Related Documents* (OECD, 2011), 14, 15 (para 9), available at <http://www.oecd.org/daf/anti-bribery/ConvCombatBribery_ENG.pdf> last visited 12 February 2017.

[42] See Wouters et al, above n 6, 239.

[43] Recommendation of the Council for Further Combating Bribery of Foreign Public Officials in International Business Transactions, 26 November 2009, para 6; Recommendation of the Council on Tax Measures for Further Combating Bribery of Foreign Public Officials in International Business Transactions, 25 May 2009, para 1.

[44] The UK's Bribery Act 2010 makes no provision for them.   [45] Rose, above n 37, 72.

[46] 15 USC § 78dd-1(g)(1).   [47] Snider and Kidane, above n 1, 719.

to the same extent as attempt or conspiracy to bribe a domestic official is criminal, a restricted obligation avoidable by parties that do not recognize attempts and/or conspiracy as part of their general principles of criminal liability. Nevertheless, difficulties of proof in a chain of corruption make conspiracy an important principle. In *R v Karigar*,[48] for example, prosecuting authorities in Canada (in which the company offering the bribe was domiciled) were not able to ascertain whether or not the accused who was the company's agent in India actually paid the Air India official in India for whom the bribe was intended, so they relied on a conspiracy between the company officials and the agent. On appeal, the Ontario Court of Appeals noted that the relevant section of the Canadian legislation, section 3 of the Corruption of Foreign Public Officials Act was consistent with article 1(2) of the OECD Anti-Bribery Convention, which extended criminalization to conspiracy.[49]

Guidance on sanctions for these offences is limited. Article 3(1) states that bribery of a foreign public official 'shall be punishable by effective, proportionate and dissuasive criminal penalties', which are to be determined by the party in question. It adds a further and novel obligation that these sanctions 'must be comparable' to the range of penalties available for domestic bribery of public officials and include deprivation of liberty sufficient to trigger legal cooperation (usually six months or one year).

Article 2 obliges parties to provide for the 'liability' of legal persons, but not necessarily for criminal liability. Some parties do provide for corporate criminal liability for corruption. India does so using the 'controlling mind' principle (although it has never prosecuted a legal person for bribery[50]). Non-criminal sanctions, such as monetary sanctions, are permissible under article 3(2), where the party's law does not make it possible to provide for criminal responsibility for legal persons. They may be simpler to impose but it is questionable whether the imposition of large fines, such as the nearly billion dollars paid in 2016 by the Brazilian petrochemical company Braskem SA for concealing millions of dollars of bribes paid to the Brazilian Government, are of sufficient deterrent value when no convictions of individuals result.[51]

9.6 Other Regional Anti-corruption Instruments

A number of regional anti-corruption conventions were adopted rapidly during a rash of law making in the late 1990s, tailored, however, to regional conditions. The 1997 Convention on the Fight against Corruption Involving Officials of the European Communities or Officials of Member States of the European Union[52] also criminalizes corrupt practices, but is limited in scope to EU officials and officials from EU members. The 1999 Council of Europe Criminal Law Convention on Corruption[53]

---

[48] 2013 ONSC 5199 paras 21 et seq.   [49] ibid, para 26.
[50] OECD Thematic Review Report 2010, *The Criminalization of Bribery in Asia and the Pacific*, available at <http://www.oecd.org/dataoecd/2/27/46485272.pdf> last visited 30 May 2017.
[51] US Securities and Exchanges Commission, 'Press Release: Petrochemical Manufacturer Braskem S.A. to pay $957 million to Settle FCPA Charges', 21 December 2016, available at <https://www.sec.gov/news/pressrelease/2016-271.html> last visited 17 May 2017.
[52] 26 May 1997, OJ C195/2 (1997).
[53] Strasbourg, 27 January 1999, ETS No 173, in force 1 July 2002.

is broader in scope, and largely responsible for the reform of anti-corruption laws in European states. It criminalizes thirteen different forms of corruption including trading in influence and concealment of corrupt accounting practices. Article 6, for example, criminalizes both active and passive bribery whether connected to transnational business or not. The inclusion of passive bribery was motivated by the idea that bribery affects both the economic and social development of a state, by undermining public confidence in public administration.[54] A major innovation is criminalization of active and passive bribery (under articles 7 and 8 respectively) in the private sector. Both articles require intentional commission of bribes made 'in the course of business activity'. The undue advantage, interpreted as something that would place the recipient in a better position than prior to the offence (eg, holidays, loans, food and drink, or better career prospects[55]) must be to 'any persons who direct or work for, in any capacity, private sector entities' for them 'to act, or refrain from acting, in breach of their duties', and neither offence requires a transnational element.[56] However, unlike the provisions for corruption in the public sector, these offences are still limited by the requirement that the individual acts 'in breach of their duties'. In another innovation, article 18(2) requires states parties to take the necessary steps to ensure a legal person can be held liable 'where the lack of supervision or control by a natural person has made possible the commission of ... corruption offences for the benefit of that legal person by a natural person under its authority'.[57] An Additional Protocol[58] introduces new specific offences relating to bribery of arbitrators and jurors. Both treaties rely on an innovative monitoring system—the Group of States against Corruption (GRECO).

In 2003 the African Union (AU) adopted the African Union Convention on Preventing and Combating Corruption.[59] Moving away from the FCPA model the scope is entirely domestic and the AU Convention is unique in that it doesn't cover corruption by foreign public officials. Instead it criminalizes a range of activities associated with both the domestic supply and demand dimensions of corruption but includes other more 'problematic'[60] offences such as 'influence peddling', illicit enrichment, and the concealment of proceeds.[61] The AU Convention's express emphasis on good governance is also distinctive.[62] Its measures for prevention emphasize the importance of public access to information,[63] call for non-governmental organization (NGO) involvement to hold governments to account, and encourage participation of the private sector in the fight against corruption.[64]

---

[54] Council of Europe explanatory report to the Criminal Law Convention on Corruption, Strasbourg, 27 January 1999, para 39.

[55] ibid, paras 37 and 38.

[56] The EU developed private sector anti-corruption measures in Council Framework Decision 2003/568/JHA of 22 July 2003 on combating corruption in the private sector.

[57] Section 7(1) of the UK's Bribery Act 2010 makes it an offence, eg, for a 'relevant commercial organisation' to fail to prevent bribery by a 'person associated' with it.

[58] Strasbourg, 15 May 2003, ETS No 191, in force 1 February 2005.

[59] 11 July 2003, 43 ILM 5, in force 5 August 2006. See generally J Hatchard, *Combating Corruption: Legal Approaches to Supporting Good Governance and Integrity in Africa* (Cheltenham: Edward Elgar, 2014).

[60] Snider and Kidane, above n 1, 713.   [61] Article 4.

[62] Articles 2–3. Snider and Kidane, above n 1, 716.   [63] Article 9.

[64] Article 11(2), article 12.

9.7 The UN Convention against Corruption

9.7.1 The development of the Convention

The most significant step in expanding the application of anti-corruption provisions has been taken under the auspices of the UN. This development was driven in part by the fact that the OECD Anti-Bribery Convention was limited in scope to OECD member states, thus leaving untouched activities by companies from non-OECD states without controls over foreign bribery.[65] There was also the sense that a new UN instrument could in some ways address the interests of developing states.[66] A special session on corruption was held in 1995 at the Ninth UN Congress on the Prevention of Crime and the Treatment of Offenders. Shortly thereafter in 1996 the General Assembly adopted the UN Declaration against Corruption and Bribery in International Commercial Transactions, which inter alia defined active and passive bribery and called on UN member states to criminalize bribery of foreign public officials.[67] These measures were not considered extensive enough, and pressure grew for a multilateral treaty of global scope targeting both private and public corruption. The result was adoption of the UN Convention against Corruption (UNCAC).[68] Its preamble proclaims that '[c]orruption is no longer a local matter but a transnational phenomenon that affects all societies and economies, making international cooperation ... essential'.

The UNCAC synthesizes the foreign and domestic focuses of the earlier treaties into an instrument with a very broad scope. In addition to making provision for criminalization of a broad range of activities, it provides for specialized law enforcement provisions, international cooperation, and asset recovery (discussed in Chapter 19). In also sets out a broad range of measures for the prevention of corruption,[69] including the setting up of anti-corruption bodies and appropriate procurement systems, measures for ensuring judicial and private sector integrity, the integration of civil society in anti-corruption efforts, and the regulation of the financial system.

9.7.2 Crimes

Introduction

The UNCAC does not introduce a generic definition of corruption because of the problem (common in transnational criminal law) of adopting one that is compatible with all the parties' definitions. Instead, like the earlier conventions it criminalizes various types of corruption, which differ principally according to the identity of the parties to the offence and their purposes. What distinguishes the UNCAC is that it

---

[65] A Cuervo-Cazurra, 'The Effectiveness of Laws against Bribery Abroad' 39 *Journal of International Business Studies* (2008) 634, 635.

[66] See M Joutsen, 'The United Nations Convention against Corruption' in A Graycar and R Smith (eds), *Handbook of Global Research and Practice in Corruption* (Cheltenham: Edward Elgar, 2011), 303.

[67] GA Resolution 51/191, 16 December 1996, paras 2 and 3.

[68] *United Nations Convention against Corruption*, New York, 31 October 2003, 2349 UNTS 41, in force 14 December 2005.

[69] Chapter II.

contains the broadest list of criminalization obligations of any of the corruption conventions, designed to suppress every form of corruption.

Active and passive national bribery

Using very similar language to the earlier conventions, article 15(a) plugs the gap in the OECD Anti-Bribery Convention by obliging parties to criminalize the 'intentional promise, offering or giving, to a public official, directly or indirectly, of an undue advantage, for the official himself or herself or another person or entity, in order that the official act or refrain from acting in the exercise of his or her official duties'.

Kubiciel and Rink explain just how expansive the scope of the conduct element is:[70]

> The prohibited behaviour on the active side of bribery encompasses all stages from promising to giving. This comprehensive coverage of possible bribing actions includes unilateral announcement of or bilateral agreement on the future undue advantage (promise), the briber's signal of his or her willingness to grant an undue advantage at any time (offering), and the actual transfer of this benefit (giving).

Looking more closely at the elements in article 15(a), the use of the phrase 'in order that' implies that the promising, offering, or giving of a bribe must be done with the specific intention of altering the official's behaviour. It also means that a mere intention is required and it does not have to be proved that the act or omission by the public official actually took place. It is thus irrelevant whether the public official could in fact deliver the service.[71] Although the UNCAC makes no exception for facilitation payments, the absence of this purpose has been held in some states to exclude the giving of social courtesy gifts.[72] In many common law states the use of the term 'corruptly' implies that such a bad intention is required.[73]

The bribe must be directed to a 'public' official. Article 2(a) defines such an official much more broadly than in previous conventions, in three ways:

- First, formally—as those holding public office of any kind on any basis, whether elected or appointed. The Interpretive Notes make clear that this includes any person holding a legislative (MPs, local and regional government representatives), executive (including the military[74]), administrative (prosecutors), or judicial office (judges).

- Second, functionally—those persons performing a public function or providing a public service (persons working for a public agency forming a public service).

- Third, legally—those defined as such in national law.

---

[70] M Kubiciel and AC Rink, 'The UN Convention against Corruption' in P Hauck and S Peterke (eds) *International Law and Transnational Organized Crime* (Oxford: OUP, 2016) 218, 224.

[71] ibid, 225.

[72] See Wouters et al, above n 6, 242 discussing decisions in the South Korean Supreme Court.

[73] See, eg, section 1 of Ireland's Prevention of Corruption Act 1906 as amended by section 2 of Ireland's Prevention of Corruption (Amendment) Act 2010.

[74] Report of the Ad Hoc Committee for the Negotiation of the Convention against Corruption on the work of its first to seventh sessions, Addendum: Interpretative notes for the official records (Travaux Préparatoires) of the negotiations of the United Nations Convention against Corruption, UN Doc A/58/422/Add.1, paras 3 and 4.

Although no further definition is given it has been suggested it includes officials who perform public functions unless the organization they work for operates on a normal commercial basis.[75] The definition is arguably not broad enough though. US resistance meant that corruption of members of political parties through such common practices as vote buying or unlawful campaign contributions was not included.[76] The fact that the promise etc of the bribe may take place 'directly or indirectly' implies criminal liability where bribes are made through intermediaries or agents, a crucial element in making many such transactions possible and in denying complicity in them. In addition, states often make provision for the liability of the agents themselves.[77] The Legislative Guide to the UNCAC notes that the undue advantage, which is not defined in the UNCAC, must be the ultimate aim of promising etc these bribes, and may be tangible or intangible, pecuniary or non-pecuniary, and does not have to be given immediately or to the person directly.[78] Finally, 'in the exercise of his or her official duties' does not actually require that the official breach of promise to breach their duties. A passport official who will only stamp a passport if paid a bribe to do so is still soliciting a bribe in terms of article 15.

Article 15(b) obliges criminalization of the intentional 'solicitation or acceptance' of bribes by national public officials. It uses the same elements but from the perspective of the bribe taker to make possible criminalization of demand, and to complete the coverage of the domestic cycle of bribery.

Active and passive transnational bribery

Article 16(1) is a mandatory provision in very similar terms to article 1(1) of the OECD Anti-Bribery Convention in its definition of the making of bribes to foreign public officials and officials of public international organizations in the conduct of international business (thus excluding making bribes for private purposes such as acquiring residence in a country). Again it is distinctive in that officials are defined expansively and in detail. A 'foreign public official' is defined in article 2(b) as 'any person holding a legislative, executive, administrative or judicial office of a foreign country, whether appointed or elected; and any person exercising a public function for a foreign country, including for a public agency or public enterprise'. This broad definition is particularly important in regard to individuals such as an employee of a private/public enterprise or parastatal. The party's law and practice is the touchstone here and the importance of reliance on it is illustrated in the definition of a 'state official' in the corruption prosecutions arising from the Lesotho Highlands Water Project (a dam-building project funded by the World Bank to provide water for Lesotho and South Africa). The trial of the CEO of the Lesotho Highlands Development Authority in Lesotho for common law bribery revealed that he had received millions of US dollars in bribes from various

---

[75] See Wouters et al, above n 6, 248.   [76] See Wouters et al, above n 6, 244.

[77] See, eg, sections 38 and 39 of Kenya's Anti-Corruption and Economic Crimes Act 2003.

[78] UNODC, *Legislative Guide for the Implementation of the United Nations Convention against Corruption* (New York: UN, 2006, UN Pub Sales No E.06.IV.16), paras 196–97.

foreign companies through intermediaries.[79] The judge explored whether for the purposes of the offence the accused was a 'state official'.[80] Even though he had been on secondment from the public service he was still found to have held the post as a 'public officer' because although his public service salary and pension had been suspended, they had been preserved and were immediately reinstated after he left the authority.[81] Finally, an 'official of a public international organization' is defined in article 2(c) as 'an international civil servant or any person who is authorized by such an organization to act on behalf of that organization'.

Article 16(2), however, develops the law by shifting attention to the bribe taker in transnational bribery although it only obliges parties to consider criminalizing the intentional

> solicitation or acceptance by a foreign public official or an official of a public international organization, directly or indirectly, of an undue advantage, for the official himself or another person or entity, in order that the official act or refrain from acting in the exercise of his or her official duties.

This unique provision is non-mandatory because it involves the prosecution of public officials in other states. It involves establishment of extraterritorial jurisdiction over such actions, which provided it is based on one of the heads of jurisdiction such as territoriality in article 42 of the UNCAC, other states parties to the UNCAC can be taken to have consented to and cannot complain it is a violation of their sovereignty. It may, however, depending on the status of the official, raise issues of their material or personal immunity from prosecution.[82] The UNCAC does not define an undue advantage; it is a matter for the domestic law of the prosecuting state, and need not take into account laws and customs in the foreign state.[83]

Embezzlement, misappropriation, or other diversion of property

The UNCAC also obliges parties to criminalize embezzlement, misappropriation, or other diversion of property (broadly defined to include anything of value) by a public official in article 17. The focus of this offence is the link between the public official and the property (private or public), which must have been placed in their protection because of their position.[84] Criminalization of these actions is aimed at supporting good governance at a national level, and they may not have and thus do not require a transnational aspect. They are covered at a domestic level primarily by existing domestic offences such as theft, fraudulent conversion, or fraudulent misappropriation.

Trading in influence

A number of UNCAC offences address the complexity of corruption by recognizing its many forms and avoid the inherently limiting equation of corruption with bribery, but

---

[79] *Rex v Masupha Ephraim Sole*, High Court of Lesotho, 20 May 2002, CRI/T/111/9799.
[80] ibid, 18 et seq.   [81] ibid, 22.   [82] Kubiciel and Rink, above n 70, 227.
[83] ibid, 228.   [84] ibid, 230.

because they extend criminalization into areas not universally recognized as wrong-ful, they are discretionary in nature. Article 18 is concerned with active and passive 'trading in influence', an offence designed to reach influence peddlers who are outside the decision circles but try to influence individuals with decision-making power in an improper way (as opposed to lobbyists as the latter have no corrupt intention because they are not trying to 'abuse' their influence) for the benefit of others, in return for some benefit. It obliges parties to consider criminalizing the actions of the person who instigates such trading as well as the trader themselves. In terms of article 18(1), the accused must promise, offer, or give to a public official or other person an undue advantage 'in order that the public official or the person abuse his real or supposed influence with a view to' getting an undue advantage for the person who instigates the act or some other person. In terms of article 18(2), the accused must solicit or accept the undue advantage for the same purpose.

These crimes are designed to reach those situations not quite covered by bribery because there is no requirement that either the official or other person have influ-ence (they may be fraudulent) or the official be proved to have acted or refrain from acting (no action may result); all that is required is the instigator have the purpose of getting them to exert their real or supposed influence. Section 10 of the Prevention of Corruption Act 2002 of Mauritius is illustrative. It criminalizes three separate forms of active trading in influence: the first an offer of a gratification to another person 'to cause a public official' to use his influence to 'obtain work, employment, contract or other benefit' from a public body;[85] the second where the gratification is directed at 'another person to use his influence';[86] and the third where the grati-fication is offered directly to the 'public official'.[87] There are two variations of pas-sive trading in influence: in the first it is 'any person' who solicits; in the second 'any public official'.[88]

Abuse of functions

Under article 19 of the UNCAC parties promise to consider criminalizing the inten-tional commission of the 'abuse of functions or position', described as 'the perform-ance of or failure to perform an act, in the violations of laws, by a public official, in the discharge of his or her functions, for the purpose of obtaining an undue advantage for himself or herself or for another person or entity'. An official might, for example, direct public funding towards an organization which they have some private, secret, pecuni-ary interest. The target is the official acting or omitting to act in order to gain advantage for themselves or another. The undue advantage thus need not actually be obtained. The undue advantage is broader than the payment of financial reward. No action in the form of bribe, etc is required by another person. It is broader than the taking of a bribe under article 15(b) because it must be 'in violation of laws' separate from the anti-bribery provisions that found accountability under article 15(b). This also means that

---

[85] Section 10(1).   [86] Section 10(2).   [87] Section 10(3).   [88] Section 10(4) and (5).

breaches of non-binding codes cannot trigger this offence. In common law countries such conduct falls within the offence of misconduct in a public office.[89]

Illicit enrichment

Article 20 provides for an obligation to consider enacting an intentional offence of 'illicit enrichment', defined as 'a significant increase in the assets of a public official that he or she cannot reasonably explain in relation to his or her lawful income'. Initially used in Latin America, states from other regions have also taken this option. For example, section 10 of Hong Kong's Prevention of Bribery Ordinance (Cap 201), criminalizes possession of unexplained wealth and requires the offender to explain evidence of a standard of living incommensurate with the alleged offender's income, or control of property disproportionate to that income. This is an intrusive provision into human rights, and therefore the obligation is also subject to the constitutional and the fundamental principles of the party's legal system. Article 30(6) of the UNCAC reminds parties of their obligation to respect 'the principle of the presumption of innocence', at least in relation to accused public officials. In Hong Kong, the reverse onus has survived constitutional challenge where balancing the interests of the individual against those of society in eradicating corruption tipped in favour of society.[90] It is doubtful, however, whether a crime that undermines one of the principles of the rule of law has any place in a system supposedly designed to uphold good governance and the rule of law. It is open to abuse by the kind of political leader against whom the UNCAC is aimed.[91] The UK has opted for measures short of criminalization of illicit enrichment, adopting, as an alternative a civil measure allowing enforcement agencies to obtain an 'unexplained wealth order' (UWO) against individuals (politically exposed persons[92] or individuals involved in serious crime) whose assets (with a threshold value of £50,000) appear disproportionate to their known income. If the individual cannot discharge a rebuttable presumption that the assets were funded by criminality, the investigating agency can obtain the UWO, which freezes the assets for a period of time to allow the authorities to gather evidence.[93]

Private sector corruption

The authors of the UNCAC also took the novel step of taking measures against corruption in the private sector. Article 21, entitled 'Bribery in the Private Sector', only requires parties to consider criminalizing the intentional commission 'in the course of economic, financial or commercial activities', of 'the promise, offering or giving'

---

[89] J Hatchard, 'Corruption' in N Boister and R Currie (eds), *The Routledge Handbook of Transnational Criminal Law* (Abingdon: Routledge, 2015), 347, 356.

[90] *AG v Hui Kin-hong* [1995] 1 HKCLR 227.

[91] See generally N Kofele-Kave, *Combating Economic Crimes: Balancing Competing Rights and Interests in Prosecuting the Crime of Illicit Enrichment* (Abingdon: Routledge, 2012), particularly at section 1.1.2.4.

[92] Foreign public office holders.

[93] Section 1 of the Criminal Finances Act 2017 inserting section 362A into the Criminal Proceeds Act 2002.

and 'the solicitation or acceptance' of an undue advantage.[94] The scope thus covers the full set of supply- and demand-driven actions. The requirement that these must be in the course of commercial activities is an attempt to cut out purely private relations such as gifts not given to seek advantage in commercial activities. These actions must be directed to or taken by a 'person who directs or works, in any capacity for a private sector entity' (therefore including agents of those entities) and who is 'in breach of his or her duties'. Article 21 is complemented by article 22 in which states parties promise to consider criminalizing embezzlement of property in the private sector.

Ancillary offences and related penal provisions

The UNCAC's corruption offences are complemented by a broadly drawn money laundering provision in article 23. Article 24 provides for an analogous offence of 'concealment', viz the intentional 'concealment or continued retention of property when the person involved knows that such property is the result of any of the' UNCAC offences. Accessorial in nature, this obligation is limited to those who have not participated in the UNCAC offences. Article 25 criminalizes the obstruction of justice, an offence common in the context of corruption where it is used to frustrate investigation and prosecution. Article 27 criminalizes participation in and attempts to commit the UNCAC offences, but a significant omission from the UNCAC is any mention of the crime of conspiracy. The provision in article 28 that knowledge, intent, and purpose can be inferred from the facts is of obvious importance because many of the UNCAC offences depend on performing particular actions with specific purposes, and all investigators may be able to show is a series of unusual 'red flags' pointing towards an advertent state of mind.

Liability of legal persons

Article 26 obliges parties to establish, 'consistent with their legal principles', the liability of legal persons for the UNCAC offences, but this may be criminal, civil, or administrative liability. One of the problems common to criminal liability of companies that arose in the Lesotho Highlands corruption scandal was the prosecution of a company for a crime requiring *mens rea*. It was resolved through reliance on section 338 of Lesotho's Criminal Procedure and Evidence Act 1991 which deemed the *mens rea* of the company's servants—the intention to pay the bribers—to be the *mens rea* of the company.[95] The UK's Bribery Act 2010 avoids *mens rea* by introducing a new strict liability offence of corporate failure to prevent bribery, in terms of which UK and non-UK-based companies[96] will be held responsible for bribery irrespective of where it takes place committed by anyone acting on its behalf, defined as 'associated persons' who 'performs services for or on behalf of' the organization, even in the absence of knowledge on the part of senior management.[97]

---

[94] Article 21(a) and (b) respectively.
[95] *R v Acres International*, High Court of Lesotho, 13 September 2002, CRITCRI/T/2/2002, 2425.
[96] Section 12. [97] Sections 7 and 8.

9.7.3 Penalties

Article 30(1) of the UNCAC provides only that the parties are obliged to make the commission of UNCAC offences open to sanctions 'that take into account the gravity of that offence'. Article 26(4) also obliges parties to 'ensure that legal persons held liable in accordance with this article are subject to effective, proportionate and dissuasive criminal or non-criminal sanctions, including monetary sanctions'. Given that corruption may involve large amounts of money, a proportional response suggests high maximum penalties. The FCPA sets a trend towards severity by providing, for example, that a company can be fined up to US$2 million per violation, while culpable individuals can face imprisonment of up to five years or a fine of up to US$250,000 per violation.[98] All corruption offences tend to carry severe penalties in national law. Mauritius, for example, makes trading in influence subject to a maximum ten-year penalty.[99] China, a party to the UNCAC, applies a range of penalties for embezzlement from not less than ten years for cases involving 100,000 yuan, and in especially serious circumstances the death penalty is available and has been applied.[100] Bribery in the private sector does not carry such heavy penalties. In Russia, for example, passive bribery of a public official carries a maximum penalty of twelve years or a million rouble fine[101] while passive bribery in the private sector only carries a 300,000 rouble fine without the possibility of imprisonment.[102]

Article 30(2) of the UNCAC obliges parties to take the gravity of the offence into account as a condition for early release or parole. Article 30(6) also asks parties to consider removing, suspending, or reassigning a public official accused of an UNCAC offence and article 30(7) provides that where the gravity of the offence warrants it, parties must consider disqualification of the convicted persons from holding public office or office in a state-owned enterprise. Section 64(1) of Kenya's Anti-Corruption and Economic Crimes Act 2003 provides, for example, that a person 'convicted of corruption or economic crime shall be disqualified from being elected or appointed as a public officer for ten years after the conviction'. In addition to conventional sanctions, article 34 allows parties to take measures to address the 'consequences' of corruption including taking corruption into consideration 'in legal proceedings to annul or rescind a contract, withdraw a concession or other similar instrument or take any other remedial action'. Inter-governmental organizations such as the World Bank disbar companies implicated in corruption from applying for any other World Bank-funded projects for a specified time, and various states have followed suit with similar national measures.[103]

9.8 The Effectiveness of the Anti-corruption Conventions

The anti-corruption conventions make provision for a range of measures to encourage investigation of corruption. One of the most important provisions in the UNCAC,

---

[98] 15 USC §§ 78dd-1.   [99] Section 10 of the Mauritius Prevention of Corruption Act 2002.
[100] Article 382 of the Criminal Law of the People's Republic of China 1979.
[101] Article 290 of the Criminal Code.   [102] Article 204.4 of the Criminal Code.
[103] See Chapter 6 of South Africa's Prevention and Combating of Corrupt Activities Act no 12 of 2004.

for example, is article 33 which requires parties to consider incorporating protections against unjustified treatment of individuals who report an UNCAC offence in good faith and on reasonable grounds. Such treatment distinguishes the situation from witness protection and may include unjustified dismissal of anyone and not just insiders. But some countries have not taken this step and others have provisions that lack detail.[104] And even when in place, whistle-blower laws are sometimes not well known or used effectively.[105] A further example of how measures designed to protect the integrity of a single state's transnational trading system, the FCPA, have not translated well to the regional or global level is the FCPA's compliance prevention measures requiring record keeping to which are attached severe civil and criminal penalties.[106] Some corruption suppression conventions only carry weak preventive measures requiring the maintenance of, for example, accounting systems that are subject to audit, and do not impose any criminal offences for non-compliance.[107] The UNCAC is an exception obliging parties in article 12(1) to take measures to enhance accounting and auditing standards in the private sector and 'where appropriate, provide effective, proportionate and dissuasive civil, administrative or criminal penalties for failure to comply with such measures'.

Overall, however, in spite of the system of treaty obligations and the revision of domestic laws to meet those obligations, globally the numbers of corruption prosecutions remain low. While the US has consistently ramped up prosecutions under the FCPA effectively becoming the global corruption policeman, elsewhere there are few complaints, few investigations, and few prosecutions. A study by the anti-corruption NGO Transparency International in 2014 found that only four parties (the US, UK, Germany, and Switzerland) actively enforced the OECD Anti-Bribery Convention, another five moderately enforced it, while eight engaged in limited enforcement, and twenty-two in little or no enforcement at all.[108]

While this lack of enthusiasm from among the globe's major exporters may be because of a range of factors, including the low pay of investigators, poor training, and slow and inefficient investigation, political will is a major problem. Efforts to monitor the conventions have been led by the example of the OECD's Working Group on Corruption,[109] which developed a peer review mechanism that adopted a four-phase review of the quality of implementing legislation, the application of implementing legislation, the enforcement of law and detection, and other enforcement issues. This forensic process has allowed the Working Group to target recalcitrant parties. For

---

[104] Transparency International, *Whistleblower Protection and the UN Convention against Corruption* (Transparency International, 2013), 8, available at <http://www.transparency.org/whatwedo/publication/whistleblower_protection_and_the_un_convention_against_corruption> last visited 17 May 2017.

[105] E Oyamada, 'Anti-corruption Measures the Japanese Way: Prevention Matters' 4(1) *Asian Education and Development Studies* (2015) 24, 31.

[106] Schroth, above n 12, 599.

[107] While the AU Convention is silent in this regard, the OECD Convention does call for an enforcement mechanism in article 3(2).

[108] Transparency International, *Exporting Corruption: Progress Report 2014: Assessing Enforcement of the OECD Convention on Combating Foreign Bribery* (Transparency International, 2014), 2 available at <https://www.transparency.org/whatwedo/publication/exporting_corruption_progress_report_2014_assessing_enforcement_of_the_oecd> last visited 5 March 2018.

[109] Established in terms of article 12 of the OECD Anti-Bribery Convention.

example, an increasingly hostile attitude from the OECD's Working Group pressured the UK into adopting the Bribery Act 2010. Prior to that the UK, a party to the convention since 1997, had had a poor record in regard to corruption, a result of the strength of the British business lobby, and had failed to pass the necessary laws to prevent British companies from engaging in foreign corruption. The UK's ineffectual response drew strong criticism from the Working Group on Bribery, whose Chairman, frustrated at the long rearguard action resisting change by the Chamber of British Industries eventually threatened the UK with sanctions (a power the Convention did not actually provide for).[110]

The problem was highlighted by the Al Yammah arms deal scandal, a debacle involving the suspension of the investigation into the British weapons manufacturer BAE Systems' allegedly paying bribes in order to secure Saudi Arabian defence contracts (if true, an offence under sections 108–110 of the Anti-Terrorism, Crime and Security Act 2001, which gives effect to the OECD Convention). The UK's Serious Fraud Office (SFO) halted its investigation after the British Prime Minister Gordon Brown intervened because of national security concerns: the SFO investigators were told that if they went into Saudi-held Swiss bank accounts Saudi Arabia would stop cooperation on anti-terrorism. Pulling the prosecution for these reasons appears to be in direct violation of article 5 of the OECD Anti-Bribery Convention which provides:

> Investigation and prosecution of the bribery of a foreign public official shall be subject to the applicable rules and principles of each Party. They shall not be subject to considerations of national economic interest, the potential effect upon relations with another State or the identity of the natural or legal persons involved.

A review court held that the SFO had acted unlawfully in dropping the investigation but the House of Lords reversed the decision.[111] Lord Bingham held:

> 46. The clear effect of article 5 is to permit national investigators and prosecutors to act in accordance with the rules and principles applicable in their respective states, save that they are not to be influenced by three specific considerations: (i) national economic interest, (ii) the potential effect upon the relations with another state, and (iii) the identity of the natural or legal persons involved. It is obvious why the parties wished to prohibit the paying of attention to (i): a bribery investigation or prosecution may very probably injure commercial, and thus economic, interests. The reason for excluding consideration of (iii) is also obvious: investigators and prosecutors should not be deterred from acting by the high ministerial office or royal connections of an allegedly corrupt person. The ambit of consideration (ii) is more doubtful. Clearly the investigator or prosecutor is not to be deterred by the prospect or occurrence of a cooling of relations between his state and that of the allegedly corrupt official, even if this escalates into a diplomatic stand-off involving (for instance) the denial of visas, the cutting off of cultural and sporting exchanges, the obstruction of trading activities, the expulsion of diplomats and the blocking of bank accounts. But can

---

[110] Rose, above n 37, 83 et seq.
[111] *R (On the Application of Corner House Research and Others) v Director of the Serious Fraud Office* [2008] UKHL 60, on appeal from [2008] EWHC 246.

the negotiators have intended to include multiple loss of life within the description 'potential effect upon relations with another State'?

The Attorney General, Lord Goldsmith had answered in the negative, opining that no state would have signed the convention if they thought article 5 meant they were abandoning their ability to have regard to national security.[112] The House of Lords concluded that it was not critical to decide this question because it was within the SFO Director's discretion under national law to stop the investigation and he had done so. Lord Bingham left it to an international court to decide whether the UK was in breach of its treaty obligation under article 5, a prospect of judicial resolution that was highly unlikely given the OECD Convention's implementation system (discussed in Chapter 21). In 2009 corruption charges against BAE Systems were laid by both the SFO and US Department of Justice for corruption in regard to contracts in Saudi Arabia and the Czech Republic and South Africa, and in early 2010 BAE settled, agreeing in a plea-bargain to pay £400 million, thus 'sweeping Britain's biggest corruption charges under the carpet'.[113] The UK passed the new Bribery Act in 2010.

Political will is absent elsewhere. The UNCAC, for instance, has been criticized as not being fully implemented in parties with a history of grand corruption.[114] Politically exposed persons can make investigation extremely difficult. For example, in an investigation into misappropriation of funds to 1MDB, a fund established by the Malaysian Prime Minister Najib Razak, the Member of Parliament who blew the whistle was jailed for 18 months for publicly disclosing classified information (a Public Audit Report reclassified as secret by the government), the Attorney General and Deputy Prime Minister who had been critical of Razak's involvement were replaced, the new Attorney General ordered that the anti-corruption agency close the investigation, and when the Swiss Attorney General made a request for mutual legal assistance in regard to evidence held in Malaysia about money from 1MDB being banked in Switzerland, the Malaysian authorities declined the request because the matter was still under investigation.[115] Faced with this level of resistance it is little wonder that some critics have suggested turning to the International Criminal Court in desperation as a solution to grand corruption. It has been argued, for example, that in certain circumstances corrupt practices performed in relation to the commission of atrocities by act or omission (the failure to deliver medical care) can become a crime against humanity if the necessary *mens rea* is present.[116] However, this option is limited by the structural requirements of crimes against humanity to a very small number of provable cases.

---

[112] 1 February 2007 (689 HL Debates, Hansard, part 38, col 378).

[113] 'BAE Systems Pays $400m to Settle Bribery Charges', *The Independent*, 6 February 2010, available at <http://www.independent.co.uk/news/business/news/bae-systems-pays-400m-to-settle-bribery-charges-1891027.html> last visited 17 May 2017.

[114] Kubiciel and Rink, above n 70, 237.

[115] B Zagaris, 'Malaysia again Rejects Swiss Evidence Gathering Request in Swiss 1MDB Investigation as Court Sentences Legislator for Discussing Information from Official Audit' 32(11) *International Enforcement Law Reporter* (2016), 426, 430.

[116] I Bantekas, 'Corruption as an International Crime and Crime against Humanity' 4 *Journal of International Criminal Justice* (2006) 466, 474.

To some extent provision to permit political weakness to limit taking effective action against corruption is actually built into the corruption suppression conventions. The UNCAC, for example, has been criticized as being weaker than earlier instruments because of its explicit recognition of protection of sovereignty against interference in article 4 and the recommendatory nature of, or get out clauses in, many of its criminalization and enforcement provisions.[117] Rose gives as an example, the attempt by the Costa Rican Government in the *Alcatel* case to argue before a US Federal District Court that its concept of 'social damage' falls under article 35's provision for compensation to victims.[118] The Costa Rican Government argued that it was entitled to compensation for social damage despite heavy official implication in the bribes paid by the French Telecom Alcatel to Costa Rican officials to get government contracts. The Court rejected the suit on the grounds that Costa Rica was too closely entwined in the corruption to in effect be treated as a separate victim. Rose notes that an earlier draft of article 35 would have precluded this argument completely because it made clear that those involved in the corruption could not be compensated.[119] This raises the difficult issue of compensation to a people that cannot be paid for obvious reasons to their corrupt agents, their government. It also points to one of the overall problems for the effectiveness of anti-corruption offences: their enforcement is often carried out by the individuals at whom they are directed, something which calls for strictly independent investigating authorities.

9.9 The Increasing Resort to Soft Law

Not surprisingly, anti-corruption efforts have increasingly eschewed direct criminalization and turned to soft law as a more effective tool to prevent and detect corruption because it is more precise, focussed, and flexible. The OECD, for example, has engaged in soft law supplements such as the Anti-Corruption Action Plan for the Asia Pacific,[120] which implements OECD Anti-Bribery Convention norms in non-party states. The Council of Europe has also adopted soft law instruments to supplement treaty action including, for example, the Codes of Conduct for Public Officials.[121] A more unusual example is the Extractive Industries Transparency Initiative,[122] an effort driven by the UK to level the playing field among oil companies by producing regularly updated standards, to which these companies have to comply by inter alia disclosing material payments in order for the state concerned to be regarded as 'compliant' after an independent review process signed off by a Board composed of members from the state, corporate and civil society sectors.[123] The main sanction is suspension, which has been

---

[117] Rose, above n 37, 105 et seq.
[118] *US v Alcatel Lucent SA*, Case no 10-CR-20906-MGC1 and 10-CR-20907-MGC1, see Transcript of Change of Plea and Sentencing, Case 10-20906-CR-COOKE, 1 June 2011.
[119] Rose, above n 37, 115 et seq.
[120] Tokyo, 30 November 2001, available at <https://www.oecd.org/site/adboecdanti-corruption initiative/meetingsandconferences/35021642.pdf> last visited 17 May 2017.
[121] Recommendation Rec(2000)10, Adopted by the Committee of Ministers of the Council of Europe on 11 May 2000.
[122] See the EITI Standards 2016, available at <https://eiti.org/document/standard> last visited 17 May 2017.
[123] Rose, above n 37, 135 et seq.

used.[124] The shortcoming of revenue transparency systems like this is that they do not reveal how licences were negotiated or how revenue is spent.[125] Interestingly, however, the model has been copied by the EU which adopted a transparency directive,[126] requiring companies involved in logging and extraction to make public the payments made to governments.

9.10 Conclusion

Part of the purpose of the criminalization of corruption through the regional anti-corruption conventions and the UNCAC has been to establish a predictable response so that corruption is not normal business in one state, an administrative matter in another, and a crime in another, but a crime in all three. The criminalization of a range of forms of behaviour built around the nucleus of giving and taking a bribe is critical to this purpose. It forms the centrepiece of steps at asset retrieval. One of the difficulties of using these crimes against corruption is that it can take unique forms in different societies that do not fall comfortably within the scope of these crimes. In Japan, for example, post-war corruption is built around the 'iron triangle' of collusion between politicians, bureaucrats, and the business sector and practices such as guarantees of *amakudari* (descent from heaven), jobs for retired politicians and bureaucrats in the private or public sector after retirement.[127] Preventative steps have to be tailored to these particular societal forms, and criminal laws derived from general obligations in corruption suppression conventions can only play a limited role. It is, however, the political will to enforce these criminalization measures that is, as we have seen, the real difficulty. The US began the task of transnational policing of corruption and to date it has few real allies among other states in this regard.

---

[124] ibid, 163.   [125] ibid, 154.
[126] Directive 2013/50/EU of 22 October 2013 amends a number of directives in this regard.
[127] Oyamada, above n 105, 35.

10

Money Laundering

10.1 Introduction

The crime of money laundering is a recent innovation of an unusual kind, in that it involves conduct that occurs after the commission of another, 'predicate', offence, and is both dependent upon and independent of that offence. The crime has become increasingly important as a method for suppressing the practice of both money laundering and the predicate offence, and also because it anchors the Anti-Money Laundering (AML) regime that imposes a web of onerous regulatory obligations on financial institutions and provides a substantive basis for asset recovery (discussed in Chapter 19). This chapter discusses the nature of the conduct involved and the reasons for criminalization, as well as the forerunner offences in national law, before analyzing the substantive offence itself from its initial limitation to drug money laundering to 'all crimes' laundering. It then briefly examines the importance of the liability of legal persons and comments on the punishment applied to money laundering, before finally turning to the main institution for coordination of the global anti-money laundering regime, the Financial Action Task Force (FATF), as a prelude to commenting upon the effectiveness of the criminalization of money laundering.

10.2 The Nature of Money Laundering

Money laundering—a term apparently originating in Mafia 'laundering' of criminal proceeds by intermingling them with licit profits through laundromats during prohibition in the US—is the attempt to convert, conceal, transfer, or disguise the proceeds of crime and render them reusable. It conventionally comprises three stages (although not every stage occurs in every case[1]):

- 'placement'—the physical introduction of the proceeds of crime (defined in the United Nations Convention against Transnational Organized Crime (UNTOC) as 'any property derived from or obtained, directly or indirectly, through the commission of an offence'[2]) into the financial system through, for example, a cash deposit in a bank account;

- 'layering'—the disguise of the origins of the proceeds by creating complex layers of financial transactions such as the wiring of funds to banks around the world; and

---

[1] L de Koker and M Turkington, 'Transnational Organised Crime and the Anti-Money Laundering Regime' in P Hauck and S Peterke (eds), *International Law and Transnational Organized Crime* (Oxford: OUP, 2016), 241, 242.
[2] Article 2(e).

- 'integration'—the integration of the layered funds back into the economy as legitimate funds by, for example, the purchase of real estate.

Money laundering legitimates the proceeds of a previous, distinct, predicate criminal activity.[3] These 'up-stream' criminal activities range from the illegal sale of alcohol in the early twentieth century (in the US), through tax offences, corruption, illegal gambling, drug trafficking, to more recently human trafficking, piracy, migrant smuggling, cybercrime,[4] and now potentially any transnational crime that produces illicit proceeds. Criminals began to actively engage in laundering as increases in profit necessitated active fiscal management of these proceeds. The globalization of the financial system made this task easier because it made it possible to launder the proceeds of crime globally.[5] It is difficult to know just how much money is laundered although the United Nations Office on Drugs and Crime currently estimates the amount is somewhere between two and five per cent of global gross domestic product (GDP) (US$800 billon to US$2 trillion).[6]

The range of money laundering methods or typologies is very broad. They include the exchange of cash in small or massive amounts, the smuggling of cash, the purchase of bearer instruments (bearer bonds, money orders, etc), the wire transfer of funds through local and foreign banks, trusts, shell corporations (companies with no substantive business), and brokerage houses, the use of internet transactions, the over-, under-, and multiple-invoicing of goods and services, the false description of goods and services, the use of high cash turnover businesses such as laundromats, real estate, and insurance, the purchase and sale of high-value movable goods (art, stamps, diamonds, gold, etc), and the use of traditional remittance schemes such as *hawala* (an ancient Middle Eastern informal alternative value transfer system where payment to a broker in one state can be retrieved from another in another state without any movement of money). Many of these schemes have a transnational aspect. For example, in the famous *Pizza Connection* case Sicilian Mafiosi smuggled heroin into the US and laundered the profits through various pizza parlours in New York.[7] In the more recent *Bosporus* case, the cash profits of a Kurdish heroin wholesaler were laundered in a sophisticated scheme through an Iranian-owned bureau de change which deposited the cash into German banks; the money was transferred by wire to money changers in New York, then diverted to Dubai and, if required, returned to Germany and Turkey.[8] *Liaquat Ali, Akhtar Hussain and Mohsan Khan Shahid Bhatti v R*[9] involved the use of *hawala* by travel agents to launder the profits of drug trafficking in the UK back to Asia.

---

[3] AVM Leong, *The Disruption of International Organized Crime: An Analysis of Legal and Non-Legal Strategies* (Aldershot: Ashgate, 2007), 30.

[4] M Levi and P Reuter, 'Money Laundering' 34 *Crime and Justice* (2006) 289, 314.

[5] G Stessens, *Money Laundering: A New International Law Enforcement Model* (Cambridge: CUP, 2000), 9.

[6] UNODC, 'Money Laundering and Globalization', available at <https://www.unodc.org/unodc/en/money-laundering/globalization.html> last visited 2 June 2017.

[7] RJ Kelly, *The Upperworld and the Underworld: Case Studies of Racketeering and Business Infiltration in the United States* (New York: Kluwer, 1999), 122.

[8] Levi and Reuter, above n 4, 316.   [9] [2005] EWCA Crim 87.

A range of actors/agents provide money-laundering services to criminals. Financial institutions and particularly banks may be consciously involved or be used as instruments by others. Lawyers, financial advisors, stockbrokers, insurance agents, real estate agents, accountants, car dealers, money exchangers, jewellers, pawnbrokers, casinos, art dealers, indeed any business providing financial services or handling valuable goods, can engage in money laundering. Frequently, the perpetrators of the predicate offence carry out the task themselves. States facilitate money laundering by providing legal guarantees of bank secrecy and weak regulation to create financial secrecy havens that offer money launderers an array of opportunities. All of these actors are financially motivated; even states that provide a legal haven for launderers benefit from the licensing of shell banks.

From a law enforcement perspective 'going after the money' has many attractions. It allows law enforcement to suppress the activities of those who provide laundering services. It can also lead back to the criminals who organize and commit predicate offences (although in fact most investigations begin with the predicate offence and then move to money laundering[10]). It can be used as a surrogate charge for the predicate offence when the predicate offence cannot be proved or it can serve as one of multiple charges.[11] It also allows states to establish jurisdiction over money laundering within their territories in situations where they don't have jurisdiction over predicate offences that take place outside their territories. For all of these reasons, it is particularly useful against organized crime.[12] This kind of reasoning has led to the expansion of measures used against money laundering to suppress other forms of 'threat finance' such as tax evasion, corruption, terrorist finance, and the financing of the proliferation of weapons of mass destruction.

10.3 The Rationale for Criminalizing Money Laundering as a Separate Offence

Money laundering was first detached from drug trafficking in the US in the 1980s. Prior to the criminalization of money laundering the only crime a drug dealer who dealt with the profits of their crime by, for example, changing the cash at a money changers, would have committed was drug trafficking. Someone else changing the funds for the dealer would at most have been liable (at least in common law systems) as an accessory after the fact (the principal offender could not be an accessory to their own offence). The invention of money laundering as an offence reconceptualized this conduct as liability for an entirely separate offence.

Status as a separate offence suggests that money laundering is per se harmful, and that there is a general public interest in its suppression and specific denunciation. The perception that money laundering creates a separate harm arose because of evidence in the US of the laundering of alarmingly large amounts of 'dirty' money.[13] Money laundering is now considered to have particular negative economic, security, political,

---

[10] Levi and Reuter, above n 4, 338.
[11] See N Abrams, 'The New Ancillary Offences' 1 *Criminal Law Forum* (1989) 1, 3.
[12] Stessens, above n 5, 9.   [13] Abrams, above n 11, 9.

and social consequences. These harmful consequences range from the re-financing of crime, the penetration of the licit economy, and the corruption of government, to the destabilization of the international financial system because of the rapid and unpredictable movement of enormous profits through the system.[14] These concerns are reflected in paragraph 5 of the preamble of the 1988 UN Drug Trafficking Convention, which states that the authors of the Convention are 'aware that illicit traffic generates large financial profits and wealth enabling transnational criminal organisations to penetrate, contaminate and corrupt the structures of government, legitimate commercial and financial business, and society at all its levels'.

However, the moral justifications for the separate criminalization of money laundering have been questioned by Alldridge.[15] He notes that removal of incentive for further commission of predicate crimes is an unproven empirical claim that is not self-evident (the high profits would still provide sufficient incentive). The notion that money laundering involves complicity in the predicate offence is open to the difficulty of specifying which predicate offence the launderer is complicit in (eg drug possession or drug possession for the purposes of supply or drug supply, or drug cultivation?) and the fact that in practice courts pay little attention to the predicate offence when setting penalties. Arguments that money laundering reaches the criminal kingpins are vulnerable because in the absence of evidence linking them to the predicate offences there is no justification for using money laundering against them either.[16] A more plausible rationale for taking action against money laundering is its negative impact on the global economy as a whole. It causes macroeconomic harm because it undermines the efficiency of markets as money ends up in places where regulation is poor rather than production is efficient.[17] It causes microeconomic harm through the subsidy of uncompetitive business, the corruption of professionals, and consequential harms to the banking system (through bank collapse). But Alldridge argues that even if it is accepted that there are negative economic effects, that is not enough to justify criminalization, a measure of last-resort, if there were viable alternates such as better confiscation given the miniscule contribution that any particular money launderer makes to these effects.[18]

10.4 The Domestic Roots of the Money Laundering Offence

Global action against money laundering has its roots in US law. In 1986 the US enacted the Money Laundering Control Act (MLCA),[19] which created three main offences. The first, the domestic laundering of monetary instruments, is provided for in section 1956(a)(1):

> Whoever, knowing that the property involved in a financial transaction represents the proceeds of some form of unlawful activity, conducts or attempts to conduct

---

[14] V Tanzi, *Money Laundering and the International Financial System*, IMF Working Paper No 96/55 (Washington: IMF, 1996), 6–7.

[15] P Alldridge, 'The Moral Limits of Money Laundering' 5 *Buffalo Criminal Law Review* (2001–2) 286.

[16] ibid, 288–90.   [17] ibid, 305 et seq.   [18] ibid, 316.

[19] Subtitle H of the Anti-Drug Abuse Act of 1986, incorporated as part of chapter 53 of Title 31.

such a financial transaction which in fact involves the proceeds of specified unlawful activity—

(A) (i) with the intent to promote the carrying on of specified unlawful activity; or

    (ii) with intent to engage in conduct constituting [tax evasion]; or

(B) knowing that the transaction is designed in whole or in part: (i) to conceal or disguise the nature, the location, the source, the ownership, or the control of the proceeds of specified unlawful activity; or (ii) to avoid a transaction reporting requirement under State or Federal law, … [commits an offence].

The offence has four elements:

a) property that represents proceeds[20] derived from a specified unlawful activity (any one of a list of predicate crimes);

b) knowledge that the property is the proceeds of a predicate unlawful activity (although the prosecution need only establish that the accused knew that the property was the proceeds of 'some form of unlawful activity' and not what that activity was[21]);

c) a financial transaction (it must either involve one or more monetary instruments, the movement of funds by wire or other means, the transfer of title to real property, or the use of a financial institution); and

d) one of the four listed forms of *mens rea*, (i) the intent to promote the carrying on of a specified unlawful activity, (ii) the intent to engage in tax fraud or tax evasion, (iii) knowledge that the transaction was designed to conceal or disguise the nature, the location, the source, the ownership, or the control of the proceeds, or (iv) knowledge that the transaction was designed to avoid a currency transaction reporting requirement.[22]

The third form of *mens rea* requires knowledge of a concealment design,[23] which has been interpreted as importing a 'design requirement' that separates the offence from mere spending of criminal proceeds. The US Supreme Court held in *Cuellar v United States*[24] that the fact the defendants concealed US$81,000 in a hidden compartment in a car driven through Texas to Mexico was insufficient to sustain a conviction, and it had to be proved he knew that the purpose of taking the funds to Mexico, rather than simply its effect, was to conceal or disguise the funds' nature, location, source, ownership, or control.

The second offence under section 1956(a)(2) criminalizes transnational money laundering transactions by criminalizing the transport, transmission, or transfer of funds across the border (this can be by any means of wire transfer or transfer of monetary instruments which either originates or terminates in the US) with one of the four listed forms of intention (ie, promoting, concealing, or avoiding reporting requirements). A third offence, under section 1956(a)(3) aims to suppress either attempts to

---

[20] In *US v Santos*, 533 US 507 (2008), the Supreme Court decided proceeds in 18 USC §1956(a)(1)(A)(i) must be 'profits' not just gross receipts.

[21] 18 USC §1956(c)(1).   [22] *United States v Brown*, 186 F3d 661, 667–8 (5th Circuit 1999).

[23] 18 USC §1956(a)(1)(B)(i).   [24] 553 USC 550 (2008).

or the actual conduct of money laundering transactions when the money has in fact been provided by the authorities in a sting operation.

The scope of money laundering was expanded by a further major offence in the MLCA, engaging in monetary transactions in property derived from specified unlawful activity. Section 1957(a) prohibits someone from knowingly engaging or attempting to engage in a monetary transaction in criminally derived property of a value greater than US$10,000 and which is derived from specified unlawful activity. Like the section 1956(a) offences it requires: (a) the proceeds of a crime; (b) knowledge of unlawful derivation; but (c) the financial transaction need only reach a stipulated monetary threshold. A specific purpose is not required.

In the MLCA model, which has been internationalized in a range of treaties beginning with the 1988 Drug Trafficking Convention, the money laundering offence has two major features: (a) its ancillary nature and (b) the 'internal' conduct and mental elements involved in the offence itself. A feature of the US model, which as we shall see, has been slowly abandoned, is the requirement of 'design', which limited the scope of the offence to deliberate laundering of criminal proceeds.

10.5 The 'External' Elements of the Money Laundering Offence—The Predicate Offence

10.5.1 From laundering drug trafficking proceeds to 'all crimes' laundering

Money laundering is a special kind of ancillary or derivative offence,[25] distinct from but predicated upon the crime that produces the money, the predicate offence (there should be evidence of this crime, although there is no necessity for a conviction in order to make a conviction for money laundering possible). The US MLCA enumerates the predicate crimes, and the first step in the development of transnational penal responses to money laundering, the requirement to criminalize different forms of laundering of the proceeds of drug trafficking through article 3(1) of the 1988 Drug Trafficking Convention, followed suit. In the 1988 Convention the predicate offences are the drug trafficking offences set out in article 3(1)(a), while the ancillary money laundering offences are provided for in article 3(1)(b) and (c).

The emphasis in transnational criminal law since 1988 has been on the expansion of the range of predicate offences to 'all crimes' money laundering. In terms, for example, of article 1(e) of the 1990 Council of Europe Convention on Laundering, Search, Seizure and Confiscation of the Proceeds of Crime[26] (the Strasbourg Convention), the crime of money laundering applies to the proceeds of 'any criminal offence'. In its Recommendations,[27] the FATF, the main institution for suppressing money laundering (examined further below), also recommends extension of money laundering to

---

[25] Abrams above n 11, 5–6.   [26] 8 November 1990, ETS No 141, in force 1 September 1993.
[27] The FATF Recommendations: International Standards on Combating Money Laundering and the Financing of Terrorism and Proliferation, 16 February 2012, updated October 2016, available at <http://www.fatf-gafi.org/media/fatf/documents/recommendations/pdfs/FATF_Recommendations.pdf> last visited 2 June 2017.

'all serious offences, with a view to including the widest range' of predicate offences.[28]
There are various reasons for this expansion: the fact that the global AML regulatory
regime could only be applied to the laundering of money from predicate offences, the
difficulty of extracting the profits of drug trafficking when they are intermingled with
other offences, and more recently the use of money laundering as a fallback crime
because of the failure to provide a comprehensive definition of organized crime in the
UNTOC.[29]

However, there are various potential problems with expansion to 'all crimes' laundering. The range of predicates to which money laundering applies dictates the scope
of the offence of money laundering, and its application to the laundering of the proceeds of trivial offences has the potential to result in over-criminalization. Requests for
cooperation in regard to very trivial offences have the added potential to undermine
international cooperation in suppressing serious criminal activity. For these reasons
various methods have been used to limit predicate offences to serious offences, such
as the enumeration of predicate offences and the imposition of evaluative thresholds.

The UNTOC, for example, expands the range of predicates to 'any offence as a result
of which proceeds have been generated',[30] but includes a threshold requirement of seriousness in respect of the predicate offences to which it is to apply. Article 6(2)(b) provides
that money laundering predicate offences include (in addition to those offences in articles 5, 8, and 23) at a minimum all 'serious crime as defined in article 2', while article
2 defines 'serious crime' as 'conduct constituting an offence punishable by a maximum
deprivation of liberty of at least four years or a more serious penalty'. It follows that if
a party imposes anything less than a four-year maximum penalty that party considers
the offence in question not to be serious enough to serve as predicate offences for the
article 6 money laundering offences.

This crude measure of seriousness of offences can be compared to the complex
attempt by the FATF to ensure some parity in the scope of money laundering among
states. FATF's Recommendation 3 recommends the application of money laundering 'to all serious crime', but FATF notes that '[p]redicate offences may be described
by reference to all offences; or to a threshold linked either to a category of serious
offences; or to the penalty of imprisonment applicable to the predicate offence (threshold approach); or to a list of predicate offences; or a combination of these approaches'.

However, echoing the UNTOC it points out that if a state uses the latter it should
either include all serious offences in its law, or offences punishable by a maximum
penalty of more than one year, or for those countries that use a minimum threshold
all offences punished by a minimum penalty of more than six months. The FATF also
notes that each country should at a minimum include a range of offences within each
of the 'designated categories of offences', which include the following transnational
crimes: organized crime, terrorism, human trafficking, migrant smuggling, drug trafficking, arms trafficking, corruption, counterfeiting, environmental crime, hostage-
taking, and piracy.[31]

---

[28] Recommendation 3.   [29] See Chapter 8.   [30] Article 2(h).
[31] Interpretive Note to Recommendation 3 of the 2012 Recommendations, 34, paras 2, 3.

The EU has taken a variety of approaches to the problem of which predicates result in money laundering. While the First EU Money Laundering Directive (1991)[32] limited money laundering to drug trafficking offences, and the Second EU Directive[33] simply expanded the list of predicates to include serious crimes such as drug trafficking, transnational organized crime, and corruption, the EU Money Laundering Framework Decision of 26 June 2001[34] switched to an evaluative approach based on a one-year punishment threshold and the Third EU Directive[35] followed suit. The Fourth Directive uses both an evaluative and enumerative approach.[36] Some EU member states also use a mixed approach. Article 368 of the Portuguese Penal Code provides, for example, for a general predicate—all offences with a six months' penalty—and then lists predicate crimes: pimping, sexual abuse, species trafficking, extortion, corruption, drug trafficking, influence peddling, organ trafficking, tax fraud, and weapons trafficking. Germany also limits predicates for money laundering to felonies and certain listed misdemeanours.[37] Globally, many states still limit the list of predicate crimes either through their domestic law excluding those considered unimportant domestically or limiting predicate crimes to crimes carrying a maximum penalty above a certain threshold.[38]

10.5.2 Extraterritorial predicates

The ancillary nature of money laundering creates a jurisdictional problem where the predicate offence occurs extraterritorially and the money laundering territorially. Certain states simply apply the general principle that the money laundering constitutes an individual part of the course of mostly extraterritorial conduct that occurs territorially. Other states require that the predicate offence occur within their criminal jurisdiction in order for them to establish jurisdiction over the laundering of the proceeds of that offence. This problem can only be resolved by a change to their jurisdictional laws allowing them to establish jurisdiction over the laundering even when the predicate offence takes place in another jurisdiction.

While it was unclear whether the 1988 Drug Trafficking Convention requires parties to extend the scope of the money laundering offence to cover extraterritorial predicates, the UNTOC and United Nations Convention against Corruption (UNCAC)[39]

---

[32] Council Directive 91/308/EEC of 10 June 1991 on the prevention of the use of the financial system for the purpose of money laundering, OJ L 166, 28 June 1991, 77.

[33] Directive 2001/97/EC of the European Parliament and of the Council of 4 December 2001 amending the Council Directive 91/308/EEC on the prevention of the use of the financial system for the purpose of money laundering, OJ L 344, 28 December 2004, 76.

[34] OJ L 182, 5 July 2001, 1.

[35] Directive 2005/60/EC of the European Parliament and of the Council of 26 October 2005 on the prevention of the use of the financial system for the purpose of money laundering and terrorist financing, OJ L 309, 25 November 2005, 15.

[36] Article 3(4), Directive 2015/849 of the European Parliament and of the Council of 20 May 2015 on the prevention of the use of the financial system for the purposes of money laundering or terrorist financing, OJ L 141, 73.

[37] Section 261(4)(b) Deutsches Strafgesetzbuch (StGB).

[38] M Arnone and L Borlini, 'International Anti-money Laundering Programs' 13(3) *Journal of Money Laundering Control* (2010) 226, 249.

[39] Article 23(2)(c).

do so expressly. Article 6(2)(c) of the UNTOC attempts to provide a model for national law reform by requiring parties to take jurisdiction over accessory offences when the predicate offence occurs extraterritorially subject to two conditions: (i) that the 'relevant conduct' is an offence in the other state where it is committed; and (ii) that it would be an offence if it occurred in the party establishing jurisdiction. FATF Recommendation 1 follows suit. The Canadian Criminal Code makes the necessary provision for this double criminality test in section 462.3 which includes within the definition of 'proceeds of crime' 'any property, benefit or advantage, within or outside Canada, obtained or derived ... as a result of ... (b) an act or omission anywhere that, if it had occurred in Canada, would have constituted a designated offence'.

10.5.3 Self-laundering

The ancillary nature of money laundering also suggests that the money launderers are not the same people who commit the predicate offence (ie laundering is carried out by a third party). In many instances, however, the same person who commits the predicate offence launders the proceeds (self-laundering). In numerous legal systems even if the accused is acquitted of the predicate crime, the accused can still be prosecuted for and convicted of money laundering.[40] While expedient, criminalizing self-laundering raises the problem of cumulative convictions and double jeopardy. The principle of subsidiarity which applies in many legal systems, including Germany's, does not permit a party to the predicate offence to be liable for assistance after the fact—self-launderers must be prosecuted for the predicate.[41] Article 6(2)(e) of the UNTOC acknowledges this approach by allowing parties to avoid applying the money laundering offence to those persons who have committed the predicate offence if their 'fundamental principles' do not permit them to do so. Article 23(2)(e) of UNCAC and the FATF Recommendations[42] follow suit. The FATF, however, presses members to prosecute self-laundering as a separate offence in all cases. In its evaluation of New Zealand it argued that self-money laundering through the use by the receiver of the proceeds was not hit by double jeopardy because it involves 'active behaviour' that was not hit by the prohibition on being punished twice for receiving the property.[43]

10.5.4 Terrorist offences as predicate offences

Finally, it is worth noting that the terrorist financing crimes discussed in Chapter 8 are similar to money laundering in that they require the raising of the finance for a subsequent action, and thus have an ancillary nature. Terrorism can and frequently does function as a predicate offence. China, for example, criminalizes the laundering of the proceeds of terrorism in article 191 of its Criminal Code. But terrorist financing

---

[40] See, eg, article 174 of the Russian Criminal Code.
[41] Section 261(9)(2) of the *Strafgesetzbuch (StGB)* (see also section 275(3)).
[42] Interpretative Note 3(6) of the FATF Recommendations.
[43] FATF, 'Mutual Evaluation Report: Anti-Money Laundering and Combating the Financing of Terrorism: New Zealand', 16 October 2009, para 157, <http://www.fatf-gafi.org/media/fatf/documents/reports/mer/MER%20New%20Zealand%20ful.pdf> last visited 2 June 2017.

offences differ conceptually from money laundering in that raising money in order to finance an act of terrorism may not involve criminal proceeds and may be gathered innocently as donations of untainted property. Terrorist financing derives its criminality not from a predicate but from its subject—the subsequent terrorism offence, which the funds are supposed by the accused to be going to be used for (they do not actually have to be used for that purpose)—the inverse of the structure of the money laundering offence. FATF Recommendation 5, which calls upon countries not only to criminalize terrorist financing but also to ensure that 'such offences are designated as money laundering predicate offences', envisages a money laundering offence that occurs when after provision or collection of funds with the necessary intention that they should be or knowledge that they are to be used to carry out terrorist acts[44] some effort is made to convert or transfer, conceal or disguise, or take possession of such funds. In other words, the predicate is an offence the criminality of which is derived from the putative act of terrorism in the mind of the collector or provider, which in an excessively strained fashion is in turn used to justify criminalizing laundering of those funds. Nevertheless evaluative approaches to predicate crimes in state practice will enable terrorist financing to serve as a predicate to money laundering, because terrorist financing is invariably regarded as a serious crime and carries heavy penalties.

10.6 The 'Internal' Elements of the Money Laundering Offence

10.6.1 Introduction

Article 3(1) of the 1988 Drug Trafficking Convention was the first major multilateral penal measure against money laundering. Article 6 of the UNTOC and article 23 of the UNCAC are in very similar terms. They oblige parties to create three new offences aimed at global curtailment of drug-money laundering. Article 3(1) of the 1988 Convention reads:

(b) (i) The conversion or transfer of property, knowing that such property is derived from any offence or offences established in accordance with subparagraph (a) of this paragraph, or from an act of participation in such offence or offences, for the purpose of concealing or disguising the illicit origin of the property or of assisting any person who is involved in the commission of such an offence or offences to evade the legal consequences of his actions;

   (ii) The concealment or disguise of the true nature, source, location, disposition, movement, rights with respect to, or ownership of property, knowing that such property is derived from an offence or offences established in accordance with subparagraph (a) of this paragraph ...

(c) ...

   (i) The acquisition, possession or use of property, knowing, at the time of receipt, that such property was derived from an offence or offences established in

---

[44] Article 2(1) of the Terrorist Financing Convention.

accordance with subparagraph (a) of this paragraph or from an act of participation in such offence or offences.

Although they do not use the term 'money laundering' these three distinct parts of article 3(1) describe the conduct and mental elements of money laundering, and this three-part categorization has been followed in later treaties.[45] Each offence involves dealing with the proceeds of crime, defined in article 1(p) as property obtained, directly or indirectly, through the commission of an article 3(1) trafficking offence. Article 1(q) defines 'property in turn as assets of every kind, whether corporeal or incorporeal, moveable or immovable'. The FATF more broadly recommends that illicitly derived property in money laundering include 'any type of property, regardless of its value, that directly or indirectly represents the proceeds of crime'.[46]

10.6.2 Placement

Article 3(1)(b)(i) covers 'placement', the introduction of the illicitly derived property into the licit financial system.[47] The material element required is the conversion/transfer of property, for example the converting of cash into property or the transfer of cash. The mental element has two parts: (i) knowledge of the illicit derivation from drug offences of the property (ii) with the specific purpose of either concealing/disguising such illicit derivation or assisting an offender to evade justice. Some domestic offences, such as section 327 of the UK's Proceeds of Crimes Act 2002 roll these forms of conduct and the next, so-called layering, into one offence.

10.6.3 Layering

Article 3(1)(b)(ii) requires parties to criminalize 'layering', disguising the illicit origins of these proceeds once they are in the licit financial system.[48] The material element required is either concealing or disguising the true nature, source, location, disposition, movement, rights with respect to, or ownership of property. The mental element is knowledge of the illicit derivation of the property. This provision echoes the use of conceal and disguise in section 1956 of the MLCA. Concealment can take many forms. In *US v Barber*,[49] for example, an expert witness explained that even the relatively straightforward deposit and then withdrawal of cash from cannabis dealing into a bank account concealed its illicit origins at several levels:

> First, because the deposit slip does not show the bills' denominations, it cannot later be determined that a large number of small bills was deposited. Second, because bills used for buying drugs often retain traces of drugs, the deposit eliminates the possibility of linking the money to the drug trade. Third, depositing drug money into an account that contains legitimate income 'lends credence or credibility to the

---

[45] Eg, article 6(1) of the 1990 Council of Europe Convention and article 6(1) of the UNTOC.
[46] Interpretive note 3(4) of the FATF Recommendations.
[47] Article 6(1)(a)(i) of the UNTOC; article 23(1)(a)(i) of the UNCAC.
[48] Article 6(1)(a)(ii) of the UNTOC; article 23(1)(a)(ii) of the UNCAC.
[49] 80 F3d 964 (4th Cir. 1996), at 970.

[drug] money.' And, finally, withdrawals of large bills facilitate physical concealment because one large bill is easier to conceal than several small ones.

10.6.4 Integration

Article 3(1)(c)(i) requires parties to criminalize 'integration', the acquisition/possession/use of the illicitly derived property knowing of its illicit derivation (an obligation subject to the basic concepts of the party's legal system because it covers the most passive forms of cooperation with the perpetrator of the predicate offence).[50] It breaks downs as follows: the material element is the acquisition, possession, or use of the property, and the mental element is again knowledge of the illicit derivation of the property. Despite its difficulties, parties have met this obligation. Section 329 of the UK's Proceeds of Crimes Act 2002, for example, criminalizes the acquisition, use, and possession of criminal property.

10.6.5 The mental element

The layering and integration offences rely only on 'knowledge' even though it is not usually used as the sole foundation of criminal liability because it places too onerous a burden on those engaged only in commercial activities. Moreover, the provisions in the treaties only provide for minimum standards,[51] while article 3(3) of the 1988 Convention which provides that 'knowledge, intent or purpose' can be inferred from objective circumstances eases the burden on the prosecution, particularly where sophisticated money laundering typologies are used and the accused denies intention or knowledge.[52]

The trend in state practice is to lighten the burden on the prosecution even further (and broaden the scope of the offence) by loosening *mens rea* requirements. Someone commits the offence of money laundering in terms of section 327 of the UK's 2002 Proceeds of Crime Act, for example, if they conceal, disguise, convert, transfer, or remove (from any part of the UK) 'criminal property'. Property is 'criminal' in terms of section 340(3) if '(a) it constitutes a person's benefit from criminal conduct or it represents such a benefit (in whole or part and whether directly or indirectly); and (b) the alleged offender knows or suspects that it constitutes or represents such a benefit'. There is no purposive *mens rea* requirement in respect of the concealment or conversion of the property; the scope of the UK Act is more extensive than the suppression conventions because knowledge or suspicion renders the property 'criminal'. The suspicion does not have to be on reasonable grounds, but the possibility has to be 'more than fanciful'.[53] Article 261(5) of the German Criminal Code goes further, basing the crime on *leichtfertigkeit* (thoughtlessness).[54] The Organization of American States' CICAD Model Regulations Concerning Money Laundering Offences Connected to

---

[50] Article 6(1)(b)(i) of the UNTOC; article 23(1)(b)(i) of the UNCAC.
[51] See, eg article 24 of the 1988 Drug Trafficking Convention.
[52] See also Interpretive Note 3(7)(a) of the FATF Recommendations.
[53] *R v Da Silva* [2007] 1 WLR 303, 309.   [54] Section 261(5) of the *Strafgesetzbuch*.

Illicit Drug Trafficking and Related Offences[55] uses the terms 'know or should have known, or intentionally ignorant'. Article 9(3) of the updated 2005 Council of Europe Convention on Laundering, Search, Seizure and Confiscation of the Proceeds from Crime and on the Financing of Terrorism[56] (the Warsaw Convention) expressly gives parties the option of using an objective standard: where they 'ought to have assumed the property was proceeds'. Hong Kong extends liability to 'reasonable grounds to believe'[57] as does the Bahamas,[58] while South Africa also adds an objective test.[59] Criminalization of inadvertent money laundering expands the scope of the offence and makes it easier to prosecute but raises concerns. Criminalizing risk, it includes within the scope of the offence those who do not enquire as to the customer's or beneficial owner's identity when they should have, even if they honestly believed the funds to be derived from a non-criminal source. Critics have pointed to the 'risk of punishing everyday behaviour in cases where there is neither intention nor knowledge of money laundering'.[60]

10.6.6 Inchoate laundering and participation

Because money laundering is a stand-alone crime it can also have inchoate versions and different levels of participation. Thus article 6(1)(b)(ii) of the UNTOC requires parties, 'subject to the basic concepts' of their legal systems, to criminalize '[p]articipation in, association with or conspiracy to commit, attempts to commit and aiding and abetting, facilitating and counselling the commission of any of the' article 6 money laundering offences. States have had little difficulty in this regard. Section 3 of India's Prevention of Money Laundering Act 2002 provides that '[w]hosoever directly or indirectly attempts to indulge or knowingly assists . . . in any process or activity connected with the proceeds of crime and projecting it as untainted property shall be guilty of the offence of money laundering'.

10.7 Criminal Liability for Legal Persons

The financial institutions through which money is laundered are frequently corporations or some other form of legal person. If money is laundered through such an organization, it is often very difficult to identify an individual who is subjectively aware of what is going on and who can be held criminally responsible. Moreover, prosecution of low-level employees does not reach into the boardroom. The suppression conventions therefore provide a number of obligations on parties to ensure that it is possible to impose criminal liability on legal persons for money laundering.[61] These obligations

---

[55] CICAD is the OAS's Inter-American Drug Abuse Control Commission. The model law was adopted in 1997.
[56] 16 May 2005, CETS 198, in force 1 May 2008.
[57] Section 25 of Organized and Serious Crimes Ordinance (Cap 455).
[58] Section 43 of the Proceeds of Crime Act 2000.
[59] Section 4 of the Prevention of Organized Crime Act 1998.
[60] Arnone and Borlini, above n 38, 257.
[61] See, eg, article 10 of UNTOC and article 26 of the UNCAC.

are usually subject to the basic legal principles of the party, and liability can be criminal, civil, or administrative so as to cater for states that do not apply criminal liability to legal persons. Paragraph 7(c) of the Interpretive Note to FATF Recommendation 3, for example, provides that countries should ensure that 'criminal liability, and, where that is not possible, civil or administrative liability, should apply to legal persons'. In practice, however, the FATF has taken a very restrictive view in recent years of when civil liability only is acceptable, thus compelling certain mainly civil law states to use criminal liability for companies. In 2010, for example, the FATF evaluation of Luxembourg singled it out for not providing for criminal liability for legal persons and it responded by immediately enacting a new law to make this possible.[62]

Article 10 of the Council of Europe's Warsaw Convention points the way to how this can be done. It obliges parties to ensure that legal persons can be held liable for money laundering

> committed for their benefit by any natural person, acting either individually or as part of an organ of the legal person, who has a leading position within the legal person, based on: a. a power of representation of the legal person; or b. an authority to take decisions on behalf of the legal person; or c. an authority to exercise control within the legal person . . . .

This provision sets out different doctrinal options that parties may adopt to ensure the legal liability of juridical persons where the juridical person is identified with those who exercise control based on representation, decision-making authority, or controlling authority. The Convention also provides for a separate obligation to ensure that a legal person can be held liable where the lack of supervision or control by a natural person makes possible the commission of money laundering offences 'for the benefit of that legal person by a natural person under its authority'.[63]

10.8 Punishment for Money Laundering

As with the other transnational crimes, parties to the suppression conventions that contain money laundering offences are only obliged to ensure that these offences are subject to adequate punishment or punishment that takes into account the gravity of the offence.[64] Although most states apply a full range of penalties, the US set a standard of severe punishment in the MLCA. Section 1956(a), for example, carries a maximum penalty of not more than US$500,000 or twice the value of the property involved in the transaction, whichever is greater, or imprisonment for not more than twenty years, or both.[65] Other states have followed this trend towards harsh deterrence. Barbados, for example, applies a maximum penalty of twenty-five years and/or a fine of BDS$2million (US$4 million) to conviction of money laundering on indictment.[66]

---

[62] Law of 3 March 2010; see FATF, 'Sixth Follow-up Report, Mutual Evaluation of Luxembourg', February 2014, (FATF/OECD, 2014), 8, available at <http://www.fatf-gafi.org/media/fatf/documents/reports/mer/FUR-Luxembourg-2014.pdf> last visited 2 June 2017.
[63] Article 10(2).   [64] See, eg, article 30(1) of the UNCAC.   [65] 18 USC §1956(b).
[66] Section 6(b) of the Money Laundering and Financing of Terrorism (Prevention and Control) Act 2011.

Germany takes a more modulated approach applying a punishment range of three months to five years for ordinary cases, up to ten years in serious cases involving money laundering on a commercial basis or by a gang, and not more than two years or a fine when the *mens rea* is *culpa*.[67] Punishment for legal persons is usually financial and heavy in order to induce them to get their house in order but this is not always the case. In Japan, for example, the heaviest available fine is 10 million Yen (US$94,500), which the 2008 FATF mutual evaluation of Japan did not consider dissuasive.[68]

10.9 The Role of the Financial Action Task Force

Anomalously, in the development of transnational criminal law there is no separate global treaty on money laundering, despite the express call for the negotiation of such a treaty by the UN's High Level Panel on Threats, Challenges and Change.[69] Instead the formation of the FATF was proposed at the G7 summit in 1988 because of its distrust of the UN's capacity to regulate the financial industry, a far more complex task than criminal law making.[70] Independent of the Organisation for Economic Co-operation and Development (OECD) (where it is housed), it behaves like an inter-governmental organization but isn't one because it's not a creature of treaty; it describes itself as an international intergovernmental body.[71] It is thus not universal, not a legal person, and has no rights and duties separate from the states creating it.

Originally composed of the G7, the EU Commission and eight other OECD states, the FATF's membership has expanded to include other countries that meet the condition that they be of 'strategic importance' in global finance (countries with strong banking sectors and GDPs), although it is not global. FATF Style Regional bodies (FSRBs)[72] are used to bring non-members into the system.[73] The Caribbean Financial Action Task Force (CFATF), for example, was established in 1990 and has adopted and monitors the implementation of the FATF Standards. Members of the FSRBs hold associate membership in FATF but the quid pro quo is FATF's membership of these

---

[67] Section 261(1), (4), and (5) respectively of the *Strafgesetzbuch*.

[68] FATF, 'Mutual Evaluation of Japan, Executive Summary', 17 October 2008, para 9, available at <http://www.fatf-gafi.org/media/fatf/documents/reports/mer/MER%20Japan%20ES.pdf> last visited 1 June 2017.

[69] 'A More Secure World: Our Shared Responsibility', The Report of the High Level Panel on Threats, Challenges and Change, UN Doc A/59/565 and corr 1, para 174.

[70] M Pieth, 'International Standards against Money Laundering' in M Pieth and G Ailofi (eds), *A Comparative Guide to Money Laundering: A Critical Analysis of Systems in Singapore, Switzerland, the UK and USA* (Cheltenham: Edward Elgar, 2004), 3, 8.

[71] C Rose, *International Anti-Corruption Norms: Their Creation and Influence on Domestic Legal Systems* (Oxford: OUP, 2015), 183–85.

[72] The Asia/Pacific Group on Money Laundering (APG); the Caribbean Financial Action Task Force (CFATF); the Eurasian Group (EAG); Eastern and Southern Africa Anti-Money Laundering Group (ESAAMLG); the Council of Europe Committee of Experts on the Evaluation of Anti-Money Laundering Measures and the Financing of Terrorism (MONEYVAL); the Financial Action Task Force on Money Laundering in South America (GAFISUD); Inter Governmental Action Group against Money Laundering in West Africa (GIABA); the Middle East and North Africa Financial Action Task Force (MENAFATF); and the Central African Group on Money Laundering (GABAC).

[73] Rose, above n 71, 178.

FSRBs which enables it to maintain a guiding hand over the direction of the system globally.[74]

Once established the FATF proved a flexible instrument for enforcing existing treaty obligations and expanding upon them; an attempt by Council of Europe members to reduce FATF's original Forty Recommendations adopted in 1990 to treaty obligations in the negotiation of the Warsaw Convention in 2005 was resisted by FATF members. The recommendations are based on majority support rather than the lowest common denominator provisions adopted by consensus in treaty making.[75] Although avowedly a policy-making organization, the FATF's membership criteria and sanctions mechanism actually give its recommendations a binding force much greater than suppression conventions.[76] Members of FATF consent in writing to adopt and implement its recommendations. Without a treaty obligation to do so this amounts to a strong 'political commitment' to implement, something reflected in the fact that although the FATF recommends that countries 'should' adopt its recommendations, 'should' is to be read as 'must' implement according to the glossary of the 2012 Recommendations. In effect, the FATF compels them to do so.[77] This occurs primarily through the evaluation process (discussed in detail in Chapter 22). The FATF recommendations have also been endorsed by UN organizations; Security Council Resolution 1617 of 2005, for example, strongly urges all UN member states to implement the FATF recommendations.

As noted, the FATF has slowly expanded its mandate from drug money laundering in 1989, to all crimes laundering in 1991, terrorist financing in 2001, and proliferation of weapons of mass destruction in 2008. The FATF was designed to prevent the banking system from being used for money laundering.[78] The model it uses is based on three pillars:

i)   criminalization of money laundering and terrorist financing as a separate offence(s);

ii) holding participants in the financial system responsible for policing AML within the system; and

iii) centralizing knowledge in Financial Information Units (FIUs[79]).

Criminalization of money laundering and terrorist financing provided the foundation for the expansion of regulatory AML activity designed to prevent the use of the financial system to commit these crimes. Initially the focus of this preventive action was on banking regulation. However, it slowly became clear that effective supervision of the system requires knowledge of financial transactions and ownership structures, knowledge that only participants in the system could gather through adopting customer due diligence (CDD) programmes. The background to the FATF's adoption of CDD obligations reveals that initially the US resisted this Swiss notion as placing too much of an administrative burden on banks, preferring to rely on banks

---

[74] ibid, 48–49.

[75] FATF, 'Financial Action Task Force on Money Laundering, Report' (1990), 16, available at <www.fatf-gafi.org> last visited 3 June 2017.

[76] Rose, above n 71, 177.   [77] ibid, 193.   [78] de Koker and Turkington, above n 1, 244.

[79] See Chapter 17.

recording and reporting of financial transactions over certain amounts to block the flow of illegal funds into the banking system.[80] It changed its position during negotiation of the Forty Recommendations, but on condition that the Recommendations would reinforce the criminalization requirements in article 3 of the Drug Trafficking Convention. As adopted by the FATF, CDD has three components: (i) identification of the customer and verification of their identity through independent sources, (ii) identification and verification of the beneficial owner of the customer to ensure that ownership and control is fully understood, and (iii) understanding of the nature and purpose of the intended business relationship.[81] The FATF currently uses a risk-based approach to provide flexible self-regulation in the highly complex financial sector with its range of potential entry points for illicit proceeds.[82] In essence this requires member countries and by extension all financial actors to take measures proportionate to specific risks. Apart from criminalization and cooperation its general preventative measures emphasize ongoing financial due diligence,[83] while it suggests specific measures such as appropriate measures and enhanced monitoring of politically exposed persons (individuals entrusted with prominent public functions).[84]

A range of other international organizations reinforce AML, including the International Association of Insurance Supervisors (IAIS), the International Organization of Securities Commissioners (IOSC), and the Group of International Finance Centre Supervisors (GIFCS) (formerly the Offshore Group of Banking Supervisors, OGBS). The World Bank and International Monetary Fund are active in regard to the suppression of money laundering, assessing many countries' compliance with the FATF standards and requiring recipients of financial assistance to institute AML programmes.

10.10 Implementation of Money Laundering Offences

Legislative reform to criminalize money laundering is carefully monitored by the FATF. States have as a result been fairly active in enacting anti-money laundering offences and preventative measures. They have had technical support from tools such as the UN's International Monetary Laundering Information Network (IMoLIN), which provides a variety of examples of model legislation.

When it comes to actual implementation through prosecution, the US remains the stand out. In 2016 there were 1,201 federal investigations of money laundering, and 668 convictions, a figure that is largely in line with the previous three years.[85] However, Levi and Reuter's criticism that 'in many countries there appears to be minimal use of criminal statutes for AML purposes'[86] still appears fair in many cases. The FATF responded to criticism that it was only engaged in monitoring paper compliance[87] by expanding its focus in its fourth round of mutual evaluations after 2012 to include both (i) technical compliance and (ii) the effectiveness of a country's anti-money laundering/

---

[80] de Koker and Turkington, above n 1, 245.   [81] ibid, 241, 256–57.
[82] Recommendation 1.   [83] Recommendation 10.   [84] Recommendation 12.
[85] See 'Statistical Data Money Laundering and Bank Secrecy Act, Federal Years 2014, 2015, and 2016', US Internal Revenue Service, available at <https://www.irs.gov/uac/statistical-data-money-laundering-bank-secrecy-act-bsa> last visited 6 June 2017.
[86] Levi and Reuter, above n 4, 333.   [87] de Koker and Turkington, above n 1, 260.

counter terrorism financing framework inter alia through detection and disruption of money laundering/terrorist financing, sanctioning of criminals, and asset recovery.[88] Now even strategic jurisdictions like Singapore come in for criticism in this regard from FATF. In its 2016 mutual evaluation of Singapore the evaluator noted:[89]

> 164. While Singapore has a very strong ML investigative framework … Singapore did not demonstrate it is using this framework sufficiently to combat ML. In particular, Singapore is not adequately identifying or investigating ML relating to foreign predicates. While 66% (665 out of 1 008) of Singapore's investigations relate to foreign predicates, they almost all relate to Singaporean money mules and shell companies that allow their bank accounts to be used to receive the proceeds of foreign wire transfer frauds. Singapore did not demonstrate that it was sufficiently identifying the more complex and sophisticated forms of ML it is likely exposed to by virtue of its large financial sector and position as a trade / transport hub.

Critics have also attacked compliance records on measures designed to prevent the proceeds of crime from entering the system or their detection and reporting, with one study showing that when asked nearly half of corporate service providers that sell shell companies did not ask for proper details identifying customers while 22 per cent did not ask for any identification at all.[90]

10.11 Conclusion

The criminalization of money laundering through transnational criminal law means that today there is a growing global acceptance that it constitutes a harmful criminal activity separate from the predicate offences that produce criminal proceeds. Those prosecuted and punished for money laundering might legitimately complain, however, of violation of fair labelling, cumulative convictions, and over-criminalization as the initially narrowly drawn offence has been expanded from deliberate dealing with illicit proceeds to any dealing with those proceeds. The effectiveness of these new offences has been heavily touted but remains under question. There is still no empirical evidence that greater enforcement and prevention under the umbrella of a strategic commitment to risk assessment and cooperation will protect the financial system from abuse by criminals. It may be that the system serves other purposes, such as simply making it possible to engage in surveillance of illicit usage, something undermined, however, by simply shutting individuals out of the system (denial of service to high risk customers is now common).[91] One banking insider suggested to the author

---

[88] FATF, Methodology for Assessing Technical Compliance with the FATF Recommendations and the Effectiveness of AML/CoFT Systems, (FATF 2014), paras 42–43.

[89] FATF, 'Anti-money laundering and counter-terrorist financing measures: Singapore Mutual Evaluation Report, September 2016' (FATF: 2016), 56, available at <http://www.fatf-gafi.org/media/fatf/documents/reports/mer4/MER-Singapore-2016.pdf> last visited 9 June 2017.

[90] M Findley, D Nielson, and J Sharman, *Global Shell Games: Testing Money Launderers' and Terrorist Financiers' Access to Shell Companies* (Griffith University Centre for Governance and Public Policy, 2012), 3, available at <http://www.gfintegrity.org/wp-content/uploads/2014/05/Global-Shell-Games-2012.pdf> last visited 26 May 2017.

[91] de Koker and Turkington, above n 1, 261–62.

that the real purpose of the system is surveillance of licit financial flows in the global financial system as a whole for business purposes (intelligence). It certainly has the necessary reach. Tham labels the privatization of AML regulation in Australia, for example, the 'deputization of the entire finance sector'.[92]

---

[92] J-C Tham, 'A Risk-Based Analysis of Australia's Counterterrorism Financing Regime' 34(2) *Social Justice* (2007) 138, 144.

11

Cybercrimes

11.1 Introduction

As the Internet has grown, so has criminal activity that uses the Internet as a tool. Computers are used to harm other computers through computer viruses, phishing for data, malware, spamming, ransomware, and so forth. Computers are used to carry out new variants of old offences such as theft of information, fraud, ticketing scams, and laundering. Computers are used to sell/transfer all sorts of illicit goods from child pornography to lists of stolen credit card numbers. The incidence of these offences is burgeoning. Industry commentators noted in 2015 that the use of ransomware was reaching 'epidemic' proportions.[1] One reason for the key to the boom in cybercrimes is the deliberately unregulated nature of cyberspace; its control is in private hands. Human immersion into the digital age and human ingenuity provide the other ingredients for harmful exploitation of this space. The state has been forced into assuming a regulatory role over this privately run infrastructure because scarcely a day goes by without a report of some major global cybercriminal activity. Recent news-grabbing events range from interference in the US election of 2016[2] to the spate of ransomware attacks of early 2017, one of which was going on as this was being written.[3] The exact value of cybercrime is unknowable but costs of meeting the threat are estimated to be climbing into the trillions.[4] Focussing on the substantive criminalization of cybercrime, this chapter briefly examines the nature of cybercrime and why it calls for a transnational response, before analysing in depth the offences spelled out in the leading multinational treaty, the Council of Europe Convention against Cybercrime.[5] It then comments on the contributions made by other international instruments, before closing with a discussion of the promises and prospects of a broader UN Cybercrime Convention.

---

[1] K Savage, P Coogan, and H Lau, *The Evolution of Ransomware*, 6 August 2015, available at <https://www.symantec.com/content/dam/symantec/docs/security-center/white-papers/the-evolution-of-ransomware-15-en.pdf> last visited 2 July 2017.

[2] See US Department of Homeland Security and FBI Joint Report, *Operation Grizzly Steppe—Russian Malicious Cyber Activity*, 29 December 2016, available at <https://www.us-cert.gov/sites/default/files/publications/JAR_16-20296A_GRIZZLY%20STEPPE-2016-1229.pdf> last visited 30 June 2017.

[3] 'Global Ransomware Attack Causes Turmoil', *BBC News*, 28 June 2017, available at <http://www.bbc.com/news/technology-40416611> last visited 30 June 2017.

[4] S Morgan, 'Costs of Cybercrime Estimated to Reach $2 trillion by 2019', *Forbes* online, 17 January 2016, <https://www.forbes.com/sites/stevemorgan/2016/01/17/cyber-crime-costs-projected-to-reach-2-trillion-by-2019/#5afe885b3a91> last visited 28 June 2017.

[5] See below.

11.2 The Nature of Cybercrime

Cybercrime is a container term of convenience describing a collection of acts or a field of criminal activity, rather than a single concept. Its core meaning tends to be constituted by acts where the *object* of the offence is a computer, computer system, data etc; whereas some of the more disparate set of actions where the *modus operandi* of the offence involves the use of computers but the object is personal gain or the like are less comfortably constrained within the definitional boundaries of cybercrime.[6] The conceptual puzzle is spelling out what cybercrime encompasses now so as to enable the scope of the special regulatory response to be set appropriately. Legislators may be tempted to add a whole string of offences to the field simply because they involve the use of a computing device. The question whether these offences are validly part of 'cybercrime' depends on the centrality of the use of a computer system to carry them out. Relying on a centrality test though may be a chimera as with growing Internet connectivity nearly all crime will soon find itself in this category, and it may become necessary to address the cybercrime features of particular types of transnational crime.

One feature common to nearly all cybercrime is transnationality. This flows from the rapid movement of information backward and forward across national boundaries even in the most trivial online interaction, such as sending an email. Clough points out one of the implications: 'At a more fundamental level, the nature of modern communications is such that even where offender and victim are in the same jurisdiction, evidence of the offending is almost certain to have passed through, or to be stored in, other jurisdictions.'[7]

This causes another headache for regulators, jurisdictional proliferation. Jurisdictional impact can, however, be mapped in geographical terms[8] and as discussed in Chapter 16, the level of difficulty of the problems of state regulation that are said to arise because of the incompatibility of orthodox principles of state jurisdiction with the unbounded nature of the Internet [9] is probably overstated.

There are, however, a range of other regulatory features of cybercrime that present challenges in trying to police activity on the Internet. These include the volatility of data, which can easily be overwritten and lost, the anonymity of users, increasing use of cryptography, and strong multiplier effects.[10] Moreover, cybercime is organized crime; some suggest by upwards of 80 per cent.[11]

---

[6] UNODC, *Comprehensive Study on Cybercrime* (Vienna: UN, 2013), 11 et seq. See also D Brodowski, 'Transnational Organised Crime and Cybercrime' in P Hauck and S Peterke (eds), *International Law and Transnational Organised Crime* (Oxford: OUP, 2016), 334–35; C Ram, 'Cybercrime' in N Boister and R Currie (eds), *The Routledge Handbook of Transnational Criminal Law* (Routledge, 2014), 379–80.

[7] J Clough, 'A World of Difference: The Budapest Convention on Cybercrime and the Challenges of Harmonisation' 40 *Monash University Law Review* (2014) 698, 700.

[8] Brodowski, above n 6, 336.

[9] N Dalla Guarda, 'Governing the Ungovernable: International Relations, Transnational Cybercrime Law, and the Post-Westphalian Regulatory State' 6(1) *Transnational Legal Theory* (2015) 211, 215, 237, 238.

[10] Brodowski, above n 6, 336.   [11] UNODC, above n 6, 39.

11.3 Towards a Global Response that Respects Human Rights

These challenges have fostered a growing consensus that harmonizing global legal responses to cybercrime is critically important. Underlying differences in laws make cooperation difficult. Double criminality in extradition becomes difficult for example, in relation to child pornography offences, if the age of minority in cooperating states in regard to these offences is defined differently. Differences of this kind also threaten legality. Prosecutions have occurred, for example, of a national of country A for posting material on the Internet considered criminal in Country B but not in Country A, when the individual visited Country B.[12] Concern about erosion of, in particular, rights of privacy by official action against cybercrime is also rising. It is implicit in a recommendation made by the Council of Europe's Commissioner for Human Rights in 2014:

> 7. States parties to the Council of Europe Convention on Cybercrime must fully comply with their international human rights obligations in anything they do (or do not do) under the convention, be that in defining the relevant crimes (and elements, exceptions and defences relating to them), in any criminal investigations or prosecutions, or in relation to mutual legal assistance and extradition.[13]

Legislators need to strike a balance between their duty to protect the rights of individuals from cybercrimes and to protect the rights of individuals from unjustifiable invasion of their rights by enforcement action against cybercrime.

11.4 The Council of Europe Cybercrime Convention

11.4.1 Introduction

Domestic responses against cybercrime originated in legislative action in the US and Canada, Japan, and a number of European countries in the 1970s.[14] Work on a multi-lateral instrument began in 1997 in the Council of Europe and led to adoption of the 2001 Council of Europe Convention on Cybercrime.[15] The Cybercrime or Budapest Convention, is largely the work of Western states. States that are not members of the Council of Europe may join the treaty but must be invited,[16] a cumbersome process which some have found off-putting. The Convention has, however, set the benchmark for substantive criminalization of cybercrimes. Although it does not define 'cyber-crime', it spells out different categories of cybercrime offences around broad definitions of 'computer systems' and 'computer data' that are technology neutral and thus adaptable to emerging technologies and software.[17] These offences broke new ground when they were adopted. Commentators pointed out at the time that many were

---

[12] Judgment of the German Bundesgerichtshof of 1 December 2000 (1 StR 184/00, please see BGH MMR 2001, pp.228 et seq) cited UNODC above n 6, 56.

[13] *The Rule of Law on the Internet and in the Wider Digital World* (Strasbourg: Council of Europe, 2014), 43.

[14] Ram, above n 6, 385.   [15] Budapest, 23 November 2001, ETS No 185, in force 1 July 2004.

[16] Article 37(1)(a).   [17] Brodowski, above n 6, 342.

drawn too broadly, beyond the scope upon which there was real agreement.[18] Hence, provision was made to permit reservations.

11.4.2 Confidentiality, integrity, and availability offences

The first category of offences contains novel crimes 'against the confidentiality, integrity and availability of computer data and systems', or so-called CIA offences. These are offences where the object of the crime is the computer data or system.

Illegal access

Article 2, the 'computer hacking' offence, obliges parties to criminalize illegal access, the intentional access without right of the whole or part of a computer system (a device that processes data automatically pursuant to a program[19]). Commission of this foundation offence often leads to other CIA offences and other computer-related and content-related offences. It infringes interests in confidentiality and usually results in significant efforts from the victim to reinstate the integrity of their system. Gaining access requires interaction with the system so that it is reacting to commands or requests. Simply sending data to a system such as by email or attempts to get such interaction that are incomplete or fail do not constitute access and do not have to be criminalized.[20] 'Pure' or 'mere' illegal access to a computer system does not, however, require that the offender accesses system files or other stored data. The Polish Penal Code, for example, used to require that after gaining access the accused gain access to data they were not entitled to, but an amendment in 2008 means that now 'pure' access is criminalized in Poland.[21] The Convention permits parties to further require that the offence be committed by infringing security measures, or with a specific intent of obtaining data or some other dishonest intent, or in relation to a computer system connected to another computer system.[22] Rights of access may be given by holders of rights in the computer system or may be implied from the design of the system such as through use of common operating practices.[23]

Illegal interception

The illegal interception offence in article 3 protects data privacy during the movement of that data (but not its storage) by criminalizing the intentional interception without right by technical means of 'non-public' transmissions of computer data (any representation of facts, information, or concepts in a form suitable for processing in a

---

[18] AM Weber, 'The Council of Europe's Convention on Cybercrime' 18 *Berkeley Technology Law Journal* (2003) 436, 442–43.

[19] Article 1(a).

[20] Council of Europe, *Explanatory Report to Council of Europe Cybercrime Convention ETS No. 185* (Strasbourg: Council of Europe, 2001), para 47.

[21] See Article 267(1) of the Polish Penal Code, Revised 2015. See generally A Adamski, 'Cybercrime Legislation in Poland', available on ResearchGate, June 2015, at <https://www.researchgate.net/publication/279191115_CYBERCRIME_LEGISLATION_IN_POLAND> last visited 2 June 2017.

[22] Council of Europe Explanatory Report, above n 20, para 44.   [23] ibid, para 48.

computer system) from or within a computer system, including electromagnetic emissions from a computer system carrying such computer data. There must be an interception and it must be intentional. The offence does not cover the situation where someone mistakenly sends data to the wrong endpoint, even if that endpoint is a fake banking site that has lured them in. Transmission implies that the data should not have reached its endpoint.[24] The purpose of limitation to interception by technical means is preventing over-criminalization. Again, parties may require that the offence be performed with a dishonest intent or that it occur in relation to a computer system connected to another computer system, in order to narrow the scope of the offence.

Illegal data or systems interference

Articles 4 and 5 provide for interference offences, similar in concept to the older offence of malicious damage to property because they protect the integrity of computer data and systems rather than the confidentiality of that data (which may be publically viewable). These older offences may not cover the illegal interference because of the non-tangible nature of the property involved. Article 4 criminalizes data interference, the intentional 'damaging, deletion, deterioration, alteration or suppression of computer data without right'. Adding data is not in itself criminal unless it causes one of these results.[25] Again parties may require that such conduct result in serious harm before they criminalize it. Article 5 obliges parties to criminalize system interference, the intentional 'serious hindering without right of the functioning of a computer system by inputting, transmitting, damaging, deleting, deteriorating, altering or suppressing computer data'. Bulk-messaging (spamming) would thus not fall within the scope of this offence unless the aggregation of spam caused such a 'serious' result. The cutting of the electricity supply to the system and other forms of external sabotage are also not included because the listed actions all involve internal processes.[26]

Computer misuse tools

Article 6 is directed at the computer hacker's tools. It is designed in part to suppress the markets that exist for passwords and access codes but also to suppress the development and supply of the software and devices used for these purposes. Article 6(1)(a) criminalizes the intentional production, sale, procurement for use, import, distribution, or otherwise making available of two kinds of items: (i) a device including a computer program designed for the purpose of committing the access, interception, or interference offences in articles 2–5; and (ii) a password, access code, or similar data allowing access to a computer system with the specific intent of committing those same offences. Article 6(1)(b) criminalizes intentional possession of either device or password with the specific intent of committing those same offences (although a state party is permitted to require that a certain number of such items be possessed before criminal liability attaches). These are controversial offences, not least because like

---

[24] Brodowski, above n 6, 344.   [25] ibid, 344.   [26] ibid, 344.

all possession offences it is not always clear when the accused has sufficient intent
to become liable. Moreover, there is a danger that information and communications
technology (ICT) security specialists whose job involves many of these activities will
also commit these offences.[27] Section 202c of the German Penal Code tries to limit
imposing liability in these circumstances by requiring that the accused prepare for
the commission of the offence of data espionage (unauthorized access) 'by producing,
acquiring for himself or another, selling, supplying to another, disseminating or making otherwise accessible' software or passwords 'for the purpose of the commission
of such an offence'. In spite of the potential danger for over-criminalization in the
offence, a danger restricted only by *mens rea*, a United Nations Office on Drugs and
Crime (UNODC) study has noted that a number of states have expanded the scope of
these offences by criminalizing these actions where the purpose of the tool was computer access rather than the purpose of the individual.[28] Parties may reserve the right
not to apply article 6(1), but this reservation cannot concern the sale, distribution,
or otherwise making available of passwords and access codes or other data allowing
access.[29]

11.4.3 Computer-related offences

The second category of cybercrime offences set out in the Cybercrime Convention
contains versions of established crimes where the *modus operandi* for commission of
the offence involves the use of computers. Here the interests protected are in property,
financial assets, and the authenticity of documents,[30] and the goal is to suppress illicit
e-commerce.[31]

Computer-related forgery

Article 7 obliges parties to criminalize computer-related forgery—the intentional
input, alteration, deletion, or suppression of computer data without right, resulting in
inauthentic data. These alternative forms of conduct all relate to actions in regard to
computer data, and thus the offence differs from the conventional form of forgery in
that it doesn't necessarily require visual representation. These different actions must
be accompanied by a specific intent that this inauthentic data be considered or acted
upon for legal purposes as if it were authentic. Again, a party may require an intent to
defraud, or similar dishonest intent, before criminal liability attaches.

Computer-related fraud

Article 8 obliges parties to criminalize computer-related fraud—the intentional causing of loss of property by another without right through two distinct means: (i) any
input, alteration, deletion, or suppression of computer data or (ii) any interference with
a computer system's functioning, accompanied by the fraudulent or dishonest intent

[27] ibid, 345.   [28] UNODC, above n 6, 95.   [29] Article 6(3).
[30] UNODC, above n 6, 96.   [31] Brodowski, above n 6, 338.

of procuring, without right, an economic benefit for oneself or another. Again the offence differs from conventional fraud in that it doesn't require deception of a person; the emphasis here is on manipulation of data or interference with the functioning of a computer system with the necessary fraudulent or dishonest specific intent.

11.4.4 Content-related offences

The third category of offences in the Cybercrime Convention are again offences where computers are used to carry out the *modus operandi* of the offence, although here the harm flows from the content of the computer data.

Child pornography

Article 9 prohibits various activities relating to child exploitation material. Its purpose is to protect minors, disrupt markets in child pornography, and deter the making of child pornography.[32] A key circumstance element in the article 9(1) offence requires that it must involve minors defined quite broadly as individuals under 18, although a party may set a lower age-limit although it shall not be less than 16,[33] which would narrow the scope of the offence. The second circumstance element required by article 9(1) is that it must involve child 'pornography', defined as pornographic material that visually depicts (thus excluding audio representation): (a) a minor engaged in sexually explicit conduct; (b) a person appearing to be a minor engaged in sexually explicit conduct; (c) realistic images representing a minor engaged in sexually explicit conduct. Not all states include within the scope of their relevant offences pornography involving adults who appear to be minors or fictitious virtual representations of minors, and parties may thus make a reservation to (b) and (c).[34] Finally, article 9(1) criminalizes the following conduct in regard to child pornography when intentional and without right: (a) production for the purpose of distribution through a computer system; (b) offering or making available through a computer system; (c) distributing or transmitting through a computer system; (d) procuring through a computer system for oneself or another (ie downloading it); (e) possessing in a computer system or on a computer-data storage medium. The requirement of procuring or possession means that mere viewing of child pornography on the Internet with downloading and storing is not criminalized by this provision. Attempts at offering, procuring, or possession of child pornography do not have to be criminalized.[35] Parties may make reservations to the procuring and possessing offences. Japan's Law on Punishment of Activities Relating to Child Prostitution and Child Pornography, and for the Protection of Children[36] follows the structure of the Convention but expands on the definition of child pornography in article 2(3) in a fashion that may be hoping to avoid the casting of the criminal net too broadly to include innocent family activities:

> The term 'child pornography' as used in this Act shall mean photographs, recording media containing electromagnetic records any record which is (produced by

[32] UNODC, above n 6, 100.   [33] Article 9(3).
[34] Article 9(2). Denmark, eg, made such a reservation to article 9(2)(b) on 21 June 2005.
[35] Article 11(2).   [36] Act No 52 of 26 May 1999, as amended.

electronic, magnetic or any other means unrecognizable by natural perceptive functions and is used for data-processing by a computer; the same shall apply hereinafter or any other medium which depicts the pose of a child) which falls under any of the following items, in a visible way: (i) Any pose of a child engaged in sexual intercourse or any conduct similar to sexual intercourse; (ii) Any pose of a child having his or her genital organs touched by another person or of a child touching another person's genital organs, which arouses or stimulates the viewer's sexual desire; (iii) Any pose of a child wholly or partially naked, which arouses or stimulates the viewer's sexual desire.

The Act criminalizes a range of different activities relating to the making, supply, and possession of child pornography, and in particular article 7(1) criminalizes any person 'who provides electromagnetic records or any other record which depicts the pose of a child'.

Copyright infringement

Article 10 obliges parties to suppress computer-based infringements of intellectual property rights. Article 10(1) criminalizes use of a computer system to engage in the infringement (i) of copyright and (ii) of related rights, when committed wilfully and on a 'commercial scale'. In both cases the property right infringed is that defined under national law pursuant to international obligations with the exception of any moral rights conferred by such conventions. Parties are likely to have difficulties with these offences. For one thing, the question of what is a commercial scale infringement of intellectual property (IP) is not settled and has caused dispute in the World Trade Organization (see Chapter 15's discussion of IP offences). This condition also ensures the offence is directed at the 'supply' of copyright infringing works, not the consumption. Parties may reserve the right not to criminalize 'in limited circumstances, provided that other effective remedies are available', and such reservations do not derogate from their obligations in the intellectual property treaties.[37]

11.4.5 Ancillary crimes and related provisions

Provision is also made in article 11(1) for the intentional aiding and abetting all of the offences in the Convention. However, article 11(2) only obliges parties to criminalize the attempt to commit a selection of the offences. Attempts to commit illegal access under article 2, and misuse of devices under article 6, and offering, procuring, or possessing of child pornography, do not have to be criminalized, because they were considered conceptually difficult to attempt or because some legal systems limit the offences which can be attempted.[38] Despite these limitations, article 11(3) goes one step further and permits parties to declare that they will not apply article 11(2) in

---

[37] Article 10(3).   [38] Council of Europe Explanatory Report, above n 20, para 120.

whole or in part, because of the wide variation in state practice in this regard.[39] Article 12 obliges parties to provide for criminal liability for legal persons for the Convention offences.

11.4.6 Penalties

The Cybercrime Convention also makes provision for the imposition of effective, proportionate, and dissuasive sanctions (including for legal persons), which include deprivation of liberty.[40] In this regard the Convention's more novel offences have failed to achieve harmonization when implemented at the domestic level. In 2013 the UNODC Cybercrime study concluded that,[41] 'The area of cybercrime offence penalties well exemplifies divergences in national approaches to cybercrime acts. Examination of just one crime—illegal access—shows considerable difference in its perceived degree of seriousness.'

11.4.7 The Cybercrime Convention's substantive shortcomings

Although the Cybercrime Convention set the standard for multilateral responses to cybercrime it constituted a snapshot of the concerns current in 1990. A number of new CIA, computer-related crimes, and content crimes, have emerged since then which do not fall within its scope. The Convention does not make specific provision for the confidentiality of data, and does not therefore criminalize data espionage as such (although it may well involve a CIA offence)[42] or the unauthorized use of valid data for gain.[43] The authors of the Convention did not anticipate the involvement of minors as offenders or the popularity of peer-to-peer software as the distribution method of choice for child pornographers. The Convention does not cover subsequent developments such as 'cyberbullying', 'sexting', the use of social networking sites, the posting of revenge porn, and online sexual exploitation[44] such as computer-aided solicitation of minors.[45] The responsibility of Internet service providers (ISPs) is not clear in the Convention. The Convention also does not criminalize bulk-messaging or spamming, a burden on recipients and potential entry point for criminal activity.[46] Nor does it make provision for identity-related crimes such as theft of identity-related information by computer.[47]

Domestic practice has tried to keep up. The prevalence of lottery scams being run in and from Jamaica, for example, led to the enactment of the Fraudulent Transactions Special Measures Act 2013, which contains a range of related offences designed to respond to every aspect of 'scamming' activity. Offences criminalizing the trafficking

---

[39] ibid, para 122.   [40] Article 13.   [41] UNODC, above n 6, 56.
[42] Brodowski, above n 6, 345.   [43] UNODC, above n 6, 98.
[44] See, eg, section 172.1 of the Canadian Penal Code; *R v Legare* 2009 SSC 56.
[45] Article 23 of the Council of Europe Convention for the Protection of Children against Sexual Exploitation, 25 October 2007, CETS 201; in force 1 July 2010; UNODC, above n 6, 103.
[46] UNODC, above n 6, 95.
[47] See, eg, article 14A of the International Telecommunications Union/CARICOM, CTU Model Legislative Texts.

in computer passwords such as in section 6(4) of the Nigerian Cyber Crimes Act,[48] are becoming more common. However, responding to developments such as the increasing use of crypto currencies like Bitcoins to facilitate crime on the Darknet is still way beyond the scope of much national legislation.

Criminalization of the use of computers for racism and the distribution of xenophobic material, which proved impossible in the Convention, was addressed in the 2003 Additional Protocol.[49] It obliges parties to criminalize the use of computer systems to disseminate racist and xenophobic material, make racist and xenophobic threats or insults, and to deny, grossly minimize, approve, or justify genocide or crimes against humanity.[50] This expansion of criminalization, however, tends to expose the slowness of the multilateral response. The pace of change in harmful ways of using the Internet is outstripping the pace of law-making.

At the same time further expansion of criminalization may impact negatively on individual rights. The potential for restriction of individuals' rights by implementing laws and more particularly the use of suppression of crime as a vehicle for censorship and state control of freedom of expression has been a source of concern in the development and implementation of the Cybercrime Convention. Article 15 of the Convention reflects this tension when it provides that implementation must meet domestic and international human rights standards and 'the principle of proportionality'. The concern is justified but must be balanced against concern for the human rights of victims of cybercrime.

11.5 Other Regional Developments

A range of other regional instruments have been developed to combat cybercrime, none as comprehensive as the Cybercrime Convention, but sometimes offering novel provisions, which show a clear trend to the expansion of criminalization, although not necessarily in a systematic or principled way.

Africa has often been considered something of a safe haven for cybercriminals because of the absence of effective suppression. The 2011 Directive on Fighting Cybercrime within the Economic Community of West African States[51] is broader in scope than the Cybercrime Convention as it applies to all crimes the detection of which requires electronic evidence. A novel addition to the list of CIA offences is the offence of illegally remaining in a computer system.[52] The Directive also does not limit criminalization of interference with a computer system to internal interference but criminalizes any impeding or altering.[53] It also criminalizes the knowing use of forged data.[54] The illicit manipulation of data may occur even through negligence.[55] The computer misuse tools offence has, however, been limited by a requirement that it must be 'without legitimate reason', suggesting a get-out for security experts.[56] The 2014 African Union (AU) Convention on Cyberspace Security and Protection of

---

[48] Cybercrime (Prohibition, Prevention) Act 2015.
[49] Strasbourg, 28 January 2003, ETS No 189, in force 1 March 2006.
[50] Articles 3, 4, 5, and 6.   [51] C/DIR/.1/08/11, 1 September 2011.   [52] Article 5.
[53] Article 6.   [54] Article 13.   [55] Article 12.   [56] Article 14.

Personal Data[57] makes similar provision for a list of substantive crimes in article 29 but goes even further in some respects. For example, it obliges AU member states to criminalize attempts to gain access to computer systems.[58]

In Asia the Commonwealth of Independent States (CIS) and Shanghai Cooperation Organisation (SCO) promote a culture of shared cyber security among parties that diverges from the cooperative regime undertaken by Council of Europe.[59] The CIS Agreement on Cooperation in Combating Offences Related to Computer Information adopted in 2001[60] takes a *sui generis* approach to criminalization in article 3, which fuses illegal access with data and systems interference. The SCO Agreement on Cooperation in the field of International Information Security adopted in 2011[61] has a very broad concept of information crime which includes the militarization of cyber-space, which blurs criminal and national cyber security provisions.

The League of Arab States has taken a more conventional approach in its Arab Convention on Combating Information Technology Offences.[62] Although its scope is expressly limited to offences with a transnational element,[63] it generally expands criminalization. It inflates CIA offences for example by criminalizing 'illicit access to, presence in or contact with' ICT[64] and provides for the aggravation of illegal access if it leads to the 'obliteration, modification, distortion, duplication, removal or destruction of saved data, electronic instruments and systems and communication networks, and damages to the users and beneficiaries, or to the acquirement of secret government information'.[65] This provision may lead to accumulation of charges if it overlaps with other separate offences. The Arab Convention also introduces a number of unique offences including criminalization of production and distribution of pornographic material,[66] the dissemination of the ideas and principles of terrorist groups,[67] facilitation of communication between terrorist organizations,[68] and diffusion of religious fanaticism or religious dissent.[69] It calls for criminalization of offences related to transnational organized crime committed by means of a computer.[70] The Arab Convention also calls for aggravation of punishment of traditional offences when committed using a computer.[71]

The EU Directive 2013/40/EU of the European Parliament and of the Council of 12 August 2013 on attacks against information systems[72] is limited to the CIA offences (other EU measures deal with other crimes), though with some subtle limitations. Member states have the discretion to limit the scope of the access offence to 'cases that are not minor'. Illegal system interference is extended to interruption of systems and the offence may be committed by rendering data inaccessible.[73] The Directive also provides for aggravation of the interference offences when the real identity of the perpetrator is concealed or if they involve organized crime or use tools designed to attack a significant number of information systems or critical systems.[74]

---

[57] Adopted 27 June 2014.   [58] Article 29(1)(a).   [59] Dalla Guarda, above n 9, 231.
[60] Signed 1 June 2001.   [61] June 2011.
[62] Adopted 21 December 2010; in force 15 February 2012.
[63] Article 3 uses the definition of transnational in article 3 of the UNTOC.   [64] Article 6(1).
[65] Article 6(2).   [66] Article 12(1).   [67] Article 15(1).   [68] Article 15(2).
[69] Article 15(4).   [70] Article 16.   [71] Article 21.   [72] OJ L 218, 14 September 2013.
[73] Article 4.   [74] Article 9.

Broader systems such as the Commonwealth rely only on the soft guidance provided by the Commonwealth Model Law on Computer and Computer Related Crime, which suggests extension of criminalization by recommending the data or systems interference acts be criminalized if committed 'recklessly',[75] an invitation that has apparently not generally been taken up by member countries.[76]

11.6 A UN Cybercrime Convention?

While the UN General Assembly called for the elimination of 'safe havens' for those 'who criminally misuse information technologies' in early 2001,[77] there is currently no treaty with global reach against cybercrime.[78] A Russian proposal for a broader-based UN Cybercrime Convention was discussed at the 2010 UN Crime Congress held in Brazil. It gathered support from developing states including China eager to get some control in this area, but was resisted by the US, Canada, the UK, and the EU. They preferred to continue support for the fairly well established European Convention on Cybercrime, fearing that lengthy negotiation of a new convention would derail progress made in legislative reform and capacity building in many states. There was also disagreement over sovereignty issues such as whether law enforcement agencies in one state should be able to access computer systems housed in others, and concerns for human rights.[79] Late in 2010 the UN General Assembly requested the Commission on Crime Prevention and Criminal Justice to establish an expert group to conduct a study on the problem of cybercrime and responses to it by member states,[80] which resulted in a comprehensive study on cybercrime undertaken by the UNODC that was completed in 2013.[81] The UNODC study identified a number of countries with significant gaps in their cybercrime legislation or no legislation at all.[82] A key finding was that:[83]

> Fragmentation at the international level, and diversity of national cybercrime laws, may correlate with the existence of multiple instruments with different thematic and geographic scope. While instruments legitimately reflect socio-cultural and regional differences, divergences in the extent of procedural powers and international cooperation provisions may lead to the emergence of country cooperation 'clusters' that are not always well suited to the global nature of cybercrime.

Of particular relevance to substantive criminalization was that '[a]nalysis of available national legal frameworks indicates insufficient harmonization of "core" cybercrime offences, investigative powers, and admissibility of electronic evidence'.[84] The study listed the development of a comprehensive multilateral instrument on cybercrime as one option to remedy the shortcomings in the global response.

---

[75] Article 6.   [76] UNODC, above n 6, 91.
[77] UN GA Res 55/63 of 22 January 2001, para 1(a).   [78] UNODC, above n 6, 68.
[79] Report of the Twelfth United Nations Congress on Crime Prevention and Criminal Justice, Salvador, Brazil, 12–19 April 2010, 18 May 2010, UN Doc A/Conf.213/18, paras 202–04.
[80] Resolution 65/230 of 21 December 2001, para 9.   [81] UNODC, above n 6.
[82] ibid, 80.   [83] ibid, xi.   [84] ibid, xi.

Most Western states are not supportive. They believe that negotiation of a further Convention would waste time and resources. They argue that the Budapest Convention can serve the role of providing a global standard as it is open to accession by non-member states of the Council of Europe. They point to the fact that it is widely ratified and its elements have been incorporated into the legislation of dozens of countries outside the Council of Europe which have not ratified. The problem is that the Budapest Convention has a considerable baggage which has meant that it has not succeeded as a global instrument for suppressing cybercrime. Many states are resistant to it because of controversial provisions for cooperation in extraterritorial searches.[85] Russia, China, and many G77 states argue that they were not involved in its negotiation, it is oriented towards the specific interests of Western countries, and is already out of date. A UN Convention offers the promise of a broader scope, a more representative negotiating process, and an opportunity to improve on the Budapest Convention. However, it would take a long time to develop and if existing standards in the Budapest Convention are lowered it would be unlikely to get Western support.[86] Moreover, the proposed convention is perceived by some states as a possible mechanism for international cooperation in control of the content on and use of the Internet for national security purposes, while others see it as a legal basis for gaining greater access to technical assistance to develop their response to cybercrime.[87] These sorts of issues are likely to continue to stymie negotiations.

11.7 Conclusion

Developments in connectivity mean that in the future all crime is likely to have a 'cyber' element to it. Types of cyber criminality are likely to proliferate exponentially. One difficulty will be discriminating issues of enforcement of ordinary crimes from crimes that require specific substantive definitional elements that involve electronic activity. Whether a multilateral treaty system with fixed offences which are difficult to amend is really the correct mode of cooperation for keeping up with this evolving problem is open to question. It may be that soft law along Financial Action Task Force recommendation lines allowing flexible alteration of standards which address evolving features of the commission of crimes in cyberspace will be considered by some to be a more viable proposition, but there will be objections on the basis of legitimacy issues already extant in current responses to cybercrime. Another difficulty may be over-criminalization—legislators in many countries are wary of pressure, for example, to criminalize possession, production and dissemination of content protected by free expression that other states may wish to criminalize as breaches of laws against blasphemy, hate laws, or threats to national security.[88] These base-lines still have to be settled, and the current fractured system of regulation is likely to persist for some time.

---

[85] Brodowski, above n 6, 339, 342, noting that this is Russia's main problem with the Convention.
[86] Clough, above n 7, 728–29.   [87] Ram, above n 6, 386.   [88] ibid, 382.

12

Environmental Crimes

12.1 Introduction

Environmental crime has been defined by the United Nations Office on Drugs and Crime (UNODC) as 'criminal conduct that may have negative consequences for the environment'.[1] It is a broad concept that covers a range of different and disparate activities. It has been placed by the UNODC into two broad categories: natural resource crimes and pollution crimes,[2] although another division commonly used is between wildlife crimes and pollution crimes.[3] Natural resource crimes involve the trafficking of valuable natural resources through, for example, the illegal trade in flora and fauna, illegal fishing, and illegal logging. Pollution crimes involve polluting activities such as the smuggling of ozone-depleting substances and the illegal movement and disposal of hazardous waste.

The scale depends on the activity but in 2005 the UN Development Programme made the general assessment of both scale and impact, commenting that environmental crime is

> a big and increasingly lucrative business—a multi-billion dollar global enterprise. Local and international crime syndicates worldwide earn an estimated US$ 22–31 billion dollars annually from hazardous waste dumping, smuggling proscribed hazardous materials, and exploiting and trafficking protected natural resources. Illegal international trade in 'environmentally-sensitive' commodities such as ozone depleting substances (ODSs), toxic chemicals, hazardous wastes and endangered species is an international problem with serious consequences: it directly threatens human health and the environment, contributes to species loss, and results in revenue loss for governments. Moreover, illegal trade in such commodities strengthens criminal organizations that also traffic in drugs, weapons and prostitution. [4]

A report released in mid-2016 by the UN Environmental Programme (UNEP) and Interpol comments on environmental crime's annual growth of five to seven per cent

---

[1] UNODC, *The Globalization of Crime: A Transnational Organized Crime Threat Assessment* (Vienna: UN, 2010), 149, available at <http://www.unodc.org/documents/data-andanalysis/tocta/TOCTA_Report_2010_low_res.pdf> last visited 27 June 2017.

[2] UNODC, *Transnational Organised Crime in the Fishing Industry* (Vienna: UN, 2011), 95, available at <http://www.unodc.org/documents/human-trafficking/Issue_Paper_-_TOC_in_the_Fishing_Industry.pdf> last visited 27 June 2017.

[3] R White, 'Environmental Theft and Trafficking' in N Boister and R Currie (eds), *Routledge Handbook of Transnational Criminal Law* (Abingdon: Routledge, 2015), 278, 296.

[4] UNDP, 'Green Customs Initiative Targets Environmental Crime' UNDP Online Press Release, 14 November 2005, available at <http://www.unep.org/Documents.Multilingual/Default.asp?DocumentID=457&ArticleID=5030&l=en> last visited 27 June 2017.

and estimates that its current value is in the range of US$91 billion to US$258 billion.[5] Usually transnational in nature, environmental crime is facilitated by weak regulation and corruption, and impacts negatively on both the environment and economy in developed and developing states.

The apparent scale and transboundary impact of the problem has not, however, occasioned a proportionate or coherent global response. Although calls have been made since the early 1990s for the development of a global transnational environmental crime prohibition regime,[6] this call has largely gone unheeded by a society of states wary of coordinating their efforts in this regard. It has been suggested that at least in the Asia Pacific region (both the market and source of supply for many natural resource and wildlife crime products) this is because the problem is not as well represented or understood as other transnational crimes and political elites do not take the problem seriously unless they or their interests are directly affected.[7]

Megrét's analysis of why criminal law has only been used reluctantly at the international level to enforce environmental standards is compelling.[8] He points to the difficulties associated with the nature of the subject matter, the environment, and the complex interests involved. He also notes that the primary norms of environmental law are mainly 'soft' in nature and their breadth and vagueness means they do not make comfortable foundations for crimes (there are over 270 multilateral environmental instruments[9]). Criminal law has also not been considered a suitable tool to use to suppress activities that do have costs but also have benefits to society, are diffuse and cause incremental damage, are frequently committed negligently rather than intentionally, and involve large numbers of actors. Nevertheless, he argues that a range of factors favour criminalization: the inadequacy of current approaches, the gravity of harm both to humans and the environment caused by this conduct, the difficulty of pointing to specific victims (which suggests a stronger role for state intervention), the utility of criminal law in reaching individuals who commit many of these offences, the key positions of some individuals (thus justifying holding them to standards of negligence), and the need to deter specific forms of behaviour through individual punishment.

International regulation has developed in two stages. Initially states adopted measures to prevent the legal pursuit of these activities. Then they slowly began to follow this up with the application of penal measures to non-state actors within international legal frameworks.[10] However, as we shall see, these developments have been sectoral

---

[5] See C Nellemann et al (eds), *The Rise of Environmental Crime* (UNEP–Interpol, 2016), 7, available at <http://www.unep.org/environmentalgovernance/erl/resources/publications/rise-environmental-crime> last visited 6 June 2017.

[6] E Nadelmann, 'Global Prohibition Regimes: The Evolution of Norms in International Society' 44 *International Organisation* (1990) 479, 523. UN affiliated agencies and Interpol have also focussed on these activities since then—see Batongbacal, below n 51, 298–99.

[7] See L Elliot, 'Transnational Environmental Crime in the Asia Pacific: An (under)securitised Security Problem' 20 *The Pacific Review* (2007) 499, 501, 513.

[8] At F Megrét, 'The Problem of an International Criminal Law of the Environment' 36 *Columbia Journal of Environmental Law* (2011) 195, 212 et seq, 221 et seq.

[9] White, above n 3, 282.

[10] See generally A Cardesa-Salzmann, 'Multilateral Environmental Agreements and Illegality' in L Elliot and WH Schaedla (eds), *Handbook of Transnational Environmental Crime* (Cheltenham: Edward Elgar, 2015), 299.

and partial rather than comprehensive, indicative of a high degree of sovereign sensitivity in this regard.

12.2 Illegal, Unregulated, and Unreported Fishing

Illegal, unregulated, and unreported (IUU) fishing occurs when fishing violates the laws and regulations that apply to fisheries in territorial waters, exclusive economic zones, or high seas fisheries. IUU fishing is a million dollar industry with its own fully developed chains of supply to fish markets that threatens to undermine already vulnerable fish stocks with serious economic, social, and environmental consequences. One of the many drivers of the decline of global fish stocks, IUU fishing is estimated to account for 35 per cent of the wild marine catch annually, with losses of as much as US$23.5 billion.[11]

The impact of IUU fishing on increasingly scarce fish stocks began to generate international alarm in 1997 when the Sixteenth Meeting of the Commission of the Convention on the Conservation of Antarctic Marine Living Resources (CCAMLR) drew attention to the problem.[12] In 2009 the UN General Assembly drew attention to the link between IUU fishing and organized crime.[13] In 2010, 'illegal fishing' was identified as a 'new trend in crime' in the Salvador Declaration of the Twelfth United Nations Congress on Crime Prevention and Criminal Justice.[14]

Regional steps to distinguish permissible from impermissible fishing have a lengthy history. In 1952, for example, the US, Canada, and Japan adopted the International Convention for the High Seas Fisheries of the North Pacific Ocean[15] and agreed to prohibit their nationals and vessels from engaging in 'the exploitation, … loading, processing, transporting or possessing' of fish from stocks that they had to agree to abstain from fishing, and from 'engaging in fishing activities' in certain waters in regard to fish stocks that they had agreed to subject to conservation measures.[16] However, they left unstipulated the precise form this prohibition should take. In the 1978 Protocol Amending the International Convention for the High Seas Fisheries of the North Pacific Ocean,[17] the parties agreed to enforce the Convention within their 200nm exclusive fishery zone and to permit any party to take enforcement action outside those zones by search and seizure of the fishing vessels of other parties.[18] However, only the authorities of the flag or nationality state are permitted to try the offence and impose penalties. In terms of article 9(2) the parties promised to enact and enforce necessary laws with appropriate penalties for violation, but, frustrated by

---

[11] Global Ocean Commission, 'Drivers of Decline' available at <http://www.some.ox.ac.uk/research/global-ocean-commission/drivers-of-decline/> last visited 2 July 2017.

[12] Report of the Sixteenth Meeting of the Commission, paras 5 and 8, available at <https://www.ccamlr.org/en/system/files/e-cc-xvi.pdf> last visited 2 July 2017.

[13] Paragraph 61 of GA Res 64/72, 4 December 2009.

[14] UNODC, 'Activities of the United Nations Office on Drugs and Crime to Address Emerging Forms of Crime' CTOC/COP/2010/3, 4 August 2010, paras 162 and 290, available at <http://www.unodc.org/documents/treaties/organized_crime/COP5/CTOC_COP_2010_3/CTOC_COP_2010_3_E.pdf> last visited 2 July 2017.

[15] Tokyo, 9 May 1952, 205 UNTS 65, in force 12 June 1953.   [16] Article 9.

[17] Tokyo, 25 April 1978, 1207 UNTS 325, in force 15 February 1979.   [18] Article 9(1).

freedom of the high seas, lack of effective control of fishing vessels by flag states, and their non-application to fishing by vessels registered in non-participating states (flags of non-compliance), it does not appear that these provisions are enough to deal effectively with IUU fishing.

Today the foundation for control of fishing is set by articles 118 and 119 of the 1982 UN Convention on the Law of the Sea (UNCLOS),[19] which establish a general obligation on parties to cooperate in the conservation and management of high seas living resources. Respect for this obligation has led to the development of marine management and conservation measures. The 1995 UN Fish Stocks Agreement[20] provides the strongest provisions for compliance. Article 18(3)(b)(ii) obliges flag states 'to prohibit fishing on the high seas by vessels which are not duly licensed or authorized to fish, or fishing on the high seas by vessels otherwise in accordance with the conditions of a license, authorization or permit'. Article 18(3)(b)(iii) requires parties to ensure that their flag-vessels do not 'conduct unauthorized fishing within areas under the national jurisdiction of other states'. Importantly, however, the Fish Stocks Agreement obliges parties that are not members of Regional Fishing Management Organizations (RFMOs) to cooperate with them.[21] RFMOs such as CCAMLR coordinate management of fishing in specific regions. The Port State Measures Agreement, a UN Food and Agriculture Organization (FAO) treaty, also provides for the closure of ports to suspected IUU fishing vessels.[22] The FAO highlights these obligations in its International Plan of Action to Prevent, Deter and Eliminate Illegal, Unreported and Unregulated Fishing.[23] It provides an outline of the nature and scope of IUU fishing in article 3, a provision which reveals the legal complexity of the primary regulations:

3.1 Illegal fishing refers to activities:
  3.1.1 conducted by national or foreign vessels in waters under the jurisdiction of a State, without the permission of that State, or in contravention of its laws and regulations;
  3.1.2 conducted by vessels flying the flag of States that are parties to a relevant regional fisheries management organization but operate in contravention of the conservation and management measures adopted by that organization and by which the States are bound, or relevant provisions of the applicable international law; or
  3.1.3 in violation of national laws or international obligations, including those undertaken by cooperating States to a relevant regional fisheries management organization.

[19] Montego Bay, 10 December 1982, 1833 UNTS 3, in force 16 November 1994.
[20] United Nations Agreement for the Implementation of the Provisions of the United Nations Convention on the Law of the Sea of 10 December 1982 relating to the Conservation and Management of Straddling Fish Stocks and Highly Migratory Fish Stocks, 8 September 1995, UN Doc A/Conf.164/37, in force 11 December 2001.
[21] Article 20(1).
[22] Agreement on Port State Measures to Prevent, Deter and Eliminate, Illegal, Unreported and Unregulated Fishing, 22 November 2009; in force 5 June 2016, available at <http://www.fao.org/Legal/treaties/037s-e.htm> last visited 14 August 2017.
[23] 2 March 2001, available at <http://www.fao.org/docrep/003/y1224e/y1224e00.HTM> last visited 2 July 2017.

3.2 Unreported fishing refers to fishing activities:

    3.2.1 which have not been reported, or have been misreported, to the relevant national authority, in contravention of national laws and regulations; or

    3.2.2 undertaken in the area of competence of a relevant regional fisheries management organization which have not been reported or have been misreported, in contravention of the reporting procedures of that organization.

3.3 Unregulated fishing refers to fishing activities:

    3.3.1 in the area of application of a relevant regional fisheries management organization that are conducted by vessels without nationality, or by those flying the flag of a State not party to that organization, or by a fishing entity, in a manner that is not consistent with or contravenes the conservation and management measures of that organization; or

    3.3.2 in areas or for fish stocks in relation to which there are no applicable conservation or management measures and where such fishing activities are conducted in a manner inconsistent with State responsibilities for the conservation of living marine resources under international law.

This is poor stuff on which to base criminalization. For one thing, the question whether many of these activities are of sufficient seriousness to warrant criminalization arises. It has been suggested that only the activities of habitual and repeat offenders really qualify as transnational organized criminal activities.[24] The UNODC has pointed out some of the other inadequacies from a criminal law point of view of the concept of IUU fishing:[25]

> IUU fishing is a concept that has emerged in the context of FAO soft law to counter non-compliance with fisheries management regulations, particularly by vessels operating under flags of convenience. Many fishing vessels engaged in IUU fishing do so by avoiding conservation and management rules and regulations, but they do not necessarily operate in contravention of them. In other words, the term 'IUU fishing' includes conduct that is not necessary illegal. The concept of IUU fishing is moreover potentially problematic because its focus is largely on the activities of fishing vessels. From a crime perspective this focus may become too narrow since criminal activities may also arise in the context of for instance aquaculture. Moreover, the definition does not seem to include criminal activities up- and downstream of the illegal fishing activities such as money laundering, corruption, document fraud or handling of stolen goods.

National control of IUU fishing is plagued by weak penalties such as the use of fines and by law enforcement difficulties. Without a more comprehensive criminal law approach, shifting flags, transferring of catch, the use of ports of convenience, and so forth, will mean that suppression of these forms of fishing will remain largely ineffective.

---

[24] T Phelps Bondaroff, W van der Werff, and T Reitano, *The Illegal Fishing and Organized Crime Nexus: Illegal Fishing as Transnational Organized Crime* (Geneva: Global Initiative against Organised Crime/Blackfish, 2015), 37, available at <http://theblackfish.org/Fishing_Crime.pdf> last visited 2 July 2017.

[25] UNODC, *Transnational Organized Crime in the Fishing Industry* (Vienna: UN, 2011), 96.

12.3 Illegal Trading in Endangered Species

There has been a resurgence in the illegal wildlife trade, with poaching in particular reaching unprecedented levels.[26] Elephant poaching in Africa, for example, reached nearly seven and a half per cent of the population in 2012.[27] These levels spell prospective extinction in the wild for many species in the shorter term. Moreover, poaching and wildlife trafficking have been cited by the Security Council as fuelling the crisis in the Central African Republic[28] and the Great Lakes Region.[29]

Taking effective steps against this trade is difficult. Illicit supply lines are complex and specific to the particular animal and countries involved. In South Africa, for example, Miliken and Shaw describe one particular chain of supply as follows:[30]

> Illicit rhino horn trade occurs along a trade chain that extends from the poacher at the site level in Africa through a series of middlemen buyers, exporters and couriers at local and international levels to an end-use consumer in a distant country, which today is usually Viet Nam. Using a conceptual framework to map criminal relationships, the South African National Wildlife Crime Reaction Unit has identified five distinct levels at which rhino horn trade syndicates are operating within and outside of Africa. The first three levels function nationally and represent the illegal killing of rhinos (Level 1), local buyers and couriers who receive the horns from the poachers (Level 2), and national couriers, buyers and exporters who consolidate horns from all sources: poaching, stockpile sales, thefts and illegal de horning, as well as 'pseudo-hunting' activities (Level 3). Linking Africa to distant markets, international buyers, exporters, importers and couriers (Level 4) are then responsible for the movement of horn to rhino horn dealers and consumers in the end-use markets (Level 5). These rhino crime syndicates are typically multi-national operations that also engage in criminal activities such as drug and diamond smuggling, human trafficking and trading other wildlife products like elephant ivory and abalone.

Suppression of these activities is also plagued by inadequate law, poor law enforcement capacity, weak political will, corruption, and poor international cooperation.

Again, with few exceptions, the non-specific nature of the primary obligations do not make resort to transnational criminal law a simple task. Early conventions protected threatened species but provided for only very general penal obligations. In the 1957 Interim Convention on Conservation of North Pacific Fur Seals,[31] for example, the parties promised to 'enact and enforce such legislation as may be necessary to guarantee the observance of this Convention and to make effective its provisions with appropriate penalties for violation thereof'.[32] Today the extraordinarily diverse

---

[26] K Lawson and A Vines, *Global Impacts of the Illegal Wildlife Trade: The Costs of Crime, Insecurity and Institutional Erosion* (London: Chatham House, 2014), 4.

[27] ibid, 5.   [28] SC Res 2127, 2013, preamble.   [29] SC Res 2136, 2014, preamble.

[30] T Miliken and J Shaw, *The South Africa–Viet Nam Rhino Horn Trade Nexus: A deadly combination of institutional lapses, corrupt wildlife industry professionals and Asian crime syndicates* (Johannesburg: Traffic, 2012) 14, available at <http://www.npr.org/documents/2013/may/traffic_species_mammals.pdf> last visited 7 July 2017.

[31] 9 February 1957, 314 UNTS 105, in force 14 October 1957.   [32] Article 10.

and lucrative licit commerce in endangered species is regulated primarily by the 1973 Convention on International Trade in Endangered Species of Wild Fauna and Flora (CITES).[33] It institutes a licensing system for import and export control of the wildlife trade, 'the import, export and re-export of live and dead animals, fish and plants, and their parts and derivatives'. 'Specimens', arranged in three extensive lists in appendices, are subject to different levels of control, dependent on the degree of threat to the particular species (those in appendix I are threatened with extinction, those in appendix II may become so, and those in appendix III are subject to regulation in some parties). This system is backed by penal sanction. Article 8(1) provides:

> 1. The Parties shall take appropriate measures to enforce the provisions of the present Convention and to prohibit trade in specimens in violation thereof. These shall include measures:
>   (a) to penalize trade in, or possession of, such specimens, or both; and
>   (b) to provide for the confiscation or return to the State of export of such specimens.

Parties have implemented this provision through enacting legislation such as the US's Endangered Species Act 1973,[34] which elaborates a comprehensive range of crimes involved in the import, export, and trafficking of endangered species, including possession.[35] Some parties, however, have not engaged in law reform and have been sent written cautions by the Conference of Parties.[36] Strydom notes that from the data compiled by the secretariat on implementation just over 48 per cent of the parties had adequate legislation while 27 per cent had partially inadequate legislation and 21 per cent general inadequate legislation, and a small percentage had pending legislation.[37] He points out that a number of enforcement issues have arisen including 'the raising of the combating of the illegal wildlife trade as a matter of high priority; the proper training and equipping of law enforcement officials; [and] the effective punishment of violators'.[38] The problems begin, it is suggested, with article 8 itself which should be developed into a number of separate provisions providing a guide as to the material and mental elements associated with criminalizing different links in the chain of supply and adequate punishment provisions. Reliance could be placed much more easily on the United Nations Convention against Transnational Organized Crime (UNTOC) to provide a framework for international cooperation if the offence provision met the UNTOC's article 2(b) threshold for serious crime: that is, it recommended the offence carry a penalty of four years or deprivation of liberty (see Chapter 8).

---

[33] Washington, 3 March 1973, 993 UNTS 243, in force 1 July 1975.   [34] 16 USC §§ 1531–1544.
[35] 16 USC § 1538(a)(1).
[36] See Interpretation and Implementation of the Convention: Compliance and Enforcement: National Laws for Implementation of the Convention, Fifteenth Meeting of the COP, Doha 13–25 March 2010, Cop 15 Doc.20, para 11 available at <http://www.cites.org/eng/cop/15/doc/E15-20.pdf> last visited 5 July 2017.
[37] H Strydom, 'Transnational Organised Crime and the Illegal Trade in Endangered Species of Wild Fauna and Flora' in P Hauck and S Peterke (eds), *International Law and Transnational Organised Crime* (Oxford: OUP, 2016), 264, 272.
[38] ibid.

12.4 Illegal Logging

Logging and sale of logs is illegal when it does not conform to national laws about who owns trees and who can log them. The unlawful harvest, transport, sale, and purchase of timber was estimated by the World Bank in 2006 to produce US$15 billion annually[39] and in 2016 those estimates were revised upwards by the UNEP and Interpol to somewhere between US$50 and US$152 billion annually.[40]

There is little in the way of penal frameworks at an international level to control this traffic. The International Tropical Timber Agreement[41] is a regulatory instrument which does not provide for penal measures. Limited provision is made in the 1973 CITES Convention, discussed above, because the prohibition on the trade in 'specimens' includes a list of plants.[42] National law is broader in scope, attempting to include within its scope all of the links in the chain of supply. In the US, for example, the Lacey Act[43] prohibits the illegal trade in plants that have been illegally taken, possessed, transported, or sold. Section 3371 of title 16 of the US Code provides that it is unlawful for any person

> '(2) to import, export, transport, sell, receive, acquire, or purchase in interstate or foreign commerce— (B) any plant—
>   (i)   taken, possessed, transported, or sold in violation of any law or regulation of any State, or any foreign law, that protects plants or that regulates—(I) the theft of plants; (II) the taking of plants from a park, forest reserve, or other officially protected area; (III) the taking of plants from an officially designated area; or (IV) the taking of plants without, or contrary to, required authorization;
>   (ii) taken, possessed, transported, or sold without the payment of appropriate royalties, taxes, or stumpage fees required for the plant by any law or regulation of any State or any foreign law; or
>   (iii) taken, possessed, transported, or sold in violation of any limitation under any law or regulation of any State, or under any foreign law, governing the export or transshipment of plants; ...'

'Plants' include trees[44] and the 'taking' of a plant includes its harvesting, cutting, logging, or removal.[45]

Reliance has also been placed on extant framework conventions. In 2007, for example, the United Nations Commission on Crime Prevention and Criminal Justice adopted Resolution 16/1 entitled 'International cooperation in preventing and combating illicit international trafficking in forest products, including timber, wildlife and other forest biological resources', which strongly encourages states to cooperate at bilateral, regional, and international levels to prevent, combat, and eradicate these

---

[39] D Brack, *Illegal Logging* (London: Chatham House Energy Environment and Development Programme, 2006), 2.

[40] Nellemann et al, above n 5, 7.

[41] 1 February 2006; in force 7 December 2011, available at International Tropical Timber Association, <http://www.itto.int/itta/> last visited 2 July 2017.

[42] Article 8.   [43] 16 USC §§ 3371–3378.   [44] § 3371(f).   [45] § 3371(j)(1).

forms of trafficking by applying the UNTOC and the United Nations Convention against Corruption. Application of the UNTOC will, as noted above, depend on whether the traffic in timber is a serious offence under national law (ie with a penalty of four years or more), which seems unlikely in most states. One of the difficulties with policing the illegal logging traffic is determining whether harvesting was illegal in the first place; commentators note that 'ownership' of the logs or the right to harvest them can be highly ambiguous and frequently takes little account of customary claims to title or informed consent of owners.[46]

12.5 Pollution

The international framework for control of pollution has been more adept at making use of the criminal law than natural resource crimes. The 1973 International Convention for the Prevention of Pollution from Ships (MARPOL)[47] obliges parties to prohibit violations, wherever committed, of prescribed anti-pollution standards, equipment requirements, and operating procedures and calls for penalties of 'adequate severity' sufficient to discourage violation.[48] However, under article 230 of the UNCLOS only monetary penalties can be imposed except in the case of a 'wilful and serious act of pollution in the territorial sea'. The 1972 London Convention on the Prevention of Marine Pollution by Dumping of Wastes and Other Matter[49] (and amending London Protocol intended to replace it) specifically prohibit the disposal into the seas 'of any wastes or other matter in whatever form or condition'.[50] The Convention lists those substances which cannot be disposed, while the Protocol is tougher listing those that can and prohibiting disposal of all others.[51] The Convention obliges the taking of appropriate measures 'to prevent and if necessary to punish' conduct in contravention of the Convention.[52] Control of the production of ozone-depleting substances by the Montreal Protocol on Substances that Deplete the Ozone Layer[53] spawned an illegal trade in chlorofluorocarbons (CFCs), which resulted in the amendment of the Protocol to oblige parties to criminalize the illegal export and import of CFCs.[54]

12.6 Illegal Transboundary Movement of Waste

Pollution that originates in one area and impacts in another is a difficult enough problem, but it becomes a criminal problem when it involves deliberate trans-boundary

---

[46] P Green, T Ward, and K McConnachie, 'Logging and Legality: Environmental Crime, Civil Society and the State' 34(2) *Social Justice* (2007) 94, 96.
[47] 2 November 1973, 1340 UNTS 184. Combined with the 1978 Protocol it entered into force 2 October 1983.
[48] Article 4(2) and (4).   [49] 29 December 1972, 1046 UNTS 120, in force 30 August 1975.
[50] Convention and Protocol, article 4(1).
[51] JL Batongbacal, 'Environmental Degradation: The Dumping of Pollution as a Transnational Crime' in N Boister and R Currie (eds), *Routledge Handbook of Transnational Criminal Law* (Abingdon: Routledge, 2015), 302.
[52] Article 7.   [53] 16 September 1987, 1522 UNTS 3, in force 1 January 1989.
[54] Article 4(a).

smuggling and dumping of waste. Batongbacal notes that transnational 'dumping of pollution' involves 'an intentional act of transferring pollution away from one state's jurisdiction and into another's, or into areas beyond national jurisdiction'.[55] In his view it is the purposeful nature of the cross-border discharge rather than some indiscriminate and undirected discharge which make a penal response more appropriate. Batongbacal notes that the more stringent regulation of pollution by states since the 1970s has had the unintended consequence of encouraging an illegal traffic of waste and pollutants out of states with high standards to other states with laxer standards.[56]

The international community responded by adopting the Basel Convention on the Control of Transboundary Movement of Hazardous Wastes and their Disposal in 1989.[57] The Convention sets up a regulatory system based on the principle that states of import and transit should give their prior informed consent before an export of waste can take place. It recognizes that parties have the sovereign right to prohibit the importation of hazardous substances or other waste for disposal.[58] The system involves inter alia a notification procedure, the environmentally sound management of the export of wastes, the duty to reimport where the provisions of the Convention are not complied with and the duty not to export to non-parties. Waste may not be exported even with consent to non-parties or to an area south of 60 degrees latitude.[59] Article 4(1)(b) obliges parties to prohibit or disallow the export of such wastes to those states that exercise that right. In terms of article 4(2) all parties also 'consider that the illegal traffic in hazardous wastes or other wastes is criminal' and are obliged to take legal, administrative and other measures for enforcement including in terms of article 4(4) 'measures to prevent and punish conduct in contravention of the Convention'. It is thus not all trade that is illegal, but only unauthorized trade in hazardous waste.[60]

The provisions of the Bamako Convention on the Ban of the Import into Africa and the Control of Transboundary Movement and Management of Hazardous Wastes within Africa[61] are substantially in line with the Basel Convention. Its penal provisions are, however, more explicit. Article 9(1) deems 'any transboundary movement of hazardous wastes' as 'illegal traffic' if it is carried out 'without notification ... to all States concerned' or 'without the consent ... of a State concerned' or if 'consent is obtained from States concerned through falsification, misrepresentation or fraud' or 'if it does not conform in a material way with the documents' or 'if it results in deliberate disposal of hazardous wastes' in contravention of the convention or international law. Article 9(2) then requires each party to criminalise all those who 'have planned, carried out, or assisted in such illegal imports', imposing penalties 'sufficiently high to both punish and deter such conduct'. Hazardous wastes are those defined as such in the convention, in national law or in other treaties controlling radioactive waste. 'Transboundary movement' is further defined in article 1(4) as 'any movement of hazardous wastes from an area

---

[55] Batongbacal, above n 51, 297–98.   [56] ibid, 305.
[57] 22 March 198, 1673 UNTS 57; in force 5 May 1992.   [58] Article 4(1)(a).
[59] Article 4(5) and (6).
[60] Batongbacal, above n 51, 306, fn 91, citing P Birnie, A Boyle, and C Redgwell (eds), *International Law and the Environment*, 3rd edn (Oxford: OUP, 2009), 473–77.
[61] Mali, 30 January 1991, in force 22 April 1998.

under the national jurisdiction of any State to or through an area under the national jurisdiction of another State, or to or through an area not under the national jurisdiction of another State, provided at least two States are involved in the movement.' Areas under national jurisdiction are defined in article 1(1) as 'any land, marine area or airspace within which a State exercises administrative and regulatory responsibility in accordance with international law in regard to the protection of human health or the environment.' Domestic legislation in African states has largely followed the Bamako Convention, although expanding on it to include purely domestic problems. Kenya's Environmental Management and Coordination Act,[62] for example, provides in section 141:

> 141. Offences relating to hazardous wastes, materials, chemicals and radioactive substances
>
> Any person who— ... (a) fails to manage any hazardous waste and materials in accordance with this Act; (b) imports any hazardous waste contrary to this Act; (c) knowingly mislabels any waste, pesticide, chemical, toxic substance or radioactive matter; (d) fails to manage any chemical or radioactive substance in accordance with this Act; (e) aids or abets illegal trafficking in hazardous waste, chemicals, toxic substances and pesticides or hazardous substances; (f) disposes of any chemical contrary to this Act or hazardous wastes within Kenya; (g) withholds information or provides false information about the management of hazardous wastes, chemicals or radioactive substances, commits an offence and shall, on conviction, be liable to a fine of not less than one million shillings, or to imprisonment for a term of not less than two years, or to both.

The minimum sentence speaks to the seriousness the problem presents.

12.7 Future Development of Environmental Crimes

The main target of criticism in regard to environmental crimes is usually poor enforcement of these laws.[63] There are many difficulties in operationalizing existing offences, particularly for developing states with limited resources, but inter-governmental organizations like the UNEP (Secretariat of the Basel Convention) are repositories of expertise and there are a number of non-governmental organizations working in the field such as the Environmental Investigation Agency which may provide assistance. However, the international laws framing these crimes are also inadequate to the task because (i) what is illicit and what is criminal are not adequately clarified and (ii) the material and mental elements of these crimes are not outlined in sufficient detail to provide for the kind of coordinated approach required to suppress the target activities. Following the sectoral nature of treaties built around specific environmental concerns, states tend to approach environmental offences individually rather than comprehensively. In Canada, for example, prosecutions are made under shipping legislation,

---

[62] [Rev 2012] Cap 387.
[63] See the discussion of law enforcement problem at White, above n 3, 288 et seq.

environmental protection legislation, wildlife legislation, and for simple fraud. The Council of Europe's 1998 Convention on the Protection of the Environment through Criminal Law,[64] which provides for a number of offences,[65] although it never entered into force, suggested at least a desire to establish a more coherent approach. Article 2 set out a comprehensive list of intentional pollution offences while article 3 required parties to criminalize negligent commission of those same forms of conduct. Article 4 added a number of other offences including trafficking in transboundary waste and protected flora and fauna, and provision was made for secondary participation, criminalization of legal persons and adequate penalties. After some false starts[66] the EU followed this example, with a Directive in 2008 on the protection of the environment through criminal law[67] designed to eliminate differences among the criminal laws of member states that give effect to the EU's environment protection requirements. Article 3 provides a single list of environmental crimes committed intentionally or with serious negligence, all of which are to be subject to effective proportionate and disuassive sanctions. This more coherent approach goes a long way to simplifying the normative terrain, making national laws more compatible, and thus enabling better cooperation.

---

[64] Strasbourg, 4 November 1998, ETS No 172, not in force.   [65] Articles 2 and 3.
[66] Council Framework Decision 2003/80/JHA of 27 January 2003 on the protection of the environment through criminal law, OJ L 029, 5 February 2003, which was struck down by the European Court of Justice.
[67] Directive 2008/99/EC of the European Parliament and of the Council of 19 November 2008 on the protection of the environment through criminal law, OJ L 328, 19 November 2008.

13

Firearms Trafficking

13.1 Introduction

Small arms and light weapons (SALW) are crucial to the violence implicit and explicit in much transnational crime. As Fellmeth points out: 'Narcotics and human traffickers, pirates and terrorists in particular use small arms and light weapons ... such as automatic rifles and handguns, to protect their income sources and leadership, suppress rival groups, kidnap for ransom, and intimidate state law enforcement officers.'[1]

SALW are as critical to enforcing illicit 'contracts' as the law is in enforcing licit contracts. However, suppressing the traffic in firearms is very difficult, as Drummond and Cassimatis note:

> The international arms trade is characteristically difficult to regulate because of the ready availability of small arms and light weapons; their easy portability, concealment and their relative inexpensiveness; the notorious dexterity of broker's exploitation of loopholes; production of free use or fake end-user certificates; evasion of airport controls, customs and radar trafficking; the overlap between black market illicit transfers and grey market government-complicit transactions; and the related lack of States' political will to implement and monitor tighter regulations and build concerted networks of international cooperation.[2]

This difficulty is compounded by the legality of private gun ownership and the manufacturing and sale of SALW in many states.[3] There is, for example, no Federal law in the US that criminalizes trafficking in firearms.[4] US prosecutors must rely on Federal laws that make it an offence to use false documents or make a false statement when purchasing weapons,[5] and which restrict the importing, manufacturing, and dealing in firearms to licensed individuals 'engaged in the business' of selling weapons,[6] even though the latter does not include those individuals engaged in occasional sales or sales from private collections.[7] Stringent lobbying by pro-gun ownership NGOs like the National Rifle Association means that the US, the architect of much modern transnational criminal law, is not a significant player in transnational arms control. Ironically, one of the peculiar features of the Mexican drug wars is that many of the guns were purchased by buyers from the drug cartels on the open market in the US.[8]

---

[1] AX Fellmeth, 'The UN Protocol Against the Illicit Manufacturing and Trafficking in Firearms, Their Parts and Components, and Ammunition 2001' in P Hauck and S Peterke (eds), *International Law and Transnational Organised Crime* (Oxford: OUP, 2016), 197.

[2] CE Drummond and AE Cassimatis, 'Weapons Smuggling' in N Boister and R Currie (eds), *The Routledge Handbook of Transnational Criminal Law* (Abingdon: Routledge, 2015), 247, 255.

[3] Fellmeth, above n 1, 198.

[4] M Krantz, 'Walking Firearms to Gunrunners: ATF's Flawed Operation in a Flawed System' 103 *Journal of Criminal Law and Criminology* (2013), 585, 592.

[5] 18 USC §§ 922 and 944.   [6] 18 USC § 922(a)(1)(A).   [7] 18 USC § 921(a)(21)(C).

[8] *United States v Hernandez*, 633 F3d 370 (5th Cir 2011), 372. See Krantz, above n 4, 604.

The range of weapons available for sale on the illicit market is astonishing. The infamous Tajik arms dealer Viktor Bout, who was caught in a US sting operation in Thailand in 2008, discussed selling the following weapons to undercover US agents:[9]

(1) 700 to 800 surface-to-air missiles; (2) 5,000 AK-47 firearms; (3) millions of rounds of ammunition; (4) various Russian spare parts for rifles; (5) anti-personnel land mines and C-4 explosives; (6) night-vision equipment; (7) 'ultralight' airplanes, which could be outfitted with grenade launchers and missiles; (8) unmanned aerial vehicles, which have a range of 200 to 300 kilometres; and (9) two cargo planes for arms deliveries.

However, because there was no weapons trafficking law in the US at the time, Bout had to be charged as a co-conspirator to kill US nationals with the 'members' of the FARC in Colombia to whom he thought he was supplying weapons (the undercover US agents).[10]

The illicit traffic in SALW is estimated to be worth US$1.7 billion to US$3.5 billion per annum.[11] The individual price of a weapon rises with the level of political instability, the further the distance the weapon has to travel, the greater the level of government control, and also depends on local perceptions of the quality of the place of manufacture.[12] Drawing a legal line between this traffic and the licit trade in SALW, estimated to be worth US$17.3 billion, has taken a long time and is still incomplete.

13.2 Background to the Firearms Protocol

The earliest multilateral instrument on control of the illicit traffic in SALW is the 1997 Inter-American Convention against the Illicit Manufacturing of and Trafficking in Firearms, Ammunition, Explosives and other Related Materials.[13] Its purpose as spelled out in article 2 is 'to prevent, combat, and eradicate the illicit manufacturing of and trafficking in firearms, ammunition, explosives, and other related materials' and to provide for international cooperation and information exchange in this regard. The provisions that were later to have the most impact on the content of the UN Firearms Protocol (see below) were the definitions of firearms as barrelled weapons using explosions to expel a projectile (although the definition also included 'any other weapon or destructive device such as any explosive, incendiary or gas bomb, grenade, rocket, rocket launcher, missile, missile system, or mine'),[14] and the expansive definitions of ammunition and 'illicit manufacturing' and 'illicit trafficking' in article 1:

1. 'Illicit manufacturing': the manufacture or assembly of firearms, ammunition, explosives, and other related materials:
   a. from components or parts illicitly trafficked; or

---

[9] *United States v Bout*, No 08 Cr 365 (SAS), 2011 WL 2693720, at 2 (SDNY July 11, 2011). See Krantz, above n 4, 605.

[10] Krantz, above n 4, 606.

[11] C May, *Transnational Crime and the Developing World* (London: Global Financial Integrity), 27 March 2017, 14, available at <http://www.gfintegrity.org/report/transnational-crime-and-the-developing-world/> last visited 4 July 2017.

[12] ibid, 14–15.   [13] 14 November 1997, 37 ILM 143 (1998); in force 1 July 1998.

[14] Article 1(3)(a) and (b).

   b. without a license from a competent governmental authority of the State Party where the manufacture or assembly takes place; or

   c. without marking the firearms that require marking at the time of manufacturing.

2. 'Illicit trafficking': the import, export, acquisition, sale, delivery, movement, or transfer of firearms, ammunition, explosives, and other related materials from or across the territory of one State Party to that of another State Party, if any one of the States Parties concerned does not authorize it.

The Inter-American Firearms Convention also made provision for criminalization of these actions as well as, subject to conformity with basic and constitutional laws, 'participation in, association or conspiracy to commit, attempts to commit, and aiding, abetting, facilitating, and counselling' their commission.[15] The regional limitations of the treaty meant that it was of limited global impact, however, and some Organization of American States members including the US have not ratified it. However, it did provide a model for further global action, which had already begun to gather steam.

In 1995, the UN Crime Congress in Cairo asked the United Nations Economic and Social Council to consider measures to prevent the 'transnational illicit trafficking in firearms, with a view to suppressing the use of firearms in criminal activity'.[16] In March 1997 a Group of Experts set up to study the problem by the UN Secretary-General recognized that global networks for smuggling SALW were becoming much more sophisticated and there was growing concern for control by transit states, destination states, and states of origin.[17] The study concluded that control of imports and exports was insufficient to control the traffic in SALW, and what was required was effective domestic regulation and international control.[18] In 1997 the UN General Assembly resolved to commence negotiation of a draft Protocol to the United Nations Convention against Transnational Organized Crime (UNTOC).[19] The negotiation process of the UNTOC undertaken by an ad hoc committee provided an opportunity for the development of the Protocol against the Illicit Manufacturing of and Trafficking in Firearms, their Parts and Components and Ammunition, supplementing the United Nations Convention against Transnational Organized Crime (the Firearms Protocol), which was adopted in 2000.[20]

13.3 Scope and Purpose of the Firearms Protocol

Although the Firearms Protocol draws heavily on the 1997 Inter-American Firearms Convention, its scope is more restricted. It is limited to portable firearms (borrowing

---

[15] Article 4(1) and (2).

[16] Report of the Ninth UN Congress on the Prevention of Crime and Treatment of Offenders, Cairo, 29 April–8 May 1995, UN DOC.A/CONF.169/16/Rev.1, 30.

[17] On the development process see J Hayes, 'The United Nations Firearms Protocol' in D Préfontaine (ed), *The Changing Face of International Criminal Law: Selected Papers* (Vancouver: The International Centre for Criminal Law Reform and Criminal Justice Policy, 2002), 125–36.

[18] Report of the Secretary-General on criminal justice reform and strengthening legal institutions and measures to regulate firearms, UN DOC.E/CN.15/1997/4, para 2.

[19] GA Res 53/111, 20 January 1999.

[20] New York, 31 May 2001, 2326 UNTS 208, in force 3 June 2005.

their definition as barrelled weapons that expel projectiles by 'explosive force' from the Inter-American Convention) and ammunition, their parts, and components, and excludes explosive devices like grenades.[21] It thus covers only light weapons that use cartridge-based ammunition and can be moved or carried by one person.[22] It also has a limited purpose: the distinction of the licit trade from the illicit traffic, and the suppression of the latter, not the suppression of the trade as a whole.[23] Although most illegal arms originate in government stockpiles, the Protocol specifically excludes 'state-to-state transactions or ... state transfers in cases where the application of the Protocol would prejudice the right of a State Party to take action in the interest of national security consistent with the Charter of the United Nations'.[24] The scope of the Protocol is thus limited to crime control rather than regulating the arms trade as a whole.[25]

13.4 Crimes and Punishments

The Firearms Protocol is designed to suppress two stages in the illicit supply of weapons, manufacturing and trafficking, but complements these offences with additional provisions. The scheme is as follows:

a) Manufacturing: Article 5(1)(a) of the Protocol requires parties to criminalize the illicit manufacturing of firearms, their parts, components, and ammunition—but illicit manufacturing is further defined in terms of article 3(d) as three different forms of conduct: (i) manufacturing from illicitly trafficked parts; (ii) manufacturing without a licence or authorization; and (iii) manufacturing without marking (required by the Protocol).[26]

b) Trafficking: Article 5(1)(b) criminalizes the illicit trafficking in firearms, etc, and again article 3(e) further defines illicit trafficking as their import, export, acquisition, sale, delivery, movement, or transfer from or across the territory of one party to that of another (i) if not authorized by either party or (ii) if the firearms are unmarked.

c) Tampering: Article 5(1)(c) supplements these two offences by obliging parties to criminalize tampering with firearms by falsifying or illicitly obliterating, removing or altering the markings on firearms required by the Protocol.

d) Ancillary offences: A range of ancillary offences back these provisions up. Article 5(2) obliges parties to criminalize accomplice liability and organizing, directing, aiding, abetting, facilitating, or counselling article 5(1) offences.

The distinction between these offences is fine. The United Nations Office on Drugs and Crime (UNODC) notes, for example, that 'knowingly marking a firearm with the same number as another firearm would fall within the manufacturing offence ... whereas

---

[21] Article 4(1) and 3(a); compare Article 1(3) of the 1997 Inter-American Convention.
[22] Drummond and Cassimatis, above n 2, 247, 260.   [23] Preambular para 1.
[24] Article 4(2).
[25] See UNODC, Travaux Préparatoires of the Negotiation for the Elaboration of the United Nations Convention Against Transnational Organized Crime and the Protocols thereto (UN: New York, 2006), Interpretive Note to Article 4; Fellmeth, above n 1, 211.
[26] Article 8.

affixing a marking that was unique but that gave a false country or place of manufacture ... would fall within the tampering offence'.[27] Other offences may be difficult for some states. The inchoate offence of counselling in article 5(2), common in many common law states, may run into human rights objections in the US on the basis of violation of freedom of expression.[28]

The definition of illicit trafficking in article 3(e) includes both intra-state and cross-border trafficking. However, article 4(1) requires transnationality and the involvement of an organized criminal group for the Protocol's application to these offences, although not as elements of these offences. Transnationality and Organised Criminal Group (OCG) involvement will also bring the participation in an OCG offences in article 5 of the UNTOC into potential application.

Article 5 is silent on penalties; however, we should bear in mind that article 11(1) of the UNTOC provides that the parties shall make the commission of its offences 'liable to sanctions that take into account the gravity of that offence'. Article 6 of the Firearms Protocol provides for confiscation of illicit firearms 'to the greatest extent possible within their domestic legal systems' but does not oblige parties to destroy them, permitting other methods of disposal.

13.5 Preventing Diversion from the Licit Trade

The Protocol provides for a number of special control measures designed to prevent diversion from the licit trade in SALW into the illicit traffic. These include obligations on parties to maintain records on firearms markings, their parts, and ammunition necessary; to be able to trace those firearms; as well as to keep records of international transactions.[29] The Protocol also requires parties to mark firearms at the time of manufacture, of import, or of transfer from government stocks, for the purposes of identification with a unique marking that provides details such as the place of manufacture, makers of the weapon, and so forth.[30] One of the central planks of the Protocol, article 10, requires parties to set up a system of export, import, and transit state authorization for the transfer of firearms and ammunition. Finally, the Protocol also requires parties to adopt measures to secure SALW shipments.[31] It has been pointed out, however, that these provisions provide little guidance to states on how they should undertake these activities, not spelling out, for example, precisely how marking should be undertaken or what information should be retained other than marking information.[32]

Perhaps the greatest weakness of the Protocol relates to brokering. Arms brokers are the intermediaries who bring parties together to facilitate the transfer of SALW, and thus play a key role in the traffic.[33] Their actions may be lawful, or unlawful, depending on the national law of the jurisdiction in which they are operating. International regulation of their conduct has been notoriously light and the Firearms Protocol is

---

[27] UNODC, Legislative Guide for the Implementation of the Protocol Against the Illicit Manufacturing of and Trafficking in Firearms, Their Parts and Components and Ammunition, Supplementing the United Nations Convention Against Transnational Organized Crime (2005), para 221.
[28] Fellmeth, above n 1, 208.   [29] Article 7.   [30] Article 8.   [31] Article 11.
[32] Fellmeth, above n 1, 208–09.   [33] Drummond and Cassimatis, above n 2, 255.

no exception. Article 15 only requires states parties that have not already established a system regulating firearms brokers to 'consider' doing so. Yet despite this relatively unobtrusive approach, major arms manufacturing states have not signed up to the Protocol. For example, while the EU has done so the US and Russia have neither signed nor ratified it, whereas China[34] and the UK have signed[35] but have not ratified.

13.6 The UN Programme of Action

The Conference of the Parties to the Protocol has picked out poor implementation of certain offences such as criminalization of marking.[36] Resort has thus been had by the UN to other softer instruments to supplement the Protocol, block gaps, and make for more effective control.

The UN Programme of Action to Prevent, Combat and Eradicate the Illicit Trade in Small Arms and Light Weapons in All Its Aspects adopted in 2001[37] provides a policy framework for further state action against SALW. It aims to promote the convergence of national legislation and to offer a foundation for multilateral activities. The Programme outlines a set of minimum international guidelines for effectively addressing the illicit arms trade, which are to be adapted by states. The exact nature of implementation of the Programme's guidelines as national obligations is left to the interpretation of each state.

The Programme provides for various guidelines relating to the illicit traffic. It urges states to review national legislation and implement reforms preventing the 'illegal manufacture of and illicit trafficking in small arms and light weapons or their diversion to unauthorized recipients'.[38] It calls in particular upon states to criminalize (it is assumed in accordance with the Protocol) 'the illegal manufacture, possession, stockpiling and trade of small arms and light weapons within their areas of jurisdiction, in order to ensure that those engaged in such activities can be prosecuted under appropriate national penal codes'.[39] In accordance with these offences, states are urged to identify and prosecute groups or individuals involved in associated acts of criminal behaviour.[40]

The Programme also sets out measures suggesting prohibiting the manufacture, stockpiling, transfer, and possession of any unmarked or inadequately marked weapons.[41] These measures include ensuring appropriate marking of SALW and the accurate recording of this information for as long as reasonably possible.[42] It also recommends that transfer authorizations should only be issued once the application has been assessed in accordance with the relevant international obligations.[43] It suggests that states make provision for the seizure and destruction of trafficked weapons.[44]

Finally, it tries to repair the lacunae in the Firearms Protocol in regard to regulation of brokering by suggesting regulation of brokers through registration, licensing, or authorization of 'brokering transactions as well as appropriate penalties for all illicit brokering activities performed within the State's jurisdiction and control'.[45]

---

[34] 9 December 2002.   [35] 6 May 2002.   [36] Fellmeth, above n 1, 215.
[37] 21 July 2001, UN Doc A/CONF.192/15.   [38] Para 2.   [39] Para 3.   [40] Para 6.
[41] Para 8.
[42] Paras 7 and 9.   [43] Paras 11 and 12.   [44] Para 16.   [45] Para 14.

While a welcome tool to facilitate implementation of the Firearms Protocol, the Programme does not compensate for the other conspicuous weakness in the Firearms Protocol, absence of provision for suppression of state transactions in firearms. The Programme stops short of establishing any further legal obligations within the framework developed by the Convention and Protocol. Implementation of the Programme has been uneven.[46]

13.7 The Tracing Instrument

The International Instrument to Enable States to Identify and Trace, in a Timely and Reliable Manner, Illicit Small Arms and Light Weapons (the Tracing Instrument), which was approved by the UN General Assembly in 2005,[47] is like the Programme of Action, designed to be complementary to the Firearms Protocol.[48] The purpose of the Tracing Instrument is to 'enable States to identify and trace, in a timely and reliable manner, illicit small arms and light weapons' and to engage in international cooperation in this regard, but explicitly not to acquire, transfer, retain, or manufacture SALW.[49] The Tracing Instrument defines 'tracing' as 'the systematic tracking of illicit small arms and light weapons found or seized on the territory of a State from the point of manufacture or the point of importation through the lines of supply to the point at which they became illicit'. Detailed guidance is given in regard to marking suggesting inter alia that while marking has to be on an exposed surface of the weapon the method used is up to the state concerned.[50] In an echo of the Firearms Protocol, the Tracing Instrument then provides further guidance as to tracing of SALW including unique marking at time of manufacture, import, transfer from Government stocks, and in Government possession, while encouraging manufacturers to develop measures against removal of marks.[51] Illicit weapons are to be marked when recovered or otherwise destroyed.[52] It also recommends further amplification of record keeping for extended periods of time[53] as well as the adoption of a system to enable international cooperation to ensure states are capable of responding to tracing requests in a timely manner.[54] One of the peculiarities of this system is that the Tracing Instrument recognizes that states maintain the right to decline or restrict the information sought by other states if doing so 'would compromise ongoing criminal investigations or violate legislation providing for the protection of confidential information', or the requesting state 'cannot guarantee the confidentiality of the information', or 'for reasons of national security consistent with the Charter of the United Nations'.[55] While a state refusing to provide such information must give its reasons for refusal,[56] the broad discretion implicit in the provision suggests a continued disinclination to allow any interference in the interstate arms trade.

---

[46] Report of the United Nations Conference to Review Progress Made in the Implementation of the Programme of Action to Prevent, Combat and Eradicate the Illicit Trade in Small Arms and Light Weapons in All its Aspects, UN Doc A/CONF.192/2012/RD/4, 18 September 2012, para 9.

[47] Annexed to GA Res 55/255, 8 December 2005.   [48] Preambular para 5.

[49] Paras 1–3.   [50] Para 7.   [51] Para 8.   [52] Para 9.   [53] Paras 11–13.

[54] Para 14.   [55] Para 22.   [56] Para 23.

13.8 Controlling the Licit Trade: The Arms Trade Treaty

Apart from commercial transfer between state-owned entities, the Firearms Protocol does not regulate the transfers of SALW between states. As noted, at a regional level, the Inter-American Convention is stronger than the Protocol in that it obliges parties to inter alia adopt a manufacturing and import export licensing regime. At a sub-regional level, the 2006 Economic Community of West African States (ECOWAS) Convention on Small Arms and Light Weapons and Other Related Materials[57] is also stronger in that it bans all transfers in the absence of collective authorization, and states have to seek exemptions from the ban for the purpose of imports for national security needs.[58]

In a reversal of the normal process of development of a global prohibition regime, the lawful transfer of conventional weapons only came under greater formal legal regulation at a global level after measures had been developed targeting the illicit trade. Initially regulation of the arms trade was conducted through informal measures such as the Wassenaar Arrangement on Export Controls for Conventional Arms and Dual-Use Goods and Technologies.[59] Negotiations of a general arms trade treaty incorporating some of the measures in this multilateral export control regime were precipitated by the UN General Assembly in 2008 when in Resolution 64/48 it recommended development of a 'legally binding instrument on the highest possible standards for the transfer of conventional arms'. Despite the fact that the General Assembly explicitly recognized the 'right of all States to manufacture, import, export, transfer and retain conventional arms for self-defence and security needs and in order to participate in peace support operations',[60] negotiation of the treaty was marked by the non-participation of major SALW manufacturing states. This negotiation process finally bore fruit with the adoption of the Arms Trade Treaty (ATT) in 2013.[61]

The Preamble of the ATT notes that regulation of lawful transfers has the potential to address the illicit trade.[62] Article 1 expands that the purpose of the ATT is to 'establish the highest possible common international standards for regulating or improving the regulation of the international trade in conventional arms' in order to 'prevent and eradicate the illicit trade in conventional arms and prevent their diversion'. The material scope of the ATT includes a full range of conventional weapons including SALW and ammunition.[63] Key to the ATT is the 'national control system' for transfers of conventional arms, ammunition, and components to be implemented for controlling the licit trade.[64] Certain exports are absolutely prohibited. Thus parties are obliged not to authorize a transfer if at the time they know that the arms will be used to commit genocide, crimes against humanity, grave breaches of the Geneva Conventions, or war crimes.[65] Others must be assessed for the risk of negative consequences outlined in the ATT and parties are obliged to refuse to authorize exports where there is an

---

[57] Signed on 14 June 2006, in force 20 November 2009, available at ECOWAS <www.ecosap.ecowas. int>. See articles 1, 3, and 4(1).

[58] *Travaux Préparatoires*, above n 25, 627.

[59] See The Wassenaar Arrangement, <http://www.wassenaar.org/> last visited 4 July 2017.

[60] Preambular para 6.

[61] Adopted by UN GA Res 67/234B on 2 April 2013; in force 24 December 2014.   [62] Para 4.

[63] Articles 2 and 3.   [64] Article 5.   [65] Article 6(3).

'overriding risk' that the exports could be used to 'commit or facilitate' international crimes, serious human rights violations, or 'an act constituting an offence under international conventions or protocols relating to transnational organized crime to which the exporting state is a party'.[66]

The ATT does not, however, explicitly prohibit arms transfers destined to criminal groups.[67] There are other weaknesses. The ATT obliges a party to regulate brokering of conventional arms within its jurisdiction, but only suggests that such measures may include registering of brokers or written authorization prior to brokering a deal, thus sustaining the weakness in this regard of the Firearms Protocol.[68] The ATT obliges parties to take steps to prevent diversion into the illicit traffic, including in similar fashion to the Tracing Instrument measures for national regulation, international cooperation, and information sharing. While the treaty sets out a series of obligations to control the licit trade, it leaves states a significant amount of latitude in the choice of how to do so, and does not oblige them to use criminalization.[69]

13.9 Conclusion

In 2013, the UN Security Council adopted its first Resolution in SALW.[70] In doing so, it recalled

> the close connection between international terrorism, transnational organized crime, drugs trafficking, money-laundering, other illicit financial transactions, illicit brokering in small arms and light weapons and arms trafficking, and the link between the illegal exploitation of natural resources, illicit trade in such resources and the proliferation and trafficking of arms as a major factor fuelling and exacerbating many conflicts.[71]

The Security Council specifically linked UNTOC, the Firearms Protocol, the Programme of Action, and the Tracing Instrument as crucial instruments in countering the 'illicit transfer, destabilizing accumulation and misuse' of SALW.[72] It is difficult, however, to get a clear idea of just how effectively these instruments are working together to suppress the illicit traffic. Data is uneven. A 2012 United Nations Office on Drugs and Crime study for the Conference of the Parties noted, for example, a significant variation in reports of the numbers of firearms confiscated from dozens in some states to tens of thousands in others, and reports of confiscation of a few rounds of ammunition to millions.[73] Prosecutions of high-profile commercial-scale traffickers like Viktor Bout are, however, quite rare. Efforts to distil complicity in core international crimes such as crimes against humanity and war crimes as a way of reaching and holding individual arms suppliers and brokers responsible for their actions[74] are mute testimony to the failure of transnational criminal law to control the illicit traffic in SALW.

---

[66] Article 7(3).
[67] Fellmeth, above n 1, 217.   [68] Article 10; Drummond and Cassimatis, above n 2, 255.
[69] Drummond and Cassimatis, above n 2, 260.   [70] SC Res 2117, 26 September 2013.
[71] Preambular para 8.   [72] Preambular para 19.
[73] Work of the United Nations Office on Drugs and Crime on conducting a study of the transnational nature of and routes used in trafficking in firearms, CTOC/COP/2012/12, 8 August 2012, para 16.
[74] Drummond and Cassimatis, above n 2, 256 et seq.

14

Illicit Trafficking in Cultural Artefacts

14.1 Introduction

The trafficking of works of art and other movable cultural artefacts[1] has grown steadily more notorious, particularly through reports that the Islamic State in Iraq and the Levant (ISIL) has been supplementing funding from oil revenues with the excavation and trafficking of antiquities from Iraq and Syria.[2] Trafficking in cultural artefacts is not, however, a new undertaking, having been intimately associated in modern times with European colonialism. It impacted heavily in the past on the heritage of particular cultures and of humanity generally, and continues to do so today.

Responses to this traffic using penal law have thus far been very limited both in scope and nature. Traditional laws prohibiting smuggling have proved to be ineffective in guarding national treasures. They have been avoided by corruption, poor implementation, sophisticated schemes to avoid detection, or through the laws themselves not being clear that the export or import of a particular artefact is in fact prohibited. International efforts to suppress the illicit traffic in cultural property have struggled to distinguish the illicit traffic from the licit trade. The difficulty, as Visconti puts it, is that 'the arts and antiquities market is intrinsically opaque, so much so that we should think in terms of a "grey market" with licit and illicit dealings closely interwoven.'[3] Cultural artefacts of all kinds—paintings, statuary, pottery, books—are looted or stolen in producer/source states only to find themselves 'lawfully' for sale on the antiques or art market in collector states. Artefacts are easily disguised as lawfully obtained and efforts to restore property are stymied by a web of national laws which protect the rights of owners and other bona fide purchasers.[4]

This chapter sets out the nature of the illicit traffic in cultural artefacts, before examining the most significant international instruments which have been adopted in the effort to control if not to suppress this traffic, with a particular focus on measures with a specific criminal content.

14.2 The Nature of Illicit Trafficking in Cultural Property

In an informal sense illicit trafficking in cultural artefacts involves the removal (whether by theft or looting), the transport, and the sale of movable objects of cultural

---

[1] A Visconti, 'Cultural Property Trafficking' in N Boister and R Currie (eds), *The Routledge Handbook of Transnational Criminal Law* (Abingdon: Routledge, 2014), 264, 265.

[2] J Pipkins, 'ISIL and the Illicit Antiquities Trade' 24 *International Affairs Review* (2016), 100, 101.

[3] Visconti, above n 1, 267.

[4] JN Lehman, 'The Continued Struggle with Stolen Cultural Property: The Hague Convention, The UNESCO Convention, and the Unidroit Draft Convention' 14 *Arizona Journal of International and Comparative Law* (1997) 527, 529.

value. Campbell suggests that the illicit supply chain involves four stages with four different roles: 'looter, early stage middleman or intermediary, late stage intermediary, and collector'.[5] He notes that individuals may be involved in more than one stage of the process but that each role requires different skills:

- looters, specific local knowledge of the location of potentially valuable artefacts;
- early stage middle men, such as transport specialists/document forgery experts/ bribe makers, how to get the artefacts across country and past potential hazards such as border posts;
- last-stage intermediaries, such as specialists at laundering, how to allay the fears of collectors that the artefacts are not 'illicit'.

These supply chains may be entirely intra-state although in many cases they cross borders (whether by smuggling or legally) and thus become transnational. The market is also said to be heavily penetrated by organized crime although the extent of this penetration is unknown.[6]

The harms that occur are varied. The introduction of a cultural artefact into the illicit chain of supply may involve a range of activities from vandalism of nationally significant archaeological sites by locals to the well-organized theft of artworks from public or private collections. Whether these activities make a significant impact on the cultural heritage of a particular culture or nation will depend on a wide variety of factors not least the cultural importance of the particular item. However, large-scale looting and trafficking can lead rapidly to the depletion of an entire national cultural heritage.

How much the individuals who operate each link in the chain of supply profit from their actions depends on their specific role. Looting of an individual artefact exposes that individual to a great deal of risk but usually does not generate much in the way of profit for the individual looter, while art 'heists' of major works may generate significantly more for the thief (although these are comparatively rare). Intermediaries especially late-stage middle men such as a range of professionals in the art trade— second-hand art dealers, retailers, and antiques dealers—stand to gain more handsomely because as the product moves down the chain of supply the specialist art knowledge required increases. While estimates of values between US$1.2 billion and US$1.6 billion have been made,[7] there are no reliable statistics on the value of the global illicit market in cultural artefacts as a whole largely because of its clandestine nature,[8] although the point has been made by many commentators that the illicit market supplies a significant proportion of the cultural artefacts being traded on the 'licit' antiquities market (a market which had a value of US$63.8 billion in 2015).[9]

---

[5] PB Campbell, 'The Illicit Antiquities Trade as a Transnational Criminal Network: Characterizing and Anticipating Trafficking of Cultural Heritage' 20 *International Journal of Cultural Property* (2013) 116.

[6] Visconti, above n 1, 268.

[7] C May, *Transnational Crime and the Developing World* (London: Global Financial Integrity), 35, available at <http://www.gfintegrity.org/report/transnational-crime-and-the-developing-world/> last visited 4 July 2017.

[8] Visconti, above n 1, 267.   [9] May, above n 7, 36.

14.3 Measures against Trafficking of Cultural Property in Wartime: The 1954 Hague Convention and its Protocols

Destruction and appropriation of cultural artefacts are a consequence of war. Although the problem is ancient, it was the Nazis' organized large-scale looting during the Second World War that led to the adoption under the auspices of the United Nations Educational, Scientific and Cultural Organization (UNESCO) of the 1954 Hague Convention for the Protection of Cultural Property in the event of Armed Conflict.[10] It defines 'cultural property' in article 1 as 'movable . . . property of great importance to the cultural heritage of every people'.[11] A response within the *ius in bello* to looting in armed conflict, it only applies to armed conflict and much of the Hague Convention is concerned with protection of cultural property during wartime. Its most relevant provision to suppression of the illicit traffic as a transnational crime is an obligation to 'prohibit ... any form of theft, pillage or misappropriation'.[12] It also calls for each party to impose penal sanctions against violators,[13] although it fails to enumerate or describe specific criminal offences. A First Protocol to the Convention is concerned about protection, custody, and return of cultural property.[14] Detailed criminalization provisions were only introduced in a Second Protocol to the Convention in 1999.[15] Article 9(1) of the Second Protocol provides that an occupying party:

> shall prohibit and prevent in relation to the occupied territory: (a) any illicit export, other removal or transfer of ownership of cultural property; (b) any archaeological excavation, save where this is strictly required to safeguard, record or preserve cultural property; (c) any alteration to, or change of use of, cultural property which is intended to conceal or destroy cultural, historical or scientific evidence.

Although article 15 introduces a range of core international crimes such as making cultural property an object of attack, it also includes its 'theft, pillage and misappropriation'.[16] The less exacting article 21 addresses some aspects of the illicit traffic other than the looting, requiring parties 'to suppress when committed intentionally' through legislative, administrative, or disciplinary measures any 'illicit export, other removal or transfer of ownership of cultural property from occupied territory in violation of the Convention or this Protocol'.[17] The limitations of this provision to export of cultural artefacts appropriated into the illicit traffic from occupied territory make it of limited value against the illicit traffic as a whole.

---

[10] 14 May 1954, 249 UNTS 240 (1956), in force 7 August 1956.   [11] Article 1.
[12] Article 4.   [13] Article 28.
[14] Protocol for the Protection of Cultural Property in the Event of Armed Conflict, The Hague, 14 May 1954, 249 UNTS 251; in force 7 August 1956.
[15] Second Protocol to the Hague Convention of 1954 for the Protection of Cultural Property in the Event of Armed Conflict, 26 March 1999, 2253 UNTS 172; in force 9 March 2004.
[16] Article 15(1)(e).   [17] Article 21(b).

14.4 Regulating Supply to the Market: The UNESCO Conventions

The UNESCO Convention on the Means of Prohibiting and Preventing the Illicit Import, Export, and Transfer of Ownership of Cultural Property[18] was adopted in 1970 in order to suppress trafficking in cultural property during peacetime. Article 1 provides for an expanded definition of 'cultural property' as 'property which, on religious or secular grounds, is specifically designated by each State as being of importance for archaeology, prehistory, history, literature, art or science' and which belongs to one of a specified range of categories: rare collections, property relating to history, products of archaeological excavations, elements of dismembered monuments, antiquities, objects of ethnological interest, and properties of artistic interest. Article 3 declares 'illicit' the 'import, export or transfer of ownership of' such property in contravention of the Convention. The Convention's provisions in this regard are elaborate. The parties agree to prohibit the unauthorized export of cultural property (ie without an export certificate)[19] and import of stolen cultural property,[20] to 'impose penalties or administrative sanctions' on infringements,[21] and return illegally imported property and, upon a fully documented claim, pay compensation.[22] Each party is also obliged to require dealers to keep a transaction register (enforced by penal or administrative sanction) recording the details of supply and sales including names of those involved, and to warn purchasers of any relevant export prohibition.[23] Western collector states, concerned about the protection of bona fide purchasers, were hesitant to ratify. When the US ratified in 1983 it declared that it understands article 3 'not to modify property interests in cultural property under the laws of the States parties'.[24]

The 2001 UNESCO Convention on the Protection of the Underwater Cultural Heritage[25] is limited to underwater cultural artefacts and takes a similarly equivocal position to the 1970 UNESCO Convention on criminal suppression. Article 14 obliges parties to 'take measures to prevent the entry into their territory, the dealing in, or possession of, underwater cultural heritage illicitly exported and/or recovered, where recovery was contrary' to the Convention itself. These measures may be enforced through criminalization,[26] as they have to be enforced in terms of article 17 through sanctions 'adequate in severity to be effective in securing compliance and to discourage violations wherever they occur'. National laws must also seek to 'deprive offenders of the benefit deriving from their illegal activities'.

There is no specific obligation to criminalize the various forms of conduct involved in the illicit chain of supply, however, in either of the UNESCO conventions, and reports suggest that preventive measure like the registration of transactions have not

---

[18] 14 November 1970, 823 UNTS 231; in force 24 April 1972.   [19] Article 6(b).
[20] Article 7(b).   [21] Article 8.   [22] Article 7.   [23] Article 10.
[24] Declaration on ratification, 2 September 1983, available at <http://portal.unesco.org/en/ev.php-URL_ID=13039&URL_DO=DO_TOPIC&URL_SECTION=201.html#RESERVES>   last   visited   2 June 2017.
[25] 2 November 2001, 41 ILM 40 (2002), in force 2 January 2009.   [26] Visconti, above n 1, 275.

been enforced in many states. May notes:[27] 'The vast majority of countries also do not regulate the sale of art, unlike the sale of other high-value items such as real estate and automobiles. There is no transaction record, no reporting to authorities, and no recorded transfer of title.'

14.5 Criminal Suppression: The Failed 1985 European Convention and the 2017 Nicosia Convention

The 1985 European Convention on Offences Relating to Cultural Property [28] took a more direct approach to the use of criminal laws to suppress the illicit traffic. The Convention, which never came into force, applied to 'cultural property', defined in a very detailed list in Appendix II(1).[29] Article 3(1) criminalized the forms of conduct listed in Paragraph 1 of Appendix III, viz theft, appropriation through violence or menace, and receiving regardless of where the theft or appropriation occurred. These measures did not cover every stage in the supply chain. However, article 3(2) permitted the parties to criminalize (other parties cannot therefore object) a very detailed range of supply chain activities (including activities that involve the introduction of the property into the illicit supply chain such as theft and fraud, destruction, or damage, to activities touching aspects of the work of intermediaries such as different forms of handling, concealment, exportation, or attempted exportation, to activities at the supply end of the chain including alienation, acquisition in a grossly negligent manner, and acquisition of inalienable property or conditionally alienable property, etc).[30] In addition, article 12 provided for 'the necessary measures for adequate sanctioning'. A significant part of the Convention was given over to measures designed to reduce barriers to international cooperation against these offences and to respect the general duty in article 6 to cooperate in restitution of the property discovered in its territory subsequent to an offence (which would include the mandatory as well as optional offences in the Convention).

Revisiting this ground in 2017, the Council of Europe replaced the 1985 Convention with the in some ways broader but still modest Convention on Offences Related to Cultural Property, which was opened for signature on 27 May in Nicosia.[31] It specifically aims to fill the criminalization gap left by other treaties dealing with cultural property,[32] by providing for criminalization of certain acts, strengthening crime prevention and criminal justice responses and promoting international cooperation in order to increase the protection of cultural property.[33] With a broad definition of cultural property that draws on the earlier conventions to include both movable and immovable property,[34] the offences in Chapter II try to cover all the links in the illegal chain of supply. Covering the supply end article 3 requires criminalization of 'theft and other forms of unlawful appropriation' to movable cultural property, while article 4(1)

---

[27] May, above n 7, 37.   [28] Delhi, 23 June 1985, ETS No 119; not yet in force.
[29] Article 2.   [30] Listed in para 2 of appendix III.
[31] 27 May 2017, CETS 221; not in force.
[32] Explanatory Report to the Council of Europe Convention on Offences Related to Cultural Property, Council of Ministers 27 May 2017, CM(2017)32, para 17.
[33] Article 1.   [34] Article 2.

criminalizes intentional excavation, removal, and retention (whether excavation was authorized or not), although article 4(2) allows states to declare that they will apply non-criminal sanctions. Shifting focus to supply, article 5(1) criminalizes intentional illegal importation of movable cultural property spelling out that such illegality may arise through theft, illegal excavation and retention, illegal export (although with the caveat that the export offence must require *mens rea* in the form of knowledge), although again article 5(2) allows states to declare that they will apply non-criminal sanctions. Article 6(1) criminalizes the analogous offence of intentional illegal importation of movable cultural property, but again article 6(2) provides the non-criminalization option. Remarkably, the Convention also targets the consumption end of the market. Article 7(1) requires criminalization of acquisition of such stolen, illegally excavated, exported, or imported property provided *mens rea* in the form of knowledge of unlawful provenance is present. Then in addition article 7(2) requires parties to consider criminalization on a 'should have known' basis if the accused 'had exercised due care and attention in acquiring the cultural property' in article 7(2). Perhaps the most interesting offence is that in article 8(1), which criminalizes 'placing on the market' of stolen, illegally excavated, exported, or imported movable cultural property with knowledge of unlawful provenance, and again article 8(2) requires parties to consider applying a should have known standard if they had exercised due care and attention. Article 9 criminalizes the falsification of documents so long as there is intention to present the property as licit in provenance. Article 10 is the only offence that deals with both movable and immovable property. Article 10(1) criminalizes destruction and damage, removal (in whole or part) with a view to importing, exporting, or placing on the market, although this time under article 10(2) parties may declare they simply do not wish to criminalize without any substitute measure or to apply it only in the absence of the owner's consent. Provision is also made for aiding, abetting, and attempts in article 11, although qualified where necessary by the qualifications in the primary offences.

In regard to penalties, article 14(1) spells out in customary fashion that natural persons should be 'punishable by effective, proportionate and dissuasive sanctions, which take into account the seriousness of the offence'. It adds that these sanctions shall include penalties of deprivation of liberty that may give rise to extradition (except for excavation and importation of illegal exported property offences). Targeting legal persons, the more innovative article 14(2) provides similarly for 'effective, proportionate and dissuasive sanctions' applied to legal persons including criminal or non-criminal monetary sanctions' suggesting also 'other measures' such as 'temporary or permanent disqualification from exercising commercial activity', 'exclusion from entitlement to public benefits or aid', 'placing under judicial supervision', or a 'judicial winding-up order'. Article 15 also provides for aggravating circumstances, including commission of the offence abusing the trust placed in them as professionals, commission by a public official tasked with conservation or protection, commission in the framework of a criminal organization, and previous convictions for these offences.

The rest of the Convention is given over to prevention and cooperation measures. The Convention certainly fills a gap. Most remarkably, it restricts the criminalization provisions in regard to the supply side of the chain of supply, but not the demand side.

It makes sense to do so given the increasing involvement of technical specialists and parallel increase in profit as one progresses along the chain. At this stage it is difficult to comment on its prospects for success, but this may be perceived rightly or wrongly as an imbalance by some states.

14.6 Recovery and Restitution under Private Law: The UNIDROIT Convention

Adopted in 1995, the Convention on the International Return of Stolen or Illegally Exported Cultural Objects,[35] which was developed by the International Institute for the Unification of Private Law (UNIDROIT), is not concerned with criminalization but with the 'restitution' of stolen cultural objects or the 'return' of illegally exported ones. It is designed to increase 'international cultural cooperation' and its authors were aware that these actions could not take the place of suppression under the criminal law.[36]

14.7 Attempting to Plug the Gaps in the Effective Suppression of Illicit Trafficking in Cultural Property

Generally the international system has thus far been better at providing for inter-state remedies for the return of unlawfully removed cultural artefacts[37] than it has been at constructing a prohibition regime in regard to trafficking in cultural artefacts. Whether the 2017 Nicosia Convention comprehensively fills this gap and leads to a significant change in the domestic legal position of the trade/traffic in cultural arte-facts is not yet clear. Given it is a Council of Europe Convention it will be difficult to apply globally.

Some attempt has been made to encourage bilateral cooperation globally against the illicit traffic through development under the Commission on Crime Prevention and Criminal Justice (CCPCJ) of the Model Treaty for the Prevention of Crimes that infringe on the Cultural Heritage of Peoples in the form of Movable Property.[38] It uses a definition of movable cultural property very similar in scope to that in the UNESCO Convention.[39] It then spells out a suggested list of prohibitions designed to suppress different elements of the illicit traffic including export and import, acquisition and dealing in illicitly exported artefacts as well as specific measures to ensure that individuals who acquire such property are not considered to have done so 'in good faith'.[40] Article 3 provides specifically that the parties agree to 'impose sanctions' on

---

[35] Rome, 24 June 1995, 34 ILM 1322 (1995); in force 1 July 1998.   [36] Preambular para 7.

[37] See, eg, in the EU, Directive 2014/60/EU of the European Parliament and of the Council of 15 May 2014 on the return of cultural objects unlawfully removed from the territory of a Member State and amending Regulation (EU) No 1024/2012, OJ L 159/11.

[38] Eighth United Nations Congress on the Prevention of Crime and the Treatment of Offenders, Havana, 27 August–7 September 1990: report prepared by the Secretariat (UN Pub Sales No E.91.IV.2), chap I, sect B.1, annex.

[39] Article 1.   [40] Article 2.

(a) Persons or institutions responsible for the illicit import or export of movable cultural property; (b) Persons or institutions that knowingly acquire or deal in stolen or illicitly imported movable cultural property; (c) Persons or institutions that enter into international conspiracies to obtain, export or import movable cultural property by illicit means.

The remaining recommendations relate to international cooperation procedures for the recovery and return of illicitly trafficked cultural artefacts. In spite of the pliability of language such as 'sanctions', it is the only UN Model Law not to be adopted as a General Assembly Resolution and thus effectively remains in draft form.[41]

Taking a different tack, in Resolution 5/7[42] the 2010 United Nations Convention against Transnational Organized Crime (UNTOC) Conference of the Parties (COP) invited parties to consider criminal offences against cultural property as 'serious crimes' in terms of article 2(b) of the UNTOC by ensuring a 'maximum penalty of deprivation of liberty of at least four years or more'.[43] This approach was approved by the UN General Assembly in Resolution 66/180 of 19 December 2011, which invites UN member states

> to make trafficking in cultural property, including stealing and looting at archaeological and other cultural sites, a serious crime, as defined in article 2 of the United Nations Convention against Transnational Organised Crime, with a view to fully utilising that Convention for the purpose of extensive international cooperation in fighting all forms and aspects of trafficking in cultural property and related offences.

Commentators have expressed caution, however, about whether it would be apt to make every such offence 'serious' in these terms simply to bring them in the scope of the UNTOC, because different states have very different offences and in regard to some more trivial offences it may involve over-penalization.[44]

Finally, the United Nations Office on Drugs and Crime has drafted a set of non-binding International Guidelines on Crime Prevention and Criminal Justice Responses with respect to trafficking in Cultural Property and Other Related Offences, which were adopted by the UN General Assembly in 2014.[45] Composed mainly of suggested measures on prevention and international cooperation, Chapter II on 'Criminal Justice Policies' does point to the adoption of penal offences that may serve the purpose of better harmonization of crimes in regard to illicit trafficking of cultural artefacts. Again, however, supply is more obviously the target than demand. After suggesting again adoption of domestic legislation that will make possible use of the UNTOC,[46] guideline 16 suggests criminalizing as 'serious' offences a number of different activities in regard to cultural property. These include trafficking, illicit

---

[41] Visconti, above n 1, 277.

[42] Conference of the Parties to the United Nations Convention against Transnational Organized Crime, Report of the Conference of the Parties to the United Nations Convention against Transnational Organized Crime on its fifth session, held in Vienna from 18 to 22 October 2010, CTOC/COP/2010/17.

[43] An invitation that has since been repeated at the 2012 CCPCJ, Report on the twenty-second session (7 December 2012 and 22–26 April 2013), E/CN.15/2013/27, at 7.

[44] Visconti, above n 1, 278.   [45] They are annexed to GA Res 69/196 of 18 December 2014.

[46] Guideline 13.

export and import, theft, looting, conspiracy, or participation in an organized criminal group to traffic in cultural property or related offences (in terms of article 5 of the UNTOC), and laundering of trafficked cultural property. Guideline 17 suggests states consider criminalizing damaging or vandalizing cultural property or acquiring it with conscious avoidance of its legal status, but only when such offences are 'related to trafficking in cultural property'. The Guidelines also recommend a reporting obligation of suspected cases of trafficking and, more interestingly, criminalization for failure to do so.[47] The heavily qualified guideline 19 attempts to confront the diligence in ignorance that accompanies much laundering of cultural artefacts onto the international antiquities trade:

> Guideline 19. States should consider making it possible, in a way not contradictory to their fundamental legal principles, to infer a perpetrator's knowledge that an object has been reported as trafficked, illicitly exported or imported, stolen, looted, illicitly excavated or illicitly traded, on the basis of objective factual circumstances, including when the cultural property is registered as such in a publicly accessible database.

The Guidelines go on to suggest application of 'proportionate, effective, and dissuasive sanctions' to these suggested offences,[48] as well as custodial sentences for certain offences so that they meet the UNTOC threshold for serious crime.[49] They also recommend bans, disqualifications, and licence revocations, which may prove more effective options against dealers.[50] These are followed by a multitude of provisions on liability for legal persons, jurisdiction, seizure, and confiscation and so forth.

The Guidelines in effect present a blueprint for a UN treaty. However, despite the availability of these soft measures to guide national practice, responding appropriately through transnational criminal law to the trafficking in cultural property remains a highly sensitive issue, which a number of developing countries keep raising. In debate at the UN CCPCJ they have suggested that a new Protocol to the UNTOC be considered.[51] Nothing has yet come of these calls, and support from Council of Europe members for the Nicosia Convention may have a dampening effect on action under the auspices of the UN.

14.8 Conclusion

Global criminal justice policy has not yet converged in regard to the trafficking in cultural objects.[52] Although there are some promising new developments, private law and administrative law are still relied upon in practice to control the illicit market in cultural artefacts, even though the actual trafficking itself involves criminal activities.[53] The difficulty is that not every link in the chain of supply is treated as a criminal offence in every state. The existing legal obligations are not sharp enough to

---

[47] Guideline 18.   [48] Guideline 20.   [49] Guideline 21.   [50] Guideline 22.
[51] UNCCPCJ, *Report of the Nineteenth Session*, 4–9 December 2009 and 17–21 May 2010, UN Doc E/2010/30, 84.
[52] Visconti, above n 1, 276.
[53] S Manacorda, 'Criminal Law Protection of Cultural Heritage: An International Law Perspective' in S Manacorda and D Chappell, *Crime in the Arts and Antiquities World* (New York: Springer, 2011), 17, 32.

respond adequately to every link in the chain and to the peculiarly opaque nature of the intermeshed licit and illicit trade/traffic. Resort to soft law suggests an underlying political ambivalence from the usual Western supporters of tougher coordinated action within transnational criminal law, perhaps because the markets for these artefacts are in the West. It is hoped that the adoption in 2017 of the Nicosia Convention will signal a fundamental shift in this regard.

15

Emerging Transnational Crimes

15.1 Introduction

Transnational criminalization follows the development of markets that meet the demand for new products and services that come to be considered undesirable and thus subject to demands for suppression. Not all such markets are new. Some transnational crimes are making a comeback. The International Convention for the Suppression of Counterfeiting Currency was adopted in 1929,[1] but the crime itself has recently undergone a rebirth exacerbated by globalization and the accessibility of printing technology. Some are novel and have met little response. Transnational tax offences, for example, are common but rather than directly regulated by international law—double taxation agreements allow for the exchange of information to prevent evasion but do not create penal offences—law enforcement relies on indirect suppression through money laundering offences. This chapter, however, turns the spotlight on a selection of emerging transnational crimes.

Some of these offences are already fairly well established; others are at an earlier stage of development. Most are evolving in discrete prohibition regimes unconnected to the existing UN framework treaties, the United Nations Convention against Transnational Organized Crime (UNTOC) and United Nations Convention against Corruption (UNCAC). There are various reasons for the lack of consolidation. Regulation of the licit forms of these activities may have long been undertaken in an already developed legal regime such as in regard to intellectual property or a specific inter-governmental organization may have an existing mandate in that area (the World Health Organization (WHO) in regard to tobacco control) and be wary of ceding territory. In both cases the existing regime takes on criminalization as an additional form of regulation rather than turn to UN's existing instruments.

Many ideas for entirely new conventions that do fall within the UN criminal justice mandate never bear fruit mainly through lack of sufficient support or because of resistance from a specific group of states, perhaps because existing instruments already in large part cover these activities. Post-UNTOC enthusiasm for instruments on trafficking in stolen vehicles, trafficking in body parts, and sports-related crime have never received much traction. 'Convention fatigue' has also set in in Vienna, with fewer experts appearing at the UN's functional crime commissions and resident diplomats doing the 'negotiating', something which has a chilling effect on new developments. Preoccupation with cost and effective implementation of existing transnational crime conventions has contributed to this stultification.

---

[1] 20 April 1929, 112 LNTS 371, in force 22 February 1931.

15.2 Anti-competitive Conduct

The resort to criminalization of anti-competitive conduct is a relatively recent global phenomenon, which is in its early stages.[2] The US has long pursued prosecution
of anti-trust offences both at home and controversially by establishing a broad extraterritorial jurisdiction. Section 1 of the US's Sherman Antitrust Act of 1890[3] prohibited collusive conduct to restrain trade a misdemeanour with maximum punishment
of a year in prison. The US only upgraded the offence to a felony in 1974 but penalties
have increased sharply since then. Moreover, what was a fairly isolated step against
cartel behaviour is steadily becoming the norm as more and more states criminalize.
Section 45 of Canada's Competition Act 1985 is comprehensive and potentially highly
punitive:[4]

> 45 (1) Every person commits an offence who, with a competitor of that person with
>   respect to a product, conspires, agrees or arranges
>   (a) to fix, maintain, increase or control the price for the supply of the product;
>   (b) to allocate sales, territories, customers or markets for the production or
>   supply of the product; or
>   (c) to fix, maintain, control, prevent, lessen or eliminate the production or
>   supply of the product.
>   (2) Every person who commits an offence under subsection (1) is guilty of an
>   indictable offence and liable on conviction to imprisonment for a term not
>   exceeding 14 years or to a fine not exceeding $25 million, or to both.

Other states have chosen to criminalize only bid rigging[5] or price fixing[6] while many
still opt for civil penalties or have not taken any action at all. The emphasis in the US
has been on increasing the effectiveness of enforcement. In 1993 the US granted automatic immunity to witnesses who were prepared to give evidence against commercial
cartels, a tactic which resulted in a surge of applications for prosecutorial immunity
and proved very cost effective. In an effort to deter rather than censure it imposes huge
fines. But the increase in global criminalization has made it possible to increase extraditions and other forms of international cooperation. In *R v Whittle (Peter)*,[7] the so-
called 'marine hose cartel' involving allocation of markets and price fixing globally for
marine hose, the accused pleaded guilty to offences in the UK as part of a plea bargain
deal with US Federal authorities in order to allow them to return to the UK from the
US and cooperate with authorities there.

Efforts at an international level to develop a global instrument to foster a greater uniformity of approach to criminalization and cooperation against commercial cartels are
already in evidence. The Organisation for Economic Co-operation and Development
(OECD)'s 2014 Recommendation concerning International Co-operation on

---

[2] See generally A Stephan, 'An Empirical Evaluation of the Normative Justifications for Cartel
Criminalisation' *Legal Studies*, published online 21 May 2017 at <http://onlinelibrary.wiley.com/doi/
10.1111/lest.12165/full> last visited 23 June 2017.
[3] 15 USC §§ 1–7.   [4] c34.   [5] Section 298 of the *Srafgesetzbuch*, Germany.
[6] Brazil's Economic Crimes Law, Law No 8137/90.   [7] [2008] EWCA Crim 2560.

Competition Investigations and Proceedings[8] is the latest iteration in a line of soft law instruments that structure international cooperation in the investigation of anti-competitive behaviour. It does not define anti-competitive practice except to point to the particular definition in domestic law.[9] It does, however, following normal OECD practice, make a number of recommendations relevant to enforcement cooperation. In Recommendation 1, for example, the OECD: 'Recommends that Adherents commit to effective international co-operation and take appropriate steps to minimise direct or indirect obstacles or restrictions to effective enforcement co-operation between competition authorities.'

The substance of the instrument is designed in larger part to try to reconcile different systems in order to make sure that they do not get in each other's way during these investigations and in smaller part to foster cooperation through information exchange etc. Regional bodies have taken matters further. Articles 101 and 102 of the Treaty for the Functioning of the EU[10] prohibit anti-competitive behaviour and article 103 authorizes a mechanism for the imposition of fines. There is no indication as yet of a global initiative of a more strongly normative kind, although the use of labels such as 'hard core cartels' by the OECD[11] suggests fertile moral soil for further initiatives.

15.3 Intellectual Property Offences

Theft of intellectual property rights by counterfeiters or intellectual property (IP) pirates is one of the more controversial of the emerging transnational crimes. The value of counterfeit goods was estimated at $250 billion annually by the OECD in 1998[12] and this figure is still bandied about. Criminalization of copyright infringement is not, however, a new concept. Driven by complaints of loss of revenue and recognizing the inadequacy of civil injunctions and damages against the financially irresponsible and transient, the US has since 1909 used criminalization as a weapon against copyright infringement. It has steadily tightened the provisions in its copyright legislation, raising the penalties and broadening the scope of offences.[13] In the era of IP 'maximilization'—the relentless seeking of ever higher standards of IP protection to protect private revenue and tax receipts[14]—enforcement of criminalization has become a priority within the US. This punitive turn has been particularly directed towards copyright violation taking place on the Internet and particularly those who facilitate such violation. The prosecutions in the US of Internet file sharers

---

[8] 16 September 2014 [C(2014)108].   [9] Paragraph 1.

[10] 13 December 2007, 2008/C 115/01.

[11] OECD, Recommendation of the Council Concerning Effective Action against Hard Core Cartels, C(98)35/final, 25 March 1998.

[12] OECD, The Economic Impact of Counterfeiting, OECD: Paris 1998, available at <https://www.oecd.org/sti/ind/2090589.pdf> last visited 17 June 2017.

[13] See generally 'The Criminalization of Copyright Infringement in the Digital Era' 112 *Harvard Law Review* (1999) 1705 et seq for a review of the legislative development in the US.

[14] See generally SK Sell, 'The Global IP Upward Ratchet, Anti-Counterfeiting and Piracy Enforcement Efforts: The State of Play' *PIJIP Research Paper Series*, no 15, 1 October 2010, available at <http://digitalcommons.wcl.american.edu/cgi/viewcontent.cgi?article=1016&context=research> last visited 23 June 2017.

that facilitate the deliberate or reckless trade in copyright infringing material such as Napster, Grokster, Kazaa, Bit-torrent, and Pirate Bay[15] exemplify this punitive approach. Intellectual property holders such as the US-based entertainment industry, consider themselves to be the victims of this file-sharing and through their significant political influence they have placed their interests at the centre of US criminal policy making. Unfortunately for the US its territorial control has not always equalled its level of control outside of the US, and IP rights are territorial. This has forced the US and other states with major IP interests to pursue the transnationalization of criminal copyright laws.

Criminalization of copyright infringement is found in a number of multilateral international instruments. Article 61 of the Agreement on Trade-Related Aspects of Intellectual Property Rights (TRIPS Agreement)[16] adopted in Marrakesh in 1994, set the tone:

> Members shall provide for criminal procedures and penalties to be applied at least in cases of wilful trademark counterfeiting or copyright piracy on a commercial scale. Remedies available shall include imprisonment and/or monetary fines sufficient to provide a deterrent, consistently with the level of penalties applied for crimes of a corresponding gravity. In appropriate cases, remedies available shall also include the seizure, forfeiture and destruction of the infringing goods and of any materials and implements the predominant use of which has been in the commission of the offence. Members may provide for criminal procedures and penalties to be applied in other cases of infringement of intellectual property rights, in particular where they are committed wilfully and on a commercial scale.

Footnote 14 to Article 51 provides:

> (b) 'pirated copyright goods' shall mean any goods which are copies made without the consent of the right holder or person duly authorised by the right holder in the country of production and which are made directly or indirectly from an article where the making of that copy would have constituted an infringement of a copyright or a related right under the law of the country of importation.

What is meant by 'commercial scale' was explored when the US initiated a trade dispute against China under the World Trade Organization (WTO) because Chinese courts had adopted a rule that individuals could avoid criminal liability if they were found in possession of fewer than 500 copies of an IP-infringing item.[17] Finding China was not in violation, the panel concluded that 'commercial scale' meant counterfeiting or piracy typical of the particular product in the particular market,[18] as Grosse Ruse-Khan put it a 'relative situation specific interpretation ... which leaves

---

[15] G Urbas, 'Copyright, Crime and Computers: New Legislative Frameworks for Intellectual Property Rights Enforcement' 7 *Journal of International Commercial Law and Technology* (2012), 11, 11.

[16] Marrakesh Agreement Establishing the World Trade Organization, Annex 1C, 15 April 1994, 1867 UNTS 3, in force 1 January 1995.

[17] Panel Report, *China—Measures Affecting the Protection and Enforcement of Intellectual Property Rights (China-IPRs)*, (WT/DS3262/R), 26 January 2009, at 7.396–7.479, 7.480–7.482.

[18] ibid, 7.577.

considerable discretion to national legislators to set thresholds on the basis of products and markets'.[19]

The 1996 World Intellectual Property Organization (WIPO) Copyright Treaty,[20] which extends the Berne Convention's protection of copyright to include various digital media, provides generally in article 14(1) that states parties are obliged to adopt national laws to implement the treaty's obligations and more specifically in article 14(2) as follows:

> Contracting Parties shall ensure that enforcement procedures are available under their law so as to permit effective action against any act of infringement of rights covered by this Treaty, including expeditious remedies to prevent infringements and remedies which constitute a deterrent to further infringements.

The US and EU member states developed the Anti-Counterfeiting Trade Agreement (ACTA)[21] outside of the auspices of the UN or WTO in order to create a more effective (and more controversial) system for the control of IP. Although not yet in force the ACTA creates a range of new counterfeiting crimes covering all intellectual property rights included in TRIPS. Article 23, for example, echoes TRIPS by requiring criminalization of 'wilful trademark counterfeiting or copyright or related rights piracy on a commercial scale', and clarifies that this involves 'commercial activities for direct or indirect economic advantage', which appears much broader than the TRIPS threshold. Advantage need only be indirect, and it is uncertain whether what matters is the scale of these activities or the intention of the accused.[22] Secondary participation is criminalized, and penalties must include imprisonment as well as fines. Specific provision has also been made in other prohibition regimes to suppress conduct enabling counterfeiting. For example, as noted in Chapter 11, article 10(1) of the 2001 Council of Europe Convention on Cybercrime[23] obliges parties to criminalize the wilful commercial-scale use of a computer system to engage in the infringement of copyright.

US law provides the legislative model for national implementation of these multilateral provisions. Title I of the US's Digital Millennium Copyright Act (DMCA),[24] for example, implements the WIPO Copyright Treaty. A global wave of US-inspired legislative action has followed. In 1997 Aoki commented wryly that the US international agenda was more concerned with the protection of private intellectual property rights in developing states than the protection of fundamental human rights.[25]

---

[19] H Grosse Ruse-Khan, 'Intellectual Property Offences' in N Boister and R Currie (eds), *The Routledge Handbook of Transnational Criminal Law* (Abingdon: Routledge, 2015), 312, 320.

[20] 20 December 1996; in force 6 March 2002, available through WIPO Collection of Laws for Electronic Access at <http://www.wipo.int/export/sites/www/treaties/en/ip/wct/pdf/trtdocs_wo033.pdf> last visited 23 June 2017.

[21] 1 October 2011, available at <http://www.international.gc.ca/trade-agreements-accords-commerciaux/assets/pdfs/ACTA_text_Nov_15-eng.pdf> last visited 12 February 2012.

[22] Grosse Ruse-Khan, above n 19, 322.

[23] Budapest, 23 November 2001, ETS No 185, in force 1 July 2004.

[24] Public Law 105–304, 28 October 1998; 112 Stat 2860 codified in particular at 17 USC § 512, § 1201.

[25] K Aoki, 'The Stakes of Intellectual Property Law' in D Kairys (ed), *The Politics of Law: A Progressive Critique*, 3rd edn (New York: Basic Books, 1998), 259, 271.

The centrepiece of US policy has been to try to ensure that wherever they operate from copyright violators will face the certainty of punishment. David notes:

> Linking file-sharing with commercial counterfeiting, bootlegging and piracy—and then linking all of these with terrorism, drugs, drug dealing, illegal immigrants ... seeks to engender both a moral rejection of copyright infringing file-sharing and the belief that both the chance and the cost of getting caught are very high. These claims are tenuous at best ...[26]

Unfortunately for the advocates of criminal suppression, violation of copyright on the Internet is not always easily suppressed. Despite this global moral and legal proselytism there remains a mismatch between the expectations of producers of the allegedly copied material and those of users whose voracious appetite for knock-offs of the latest movie or handbag is driving this market.[27]

15.4 Counterfeiting of Medicines

Counterfeiting of medicines is a particular type of IP offence which has negative effects for both property rights and more importantly health rights, and thus has received special attention at the global level. In 1992 a WHO expert group defined counterfeit medicines as follows:[28]

> A counterfeit medicine is one which is deliberately and fraudulently mislabelled with respect to identity and/or source. Counterfeiting can apply to both branded and generic products and counterfeit products may include products with the correct ingredients or with the wrong ingredients, without active ingredients, with insufficient (inadequate quantities of) active ingredient(s) or with fake packaging.

Although there have been estimates of deaths because of the use of fake medicine ranging from the hundreds of thousands to millions per annum,[29] the true extent of the problem is not known. In 1998 the WHO's Declaration of Rome[30] identified counterfeiting of medicines as a global activity of specific concern, and in 2010 the UN Commission on Crime Prevention and Criminal Justice (CCPCJ) advocated criminalization and cooperation.[31] The most significant development thus far, has been adoption by the Council of Europe of the Convention on the Counterfeiting of Medical Products and Similar Crimes Involving Threats to Public Health (Medicrime

---

[26] M David, *Peer to Peer and the Music Industry: The Criminalization of Sharing* (London: Sage, 2009), 7.

[27] D Calhoun, 'Kim Dotcom: Cyber Policing Overreach or Just Desserts for a Digital Pirate?' [2012] *New Zealand Intellectual Property Journal* 877, 882.

[28] Guidelines to develop measures to combat counterfeit drugs, WHO/EDM/QSM 99.1 (1999) <http://whqlibdoc.who.int/hq/1999/WHO_EDM_QSM_99.1.pdf> last visited 17 June 2017.

[29] See A Ossola, 'The Fake Drug Industry is Exploding and We Can't do Anything About it' *Newsweek*, 7 September 2015, available at <http://www.newsweek.com/2015/09/25/fake-drug-industry-exploding-and-we-cant-do-anything-about-it-373088.html> last visited 17 June 2017.

[30] WHO International Conference, Combating Counterfeit Drugs: Building Effective International Collaboration, 'Declaration of Rome', 18 February 2006, paras 1 and 2.

[31] UNCCPCJ, *Report on the Twentieth Session* (3 December 2010 and 11–15 April 2011), UN Doc E/CN.15/2011/21.

Convention).[32] The purposes of the Convention are to criminalize, to protect the rights of victims, and to promote cooperation.[33] Its focus is on counterfeit medical products, substances, and related material, defined in article 4j as products in which 'a false representation' has been made 'as regards identity and/or source'.

Article 5(1) requires each party to criminalize 'the intentional manufacturing of counterfeit medical products, active substances, excipients, parts, materials and accessories', while (in language redolent of article 36(1) of the 1961 Single Convention on Narcotic Drugs) article 6(1) requires each party to criminalize 'the supplying or the offering to supply, including brokering, the trafficking, including keeping in stock, importing and exporting of counterfeit medical products, active substances, excipients, parts, materials and accessories'. Falsification of documents and various offences of unauthorized manufacturing and stockpiling are also to be criminalized, along with accessory and inchoate liability in all of these offences.[34]

All of the offences are to be subject in terms of article 12(1) to 'effective, dissuasive and proportionate sanctions including criminal or non-criminal monetary sanctions' and unusually, article 13 provides for a number of aggravating circumstances worth repeating in full because they sketch the contours of the illicit market:

a. the offence caused the death of, or damage to the physical or mental health of, the victim;

b. the offence was committed by persons abusing the confidence placed in them in their capacity as professionals;

c. the offence was committed by persons abusing the confidence placed in them as manufacturers as well as suppliers;

d. the offences of supplying and offering to supply were committed having resort to means of large scale distribution, such as information systems, including the Internet;

e. the offence was committed in the framework of a criminal organisation;

f. the perpetrator has previously been convicted of offences of the same nature.

Provision is also made for preventive measures, international cooperation, and protection of victims.

The Medicrime Convention remains the only multilateral instrument in this field. At the UN CCPCJ efforts have been limited to a Resolution in 2011 urging[35]

... Member States to prevent trafficking in fraudulent medicines by introducing legislation, as appropriate, covering, in particular, all offences related to fraudulent medicines, such as money-laundering, corruption and smuggling, as well as the confiscation and disposal of criminal assets, extradition and mutual legal assistance, to ensure that no stage in the supply chain of fraudulent medicines is overlooked.

---

[32] 28 October 2011, CETS No 211; opened for signature on 28 October 2011. See generally S Negri, 'The Medicrime Convention: Combating Pharmaceutical Crimes through European Criminal Law and Beyond' 7 *New Journal of European Criminal Law* (2016) 350.
[33] Article 1(1).   [34] Articles 8 and 9.   [35] Resolution 20/6 para 2.

The United Nations Office on Drugs and Crime (UNODC) has engaged in developing model legislation while the UNTOC Conference of the Parties has urged advocating the use of the UNTOC against various aspects of the trade in counterfeit medicines.[36]

15.5 Identity Fraud

Identity-related crime is also of growing interest. A UN Expert Group[37] found that it has two pillars—identity theft and identity fraud—and although traditional offences of theft and fraud are available, it is arguable that identity crime constitutes a separate kind of social harm because it victimizes the person whose identity is stolen through their being as a result suspect of offences, blacklisted for credit purposes, and so forth. Discussion at the 2010 UN Crime Congress revealed that some states want a global instrument while others are opposed.[38] Since then a string of ECOSOC resolutions originating in the CCPCJ have urged cooperation against identity-related crime, and the UNODC has worked on developing model legislation, but no binding formal treaty obligations have either been agreed or indeed appear to be likely.

15.6 Offences against Children

The difficulty of deciding whether a new treaty is necessary is well illustrated by child exploitation.[39] Against a background of absence of national recognition of specific crimes such as child sex tourism, 'the exploitation of children by travelling child sex offenders',[40] the Convention on the Rights of the Child[41] separated requirements for domestic responses to the trafficking of and exploitation of children in articles 34 and 35, recognizing that while trafficking may involve exploitation for sexual purposes it would not necessarily do so. Child pornography and the sale and prostitution of children generally is already suppressed by article 1 of the Optional Protocol to the Convention on the Rights of the Child on the Sale of Children, Child Prostitution and Child Pornography,[42] which obliges parties to prohibit these activities. Criminalization is provided for in article 3:

    1. Each State Party shall ensure that, as a minimum, the following acts and activities are fully covered under its criminal or penal law, whether such

---

[36] 'Experts apply organized crime Convention in fight against fake medicines', 13 October 2014, UNODC Website, available at <https://www.unodc.org/unodc/en/frontpage/2014/October/experts-apply-organized-crime-convention-in-fight-against-fake-medicines.html> last visited 17 June 2017.
[37] Established by ECOSOC Res 2004/26 of 21 July 2004.
[38] The Salvador Declaration on Comprehensive Strategies for Global Challenges: Crime Prevention and Criminal Justice Systems and Their Development in a Changing World, 2010, paras 15, 41, 42, available at <https://www.unodc.org/documents/crime-congress/12th-Crime-Congress/Documents/Salvador_Declaration/Salvador_Declaration_E.pdf> last visited 7 August 2017.
[39] See L Buckingham, 'Child Sex Tourism' in N Boister and R Currie (eds), *The Routledge Handbook of Transnational Criminal Law* (Abingdon: Routledge, 2015), 210.
[40] ibid.   [41] 20 November 1989; 1527 UNTS 3; in force 2 September 1990.
[42] 25 May 2000, 2171 UNTS 227, in force 18 January 2002.

offences are committed domestically or transnationally or on an individual or organized basis:

(a) In the context of sale of children as defined in article 2:
    (i) Offering, delivering or accepting, by whatever means, a child for the purpose of:
        a. Sexual exploitation of the child;
        b. Transfer of organs of the child for profit;
        c. Engagement of the child in forced labour;
    (ii) Improperly inducing consent, as an intermediary, for the adoption of a child in violation of applicable international legal instruments on adoption;
(b) Offering, obtaining, procuring or providing a child for child prostitution, as defined in article 2;
(c) Producing, distributing, disseminating, importing, exporting, offering, selling or possessing for the above purposes child pornography as defined in article 2.

There are obviously significant overlaps with the scope of the offences in the Human Trafficking Protocol, but the Optional Protocol's narrow focus on the plight of children as victims of exploitation justifies the special measure which is of similar vintage to the Human Trafficking Protocol. A set of more narrowly focused measures are provided for in the 2007 Council of Europe Convention on the Protection of Children against Sexual Exploitation and Sexual Abuse,[43] which criminalizes various forms of sexual abuse of children, including such abuse committed in the home or family, with the use of force, coercion, or threats. These criminalization provisions are backed up by a range of specially tailored protections and preventive measures, not generally available.

15.7 The Necessity of Further Suppression Conventions

Activities like global organ trafficking—the harvesting, supply, and placing of essential organs—are areas beginning to draw international attention. There is evidence of coerced supply,[44] national legislation such as the UK's Human Tissue Act 2004 criminalizes donors, brokers, surgeons, etc,[45] and there have been successful national prosecutions of suppliers[46] and of hospitals.[47] The UN General Assembly has urged states 'to adopt the necessary measures to prevent, combat and punish the illicit removal of and trafficking in human organs'.[48] Is a new instrument necessary to specifically

---

[43] 25 October 2007, CETS No 201, in force 1 July 2010.
[44] D Marty, 'Inhuman Treatment of People and Illicit Trafficking in Human Organs in Kosovo', Council of Europe draft report, available at <http://www.assembly.coe.int/CommitteeDocs/2010/ajdoc462010prov.pdf> last visited 7 February 2017.
[45] Section 32.
[46] In *R v Tuck* English authorities successfully prosecuted a man who tried to sell his own kidney over the Internet—see 'Body Parts Sale Man Avoids Jail', *BBC News*, 11 May 2007, available at <http://news.bbc.co.uk/2/hi/uk_news/england/west_midlands/6646467.stm> last visited 17 June 2017.
[47] 'South African Hospital Pleads Guilty to Organ Trafficking Case', *Daily Telegraph*, 17 June 2017.
[48] GA Res 59/156 of 20 December 2004.

suppress this activity? As pointed out in Chapter 4, trafficking in body parts is already covered under the Human Trafficking Protocol. Various aspects of the trade in organs including, for example, engaging in 'health tourism', travelling abroad to buy organs that may have been trafficked, do not, however, fall comfortably into the scope of the Protocol, and domestic legislation has jurisdictional inadequacies.[49] However, these shortcomings probably do not justify a full-scale treaty making process and can be dealt with through soft law.

The point of some new treaties (or at least some of their provisions) is open to question. Increased international legal regulation of the smuggling of tobacco products was kicked off by the adoption of article 15 of the WHO Framework Convention on Tobacco Control,[50] in which the parties recognize: 'that the elimination of all forms of illicit trade in tobacco products, including smuggling, illicit manufacturing and counterfeiting, and the development and implementation of related national law, in addition to subregional, regional and global agreements, are essential components of tobacco control'.

The 2012 Protocol to Eliminate Illicit Trade in Tobacco Products[51] was developed under the auspices of the WHO to flesh out the general obligations in article 15. Its substance is concerned with supply chain control. It makes provision for the licensing of the manufacture of and import and export of tobacco products,[52] due diligence obligations on those engaged in the supply chain,[53] provisions for tracking and tracing of tobacco products,[54] and related provisions. Some of the provisions of the Protocol are delicate compromises, indicative of the wariness of parties about the necessity of making a new agreement in this regard. Article 14(1) obliges states parties to prohibit as unlawful an extremely detailed range of activities covering the full tobacco supply-chain, as well as a range of ancillary activities used to avoid enforcement. Many of these actions are at most administrative offences in many states. The failure of states to agree on which of these forms of conduct were serious enough to be worthy of criminalization and thus of international cooperation, led to the vacant arrangement in article 14(2), which leaves it to each party to decide which of these various forms of conduct to criminalize, something that will not lead to an even playing field in regard to criminalization of these forms of conduct. The residual application of the UNTOC to serious crime committed by Organized Criminal Groups discussed in Chapter 8, means arguably that if criminalized by a state party with a penalty of four years or more[55] these tobacco smuggling offences are already covered by the UNTOC in any case of tobacco smuggling which really matters. It makes one wonder about the point of article 14.[56]

---

[49] Section 32 of the UK Human Tissue Act, has, eg, no explicit extraterritorial application.

[50] 21 May 2003, 42 ILM 518 (2003), in force 27 February 2005.

[51] See Conference of the Parties to the WHO Framework Convention on Tobacco Control, *Draft Protocol to Eliminate Trade in Tobacco Products*, FCTC COP/5/6, 11 May 2012.

[52] Article 6.   [53] Article 7.   [54] Article 8.   [55] Article 2(b).

[56] See N Boister, 'The (Un-)Systematic Nature of the UN Criminal Justice System: The (Non) Relationship Between the Draft Illicit Tobacco Trade Protocol and the UN Convention Against Transnational Organised Crime' (2010) 21 *Criminal Law Forum* 361.

The same argument goes for a range of proposed new offences that meet the UNTOC's conditions for application; the UNTOC was after all supposed to make future treaty making unnecessary, and should an offence reach a threshold significant enough to generate a consensus about criminalization, if it involves organization of crime it seems logical that it should be adopted as a Protocol to the UNTOC, rather than as a separate treaty.

PART III

ENFORCEMENT

The investigation, prosecution and suppression of crime for the protection of the citizen and the maintenance of peace and public order is an important goal of all organized societies. The goal cannot realistically be confined within national boundaries.

United States of America v Cotroni [1989] 1 SCR 1469 at 1470

16

Jurisdiction over Transnational Crime

16.1 Introduction

Criminalization of the activities described in preceding chapters is of limited practical effect unless the state enacting the crime establishes an adequate criminal jurisdiction over that crime. Cross-border crime, however, raises issues crossing sovereign jurisdictional orders. Jurisdiction over crime is coextensive with, and incidental to, but limited by, a state's sovereignty.[1] If a state assumes jurisdiction outside the limits of its sovereignty, it comes into conflict with the sovereignty of other states. International law guides the application of jurisdiction over transnational crime in the sense of spelling out limits on national criminal jurisdiction; but it is national law which actually establishes and enforces the particular jurisdiction.

The establishment by states of competence over crimes is fundamental to criminal law, and occurs concurrently with criminalization itself. 'Jurisdiction' derives from *juris* (law) and *dictio* (saying); the state 'says' that it is against its law to perform a particular action (criminalization) in a particular place (jurisdiction). Only once states have prescribed in their national laws the reach of these laws (prescriptive or legislative jurisdiction) over the particular form of conduct, can this rule-making jurisdiction be enforced by law enforcement agents (enforcement jurisdiction in the narrow sense) or adjudicated by courts (adjudicative jurisdiction).

Falk's view that 'a rigid territorial allocation of jurisdictional competence creates an impunity umbrella for those who act from abroad to achieve their "illegal" domestic objectives' is now generally accepted.[2] This chapter is thus principally concerned with the role transnational criminal law plays in the extraterritorial expansion by states of their jurisdiction in order to suppress crimes that occur, in whole or in part, abroad. It examines the various principles embodied in provisions of the suppression conventions and used as the basis for that extension: territoriality and its variations, nationality, passive personality, protective jurisdiction, jurisdiction conditional on non-extradition, and (controversially) universality. Finally it looks at problems of concurrent jurisdiction and immunity from jurisdiction. The chapter begins, however, by looking at the distinction between establishing and enforcing jurisdiction and limitations on jurisdiction over transnational crime.

---

[1] FA Mann, 'The Doctrine of Jurisdiction in International Law' 111 *Recueil des Cours* (1964) 1, 15. Historically jurisdiction preceded sovereignty and territory—M Hildebrand, 'Extraterritorial Jurisdiction to enforce in Cyberspace? Bodin, Schmitt, Grotius in Cyberspace' 3 *University of Toronto Law Journal* (2013) 196, 205.

[2] RA Falk, 'International Jurisdiction: Horizontal and Vertical Conceptions of Legal Order' 32 *Temple Law Quarterly* (1959) 295, 303.

16.2 Establishing and Enforcing Jurisdiction

The Permanent Court of International Justice (PCIJ) in 1927 in the *Lotus* case[3] distinguished between establishing and enforcing extraterritorial criminal jurisdiction. The establishment of extraterritorial jurisdiction spells out the ambit of a law. It is the logical precursor of the enforcement of that jurisdiction through either (i) investigation, arrest, prosecution, adjudication, and punishment if the alleged offender is within the state's custody or (ii) extradition if the alleged offender is in another state. The distinction between establishment and enforcement of jurisdiction is only rarely drawn in common law countries[4] though it is a sharp distinction in civil law countries.[5]

Jurisdiction is sometimes expressly established in national law, but often it must be implied from legislative intent. Most US criminal laws are, for example, silent on the question of jurisdiction and presumed to be territorial in application; extraterritorial jurisdiction has to be implied from the nature of the criminal activity proscribed by the particular law. Even if a law expressly prescribes its jurisdiction, it will not usually provide expressly for the enforcement of that jurisdiction, which must be implied from the establishment of jurisdiction. The scope of the jurisdiction established, however, is generally coterminous with the scope of its enforcement because courts and police enforce their state's laws.[6] The establishment of extraterritorial jurisdiction must be distinguished from effects that domestic steps have abroad. If X is, for example, prevented from sending a drug into Singapore from China by Singapore's action at its border, that action will have an effect in China, but it will not involve the establishment of Singapore's extraterritorial jurisdiction in China.[7]

The jurisdictional principles applied today in national law in order to establish and enforce jurisdiction are considered customary international law (although some are more secure than others) and originate in the seventeenth century. Prior to this, jurisdiction in Europe at least was primarily *ratione personae* because all Christians were considered one nation. After the Treaty of Westphalia (1648) and the rise of the nation state, criminal jurisdiction of states was *ratione loci*, that is over the *loco delicto* (the place where the crime was committed). Beccaria rationalized that 'the place of punishment can certainly be no better than that where the crime was committed; for the necessity of punishing an individual for the general good, subsists there, and there only'.[8] Common law states were wedded to territoriality for reasons of sovereignty and practicality: the territorial state had the strongest interest in the matter and was

---

[3] (1927) PCIJ Reports Series A No 10, 18–20.
[4] *Treacy v Director of Public Prosecutions* [1971] AC 537, 559.
[5] See, eg, the provisions for jurisdiction in articles 3–9 of the Swiss Criminal Code of 1937, which are part of the General Part of the Code.
[6] Council of Europe's European committee on crime problems, 'Extraterritorial Criminal Jurisdiction' (Strasbourg: CoE, 1990) reproduced in 3 *Criminal Law Forum* (1992) 441, 458. But see RS Clark, 'Some Aspects of the Concept of International Criminal Law: Suppression Conventions, Jurisdiction, Submarine Cables and the Lotus' 22 *Criminal Law Forum* (2011) 519, 522, 525, for examples where states appeared to enforce jurisdictions they had not previously established over slaving on the high seas.
[7] T Scassa and RJ Currie, 'New First Principles? Assessing the Internet's Challenges to Jurisdiction' 42 *Georgetown Journal of International Law* (2010–11) 1017, 1070.
[8] C Beccaria, *An Essay on Crimes and Punishments*, 2nd edn (1819; Academic Reprints, 1953), 135.

more able to secure the evidence than another interested state.[9] While also relying on territoriality, civil law states were more likely to establish extraterritorial jurisdiction because the mobility of their inhabitants through Europe made it more practical to base jurisdiction on the *loco originis* (place of birth of offender), the *loco domicile* (place of habitation of offender), or *locus deprehensionis* (place of apprehension).

The modern versions of these principles are extrapolations developed in an uneven and unsystematic way in response to specific problems.[10] The rise of digitally based transnational crime has led to questions about their suitability because of the speed and complexity of movement of digital information which makes it difficult to say that particular events happen anywhere, or are directed by anyone against any victim.[11] This scepticism reinforces an already growing tendency to establish less territorially rooted principles of jurisdiction. Balance will be required to ensure that states do not develop principles that permit jurisdictional over-reach over cybercrime, or any transnational crime, in a way that subverts the laws of the territorial state.[12]

16.3 Limitations on Jurisdiction over Transnational Crime

16.3.1 The permissive approach versus sovereignty

The PCIJ in the *Lotus* case also recognized that extraterritorial jurisdiction is restricted by three international law principles later codified in the UN Charter as the 'sovereign equality of states, territorial sovereignty and non-intervention'.[13] Although the PCIJ was clear that a state could not enforce its jurisdiction in the territory of another state in the absence of some pre-existing legal rule permitting it to do so, such as the consent of the requested state, it held that states enjoyed 'a wide measure of discretion' to establish their jurisdiction over persons, property, and acts outside their territory, limited only in certain cases by pre-existing 'prohibitive rules' of international law.[14] They were then free to exercise that established extra-territorial jurisdiction in their own territory. The permissive nature of this approach was justified on the basis that states were simply exercising sovereignty and because it was practically impossible to cite a universally accepted rule in order to support entitlement to jurisdiction. Later decisions cast doubt on whether this 'laissez-faire' approach to the establishment of extraterritorial jurisdiction still pertains[15] and commentators deny that it ever did, arguing that the record of state practice illustrates that states challenge the establishment of

---

[9] G Mullan, 'The Concept of Double Criminality in the Context of Extraterritorial Crimes' [1997] *Criminal Law Review* 17.

[10] L Farmer, 'Territorial Jurisdiction and Criminalization' 63 *University of Toronto Law Journal* (2013) 225, 241.

[11] See DR Johnson and DB Post, 'Law and Borders: The Rise of Law in Cyberspace' (1996) 48 *Stanford Law Review* 1367.

[12] See, eg, *The Rule of Law on the Internet and in the Wider Digital World: Issues Paper published by the Council of Europe Commissioner for Human Rights* (Council of Europe, 2014), 78, available at <https://wcd.coe.int/com.instranet.InstraServlet?command=com.instranet.CmdBlobGet&InstranetImage=2933488&SecMode=1&DocId=2262340&Usage=2> last visited 6 June 2017.

[13] Article 2(1), 2(4), and 2(7) of the UN Charter respectively.   [14] Above n 3, 19.

[15] *Arrest Warrant of 11 April 2000 (Democratic Republic of the Congo v Belgium)*, ICJ Reports 2002, Joint Separate Opinion of Judges Higgins, Buergenthal, and Kooijmans, 78, para 51.

extraterritorial jurisdiction by other states by asserting they have no right to do so, and leave it to the state making the claim to prove entitlement to do so.[16]

While extraterritorial criminal jurisdiction is in fact relatively rare, more powerful states have expanded their 'long-arm' criminal jurisdiction to suppress transnational crime, leading to conflicting interests with other states. Although US law, for example, has operated under the presumption that jurisdiction is territorial,[17] in 1922 in *United States v Bowman*,[18] the US Supreme Court anticipated the need to expand jurisdiction over transnational crime reasoning that to restrict jurisdiction to territoriality 'would be greatly to curtail the scope and usefulness' of the particular criminal law. In the post-war period the US has taken the lead in unilaterally expanding its criminal jurisdiction. Other states are wary of such expansions, viewing them as encroaching on the rights of territorial states and as unfair to the foreigners who have no legal rights in the state establishing jurisdiction and thus no influence on the making of that law to which they are now subject.

16.3.2 Limitations on the expansion of jurisdiction

Various methods have been proposed to try to control these expansions, most popularly by insistence on some kind of link between the object of the jurisdiction and the interests of the state taking jurisdiction, a notion borrowed from private international law.[19] The nature of this link is characterized in various ways: the establishment of extraterritorial jurisdiction is permissible if the establishing state can show a 'reasonable', 'proportional', or 'substantial' connection with its interests.[20] In *Libman v The Queen*,[21] for example, the Canadian Supreme Court held that extraterritorial jurisdiction was lawful if there was a 'real and substantial link' between the offence and Canada. Establishing such a link implies both identification of points of connection and evaluation of the strength of those connections,[22] something that can be done by assessing the extent of the extraterritorial activities, the degree of regulation, the fairness to the accused and the victims, the values under threat, and the territorial and international support for suppression.[23]

A related restraint emphasizes the necessity of proportionality between the expanded jurisdiction and the state's interests. Jeschek argues that it is a general principle recognized by all civilized nations 'that a state may not arbitrarily subject to its own criminal power acts which either occurred abroad or were committed by a

---

[16] V Lowe and C Staker, 'Jurisdiction' in M Evans (ed), *International Law*, 3rd edn (Oxford: OUP, 2010), 315, 319, 330; C Ryngaert, *Jurisdiction in International Law* (Oxford: OUP, 2008), 21.

[17] *Murray v Schooner Charming Betsy*, 6 US (2 Cranch) 64 (1804). See more recently *Morrison v National Bank of Australia* 561 US 247 (2010) where the Supreme Court made it clear at 255 that 'when a Statute gives no clear indication of an extraterritorial application, it has none'.

[18] 260 US 94 (1922) at 98.

[19] *Barcelona Traction, Light and Power Company, Limited (Belgium v Spain)*, Separate Opinion of Judge Sir Gerald Fitzmaurice, [1970] ICJ Reports 103, 105.

[20] Mann, above n 1, 44–45.   [21] [1985] 2 SCR 174 at 213.

[22] Scassa and Currie, above n 7, 1048.

[23] Section 403(2)(a)–(h) of the Third Restatement of US Foreign Relations Law, American Law Institute, 1987.

foreigner unless there exists a meaningful point of relation which rationally connects the factual context of the act to the legitimate interests of the prosecuting state'.[24] He implies that these expansions of penal power should not be out of proportion to a state's legitimate interests.

Respect for international comity in the sense of an 'attitude of moderation and restraint vis-à-vis the other participants in laying claims to exercise state authority outside its own national territory'[25] also limits the establishment of extraterritorial criminal jurisdiction. It implies a balancing of the interests of the prosecuting state and other states.

These restraints are of limited effect, however, if applied unilaterally by the authorities of the prosecuting state on a case-by-case basis.[26] But if laid down as a general requirement by the courts they can frustrate jurisdictional over-reach in the cause of policing the world.[27] Challenges to the establishment of 'long-arm' jurisdiction over transnational crimes are relatively rare, although not as we shall see unknown.

16.3.3 Legality as a limitation on jurisdiction over transnational crime

The establishment of jurisdiction is a legislative act more properly considered to be part of the applicability of the substantive criminal norm, distinguishable from the process of enforcement of that established jurisdiction.[28] Reliance on setting the ambit of an established jurisdiction by reference to the *actus reus* or *mens rea* of the particular offence tends to confirm this substantive nature.[29] It follows that the establishment of jurisdiction over transnational crime, and in particular extraterritorial transnational crime, is subject to the controlling principles of legality in domestic criminal law doctrine rather than left to procedure where these principles do not apply. Jurisdiction should therefore be spelled out clearly and precisely in law and changes in jurisdiction should not be applied retroactively. Fair warning to those abroad is difficult. Individuals cannot consciously conform to a foreign law of which they are ignorant, a difficulty compounded when subject to multiple jurisdictions.[30] As the European Committee on Crime Problems notes:

[24] HH Jeschek, 'International Criminal Law: Its Object and Recent Developments' in MC Bassiouni and VP Nanda (eds), *A Treatise on International Criminal Law: Volume I Crimes and Punishment* (Springfield, IL: Charles C Thomas, 1973), 49, 51
[25] Council of Europe, above n 6, 448.   [26] ibid, 464.
[27] Fabiarz argues that US Federal District Court requirement of a jurisdictional nexus to meet due process requirements first laid down in *US v Davis* 905 F2d 245 (9th Cir 1990) is not required to meet the concerns of cooperating states because this is a matter for the executive and is not an issue of individual rights except in cases where there is an actual conflict of jurisdiction (ie there is no double criminality)— see M Fabiarz, 'Extraterritorial Criminal Jurisdiction' 114 *Michigan Law Review* (2016) 507, 519.
[28] G Hallevy, *A Modern Treatise on the Principle of Legality in Criminal Law* (New York: Springer, 2010), 82.
[29] See, eg, *R v Keyn* (1876–7) LR 2 Ex D 63 where the accused's lack of intention to damage the British-registered ship *Franconia* was held to mean that no act was done in England and it did not enjoy jurisdiction.
[30] A Petrig, 'The Expansion of Swiss Criminal Jurisdiction in the Light of International Law' 9(4) *Utrecht Law Review* (2013) 34, 35.

... it would be unreasonable to require that rules on extraterritorial jurisdiction be published abroad by the legislating state. There is arguably no problem where the offence is also a criminal offence under the law of the state of the locus delicti. Where this is not the case, however, some balance may be necessary by providing for a wider application of the defence based on error iuris.[31]

Although double criminality preserves legality and thus should be a condition for the establishment of jurisdiction that has an extraterritorial impact, its application is controversial.[32] Common law states tend to ignore it. In *United States v Al Kassar*[33] the supply of missiles to terrorists in Colombia to shoot down US military personnel was considered by the court to have met the fair warning requirement because it was 'self-evidently criminal'. Civil law states do not generally require double criminality when reliance is placed on territoriality and the protective jurisdiction, although some do when using nationality and passive personality. International law is uncomfortably silent on this point and on the application of legality to jurisdiction as a whole. Ignorance or mistake of law should be a tenable defence in the absence of a reasonable basis for assuming knowledge. The existence of a suppression convention does not by itself provide such a reasonable basis; they are inter-state agreements not intended as a means of publication of laws binding individuals.

16.4 Extensions of Jurisdiction Recognized by the Suppression Conventions

The suppression conventions provide vehicles for the reasonable extension of states parties' jurisdiction vis-à-vis other states parties with their agreement, thus avoiding controversial unilateral assertions of jurisdiction.[34] Treaty rules mandate but do not oblige long-arm jurisdiction. By adopting a particular convention the parties make reciprocal grants of special competence on the jurisdictional principles listed in the conventions and in doing so waive their rights to object to the establishment of extraterritorial jurisdiction on the basis of these principles. If the particular suppression convention makes the establishment by the party of the listed principle of jurisdiction obligatory over a particular crime, this indicates a general acceptance by the participating states of a mutual interest in suppression of these forms of criminality. Inclusion of more controversial principles only as permissions in a suppression convention serves legally to validate the use of these principles because parties are estopped from objecting when other parties rely on them to establish jurisdiction over the particular convention's offences. They can be construed as proof of an absence of a

---

[31] Council of Europe, above n 6, 454.
[32] See C van den Wyngaert, 'Double Criminality as a Requirement for Jurisdiction' in J Dugard (ed), *International Criminal Law and Procedure* (Aldershot: Dartmouth, 1996), 131.
[33] 660 F3d 108 (2nd Cir 2011).
[34] CD Ram, 'The Globalization of Crime as a Jurisdictional Challenge', paper given at the Annual Conference of the International Society for the Reform of Criminal Law, Ottawa, 7–11 August 2011, 17 et seq. The PCIJ in the *Lotus Case* above n 3, 191, recorded the function of conventions to 'limit the discretion at present left to States' by international law and thus making good jurisdictional lacunae or removing conflicting jurisdiction.

prohibition on the establishment of a particular form of jurisdiction, not authority to actually enforce that jurisdiction in the territory of other states parties without their consent. However, making them optional also reveals a general hesitancy about their legitimacy, and in implementing the conventions few parties choose to establish jurisdiction on these optional grounds because they have neither the interest in establishing such a jurisdiction nor the capacity to enforce it.[35]

Although the parties waive their objection to the establishment of criminal jurisdiction on the basis of the principles in the suppression conventions, this waiver does not extend to states not party to the conventions. If a suppression convention provides, for example, for the prosecution of nationals of a third party state for an offence committed outside the territory of a party to a convention, the convention does not legally permit a party to the convention to establish such jurisdiction because in terms of the *pacta tertiis* rule[36] the treaty cannot bind a non-party state. If a state nevertheless establishes its jurisdiction over such an individual without the consent of the state of nationality, its claim is based on custom, to which the third party states can either object or be held to acquiesce.[37] In practice, third parties appear not to have objected when this has been done.[38]

Finally, it is worth noting that common law states tend to implement the jurisdictional provisions in the suppression conventions in special legislation in regard to specific crimes, while civil law states tend to rely on their general jurisdictional provisions.[39]

16.5 Territoriality

16.5.1 Strict territoriality

National criminal jurisdiction is coterminous with sovereignty, and thus states usually require that an offence occur within their territory before they exercise jurisdiction. Territoriality is practical—that's where the harm is done, that's where the evidence is, and that's where the interest in suppression is. Provision is made in almost every suppression convention for the obligatory establishment of territorial jurisdiction, mirroring such provision in domestic law.[40] Thus, for example, article 42(1)(a) of the United Nations Convention against Corruption (UNCAC) provides:

1. Each state party shall adopt such measures as may be necessary to establish its jurisdiction over the offences established in accordance with this Convention when:

---

[35] The optional grounds for jurisdiction in article 6(2) of the Convention for the Suppression of Unlawful Acts of Violence against the Safety of Maritime Navigation (SUA Convention) (habitual residence, passive personality, etc), eg, have not been implemented by parties—see IMO, *Piracy: A Review of National Legislation*, Leg 96/7, 20 August 2009, para 3.

[36] Article 34 of the Vienna Convention on the Law of Treaties, 23 May 1969, 115 UNTS 311; in force 27 January 1980.

[37] M Akehurst, 'Custom as a Source of International Law' 47 *British Yearbook of International Law* (1974–75) 1, 44.

[38] Lowe and Staker, above n 16, 328.

[39] See, eg, article 113 of the Polish Criminal Code, 1997, as amended in 2012.

[40] See, eg, article 5(1) of Vietnam's Criminal Code, 1999.

(a) the Offence is committed in the territory of that State Party.

Territorial jurisdiction includes internal waters, territorial waters (12 nautical miles from the baseline of a coastal state)[41] and super adjacent airspace.[42] Some states also claim jurisdiction over customs and fiscal offences in a 24 nautical mile contiguous zone, and over offences pertaining to the enjoyment of their 200 nautical mile exclusive economic zones (EEZs) such as fishing offences and environmental pollution offences. Territoriality has been expanded upon in various ways to deal with these situations.

16.5.2 Quasi-territoriality

All merchant vessels must be registered in a 'flag state', which is required to exercise its jurisdiction over the ship.[43] All aircraft must be registered in a 'state of registration', which is required to exercise jurisdiction over the aircraft.[44] These forms of jurisdiction have been analogized with territoriality, although they are actually species of nationality. Some suppression conventions give specific content to these general obligations by making it obligatory for parties to establish jurisdiction over various forms of international quasi-territoriality over their flag-vessels and registered aircraft in respect of specific crimes. Article 4(1)(a) of the 1988 Drug Trafficking Convention, for example, obliges parties to establish their jurisdiction over article 3(1) offences (drug trafficking offences) when '(ii) The offence is committed on board a vessel flying its flag or an aircraft which is registered under its laws at the time the offence is committed'.

The 1970 Hague Hijacking Convention obliges the state of registration of hijacked aircraft and the territorial state through whose airspace a hijacked aircraft is flown to establish their jurisdiction. Article 4(1) introduced so-called 'landing state' jurisdiction, by obliging parties to establish their jurisdiction 'when the aircraft on board which the offence is committed lands in its territory with the alleged offender still on board'. The US which had already established jurisdiction over a broad range of criminal activities on aircraft flying into and out of the US from the time of the enactment of the Federal Aviation Act 1958,[45] expanded its jurisdiction to meet this new obligation over the commission of hijacking offences on aircraft outside US territory if the aircraft landed in the US with the alleged offender on board. No other link to the US was required, that is the flight had neither to be destined for nor originate in the US.[46] Article 8(4) of the Hague Hijacking Convention provides that the offence shall be treated, for the purpose of extradition, as if it had been committed not only in the place in which it occurred but also in the territories of the states required to establish their jurisdiction in terms of article 4(1). This fiction expands territory to include the location of acts that take place on aircraft that land in that party for the purposes of

---

[41] Article 3 of the UNCLOS—see Chapter 3.
[42] Article 1 of the Chicago Convention on Civil Aviation, 7 December 1944, 15 UNTS 295, in force 4 April 1947.
[43] Articles 91 and 94(1) of the UNCLOS.   [44] Article 20 of the Chicago Convention.
[45] 49 USC § 1472 and § 1301(4) and (20).   [46] 49 USC App § 1301(638)(d)(ii) (1982).

extradition treaties which provide for extradition of individuals accused of offences committed within the territory of a party.

A similar expansion of territorial jurisdiction is found in article 4(1) of the SUA Convention,[47] which applies the Convention to those offences committed on board vessels that are navigating, or scheduled to navigate, into, through, or from the waters beyond the outer limit of the territorial waters of a coastal state or offences committed in territorial waters. But there must be a jurisdictional nexus with the offender. In *Shantou Municipal People's Prosecutor v Naim and others*,[48] China established jurisdiction over the hijacking of a Taiwanese vessel that had occurred in Malaysian territorial waters but had been perpetrated by Indonesians on the basis that the accused had sailed the vessel into Chinese territorial waters. The hijackers were charged with robbery under article 263 of China's Criminal Code. The court relied on article 9 of the Criminal Code, in terms of which China establishes the jurisdictions provided for in its treaty obligations. These treaty obligations included the obligation in the SUA Convention to establish jurisdiction over the offences in article 3(1)(a), which the court held include acts of violence on board ship such as the hijacking.[49]

16.5.3 Qualified territoriality

Subjective and objective territoriality, ubiquity

Territorial jurisdiction provides a foundation out of which forms of qualified territoriality have been extrapolated, usually by judicial interpretation rather than legislative intervention. Formally principles of territorial not extraterritorial jurisdiction, they provide for a significant extraterritorial expansion of the competence of states in a fashion easier to justify than reliance on extraterritorial jurisdiction, because of the existence of the territorial link (however tenuous).[50] The US concepts of subjective and objective territoriality and effects jurisdiction have become popular to describe these extrapolations.

Subjective territoriality requires only that some of the conduct elements of the offence occur in the territory. These usually involve the initiation of the crime within the territory of the state establishing jurisdiction even if the offence terminates abroad. Even if the state in question can show no harm, there may be a state interest in suppressing the conduct because the state where the crime has its result or effect may be incapable of suppressing it.

Objective territoriality applies where a transnational crime is initiated abroad and only completed in the state wishing to establish jurisdiction. National approaches differ. In US law it is limited to those cases where the result is an element of the offence[51] whereas in France it includes effects that are not an element of the offence.[52] English law requires the last act to have occurred in England, not the result. In *Director of*

---

[47] See Chapter 3.

[48] *Shantou Municipal People's Prosecutor v Naim and ors, Decision of first instance, Shan Zhong Fa Xing Yi Chu Zi No 22*; ILDC 1161 (CN 2003).

[49] At page 13 of original judgment—see ILDC H3.   [50] Ryngaert above n 16, 208.

[51] Section 1.03 of the Model Penal Code.   [52] Ryngaert above n 16, 199.

Public Prosecutions v Doot,[53] for example, the House of Lords held that it had jurisdiction over a conspiracy to import cannabis resin into the UK where the conspiracy was agreed abroad but where several parties to the agreement had performed overt acts within England.

States increasingly follow the civil law position and roll subjective and objective territoriality up in a ubiquity doctrine where jurisdiction is established through the occurrence of any elements of an offence or the effects within their territory.[54] Article 113-2 of the French Penal Code, for example, deems an offence as having been committed in France if one of its constituent elements was committed in France. Ubiquity is justified on the basis that the conduct and consequences form a legal unity.[55] Territoriality can be expanded to include extraterritorial conduct and results and even intended results that do not eventuate.[56] Moreover, it allows civil law states such as Switzerland that require double criminality to underpin extraterritorial jurisdiction to avoid the necessity of taking foreign law into account because jurisdiction is territorial.[57]

Although subjective and objective territoriality/ubiquity have their origins in unilateral state practice and not in an express treaty obligation, some suppression conventions make the adoption of these forms of qualified territoriality an explicit obligation. For example, article 30(1) of the Arab Convention on Combating Information Technology Offences obliges a state party to extend its jurisdiction over any of the Convention's offences if it was 'committed, partly or totally, or was realized [...] in the territory of the State Party'. Nonetheless, both subjective and objective territoriality were approved of in the *Lotus* case and thus the inclusion in the suppression conventions of obligations to establish territorial jurisdiction arguably can be interpreted to include, if not an obligation to establish subjective and objective territoriality/ubiquity, at least a permission based on customary law to parties to do so.

Territorial jurisdiction can be expanded enormously using these principles; the actions within a territory justifying jurisdiction may be as limited as the electronic transmission of laundered money through a bank located in a state.[58] The US also establishes territorial jurisdiction in anti-bribery cases based on financial transactions undertaken abroad in US dollars cleared through correspondent bank accounts in the US.[59] Jurisdiction of this kind tests the reasonableness of the link between the US and the criminal conduct in question, risks disproportionality between jurisdiction and state interest, and indicates a lack of jurisdictional restraint. They also raise issues of substantive legality. In the *Magyar Telekom*[60] case, for example, the US courts rejected a requirement that in order to establish objective territoriality the authorities must show that individuals whose emails were rooted through or stored on servers located in the US were conscious that this was the case. In cases where territorial conduct is

---

[53] [1973] AC 807, 819.   [54] Council of Europe, above n 6, 445.
[55] C Ryngaert, 'Territorial Jurisdiction over Cross-Frontier Offences: Revisiting a Classic Problem in International Criminal Law' 9 *International Criminal Law Review* (2009) 187, 198.
[56] See, eg, section 9 of Germany's *Strafgesetzbuch*.   [57] Petrig, above n 30, 40.
[58] See, eg, the money laundering offence in 18 USC § 1956 (2). See G Stessens, *Money Laundering: A New International Enforcement Model* (Cambridge: CUP, 2001), 219.
[59] See NN Wilson, 'Pushing the Limits of Jurisdiction over Foreign Actors under the Foreign Corrupt Practices Act' 91(4) *Washington University Law Review* (2014) 1063, 1072.
[60] *SEC v Magyar Telekom Plc. and Deutsche Telekom AG* Case No 11 civ 9646 (SDNY).

minimal and unconscious, the claim to competence fails to meet standards of fair warning.[61]

Effects

Expanding on objective territoriality/ubiquity, certain states establish jurisdiction when no element of the offence occurs within the territory,[62] but where a significant harmful consequence of the offence is felt within that state's territory. Originating in the establishment of US jurisdiction over transnational anti-trust violations (agreements between non-US companies operating outside the US to fix prices, etc) on the basis of adverse territorial effects in the US,[63] it has been adopted by US criminal law. In the *United States v Neil*,[64] for example, the US Court of Appeals for the Ninth Circuit established jurisdiction on the basis of the effects doctrine over the sexual violation of a 12-year-old US minor on board a non-American vessel in the territorial waters of another state because the cruise began and ended in the US and the victim had sought counselling in the US. More recently the US Supreme Court has reigned in judicial extension of jurisdiction of this kind in the absence of either a clear legislative intent to apply the domestic statute extraterritorially or when the relevant conduct occurred in the US.[65] Other states have embraced the effects doctrine. In the *Yahoo!* case involving sale of Nazi memorabilia from the US on the internet in violation of the French Penal Code a French Court took jurisdiction on the basis of the effects doctrine even though those effects were not intended.[66]

Based on results, the effects principle does not lend itself comfortably to conduct-based offences like money laundering. The difference between effects on a jurisdiction and actions occurring in a jurisdiction in the case of cybercrime has also been questioned.[67] It may well be that effects jurisdiction, along with objective and subjective territoriality, will collapse into one category in the confrontation between jurisdiction and cyberspace. However, while many states are comfortable with establishment of jurisdiction where a harmful consequence of the crime is actually felt in the territory of the state establishing jurisdiction, the less substantial this consequence the more likely other states are to object to it, which limits its scope as a legitimate interpretation of the obligations to establish territorial jurisdiction in the suppression conventions.

---

[61] Wilson, above n 59, 1075.

[62] D Bowett, '"Jurisdiction": Changing Patterns of Authority over Activities and Resources' 53 *British Yearbook of International Law* (1982) 1, 7.

[63] Ryngaert, above n 16, 42.

[64] 312 F 3d 419 (9th Cir 2002); ILDC 1247 (US 2002), 10 September 2002.

[65] See *Morrison v National Bank of Australia*, above n 17; *RJR Nabisco, Inc v European Community* 136 S Ct 2090 (2016) at 2111.

[66] *La Ligue Contre le Racisme et l'Antisémitisme (LICRA) and l'Union des Etudiants Juifs de France (UEJF) v Yahoo Inc! and Yahoo France*, Trib de 1re Instance, Paris, interlocutory court orders of 22 May 2000, 22 August, and 20 November 2000. See T Schultz, 'Carving up the Internet: Jurisdiction, Legal Orders, and the Private/Public International Law Interface' 19 *European Journal of International Law* (2008) 799, 812.

[67] M Hayashi, 'The Information Revolution and Rules of Jurisdiction in Public International Law' in M Dunn et al, *The Resurgence of the State: Trends and Processes in Cyberspace Government* (2007), 74.

Applying qualified jurisdiction to inchoate crimes and secondary participation

States also engage in elaborate legal constructions of qualified territoriality to include 'participation, procuring the commission of an offence, attempted offences, planning an offence, offences of omission, continuous offences, a series of offences violating several legal interests, and connected offences' within their jurisdictions.[68]

States have had little difficulty in establishing jurisdiction over inchoate conduct such as attempts and conspiracies that occur abroad and which are intended to be completed in the state establishing jurisdiction, even where no overt conduct, result, or effect occurs in territory because they are in some way frustrated or never completed.[69] In 1980 in *United States v Ricardo*[70] the US District Court took jurisdiction over defendants charged with conspiracy to import marijuana, even though the conspiracy took place outside the US and was thwarted before any marijuana was imported. The court ruled that US drug conspiracy laws had extraterritorial reach, inter alia, as long as the defendant intended to violate those laws and to have the effects occur within the US.[71] This approach received international sanction in article 4(1)(b)(iii) of the 1988 Drug Trafficking Convention, which provides that each party may establish its jurisdiction over article 3(1)(c)(iv) offences—inchoate drug supply offences and complicity in those offences—if the offence 'is committed outside its territory with a view to the commission, within its territory[,]' of the drug supply and money laundering offences in article 3(1). Article 4(1)(b)(iii) is permissive because of the difficulties some parties have with establishing jurisdiction when the conspiracy takes place abroad and is wholly frustrated before any negative effect occurs within the territory.

Nevertheless, other states have followed the US example. In 1990 in *Liangsiriprasert v US*,[72] for example, a Thai national arrested in Hong Kong pending extradition to the US appealed to the Privy Council on the basis that the US did not have jurisdiction. He had allegedly entered a conspiracy in Thailand with an undercover US agent to import drugs into the US (Thailand did not extradite drug offenders to the US) but when he travelled to Hong Kong (which did extradite drug offenders to the US) he was arrested at the request of the US. He argued inter alia that Hong Kong law followed the then English law and did not apply to conspiracies entered into abroad where there was no impact in that territory and he had not performed any act that had an impact in the US. Lord Griffiths reasoned that inchoate actions are criminal in England, so there was no reason why extraterritorial actions should be required to be choate:

> Unfortunately in this century crime has ceased to be largely local in origin and effect. Crime is now established on an international scale and the common law must face this new reality. Their Lordships can find nothing in precedent, comity or good sense that should inhibit the common law from regarding as justiciable in England inchoate crimes committed abroad which are intended to result in the commission

---

[68] Council of Europe, above n 6, 416.
[69] See generally JDA Blackmore, 'The Jurisdictional Problem of the Extraterritorial Conspiracy' 17 *Criminal Law Forum* (2006) 71.
[70] 619 F 2d 1124 (5th Cir 1980).   [71] ibid, 1128–29.   [72] 1990 (2) All ER 866.

of criminal offences in England. Accordingly, a conspiracy entered into in Thailand with the intention of committing the criminal offence of trafficking in drugs in Hong Kong is justiciable in Hong Kong even if no overt act pursuant to the conspiracy has yet occurred in Hong Kong.[73]

English law has followed suit[74] and the same approach is followed in German law[75] but not in other civil law countries.[76] However, the approach has been criticized because the jurisdictional hook—the harmful conduct, result, or effect—is only potential.[77] It is arguably permissible if the individual concerned intends harm in the state establishing jurisdiction, although not if they do not, because of the principle of fair warning: they should consciously submit themselves to the law. This is a point that the signatories to the 1988 Drug Convention appears to have accepted in article 4(1)(b)(iii) because it requires that commission take place outside a state's territory 'with a view to' commission within a state taking jurisdiction.

The suppression conventions are silent on territorial jurisdiction over secondary parties. They generally speak only of the obligation to establish jurisdiction when 'the offence' is committed in the territory of the state party. However, inclusion of provision for criminalization of secondary criminal liability is normal in the suppression conventions and implies permission to states to engage in a congruent expansion of jurisdiction to that over principals or perpetrators. In practice, most states will only establish their territorial jurisdiction, including in the expanded sense of qualified territoriality, over secondary parties, when they have jurisdiction over the principal, but this may also be under qualified territoriality.[78]

16.6 Personality

16.6.1 Nationality/active personality

The nationality (or active personality) principle provides a state with the legal authority to establish criminal jurisdiction over the commission of a criminal offence by one of its nationals within and outside of its territory. Nationality jurisdiction has many advantages. Article 7(2) of the Swiss Criminal Code provides, for example, that nationality jurisdiction can be applied when the perpetrator is a national at the time of the offence or at the time of the trial. Moreover, diplomatic or sovereign immunity is unavailable to nationals prosecuted before their own courts. It is particularly useful against transnational offenders who enjoy immunity in the territory where the offence occurs because of legislative inadequacy, incapacity, disinterest, or corruption. The option to establish nationality

[73] ibid, 878. [74] See in English law *R v Sansom* [1991] 2 All ER 145.
[75] Section 9(i) of the *Strafgesetzbuch*. [76] Ryngaert, above n 16, 207.
[77] CL Blakesly and O Lagodny, 'Finding Harmony amidst Disagreement over Extradition, Jurisdiction, the Role of Human Rights, and Issues of Extraterritoriality under International Criminal Law' 24 *Vanderbilt Journal of Transnational Law* (1991) 1, 53.
[78] Ryngaert, above n 16, 203.

jurisdiction is now common in the suppression conventions;[79] some European treaties also make it obligatory.[80]

Nationality jurisdiction is a constitutional rule in many civil law states. Civil law states consider their nationals responsible to the state wherever they are because they benefit from its protection, owe it allegiance, and because their actions may injure its reputation. The principle's importance is increased by the fact that civil law states generally refuse to extradite their nationals. Non-civil law states have begun to increase their use of nationality jurisdiction in order to ensure that egregious transnational crimes, such as sex tourism, committed wholly outside their territories by their nationals do not go unpunished. For example, article 10 of Japan's Law for Punishing Acts Relating to Child Prostitution and Child Pornography and for Protecting Children[81] provides for extraterritorial jurisdiction over Japanese nationals who commit child sex offences. In *United States v Clark*,[82] the US Court of Appeals for the Ninth Circuit held that the nationality principle justified jurisdiction for offences under the Prosecutorial Remedies and Other Tools to End the Exploitation of Children Today Act 2003[83] for the offences of a US national apprehended having sex with minors in Cambodia. 'Chuckie' Taylor, son of former Liberian President Charles Taylor, was arrested in Florida for torture offences relying on his US nationality.[84] Some common law states have expanded its use against a range of extraterritorial transnational crimes. Section 7A of the New Zealand Crimes Act 1961, for example, applies nationality to wholly extraterritorial terrorism; dealing in people under 18 for sexual exploitation, removal of body parts, or engagement in forced labour; participation in organized criminal groups; smuggling migrants; human trafficking; money laundering; and corruption of officials. Although the establishment of nationality jurisdiction has been subject to constitutional challenge in some common law states, it has withstood that challenge.[85]

The presumption that nationals are familiar with their state's law serves as the rationale for the legality of nationality jurisdiction; global mobility and multiple nationalities undermine this rationale. For this reason a range of conditions are applied to its use in civil law states, and some of these have been taken up generally.

Certain states set explicit penalty thresholds in order to limit nationality's use to serious offences only.[86] The Swiss Penal Code does this indirectly by insisting the offence is extraditable under Swiss law to ensure that jurisdiction is not established over trivial offences.[87]

Double criminality is standard. Article 5 of the Netherlands Criminal Code provides for jurisdiction over Dutch nationals, for example, only if the offence is also 'punishable under the law of the country in which it has been committed'. The outer limits of article 5 were explored by the Netherlands Court of Cassation in

---

[79] See, eg, article 15(2)(b) of UNTOC; article 42(2)(b) of the UNCAC.

[80] See, eg, article 13(1)(d) of the European Convention relating to Offences against Cultural Property, 23 June 1985, CETS 119; not in force.

[81] Law No 52 of 1999.

[82] 435 F 3d 1100 (9th Cir 2006); ILDC 897 (US 2007), 25 January 2006.   [83] 18 USC § 2423(c).

[84] See *US v Emmanuel*, No 06-20758-CR (SD Fla 7 July 2007).

[85] See, eg, in Australia, *XYZ v The Commonwealth* [2006] HCA 25.

[86] See, eg, article 7 of the Criminal Law of the People's Republic of China, which provides for a two-year penalty threshold for its use.

[87] Articles 6 and 7 of the Swiss Penal Code.

the *Asean Explorer* case.[88] There were two grounds for appeal: (i) the offence—possession of hashish—had occurred not on the physical territory of Saint Vincent and the Grenadines, but on a vessel, the *Asean Explorer*, registered in that territory; and (ii) the accused had not been on the vessel, the hashish had. The Court held: (i) that as the offence was punishable under the law of the flag state the double criminality requirement was met as such an offence must be considered equivalent to one committed within its territory; and (ii) even those not on board fell within the flag-state jurisdiction.[89] Transnational criminal law helps to meet this double criminality condition because it ensures states have similar offences, and the condition has been built into suppression conventions that oblige parties to establish nationality.[90]

Some states insist that nationality jurisdiction is only available if the offence occurs wholly outside the state establishing jurisdiction,[91] a condition also recognized in some suppression conventions. The difficulty of this requirement in a world of different criminal actions in different states was confronted in *Eviko v Israel*.[92] Eviko was party within Israel to a conspiracy to transfer 20,000 ecstasy pills from the Netherlands to the US. An entirely external action was made criminal in Israel by the legal fiction in section 38A of Israel's Dangerous Drugs Ordinance 1973 (as revised), which states that an Israeli citizen or resident who commits an act, which, if committed in Israel, would have been considered an offence according to the Ordinance, is considered to have committed the offence in Israel. Unfortunately, Eviko's action was neither committed entirely within Israel nor entirely without Israel. On appeal, the Israeli Supreme Court dismissed his argument that Israel thus did not have jurisdiction inter alia on the basis that the appellant's interpretation would lead to the absurd result that offences wholly within and wholly without Israel would fall within Israel's jurisdiction and not offences partly within and partly without (ie many transnational offences).

Another problem occurs where the state only extends nationality jurisdiction over the principal and not secondary parties. This point is nicely illustrated by the New Zealand Supreme Court case *LM v R*[93] where the accused, a New Zealand national, was prosecuted as a secondary party to sexual conduct by a Russian national with a minor that occurred in Russia. Section 114 of the New Zealand Crimes Act 1961 made provision for jurisdiction over New Zealanders who perform conduct which would be an offence involving sexual offending against children and young people if it occurred in New Zealand. However, the Supreme Court noted that section 114 did not explicitly permit jurisdiction over secondary parties who act abroad, but over principals only, and thus because the Russian was not committing an offence in New Zealand law,

---

[88] Judgment on Appeal in Cassation, no HR 00555/01, LJN: AD9557; ILDC, 148 (NL 2002); NJ 2003/316; JOL 2002, 294, 21 May 2002.

[89] ibid, at para 4.6.

[90] Article 22(1)(d) of the Council of Europe Convention on Cybercrime, 23 November 2001, CETS 185, in force 1 July 2004.

[91] See, eg, section 73.4 of the Australian Criminal Code Act 1995 (Cth).

[92] Further hearing of a Supreme Court appeal decision, CrFH 2980/04; ILDC, 367 (IL 2004) 29 December 2005.

[93] [2014] NZSC 110.

the secondary liability of the New Zealander in New Zealand could not be derived because there had been no offence from which to derive it (he was eventually convicted as a principal).

The principal weakness of nationality as a basis for criminal jurisdiction is that there are no agreed rules for the award of nationality; international law only requires a genuine link between state and individual,[94] and states are free to adopt whatever conditions they choose. Usually they award it to natural persons on the basis of birth, parentage, naturalization, or some other criterion. Common law states tend to confer nationality on juristic persons such as companies on the basis of where they were incorporated, civil law states on where they are managed. A narrow reading of nationality ignores the reality that many of the long-term residents of states, natural or juristic, are not nationals. Permissive establishment of jurisdiction over permanent residents and more expansively over habitual residents, addresses this problem. Article 15(2)(b) of the United Nations Convention against Transnational Crime (UNTOC) provides that parties may establish jurisdiction when '[t]he offence is committed by a ... stateless person who has his or her habitual residence in its territory'. Somewhat more broadly, article 4(2)(b) of the 1988 Drug Trafficking Convention also permits states to establish jurisdiction over habitual residents, but does not require they be stateless, which means that parties may establish jurisdiction on this basis over the nationals of other parties. Nonetheless, active personality based on 'formal presence' can become tenuous and raise issues of the reasonableness and legality. In, for example, *US v Statoil*,[95] the US took jurisdiction over a Norwegian company that engaged in bribery of an Iranian public official based on nothing more than the issuing of stock by the company on a US Stock Exchange.

16.6.2 Passive personality

The passive personality principle permits states to establish jurisdiction when one of their nationals is the victim of a crime, wherever the commission of that crime takes place, no matter how many other victims of other nationalities there may have been, and whether or not the accused intended to target that particular nationality. Also popular among civil law states because of their legal relationship with their nationals,[96] it derives from their legitimate interest in their nationals' welfare, but should only be established if there is a compelling nexus between the victim's nationality and the crime.

Common law states initially rejected passive personality because of its breadth and indeterminacy, and because it overrides the sovereignty of the territorial state. More recently, they have begun to see the utility of the principle in situations where the territorial state does not act, in order to respond to the harm done to nationals abroad

---

[94] *The Nottebohm, Second Phase, Judgment*, ICJ Reports 1955, 4.
[95] ASA Docket No 06 Cr 960 (SDNY October 13, 2006).
[96] See, eg, article 113–7 of the French Criminal Code.

when the nationality of the victim was central rather than merely incidental to the commission of the offence. The US, historically an antagonist of this principle,[97] for example, now applies passive personality to selected crimes such as terrorism.[98] Its nationals have repeatedly come under attack while abroad because of their nationality. In *United States v Yunis*,[99] a US Court assumed passive personality jurisdiction over the hijacking by the accused of a Jordanian airline, even though he was Lebanese, the crime had occurred in Jordanian airspace, and the plane had landed in Jordan, because two US citizens were on board the aircraft.[100] The territorial state's consent was not sought.[101]

The passive personality principle has also been applied in suppression conventions that focus on security. Article 6(2)(b) of the 1988 SUA Convention, for example, provides that a party may establish its jurisdiction over any convention offence when 'during its commission a national of that State is seized, threatened, injured or killed'. Curiously, passive personality has also been included as an optional provision in more general suppression conventions such as the UNCAC and the UNTOC, where its use is not as easily justified.[102] It is not immediately apparent why organized criminals would commit a crime against someone because of their nationality, although an attack on a foreign judicial or law enforcement official may be what the authors of the UNTOC had in mind.

Use of passive personality raises issues of legality, particularly if the conduct is an offence in the victim's state but not in the state where it occurs. It potentially violates fair-warning because the accused will in many cases be unaware of the nationality of the victim and thus the law that they are violating. Deterrence is minimal if the offender cannot reasonably be presumed to know the law applied to them. Many states therefore condition use of the principle on the presence of the suspect in their territory (either voluntarily or by extradition), a certain level of gravity,[103] and double criminality (although some specifically exclude this).[104] Courts have relied on the inclusion of passive personality in the suppression conventions to address legality problems with its use. In *Yunis*, for example, the US Court relied explicitly on article 5(1)(d) of the Hostage Taking Convention, which permits states to use passive personality in regard to the taking of a hostage who is a national of that state. It is unclear how the accused in this case could reasonably have been expected to access the terms of this Convention.

The criteria for nationality discussed above are equally relevant here. Some Scandinavian countries take jurisdiction where the 'victim' is a private corporation or association registered in that state.[105]

---

[97] See *The Cutting Case*, 1887 Foreign Relations 751 (1888) excerpted in 2 J Moore, *International Law Digest* (1906), 228.

[98] See, eg, 18 USC §§ 2331, 2332.

[99] 681 F Supp 896 (DDC 1988); upheld by Court of Appeal 924 F 2d 1086 (DC Cir 1991).

[100] Applying 18 USC § 32(a) (Aircraft Piracy Act).

[101] A common practice—see also *US v Rezaq* 899 F Supp 697 (DDC 1995).

[102] Article 42(2)(a) of the UNCAC; article 15(2)(a) of the UNTOC.

[103] Petrig, above n 30, 42.   [104] Council of Europe, above n 6, 418.

[105] Section 1(5) of Finland's Penal Code of 1889; section 2.3 of Sweden's Penal Code of 1999.

16.6.3 Protective

The protective principle (protective personality) permits states to establish jurisdiction over specific categories of offences, which though committed entirely extraterritorially, have an impact on or threaten that state's sovereignty, security, integrity, or some other important governmental function. The protective jurisdiction is triggered by the fact that the state, and its essential interests, are actually the target of the hostage-taker's pressure. Protective jurisdiction is broader in scope than objective territoriality in that it allows the establishment of jurisdiction over conduct that poses a potential threat,[106] broader than nationality in that it applies to nationals and foreigners, and broader than passive personality in that it covers a more diffuse range of threats. It has the added virtue that the state most strongly affected has the best claim.

The protective principle appears in various forms in more recent suppression conventions. Article 5(1)(c) of the Hostage Taking Convention, for example, obliges parties to establish jurisdiction over hostage-taking when the offence is 'committed ... (c) in order to compel that state to do or abstain from doing any act'. Article 13(1) of the 1985 European Convention on Offences Relating to Cultural Property sets out a more unusual form of the principle. It obliges parties to establish their jurisdiction when 'any offence relating to cultural property' is 'f. committed outside its territory when it was directed against cultural property originally found within its territory'. Here the party establishes its jurisdiction to protect 'its' cultural property. This innovation is noticeably absent from the 2017 Council of Europe Convention on Offences relating to Cultural Property.

The rationale of the protective principle is self-help; the offence must impact directly or indirectly on the state's essential interests. There has been a growing tendency to characterize a number of transnational crimes as threats to security, particularly when other principles of jurisdiction are not available. The US took the lead in this regard in 1980, enacting the Marijuana on the High Seas Act (MHSA),[107] which in section 955(c) prohibits 'any person on a vessel within the customs waters of the United States' (parts of the high seas in regard to which by treaty or arrangement a foreign state has agreed that US may enforce its criminal law in the foreign vessel) from possessing a controlled substance with 'intent to distribute'. The US courts interpreted this provision as implying a protective jurisdiction. In *US v Gonzales*[108] the US Court of Appeals held that the US had protective jurisdiction for a violation of the Act over a Honduran vessel found 125 miles east of Florida, carrying 114 bales of marijuana, which US officials had boarded with Honduran permission (in effect ceding jurisdiction to the US).[109] According to the Court, the protective principle allowed the establishment of jurisdiction 'over a person whose conduct outside the nation's territory threatens the nation's security or could potentially interfere with the operation of its governmental functions'.[110] The Court thought reliance on protective jurisdiction by

---

[106] *US v Pizzarusso* 338 F 2d 8 (2nd Cir 1968).   [107] 21 USC § 955(a)–955(d).
[108] 776 F 2d 931 (11th Cir 1985).
[109] ES Podgor and R Clark, *International Criminal Law: Cases and Materials*, 3rd edn (Newark: Lexis Nexis, 2010), 100–02.
[110] ibid, 938.

the US Congress had been proper because of the difficulty in proving beyond reasonable doubt that a vessel on the high seas carrying contraband was headed for the US, and because the protective principle did not require proof of an actual or intended effect within the US, but only a potentially adverse effect. The final requirement was that the crime be recognized 'by nations that have reasonably developed legal systems', and drug trafficking was such a crime.[111] Three years later article 4(1)(b)(ii) of the 1988 Drug Trafficking Convention made provision for an optional form of protective jurisdiction over vessels on which drug trafficking offences have occurred and the party has been 'authorized to take appropriate action pursuant of article 17'. In 1986 the US enacted the Maritime Drug Law Enforcement Act,[112] which abandoned the restrictive requirements of the MHSA when it provided for jurisdiction over a 'vessel subject to the jurisdiction of the United States ... even though the act is committed outside the territorial jurisdiction of the United States'.[113] Some US courts still consider this an application of the protective jurisdiction, others not,[114] although rather than establish a jurisdiction over actions directed against US essential interests, it appears to establish a general police power over trafficking on the high seas.

US courts have used the principle in establishing jurisdiction in regard to other types of offences[115] and they have not been alone in using protective jurisdiction. The German Bundesgerichtshof established jurisdiction over a Dutch cannabis dealer operating in the Netherlands on the basis of the protective principle on the condition that a direct domestic link to Germany could be established.[116] The Court held that the dealer had violated German interests by having sold over many years a considerable amount of hashish to German nationals who had taken the drug to Germany to consume or resell it.

There are two basic limits to the protective principle. First, the interest should be particular to the state concerned. Entirely extraterritorial transnational crimes without an intention to engage in some form of trafficking within the state do not genuinely threaten a state's interests. It is difficult to understand how, for example, foreign corrupt schemes that breach US Securities Regulations are conduct 'directed at' the US.[117] Provisions in the suppression conventions such as article 30(1)(e) of the Arab Convention on the Combating of Information Technology Offences, which obliges a state party to extend its jurisdiction 'based on an overriding interest of the state', sanction potentially exorbitant claims to interest.

Second, the interests must be those of the state apparatus.[118] Traditionally these have been its security interests; extension to include the economy and public order and governmental functions may expand the principle's scope potentially excessively.

---

[111] ibid, 939–40.   [112] Codified at 46 USC §§ 70501–07.

[113] 46 USC § 70503(a)(1) and (b).

[114] For *United States v Gonzalez*, 311 F3d 440, 446 (1st Cir 2002); against *United States v Perlaza*, 439 F3d 1149, 1162 (9th Cir 2006).

[115] See, eg, *US v Ahmed* 94 F Supp 3d 394 (EDNY), in a prosecution for material support of a foreign terrorist organization.

[116] Judgment of the Federal Supreme Court, 34 BGHSt 334 [1988], 339.

[117] *SEC v Straub* 921 F Supp 2d 244 (SDNY 29 December 2011).

[118] E Kontorovich, 'Beyond the Article I Horizon: Congress's Enumerated Powers and Universal Jurisdiction Over Drug Crimes' 93 *Minnesota Law Review* (2009) 1191, 1230.

Extraterritorial drug trafficking, for example, may engage a state's population's moral, social, and medical well-being but not actually threaten the state apparatus itself.[119] Only the objections of other states appear to provide any restriction, and again these are negated if the principle finds support in a suppression convention. In *United States v Bravo and ors*[120] the US Court of Appeals noted, without referring to specific provisions, that the protective principle was supported by all three modern drug conventions as well as UNCLOS.[121]

The protective principle is considered a practical solution to deal with jurisdictionally difficult offences such as cyberterrorism.[122] Offences with multiple, obscure points of origin, which affect multiple victims in multiple jurisdictions and lead to potentially massive concurrent jurisdiction and forum shopping by criminals for the weakest laws, make an argument for a jurisdiction based on self-defence appealing. This reasoning is applicable to many transnational crimes facilitated by the Internet and suggests that the protective principle will become increasingly popular in the war on transnational crime. Issues of legality are not as troublesome when someone undertakes conduct deliberately intended to strike or occur within a number of different jurisdictions; but when they are ignorant of these effects fair warning as to which state's laws they are potentially going to violate is an issue.

16.7 *Aut Dedere Aut Judicare*

Suppression conventions commonly provide for extraterritorial jurisdiction based on the *aut dedere aut judicare* (extradite or prosecute) principle. It requires the state establishing jurisdiction to do so because the individual implicated in an offence is in its territory and it does not extradite them. It usually operates as follows: Party A establishes its jurisdiction over a particular offence in a suppression convention (this could be on any basis; the offence may not in fact be an offence in the territory where it occurs). Party B then discovers the alleged offender is present on their territory. Party B, aware of Party A's jurisdiction, must either extradite the offender or prosecute that offender if it fails to extradite. But the obligations are not necessarily sequential in the sense that Party A must make an extradition request, Party B must refuse to extradite, and only then must Party B establish its jurisdiction. Some conventions do require Party A to make an extradition request and Party B to refuse to comply.[123] Most accord no priority to either Party A or Party B's prosecution; they permit Party B to choose to prosecute if the alleged offender is found in its territory.[124] Reliance on this principle requires parties to (i) establish their criminal jurisdiction over an alleged offender who is within their territory and then (ii) exercise that jurisdiction if they do not extradite that offender. No other jurisdictional link is required.

---

[119] ibid, 1231.   [120] 489 F 3d 1 (1st Cir 2007); ILDC 1061 (US 2007).   [121] ibid, 7.
[122] PN Stockton and M Golabek-Goldman, 'Prosecuting Cyberterrorists: Applying Traditional Jurisdictional Frameworks to a Modern Threat' 25 *Stanford Law and Policy Review* (2014) 211, 230 et seq.
[123] Article 16(10) of the UNTOC.
[124] See M Plachta, 'Aut dedere aut judicare: An Overview of Modes of Implementation and Approaches' 6 *Maastricht Journal of European and Comparative Law* (1999) 331, 335.

The first requirement that the individual is 'found in' a jurisdiction is usually unproblematic. In the Dutch case of *Anonymous v Public Prosecutor*[125] one of the 2004 Madrid bombers was only suspected of being in the Netherlands and was identified using an allegedly illegal wire-tap. Article 4(13) of the Netherlands Penal Code, the implementation in Dutch law of the *aut dedere aut judicare* principle provided for in article 6(4) of the Terrorist Bombings Convention, was available to establish jurisdiction and thus authorize the execution of that jurisdiction through the wire-tap. Citing a legislative memorandum that the Convention must be interpreted expansively and that the implementing law was designed to reach terrorists who flee to another state, the Court interpreted the phrase 'being in the Netherlands' in article 4(13) expansively and found that the Netherlands had had jurisdiction and was justified in tapping the phone. The Netherlands Supreme Court decision in *Bouterse*[126] provided authority that when the suspect was found in the Netherlands it had, at that moment, jurisdiction. In *FE alias NY v DS*[127] the Belgian Court found that the obligation to extradite or prosecute in the 1977 European Terrorism Convention only required that the accused be found in Belgian territory; it did not imply 'remain in', allowing Belgium, which can prosecute in absentia in terms of its domestic laws, to do so.

The second requirement, non-extradition, may be because the state establishing jurisdiction either refuses an extradition request or because it understands no such request will be made. Refusal to extradite may be based on a wide variety of grounds, as discussed in Chapter 20.

Agreement to subject the particular offence to suppression in the treaty indicates that it is sufficiently serious to justify this tenuous form of jurisdiction. The 1970 Hague Hijacking Convention was the first suppression convention to make it obligatory to establish jurisdiction unless extradition was granted to some other party. Article 4(2) provides:

> Each Contracting State shall likewise take such measures as may be necessary to establish its jurisdiction over the offence in the case where the alleged offender is present in its territory and it does not extradite him pursuant to Article 8 to any of the States mentioned in paragraph 1 of this Article.

In many suppression conventions, however, the provision to establish jurisdiction is obligatory when it involves the refusal to extradite nationals but still only permissive when it involves non-nationals. Thus while article 4(2)(a) of the 1988 Drug Trafficking Convention obliges parties to establish jurisdiction when the alleged offender is present and the party does not extradite them because the party has territorial or nationality jurisdiction, article 4(2)(b) provides that a party 'may' establish jurisdiction when the party's failure to extradite is on some other ground. In the former case, the party has a strong jurisdictional connection and thus must enforce it; in the latter it may not have any other jurisdictional connection so the provision permits it to choose whether to establish jurisdiction or not. In such a situation the state may have valid

---

[125] Preliminary decision, Case no 10/000218-04; ILDC 853 (NL 2005) LJN AS5609; (2005) NJ 185, 8 February 2005.

[126] Judgment on appeal, LJN AB1471; ILDC 80 (NL 2001); (2002) NJ, 18 September 2001.

[127] Final appeal judgment, Case No P.07.0571.N, ILDC 1117 (BE 2007), 18 September 2007, para 15.

grounds such as triviality or difficulty in obtaining evidence for refusing extradition and declining jurisdiction.

A state implementing an extradite or prosecute provision must both make it possible to prosecute rather than extradite and to establish its own jurisdiction in such a case. This is apparent, for example, in section 35(2) of South Africa's Prevention and Combating of Corrupt Activities Act, designed to implement article 44(4) of the UNCAC, which deems the offence that occurs abroad to have been committed in South Africa if the alleged offender is 'found in' South Africa and 'for one or other reason not extradited by South Africa or if there is no application to extradite that person'. Once jurisdiction is established, the duty to exercise it is limited. Most conventions usually only provide for a duty to 'submit' the case to the prosecutorial authorities leaving any discretion as to whether to prosecute intact.[128]

This principle of jurisdiction is sometimes termed 'subsidiary' or 'secondary' universality for two reasons: it is universal in that in theory if the treaty is universally adhered to it can close all jurisdictional gaps in the system, and it is subsidiary in that it is subsidiary/secondary to another state's jurisdiction. But to call it universal jurisdiction is difficult because the principle is neither part of custom nor *ius cogens*; it is based solely on a treaty.[129] Moreover, its application involves the representation of another more directly concerned state.[130] It is more properly a form of 'representative or vicarious administration of justice' based on territorial jurisdiction over the presence of the alleged offender, the establishment of which is triggered by their non-extradition.[131] Indeed, double criminality is expressly required by certain states because the state establishing jurisdiction is acting on behalf of another state.[132] By joining a particular suppression convention Party A delegates its jurisdiction to Party B so that it can take jurisdiction on Party A's behalf, vicariously or in a representative fashion. It doesn't delegate this jurisdiction to all states/the international community, which is what distinguishes this form of jurisdiction from absolute universality jurisdiction. Its representative nature is clear, for example, in article 8 of the 1936 Convention for the Suppression of the Illicit Traffic in Dangerous Drugs,[133] which provides that a foreigner in the territory of a party who has committed offences abroad 'shall be punished as though the offence had been committed in that territory' if there had been a failure to extradite them. State B's action is not entirely selfless, however; it is in its own interests not to have a transnational criminal in its jurisdiction going unpunished.

Almost inevitably, the application of this principle gives rise to a conflict of interests with a state that has a stronger jurisdictional link and would prefer extradition. The Belgian case *FE alias NY v DS*,[134] for example, involved the obligation to extradite or prosecute in articles 6 and 7 of the 1977 European Terrorism Convention,

---

[128] See, eg, article 8(1) of the 1979 Convention against the Taking of Hostages.
[129] Contra Bassiouni but following Wise in MC Bassiouni and EM Wise, *Aut dedere aut judicare: The Duty to Extradite or Prosecute in International Law* (Dordrecht: Martinus Nijhoff, 1995).
[130] Council of Europe above n 6, 419.
[131] See *Arrest Warrant Case* (Joint Separate Opinion), above n 15, 75, para 41.
[132] Petrig, above n 30, 44.
[133] LNTS No 4648, volume 198, p 301, signed 26 June 1936, never in force.
[134] Final appeal judgment, Case No P.07.0571.N, ILDC 1117 (BE 2007), 18 September 2007.

implemented in Belgium by article 2 of a Law of 2 September 1985. A Belgian Court had earlier refused to extradite the accused, a member of a Turkish Marxist Organization DHKP-C, to Turkey for the murder of a Turkish businessman on the grounds it was a political offence. When, however, Belgium established its jurisdiction over the offence, the accused challenged it, inter alia, because two further Turkish extradition requests were pending and the accused had not been in Belgium when the judgment was rendered. The Belgian Court of Cassation held the existence of further extradition requests irrelevant so long as the Court had not changed its mind about refusal of the first request as this is what triggered its jurisdiction.[135] The requesting state cannot therefore prevent the establishment of the jurisdiction by continuing to lay extradition requests after an initial refusal.

The duty to extradite or prosecute has been touted as the solution to situations where states cannot extradite inter alia because of the nationality exception or death penalty exception. Yet it is not a panacea. Support for the principle in many suppression conventions has only led to patchy national implementation.[136] States that do not extradite their nationals do not prioritize requests for vicarious prosecution either. There are practical difficulties in gathering evidence from abroad. States that request extradition lose interest in a prosecution they cannot control. US efforts, for example, to support vicarious prosecution of Mexican drug traffickers from the 1960s to the 1980s by the Mexican authorities largely failed,[137] although the early 1990s reveal an increase in its use.[138] During the negotiation of the 1988 Drug Trafficking Convention the UK cited the difficulties of extraterritorial prosecution without direct access to evidence and of case load, in support of its view states that extradite their nationals should do so, and those states that do not extradite their nationals should establish jurisdiction on the basis of nationality 'and then deal with the evidential and procedural problems in the way provided by their own legal system'.[139] The UK also voiced concerns that vicarious prosecution could be used to block extradition because it might result in acquittal and a plea of double jeopardy to further prosecution in another state. Although the UK was unsuccessful in preventing incorporation of the principle in the 1988 Convention, article 6(9)(b) does permit a party requesting extradition to ask a requested party permitted to take jurisdiction on the basis of *aut dedere aut judicare* to refrain from doing so, in order to preserve the requesting party's legitimate jurisdiction. The UNTOC's authors, and in particular the US, were similarly concerned to prevent either a decision not to prosecute being made on inadequate grounds or an ineffective prosecution.

---

[135] ibid, para 12.
[136] See *The Report of the IBA Legal Practice Division Task Force on Extraterritorial Jurisdiction* (2009), 155, available at <https://documents.law.yale.edu/sites/default/files/Task%20Force%20on%20Extraterritorial%20Jurisdiction%20-%20Report%20.pdf> last visited 4 December 2017. In its limited survey of twenty-seven states only eight applied this form of jurisdiction.
[137] E Nadelmann, *Cops Across Borders: The Internationalization of US Law Enforcement* (University Park, PA: Penn State University Press, 1993), 434–36.
[138] See R Labardini, 'Extraterritorial Jurisdiction and Prosecution in lieu of Extradition' 22 *International Law Enforcement Reporter* (2006) 33.
[139] *United Nations Conference for the Adoption of a Convention against Illicit Traffic in Narcotic Drugs and Psychotropic Substances, Official Records, Volume II* (New York, 1991) UN Doc E/CONF.82/16/Add.1, UN Publication Sales No E.91.XI.1, 137.

The second sentence of article 16(10) of the UNTOC thus contains a safeguard obliging the authorities of the party refusing extradition to 'take' the decision on whether or not to prosecute, and if they do prosecute, to conduct the proceedings, 'in the same manner as in the case of any other offence of a grave nature under the domestic law of that state party'.

Even though the *aut dedere aut judicare* principle reflects a form of representative jurisdiction and thus should preclude double jeopardy for the same conduct, this is not the view of US courts. *United States v Rezaq*[140] dealt inter alia with whether the US had jurisdiction over Rezaq for a hijacking in which two US citizens had been killed. When the hijacked aircraft landed in Malta, Malta did not extradite. It convicted him and sentenced him to serve a twenty-five year sentence. Upon his release after serving seven years, he was extradited to the US to face further different charges arising from the same matter. He argued that the extradite or prosecute obligation in article 4(2) of the Hague Hijacking Convention precluded US jurisdiction over the offence. On appeal, the US court allowed jurisdiction because there was no express prohibition on double jeopardy in the Convention and it had been explicitly rejected in the negotiations.[141] In both *Rezaq* and the Belgian Case *FE alias NY v DS* an unwillingness to extradite did not result in a failure to prosecute at all, only a failure to prosecute in the US and Turkey, the states that had originally established their jurisdiction, which goes to the heart of the problem with the effectiveness of this principle of jurisdiction—for such states, vicarious prosecution by other states does not satisfy their penal interests.

16.8 Absolute Universality

The principle of absolute universality confers jurisdiction on all states to try certain crimes regardless of where the offence was committed, who committed it, and where the alleged offender is located. It has two rationales. First, because these offences shock humanity's shared conscience or disturb the international order. Second, because these offences occur outside an effective jurisdiction, either on the high seas or in states unable or unwilling to prosecute.

Under customary law, crystallized in article 105 of the UNCLOS, states enjoy a permissive universal jurisdiction on the high seas over pirates because they are considered the enemy of all.[142] This returns us to the question discussed in Chapter 3 whether piracy is a core international crime and pirates are enemies of all, or whether particular pirates are enemies of particular states which use this (spatially limited) permissive universal jurisdiction for their own ends. Rubin comments on the origins of this universal standing:

> British expanding and aggressive mercantilist interest, overwhelming naval dominance, and self-perception as a law-abiding 'race' bringing 'justice' to benighted parts of the globe from the time of the end of the Napoleonic Wars to the World War of 1914–1918, brought together a combination of factors making universal 'standing'

---

[140] 134 F 3d 1121 (DC Cir 1998); ILDC 1391 (US 1998), 6 February 1998.   [141] ibid, 1128–30.
[142] P Birnie, 'Piracy: Past, Present and Future' 11 *Marine Policy* (1987) 163, 164.

under the law, with Great Britain the only country likely to be able to exercise it, seem a compelling legal rationale for police actions.[143]

In his view universality's application to piracy owes more to its practical utility to maritime powers than to a desire to develop global solidarity. Unsurprisingly, weaker states have struggled with the application of universality to piracy in the situation off Somalia.[144]

Absolute universality is not generally applied to transnational crimes by analogy to the core international crimes because they are considered to serve different interests. In the *United States v Yousef*[145] the US Court of Appeals for the Second Circuit held that the list of crimes to which universality applies cannot be added to by reliance on the supposed interests of the international community or by analogy, particularly when the crime—in this instance terrorism—was still a powerfully charged loosely deployed term.[146] Nevertheless, universality has been applied by some states to crimes derived from the suppression conventions. Switzerland, for example, applies it to a range of offences including sexual offences and human trafficking if the victim is a minor.[147] Section 6 of the German Criminal Code provides for jurisdiction over a number of crimes when committed abroad including human trafficking, counterfeiting, and drug trafficking, irrespective of the law of the place where the offence was committed. In 1987 in the *Universal Jurisdiction over Drug Offences Case*[148] the German Federal Supreme Court held that section 6(5) grounds jurisdiction for prosecution of illicit traffic in all kinds of controlled drugs on the principle of universality. In 1999, however, the same Court introduced the requirement of a 'legitimizing connection' to Germany, such as former domicile in Germany, before jurisdiction grounded in section 6(5) was established.[149]

Universality does provide powerful states with a powerful tool against transnational crime. Kontorovich shows how in the Maritime Drug Law Enforcement Act the US in effect extended universal jurisdiction without constitutional warrant over drug traffickers on the high seas who are not US citizens, not on US vessels and not heading towards the US.[150] Article I of the US Constitution gives the US power over piracy on the high seas; drug trafficking has been analogized with piracy by US courts without meeting the requirement that the exercise of universal jurisdiction must be applied to offences recognized by the law of nations, that is core international crimes. Yet in the *United States v James-Robinson*[151] the US District Court for Florida found that drug trafficking is not a crime justifying universal jurisdiction.

---

[143] AP Rubin, *The Law of Piracy*, 2nd edn (The Hague: Brill, 1998), 386.
[144] See, eg, the Kenyan case *In Re Hashi et al* [2009] eKLR (HCK).
[145] 327 F 3d 56, overruling the district court decision in 927 F Supp 673.
[146] At para 125 et seq.
[147] Article 5 of the Swiss Criminal Code 21 December 1937 as amended.
[148] 27 BGHSt 30, 32; (1987) 74 ILR 166, 168.
[149] *Judgment of the Federal Supreme Court*, Unpublished, 30 April 1999, 3 STR215/98.
[150] Kontorovich, above n 118, 1195, 1123.
[151] 515 F Supp 1340 (DC Fla 1981), 1344 fn 6; see also *United States v Marino-Garcia*, 679 F 2d 1373 (11th Cir 1982), 1382, fn 16.

Haphazard analogies with core international crimes will not serve to justify the use of universal jurisdiction against a transnational crime. To provide a reasonable link, a state must show that more than its interests are at stake, and that it is enforcing an international community interest. This dilemma is nicely illustrated in *Spain v Alvaro and ors, Appeal judgment on admissibility*,[152] where the Spanish Supreme Court dealt with the question of whether Spain (in the absence of a better basis for jurisdiction) had established universal jurisdiction over a boat of alleged migrant smugglers found outside Spanish territorial waters though heading towards Spain, in order to stop and search the boat and prosecute the smugglers for the crime of migrant smuggling under article 318*bis* of the Spanish Criminal Code 1995. Article 23(4) of Spain's 1985 Organic Law of the Judicial Power vested Spain with universal jurisdiction to prosecute certain crimes but not migrant smuggling. However, the Supreme Court, noting that migrant smuggling was a serious crime subject to international suppression, effectively read the provisions in the Migrant Smuggling Protocol as inserting migrant smuggling into article 23(4), and held that Spain had universal jurisdiction over migrant smuggling. Article 23(4) was later specifically amended to establish such jurisdiction. It is open to question whether Spain was invoking universality against migrant smugglers whilst acting for itself or for the international community. Transnational crimes are generally not sufficiently shocking to the human conscience to justify dispensing with a reasonable jurisdictional link and the requirement of fair warning, the rationale usually associated with doing so when applying absolute universality.

16.9 Concurrent Jurisdiction

National implementation of the jurisdictional principles in the suppression conventions leads to problems of overlapping national jurisdictions over transnational crime. Consider the jurisdictional problems that arose from, for example, the hijacking of a Russian passenger plane in March 2001 by Chechen hijackers who were detained by Saudi Arabian authorities in Saudi Arabia after killing a Turkish passenger and a Russian crew member.[153] Nearly every principle of jurisdiction discussed above was potentially relevant, including the special landing aircraft jurisdiction of the Hague Hijacking Convention. Concurrent jurisdiction raises two issues: which state has precedence and can more than one state prosecute for the same offence in violation of *ne bis in idem*?

General international law does not provide a hierarchy of application of jurisdictional principles and nor do the suppression conventions. They accept that more than one party will have a valid jurisdiction, and that it is for parties simply to take their turn. In the *United States v Pendleton*,[154] for example, a US District Court held that the extraterritorial jurisdiction established over the actions of a US national who had sex with minors abroad[155] was not precluded by Germany's jurisdiction for the same

---

[152] Case no 582/2007; ILDC 994 (ES 2007), 21 June 2007.

[153] M Warren, '20 Freed, 15 Escape after Chechens Hijack Jet', *The Daily Telegraph*, 16 March 2001.

[154] *Decision on Motion to Dismiss Indictment*, No 08-111-GMS (DDe 2009); ILDC 1382 (US 2009), 11 February 2009.

[155] 18 USC § 2423(c) and § 2423(f)(1).

activity.[156] The suppression conventions have been limited to requiring states to consult. Article 4(3) of the Organisation for Economic Co-operation and Development Anti-Bribery Convention, for example, provides that '[w]hen more than one Party has jurisdiction over an alleged offence described in this Convention, the Parties involved shall, at the request of one of them, consult with a view to determining the most appropriate jurisdiction for prosecution'. This does not preclude jurisdiction by a state that does not make such a request, even if it has given indications that it would not prosecute because another state had already done so.[157]

A practical limitation is set by the fact that one state has custody of the individual concerned. In regard to some crimes this sets the legal precedent. For example, in regard to piracy, article 4(6) and (7) of the Djibouti Code provide that the capturing state has the primary right to exercise jurisdiction, in line with article 105 of UNCLOS.

In general the only 'legal' limitation is international comity, which cautions against reliance on jurisdictional principles that might be construed as invasive of another state's sovereignty or which conveys a mistrust of another state's criminal justice system. In *Adamov v Federal Office of Justice*,[158] for example, Switzerland was faced with competing requests, first from the US and then Russia, for the extradition of Adamov, a former Russian Minister for Nuclear Energy, for various offences including corruption. The Swiss Court prioritized the Russian request because of the fact the offences had been committed whilst working in an official capacity for the Russian State and thus it was the most seriously affected by this abuse of office. The Court, noting that there is no blanket permission to impose domestic criminal law extraterritorially, implied that the US was interfering in activities that were not its business and noted that Russia had taken steps to prevent extradition to the US and had complained to Switzerland for even entertaining the US request.[159]

Arguably, states with territorial jurisdiction should have the better claim as that is where the impact of the crime is felt. This 'priority' is faintly reflected in the obligatory nature of territoriality in the suppression conventions, while other principles are permissive. It is generally considered more pragmatic, however, to adopt the conflicts of laws approach that prefers the jurisdiction of the state with the better centre of gravity, that is the state where the victims are and the harm is and where the evidence is, and which has the capacity to and has made progress in investigation, and which has the better laws.[160] One way for this to be applied is for domestic courts to apply the doctrine of *forum non-conveniens* when it is clear that a court in another state has a much stronger jurisdictional connection and greater practical capacity through access to witnesses and evidence to conduct a successful case. There is a perceptible movement towards this approach in transnational criminal law. In *Ze'ev Rosenstein v Israel*[161] Israel's Supreme Court had to decide whether an Israeli national accused of being party to a conspiracy to traffic drugs into the US, where the conspiracy was hatched in

---

[156] Above n 154, para 24.
[157] See, eg, *United States v Jeong*, 624 F3d 706; ILDC 1579 (US 2010), 22 October 2010.
[158] Appeal judgment, No 1A 288/2005; ILDC 339 (CH 2005), 22 December 2005.
[159] ibid, para 3.4.3.   [160] *Spiliada Maritime Corp v Cansulex Ltd* [1987] AC 460, 476.
[161] Appeal judgment, Crim A 4596/05; ILDC 159 (IL 2005), 30 November 2005. See also *United States v Cotroni* [1989] 1 SCR 1469, paras 36, 46, 61.

Israel, should be tried in Israel or extradited to the US. The Court began by recalling that the priority of the drug conventions was that he should stand trial and not where he should stand trial. It discounted prioritizing nationality because in the global village the idea of the necessity of protecting nationals against justice meted elsewhere had become anachronistic; it discounted territoriality when the offence was committed in more than one state. So the Court adopted the centre of gravity approach—the state with the most interests in prosecution—as offering an efficient rule of preference. In the particular case the centre of gravity was in the US because that is where the crime was to be consummated, where the potential victims were, and where the effort had been made to investigate the crime. The Court appears to have considered the effectiveness of enforcement of jurisdiction a trump card in deciding preference of concurrent jurisdictions.

The Eurojust guidelines on jurisdictional preference[162] support a centre of gravity approach, while an EU Green Paper suggests two approaches: the balancing of reasonableness of different claims against each other and an approach which applies subsidiarity prioritizing those states with claims based on territory and perhaps nationality over other claims.[163] The International Association of Prosecutors advocates an approach that takes into account the complexity of factors, practical and legal, in pursuit of a 'realistic prospect' of success.[164] These include factors such as the locus of the offence and location of accused, evidence, witnesses, and victims, but also include factors relating to the capacity for comprehensive prosecution, the state best connected in terms of mutual legal assistance, the credibility of the criminal justice system, the capacity to engage in deterrent sentencing as well as respect for due process rights and fair trial standards, and stronger state interest in prosecution. The explicit message is that coordination among prosecutors who trust each other is necessary to achieve this effective outcome but the factors also speak to the crime control interests of more powerful states because of their emphasis on capacity.

The priority of a jurisdictional interest is a political as much as a legal problem; which state proceeds first is usually a matter of negotiation. Provisions in recent suppression conventions, such as article 15(5) of the UNTOC, oblige parties in cases of jurisdictional conflicts to cooperate to resolve these conflicts. In contentious cases the party with custody may as a practical matter have the upper hand, but negotiation will be essential when it has weak grounds for jurisdiction. The European Framework Decision on Combating Terrorism goes further and obliges Member States that have jurisdiction to 'decide which one of them will prosecute with the aim, if possible, of centralising proceedings in a single member state'.[165]

---

[162] Eurojust, Guidelines for Deciding 'Which Jurisdiction should Prosecute?' in Eurojust *Annual Report 2016*, at 54. Available at <http://www.eurojust.europa.eu/doclibrary/corporate/eurojust%20Annual%20Reports/Annual%20Report%202016/AR2016_EN.pdf> last visited 8 February 2018.

[163] European Commission, Conflicts of Jurisdiction and the Principle Ne Bis In Idem in Criminal Proceedings (Green Paper) Com (2005) 696 final, 8.

[164] International Association of Prosecutors, *Prosecutorial Guidelines for Cases of Concurrent Jurisdiction: Making the Decision—'Which Jurisdiction Should Prosecute?'* (The Hague: IAP, 2013), 7.

[165] 2002/475/JHA, article 9(2).

As noted, concurrent jurisdiction also raises issues of double jeopardy. The prohibition on multiple prosecutions for the same offence in article 14(7) of the International Covenant on Civil and Political Rights is treated as being limited to the laws of a particular state, the interpretation preferred by the Human Rights Committee.[166] Article 3(d) of the UN Model Extradition Treaty, however, recommends prohibition on extradition if a final judgment had been rendered against the requested person in the requested state. Nevertheless, while pleas of *autrefois convict* or *acquis* may operate in regard to some states[167] they do not deter many states from prosecuting for the same conduct. The EU's 2009 Framework Decision on preventing such conflicts of jurisdiction[168] emphasizes consultation with the aim of preventing violation of this principle with reference to Eurojust if the matter cannot be resolved. Transnational criminal law implies recognition of the criminal justice interests of other states; it cannot be just if those states do not recognize the potential for multiple prosecution for the same conduct and guard against it by prohibiting transnational double jeopardy.

16.10 Immunity from Jurisdiction over Transnational Crime

16.10.1 Introduction

Even if a state has established jurisdiction over a transnational crime, it may be unable to enforce it if the individual or action concerned is immune from that jurisdiction.[169] Immunity from jurisdiction over transnational crime is not as common a problem as immunity from jurisdiction over the core international crimes because while commission of the core international crimes is usually the result of official or state action, transnational crime is not. There are, however, occasionally cases where sovereign or diplomatic immunity is raised against criminal charges for transnational crimes allegedly committed by officials of another state or by individuals working for an international organization.

16.10.2 Sovereign immunity

The principle of sovereign immunity, provided for in general international law, is to the effect that a court may not entertain a prosecution of a foreign official; it is not an assertion that the official is not in fact criminally liable. In the *Belgian Arrest Warrant Case* the International Court of Justice (ICJ) held that treaty obligations to establish extraterritorial jurisdiction and extradite offenders had not altered this customary immunity.[170] Personal immunity (immunity *ratione personae*), a consequence of the

---

[166] Human Rights Committee, *Views: Communication No 204/1986*, 21st Sess, UN Doc CCPR/C/Op/2 (1990) 67, para 7.3.

[167] See, eg, section 10a of the Danish Criminal Code.

[168] EU Council Framework Decision 2009/948/JHA of 30 November 2009 on the prevention and settlement of conflicts in the exercise of jurisdiction in criminal proceedings, [2009] OJ L 328.

[169] International Law Commission, 'Preliminary Report on Immunity of State Officials from Foreign Criminal Jurisdiction by Ramon Kolodkin, Special Rapporteur', Sixtieth Session, 29 May 2008, UN Doc no A/CN.4/601.

[170] See *Arrest Warrant Case*, above n 15, Judgment, paras 51, 54, 59. See also *Certain Questions of Mutual Assistance in Criminal Matters (Djibouti v France)*, Judgment, ICJ Reports 2008, 177; [2008] ICJ

principle that one state may not sit in judgment of another, provides that the high-ranking status of certain foreign officials who embody the state renders them immune from foreign criminal jurisdiction. Functional immunity (immuity *ratione materiae*), which exists to facilitate international relations, protects government acts of one state from being adjudicated before the court of another state and thus only incidentally confers immunity on the individual. According to the similar but distinctive act of state doctrine, common law courts refuse to pass judgment on the actions of foreign states performed within their jurisdiction, seeing it as an exercise of executive power and thus in violation of separation of powers doctrine. There are three conditions for these immunities.

First, the entity which the accused represents must be sovereign. Personal immunity has been denied to heads of sub-state entities within a federal state's system accused of transnational crimes such as corruption.[171] In *Italy v D M (Djukanovic)*[172] the Italian Court of Cassation overturned a lower-court decision that Milo Djukanovic, Montenegro's Prime Minister, enjoyed personal immunity from a charge for involvement in smuggling tobacco into Italy because it found that at the time of the commission of the offence Montenegro, then in a union with Serbia, was not sovereign (it became independent in 2006).

Second, to enjoy personal immunity the accused must be the current leader or occupy a senior role in this sovereign entity such as the serving head of state. *R v Bow Street Metropolitan Stipendiary Magistrate, ex p Pinochet Ugarte (No 3)*[173] confirmed the availability of personal immunity for serving heads of state. The ICJ affirmed this position in the *Belgian Arrest Warrant Case*[174] and the French Court of Cassation confirmed the incumbent head of state's immunity from prosecution in regard to Muammar Khaddafyi's alleged involvement in the bombing of a UTA flight in 1989 over the Sahara which killed 170 people.[175] The *Belgian Arrest Warrant Case* took a functional approach based on an official's involvement in international affairs of the state and extended the scope of personal immunity to include ministers for foreign affairs, and some states have followed suit.[176] This functional approach potentially expands the scope of the immunity significantly. In the earlier US case, *United States v Noriega*,[177] for example, the US District Court held that the acts of drug trafficking committed did not attract personal immunity because General Noriega had only been the de facto leader of Panama. On the functional approach, however, it appears that

---

4 para 170; *Jurisdictional Immunities of the State (Germany v Italy: Greece intervening), Judgment,* ICJ Reports 2012, p 99; [2012] ICJ 10 paras 81–97.

[171] See *R (on the application of Alamieyeseigha) v Crown Prosecution Service,* (2005) All ER (D) 348; ILDC 93 (UK 2005).

[172] Final appeal on preliminary question, Court of Cassation, no 49666; ILDC 74 (IT 2004), Diritto e giustizia 30 (11/2005) (in Italian), 28 December 2004.

[173] (2000) 1 AC 147.   [174] Above n 170, Separate Opinion of Judge Bula-Bula at 121, para 62.

[175] *Court of Cassation,* Criminal Chamber, Appeal No 00-87215, Appeal judgment, Decision No 64; ILDC 774 (FR 2001), 13 March 2001.

[176] *Re: Bo Xilai,* Bow Street Magistrates' Court, (unpublished), 8 November 2005, it was extended by an English Court to a Chinese Minister of Commerce.

[177] 746 F Supp 1510, 1519 (SD Fla 1992); upheld *United States v Noriega* 117 F 3d 1206, 1212 (11th Cir 1997).

his actions should have attracted immunity. In *Teodoro Nguema Obiang Mangue*[178] the French Court rejected a petition to have a case of money laundering and corruption laid against the First Vice-President of Equatorial Guinea and son of the president dismissed on grounds of diplomatic immunity. The French Court of Cassation held that immunity was limited to heads of state, heads of governments, and foreign ministers, and at the time of the alleged corruption he was Minister of Agriculture.[179] Many of these questions will have to be relitigated in *Immunities and Criminal Proceedings (Equatorial Guinea v France)*[180] where Guinea is challenging French criminal jurisdiction over Obiang. One of Guinea's arguments is that the French action violates Guinean sovereignty in breach of article 4 of the UNTOC, which requires parties to carry out their obligations consistently with the principles of sovereign equality, territorial integrity, and non-intervention, and more specifically provides that the UNTOC does not entitle the exercise of extraterritorial jurisdiction inside another state's territory.

16.10.3 Diplomatic immunity

Transnational criminals may also benefit from diplomatic immunity, a form of immunity *ratione personae* embodied in treaty obligations, which covers both acts performed in an official capacity and acts performed in a private capacity while the individual holds the particular post. The 1961 Vienna Convention on Diplomatic Relations[181] provides complete immunity to the diplomat and their family from detention (at, eg, border posts), search, arrest, and prosecution in the receiving state.[182] Unsurprisingly, diplomatic passports have been found in the possession of suspected drug traffickers.[183] A diplomatic mission's administrative and technical staff enjoy these same rights but only while performing official diplomatic business.[184]

Inviolability extends to diplomatic premises,[185] and they have been used for acts of terrorism. In 1984, for example, shots were fired into a demonstration from inside the Libyan Embassy in London, killing a policewoman. After the UK severed diplomatic relations with Libya, the occupants of the Embassy returned to Libya. A search of the premises revealed a submachine gun and seven handguns.[186]

---

[178] Court of Appeal of Paris, *Pôle* 7, Second Investigating Chamber, judgment of 13 June 2013; application for annulment, judgment of 16 April 2015.

[179] Cour de cassation, chambre criminelle, Audience publique du mardi 15 décembre 2015, N° de pourvoi: 15-83156.

[180] See Press Release <http://www.icj-cij.org/docket/files/163/19028.pdf> last visited 2 June 2017.

[181] 18 April 1961, 500 UNTS 95, in force 24 April 1964.

[182] Articles 29–31, 37. See also article 31(1) of the Vienna Convention on Special Missions, 1400 UNTS 23431 which provides immunity for a special mission from one state in another. Articles 30(1) and 60(1) of the Vienna Convention on the Representation of States in their Relations with International Organizations of a Universal Character, UN Doc A/Conf.67/16, 14 March 1975, although not in force, provide for diplomatic immunity in the host state of the UN or one of its functional organizations.

[183] J Njoroge, 'Drug Traffickers Arrested with Diplomatic Passports' *Daily Monitor* (Kampala), 14 September 2010.

[184] Convention on Diplomatic Relations, above n 181, article 37.   [185] ibid, article 22.

[186] I Cameron, 'First Report of the Foreign Affairs Committee of the House of Commons' 34 *International and Comparative Law Quarterly* (1985) 610.

Originally intended to provide secrecy to communications between the sending state and its officials, the inviolability of the diplomatic bag (not an actual bag but an authority to declare things inviolable)[187] is open to abuse and it has been used to smuggle drugs, weapons, and cultural artefacts. In 1980 a Moroccan diplomatic crate, accidentally dropped during offloading at a British airport, split open to reveal £500,000 worth of cannabis.

The host state has limited options should such a crime be fortuitously revealed. It may request the sending state to waive the diplomat's immunity[188] and in more extreme cases it may declare the diplomat in question *persona non grata*, precipitating their recall.[189] But without permission, search of the diplomatic bag taints any evidence revealed. In *JKO v Public Prosecutor*,[190] for example, a Surinamese national argued that a search of postbags marked as the diplomatic pouch of Surinam by Dutch officials was unlawful and thus the evidence against him, a large quantity of cocaine, was unlawfully obtained. The Netherlands Court ascertained after the search that the claimed diplomatic status of the bags was false and dismissed the argument, retrospectively curing what was at the time at face value an unlawful search. Bilateral arrangements can vary the 1961 Vienna Convention, allowing diplomatic bags to be opened in the presence of the official from the sending state.

16.10.4 Immunity of officials from inter-governmental organizations

Examples such as the engagement of UN peacekeepers in human trafficking in Bosnia[191] raise the question of the legal immunity from criminal jurisdiction of members of inter-governmental organizations, the subject of an extensive UN report.[192] The basic distinction is that high-ranking UN officials are accorded diplomatic immunity while lower-ranking officials only consular immunity.[193]

16.10.5 Immunity of officials under their own national law

An equally difficult legal shield against jurisdiction is the immunity of senior officials and political leaders within a state to that state's criminal jurisdiction. Section 308(1)(a) of the Nigerian Constitution, for example, provides that 'no civil or criminal

---

[187] Convention on Diplomatic Relations, above n 181, article 27.

[188] ibid, article 32. In *United States v Guinand* 688 F Supp 774 (DDC 1988) the Peruvian Government terminated its employment of an embassy official accused of cocaine trafficking in the US, and after he failed to leave the US he lost diplomatic immunity to prosecution.

[189] ibid, article 9.

[190] Judgment on appeal, 23-003075-01; ILDC 147 (NL 2002); LJN: AF1037, 19 November 2002.

[191] Human Rights Watch, 'Hopes Betrayed: Trafficking of Women and Girls to Post-Conflict Bosnia and Herzegovina for Forced Prostitution' 14 (9D) *Human Rights Watch* (2002), 49.

[192] A Comprehensive Strategy to Eliminate Future Sexual Exploitation and Abuse in United Nations Peacekeeping Operations, UN Doc A/59/710, 24 March 2005.

[193] Articles 18 and 19 of the Convention on the Privileges and Immunities of the United Nations, 13 February 1946, 1 UNTS 16, in force 17 September 1946.

proceedings shall be instituted or continued against a person to whom this section applies during his period of service' (this includes the president, vice president, governor, or deputy governor).

16.10.6 Removal of immunity for criminal acts

It is arguable that criminal acts do not attract functional immunity if they are considered *ultra vires* the official duties of an individual. The position is, however, confused. The House of Lords in *Pinochet*, for example, limited functional immunity for former heads of state accused of in this case torture because criminal acts condemned in a treaty could not qualify as official acts. In *Noriega*, the US Court held that functional immunity did not attach to his actions because they were committed in violation of the sovereign's position and not in pursuance of it.[194] Then again in *Al Adsani v the United Kingdom* the Grand Chamber of the European Court of Human Rights held that Kuwait could rely on state immunity against a claim bought in the UK concerning acts of torture allegedly committed by a member of the Kuwaiti Government.[195] In *Jones v Ministry of Interior Al-Mamlaka Al-Arabiya AS Saudiya (the Kingdom of Saudi Arabia) and others*[196] the Law Lords accepted that torture was an official act and that functional immunity for torture extended to state officials, servants, or agents. They read *Pinochet* as permitting the removal because of the 'consent' of Chile through its adherence to the Torture Convention, the purpose of which would be defeated if immunity was not impliedly removed. The ICJ, however, rejects even this narrow reading, holding that immunity remains completely intact because immunity is not a substantive question but a procedural matter—whether the courts of one state may exercise jurisdiction over another state.[197] Moreover, signing a suppression convention cannot be construed as consent to the removal of immunity for the transnational crime in question unless expressly provided for or a necessary implication. The debate whether this exception exists has generally been related to true international crimes involving *erga omnes* obligations, and not transnational crimes.[198] Nevertheless some national courts have rejected the application of immunity to terrorist acts that involve death and destruction[199] and more recently to corruption which involved abuse of an individual's status as an official and caused economic harm to the state (echoing civil judgments[200] where personal enrichment was held not to be shielded by the immunity of state officials).

---

[194] Following *Jimenez v Aristeguieta* 311 F 2d 547 (5th Cir 1962).

[195] Judgment of 21 November 2001, App No 35763/97, [2001] ECHR 761.

[196] [2006] UKHL 26. See para 57.

[197] The *Belgian Arrest Warrant Case* above n 15; *Jurisdictional Immunities of the State (Germany v Italy: Greece Intervening)* ICJ Reports, 3 February 2012, paras 92–97.

[198] See ILC, Fifth Report on Immunity of State Officials from Foreign Criminal Jurisdiction, by Concepción Escobar Hernández, Special Rapporteur, UN Doc A/CN.4/701, 14 June 2016, page 87, paras 219 –21.

[199] *R v Mafart and Prieur* (Rainbow Warrior Case) New Zealand High Court Auckland, November 1985, 74 ILR 241.

[200] Eg, *Trajana v Marcos* 978 F 2d 493 (9th Cir 1992).

While the suppression conventions do not explicitly attempt to alter sovereign or diplomatic immunity under international law, they do try to get states parties to exercise self-restraint in this regard. Article 30(2) of the UNCAC, for example, provides:

> 2. Each State Party shall take such measures as may be necessary to establish or maintain, in accordance with its legal system and constitutional principles, an appropriate balance between any immunities or jurisdictional privileges accorded to its public officials for the performance of their functions and the possibility, when necessary, of effectively investigating, prosecuting and adjudicating offences established in accordance with this Convention.

The aim of this provision is to 'eliminate or prevent' the use of immunity by corrupt officials as far as possible,[201] and is directed at immunity given to public officials under national law rather than to immunity under international law. It does not require the elimination of national immunity per se but does oblige parties to balance the effectiveness of criminal justice measures against immunity required to perform official functions. An interpretive note from the UNCAC *travaux préparatoires* makes it clear that the balance should be both in law and in practice.[202] A similar provision is found in article 7(5) of the African Union Convention on Preventing and Combating Corruption: 'Subject to the provisions of domestic legislation, any immunity granted to public officials shall not be an obstacle to the investigation of allegations against and the prosecution of such officials.'

The opening condition nullifies the impact of this apparent obligation to not permit immunity to get in the way of investigation and prosecution. Perhaps the most important immunity to prosecution for transnational crime whether at home or abroad is the political immunity that members of political, social, economic, and military elites enjoy in many states parties to suppression conventions.

16.11 Conclusion

The apparently inexorable expansion of criminal jurisdiction is driven by the perception that offenders may use jurisdictional gaps to escape justice. Extraterritorial jurisdiction throws up the problem of a state establishing its jurisdiction over actions that occur in the territory of another state. In their practice states usually try to establish a reasonable jurisdictional connection with the person/conduct. Often they use jurisdictional principles in combination rather than alone. A few are adventurous in their assertion of 'long arm' jurisdiction; most are restrained taking only the jurisdiction the suppression conventions oblige them to and eschewing the optional provision, thus subtly opposing these 'long-arm' provisions. Sovereign push and sovereign resistance therefore set the limits of the establishment of jurisdiction over crime. The

---

[201] See UNODC, *Legislative Guide for the Implementation of the UN Convention Against Corruption* (New York: UN, 2006, UN Pub Sales No E.06.IV.16), 132, para 387.
[202] ibid, para 388, citing UN Doc/A/58/422/Add.1 para 34.

legality of that jurisdiction from the point of view of fair warning to individuals about jurisdiction remains, however, almost entirely neglected in transnational criminal law. Immunity, while potentially a procedural shield behind which certain high-ranking transnational criminals may hide, is of relatively limited impact upon jurisdiction because of its limited personal and material scope.

17

International Law Enforcement Cooperation

17.1 Enforcing an Established Jurisdiction

When a state establishes its criminal jurisdiction over a particular transnational crime, that prescription renders a particular action potentially criminal. To have a concrete effect, that jurisdiction once established must be enforced through investigation and trial of the particular offence. This chapter explores the state's enforcement of its jurisdiction over transnational crime through the work of its law enforcement agencies, and focuses in particular on law enforcement cooperation with other states because of the inherent difficulties of extraterritorial law enforcement. It covers both police cooperation and other forms of mutual assistance in administrative matters which have an investigative and crime prevention function. Chapters 18 (legal assistance), 19 (asset recovery), and 20 (extradition) examine the more formal legal relationships necessary for enforcement cooperation between states.

17.2 Territorial Enforcement against Transnational Crime

Territorial law enforcement against transnational crime is not complicated by the necessity of cooperation with other states if the suspects and evidence are in the enforcing state's territory. Many states, however, have poorly organized, trained, paid, or motivated police working in poorly coordinated systems where corruption is common, factors that make cooperation with these states difficult.

Efforts to develop police expertise transnationally within treaty frameworks can be traced at least to articles 12–15 of the 1929 International Convention for the Suppression of the Counterfeiting of Currency, which suggested the establishment within states of a centralized anti-counterfeiting office able to cooperate internationally with other central offices.[1] Modern suppression conventions emphasize the establishment of independent law enforcement bodies with their own power to investigate and prosecute. Article 36 of the United Nations Convention against Corruption (UNCAC), for example, obliges parties to establish independent bodies to combat corruption. Hong Kong's Independent Commission against Corruption (ICAC), which is largely separate from public service and has its own prosecutorial power, provides an influential model of an organization considered free from political interference. In South Africa, a 2011 Constitutional Court decision ruled that the Government is constitutionally obliged to set up an independent anti-corruption commission, although the

---

[1] [1929] PITSE 3, signed 20 April 1929, in force 22 February 1931.

Court later determined that such an organization can be set up within the police if there is adequate independence.[2]

The conventions encourage parties not to use prosecutorial discretion in a way that may frustrate the suppression of transnational crime. For example, article 11(2) of the United Nations Convention against Transnational Organized Crime (UNTOC), which provides that parties shall endeavour to ensure that any 'discretionary' prosecutorial powers be exercised to maximize law enforcement effectiveness, is aimed at restricting practices such as plea-bargaining so that its use does not defeat effective law enforcement, rather than out of principled objection to these practices. Indeed, article 37(1) of UNCAC provides that parties should make provision to encourage individuals implicated in corruption to assist law enforcement through 'appropriate measures', while article 37(2) asks parties to consider mitigation of punishment, and article 37(3) suggests immunity from prosecution for those who provide substantial help.

17.3 The Necessity for and Legal Nature of International Cooperation against Extraterritorial Crime

A state has limited options if the witnesses and the evidence necessary to establish that an offence has occurred are located in another state's territorial jurisdiction. This is primarily because criminal law enforcement in the territory of another state is a violation of that state's sovereignty. In the *Lotus Case* the PCIJ was clear:

> Now the first and foremost restriction imposed by international law upon a State is that—failing the existence of a permissive rule to the contrary—it may not exercise its power in any form in the territory of another State. In this sense jurisdiction is certainly territorial; it cannot be exercised by a State outside its territory except by virtue of a permissive rule derived from international custom or from a convention.[3]

The suppression conventions reiterate this rule. Article 4(1) of the UNTOC, for example, obliges parties when carrying out the UNTOC's obligations to do so consistently with the principles of sovereign equality, territorial integrity, and non-intervention, while article 4(2) obliges parties not to carry out in the territory of another party either the exercise of extraterritorial jurisdiction or the performance of functions exclusively reserved to that other party by its domestic law. These provisions clarify that parties that unilaterally exercise extraterritorial jurisdiction by, for example, engaging in investigations within another party's territory without consent, will be acting unlawfully. A state that engages in law enforcement action in the territory of another state without permission, even in regard to transnational crimes derived from suppression conventions to which they are both parties, commits an internationally wrongful act that violates the other state's sovereignty and may result in their agents facing arrest and the state facing a claim of state responsibility. In 2009, for example, twenty-two

---

[2] *Hugh Glenister v President of the Republic of South Africa and ors* (2011) ZACC 6; *Helen Suzman Foundation v President of the Republic of South Africa and Others; Glenister v President of the Republic of South Africa and Others* [2014] ZACC 32.

[3] (1927) PCIJ Reports Series A No 10, at 18–19.

CIA agents were convicted and sentenced in absentia by an Italian Court for the kidnapping and illegal rendition to Egypt of the Muslim cleric Osama Nasr in 2003.[4]

The enforcement of a jurisdiction against transnational crime may be a sovereign exercise, but because it usually involves suspects or evidence located elsewhere, it must of necessity involve international cooperation. Transnational criminal law enforcement cooperation is not a conflict of laws situation involving choice of law or recognition of foreign judgments.[5] States apply their law to help other states; they do not apply the other state's laws. Where State A is attempting to police activities that occur in State B, even where State B cooperates, the ultimate source of coercive authority is in State A. However, the cooperating state, State B, may be called upon by State A to use its coercive powers on behalf of State A. At this point, the local law in State B governs as a matter of sovereignty. The exercise of State B's law has roots in State B's public order interest and in State B's inhabitants' interest in the normal domestic protection of their rights and not to be subject to law enforcement processes that are foreign and unfamiliar. State B must, however, seek justification for the use of its coercive powers by relying on information from State A.

All forms of procedural cooperation throw up the problem of what conditions to impose on this reliance. Transnational criminal law attempts to lay down a broad framework for that process of reliance, setting out where it can be informal and where it must be juridically sanctioned, and what conditions must be met. As a rule of thumb, the more coercive the power requested, the more formal the legal power required, and the more formal the authorization for the request must be in order to be consistent with local laws. Thus, for example, while extradition insists on dual criminality, cooperation in investigation may not. From a police point of view, the more formal the requirements insisted on by the requested state, the more difficult they are to meet (a strong incentive to keep relations informal). Disputes usually relate to whether what occurred was agreed on or if the agreement has been exceeded. This is well illustrated by the 1925 international arbitral decision in *Arrest and Repatriation of Savarkar.*[6] It dealt with the escape of an Indian nationalist sent back to India to serve out sentences for conspiracy to wage war against the king and with abetting murder by providing weapons used to assassinate a British civil servant. He escaped from a ship he was travelling on under escort back to India at Marseilles, and was rearrested by a French Gendarme with some assistance from two Indian policemen and delivered back to the ship. France later objected to the British assistance in his removal and argued he should be returned. The arbitral tribunal, relying on formal requests for assistance from the British prior to the trip and assurances by French officials of its availability,

---

[4] J Hooper, 'Italian Court Finds CIA Agents Guilty of Kidnapping Terrorism Suspect', *The Guardian* 4 November 2009.

[5] MD Dubber, 'Criminal Law in Comparative Context' 56 *Journal of Legal Education* (2006) 433, 434. Arguments that a choice of law approach should be adopted in the enforcement of extraterritorial jurisdiction such as that proposed in M Fabiarz, 'Extraterritorial Criminal Jurisdiction' 114 *Michigan Law Review* (2016) 507, 535, suggest that if there is no real conflict of criminal law in such a situation, there is no legitimate reason for a foreign state to object to extraterritorial jurisdiction, ignoring they may have sovereign reasons for doing so.

[6] *Arrest and Repatriation of Savarkar, award of 25 October 1925*, 11 NRI 243. See B Zagaris, *White Collar Crime*, 2nd edn (Cambridge: CUP, 2016), 615.

found there had been no fraud or force in his re-arrest, and although their actions were irregular those involved had acted in good faith and had not violated the sovereignty of France, and there was no duty on Britain under international law to restore him in these circumstances.

Most of the more modern suppression conventions provide for general obligations to cooperate in law enforcement. Article 9(1) of the 1988 Drug Trafficking Convention's general obligation to cooperate is typical but, also typically, it is subject to the condition that the measures requested are appropriate and consistent with the requested party's legal system. Article 9 does not impose conditions such as double criminality (the offence is a crime under both requesting and requested party's laws) because police may not know what particular offence has been committed at the investigative stage; any conditions are at the discretion of requested states. Nor does it specify the mode of cooperation. As we shall see, however, later treaties have become more specific in regard to obligations to exchange data and have even provided for limited obligations to cooperate in operational law enforcement.

17.4 The Development of Direct Police to Police Contact

Usually the police make the request for cooperation. New national agencies with law enforcement powers are, however, entering the arena of law enforcement cooperation: competition watchdogs, tax authorities, security agencies, giving it an administrative complexion.

In the mature phases of a transnational criminal investigation, mutual legal or judicial assistance is required in order to gather admissible evidence in the other state. The formal processes of legal assistance are unnecessary in the early phases of an investigation when law enforcement agents are trying to identify the criminal activity and the criminals involved. Law enforcement cooperation departs from the classical scheme for legal assistance in that it often involves direct communication fostered by informal connections made through police forums, through education, and through training. These direct communications are not sanctioned by some higher prosecutorial or judicial authority and do not meet conditions such as double criminality.

Law enforcement cooperation is used to prepare the ground for formal cooperation. Mutual legal assistance may be inappropriate in the early stages of an investigation mainly because it is too slow.[7] A Canadian investigator complained, for example, that he had waited five years for banking records from the US without getting them.[8] Law enforcement cooperation also has the virtue of being technical and non-political. It can avoid problems like the reluctance of Latin American police to use foreign affairs departments to handle mutual assistance requests because of apprehension about political interference.[9] It also makes more sense to share information multilaterally than bilaterally because it picks up pieces of the puzzle.

---

[7] ME Beare, 'Shifting Boundaries—between States, Enforcement Agencies, and Priorities' in HG Albrecht and C Fijnaut (eds), *The Containment of Transnational Organized Crime* (Freiburg: Iuscrim, 2002), 171, 189.
  [8] ibid, 190.   [9] ibid.

Law enforcement cooperation still faces formidable practical problems including differences in language, methods, and powers. The covert investigative powers of many federal US law enforcement agencies are, for example, significantly greater than those of police in most other states. Customs authorities in India have the power to arrest,[10] while in other states customs authorities only have administrative sanctions at their immediate disposal and must rely on the police for arrest.[11] It may be very difficult for a law enforcement agent in one state even to identify the competent law enforcement authority in another. The suppression conventions provide some solutions to these problems. Article 9(1)(a) of the 1988 Drug Trafficking Convention, for example, obliges parties to 'establish channels of communication between competent agencies' regarding article 3(1) drug trafficking offences. The use of 'competent agencies' rather than 'police' reflects the difference between common law and civil law traditions; while in the former, police are independent and enjoy substantial discretionary authority, in the latter, the judiciary controls investigation (and is often unwilling to deal with foreign police directly). Perhaps the most critical problem though is trust. Its importance in law enforcement cooperation has been heavily emphasized.[12] Sometimes it is absent because of fears about who is actually being dealt with. As a Senior Official in the UK's Serious Organised Crime Agency noted: 'The sad truth is I am not going to share my best, most delicate information with the Russian or Mexican police departments'.[13] It is also reflected in the unwritten rule of information exchange that if officials from State A send information to officials in State B, they will not, without permission send it to officials in State C.

During the investigation of an offence law enforcement officials may need access to information held by other states. The suppression conventions provide a partial framework for limited cooperation with other police forces in the exchange of information and in operational matters. The detail is provided in regional or bilateral arrangements.

17.5 Information Storage and Exchange

17.5.1 Introduction

Some states keep almost no information of use in the suppression of crime while others have elaborate systems for storage of such information. Gathered for official purposes or by private networks such as those involved in financial transactions, this information ranges from the mundane (such as birth and death records) to the sensitive (such as DNA records, records of previous convictions, and suspicions about as yet unproven criminal activity). States also retain strategic or tactical information on

---

[10] Section 104 of the Indian Customs Act 1962.
[11] Eg, section 32C of the New Zealand Customs and Excise Act 1996.
[12] See generally S Hufnagel and C McCartney (eds), *A Question of Trust: Socio-legal Imperatives in International Police and Justice Cooperation* (Oxford: Hart-Bloomsbury, 2017).
[13] M Naim, 'Mafia States: Organized Crime Takes Office' 91 *Foreign Affairs* (2012) 100, 109.

new enforcement techniques, new crime trends, and the means or methods used to commit offences. The gathering of intelligence on modus operandi, dates and value of financial transactions is particularly important in individual cases. The supervised exchange of this information is critical in the suppression of crime that crosses jurisdictions. Law enforcement officials seek fast and depoliticized ways to transfer it across borders. The suppression conventions provide a legal structure for the transfer between parties of these types of information in regard to the specific offences criminalized in the particular convention.

17.5.2 Treaty provisions for information exchange

Measures such as article 22 of the 1959 European Convention on Mutual Assistance in Criminal Matters,[14] which provides for the transfer of information on previous convictions, were largely absent in the early suppression conventions. Article 35(f) of the 1961 Single Convention on Narcotic Drugs, for example, only makes provision for the furnishing of information on the illicit traffic to the Commission on Narcotic Drugs and the International Narcotics Control Board, and not to other parties. Article 9(1) of the 1988 Drug Trafficking Convention expanded the scope of obligation to exchange information, requiring parties to:

(a) Establish and maintain channels of communication between their competent agencies and services to facilitate the secure and rapid exchange of information concerning all aspects of offences established in accordance with article 3, paragraph 1, including, if the Parties concerned deem it appropriate, links with other criminal activities;

(b) Co-operate with one another in conducting enquiries, with respect to offences established in accordance with article 3, paragraph 1, having an international character, concerning:

    (i) The identity, whereabouts and activities of persons suspected of being involved in offences established in accordance with article 3, paragraph 1;

    (ii) The movement of proceeds of property derived from the commission of such offences;

    (iii) The movement of narcotic drugs, psychotropic substances, substances in Table I and Table II of this Convention and instrumentalities used or intended for use in the commission of such offences.

Article 9(1) contains a general obligation and a more specific obligation. The (very typical) general provision obliges parties to exchange information in regard to all aspects of offences. The more specific obligation to cooperate in the conduct of enquiries enumerates information about identity, whereabouts, and activities of suspects as well as the movement of illicit substances and criminal proceeds. More recent conventions, such as the Migrant Smuggling Protocol, are even more specific in regard to types of information. Article 10 of the Protocol makes special provision for exchange of

---

[14] 20 April 1959, ETS No 30, in force 12 June 1962.

information (particularly between parties that share borders or are traversed by smuggling routes) on matters such as: (a) embarkation and destination point, routes, carriers, and means of smuggling; (b) the identities of smuggling organizations; (c) their proper travel documents and theft or misuse of such documents; and (d) means and methods of concealment and transportation of persons, the unlawful alteration, reproduction, or acquisition or other misuse of travel or identity documents and ways of detecting them. The newer conventions also typically make provision for obligations to provide where appropriate for necessary items or quantities of allegedly illicit substances for analytical or investigative purposes.[15]

Usually the suppression conventions leave the institutional arrangements for exchange to be worked out between 'the competent authorities, agencies and services' of the parties.[16] Some conventions can be more prescriptive in this regard because of the nature of the crimes they address. Article 35 of the Council of Europe Convention on Cybercrime, for example, obliges each party to designate a contact point 'available on a twenty-four hour, seven-day-a-week basis, in order to ensure the provision of immediate assistance for the purpose of investigations or proceedings concerning criminal offences related to computer systems and data, or for the collection of evidence in electronic form of a criminal offence'. The obligation assumes technical and human capacity to communicate rapidly with other parties.

In general, however, the system of information exchange in transnational criminal law rests on the bilateral and regional arrangements for information exchange; the suppression conventions only provide a framework for such exchange. Thus article 48(2) of the UNCAC provides:

> With a view to giving effect to this Convention, States Parties shall consider entering into bilateral or multilateral agreements or arrangements on direct cooperation between their law enforcement agencies and, where such agreements or arrangements already exist, amending them. In the absence of such agreements or arrangements between the States Parties concerned, the States Parties may consider this Convention to be the basis for mutual law enforcement cooperation in respect of the offences covered by this Convention. Whenever appropriate, States Parties shall make full use of agreements or arrangements, including international or regional organizations, to enhance the cooperation between their law enforcement agencies.

Arrangements for enhancing transnational law enforcement cooperation are proliferating and linking up. Europe has served as a laboratory in this regard. Twenty-six European states rely on the Schengen Information System version II (SIS II).[17] It allows access to information on a range of topics including identity and whereabouts

---

[15] Article 48(1)(c) of the UNCAC.   [16] Article 48(1)(e) of the UNCAC.

[17] It is based on the Schengen Agreement and its Application Convention. Belgium-France-Federal Republic of Germany-Luxembourg-Netherlands: Schengen Agreement on the Gradual Abolition of Checks at their Common Borders, 14 June 1985, (1991) 30 ILM 68; Convention Implementing the Schengen Agreement of 14 June 1985 Between the Governments of the States of the Benelux Economic Union, the Federal Republic of Germany and the French Republic on the Gradual Abolition of Checks at their Common Borders, signed 19 June 1990, [2000] OJ L 239/19, in force 1 September 1993. The Convention was extended to all EU member states in 1998 via the Treaty of Amsterdam and its Protocol Integrating the Schengen Acquis into the Framework of the European Union [2000] OJ L 239/1.

and also posts alerts in regard to lost firearms, stolen or fraudulent documents, and so forth. The 2005 Prüm Treaty in Europe[18] provides for a system for the exchange of biometric information and driver/vehicle data. At the Common German French Centre for Police and Customs Cooperation[19] co-located German or French officers can request their counterparts to extract information from national databases on useful topics including, for example, the validity of drivers' licences.[20] Within the EU the 2006 'Swedish Initiative'[21] provided a common legal framework to simplify the exchange of information and intelligence between law enforcement authorities. In 2010 the EU decided to standardize all DNA and fingerprint laboratories across the EU so that all member states could rely upon evidence gathered/generated by EU labs in other member states.[22] From April 2012 all European member states have had access to criminal records held by other member states through ECRIS, the EU criminal record database.[23]

At a more global level Preventing and Combating Serious Crime (PCSC) agreements[24] between the US and various partners, provide for the reciprocal exchange of biometric and biographic data and law enforcement data such as access to fingerprint records. Passenger Name Record (PNR) agreements[25] require airline carriers to submit passengers data to transit or destination state authorities.

17.5.3 Information exchange in practice

A number of hurdles in storing and sharing information limit international cooperation. Much will depend on the implementation of the particular information exchange agreement. At a practical level, the requesting agency may not, for example, be on the list of agencies recognized as being able to make such requests by agencies in other parties. Articulation between states is difficult if they are at different levels

---

[18] Convention on the Setting Up of Cross-Border Cooperation Particularly in Combating Terrorism, Cross-Border Crime and Illegal Migration, 27 May 2005; English version in Council of the European Union, Brussels, 6 December 2006, 16382/06.

[19] See the Mondorf Agreement, 9 October 1997, between Germany and France, based on article 39 of the Schengen Implementing Convention of 1990.

[20] See O Felsen, 'European Police Cooperation: The example of German-French Centre of Police and Customs Cooperation Kehl (GZ Kehl)' in S Hufnagel, C Harfield, and S Bronitt (eds), *Cross-Border Law Enforcement: Regional Law Enforcement Cooperation—European, Australian and Asia Pacific Perspectives* (London: Routledge, 2011), 73.

[21] Council Framework Decision 2006/960/JHA of 18 December 2006 on Simplifying the Exchange of Information and Intelligence between Law Enforcement Authorities of the Member States of the European Union, OJ L 386/89, 29 December 2006.

[22] Council Framework Decision 2009/905/JHA on Accreditation of Forensic Service Providers Carrying out Laboratory Activities OJ L 322, 9 December 2009, 14.

[23] Council Decision 2009/316/JHA of 6 April 2009 on the Establishment of the European Criminal Records Information System (ECRIS) in Application of Article 11 of Framework Decision 2009/315/JHA, OJ L 093, 7 April 2009, 33–48.

[24] See, eg, the Agreement between the Government of the United States of America and the Government of the Republic of Estonia on Enhancing Cooperation in Preventing and Combating Serious Crime, 29 September 2008; in force 5 November 2008.

[25] See, eg, Agreement between the United States of America and the European Union on the Use and Transfer of Passenger Name Records to the United States Department of Homeland Security, 11 August 2012, 2012 OJ L 215/5.

of development when it comes to information gathering and storage. In Australia, for example, the federal agency CrimTrac[26] manages, inter alia, separate databases on DNA, fingerprints, criminal histories, vehicles, firearms, persons subject to outstanding warrants of arrest, sex offenders, known or suspected members of organized criminal groups, and so forth.[27] Most states are not nearly as advanced. The quality of the raw data being held by states may be unverifiable—it may, for example, not distinguish between corroborated information and hearsay-based suspicions—which can lead to difficulties if it is relied on to provide evidence for conviction.

Different organizational arrangements and cultures between police forces present obstacles to effective information exchange. In one state, information may fall under judicial control, while in another it may be under police control. There will inevitably be different protocols about who may access what data. States are for good reason wary of the foreign law enforcement agents engaging in 'fishing expeditions' in their information systems. This is a particularly sensitive issue when the rules of discovery in the state seeking information are more relaxed than those in the state where discovery is to take place. In the US, for example, discovery laws relate not only to admissible evidence but to information that is reasonably calculated to lead to the discovery of admissible evidence, information which other states may object to handing over. Technical difficulties such as linking a paper-based system with a computer-based system can be overcome, but they can also be used as a proxy for unwillingness to supply the information.

In the age of mass concern about mass government surveillance, the storage and exchange of information raise significant human rights concerns. Different laws permit storage of different kinds of data for different lengths of time. A judicial line was drawn by the European Court of Human Rights about the duration for which information could be kept in *S and Marper v the United Kingdom*[28] when it ruled that the UK's indefinite retention of the applicant's fingerprints and DNA, even though they had been acquitted, breached their right to respect for their private lives under article 8 of the European Convention on Human Rights. Courts have also reinforced the right to be forgotten.[29] And in 2014 an EU Data Storage directive requiring Internet Service Providers to store data about the source, time, and duration of communications in order to facilitate the prevention and prosecution of crime was struck down by the European Court of Justice[30] because it disproportionately interfered with the right to respect for private life (article 7) and the right to protection of personal data (article 8) of the Charter of Fundamental Rights of the European Union.[31]

---

[26] See <http://www.crimtrac.gov.au/> last visited 12 February 2017.

[27] See S Hufnagel, '(In)Security Crossing Borders: A Comparison of Police Cooperation within Australia and the European Union' in S Hufnagel, C Harfield, and S Bronitt (eds), *Cross-Border Law Enforcement: Regional Law Enforcement Cooperation—European, Australian and Asia Pacific Perspectives* (London: Routledge, 2011), 198.

[28] 2008 ECHR 1581.

[29] See *Google Spain SL and Google Inc v Agencia Española de Protección de Datos (AEPD) and Mario Costeja González* Case C-131/12, 13 May 2014.

[30] *Digital Rights Ireland Ltd v Minister for Communications, Marine and Natural Resources and Others and Kärntner Landesregierung and Others*, Joined Cases C-293/12 and C-594/12, 8 April 2014.

[31] Charter of Fundamental Rights of the European Union, 18 December 2000, OJ 2000/C 264/1.

The potential exchange of sensitive information out of the jurisdiction results in that information escaping from the control of the state that originally captured it; differences in national laws for data protection then become a significant problem. The suppression conventions support the principle that national law determines what information can be shared with foreign authorities, and if it is shared, what duties of confidentiality apply. Article 10(2) of the Human Trafficking Protocol provides, for example, that the receiving party must comply with any restrictions placed on the data by the transmitting party, which may include the types of case in which the data can be used as evidence as well as ensuring that the data is not disclosed to suspects or the public. However, this causes difficulties when parties have inadequate laws protecting the privacy of sensitive information or national law requires the disclosure of exculpatory information to the defence.[32] The US's implementation of its Terrorist Financing Tracking Program (TFTP), which collects data from the Society for Worldwide Interbank Financial Telecommunications (SWIFT) based in Belgium (but with a mirror site in the US), led to concerns about violation of EU data protection laws. These concerns resulted in the conclusion of an EU–US agreement to exchange information gleaned from SWIFT data,[33] applying privacy guarantees around transparency, individual access and correction, security, enforcement, and proportionality.[34] The Organisation for Economic Co-operation and Development (OECD) Privacy Principles[35] for exchange of information provide the most commonly used framework for privacy. They are reflected in data protection legislation globally, and in essence involve a set of domestic safeguards which must be in place before cross-border exchange occurs. The EU Data Protection Directive,[36] for further example, provides that the transfer of personal data to a non-EU state if that foreign state provides for an adequate level of data protection (a principle restated in the EU's new General Data Protection Regulation of 2016[37]). However, the power of the European Commission to make a finding that such a state does have this adequate level of protection does not preclude member states from deciding otherwise, and the safe harbour provisions for transfer of data between the EU and US have, in the wake of the Snowden revelations, for example, been declared invalid,[38] leading to the

---

[32] UNODC, *Legislative Guides for the Implementation of the United Nations Convention against Transnational Organised Crime and the Protocols Thereto* (New York: UN 2004), 309.

[33] The current agreement is the EU US Terrorist Financial Tracking Programme Agreement (TFTP II), adopted by the EU 13 July 2010, in force 1 August 2010.

[34] See F Bignami and G Resta, 'Transatlantic Privacy Regulation: Conflict and Cooperation' in 78(4) *Law and Contemporary Problems* (2015) 231, 244 et seq.

[35] See OECD Guidelines on the Protection of Privacy and Transborder Flows of Personal Data, available at <http://www.oecd.org/internet/ieconomy/oecdguidelinesontheprotectionofprivacyandtransborder-flowsofpersonaldata.htm#guidelines> last visited 16 January 2017.

[36] Directive 95/46/EC of the European Parliament and of the Council of 24 October 1995 on the protection of individuals with regard to the processing of personal data and on the free movement of such data, OJ 1995 L 281/31.

[37] Article 45, Regulation 2016/679 of the European Parliament and of the Council of 27 April 2016 on the protection of natural persons with regard to the processing of personal data and on the free movement of such data, and repealing Directive 95/46/EC (General Data Protection Regulation), OJ L 119/1.

[38] *Schrems v Data Commissioner*, Case C-362/14, 6 October 2015.

development of a new EU–US agreement for exchange of data affording a high level of protection.[39]

17.6 Operational Cooperation

17.6.1 Introduction

At an operational level the law enforcement agencies of different parties have different forensic and coercive powers and different training and technological capacities. Transnational criminal law facilitates operational cooperation through provision for liaison officers and joint investigation teams (JITs), and through support for various special investigative techniques such as controlled delivery and electronic surveillance.

Many of these techniques were initially developed by US law enforcement agencies such as the Drug Enforcement Administration (DEA) domestically and then trialled in a transnational context in Latin America and Europe.[40] As part of the Nixon administration's war on drugs, they emphasized support for supply-side drug enforcement. They fostered institutional changes in local policing such as the establishment of specialized drugs police, and operational changes, such as the use of undercover operations (and, more dubiously, 'buy bust' operations), controlled delivery of illicit drug consignments, and electronic surveillance.

More recently, Europe has become a laboratory for the development of other cross-border forms of cooperation, justified by the apparent increase in transnational crime brought about by the disappearance of border controls between most European states.[41] Article 53 of the Schengen Convention, for example, provides for direct communication of requests for assistance between police without the necessity of using central authorities. The Schengen approach of refining cooperation at operational levels in respect of a range of offences was incorporated in the EU's 2000 Convention on Mutual Legal Assistance in Criminal Matters of the Member States of the European Union.[42] Articles 12–16 deal with cross-border controlled deliveries, JITs, and covert investigations, while articles 17–22 deal with the thorny issue of the interception of telecommunications.

Many of these procedures pioneered by the US and in Europe have been taken up in suppression conventions.

17.6.2 Liaison

The stationing of law enforcement agents in diplomatic missions abroad is a practice which has seen enormous development in the post-war period and particularly since

---

[39] Agreement between the United States of America and the European Union on the Protection of Personal Information Relating to the Prevention, Investigation, Detection and Prosecution of Criminal Offences, 10 December 2016, OJ L 336/3, in force 1 February 2017.

[40] See generally P Andreas and E Nadelmann, *Policing the Globe: Criminalization and Crime Control in International Relations* (Oxford: OUP, 2006), 105, 128 et seq.

[41] ibid, 177 et seq.   [42] 29 May 2000, OJ C 197, 12 July 2000.

the 1980s.[43] The Federal Bureau of Investigation (FBI)'s Legat (Legal Attaché) programme broke the ice, but many state police forces, including, for example, Brazil's Federal Police (DPF), now post police liaison officers in foreign states, and the suppression conventions provide multilateral support for liaison. Article 9(1)(e) of the 1988 Drug Trafficking Convention, for example, obliges parties to 'promote the exchange of personnel and other experts, including the posting of liaison officers'.

Police liaison officers are usually from states with markets for contraband and are posted to transit or source states. These officers serve as points of contact for information on the identities, methods, and criminal records of transnational criminals. They also commonly assume a more proactive role in the policing of particular types of crime. For example, US DEA agents operating abroad (more than 500 in drug-producing and transit states) are in a relationship of mutual dependence with host police agencies. They have no inherent legal powers within the host nations (unless specifically given them) and, in particular, cannot arrest criminals or interview or conduct enquiries. They rely on their host agencies to perform these functions in exchange for access to intelligence, funds, and expertise. They do, however, gather intelligence and provide guidance. The DEA has succeeded in this role because it has operated vicariously through local police agencies rather than attempting to expand its own freedom of operation, and ensured that local policing laws and practices harmonized with its own.[44] Uniquely, some states from the same region, such as the Nordic states, share liaison officers posted to transit and production states.[45]

17.6.3 Joint investigations

Joint investigation teams are a more enhanced form of cooperation, set up for a limited time and purpose. In 2017, for example, a joint action between Slovakia, the UK, and Europol dismantled an organized criminal group involved in trafficking Slovak women for sham marriages and sexual exploitation with simultaneous arrests in Scotland and Slovakia.[46] Sovereign sensitivities are strong, however. In 2011 the then Afghan President Hamed Karzai, for example, protested against Russian involvement in a joint US-Afghan-Russian drug enforcement operation in Afghanistan without prior authorization from or consultation with the Afghan government.[47]

Article 9(1)(c) of the 1988 Drug Trafficking Convention introduced JITs into transnational criminal law. In order to meet their obligation to cooperate in law enforcement,

---

[43] On liaison see generally M Deflem, 'International Police Cooperation in North America: A Review of Practices, Strategies, and Goals in the United States, Mexico and Canada' in DJ Koenig and DK Das (eds), *International Police Cooperation: A World Perspective* (Lanham, MD: Lexington, 2001), 71.

[44] See E Nadelmann, *Cops Across Borders: The Internationalization of U.S. Criminal Law Enforcement* (State Park, PA: Penn State University Press, 1993), 189–249.

[45] See ME Kleiven, 'Nordic Police Cooperation' in S Hufnagel, C Harfield, and S Bronitt (eds), *Cross-Border Law Enforcement: Regional Law Enforcement Cooperation—European, Australian and Asia Pacific Perspectives* (London: Routledge, 2011), 63, 65.

[46] See 'Europol Supports Joint Investigation into International Human Trafficking' *Europol Press Release*, 15 February 2017, <https://www.europol.europa.eu/newsroom/news/europol-supports-joint-investigation-international-human-trafficking> last visited 2 January 2017.

[47] B Zagaris, 'Multinational Operation Seizes $55.9 million heroin but Karzai protests' 27(1) *International Law Enforcement Reporter* (2011) 541–42.

it provides that parties shall '[i]n appropriate cases and if not contrary to domestic law, establish joint teams, taking into account the need to protect the security of persons and of operations'. It cautions, however, that '[o]fficials of any Party taking part in such teams shall act as authorised by the appropriate authorities of the Party in whose territory the operation is to take place; in all such cases, the Parties involved shall ensure that the sovereignty of the Party on whose territory the operation is to take place is fully respected'. Domestic law reform is thus necessary in most parties in order to make a JIT legally possible and to circumscribe the rules for its operation. As a result of sovereign sensitivity to foreign police within a jurisdiction, many parties have not made it possible to use JITs. States retreated a little from the 1988 commitment in later suppression conventions. Article 49 of the UNCAC,[48] for example, eschews any attempt to adopt a multilateral obligation to provide for JITs and points to adoption of a regional or bilateral basis for joint investigation (which is almost exclusively the case in practice):

> States Parties shall consider concluding bilateral or multilateral agreements or arrangements whereby, in relation to matters that are the subject of investigations, prosecutions or judicial proceedings in one or more States, the competent authorities concerned may establish joint investigative bodies. In the absence of such agreements or arrangements, joint investigations may be undertaken by agreement on a case-by-case basis. The States Parties involved shall ensure that the sovereignty of the State Party in whose territory such investigation is to take place is fully respected.

The EU's 2000 Convention on Mutual Assistance in Criminal Matters provides a regional model for the use of JITs[49] and relies on Europol to play a central supervisory and advisory role.[50] Other states have taken bilateral steps. In 2003, for example, Cambodia and Thailand signed a Memorandum of Understanding on Bilateral Cooperation for Eliminating Trafficking in Children and Women which makes provision for joint investigations of transnational human traffickers.[51]

A United Nations Office on Drugs and Crime expert group identified two broad models for JITs: (i) parallel and co-ordinated investigations (used by states from different geographical regions) that have a common goal but are not co-located and rely on law enforcement cooperation as well as formal mutual legal assistance; and (ii) an integrated model used by neighbouring states where officers are co-located, and which are either passive or active depending on the extent of law enforcement powers available to the foreign officers.[52] The latter integrated model can be structured in any number of ways depending on whether the law of the territorial state and that of the sending state allow the foreign police officers to go along on operations, to engage in arrests, to

---

[48] See also article 19 of the UNTOC.   [49] Article 13(1).

[50] On JITs in the EU see L Block, 'EU Joint Investigation Teams: Political Ambitions and Police Practices' in S Hufnagel, C Harfield, and S Bronitt (eds), *Cross-Border Law Enforcement: Regional Law Enforcement Cooperation—European, Australian and Asia Pacific Perspectives* (London: Routledge, 2012), 87.

[51] Adopted 31 May 2003 at Siem Riep.

[52] Conference of the Parties to the UNTOC 2008, Informal Expert Working Group on Joint Investigations: Conclusions and Recommendations 2–4 September 2008, Vienna, UN DOC CTOC/COP/2008/CRP.5 2 October 2008, 7, 10.

carry firearms, etc. US domestic law, for example, prohibits US drug law enforcement agents actually arresting someone even as part of a police action in another state.[53] Whether domestic constitutional protections of the sending state apply to their law enforcement officers' actions when they are participating in a joint team appears to depend on who is in control of the investigation: the sending state or receiving state. In the Canadian Supreme Court decision in *R v Hape*,[54] the appellant sought to exclude evidence gleaned from warrantless searches in the Turks and Caicos Islands by Royal Canadian Mounted Police officers (under the supervision of a Turks and Caicos police officer) because of a violation of the guarantees of security against unreasonable search and seizure in section 8 of the Canadian Charter of Rights and Freedoms. The Court held that the Charter did not generally apply to search and seizures in other states because it only applied to state agents exercising state power, and extraterritorial enforcement was itself not possible. Reasoning that the Turks and Caicos were not consenting to allow Canada to enforce its jurisdiction in the Turks and Caicos but rather actually controlling the investigation, in the Court's view the only reasonable approach was to apply the law of the state where the search was made subject to the limits of international comity and Canada's international human rights obligations.[55]

17.6.4 Hot pursuit

Unusually, parties to the Schengen Convention permit police from other member states to cross into their territories to continue observation of criminals under specific limitations subject to further bilateral or multilateral agreements. Although prior consent is usually required for more serious offences, it can be dispensed with.[56] Arrest is prohibited, although hot pursuit across borders of fleeing fugitives is possible in limited territories.[57] Sovereignty concerns make inclusion of provisions of this kind within a suppression convention that has a broad multilateral participation a political impossibility.

17.6.5 Controlled delivery

Controlled delivery across borders—permitting the delivery of a consignment of illicit drugs from one state into another in order to identify and provide evidence against traffickers—was introduced by the US into transnational criminal law. Civil law states initially found it legally problematic because their customs laws required that all imported goods must be declared and cleared, and strict application of the legality principle demanded that contraband must be seized immediately upon discovery. The DEA introduced controlled delivery into Europe through selectively informing sympathetic local drug police of such consignments. As the procedure became more widely known, the DEA assured local authorities that the courier would be arrested in the destination country and the drugs seized and substituted (so-called 'clean deliveries'). Controlled delivery was introduced to a broader audience through the 1988 Drug

---

[53] 22 USC § 2291(c)(1).   [54] [2007] 2 SCR 292, 2007 SCC 266.   [55] ibid, 340–41.
[56] Article 40 of the Schengen Convention.   [57] Article 41 of the Schengen Convention.

Trafficking Convention. Article 11 obliges parties, if their basic legal principles permit, to use controlled delivery, but only on a case-by-case basis and only on the basis of mutual agreement between the parties. It also usually requires changes in national law to permit its use. Article 67 of the French *Codes Des Douans* (Customs Code), for example, now permits the purchase, holding, transportation, and delivery of illicit substances by enforcement officers.

Controlled delivery can fail to achieve its goals if it involves illegal actions in a state of origin, such as the unsanctioned purchase of drugs by an informer or foreign law enforcement agent, and/or unlawful acts in the destination state because the law has not been changed to permit controlled delivery. In *Ridgeway v Queen*,[58] for example, the Australian High Court overturned a conviction for the importation of drugs based on a controlled delivery. The case involved the purchase of heroin in Malaysia in breach of Malaysian law by a police informer, who supplied it to the appellant who was then permitted by the Australian authorities to deliver the heroin into Australia. The appeal succeeded because the High Court held that Australian domestic law had not at that stage been altered to allow the controlled importation of drugs in terms of article 11 of the 1988 Drug Trafficking Convention and the majority of the court found that the unlawful acts of the police had tainted the conviction.

Controlled delivery is now a standard technique in many states. In 2008 in the UK, for example, Operation Caroche allowed the import of £36 million of cannabis into the UK on board the MV *Abbira*, an ocean-going tugboat, which led to arrests in the UK and Israel.[59] Its scope is broadening to include all forms of contraband. In Australia, for example, controlled operations can involve a wide variety of 'serious' commonwealth offences—and are supported in other suppression conventions,[60] which also provide an option of 'clean delivery'.[61] Further cooperation will become difficult if partners are not kept abreast of how investigations develop post the controlled delivery. Moreover, there is a danger that zealous authorities may end up becoming major importers of contraband if insufficient provision is made for oversight.

17.6.6 Undercover operations

Until the 1980s European states were generally hostile to undercover or covert investigations. They applied the principle of legality strictly and prosecuted undercover agents who pretended to commit a crime. The US, on the other hand, developed the principle that '[a]cts which would be criminal when done by a private citizen are justifiable and not criminal when done by a government agent in the reasonable exercise of law-enforcement power'.[62] The US adapted 'buy-busts' of illicit drugs to European conditions by setting up the purchase of the drugs but not completing it, allowing

---

[58] (1995) 129 ALR 41.
[59] 'Haul was enough to make 3.5 million deals', *Daily Echo*, 3 June 2009, available at <http://www.dailyecho.co.uk/news/crime/4416862.print/> last visited 22 February 2017.
[60] See, eg, article 20(1) of the UNTOC; article 50(1) of the UNCAC; FATF Recommendation 27.
[61] See Article 20(4) of the UNTOC.
[62] RI Blecker, 'Beyond 1984: Undercover in America—From Serpico to Abscam' 28 *New York Law School Law Review* (1984) 823, 855.

local police to arrest the accused for possession, and then relying on the legal presumption that possession of more than a certain amount establishes an intention to supply.

Despite qualms about such heavy government involvement in setting up the conditions for commission of a crime, sting operations of this kind have since spread to enforcement of other crimes, on the rationale that they provide information on and deter further criminal activity.[63] The optional provision in article 14 of the 2000 EU Convention on Mutual Assistance in Criminal Matters, for example, provides for agreement on a case-by-case basis between parties to 'assist one another in the conduct of investigations into crime by officers acting under covert or false identity (covert investigations)'. There is no legal obligation on parties to agree to cross-border undercover investigations. All the details—duration, conditions, the legal status of officers involved, and supervision of the investigation—are left to agreement having regard to national law. The more recent suppression conventions make a very limited endorsement of undercover operations. Article 20(1) of the UNTOC provides,[64] for example, that each party shall take necessary measures to provide for undercover operations, but this 'obligation' is heavily limited. It must be 'permitted by the basic principles' of the party's legal system, its use must be within the 'possibilities and under the conditions prescribed by' national law, and it is only to be used where the party deems it appropriate 'by its competent authorities in its territory'. It follows that all details will have to be worked out beforehand and article 20(2) encourages parties to conclude bilateral or multilateral agreements to use undercover operations 'in the context of cooperation at the international level', emphasizing the necessity of carrying out these operations strictly in accordance with the agreement and respecting sovereign equality. In the absence of agreement, article 20(3) urges use on a case-by-case basis.

In practice, although support for transnational undercover policing received a major boost from the war on terror subsequent to 9/11, many states have not made the domestic changes necessary to permit this technique, and courts are wary of them. In *Teixeira de Castro v Portugal*,[65] the European Court of Human Rights held that a 'buy bust' operation by undercover Portuguese police amounted to entrapment and a violation of the appellant's right to a fair trial under article 6(1) of the European Convention, even though the Portuguese Government pointed to the endorsement of undercover operations in the 1988 Drug Trafficking Convention. The Court justified its decision by the absence in the particular case of judicial supervision of the investigation, the absence of objective evidence to justify the suspicion that the appellant was a drug trafficker, and the essentially passive nature of his involvement as justifications for its decision.[66] In practice, some states have adopted more onerous standards for domestic than transnational undercover operations, while some states permit transnational undercover policing if a particular crime is involved.[67] However,

---

[63] See B Hay, 'Sting Operations, Undercover Agents and Entrapment' 70 *Missouri Law Review* (2005) 388 at 389.

[64] See also article 50(1) of the UNCAC.   [65] (1998) 28 EHRR 101.

[66] ibid, 115–16, paras 38–39.

[67] JE Ross, 'Impediments to Transnational Cooperation in Undercover Policing: A Comparative Study of the United States and Italy' 52 *American Journal of Comparative Law* (2004) 569.

'policing' states still sometimes act unilaterally. For example, in 1998 the US engaged in operation 'Casablanca' which involved extensive undercover investigation inter alia of Mexican banks in Mexico without Mexican permission and resulted in numerous indictments for laundering drugs proceeds.[68] Mexico protested the invasion of its sovereignty and four Mexican bankers convicted in Mexico were released in 2004 when the Mexican Supreme Court declared the operation unconstitutional.[69]

17.6.7 Electronic surveillance

Electronic surveillance covers a range of activities:

- audio surveillance through techniques such as phone tapping, listening devices and Voice over Internet Protocol (VOIP), visual surveillance through video surveillance and thermal imaging;

- tracking surveillance through mobile phones, GPS, similar techniques; and

- data surveillance through spy-ware, keystroke monitoring and surveillance of mobile phone use through cell site dumps and the use of stingray phone trackers.[70]

The goal can be surveillance of the content of exchanges or geo-location of individuals. Electronic surveillance is also identified as a special investigative technique in article 20(1) of the UNTOC, and again while in theory each party shall take necessary measures to provide for undercover operations, this 'obligation' must be 'permitted by the basic principles' of the party's legal system, its use must be within the 'possibilities and under the conditions prescribed by' national law, and it is only to be used where the party deems it appropriate 'by its competent authorities in its territory'. Many states have altered their domestic law to make these practices possible. Austria, for example, permits electronic surveillance and wiretaps of telephones, applying different sets of conditions to these activities.[71] States usually require judicial approval and some form of supervision of the procedure. Argentina, for example, follows general practice and requires court authorization.[72]

National and international guarantees of the right to privacy and to private correspondence restrict the use of surveillance.[73] The European Court of Human Rights has made it clear that domestic surveillance requires precise legal powers and judicial

---

[68] See MD Hoffer, 'A Fistful of Dollars: "Operation Casablanca" and the Impact of Extraterritorial Enforcement of United States Money Laundering Law' 28 *Georgia Journal of International and Comparative Law* (2000) 293.

[69] P Reuter and EM Truman, *Chasing Dirty Money: The Fight Against Money Laundering* (Washington, DC: Institute for International Economics, 2004), 91.

[70] UNODC, *Current Practices in Electronic Surveillance in the Investigation of Serious and Organised Crime* (New York, UN, 2009, UN Pub Sales No E.09.XI.19), 2.

[71] Interceptions of communications (phone taps) are provided for under article 149a of the Code of Criminal Procedure (*Strafprozeßordnung*) with different rules for identifying the device used, tracing the caller, and listening, recording etc. Electronic surveillance is provided for under article 149d et seq with different rules for surveillance of non-public communications where one participant is informed and those where no participants are informed.

[72] Article 236 of the Code of National Criminal Procedure (*Código Procesal Penal de la Nación*, Ley 23.984, 1991).

[73] See, eg, articles 13(2) and 10 of the Netherlands Constitution 1983; article 8 of the European Convention on Human Rights; article 17 of the ICCPR.

control.[74] The UN High Commissioner for Human Rights has clarified that this cannot be rubber stamp control and must afford effective remedies to those subject to surveillance.[75] Principle 2 of the OECD data protection principles provides that individuals about whom data has been collected must be notified as soon as the object of the police investigation will no longer be jeopardized by doing so, and this has been upheld even though there is a risk enforcement methods will be revealed.[76]

From a legal perspective cross-border electronic surveillance raises issues of cross-jurisdictional legality of gathering information in another jurisdiction. To be performed legally in the surveyed state it will usually require a formal legal assistance request for a warrant, which may require double criminality. In addition to the legal and practical limitations on cooperation, law enforcement agents will also have to cope with foreign constitutional limitations and data protection laws. Article 20(2) of the UNTOC encourages bilateral and multilateral agreements to enable transnational electronic surveillance. Parties cannot be obliged to engage in domestic surveillance or permit transnational surveillance if such surveillance is contrary to its law. Article 50(1) of the UNCAC develops the provisions of the UNTOC only slightly by also urging parties to allow for the admissibility of evidence derived from electronic surveillance. While some regional arrangements compel cooperation,[77] efforts during negotiation of the Council of Europe Cybercrime Convention to allow warrantless searching of computer files located in foreign jurisdictions failed.[78] A search is only possible where the data is 'publicly available' in terms of article 32.

Officials may resort to self-help, which some argue is legal out of necessity.[79] In the *Gorshkov and Ivanov* cases two Russian hackers were lured to the US by the FBI and arrested.[80] Using logins obtained under pretext the FBI accessed their computers in Russia obtaining large amounts of incriminating information which was used at their trial. Russia protested and charged the US agents with hacking. The defendants' attempt to argue that the US lacked jurisdiction at their trial failed because the Federal District Court applied the effects doctrine holding that the relevant legislation had an extra-territorial scope.[81] States in their domestic law and practice permit such unilateral searching but don't like it being done to them. But there is little doubt that the admissibility of evidence gleaned by self-help greatly encourages the practice. The US 'silver platter' doctrine of permitting evidence taken illegally[82] has, for example, been

---

[74] *Klass v Germany* 2 EHRR 214, IHRL 19 (ECHR 1978), 6 September 1978, where statutory provision for blanket phone interceptions was considered a violation of inter alia article 8 of the European Convention's guarantee of privacy.

[75] The Right to Privacy in a Digital Age, UN Doc A/HRC/27/37, 30 June 2014, paras 37–41.

[76] See *Weber and Savaria v Germany* [2006] ECHR 1173, 29 June 2006.

[77] See, eg, article 4 of the Agreement between the Governments of State members of the Shanghai Cooperation Organization on the cooperation in the field of ensuring the international information security of June 16, 2009.

[78] Council of Europe, *Explanatory Report to Council of Europe Cybercrime Convention ETS No 185* (Strasbourg: Council of Europe, 2001), paras 293–94.

[79] J Goldsmith, 'The Internet and the Legitimacy of Cross-Border Searches' [2001] *University of Chicago Legal Forum* 103, 104.

[80] S Brenner and B-J Knoops, 'Approaches to Cybercrime Jurisdiction' 4 *High Tech Law* (2004) 1, 21–23.

[81] *United States v Ivanov* 175 F Supp 2d 367, 6 December 2001.

[82] *Elkins v United States*, 364 US 206 (1960).

applied to these illegal cross-border searches.[83] There is a danger of retaliatory unilateral actions of a similar kind by other states. It is not clear whether if a state permits its agents to search foreign computers without permission is it estopped from complaining agents in those foreign states engage in digital searches within its territory.

17.7 Policing the High Seas

17.7.1 Enforcing flag state jurisdiction

The customary right to freedom of navigation on the high seas[84] is abused by criminals who use the high seas as a transit zone for contraband and for carrying out attacks on maritime commerce through piracy. The state of registry of a vessel enjoys jurisdiction over flag vessels and crew on the high seas,[85] and the suppression conventions entrench this with regard to specific transnational crimes.[86]

17.7.2 Enforcing jurisdiction over stateless vessels

States enforcing their criminal jurisdiction have a right of visitation of vessels not flying the flag of any state.[87] In the *United States v Marino-Garcia and ors*[88] the US Court of Appeals for the Eleventh Circuit noted that nothing in international law prohibited US jurisdiction over stateless vessels on the high seas (in this case found carrying large quantities of drugs) even when there was no evidence that the vessels were bound for the US or had any jurisdictional nexus with the US. The court held: 'Vessels without nationality are international pariahs. They have no internationally recognized right to navigate freely on the high seas.'[89] Where a vessel makes an unverifiable claim to nationality it is usually treated as stateless. In *United States v Bravo and ors*,[90] for example, the US Court of Appeals for the First Circuit affirmed US jurisdiction over a vessel which made an unverifiable claim to Colombian nationality when it was interdicted by US officials on the high seas carrying one ton of cannabis. The 1997 Agreement Between the Government of the United States of America and the Government of the Republic of Colombia to Suppress Illicit Traffic by Sea[91] required only that the US act 'within international law' in such a situation, and the US had done so according to the Court by relying on protective jurisdiction.[92]

17.7.3 Enforcing jurisdiction over foreign vessels

The United Nations Convention on the Law of the Sea (UNCLOS) permits the territorial state to engage in 'hot pursuit' of foreign vessels out of its territorial waters onto

---

[83] *United States v Verdugo-Urquidez* 494 US 259 (1990).   [84] Article 87 of the UNCLOS.
[85] Article 92(1) and 94(1) of the UNCLOS.
[86] See, eg, article 4(1)(a)(ii) of the 1988 Drug Trafficking Convention.
[87] Article 110(1)(d) of the UNCLOS.
[88] 679 F 2d 1373 (11th Cir 1982); ILDC 687 (US 1982), 9 July 1982.   [89] ibid, 1383.
[90] 489 F 3d 1 (1st Cir 2007); ILDC 1061 (US 2007), 29 May 2007.
[91] 20 February 1997, TIAS No 12835, in force 20 February 1997.   [92] Above n 91, 7.

the high seas if the territorial state has good reason to believe they have violated its laws.[93] However, the right to stop and search foreign vessels on the high seas—even slave ships—is very limited outside of wartime.[94] Under customary international law states are entitled to stop and search a foreign vessel only if that state gives its permission. In the *US v Gonzales*,[95] for example, the US Court of Appeals for the Eleventh Circuit affirmed US jurisdiction over a Honduran vessel found 125 miles east of Florida carrying 114 bales of cannabis. The Marijuana on the High Seas Act[96] criminalized possession of a controlled substance in US 'customs waters', the area of the high seas adjacent to the US coast in which the US was permitted by arrangement with the flag state to enforce that law, and Honduras's telephonic permission constituted such an arrangement. The court rejected arguments that this jurisdiction was too vague and unknowable, noting that Congress had relied on the protective principle; the reasonableness of enforcing jurisdiction that far from US territorial waters was demonstrated by Honduran consent.[97] The enactment by the US of the Maritime Drug Law Enforcement Act[98] in effect extended universal jurisdiction without constitutional authority over drug traffickers on the high seas who are not US citizens, not on US vessels, and not heading towards the US, on the basis of the flag state's consent.[99]

Flag states may give such permission on an ad hoc basis, although increasingly they adopt semiformalized systems for doing so in regard to specific transnational crimes. Article 17(3) of the 1988 Drug Trafficking Convention, for example (in an approach used in regard to other crimes[100]), develops the general duty under article 108(1) of the UNCLOS to cooperate in the suppression of drug trafficking 'by ships on the high seas contrary to international conventions'. It permits a party that has reasonable grounds for believing that a vessel 'exercising freedom of navigation' and flying the flag of another party, is engaged in the illicit traffic of drugs to request the flag state's permission to take 'appropriate measures', which in terms of article 17(4) include boarding and searching the vessel and taking 'appropriate action' if evidence of involvement in the illicit traffic is found. In order to speed up responses during interdiction the US pioneered 'shiprider agreements' with states to permit a law enforcement officer 'riding' on the ship of another state to authorize immediate enforcement action against flag vessels. Substantial reductions of economic aid were used as an inducement by the US to convince sovereign-sensitive partners of their value.[101] Shiprider agreements have also been put to use against piracy.[102] Developing this position in regard to policing illegal, unreported, and unregulated fishing, article 21 of the 1995 UN Fish Stocks Agreement[103] provides that all parties consent in advance to boarding

[93] Article 111.   [94] *Le Louis* [1817] 2 Dods 210, 243.   [95] 776 F 2d 931 (11th Cir. 1985).
[96] 21 USC § 955(a)–955(d).   [97] Above n 95, 938–39.
[98] Codified at 46 USC § 70501–70507.
[99] E Kontorovich, 'Beyond the Article I Horizon: Congress's Enumerated Powers and Universal Jurisdiction Over Drug Crimes' 93 *Minnesota Law Review* (2009) 1191, 1195 et seq.
[100] Article 8(2) of the Migrant Smuggling Protocol.   [101] Kontorovich, above n 99, 1242.
[102] Article 7 of the, the Code of Conduct Concerning the Repression of Piracy and Armed Robbery against Ships in the Western Indian Ocean and the Gulf of Aden, IMO Council Doc C 102/14, Annex (2009), 29 January 2009, (Djibouti Code of Conduct).
[103] United Nations Agreement for the Implementation of the Provisions of the United Nations Convention on the Law of the Sea of 10 December 1982 relating to the Conservation and Management

and inspection of their flag vessels to ensure compliance with Regional Fisheries Management Organization measures, and permits enforcement action where there is clear evidence of breach.[104]

Rights of visit without permission are limited to a number of crimes. Under article 110(1)(b) of the UNCLOS, an enforcing state's warship has a right of 'visit' (right to board) a foreign ship reasonably suspected of engaging in the slave trade. States also enjoy a right of visit under the article 110(1)(a) in respect of piracy, as well as additional enforcement powers. In addition to being under a general duty to cooperate in the suppression of piracy,[105] article 105 of UNCLOS provides:

> On the high seas, or in any other place outside the jurisdiction of any State, every State may seize a pirate ship or aircraft, or a ship or aircraft taken by piracy and under the control of pirates, and arrest the persons and seize the property on board. The courts of the State which carried out the seizure may decide upon the penalties to be imposed and may also determine the action to be taken with regard to the ships, aircraft or property subject to the rights of third parties acting in good faith.

It is not clear whether it is only the seizing state that may prosecute or whether it can transfer pirates to other states for prosecution, although commentators prefer the latter position.[106] Canada, Denmark, the EU, US, UK, and China have concluded agreements with Kenya for the prosecution and, potentially, the imprisonment[107] in Kenya of Somali pirates over which Kenya enjoys universal jurisdiction.[108] Law enforcement operations against suspected pirate vessels on the high seas have not been all plain sailing, however.[109] In the *Enrica Lexie Incident*, for example, two Italian marines on an Italian-flagged vessel killed two Indian fishermen by mistake off the coast of India and were detained for two and four years respectively on charges of murder before they were released on bail, leading to a souring of relations between Italy and India. The Indian criminal process against the two has been suspended and the matter has gone to the Permanent Court of Arbitration for dispute settlement, with the main dispute being whether the incident which took place twenty-one nautical miles from the Indian coast was within Indian jurisdiction or not.[110]

---

of Straddling Fish Stocks and Highly Migratory Fish Stocks, 8 September 1995, UN Doc A/Conf.164/37, in force 11 December 2001.

[104] Article 21(6) and (7).   [105] Article 100 of the UNCLOS.

[106] See M Gardner, 'Piracy Prosecution in National Courts' 10 *Journal of International Criminal Justice* (2012) 797, 804 et seq; J Ashley-Roach, 'Countering Piracy off Somalia: International Law and International Institutions' 104 *American Journal of International Law* (2010) 397, 403.

[107] See, eg, Exchange of Letters between the European Union and the Government of Kenya on the Conditions and Modalities for the Transfer of Persons suspected of Having Committed Acts of Piracy and Detained by the European Union-led Naval Force (EUNAVFOR), and Seized Property in the Possession of EUNAVFOR, from EUNAVFOR to Kenya and for their Treatment after Such Transfer, OJ L 79, 25 March 2009.

[108] See *In re Mohamud Mohammed Hashi, et al*, Kenyan Court of Appeal, Civil Appeal no 113 of 2011, 18 October 2012.

[109] See generally V P Nanada and J Bellish, 'Moving from Crisis Management to a Sustainable Solution for Somali Piracy: Selected initiatives and the Role of International Law' 46 *Case Western Reserve Journal of International Law* (2013) 43, 66 et seq.

[110] The '*Enrica Lexie*' Incident (Italy v India) PCA Case No 2015-28, at <https://pca-cpa.org/en/cases/> last visited 7 January 2017.

Vessels that seek refuge in another state's territorial waters are beyond foreign law-ful enforcement for any crime, without territorial state permission. Some shiprider agreements with territorial states allow enforcing states to enter their territorial waters in order to pursue and arrest drug traffickers.[111] Pursuit of Somali pirates into Somalia's claimed 200 nautical mile territorial waters with Somali Government per-mission was made difficult by the absence of a functional government in Somalia. The UN Security Council eventually resolved the problem in Resolution 1816 of 2008[112] when it sanctioned law enforcement in violation of Somalian sovereignty, tempor-arily authorizing those states 'cooperating' with the Government of Somalia to enter its territorial waters in order to repress piracy and to use 'all necessary means' (the use of force) to repress acts of piracy and armed robbery, while in Resolution 1851 of 2008[113] it provided that for twelve months patrolling states and regional organiza-tions 'may undertake all necessary measures that are appropriate in Somalia' for the purpose of suppressing piracy, so long as they have the consent of the Transitional Federal Government of Somalia. These resolutions have been reaffirmed annually by the Security Council ever since.[114] More recently, the same approach has been sanc-tioned by the Security Council in operations against suspected migrant smuggling vessels off Libya.[115]

17.8 Policing the Financial System

17.8.1 Introduction

The anti-money laundering/counter-terrorist financing regime (discussed in Chapter 10) serves to prevent the use of the financial system for criminal purposes[116] and to enable the investigation of money laundering and terrorist financing offences and international cooperation in this regard.[117] Part of the motivation for this devel-opment was the difficulty of the extraterritorial policing of offshore financial centres (OFCs) which guarantee legal anonymity to bank customers in order to reap the bene-fits through licensing fees. These secrecy 'products' include numbered bank accounts (originally accounts where the name of the beneficial owner was unknown to the bank but more recently where it is a closely guarded secret), shell banks (banks that have no physical presence in the country in which they operate), and companies and trusts where no information about owners or beneficiaries is kept on the public registers.

---

[111] See article 7(1)(d) of the Agreement Concerning Co-operation in Suppressing Illicit Maritime and Air Trafficking in Narcotic Drugs and Psychotropic Substances in the Caribbean Area (CRA), 10 April 2003, not yet in force (although accepted in practice).
[112] S/Res/1816 (2008), 2 June 2008, para 10.
[113] S/Res/1851 (2008), 16 December 2008, para 6.
[114] See S/Res/2316 (2016), 9 November 2016, para 14.
[115] See S/Res/2240 (2015), renewed in S/Res/2312 (2016).
[116] See Preamble of the 2012 Wolfsberg Anti-Money Laundering Principles for Private Banking, available at <http://www.wolfsberg-principles.com/pdf/standards/Wolfsberg-Private-Banking-Prinicples-May-2012.pdf> last visited 15 February 2017.
[117] 2012 FATF Recommendations: International Standards on Combating Money Laundering and The Financing of Terrorism and Proliferation, 7, <http://www.fatf-gafi.org/publications/fatfrecommendations/documents/fatf-recommendations.html> last visited 22 February 2017.

17.8.2 Globalizing risk assessment

Through customer due diligence (CDD) banks engage in risk assessment and provide a source of information to law enforcement agencies on suspicious transactions. The private sector-driven Wolfsberg AML Principles on Private Banking define CDD to include finding out the source of the wealth (how it was generated) and the source of the funds (their origin and means of transfer into the account),[118] and characterize suspicious transactions as transactions inconsistent with the account holders' banking profiles, cash transactions over a certain threshold, and rapid movement of funds.[119] The CDD measures pioneered in the US include obligations on financial institutions (banks, institutions, and professions offering financial services) to monitor and record monetary transactions involving more than US$10,000 (currency transaction reports or CTRs),[120] to abolish anonymous accounts and identify the real party in interests being operated by a nominee (know your customer or KYC obligations),[121] and to report any suspicious transactions (suspicious activity reports or SARs).[122]

Evidence of large-scale involvement of banks in laundering in the Bank of Credit and Commerce International (BCCI) case[123] gave the impetus for establishment of a global AML regime. The Financial Action Task Force (FATF) has taken the lead through its set of Recommendations. It has expanded the subjects of preventative duties beyond the banks to non-financial businesses such as lawyers, casinos, real estate, precious metal and stone dealers, trust companies, and service providers,[124] and updated customer identification by emphasizing the introduction of systems of mandatory suspicious transaction reports (STRs) and by introducing CDD on a risk-sensitive basis involving enhanced CDD of potentially suspicious persons in order to alleviate compliance costs to the financial industry.[125] The FATF's approach has been picked up in recent suppression conventions. Article 52 of the UNCAC, for example, provides for a system of improved examination of high-value bank accounts whose beneficial owners or their families or associates hold prominent public positions. Regional organizations have gone further. The EU's fourth AML/CTF Directive[126] in 2015, for example, applies enhanced CDD obligations on a risk-sensitive basis[127] to the full range of financial businesses[128] and lowers the CTR reporting level from €15,000 to €10,000 in some instances, while still obliging them to cooperate with authorities.[129] The 2005 Council of Europe Convention on Laundering, Search, Seizure and Confiscation of the Proceeds

---

[118] Principle 1.3.   [119] Principle 4.1.   [120] 31 USC §§ 5311–5322.
[121] 31 USC § 5325.   [122] 31 USC § 5318(g).
[123] *Bank of Credit and Commerce International (Overseas) Ltd v Akindele* [2000] 4 All ER 221 [2000] 3 WLR 1423.
[124] Recommendation 22.   [125] Recommendation 10.
[126] Directive of the European Parliament and of the Council of 20 May 2015 on the prevention of the use of the financial system for the purposes of money laundering or terrorist financing, amending Regulation (EU) No 648/2012 of the European Parliament and of the Council, and repealing Directive 2005/60/EC of the European Parliament and of the Council and Commission Directive 2006/70/EC, OJ L 141/73.
[127] Article 4.   [128] Chapter II, article 18.   [129] Article 33.

from Crime and on the Financing of Terrorism[130] introduced the broad strategy of prevention to members of the Council of Europe.[131]

States have embraced these provisions, although some more readily than others. In Portugal, for example, *Lei* (Law) 25 of 5 June 2008 makes provision, inter alia, for a range of financial entities to do CDD and provide STRs, as well as to cooperate with law enforcement (all the time maintaining secrecy). One difficulty has been the expansion of the duty to entities that are not traditionally considered to be involved in banking such as real estate agents, lawyers, chartered accountants, and other dealers in value. The considerable compliance expense to little effect has been another. A Law Society submission to a British Parliamentary enquiry estimated that in 2007–2008, 210,000 SARs were made in the UK, resulting in the recovery of only £135 million in criminal assets. Finally, there are still some OFCs holding out against regulation. In the British Virgin Islands, for example, those seeking the beneficial owner of an account will find them hidden behind a nominee[132] while a bewildering array of mechanisms used by investors to hide assets has been exposed by the Panama Papers.[133]

17.8.3 Removing bank secrecy

Bank secrecy has been another target of policing in the financial arena. Austria's bank secrecy law, for example, prohibits financial institutions, governors, members, employees, and any other persons acting on their behalf 'from divulging or exploiting secrets which are revealed or made accessible to them exclusively on the basis of business relations with customers'[134] and attaches criminal and civil liability to violation of these laws.[135] The US has tried to use long-arm subpoenas to breach security laws of this kind. In the *Bank of Nova Scotia* cases, for example, it attempted to force the bank to breach Cayman Islands secrecy laws by delivering documents from its Cayman Islands branch in response to subpoenas for the documents served on its Miami branch.[136] The development of obligations on states parties to the suppression conventions to remove bank secrecy began with article 5(3) of the 1988 UN Drug Trafficking Convention, which provides:

> In order to carry out the measures referred to in this article, each party shall empower its courts or other competent authorities to order that bank, financial or commercial records be made available or be seized. A party shall not decline to act under the provisions of this paragraph on the grounds of bank secrecy.

FATF Recommendation 9 provides that '[c]ountries should ensure that financial institution secrecy laws do not inhibit implementation of the FATF Recommendations'.

---

[130] 16 May 2005, CETS No 198, in force 1 May 2008.

[131] See WC Gilmore, *Dirty Money: The Evolution of International Measures to Counter Money Laundering and the Financing of Terrorism*, 4th edn (Strasbourg: Council of Europe, 2011), 187.

[132] 'License to Loot', *The Economist*, 17 September 2011, 62.

[133] L Harding, 'What are the Panama Papers? A Guide to History's Biggest Data Leak', *The Guardian*, 5 April 2016, <https://www.theguardian.com/news/2016/apr/03/what-you-need-to-know-about-the-panama-papers>.

[134] Article 38(1) of the Banking Act (*Bankwesengesetz*).

[135] Article 101 of the *Bankwesengesetz*.

[136] See, eg, *In re Grand Jury Proceedings, United States of America v The Bank of Nova Scotia* 691 F 2d 1384 (11th Circ 1982) 29 November 1982.

These laws and their analogues have allowed law enforcement to open up many secrecy laws. Austria, for example, has, under threat of FATF blacklisting and EU pressure, provided legislative gateways through its secrecy laws in order to enable conditional access to protected information upon official request, although these gateways require substantial material evidence that the conditions for access have been met and can be appealed, potentially causing delay.[137] The scope of these obligations can have an extra-territorial element. In *Jyske Bank Gibraltar v Administración del Estado*[138] the European Court of Justice ruled that Spain had the right to ask for information under EU law about the identities of customers from a Danish bank based in Gibraltar because Spain was where it carried on business although it was not registered there.

17.8.4 Financial Intelligence Units

The US Treasury Department's Financial Crimes Enforcement Network (FinCEN), established in 1990, was the first Financial Intelligence Unit (FIU). All financial institutions operating in the US file their suspicious and cash transaction reports to FinCEN, and it reviews these to gather usable law enforcement intelligence. FATF Recommendation 29 defines and supports the globalization of FIUs:

> Countries should establish a financial intelligence unit (FIU) that serves as a national centre for the receipt and analysis of: (a) suspicious transaction reports; and (b) other information relevant to money laundering, associated predicate offences and terrorist financing, and for the dissemination of the results of that analysis. The FIU should be able to obtain additional information from reporting entities, and should have access on a timely basis to the financial, administrative and law enforcement information that it requires to undertake its functions properly.

In more cryptic terms article 58 of the UNCAC makes it obligatory only to 'consider establishing a financial intelligence unit to be responsible for receiving, analysing and disseminating to the competent authorities reports of suspicious financial transactions'. In practice, some FIUs are regulatory in nature, independent of prosecutorial authorities although they have strong relations with banks and place a heavy emphasis on prevention. Others are actually part of law enforcement agencies and respond more rapidly in an investigative role but may pay less attention to preventive measures. A third type is judicial in nature, strong on oversight but not on enforcement.[139]

FIUs provide a vehicle for international law enforcement cooperation. The Egmont Group, formed in 1995 at a meeting held at the Palais d'Egmont-Arenberg in Brussels, is a collaborative forum of 152 FIUs, which seeks according to its Charter to develop more effective and practical cooperation among FIUs, especially in the area of

---

[137] See article 38(2) of the *Bankwesengesetz* and article 116 of the Code of Criminal Procedure (*Strafprozessordnung* or StPo). See further FATF, Mutual Evaluation of Austria, 2016, p 131, available at <http://www.fatf-gafi.org/media/fatf/documents/reports/mer4/MER-Austria-2016.pdf> last visited 22 February 2015.

[138] Case C 212/11, 25 April 2013.

[139] See IMF/World Bank, *Financial Intelligence Units: An Overview* (Washington, DC: IMF Publication Services, 2004), 9–17.

information exchange and sharing of expertise.[140] Information exchange must however conform to principle 3.1(a):

> All members foster the widest possible co-operation and exchange of information with other Egmont Group FIUs on the basis of reciprocity or mutual agreement and following the basic rules established in the Principles:
> 1) Free exchange of information for purposes of analysis at FIU level.
> 2) No dissemination or use of the information for any other purpose without prior consent of the providing FIU.
> 3) Protection of the confidentiality of the information.

The Egmont Secure Web (ESW) permits the secure sharing of sensitive operational information.

17.8.5 Counter-terrorist financing

The 1999 Terrorism Financing Convention makes provision for regulation of financial institutions, obliging them to disclose information on unusual and suspicious transactions.[141] The Convention was criticized as ineffective,[142] and in response to 9/11[143] the AML regime was 'rebooted' to counter the financing of terrorism. In 2001 FATF's mandate was expanded to include counter terrorist financing, and it made nine Special Recommendations on Terrorist Financing, which were fully integrated into the FATF Recommendations in 2012. The recommendations explicitly apply CDD obligations to terrorist financing.[144]

At a national level the US led the way in the Suppression of the Financing of Terrorism Convention Implementation Act 2002,[145] applying strict CDD and reporting requirements to a broad range of transactions. Other states followed suit. In Canada the Proceeds of Crime (Money Laundering) Act was rebadged in 2001 as the Proceeds of Crime (Money Laundering and Terrorist Financing) Act, and amended to apply CDD and reporting requirements to terrorist financing.

Policing the financing of terrorism is, however, a difficult undertaking because of a number of factors intrinsic to the process of fund raising for terrorism: it may involve donations through a charity or from personal funds; CDD obligations may not operate when no offence has yet occurred to arouse a bank's suspicions, or money is not moved quickly or frequently; reporting requirements may not be triggered if the amounts used are too small (the bombings in central London in July 2005, for example, cost a few hundred pounds to execute[146]).

---

[140] See generally the Egmont Group of Financial Intelligence Units Charter, 5 July 2013, available at <https://www.egmontgroup.org/> last visited 1 March 2017.

[141] Article 18(1)(b)(iii).

[142] K Roach, 'Sources and Trends in Post 9/11 Anti Terrorism Laws' in BJ Goold and L Lazarus (eds), *Security and Human Rights* (Oxford: Hart, 2007), 227, 233–34.

[143] See I Bantekas, 'The International Law of Terrorist Financing' 97 *American Journal of International Law* (2003) 315.

[144] Recommendation 10(iii).   [145] 18 USC § 2331 et seq.

[146] M Buchanan, 'London Bombs Cost Just Hundreds', BBC News, 3 January 2006, <http://news.bbc.co.uk/2/hi/uk_news/4576346.stm> last visited 1 March 2017.

17.9 Law Enforcement Training

Provisions in the suppression conventions encourage cooperation in training. Article 29 of the UNTOC, for example, obliges parties to train their own law enforcement agents (and judicial officers and prosecutors) and to assist each other in training in the following matters:

(a) Methods used in the prevention, detection and control of the offences covered by this Convention;

(b) Routes and techniques used by persons suspected of involvement in offences covered by this Convention, including in transit States, and appropriate countermeasures;

(c) Monitoring of the movement of contraband;

(d) Detection and monitoring of the movements of proceeds of crime, property, equipment or other instrumentalities and methods used for the transfer, concealment or disguise of such proceeds, property, equipment or other instrumentalities, as well as methods used in combating money-laundering and other financial crimes;

(e) Collection of evidence;

(f) Control techniques in free trade zones and free ports;

(g) Modern law enforcement equipment and techniques, including electronic surveillance, controlled deliveries and undercover operations;

(h) Methods used in combating transnational organized crime committed through the use of computers, telecommunications networks or other forms of modern technology; and

(i) Methods used in the protection of victims and witnesses.

In practice, support for the training of foreign police forces has proved difficult and requires long-term engagement and technical assistance. It may require trainees to be taken out of the country or the development of regional training centres such as the Jakarta Centre for Law Enforcement Cooperation (JCLEC)[147] or specialist centres such as the International Anti-Corruption Academy (IACA) in Austria.[148]

17.10 Human Rights in Law Enforcement Cooperation

Transnational criminals are exposed to a range of different standards of human rights protection during the process of law enforcement cooperation leaving them particularly vulnerable because of the absence in a practical sense of transnational guarantees

---

[147] See JCLEC at <http://www.jclec.com/> last visited 2 March 2017.
[148] See IACA at <www.iaca.int> last visited 2 March 2017.

of fairness.[149] For example, law enforcement agents may engage in forum shopping to find the most severe outcomes for the defendant.[150]

Specific provision for human rights protections in international agreements for law enforcement cooperation is rare. Human rights charters and domestic constitutional protections provides the only protection. The principle of state-agency—that domestic human rights restraints apply to state agents operating extra-territorially on public business—is, however, growing in acceptance in the European Human Rights regime. When they assume public powers normally associated with the territorial government they arguably operate under domestic human rights constraints whether they assume those powers completely (which as we have seen is most unusual in police cooperation)[151] or when they do so under the authority of the territorial state.[152] Human rights tribunals tend nevertheless to grant a broad margin of appreciation when dealing with protecting human rights in the policing of difficult to police areas such as the high seas. In *Medvedyev v France*,[153] for example, the crew of the MV *Winner*, a Cambodian-flagged vessel arrested by a French ship on the high seas off Cape Verde in a drug interdiction operation, were detained for nearly two weeks on board the French vessel before being brought before a judge when it reached port. The Court held that the crew had been deprived of their liberty in a procedure unsanctioned by law in breach of article 5(1) of the European Convention on Human Rights because Cambodia's written consent to the search of the vessel had made no reference to authority over the crew. Article 5(3), the right to be brought promptly before a judge, had not in the court's view been breached because of the exceptional circumstances entailed by the *Winner*'s poor seaworthiness and the fact that seizure was on the high seas. In similar tone although in a completely different context, a challenge to French legislation implementing EC Directives on money laundering which inter alia placed duties on legal professionals to inform FIUs if they 'know, suspect or have reasonable grounds to suspect' money laundering or terrorist financing is being committed or attempted as a violation of human rights because it was too vague was rejected by the European Court of Human Rights in *Michaud v France*.[154]

For the majority of individuals who find themselves beyond the range of constitutional or regional human rights regimes, trial courts become the only real venue for due process protection; in such situations the admission of evidence gleaned by unfair processes in other states reinforces the use of those unfair processes.[155]

---

[149] See S Gless, 'Transnational Cooperation in Criminal Matters and the Guarantee of a Fair Trial' 9 *Utrecht Law Review* (2013) 90.

[150] S Gless, 'Birds-Eye View and Worm's Eye View: Towards a Defendant-Based Approach in Transnational Criminal Law' 6(1) *Transnational Legal Theory* (2015) 117, 129.

[151] *Al Skeini v United Kingdom* ECtHR App no 5572/07 (Grand Chamber) para 131; *Al Jedda v The United Kingdom* ECtHR App No 27021/08 (Grand Chamber).

[152] *Jaloud v The Netherlands* ECtHR App no 47708/08 (6 February 2008) (Grand Chamber).

[153] *Medvedyev and others v France* (2010) 51 EHRR 39, paras 131–34.

[154] Application no 12323/11, 6 December 2012.

[155] See C Street, 'Streamlining the International Silver Platter Doctrine: Coordinating Transnational Law Enforcement in the Age of Global Terrorism and Technology' 49 *Columbia Journal of Transnational Law* (2010–11) 411.

17.11 International Law Enforcement Organizations

There is no global police force actively policing transnational crime; the UN Police's (UNPOL) role is limited to peace operations and diplomatic protection. Article 35(b) of the 1961 Single Convention obliges parties to 'cooperate closely with … the competent international organizations of which they are members with a view to maintaining a coordinated campaign against the illicit traffic'. This provision recognizes the role international organizations (IGOs) like the International Criminal Police Organization (ICPO or Interpol) play as intermediaries for police-to-police cooperation.[156] It is not an operational IGO with powers of arrest in different states; it is a network of national police organizations that can be used to track suspected criminals. It operates through National Central Bureaus (NCBs), and is staffed by national law enforcement officials.

Interpol's work prioritizes certain common transnational crimes—terrorism, drug trafficking, organized crime, and human trafficking. Its primary function is to serve as a conduit for requests for information from national law enforcement through their NCBs through the Interpol General Secretariat (based in Lyon) to NCBs in other member states. Although this used to be done by post, it is now automated using an encrypted Internet-based system (I-24/7). Interpol issues a kaleidoscope of notices on behalf of states: the Red Notice—wanted persons; the Blue Notice—enquiry for information about individuals; the Green Notice—warnings about criminals operating internationally; the Yellow Notice—request for missing persons; and the Black Notice—identification of a corpse. Under UN Security Council Resolution 1617 since 2005 Interpol has also issued the *sui generis* Interpol-UN Security Special Notices for the freezing of assets of suspected Islamist terrorists. Nevertheless, Interpol is not purely a conduit. Two acts are involved, for example, in the issuing of a Red Notice—the issuing of the warrant by the judicial authorities of the state and the administrative sanction of that request by Interpol. Interpol acts more purely as a conduit in regard to 'diffusion alerts', NCB requests circulated over the Interpol I-Link network but unlike the Red Notice not published by Interpol. Interpol also serves as a resource centre for the collection and distribution of data and maintains databases on names, fingerprints, DNA profiles, etc which serve as useful sources of information.

Although Interpol is generally considered effective, the informal way Interpol is constituted and the poor political control over the organization has been subject to criticism.[157] The Red Notice's 'soft' (non-binding) request to arrest pending an extradition request is, for example, widely used, widely honoured, and hard to challenge. About one third of Interpol members rely on them to justify arrest; the rest

---

[156] Interpol has no treaty basis but is recognized in customary international law as an IGO. See M Deflem and S McDonough, 'International Law Enforcement Organisations' in S Kethineni (ed), *Comparative and International Policing, Justice, and Transnational Crime* (Durham, NC: Carolina Academic Press, 2010), 127, 137–41.

[157] See generally M Anderson, *Policing the World* (Oxford: OUP, 1989); J Sheptycki, 'Brand Interpol' in S Hufnagel and C McCartney (eds), *Trust in International Police and Justice Cooperation* (Bloomsbury-Hart: London, 2017), 97.

insist on a specific diplomatic request for arrest. There are, however, reported incidences of the attempted use of Red Notices for political purposes, expressly prohibited by article 3 of Interpol's Constitution,[158] and unacceptable to many member states.[159] This has led to reforms of the Red Notice scheme such as the introduction of the Commission for the Control of Interpol's Files (CCF), which serves as an independent monitoring body of the Interpol Secretariat's issuing of notices, but the CCF only reviews selected cases and there is no entitlement to an oral hearing, meaning the legal remedies for individuals to challenge the issue of Interpol Red Notices are limited.[160]

The European Union Agency for Law Enforcement Cooperation (Europol) provides an innovative model for regional law enforcement cooperation. Established as a result of agreement in the Treaty on European Union of 7 February 1992 to make improving police cooperation in the field of terrorism, unlawful drug trafficking, and other serious crimes a common objective,[161] Europol began life as a centre for constant, confidential, and intensive exchange of information between member states' national units. It was later given the power to carry out intelligence analysis, strategic analysis of criminal threats, and to request member states to initiate, conduct, or coordinate investigations in specific cases. Today it manages the Europol computer system, which provides data on a broad range of subject matter. No longer an IGO, but one of the three EU agencies in the field of police and justice cooperation, its new legal basis in Regulation (EU) 2016/794[162] of the European Parliament and Council on the European Union Agency for Law Enforcement Cooperation, provides more detailed rules on parliamentary scrutiny and data protection. As well as representatives of EU member states, Europol also hosts liaison officers from thirteen non-EU states, including liaison officers from eleven separate US federal law enforcement agencies making the US the largest single observer.[163]

There are a large number of other international police organizations. While most are concerned with policing strategy rather than individual operational problems, there is a trend to operational cooperation on specific crimes. The Shanghai Cooperation Organisation, Regional Counter-Terrorism Structure (RATS), based in Tashkent, for example, addresses all transnational security threats and works to coordinate information sharing interoperability between civilian or military security organizations.[164]

---

[158] Article 3 of the Interpol Constitution strictly forbids Interpol from undertaking 'any intervention or activities of a political ... character'. The Constitution of 13 June 1956 (as amended) is available at <http://www.interpol.int/About-INTERPOL/Structure-and-governance> last visited 13 February 2012.

[159] See selected cases in Fair Trials International, *Cases of Injustice*, available at <https://www.fairtrials.org/campaigns/interpol-campaign/cases-of-injustice/>.

[160] Discussed in M Savino, 'Global Administrative Law meets "Soft" Powers: The Uncomfortable Case of Interpol Red Notices' 43 *NYU Journal of International Law and Politics* (2011) 263 who argues that soft restraint is apt for soft mechanisms.

[161] Deflem and McDonough above n 156, 141–44.   [162] OJ L 135, 11 May 2016.

[163] See Europol, Partners and Agreements at <https://www.europol.europa.eu/partners-agreements> last visited 4 December 2017.

[164] See the RATS website <http://ecrats.org/en/> last visited 7 June 2017.

17.12 The Emerging Transnational Law Enforcement Culture

International law enforcement cooperation is characterized by coordination of sovereign entities rather than centralization of control at an international level. International law enforcement cooperation has not led to the erosion of national control of policing or the elimination of different national styles of policing. Indeed, becoming acquainted with and working with the different styles of cooperating police forces is one of the essential requirements along with trust for successful police cooperation. The autonomy that national police officers enjoy in the transnational space has led rather to a culture of transnational policing characterized by the sharing of common values among nominally sovereign police forces, a culture that does not only engage in enforcing existing laws but also develops new laws and practices to both prevent and punish crime transnationally.[165] According to Bowling and Sheptycki, national police are being 'glocalised ... drawn into transnational networks of training and knowledge exchange predicated on the perceived need to control local manifestations of national crime and disorder'.[166] They share the same values about what transnational crime is, what causes it, and how to respond to it, and those values are mobilized in the development of transnational criminal justice policy designed to suit operational requirements. Working largely out of sight, this transnational law enforcement culture is not subject to any form of democratic accountability or authority.[167] Indeed, it avoids centralized control of cross-border law enforcement.

---

[165] See generally MD Dubber and M Valverde (eds), *The New Police Science: The Police Power in Domestic and International Governance* (Stanford, CA: Stanford University Press, 2006), 149. On global police cooperation see Ben Bowling and James Sheptycki, *Global Policing* (Sage, 2012), B Bowling and J Sheptycki (eds), *Global Policing and Transnational Law Enforcement* (Sage, 2015). See also B Bowling, 'Transnational Policing: The Globalization Thesis, A Typology and Research Agenda' 3(2) *Policing* (2009) 149, 151–52.

[166] B Bowling and J Sheptycki, 'Global Policing and Transnational Rule with Law' 6(1) *Transnational Legal Theory* (2015) 141, 146.

[167] ibid, 153.

18

Legal Assistance

18.1 Introduction

Activities requiring legal authority such as the gathering of admissible evidence, the service of legal documents, and the recovery of assets extraterritorially are exercises in enforcing jurisdiction. States cannot undertake them unilaterally; their powers are limited by the general principle that enforcement of jurisdiction is territorial. These activities require more formal cooperation than the informal police-to-police cooperation examined in Chapter 17 because they involve judicial processes. States are thus compelled to seek legal assistance (mutual legal assistance, judicial cooperation) from the territorial state to enforce their coercive powers in another jurisdiction.

This chapter briefly discusses the nature of legal assistance and its development, before examining the provisions in the suppression conventions setting out the scope of legal assistance obligations, the range of kinds of legal assistance that can be requested, the conditions for legal assistance, and the procedure for making requests. It then comments on the rights of individuals within the legal assistance process and alternative methods of acquiring evidence abroad.

18.2 The Nature of Legal Assistance

Common law states were initially hesitant to provide legal assistance because of their belief that criminal law is local and their reluctance to enforce another state's criminal law. In contrast, civil law states were more comfortable with providing legal assistance because they saw it as providing assistance to other states to enforce their own laws over criminal offences that concerned them. Today it is accepted that the provision of legal assistance does not mean that the requested state exercises the requesting state's sovereign power; rather, it uses its own power to do something for the requesting state. Again local law governs the granting of legal assistance, but local cooperation is conditioned on the provision of information from the requesting state in an acceptable form in order to justify assistance.

Like extradition, legal assistance is based on reciprocity. There is no general customary international law obligation to grant such assistance. It is regulated entirely by treaty or more informal relations. Moreover, as the International Court of Justice has noted[1]

> ... the ultimate treatment of a request for mutual assistance in criminal matters clearly depends on the decision by the competent national authorities, following the

---

[1] *Case Concerning Certain Questions of Mutual Assistance in Criminal Matters (Djibouti v France (Judgment)* [2008] ICJ Reports 177, para 123.

procedure established in the law of the requested State ... [T]he State does not thereby guarantee the outcome.

Legal assistance can be long-winded and bureaucratic, particularly when it has to deal with differences in prosecutorial culture such as the high level of discretion enjoyed by prosecutors in common law states which permits them to discontinue proceedings in the public interest, while their counterparts in civil law states are bound by a legality principle which allows little or no discretion in the early stages of the criminal process. Legal assistance can, however, be effective in today's cooperative climate. A major corporation involved in corruption, for example, may make an admission in one state that will as a result of legal assistance become available in other states, forcing it to settle everywhere that it is potentially open to prosecution.

18.3 Letters Rogatory

Conceived of as a matter of inter-state relations, legal assistance was originally bound up in diplomatic customs. The issuing of letters rogatory (rogatory letters, *lettres rogatoire*), a court to court process borrowed from international civil procedure, was the recognized way of requesting legal assistance. It involves the communication of a unilateral request for legal assistance from the judiciary of one state to the judiciary of another, the assistance to be executed by the latter's officials at their discretion. This transjudicial assistance was described by a US Court as follows:[2]

> Letters rogatory are the medium, in effect, whereby one country, speaking through one of its courts, requests another country, acting through its own courts and by methods of court procedure peculiar thereto and entirely within the latter's control, to assist the administration of justice in the former country; such request being made, and being usually granted, by reason of the comity existing between nations in ordinary peaceful times.

According to the Council of Europe such letters provide 'a mandate by the judicial authority of one country to a foreign judicial authority to perform in its place one or more specified actions'.[3] The power to issue that mandate may depend on statute or on the inherent jurisdiction of the court,[4] and sanction by the court will depend on the materiality of information sought and the unavailability of witnesses in the requesting state. The request is then passed through diplomatic channels.

The requesting state will also have to show that what is sought is discoverable within the requested state, and that this process can be undertaken while adhering to the laws and practices of the requested state. It may be limited to requests where the subject of the investigation has already been arrested and proceedings instituted against them (ie they have been indicted). It usually has to be written to be understood by lawyers within the requested state. It may have to address the particular municipal court with

---

[2] *The Signe* 37 F Supp 819, 820 (ED La 1941).
[3] *Explanatory Report to the European Convention on Mutual Assistance in Criminal Matters* (Strasbourg: Council of Europe, 1969), 14.
[4] *In re Pacific Railway Commission* 32 F 241, 12 SAWY 559 (ND Cal 1887).

jurisdiction. Hiring a local lawyer to put the request to the local court may be necessary and costly. The process is usually slow and normally requires the suspension of statutes of limitations. The formality of inter-sovereign communication therefore has the potential to frustrate the necessarily rapid investigation of offences and to allow suspected offenders to slip away.

18.4 Mutual Legal Assistance

18.4.1 The development of mutual legal assistance treaties (MLATs)

MLATs are treaty-based reciprocal obligations to provide legal assistance, developed as evidence-gathering tools in regard to specific transnational crimes. An MLAT obligation is engaged by a request from the authorities of the requesting state to the central authority of the requested state. The requested state is then obliged to use its own statutory authority on behalf of the requesting state. These local authorities execute requests under the *lex loci*; they do not allow the conduct of a transnational investigation by the requesting authorities in their jurisdiction. These treaties are usually self-executing although they can be implemented by specific statutory provisions. The conditions and grounds for refusal, even when they include discretionary clauses giving the right to refuse in the interests of the sovereignty, security, or *ordre public* of the requested state, are limited by a duty of good faith.[5] An MLAT is not usually available to the defendant for their use to discover exculpatory evidence.[6]

The Council of Europe's 1959 European Convention on Mutual Assistance in Criminal Matters[7] played a formative role in developing this procedure. Its chief innovation was to establish an obligation on parties to grant mutual legal assistance, but the provisions it made for the scope of legal assistance, conditions for legal assistance, exceptions to legal assistance, and procedures for legal assistance provided a model for subsequent treaties. Various other regional treaties have been adopted, including the 1992 Inter-American Convention on Mutual Assistance in Criminal Matters[8] and the 2004 ASEAN Treaty on Mutual Assistance in Criminal Matters.[9] In Europe the Benelux Treaty for Mutual Legal Assistance[10] was followed by the 2000 EU Convention on Mutual Legal Assistance in Criminal Matters,[11] the 2008 European Evidence Warrant (a warrant for objects, documents, and data enforceable in other EU member states without further formality),[12] and in 2017 by the European Investigation Order (EIO) (an instrument 'for the gathering of evidence' which provides for enforcement

---

[5] *Djibouti v France (Judgment)* [2008] ICJ 177, (Declaration of Judge Keith), para 6.

[6] *US v Davis*, 767 F2d 1025 (2d Cir. 1985). See also article 1(3) of US–UK MLAT, 6 January 1994.

[7] 20 April 1959, ETS 30, in force 12 June 1962. See also the Additional Protocol, 17 March 1978, ETS 99, in force 12 April 1982, and Second Additional Protocol, 8 November 2001, ETS 182, in force 1 February 2004.

[8] 23 May 1992, OASTS no 75, in force 14 April 1996.   [9] 29 November 2004.

[10] Early steps included the Benelux Treaty on Extradition and Mutual Assistance in Criminal Matters of 27 June 1962 and the Schengen Agreement of 14 June 1985.

[11] OJ C 197/3, 12 July 2000.

[12] Council Framework Decision 2008/978/JHA of 18 December 2008 on the European evidence warrant for the purpose of obtaining objects, documents and data for use in proceedings in criminal matters, [2008] OJ L 350.

of investigative measures specified by the issuing EU member with the objective of facilitating the fair determination of criminal charges throughout the EU by ensuring that the trial court has relevant available evidence wherever it might be located).[13]

At a broader level, the 1986 Commonwealth Scheme for Mutual Legal Assistance[14] provides an agreed set of recommendations for legislative provision for mutual legal assistance in Commonwealth states.

At a bilateral level, the Mutual Legal Assistance Treaty between the US and Switzerland signed on 25 May 1973[15] broke new ground in bilateral legal assistance relations between common law and civil law states. The US has followed it up with a large number of MLATs with strategic transnational crime suppression partners. The advantage of bilateral MLATs is that they can be tailored to a particular relationship and they permit states to choose their treaty partners, thus avoiding obligations to provide information to unfriendly or untrustworthy states. The UN Model Treaty on Mutual Assistance in Criminal Matters 1990[16] is an attempt to standardize provisions in bilateral treaties.

18.4.2 The inclusion of mutual legal assistance provisions in the suppression conventions

The older suppression conventions contain very limited provisions on legal assistance. Thus, for example, article 35(e) of the 1961 Single Convention on Narcotic Drugs provides only that parties should:

> Ensure that where legal papers are transmitted internationally for the purposes of a prosecution, the transmittal be effected in an expeditious manner to the bodies designated by the Parties; this requirement shall be without prejudice to the right of a Party to require that legal papers be sent to it through the diplomatic channel.

In effect this was an attempt to speed up the traditional process of letters rogatory. Article 7 of the 1988 UN Drug Trafficking Convention was the first of the mini-MLATs, a set of detailed obligations for the provision of legal assistance within a suppression convention. These mini-MLATs are now common in suppression conventions, and rely in part on existing mutual assistance arrangements, and in part provide for standalone obligations. For example, the provisions in article 18(1)–(6) of United Nations Convention against Transnational Organized Crime (UNTOC) are free standing and do not require a treaty between parties while the provisions of article 18(7)–(29) are not free standing—they apply to requests if the parties are not bound by a treaty or, if they are, the parties can choose to apply either the treaty or the UNTOC.[17] Moreover,

---

[13] Directive 2014/41/EU of the European Parliament and the Council of 3 April 2014 regarding the European Investigation Order in criminal matters, OJ L 130/1.

[14] Scheme Relating to Mutual Assistance in Criminal Matters within the Commonwealth (Harare Scheme) 1 August 1986, 12 *Commonwealth Law Bulletin* (1986) 1118 (as amended in 1990, 2002, and 2005).

[15] Treaty Between the United States of America and the Swiss Confederation on Mutual Assistance in Criminal Matters, 25 May 1973, 27 UST 209, TIAS 8302, in force 23 January 1977.

[16] Annexed to GA Res 45/117 (1990), 14 December 1990, as amended by GA Res 53/112 (1999), 9 December 1998.

[17] See, eg, article 46(7) of the UNCAC.

these mini-MLATs commonly contain a provision encouraging them to conclude bi- and multilateral agreements to enhance the mini-MLATs' provisions.[18]

18.4.3 The general duty in suppression conventions to provide mutual legal assistance

Mini-MLATs in suppression conventions usually impose a general duty on parties to provide legal assistance. In terms of article 46(1) of the United Nations Convention against Corruption (UNCAC), for example, the parties promise to 'afford one another the widest measure of mutual legal assistance'.[19] These general obligations have been imposed to overcome the reluctance of parties that otherwise take a very rigid (and negative) view of what they see as 'fishing expeditions' by other parties. However, general obligations do not guarantee that all requests for assistance will be met. As the International Court of Justice pointed out in the *Djibouti Case*:

> the ultimate treatment of a request for mutual assistance in criminal matters clearly depends on the decision by the competent national authorities, following the procedure established in the law of the requested State. While it must of course ensure the procedure is put in motion, the State does not thereby guarantee the outcome, in the sense of the transmission of the file requested in the letter rogatory.

While the requests must be dealt with in good faith, if the conditions, procedure, etc. are not adhered to, they may be refused.[20]

18.4.4 The limitation of mutual legal assistance to criminal proceedings

States differ as to how early in the criminal process they are willing to entertain a request for legal assistance. While the US is willing to provide assistance in regard to criminal investigations that have not yet reached the indictment stage,[21] other states are wary of having to assist foreign law enforcement agencies in pre-charge investigations where the police are 'fishing' for substance. Article 1 of the 1959 European Convention on Mutual Assistance obliges parties to provide assistance in regard to 'proceedings in respect of offences, the punishment of which, at the time of the request for assistance falls within the jurisdiction of judicial authorities'. It suggests that formal investigation under judicial control (such as an investigating magistrate in civil law systems) must have commenced. The broader Commonwealth Scheme responds to the fact that in common law states the greater part of investigation and evidence gathering occurs prior to the court process, by providing that requests can be made in respect of 'criminal matters' where criminal proceedings have been instituted or 'there is reasonable cause to believe that an offence in respect of which such proceedings

---

[18] See, eg, article 18(30) of the UNTOC; article 46(30) of the UNCAC.
[19] See also, eg, article 7(1) of the 1988 Drug Trafficking Convention; article 18(1) of the UNTOC.
[20] *Djibouti* case above n 1, para 123.
[21] In terms of 28 USC § 1782; see *In Re Letter Rogatory from Justice Court Dist of Montreal, Canada,* 523 F2d 562 (6th Circ) 25 June 1975.

could be instituted has been committed'.[22] Article 1(1) of the UN Model Treaty on Mutual Assistance provides for assistance 'in investigations or court proceedings' also without stipulating the necessity for judicial supervision of those investigations. The suppression conventions follow a similarly broad approach. Thus, for example, article 18 of the UNTOC provides explicitly for an obligation to afford assistance in 'investigations, prosecutions and judicial proceedings' against natural and legal persons.[23] When it comes to the meaning of 'judicial proceedings', according to the Legislative Guide to the UNTOC, a requested party retains 'discretion in determining the extent to which they will provide assistance for such proceedings, but assistance should at least be available with respect to portions of the criminal process that in some countries may not be part of the actual trial, such as pre-trial proceedings, sentencing proceedings and bail proceedings'.[24]

Provisions of this kind in the suppression conventions are thus open to fairly elastic interpretations to suit conditions in the parties and it is difficult to determine their scope precisely. More specific MLATs are usually relied on to resolve problems. Uniquely, the EIO addresses the distinct issue of the availability of legal assistance for infringements that are not crimes, as in addition to criminal proceedings it is also available for administrative infringements and other legal infringements falling with the criminal jurisdiction.[25]

18.4.5 Types of mutual legal assistance available

A broad range

The range of types of legal assistance available depends on (a) what has been agreed to in the particular suppression convention and (b) whether and if so how this has been transposed into the domestic law of the requested state. Some conventions provide for special types of assistance. The European Cybercrime Convention,[26] for example, makes provision for mutual assistance in a range of highly specialized areas such as the expedited preservation of stored computer data[27] and the expedited disclosure of preserved traffic data.[28] Article 46(3) of the UNCAC provides an example of the full range of normal types of legal assistance that may be requested:

  (a) Taking evidence or statements from persons;

  (b) Effecting service of judicial documents;

  (c) Executing searches and seizures, and freezing;

  (d) Examining objects and sites;

  (e) Providing information, evidentiary items and expert evaluations;

---

[22] Para 1(2) and para 3(1).   [23] Article 18(2).   [24] Para 465.
[25] Article 4 of the EIO Directive, above n 13.
[26] 23 November 2001 Convention on Cybercrime ETS No 185.   [27] Article 29.
[28] Article 30.

(f) Providing originals or certified copies of relevant documents and records, including government, bank, financial, corporate or business records;

(g) Identifying or tracing proceeds of crime, property, instrumentalities or other things for evidentiary purposes;

(h) Facilitating the voluntary appearance of persons in the requesting State Party;

(i) Any other type of assistance that is not contrary to the domestic law of the requested State Party;

(j) Identifying, freezing and tracing proceeds of crime in accordance with the provisions of chapter V of this Convention;

(k) The recovery of assets, in accordance with the provisions of chapter V of this Convention.

Two broad kinds of assistance are covered: assistance in gathering the evidence of crime (discussed below) and assistance in recovering the proceeds of crime (discussed in Chapter 19). Evidence gathering abroad involves a wide range of different activities from gathering genetic samples to the production of documents. Certain forms of evidence gathering abroad are, however, particularly problematic.

Witnesses

Provision for assistance in the taking of statements or evidence from witnesses and experts located in foreign states is a critical element of many transnational prosecutions. States may request that statements be taken from witnesses in the requested party. Section 7(1)(a)–(c) of Australia's Foreign Evidence Act 1994, for example, makes provision for an Australian court to order the examination of any person abroad when it 'appears in the interests of justice to do so', considering factors such as whether the person is willing to come to Australia, whether the evidence is material, and the interests of the parties. The court can order that the person be examined under oath before a judge in the foreign court or by a commission from Australia or in response to a letter of request to the foreign state's judicial authorities. Parties may also request assistance in enabling the voluntary appearance of the witness to give evidence in the requesting party. Giving evidence by video link makes this process much easier, and more recent suppression conventions encourage this process.[29] In order to make use of these provisions states making requests must make provision in their national law for the admission in evidence of documents and written materials obtained abroad.[30]

There are obvious problems in taking statements from witnesses located elsewhere. First there must usually be some kind of legal platform for making the request to do so—usually an MLAT. In practice, common law states will generally allow direct approaches to a potential witness by the officials of a foreign state (who have

---

[29] Article 18(18) of the UNTOC.
[30] See, eg, 18 USC § 3481; 18 USC § 3505 makes provision for an exception to the hearsay rule.

no authority to enforce jurisdiction), without necessarily requiring a formal treaty request. They will allow questioning (assuming the interviewee consents), the taking of statements, and video linkups, and appoint commissioners to take evidence on the foreign state's behalf, and on occasion relax their laws of evidence in the process to suit the requesting state. Civil law states generally require a formal mutual assistance request to make the interview of witnesses possible, and some will not permit it at all unless there is a specific law providing for it.

Second there are practical problems: adherence to the defendant's rights including for example the right of confrontation, testing the weight of evidence through assessing the demeanour of witnesses, adherence to the witnesses' right such as rights to immunity from prosecution which differ from state to state.

Requesting states may require that a witness appear personally in court in the requesting state. Witnesses may not, however, always be willing to give evidence in foreign states or employers may be unwilling to let them go. In these situations the requesting party may wish to serve a subpoena on a witness to appear in the requesting party. Most modern mini-MLATs within suppression conventions permit such service.[31] The position is more complicated when a requesting party wishes to enforce a subpoena through measures of compulsion such as the application of a penalty for a failure to appear. While some bilateral treaties do make provision for enforced appearance at the request of another party,[32] the suppression conventions follow general multilateral mutual assistance treaties[33] in that although they permit the service of documents to contain a penalty for non-appearance they do not oblige parties to enforce presence, which means such penalties are without force. In terms of article 18(27) of the UNTOC, for example, witnesses and experts must consent to appear, and if they do so they are given immunity for fifteen days.[34] Persons in custody in the requested party must also freely consent to transfer to a requesting party to give evidence[35] and are not open to prosecution in the requesting party unless the requested party agrees.[36]

Interception of telecommunications

Unlike general MLATs,[37] the suppression conventions usually do not make express provision for assistance in the interception of telecommunications, probably because this matter is so sensitive. It may however be covered by obligations to undertake 'searches' or the catch-all provision for 'other types' of assistance not contrary to the requested party's law. In practice, assistance in the interception of telecommunications will be subject to more detailed bilateral and regional MLATs and domestic law.[38]

---

[31] Article 18(3)(b) of the UNTOC.
[32] US–Italy Mutual Assistance Treaty, 11 September 1982, 24 ILM 1539, in force 13 November 1985.
[33] Article 8 of the 1959 European Convention on Mutual Assistance; para 15(5) of the Commonwealth Scheme.
[34] See article 46(27) of the UNCAC; article 18(27) of the UNTOC.
[35] Article 18(10)(a) of the UNTOC.   [36] Article 18(12) of the UNTOC.
[37] Article 3 of the 1959 European Convention on Mutual Assistance.
[38] See, eg, section 24 of Ireland's Criminal Justice (Mutual Assistance) Act 2008.

Records

The communication of judicial and official records on request is important to reveal vital information such as the previous convictions of the person being prosecuted. The suppression conventions oblige requested parties to convey publicly available government records, documents, and information to requesting parties but leave it to the discretion of requested parties to make available records not publicly available.[39]

More advanced forms of assistance

The EIO Directive also makes provision for the issuing of EIOs inter alia for real-time evidence gathering and covert investigations,[40] measures of cooperation not specifically contemplated in suppression conventions.

18.4.6 The conditions for and exceptions to mutual legal assistance

Introduction

Requests for legal assistance are usually subject to limited conditions and exceptions borrowed from the law of extradition. The suppression conventions have tried to limit these conditions and exceptions because legal assistance is not as serious an inroad into human rights as extradition. Some exceptions common in extradition treaties, such as the nationality exception, are simply inappropriate to legal assistance. Some reasons for refusal, such as bank secrecy, have been specifically removed by more modern suppression conventions.[41] The precise conditions and exceptions involved in regard to any particular transnational crime will depend on the contents of the suppression convention or other regional or bilateral MLAT on which the requesting party is relying. Invoking these conditions and exceptions is a matter for the requested party, acting in good faith.

Double criminality

The application of double (or dual) criminality (the requirement that the conduct be criminal in both requesting and requested states) to legal assistance has been criticized as 'an unnecessary and outmoded barrier to cooperation',[42] and is becoming less common. Under regional MLATs, such as the 1959 European Convention, double criminality is not generally required[43] except in regard to more serious inroads into personal liberty such as search and seizure of property.[44] In the Commonwealth Scheme, it is a discretionary condition for assistance.[45] Similarly, article 18(9) of the

---

[39] See, eg, article 18(29) of the UNTOC; article 46(29) of the UNCAC.
[40] See, eg, articles 28 and 29 of the EIO Directive, above n 13.
[41] See, eg, article 7(5) of the 1988 Drug Trafficking Convention; article 46(8) of the UNCAC.
[42] R Ivory, *Corruption, Asset Recovery and the Protection of Property in Public International Law: The Human Rights of Bad Guys* (Cambridge: CUP, 2014), 208, and authors cited there.
[43] Article 1(1).   [44] Articles 5 and 6.   [45] Para 7(1)(a).

UNTOC permits a party to decline assistance on the basis of double criminality if it chooses to.

There is a growing practice of not requiring double criminality unless the other party insists on it. As a result of pressure from African states during negotiations, the UNCAC provides in article 46(9)(b) that parties shall provide assistance of a non-coercive nature even in the absence of double criminality. The definition of 'offence' in section 2 of Canada's Mutual Legal Assistance in Criminal Matters Act 1985, for example, refers to the relevant treaty, which will either require double criminality or not. More recent bilateral US MLATs require assistance without regard to dual criminality. Article II(3) of the Canada–US MLAT[46] provides that 'assistance shall be provided without regard to whether the conduct under investigation or prosecution in the Requesting State constitutes an offence or may be prosecuted by the Requested State'. In result, a Canadian judge can order the issue of an arrest warrant under section 12 of Canada's Act or order evidence gathering under section 18 without considering double criminality. Financial Action Task Force Recommendation 37 provides that '[c]ountries should render mutual legal assistance, notwithstanding the absence of dual criminality, if the assistance does not involve coercive actions'. The new EIO dispenses with double criminality entirely. It provides that police in the requested EU member state have to investigate upon request from another member state, and it does not matter if it is a crime in the receiving state or not.[47]

Certain states, however, have problems with requests for assistance in regard to transnational crimes they do not recognize. In Thailand, for example, section 9(2) of the Act on Mutual Assistance in Criminal Matters[48] provides that, unless the specific MLAT stipulates otherwise, 'the act which is the cause of the request must be an offence punishable under Thai laws'. The absence of double criminality will cause difficulties if the offence in regard to which the request is made is not generally recognized. The suppression conventions do not overcome this problem entirely because, as we have seen, they often leave criminalization of certain forms of conduct optional. Even if the suppression convention in question obliges a party to criminalize the particular form of conduct to which the requests relates, double criminality will not exist if the state in question has failed to criminalize. Article 9(2) of the Organisation for Economic Co-operation and Development Anti-Bribery Convention does not, however, allow a party's own failure to implement the convention to allow it to escape the obligation to provide assistance. It provides that where a party insists on double criminality in order to make legal assistance available, it 'shall be deemed to exist if the offence for which the assistance is sought is within the scope of this Convention'. This might satisfy legal expediency but does not respect fair warning to the individual concerned.

If double criminality is a requirement, the question becomes whether the formal legal elements or only the underlying conduct need be the same in both parties (a

---

[46] Treaty between the Government of Canada and the Government of the United States of America on Mutual Legal Assistance in Criminal Matters, 18 March 1985, CTS 1990 No 19; in force 18 March 1985.
[47] See EIO Directive above n 13, Article 4(a).
[48] Act on Mutual Assistance in Criminal Matters, BE 2535 (1992).

question discussed in detail in Chapter 20 in relation to extradition). The trend is towards the latter. Article 25(5) of the European Cybercrime Convention, for example, provides that if parties require dual criminality, the sole condition shall be if the conduct underlying the offence is criminal in its laws.

Specialty

Application of the doctrine of specialty to requests for the provisions of documents means that documents can only legally be used for the request for which they are handed over. It may be necessary to preserve privacy or secrecy interests. Article 42(1) of the Council of Europe's 2005 Money Laundering Convention, for example, permits the requested party to make 'the execution of a request dependent on the condition that the information or evidence obtained will not, without its prior consent, be used or transmitted by the authorities of the requesting Party for investigations or proceedings other than those specified in the request'. Specialty conditions of this kind can also be found in article 12(3) of the Terrorism Financing Convention and in other suppression conventions.[49]

Political offence exception

The UN Model Treaty on Mutual Assistance recognizes the discretion of the requested party to refuse on political grounds,[50] a position followed in the Commonwealth Scheme,[51] although the latter makes it clear that transnational crimes are not to be considered political offences.[52] Some bilateral MLATs retain the political offence exception,[53] but as in extradition, there has been steady pressure to remove the application of the political offence exception to legal assistance. Terrorism conventions like the Terrorism Financing Convention are clear that none of the offences in the treaty are to be regarded 'as a political offence or as an offence connected with a political offence or as an offence inspired by political motives' and thus a request for legal assistance cannot be refused on these grounds alone.[54]

Military offence exception

Bilateral MLATs tend to retain the exception that mutual assistance cannot be requested for military offences that are not crimes under general criminal law,[55] although this exception has been abandoned in the suppression conventions.

---

[49] Article 18(19) of the UNTOC.   [50] Article 4(1)(b).   [51] Para 7(1)(b).
[52] Para 7(2)(4).
[53] See, eg, article 3(1)(c)(i) of the Treaty between the United States of America and Ireland on Mutual Legal Assistance, 18 January 2001, UST Doc 107-9 (2002), in force 11 August 2009.
[54] Article 12.
[55] See, eg, article 4(1) of the Treaty Between the United States of America and the Russian Federation on Mutual Legal Assistance in Criminal Matters, 17 June 1999, UST Doc No 107–13 (2002), in force 31 January 2002.

Fiscal offence exception

Older regional MLATs still permit parties to refuse a request where the party considers that it concerns a fiscal offence or an offence connected with a fiscal offence, but this condition has been removed by supplementary treaties.[56] The newer suppression conventions provide that a request may not be refused on fiscal grounds.[57]

Sovereignty, security, and public order

Following the position in most MLATs,[58] the suppression conventions commonly contain a provision entitling the requested party to refuse if it considers 'the execution of the request is likely to prejudice its sovereignty, security, *ordre public* or other essential interests'.[59] In the *Djibouti Case*, the French decision not to grant assistance to Djibouti's authorities to investigate the murder of a French judge in Djibouti was made by an investigating magistrate on grounds of national security, and the ICJ ruled it could not be challenged by Djibouti.[60]

Prohibition on carrying out the requested action in national law

Some states possess much broader investigative powers than others. As a result, article 46(21)(c) of the UNCAC entitles the requested party to refuse: '(c) If the authorities of the requested State Party would be prohibited by its domestic law from carrying out the action requested with regard to any similar offence, had it been subject to investigation, prosecution or judicial proceedings under their own jurisdiction ...'

De minimis

Some suppression conventions, quite wisely, allow refusal if the requested party does not consider the particular case important enough to warrant taking the actions requested.[61]

Incorrect procedure

The suppression conventions commonly contain a provision entitling the requested party to refuse a request if the procedural provisions in the mini-MLAT with the particular convention are not adhered to.[62]

---

[56] Article 2(a) of the 1959 European Convention on Mutual Assistance; removed by article 1 of the 1978 Protocol.

[57] See, eg, article 18(22) of the UNTOC; article 46(22) of the UNCAC.

[58] See, eg, article 2(b) of the 1959 European Convention on Mutual Assistance. See also article 4(1)(a) of the UN Model Treaty and para 7(2a) of the Commonwealth Scheme.

[59] See, eg, article 18(21)(b) of UNTOC; article 46(21)(b) of UNCAC.

[60] See the *Djibouti Case*, above n 1, para 146.

[61] See, eg, article 28(1)(c) of the 2005 Council of Europe Money Laundering Convention.

[62] Article 18(21)(a) of the UNTOC; article 46(21)(a) of the UNCAC; article 9(3) of the OECD Bribery Convention.

Nemo bis in idem

The principle *nemo bis in idem debet vexari*, that someone convicted or acquitted for the same offence cannot be charged with it again, is an optional ground for refusing legal assistance in certain suppression conventions[63] and a mandatory ground in the UN Model Treaty,[64] and is fairly common in bilateral MLATs.[65]

Human rights

States are reluctant to refuse requests for mutual legal assistance on the grounds that such assistance may result in an unfair trial in the requesting state because of the need for comity on the issue of suppression of crime and because such an assessment involves the courts in foreign policy, something that falls within executive competency.[66] Interestingly, while non-discrimination clauses are found in some MLATs[67] they have been omitted as a ground for refusing legal assistance in most suppression conventions. However, human rights obligations can be a valid ground for refusing legal assistance even though they are not explicitly contemplated in an MLAT (see the discussion under extradition in Chapter 20).

Conclusion

The parameters of these conditions and exceptions depend on their interpretation by the officials of the requested state. Effective law enforcement has to be balanced with a state's control over its jurisdiction and with the interests of the suspected or accused person. Most legal assistance treaties provide for postponement or conditional granting of a request while insisting on the giving of reasons for refusal,[68] and the suppression conventions follow suit.[69]

18.4.7 The procedure for applying for mutual legal assistance

Introduction

Regional or bilateral MLATs usually detail the procedure to be followed when making and responding to requests for legal assistance; this is used in conjunction with domestic law. If parties to a suppression convention do not have pre-existing legal assistance relations, suppression conventions like the UNTOC 'strongly encourage' parties to apply the procedural provisions in the convention's mini-MLAT.[70]

---

[63] See, eg, article 28(1)(f) of the 2005 Council of Europe Money Laundering Convention.
[64] Article 3(d).   [65] See US–Ireland, above n 53, article 3(1)(b).
[66] See *Thatcher v Minister of Justice and Constitutional Development and ors*, Decision of High Court (2005) 1 All SA 373 (C); ILDC 172 (ZA 2004) 2005 (4) SA 543 (C), 24 November 2004.
[67] Para 7(2b) of the Commonwealth Scheme; article 4(1)(c) of the UN Model Treaty.
[68] See, eg, article 4(3) and (4) of the UN Model Treaty.   [69] Article 18(23) of the UNTOC.
[70] Article 18(7).

Transmission of requests

Early suppression conventions were designed to provide for different channels for making requests for assistance. Article 16 of the 1929 Counterfeiting Convention,[71] for example, provides:

> The transmission of letters of request relating to offences . . . should be effected:
> (a) Preferably by direct communication between the judicial authorities, through the central offices where possible;
> (b) By direct correspondence between the Ministers of Justice of the two countries, or by direct communication from the authority of the country making the request to the Minister of Justice of the country to which the request is made;
> (c) Through the diplomatic or consular representative of the country making the request in the country to which the request is made; this representative shall send the letters of request direct to the competent judicial authority or to the authority appointed by the Government of the country to which the request is made, and shall receive direct from such authority the papers showing the execution of the letters of request.

Ironically, despite the formalization of the obligation to provide legal assistance, requests for assistance are still commonly made through letters rogatory. More recent provisions have tried to avoid the delay-inducing problems of letters rogatory including the use of the diplomatic channel, differences in authentication requirements between states, paper-heavy bureaucratic procedures, and strict formal adherence to national rules (a useful tool to block 'incompetent' foreign authorities' requests).

A key development has been the channelling of requests for legal assistance through national points of contact. Article 7(8) of the 1988 UN Drug Trafficking Convention obliges each party to designate a 'central authority' to receive requests and to speedily and properly execute them or transmit them to the competent authorities for execution. Parties are to notify the UN Secretary-General of these authorities. Central authorities, staffed by experienced officers with the necessary language and legal skills, have been established in many states,[72] and the United Nations Office on Drugs and Crime (UNODC) maintains an online directory of competent national authorities.[73] Unfortunately, parties may still insist that assistance requests be sent via diplomatic channels or through Interpol, while in some states, the central authority will simply pass the request to a local official unfamiliar with the agreed legal assistance procedure. One way of bridging the gap is to post national prosecutors abroad as liaison officers who can coach prosecutors in the state in which they are located in the correct way to make a request. Eurojust, the European Prosecutor's Office, takes this one step further by serving as a central hub for cooperation in prosecution thus replacing the need for liaison prosecutors.

---

[71] The International Convention for the Suppression of Counterfeiting of Currency, 20 April 1929, 112 LNTS 371, in force 22 February 1931.
[72] In the Russian Federation, eg, it is the Officer of the Procurator General.
[73] Competent National Authority (CNA) Directory, available on SHERLOC (Sharing Electronic Resources and Law on Crime) database, at <https://www.unodc.org/cld/en/v3/sherloc/cnadir.html>.

The formalities are otherwise fairly straightforward. Requests for assistance, under the UNCAC, for example, have to be in writing and in a language acceptable to that party and under conditions that enable the requested state to establish authenticity.[74] Article 25(3) of the European Cybercrime Convention permits the use of electronic means of transmission in urgent circumstances, including fax and email (encrypted if necessary for security purposes), with formal requests following only if the requested party insists.

As to the content of such requests, article 18(15) of the UNTOC, which is expressed in very similar terms to article 5(1) of the UN Model Treaty, is illustrative:

> A request for mutual legal assistance shall contain:
> (a) The identity of the authority making the request;
> (b) The subject matter and nature of the investigation, prosecution or judicial pro-
>   ceeding to which the request relates and the name and functions of the authority
>   conducting the investigation, prosecution or judicial proceeding;
> (c) A summary of the relevant facts, except in relation to requests for the purpose of
>   service of judicial documents;
> (d) A description of the assistance sought and details of any particular procedure
>   that the requesting State Party wishes to be followed;
> (e) Where possible, the identity, location and nationality of any person concerned; and
> (f) The purpose for which the evidence, information or action is sought.

The UNODC provides tools to guide states in making such requests.[75]

Execution of requests

Applying the generally accepted approach,[76] article 18(17) of the UNTOC confirms that a request is to be executed in accordance with the domestic law of the requested party and only to the extent that it is contrary to the law in accordance with the procedures specified in the request.

The suppression conventions are silent on the method of service of documents although usually service must be in a manner followed by or acceptable to the requested state. The trend towards acceptability of modern forms of communications is illustrated by the EIO which can be transmitted 'by any means capable of producing a written record under conditions allowing the executing authority to establish authenticity', and this includes transmission through the European Judicial Network.[77]

When it comes to more intrusive matters such as the examination of witnesses, the placing of witnesses under oath, the recording of testimony, the presence of an official from a requesting state at the execution of the request, and the use of modern techniques such as video conferencing,[78] the general principle is that the law of the requested state governs. The law of the requesting state will usually set conditions to

---

[74] See article 46(14).
[75] See the UNODC's Mutual Legal Assistance Request Writer Tool, available at <http://www.unodc.org/mla/en/index.html>.
[76] Article 6 of the UN Model Convention.
[77] Article 7(1) and (4) of the EIO Directive, above n 13.   [78] Article 18(18) of the UNTOC.

suit the requirements of its law of evidence and procedure, such as requiring that witnesses be put under oath and be cross-examined (ie a right of confrontation) before their evidence is admissible. It may request another party to apply these conditions in the examination of a witness on its behalf.[79] If the law of the requested state does not require an oath or permit cross-examination of witnesses, the requested state will still comply with its legal assistance obligation if it does not place the witness under oath or permit their cross-examination. The requested state cannot be obliged to grant the authorities of the requesting state better rights than those granted in domestic proceedings.[80] This ensures that individuals are not subject to foreign legal regimes with more power over them than their own state. Moreover, witnesses are usually granted the benefits applicable in either requested or requesting states. The Commonwealth Scheme, for example, clarifies that a witness may claim any privilege open to them in either the requesting or requested state[81] while the UN Model Treaty provides that a witness may refuse to give evidence if they are permitted or obliged to refuse under the law of the requesting or requested states.[82] These conditions may cause significant problems for the reception of the evidence gathered back in the courts of the requesting state.

Common law states in particular struggle to get states from other legal traditions to adhere to their arcane rules of evidence when giving assistance in order to ensure that the information supplied is admissible in a common law criminal trial. They can try to get requested states to comply (by coaching them on the necessity of compliance[83]) or they can relax their own rules of admissibility. In *R v Dorsay*,[84] for example, an inculpatory statement made by the accused in the US to a psychiatrist, which in the US would have been subject to absolute privilege, was admitted as evidence taken on commission on behalf of Canada by a US judge because the judge applied the Canadian qualified privilege to such statements. Excluded at trial in Canada, it was admitted after a successful appeal. In a further example, although the Sixth Amendment to the US Constitution insists that all criminal defendants have the right to confront the witnesses against them, which implies that evidence must be testimony given in court subject to cross-examination and cannot take the form of depositions (written statements), Rule 15 of the Federal Rules of Criminal Procedure provides that a deposition of an unavailable witness is admissible whenever 'due to the exceptional circumstances of the case it is in the interest of justice' to allow it. In the *United States v Salim*,[85] although the witness was in France and the accused in the US, the accused's attorney was allowed to submit questions in writing through the French *juge d'instruction* when the witness's evidence was taken, and the US Court of Appeals held the deposition admissible. Although non-confrontation remains exceptional under English law,

---

[79] Section 8 of Australia's Foreign Evidence Act 1994 provides that where a court orders that a letter of request be sent to a foreign state's judicial authorities for the examination of a witness under section 7(1)(c) it may include a request about any matter relating to taking that evidence including inter alia the examination, cross-examination, or re-examination of the person, whether the person's evidence is given orally, on affidavit or otherwise, and the attendance and participation of the legal representative of each party to the proceeding.

[80] See, eg, paragraph 7(3) of the Commonwealth Scheme.   [81] Paragraph 17.

[82] Article 12.   [83] Canada, eg, has posted a Liaison Officer to Brussels for this purpose.

[84] 209 CCC (3d) 184; 42 CR (6th) 155; 146 CRR (2d) 12.   [85] 855 F 2d 944 (2nd Circ 1988).

the position has since slowly relaxed in respect of certain kinds of statement in certain kinds of proceeding. Thus, for example, in *R v Foxley*[86] the English Court of Appeal held that bank documents revealing corrupt payments to the accused obtained from Italy, Norway, and Germany were admissible even though their makers were not present and could not be cross-examined. Section 24 of the Criminal Justice Act 1988 only required that the documents be made in the course of business and the information contained was supplied by someone who could reasonably be presumed to have personal knowledge thereof. Similar problems do not occur in provision of evidence for the defence because in respect of evidence for the defence the state has no right of confrontation.

Requests from civil law states to common law states do not encounter the same problems with the application of rules of evidence or the right of confrontation. In civil law states the reception of evidence is acceptable because the use of depositions is legal, and most common law states now make provision for the taking down of testimony to be used in foreign courts.

Finally, under most legal assistance arrangements, including the mini-MLATs in the suppression conventions, the requested state bears the bulk of the costs of executing requests unless they are of an extraordinary nature, in which case the states must consult one another.[87]

18.4.8 Concurrent requests for legal assistance

Suppression conventions and legal assistance treaties do not make general rules for resolving concurrent demands for legal assistance. Portugal applies a rule that in the case of concurrent requests in regard to the same case, assistance shall be afforded to the state that in the circumstances 'might better safeguard both the interests of justice and the interests of the social rehabilitation of the suspect'.[88] It affords a rare consideration for the individuals actually subject to this process.

18.5 The Rights of Individuals to Legal Assistance and in the Mutual Legal Assistance Process

Most US MLATs also expressly exclude any rights for the defence to obtain evidence in terms of the treaty.[89] So if, as was alleged in *United States v Sturman*,[90] the US Government misused the US–Swiss MLAT to get at tax records and the appellant wanted to use the treaty to rectify this, he could not. The court held that for violation of the treaty to lead to an acquittal there must be evidence of 'serious governmental misconduct'. The individual has no standing and cannot suppress evidence, which effectively avoids the normal rules of admissibility and any applicable constitutional

---

[86] [1995] 2 Cr App R 523.
[87] See, eg, article 18(28) of the UNTOC; article 46(28) of the UNCAC.
[88] Article 14(1) of the Law No 144/99, International Judicial Cooperation in Criminal Matters, as amended.
[89] See, eg, article 37 of the US–Switzerland MLAT.   [90] 951 F 2d 1466 (6th Cir 1991).

rights. This view has influenced treaty development. Individuals have no rights to ask for assistance through the mini-MLATs in the suppression conventions.

Legal assistance is designed to assist in the enforcement of criminal law not to assist individuals subject to investigation. It can be used somewhat cynically by prosecuting authorities to try to circumvent rights available to the individual in the requesting state being applied in the requested state and the MLATs provide no assistance to individuals in this regard. Some bilateral US MLATs, for example, specifically exclude 'the right of any person to take any action in the US to suppress or exclude any evidence or to obtain other judicial relief in connection with requests under this treaty'. In other words, no action can be taken in a US court to prevent the operation of the MLAT by the requested state. In the *United States v Davis*,[91] Davis was not notified of a US request for his bank records to be given up by Switzerland in terms of the US–Switzerland MLAT, so he could not exercise his right under the MLAT to attend those proceedings. But he could not challenge this in the US Court because he did not have *locus standi* and it was not the duty of the requesting state to alert him about the request; it was for the Swiss authorities to do so. His right and remedy was not where the request was made but where it was executed. In a similar division of responsibility the EIO provides that member states must 'ensure legal remedies equivalent to those available in a similar domestic case are applicable to the investigative measures indicated in the EIO' but only permits challenge to the substantive reasons for issuing of an EIO in the issuing state.[92]

The suppression conventions are almost entirely silent on the rights of the accused in the legal assistance process. The mini-MLATs also contain confidentiality provisions that may unbalance the equality of arms. The UNTOC does allow an accused to benefit indirectly from exculpatory evidence transmitted either spontaneously by another party even if it is subject to a request that it remain confidential (out of respect for prosecutorial duties to disclose such information).[93] Where the information is the product of a request, the position is the same, although the requesting party is under a duty to notify, and if necessary consult with, the requested party.[94] The requesting party may also oblige the requested party to keep confidential 'the fact and substance of the request, except to the extent necessary to execute the request'.[95] This means that individual subjects of requests may not be notified that a request concerning them is being made.

18.6 Alternative Methods of Acquiring Evidence Abroad: Getting Around the 'MLAT Problem'

18.6.1 Introduction

MLATs are usually crime specific and their execution tends to be slow. They are to some extent being overtaken by the spread of criminal activity and the speed at which digital information can be moved before the request is met. The growing perception

---

[91] 767 F 2d 1025 (2d Cir 1985).   [92] Article 14(1) and (2) of the EIO Directive, above n 13.
[93] Article 18(5) of the UNTOC.   [94] Article 18(19) of the UNTOC.
[95] Article 18(20) of the UNTOC.

that there is a difficulty in this regard with MLATs was echoed in the *Microsoft Ireland Case*[96] (discussed below) where the judge issuing the warrant referred to them as 'cumbersome'. It has stimulated resort to using various extra-treaty evidence-gathering tools, the international legality of which may be dubious.

18.6.2 'Long-arm' subpoenas

A so-called 'long-arm subpoena' is an order made by a judge under domestic law of one jurisdiction (backed by the threat of contempt of court) to enforce the delivery of evidence situated in another jurisdiction.[97] It avoids the necessity of direct contact with the foreign state because these subpoenas are usually directed at individual defendants who are in its jurisdiction, even its extraterritorial jurisdiction,[98] for delivery of documents in their possession but which are outside its territory. Although this long-arm adjudicative jurisdiction undermines existing MLATs, US courts have sanctioned its use. In the *Re Sealed Case*[99] the defendant argued that the US–Swiss MLAT provided the exclusive means for accessing records held in Switzerland subpoenaed by the US Court investigating the arms-to-Iraq affair. Although the Swiss Government supported this argument and confirmed that the use of a subpoena violated international comity, the US Court of Appeals held that the MLAT was not the only way of obtaining evidence. It recognized the importance of comity but considered that it still had the power to order any defendant within its jurisdiction to deliver up documents regardless of a foreign sovereign's views to the contrary. States respond to this US practice by insisting on specific provisions in treaties with the US that forbid the use of extraterritorial coercive methods by US courts.[100] Separation of powers, however, means that treaties are an executive matter, and US courts are not bound by them in applying domestic judicial remedies. US courts have also sanctioned the use of 'compelled consent', where prosecutors compel individuals in US jurisdiction to consent to the release of information located in foreign states. It is not protected by the right to silence because it is not testimonial in nature.[101]

18.6.3 'Long-arm' search warrants

Law enforcement reliance on domestic court orders ordering multinational companies to provide information under their control about individuals which is stored in foreign jurisdictions received a blow in the *Microsoft Ireland Case*[102] when the US Federal

---

[96] See below n 102, at para 75.
[97] *United States v Bank of Nova Scotia* 691 F 2d 1384 (11th Cir 1982).
[98] *Marc Rich and Co AG v United States* 707 F2d 663 (2nd Cir 1983).
[99] 825 F 2d 494 (DC Cir 1987); see also *Re Grand Jury Proceedings, Marsoner v US* 40 F 3d 949 (9th Cir 1994); *Marc Rich and Co AG v United States* 707 F2d 663 (2nd Cir 1983).
[100] See, eg, article 1(3) of Treaty between the [USA] and the [UK] Concerning the Cayman Islands Relating to Mutual Assistance in Criminal Matters, 3 July 1986, 26 ILM 536 (1987), in force 18 July 1990.
[101] *Doe v United States* 487 US 201 (1988).
[102] *Microsoft v United States* 829 F 3d 197 (2d Circ 2016). *See also Walsh v National Irish Bank* [2013] IESC 4, where an order to produce tax records issued in Ireland against the Irish National Bank was held not to be binding on a branch of that bank in the Isle of Man.

Court of Appeals for the Second Circuit ruled that a search warrant issued by a federal judge in the US for emails held on Microsoft servers in Ireland was void because it was not clear that the enabling legislation was intended to apply extraterritorially. A search warrant implied that Microsoft, the custodian rather than personal holder of the information, would act as an agent for the US government and search on its behalf in the US, something prohibited under international law. The issuing judge had noted that the MLAT procedure was 'cumbersome' but as Ireland pointed out in its amicus brief when a state acts unilaterally in this way in another state it bypasses the legal process for engaging in cooperation—the MLAT—and imposes different standards of data protection.[103] The US courts are, however, not unanimous as to the illegality of these kinds of actions,[104] and clarification by the Supreme Court seems likely.

18.6.4 Unsanctioned extraterritorial evidence gathering

States may go one step further and rely on a long-arm law enforcement jurisdiction to violate the sovereignty of other states and gather evidence in their territories, at the same time potentially violating the suspect's individual rights to due process.

The *United States v Verdugo Urdiquez*[105] is the best-known example of 'evidence-napping'. The defendant was arrested in the US for drug trafficking offences. The Drug Enforcement Administration, together with Mexican officials, searched his premises in Mexico and seized various items of evidence without a warrant. The defendant argued that it was a violation of his Fourth Amendment protections against unreasonable search and seizure, and was therefore inadmissible. Although the Federal District Court and the Court of Appeals agreed, the US Supreme Court per Chief Justice Rhenquist held that the Fourth Amendment does not apply to search and seizure by US agents of property owned by a non-resident alien located in a foreign country, but only protects 'the people' of the US, those nationals or persons with sufficient connections to the US, and the defendant was not one of the people. The judgment accepts that if US officials obtain evidence abroad unlawfully both in terms of US law and of foreign states' law, this evidence is admissible in the US. The Supreme Court's justification was foreign policy: 'Application of the 4th amendment could significantly disrupt the ability of the political branches to respond to foreign situations involving our national interest.'[106] An effective response to transnational crime demanded that the 'long arm' of US criminal law be coupled with the 'short arm' of US constitutional protection. International comity, Mexico's protests at the violation of its sovereignty and the fact that article 1(2) of the US–Mexico MLAT[107] expressly forbade the

---

[103] *Microsoft v US, Brief of Amicus Curiae Ireland*, available at Digital Constitution, <http://digital-constitution.com/wp-content/uploads/2014/09/Ireland-AmicusBrief.pdf> last visited 2 January 2017.

[104] See *In Re Search Warrant No. 16-190-M-01 to Google; In re Search Warrant No. 16-690-m to Google*, decision of Judge TJ Reuter, District Court Eastern District for Pennsylvania, 3 February 2017, where the judge ordered Google to comply with search warrants for emails stored outside the US, and appeal was refused.

[105] 110 USC 1056; 494 US 259 (1990).

[106] ibid, 1065.

[107] Mutual Legal Assistance Co-operation Treaty between the US and Mexico, 9 December 1987, 27 ILM (1998) 445.

exercise of sovereign power in the other's territory were all disregarded. Only if the evidence gathered 'shocks the conscience' of the court will it be excluded (earlier cases disallowed it if there was substantial US involvement). Brennan J dissented mainly on the basis that the enforcement of US criminal law abroad transforms an accused into one of the governed under US Constitutional protection, but he also argued that the US must distinguish national security interests from extraterritorial criminal law enforcement.[108]

Various methods of avoiding the conundrum of disrespect for another state's law in engaging in search and seizure abroad have been suggested including the notion of 'double illegality': if the search violates the procedural protections common to both the searching state and the searched state, the evidence should be inadmissible in the searching state,[109] although this would not cure the illegality under international law.

In *R v Governor of Pentonville Prison, ex parte Chinoy*[110] the English courts willingly cooperated in 'evidence laundering' by the US. Chinoy, a manager of Bank of Credit and Commerce International in Paris was wanted in the US for money laundering offences. US agents had gathered evidence using an illegal phone tap in France, which meant the evidence was inadmissible at an extradition hearing in France. They therefore arranged for British police to arrest Chinoy when he visited the UK, and adduced the phone-tap evidence to justify his extradition to the US. Chinoy appealed, arguing that his arrest in the UK was an abuse of process designed to circumvent French law. Nolan J dismissed the application because the abuse of process took place before the matter fell in the court's jurisdiction and therefore he had no discretion to refuse to admit the evidence. The rule was that evidence was admissible if it was obtained in the UK or elsewhere if the probative value outweighed the prejudicial effect. No reference was made to incursion into French sovereignty, and the court condoned the circumvention of treaty law for the exchange of evidence, never mind the rights of the accused under French or European law.

Explicit provisions in the suppression conventions guarantee sovereignty and territorial integrity, echoing customary international law. A party that engages in long-arm adjudicative or law enforcement jurisdiction in another party violates the terms of the suppression conventions to which both are party because those actions involve interventions in the domestic affairs of the other party or the performance of functions reserved exclusively for the authorities of the other party by its domestic law.[111]

18.7 Conclusion

The practical experience of the application of legal assistance treaties, both bilateral and multilateral, has shown that less formal, more rapid international legal assistance is possible, but that considerable obstacles remain. The key to increased cooperation has long been considered to be trust in the underlying values of the foreign legal

---

[108] See above n 105, 1068.
[109] E Bentley Jr, 'Towards an International Fourth Amendment: Rethinking Searches and Seizures Abroad After *Verdugo-Urquidez*' 27 *Vanderbilt Journal of Transnational Law* (1994) 329, 371, 378.
[110] [1992] 1 All ER 317.   [111] See article 4(1) and (2) of the UNTOC.

system being dealt with. As Fijnaut noted in 2000: 'International police and judicial cooperation—as well as cooperation between customs services—can only form the tailpiece of a transnational policy against transnational crime for the simple reasons that, generally speaking, this kind of cooperation only works between prosperous and peace loving nations that have an effective public administration.'[112]

At the global level such trust is not always forthcoming and the existence of legal obligations is not a complete replacement for trust.[113] Nevertheless, today formal legal obligations are increasingly relied upon for legal assistance with non-traditional state partners in what amounts to a slow relaxation of domestic standards for the giving and taking of legal assistance. Resort to alternative methods undermining the treaty system on which legal assistance is based is thus becoming unnecessary as the legal methods for obtaining assistance become simpler and easier to use.

---

[112] C Fijnaut, 'Transnational Crime and the Role of the United Nations' 8 *European Journal of Criminal Law and Criminal Justice* (2000) 119, 125.
[113] See, eg, the *Djibouti Case*, above n 1.

19

Asset Recovery

19.1 Introduction

Most states have long possessed the power both to confiscate the instruments that enable the perpetration of a crime and to remove and return stolen property. The proceeds of the sale of contraband, and the funds paid in bribes in cases of corruption, present more difficult problems, because of questions over ownership of the property involved. One of the purposes of criminalizing money laundering is to permit law enforcement agencies to seize and confiscate these proceeds or instruments of crime. While confiscation is considered 'a form of condign punishment' for those who engage in the predicate offences,[1] recovering 'dirty' assets is also justified as a deterrent to offenders, a preventive tool against commission of further crimes, a way of making law enforcement pay for itself, and a vehicle for restitution of property to victims. Indeed, there appears to be a discernible shift in emphasis from criminalization to asset recovery as a tool of crime suppression. The amounts recovered domestically by some states are high. US authorities seized more than US$12.6 billion between 1989 and 2010[2] and by 2014 the EU was seizing more than €2.4 billion per annum.[3] These figures pale into insignificance when compared to the United Nations Office on Drugs and Crime (UNODC)'s estimation that US$1.6 trillion was laundered in 2009.[4]

Recovery of the instruments or proceeds of crime is problematic for most states because the assets to be recovered are many steps away from the original offence, have often been transformed into other forms of property, and are held in a situation practically impossible to link to the crime, difficulties compounded when the assets are in another state. This chapter examines the international development of asset recovery laws. It looks at provision in the suppression conventions for interim measures such as seizure, criminal confiscation, and civil forfeiture, transnational asset recovery, and the dispersal of the assets. It concludes with a brief comment on the human rights implications and effectiveness of asset recovery.

---

[1] M Levi and P Reuter, 'Money Laundering' 34 *Crime and Justice* (2006) 289, 348.

[2] *Sourcebook of Criminal Justice Statistics Online*, US Department of Justice, Bureau of Justice Statistics (Albany, NY: University of Albany, Hindelang Criminal Justice Research Center, 2009), Table 4.45.2010, available at <http://www.albany.edu/sourcebook/pdf/t4452010.pdf> last visited 1 March 2017.

[3] Europol, *Does Crime Still Pay? Criminal Asset Recovery in the EU: Survey of Statistical Information 2010–2014* (The Hague: Europol, 2016), 9.

[4] UNODC, *Estimating Illicit Financial Flows Resulting from Drug Trafficking and other Transnational Organized Crimes* (Vienna: UNODC, 2011), 9.

19.2 The International Development of Asset Recovery

While prior to 1988 some states had made provision for asset recovery, most states did not have asset recovery legislation and calls were made for steps to be taken to bring the international position into line with the more advanced domestic jurisdictions. Development of a legal response through transnational criminal law has taken place in two broad phases.

The first phase—the asset forfeiture phase—was set off by the adoption of article 5 of the 1988 Drug Trafficking Convention, which was designed to attack international drug trafficking by making possible the seizure and confiscation of the proceeds that accrue from it wherever they may be held. Subsequent international provisions like article 13 of the Council of Europe's Convention on Laundering, Search, Seizure and Confiscation of the Proceeds of Crime[5] developed along the same lines, although the scope of obligations to recover laundered assets expanded as the scope of the offence of money laundering broadened to all-crimes money laundering.[6] National measures, such as article 240 of Italian Penal Code which permits authorities to confiscate the proceeds of any crime, followed suit. Regulatory development of cooperation was guided by the UN through the Optional Protocol to the Model Treaty on Mutual Assistance in Criminal Matters concerning the proceeds of crime.[7] It spells out mechanisms enabling the identification and confiscation of assets in other jurisdictions. Model legislation, such as the UN's 1999 Model Legislation on Laundering, Confiscation and International Cooperation in Relation to the Proceeds of Crime, also provides legislative prototypes with variations for states to adapt to their particular needs.[8] During this first phase of development, limited provisions for seizure and confiscation percolated from money laundering into terrorist financing. Article 8(1) of the 1999 Terrorist Financing Convention, for example, obliges parties to take appropriate measures to identify, detect, freeze, and seize any funds used in connection with terrorist activities, while article 11 provides in that such funds and their proceeds must be forfeited if they are deemed to be associated with terrorist activities.

The second phase of development—the asset recovery phase—began when it was recognized that recovering assets relates as much to the instruments and proceeds of corruption as to the proceeds of money laundering and terrorism. While asset forfeiture of money laundering was led by the global North as one means of suppressing global supply of illicit drugs and other contraband, the global South has been at the forefront of pressure for international cooperation in the recovery of corruptly acquired assets hidden in banks in the developed world. They have been

---

[5] 8 November 1990, ETS No 141, in force 1 March 1991. It has been expanded to include broader obligations—the 2005 Council of Europe Convention on Laundering, Search, Seizure and Confiscation of the Proceeds From Crime and of the Financing of Terrorism, 16 May 2005, CETS No 198, in force 1 May 2008.

[6] Article 1(e). FATF Recommendation 3 uses 'all serious offences'.

[7] Annexed to the UN Model Treaty, GA Res 45/117, 14 December 1990, 30 ILM 1434–41.

[8] Available on the IMOLIN Website at <https://www.imolin.org/imolin/ml99eng.html> last visited 1 February 2017.

spurred on by low rates of recovery of assets stolen by former leaders such as Haiti's 'Baby Doc' Duvalier, who is reported to have stolen the equivalent of approximately 1.7 to 4.5 per cent of Haiti's GDP every year that he ruled.[9] Although developing states lose up to US$40 billion per annum through corruption, in the period 1995–2010 only US$5 billion was recovered.[10] As a result of pressure by African states in particular, detailed measures drawing on models developed to forfeit the proceeds of illicit trafficking were introduced for the first time into the United Nations Convention against Corruption (UNCAC) to provide for recovery of corruptly acquired assets.[11]

19.3 Interim Measures: Identification, Tracing, Freezing, and Seizing

The suppression conventions recognize that certain interim legal steps are necessary prior to confiscation of the proceeds of crime. Article 5(2) of the Drug Trafficking Convention introduced provision, for example, for the identification, tracing, freezing, or seizing of assets, and similar provisions have been included in more recent suppression conventions. Financial Action Task Force (FATF) Recommendation 4 describes the property at which these measures are directed as:

(a) property laundered, (b) proceeds from, or instrumentalities used in or intended for use in money laundering or predicate offences, (c) property that is the proceeds of, or used in, or intended or allocated for use in, the financing of terrorism, terrorist acts or terrorist organisations, or (d) property of corresponding value.

It also details the interim measures as measures to:

(a) identify, trace and evaluate property which is subject to confiscation; (b) carry out provisional measures, such as freezing and seizing, to prevent any dealing, transfer or disposal of such property; (c) take steps that will prevent or void actions that prejudice the State's ability to recover property that is subject to confiscation; and (d) take any appropriate investigative measures.

The purpose of these provisional steps is not the gathering of evidence against an accused but restraint of the assets, thus preventing their removal and, in turn, enabling confiscation or forfeiture. Confiscation of the asset is not, however, inevitable, and a provisional measure may be used as a tactic on its own simply to immobilize the property while further investigation is undertaken. Nor is an interim order always required prior to confiscation; it depends on national law.

---

[9] MV Vlasic and G Cooper, 'Beyond the Duvalier Legacy: What New "Arab Spring" Governments Can Learn from Haiti and the Benefits of Stolen Asset Recovery' 10 *Northwestern University Journal of Human Rights* (2011–12) 19, 20. For a series of case studies on asset recovery in grand corruption cases see R Ivory, *Corruption, Asset Recovery, and the Protection of Property in Public International Law: The Human Rights of Bad Guys* (Cambridge: CUP, 2014), 38–54.

[10] O Canuto and J Devan, 'No Safe Havens for Stolen Funds', *International Herald Tribune*, 26 March 2010, 8.

[11] See Chapter V, articles 51–59 of the UNCAC.

At the investigation stage the assets are identified and located. Identification and tracing commonly runs into problems of access to the assets and banking confidentiality, and the removal of bank secrecy plays a key role in making these steps possible.

At the judicial stage, national law usually requires an interim judicial order, normally based upon the reasonable suspicion of law enforcement officers, to either freeze or seize the assets (the variety and complexity of these orders depend on national law). Freezing applies to intangibles such as money held in bank accounts. Seizing applies to tangibles such as cash, cars, houses, etc. Article 1(1) of the 1988 Drug Trafficking Convention refers to freezing and seizing as 'temporarily prohibiting the transfer, conversion, disposition or movement of property or temporarily assuming custody or control of the property on the basis of an order issued by a court or competent authority'. Freezing is less serious than seizure; it involves the stopping of all movement of funds held in an account. Delay may precipitate evaporation of the funds. These interim steps are of critical importance. In terms of section 41 of the UK's Proceeds of Crime Act 2002, for example, the Crown Court may make a restraint order 'prohibiting any specified person from dealing with any realisable property held by him'. To grant such an order the Court must be satisfied of one of a number of conditions set out in section 40 including reasonable cause that someone under investigation or being prosecuted has benefited from criminal conduct.

Seizing and freezing assets does, however, restrict basic rights to property, and should require substantial grounds and a proper procedure, and if wrongfully applied, compensation to rights' holders. Generally, domestic courts have granted governments a fairly broad margin of appreciation in this regard. Italian Supreme Court case law, for example, supports the view that third party rights are not impinged upon by seizure of the proceeds of organized crime.[12] The freezing of the funds of Islamic charities to prevent terrorist financing has in contrast been subject to heavy scrutiny for rights compliance. In 2001, for example, Yassin Abdullah Kadi and the charity Al Barakaat were added to a list of individuals and organizations designated by the UN Security Council 1267 Sanctions Committee (established by Security Council Resolution 1267) as a result of which UN member states were obliged to freeze their funds. The EU did so through an EU Council regulation. In 2008, in *Yassin Abdullah Kadi and Al Barakaat International Foundation v Council of the European Union and Commission of the European Communities*,[13] the European Court of Justice annulled the regulation inter alia because it infringed their rights to be heard, to effective judicial review, and to property. The UN 1267 Sanctions Committee (and by extension the EU regulation) made no provision for a hearing or for transmission of the grounds on which the decision to designate individuals and organizations for this treatment was made.[14] The UN Security Council responded with a more robust review mechanism

---

[12] D Piva, 'Anti-Mafia Forfeiture in the Italian System' in C King and C Walker (eds), *Dirty Assets: Emerging Issues in the Regulation of Criminal and Terrorist Assets* (Farnham: Ashgate, 2014), 71, 81.

[13] Joined Cases C-402/05 P and C-415/05 P, 3 September 2008, European Court Reports 2008 I-06351.

[14] In *Aboufasin Abdelrazik v The Minister of Foreign Affairs and the AG of Canada* [2009] FC 580 the Canadian Federal Court followed suit holding Canada's domestic measures in violation of human rights. In *Mohammed Jabar Ahmed and ors v HM Treasury* [2010] UKSC 2 the UK Supreme Court quashed

allowing an independent ombudsperson to review the listing of individuals and recommend delisting if warranted.

19.4 Conviction-based Confiscation

19.4.1 General

Most national legal systems provide for the confiscation on conviction of instruments acquired legally but then used in a crime. The same approach has been adapted for use against the proceeds of crime, and most national laws permit confiscation, following conviction, of the proceeds of that crime (criminal confiscation, *in personam* confiscation[15]). A conviction-based confiscation proceeding usually involves a two-stage process. First, it depends upon criminal conviction of the holder of the property, and second, upon proof of a link between that property and the criminal activity for which the holder was convicted.

Early international provisions allowing for confiscation of property such as article 37 of the 1961 Single Convention on Narcotic Drugs were married to the principle that confiscatable property has to be derived by the offender from the offence for which he was convicted and thus all asset recovery systems based on these conventions were conviction-based systems, usually considered to be part of the sentencing process. Conviction-based confiscation demands a criminal standard of proof and follows a trial in which the accused is usually granted all the fair trial rights. Strong on principle, it is not particularly expedient. Attaining the criminal conviction and linking it to particular assets presents problems, particularly if the predicate offence occurs abroad or where the assets are owned by individuals living or companies domiciled in foreign states. It is also not available against the property of third parties not subject to that particular prosecution. The limitations of conviction-based confiscation were revealed in *R v Cuthbertson*,[16] where the House of Lords conceded with 'considerable regret' that section 27(1) of the Misuse of Drugs Act 1971 only permitted the instruments of crime to be forfeited, and not profits from drug trafficking.

19.4.2 Reversing the onus of proof

To remedy these shortcomings, article 5(7) of the 1988 Drug Trafficking Convention urges parties to 'consider ensuring that the onus of proof be reversed regarding the lawful origin of alleged proceeds or other property liable to confiscation, to the extent that such action is consistent with the principles of its domestic law and with the nature of the judicial and other proceedings'. Other suppression conventions also encourage

---

domestic measures for freezing accounts in compliance with the UN Security Council resolutions on the basis that they were *ultra vires* the enabling Act.

[15] It is *in personam* because it is based on the authority of the court over the person and thus by extension permits steps to be taken against his property.

[16] [1981] AC 470, 479.

the adoption of reverse onus provisions of this kind.[17] Reverse onus provisions are difficult to reconcile with the presumption of innocence protected in, for example, article 14(2) of the International Covenant on Civil and Political Rights and article 6(2) of the European Convention on Human Rights, particularly if the onus shifts to the owner or possessor of the property to show its licit origins without any burden on the state to show some objective grounds for suspicion that the property is of illicit origin.

19.4.3 Value confiscation

Supported by transnational criminal law, some states have gone further and broadened their confiscation powers from conviction-based confiscation of the actual proceeds of a specific crime to confiscation of property of equivalent value. Article 5(1)(a) of the 1988 Drug Trafficking Convention makes provision for confiscation of the proceeds of drug offences 'or property the value of which corresponds to that of such proceeds'. 'Value confiscation', as this variant is known, is *in personam* because it is directed against the particular convict's property although not necessarily against the proceeds of an identifiable crime. Although it does not have the symbolic impact of confiscation of the actual proceeds, it does mean that (i) efforts to hide the actual proceeds are irrelevant and (ii) property that is held legally can be confiscated without it being necessary to shift the onus of proof of origins onto the holder or any other claimant.

The notion that criminal 'benefit' rather than identifiable proceeds can be subject to confiscation (with the aid of a reverse onus provision), sometimes labelled extended confiscation, is now supported at a regional level in the EU by article 5 of the 2014 EU Directive on the Freezing and Confiscation of Instrumentalities and Proceeds of Crime in the European Union,[18] which reads:

> 1. Member States shall adopt the necessary measures to enable the confiscation, either in whole or in part, of property belonging to a person convicted of a criminal offence which is liable to give rise, directly or indirectly, to economic benefit, where a court, on the basis of the circumstances of the case, including the specific facts and available evidence, such as that the value of the property is disproportionate to the lawful income of the convicted person, is satisfied that the property in question is derived from criminal conduct.

States may take the step of enabling a court to make a finding deeming an individual to have a 'criminal lifestyle' thus allowing the court to presume that all property currently held or obtained during a specified period prior to proceedings was obtained as a result of criminal conduct, while any expenses during that period were also met by such property.[19]

---

[17] See, eg, article 3(4) of the 2005 Council of Europe Money Laundering Convention; FATF Recommendation 4.

[18] Directive 2014/42/EU, OJ L 127/39, 3 April 2014. See generally MJ Borgers, 'Confiscation of the Proceeds of Crime: the European Union Framework' in C King and C Walker (eds), *Dirty Assets: Emerging Issues in the Regulation of Criminal and Terrorist Assets* (Farnham: Ashgate, 2014), 27, 28 et seq.

[19] FATF, *Best Practices on Confiscation (Recommendations 4 and 38) and a Framework for Ongoing Work in Asset Recovery* (Paris: FATF/OECD, 2012), 8.

Extending confiscation through these legislative devices, however, appears problematic from the point of view of the presumption of innocence. In *Her Majesty's Advocate and Her Majesty's Advocate General for Scotland v Robert McIntosh*,[20] the prosecutor asked for an order for the confiscation of gifts given to McIntosh's partner, on the basis of McIntosh's conviction for a drug trafficking offence. On appeal to the Privy Council, McIntosh contended that section 3(2) of the Proceeds of Crime (Scotland) Act 1995 was incompatible with article 6(2) of the European Convention on Human Rights, the presumption of innocence of 'a person charged with an offence'. The Act provided that while the making of a confiscation order depended on a conviction for a drug trafficking offence, the sum confiscated did not have to be the profit made from the particular drug trafficking offence of which the accused had been convicted. It included the value of the proceeds of 'drug trafficking', which was defined in terms of section 3(2) to include any payments made to anyone in connection with the drug trafficking carried out by the convict. The Act also provided that property held by him or transferred to him six years before he was indicted was presumed to be such property. The Privy Council held that he was not a 'person charged with an offence' in terms of article 6(2) of the European Convention, inter alia, because in the confiscation process he was not being charged with an offence or being accused of a crime; he had already been convicted of an offence in another process. The application was part of the sentencing procedure and did not culminate in a verdict, and the sum confiscated was not the profit made in the offence. Thus the process involved no inquiry into the commission of drug trafficking offences although it relied on the person in question having first been convicted of a drug trafficking offence. The European Court of Human Rights gave its seal of approval to this interpretation in the leading case *Phillips v The United Kingdom*[21] that a criminal confiscation order based on an unrebutted presumption that assets were the results of a convict's drug trafficking activities (he owned cars, four houses, had £17,000 in the bank but had not worked for years) was not a violation of his fair trial rights under the European Charter. In the Court's view the value confiscation procedure provided for in sections 2, 4, and 5 of the Drug Trafficking Act 1994 (England and Wales)[22] was compatible with article 6(2) of the European Convention because it was part of the sentencing process, and did not involve a criminal charge but rather an assessment of the amount at which the confiscation order should be fixed, something analogous to determining a penalty on sentence.[23]

19.4.4 Third party confiscation

One method for criminals to avoid confiscation is to transfer the proceeds of crime or any property of value into the possession or ownership of third parties such as their partners. The potential abuse of third party possession of the proceeds of crime has

---

[20] [2001] UKPC D1.   [21] [2001] ECHR 437, (2002) 11 BHRC 280.
[22] See now the Proceeds of Crime Act 2002.   [23] Above n 21, para 34.

led to further extension of criminal confiscation through the introduction of a specific obligation in the 2014 EU Confiscation Directive[24] obliging EU member states to provide for the confiscation of the proceeds of crime (or equivalent value)

> transferred by a suspected or accused person to third parties or ... acquired by third parties from a suspected or accused person, at least if the third parties knew or ought to have known that the purpose of the transfer or acquisition was to avoid confiscation, on the basis of concrete facts and circumstances, including that the transfer or acquisition was carried out free of charge or in exchange for an amount significantly lower that the market value.

This provision for third party confiscation should not however 'prejudice the rights of bona fide third parties'.

19.5 Non-conviction-based Forfeiture

19.5.1 Pursuing 'guilty' property

Despite the more flexible procedures adopted, criminal confiscation still carries inherent disadvantages because it is dependent on the outcome of an expensive and lengthy criminal trial which may result in acquittal. The alternative, non-conviction-based forfeiture (*in rem* forfeiture, civil forfeiture, civil recovery) is an old remedy, used inter alia to confiscate pirate and slaving ships. It was reintroduced in its modern form in US law through the Racketeer Influenced and Corrupt Organizations Act (RICO)[25] and Continuing Criminal Enterprise (CCE) statutes.[26] Designed to be used in situations where there was evidence of criminality but the individual criminal could not be identified, the rationale for *in rem* forfeiture was originally that the thing itself committed the offence, although this has evolved to the more supportable notion that the 'instrumentality' (which can be property as diverse as money or the vehicle in which contraband is smuggled) of crime facilitates the commission of offences.[27] The much reduced burden of only having to prove that the property in question is more likely than not to be the proceeds of crime is not the only advantage to law enforcement. The state does not have to establish the criminal guilt of the holder of the property. Indeed, the holder of the property may be in another state, or dead, or may not even be a criminal. Even if the proceeds of crime are broken up and dispersed, the state can still proceed against any part of those proceeds within its jurisdiction so long as it is able to adduce evidence of the tainted nature of the particular part. There are, however, disadvantages in using this procedure. It cannot be used to forfeit property that is not tainted. In the English case of *Director of the Assets Recovery Agency v Green and others*,[28] for example, the court noted that in civil proceedings for a 'recovery order'

---

[24] Article 6.   [25] 18 USC §§ 1961–68.   [26] 21 USC § 848 et seq.
[27] SD Casella, 'Asset Forfeiture in the United States' in SNM Young (ed), *Civil Forfeiture of Criminal Property: Legal Measures for Targeting the Proceeds of Crime* (Cheltenham: Edward Elgar, 2009), 23, 27, 43. Hence the US practice of reporting the defendant as an object, eg *United States of America v $124,700 in U.S. Currency*, 05–3295 (8th Cir 2006).
[28] [2005] All ER (D) 261.

under section 241 of the Proceeds of Crime Act 2002 it was necessary to set out the various kinds of unlawful conduct by which the property was obtained, and insufficient to rely on the defendant not having an identifiable income to justify his lifestyle. It thus cannot be used for value confiscation, and it cannot be used to forfeit tainted property that has been mingled with other untainted property because the criminal proceeds cannot be identified. In these situations it is more practical to use value confiscation if available.

Non-conviction-based forfeiture is still relatively uncommon and thus the suppression conventions do not oblige parties to provide for it, although they do permit it. Article 12(1)(a) of the United Nations Convention against Transnational Organized Crime (UNTOC), for example, provides for a general obligation 'to the greatest extent possible' to confiscate the proceeds and property of crime,[29] and article 2(g) provides that confiscation 'includes forfeiture where applicable'. Advocates of non-conviction-based forfeiture as a law enforcement panacea do pressure parties, however, to take the option, particularly given the perceived failings of criminal confiscation legislation. FATF Recommendation 4 provides that '[c]ountries may consider adopting measures that allow such proceeds or instrumentalities to be confiscated without requiring a criminal conviction'. Non-conviction-based recovery of assets is of particular importance in corruption cases, and article 53(a) of the UNCAC obliges parties to allow other parties to initiate 'civil action' in its courts to establish title to or ownership of property acquired through corruption offences.

19.5.2 Using civil process

Non-conviction-based forfeiture has been criticized for achieving penal goals while dispensing with procedural safeguards.[30] This is particularly apparent in resort to the civil process. Applied first to the proceeds of drug trafficking and then generally to other offences, the introduction of *in rem* forfeiture ushered in what Leacock aptly terms the 'civilizing' of confiscation[31] because it avoids the strictures of criminal law to reach property under the control of the organizers of criminal activity using civil procedures.[32] In non-conviction-based forfeiture, the state proceeds as plaintiff against the thing itself in a civil court in order to claim title. Those individuals with an interest in the property line up to object. The property must be shown on the civil standard of a balance of probability to be 'tainted', meaning suspected on reasonable grounds of being derived in whole or part from significant criminal activity.[33] A form of restitution, non-conviction-based forfeiture is claimed not to be a punishment although

---

[29] See also article 31(1) of the UNCAC.

[30] SNM Young, 'Introduction' in SNM Young (ed), *Civil Forfeiture of Criminal Property: Legal Measures for Targeting the Proceeds of Crime* (Cheltenham: Edward Elgar, 2009), 1, 4.

[31] CC Leacock QC, 'Internationalization of Crime' 34 *New York University Journal of International Law and Politics* (2001–02) 263, 266.

[32] *M v D* [1998] 3 Irish Reports 175 (High Court), 178.

[33] See, eg, sections 24 and 5 of New Zealand's Criminal Proceeds (Recovery) Act, 2009. In terms of section 6 'significant' criminal activity is activity carrying a penalty of more than five years' imprisonment or valued at NZ$30,000 or more.

it does have deterrent and preventive (in the sense of restricting the (re)financing of crime) rationales.[34]

Characterization as a civil process permits avoidance of criminal due process guarantees. National courts have generally rejected defence arguments that non-conviction-based forfeiture is a disguised criminal process to which these due process guarantees should apply. In *Chatterjee v Attorney General of Ontario*[35] the Canadian Supreme Court's answer to the appellant's argument that civil forfeiture is criminal because it adds to the particular criminal penalties imposed was that while forfeiture does make an incidental intrusion into the field of criminal law, it enables recovery of proceeds of crime rather than conviction, thus its dominant feature is that it involves property rights. The European Court of Human Rights considers non-conviction-based asset forfeiture as a preventive measure intended to take criminal proceeds out of circulation[36] and not as a criminal procedure under article 6 of the European Convention.[37] This conclusion is based on the fact that no one is charged with a new 'criminal offence', the procedure does not require proof of *mens rea*, and it does not involve criminal courts.[38] The US Supreme Court takes a more nuanced view that forfeiture can be purely remedial or both remedial and punitive, depending on the particular legislative purpose in the particular case.[39]

19.5.3 Forfeiture versus property rights

Another area of concern (relevant to both civil and criminal confiscation) has been the protection of the property rights of innocent third parties who have taken possession or ownership of tainted property. The suppression conventions build in limited safeguards to prevent abuse of the rights of innocent third parties in (what they think is) lawful possession of such property. Article 12(8) of the UNTOC provides generally that the provisions of article 12 which deals with asset recovery 'shall not be construed to prejudice the rights of bona fide third parties',[40] but leaves the parties to decide what this amounts to. More specifically, article 12(7) recommends that parties consider permitting an 'innocent owner' defence. This defence, derived from US law[41] but applied in some other parties,[42] provides only a partial safeguard of third-party rights because it shifts the onus onto the owner to prove that they did not know of the conduct giving rise to the forfeiture, or if they did know that they

---

[34] J Simser, 'Perspectives on Civil Forfeiture' in SNM Young (ed), *Civil Forfeiture of Criminal Property: Legal Measures for Targeting the Proceeds of Crime* (Cheltenham: Edward Elgar, 2009), 13.

[35] [2009] SCC 19, [2009] 1 SCR 624, paras 29–54.

[36] See *Butler v United Kingdom*, ECtHR, Application No 41661/98 (27 June 2002); *M v Italy* ECtHR Application No 12386/86 (15 April 1991).

[37] *Air Canada v United Kingdom* (1995) 20 EHRR 150.

[38] *AGOSI v United Kingdom* (1987) 9 EHRR 1, 62.

[39] *Austin v the United States* 509 US 602 (1993). See SD Cassella, *Asset Forfeiture Law in the United States*, 2nd edn) (Huntington, NY: JurisNet, 2007), 59.

[40] See also article 5(8) of the 1988 Drug Trafficking Convention; article 31(9) of the UNCAC.

[41] 18 USC § 983(d).

[42] See, eg, section 52 of South Africa's Prevention of Organised Crime Act 1998.

did all they reasonably could to terminate the use of those assets for that purpose. In practice third parties may still find it very difficult to prove this innocence. Article 5 of the 2005 Council of Europe Money Laundering Convention expands protections obliging parties to provide effective legal remedies for such third parties in order to preserve their procedural rights such as the right to be informed of the procedure, in addition to the right to challenge it in court.[43] Greater protection is provided by the EU-wide safeguards spelled out in article 8 of the EU's 2014 Confiscation Directive. It provides that all interested parties should have a right to be informed of freezing and possible confiscation, the reasons for doing so and of all their attendant rights, a right to be heard, a right to challenge the confiscation order when already in force in cases where they had no earlier opportunity to take legal action, a right to legal assistance and to present testimony and other evidence, and a right to review of the order by a higher court, and a right to immediate return of the property if not confiscated.

The courts have been wary of allowing property rights to frustrate the removal of tainted property. The European Court of Human Rights held, for example, in *Raimondo v Italy*[44] that preventive confiscation of a suspected Mafiosi's property was not a violation of the right to the peaceful enjoyment of their possession because it was designed in the public interest to block movements of suspect capital in an attempt to combat the organization. In similar vein the English courts justify non-conviction-based forfeiture as a proportional response that serves an overriding public interest.[45] In *Phillips* the European Court held that any interference with the right of peaceful enjoyment of possession under article 1 of the First Protocol of the European Convention on Human Rights was justified and not disproportionate.[46] Although states have a broad discretionary power to interfere with property in the suppression of crime[47] that power is not unlimited.[48] In South Africa, for example, the courts have insisted that the severity of the interference with property rights must be proportionate to the goal of forfeiture to suppress organized criminal activity.[49] Certain states have taken legislative steps to ameliorate the impact of non-conviction-based asset recovery. In England and Wales, for example, in exercising its discretion to make a recovery order, a court must take into account considerations relating to justice and equity and respect for human rights.[50]

---

[43] G Stessens, *Money Laundering: A New International Law Enforcement Model* (Cambridge: CUP, 2000), 77.

[44] 1994 ECHR 3, (1994) 18 EHRR 237.

[45] See, eg, *R v Benjafield* [2002] 1 All ER 815, where Lord Steyn called the procedure 'a fair and proportionate response to the need to protect the public interest'.

[46] Above n 21.

[47] P Aldridge, *Money Laundering Law: Forfeiture, Confiscation, Civil Recovery, Criminal Laundering and Taxation of the Proceeds of Crime* (Oxford: Hart, 2003), 115.

[48] *Lindsay v HM Customs and Excise Commissioners* [2002] EWCA Civ 267; [2002] 3 All ER 118.

[49] *Prophet v NDPP* 2006 (1) SA 38 (SCA); *Mohunram and Another v National Director of Public Prosecutions* [2007] ZACC 4 (26 March 2007).

[50] Sections 266(3)(a) and (b) of the Proceeds of Crime Act 2002.

19.5.4 International reluctance

In spite of these safeguards, states are wary of the procedure, perhaps for political rather than human rights reasons. In 2010, for example, a Bill providing for civil forfeiture was defeated in the Nigerian House of Representatives and despite subsequent Proceeds of Crime Bills being passed in the Nigerian Senate and recommendations from the Intergovernmental Action Group against Money Laundering in West Africa, Nigeria still does not have a civil forfeiture regime.[51] One way of controlling the use of non-conviction-based assets recovery is to limit authority to use it to a specialist agency. In Ireland, for example, the Criminal Assets Bureau, which is independent of the police, is able to use forfeiture while the Director of Public Prosecutions only has criminal confiscation at their disposal.[52]

19.6 Transnational Asset Recovery

19.6.1 Domestic platform

Provision for asset recovery at a national level leaves criminals with the option of removing (usually quite rapidly) their property from that particular jurisdiction in order to frustrate domestic seizure or confiscation orders directed at that property. If the illicit proceeds of a crime committed in one state are located in another, then two things are critical. First, the state seeking the money must have the powers to pursue it overseas. Kenya's asset recovery powers under section 7(1)(h) of Kenya's Anti-Corruption and Economic Crimes Act 2003, for example, give Kenyan authorities the power to institute civil proceedings against any person for the recovery of lost public property or for compensation, and to recover such property or enforce an order for compensation even if the property or the assets that could be used to satisfy the order may be outside Kenya. Second, states must establish extraterritorial jurisdiction over tainted assets in order to use domestically issued court orders to retrieve them from abroad.[53] The extent to which the ordinary principles of jurisdiction (discussed in Chapter 16) are applied to asset recovery measures depends on the specific practice of the state concerned. However, importantly, in order to enforce that jurisdiction states have to seek cooperation from other states in the asset recovery process; without it asset recovery is impossible. States have made provision for the enforceability of domestic orders abroad. In England and Wales, for example, when assets are located overseas, section 247 of the Proceeds of Crime Act 2002 permits the court to make an Interim Receiving Order. International cooperation in the asset recovery process can work. In taking down the 'Megaconspiracy' run by alleged Internet Pirate Kim

---

[51] CC Nwabuzor, 'Codifying Civil Asset Forfeiture in Nigeria', Nigerian Institute for Advanced Legal Studies' 2016, available at NIALS, <http://www.nials.edu.ng/index.php?option=com_content&view=article&id=219:codifying-civil-asset-forfeiture-in-nigeria&catid=15&Itemid=141> last visited 2 March 2017.

[52] See the Proceeds of Crime Act 1996 as amended in 2012 and 2016; Criminal Assets Bureau Act 1996 as amended in 2005 and 2013.

[53] See, eg, 28 USC § 1355(b)(2) which gives US Federal prosecutors the power to seek to enforce domestic restraint and confiscation orders over the proceeds and instrumentalities of illegal activities located in foreign states.

Dotcom, US$60 million was seized in Hong Kong and New Zealand as a result of requests made by US authorities.[54]

19.6.2 Making contact and seeking assistance

How does international cooperation to use these orders work? In its initial phases it will depend largely on the kind of informal direct communication using existing law enforcement networks described in Chapter 17 to locate the assets, before an official letter of request is actually sent.[55] At that point the general provisions for mutual legal assistance discussed in Chapter 18 are important in cooperation in both the interim and final measures of the asset recovery process. In the Lesotho Highlands Development project cases, for example, the Lesotho Government's application in 1997 to a Swiss Court for disclosure of a number of bank accounts in Switzerland, including accounts with the Union Bank of Switzerland (UBS), was resisted by a number of global companies that had contracted with the Lesotho Highlands Water Project. However, Switzerland made changes to its bank secrecy laws in 1997, and in 1999 the bank records were handed over, which provided the critical evidence necessary for the prosecution of companies and individuals who had engaged in giving and taking bribes.[56]

19.6.3 International platforms for asset recovery

The specific nature of the seizure and confiscation of illicit assets at the request of another state demands specific forms of international cooperation in pursuit of this property. The suppression conventions provide for obligations to cooperate in the investigation stage by providing information on bank accounts and banking transactions in order to make it possible to take provisional measures such as freezing or seizure.[57] When more formal assistance is necessary, in terms of article 8 of the 1986 European Convention on Offences Relating to Cultural Property,[58] for example, the parties agreed to execute letters rogatory for the purpose of procuring evidence about cultural property and in order to seize and restore cultural property removed from the requesting party's territory as a result of an offence. Article 51 of the UNCAC also points to the need for specific measures when it makes the return of assets a fundamental principle of the Convention and obliges the parties to afford one another the widest measure of cooperation and assistance in this regard.

---

[54] *Congressional Report Federal Bureau of Investigation: Pro IP Act Annual Report 2012*, available on the US Department of Justice website, 3, at <http://www.justice.gov/dag/iptaskforce/proipact/fbi-pro-ip-rpt2012.pdf> last visited 7 January 2017.

[55] See FATF, above n 19, 2. See also C Monteith and PG Pereira, 'Asset Recovery' in N Boister and R Currie (eds), *The Routledge Handbook of Transnational Criminal Law* (Abingdon: Routledge, 2015), 137, 146 et seq for a discussion of investigation strategy.

[56] *Rex v Masupha Ephraim Sole*, 20 May 2002, CRI/T/111/97.

[57] See, eg, articles 15–45 of the 2005 Council of Europe Money Laundering Convention.

[58] 23 June 1985, (1986) 25 ILM 44.

19.6.4 Interim legal measures in the requested state

Two options are available to states when they seek interim measures such as seizing or freezing the property in question. For example, article 5(4)(b) of the 1988 Drug Trafficking Convention is an obligation to provide for interim measures on the application of another party, which may be carried out by enforcing an order made by another state or granting an entirely new order at the behest of the other state. Taking these steps is also an obligation under article 54(2) of the UNCAC, for example, but the UNCAC insists that there be a 'reasonable basis' for doing so—that is some objective evidence. An issue which again depends on national law is whether the courts in the requested state are able to freeze an individual's assets on the basis of a foreign law enforcement official's allegation that they are subject to an investigation or whether a foreign court order must first be made. In *US v Opportunity Fund*,[59] dealing with a request made to freeze assets by Brazil in terms of its mutual legal assistance treaty (MLAT) with the US, the US Court of Appeals for the DC Circuit held that the relevant US law[60] only granted federal courts jurisdiction to issue temporary restraining orders to 'preserve the availability of property subject to a foreign forfeiture or confiscation judgment', implying the foreign court had to have made the order before it would be enforced in the US. It rejected arguments made by the US government that if it were not able to restrain assets before a foreign forfeiture order was made it would not be meeting its obligations under the 1988 Drug Trafficking Convention in favour of the property rights of individuals including US citizens that may be subject to such an order.

19.6.5 Final legal measures in the requested state

The same two options are available for finalizing recovery of the assets: either enforcing the foreign confiscation/forfeiture order or granting one *de novo*. The state where the assets are located must thus be legally able and prepared either to grant confiscation orders at the request of another state or enforce the requesting state's orders.[61] By the mid-1980s various states had responded by making legislative provision for international cooperation in regard to confiscation. For example, the UK's Drug Trafficking Offences Act 1986 allowed the courts to register, upon application by a designated country, a confiscation order made in another state. The first measure of support in a suppression convention for this approach was article 5(4)(a) of the 1988 Drug Trafficking Convention, which obliges a party either to submit the confiscation request of the other party to its own authorities or recognize the confiscation order made by the requesting party's authorities. Article 13(1) of the UNTOC also envisages either resubmission of the confiscation request or direct enforcement.

From the point of view of law enforcement efficiency the enforcement of the foreign order is preferable to reapplying for the order from the requested party's authorities because it avoids duplication of procedures and a waste of time and money.

---

[59] Case No 09-5065 (DC Circ 16 July 2010), 12.   [60] 28 USC § 2467(d)(3).
[61] Stessens above n 43, 385.

Exequatur proceedings of this kind (proceedings relating to the enforcement of a foreign court order) do not decide anew the merits of the foreign court's decision, they simply examine whether the conditions for granting of execution have been met. They examine whether the requesting state has provided a legal basis for asset recovery and whether one of its courts has authorized the request based on some evidence, before the requested state's judicial authorities will endorse the request. They do, however, involve the enforcement of foreign penal judgments and therefore require trust in the requesting party's system. They do not, however, provide an opportunity for the requested party to re-examine the link between asset and crime. Unsurprisingly, article 13(1) of the UNTOC affords a party the discretion to adopt this approach 'to the greatest extent possible within its domestic legal system'. Some parties have, nevertheless, followed the UK's early lead. Section 28 of Hong Kong's Mutual Legal Assistance in Criminal Matters Ordinance (Cap 525) 1997, for example, allows the registration of foreign confiscation orders.

19.6.6 General conditions and grounds for refusal of assistance

The requested party is in the more powerful position in the transnational asset recovery process as international cooperation is generally subject to its law[62] and the general grounds for refusing legal assistance may also be relied on to refuse to provide legal assistance in such cases.[63] States may insist on double criminality, for example. Ontario's Civil Remedies Act 2001 provides that actions against 'unlawful property' defined in terms of section 2 include 'an offence under an Act of a jurisdiction outside Canada, if a similar act or omission would be an offence under an Act of Canada or Ontario if it were committed in Ontario'.[64] In the recent Jamaican case of *Assets Recovery Agency v Barnes et al*,[65] which involved a without notice application by Jamaica's Assets Recovery Agency (ARA) to restrain property in Jamaica alleged to be the benefit of drug trafficking-related crimes committed in Canada by the respondents, the court made it clear that simply alleging that a Canadian drug trafficking offence had taken place was not enough to meet double criminality requirements under Jamaica's Proceeds of Crime Act 2007; an outline of the conduct alleged in Canada had to be made available to the court to decide whether the conduct was criminal in Jamaica. Moreover, there had to be evidence sufficient to substantiate the theory that criminal conduct had occurred in Canada to enable the court to decide whether the ARA had reasonable cause to believe the respondent's property in Jamaica was criminal proceeds. Simply making allegations that a respondent was an associate of a convicted drug trafficker was not enough.

The general view that double criminality is inapt for legal assistance is, however, also applied to asset recovery. Increasingly suppression conventions make provision for watering double criminality down in this context. For example, article 9(2) of the OECD Anti-Bribery Convention is to the effect that if parties insist upon double

---

[62] Article 13(4) of the UNTOC.   [63] Article 7(15) of 1988 Drug Trafficking Convention.
[64] See also section 9(4)5.b of Canada's Mutual Legal Assistance in Criminal Matters Act 1985.
[65] [2015] MSC Civ 163.

criminality it shall be deemed to exist if the offence is within the scope of the convention, and not by implication in the domestic law of the requested state (which may not have got around to enacting the offence). Article 43(2) of the UNCAC effectively obliges parties that require double criminality to accept that it has been met when 'the conduct underlying the offence for which assistance is sought is a criminal offence under the laws of both States Parties' (ie double criminality *in abstracto*).

19.6.7 International cooperation in non-conviction-based forfeiture

International cooperation in regard to non-conviction-based forfeiture orders has specific advantages. The irrelevancy of an accusation of criminality does not raise any requirement of double criminality. Recovery is not prevented by the death of the criminal. It is also straightforward to establish jurisdiction over the proceeds of crime if the proceeds have passed through that state's territory (even in situations where the predicate offences occurred elsewhere). But there are disadvantages. Many states do not recognize the procedure and thus will not enforce a foreign request to enforce it. Certain states that do recognize the procedure, such as Canada, will not permit the enforcement of foreign orders obtained by civil process.[66] MLATs limited to assistance in criminal rather than civil proceedings are useless. Most suppression conventions do not require parties to cooperate in the provision of civil forfeiture. The 2012 FATF Recommendation 38, however, emphasizes that the authority to provide assistance in response to requests by other countries 'should include being able to respond to requests made on the basis of non-conviction-based confiscation proceedings and related provisional measures, unless this is inconsistent with fundamental principles of their domestic law'. Article 23(5) of the 2005 Council of Europe Money Laundering Convention explicitly requires mandatory cooperation between states on civil recovery.

19.6.8 Practical difficulties in transnational asset recovery

A range of practical difficulties will need to be overcome to pursue assets in multiple jurisdictions. The property will have to be identified, which usually means an evaluation of the amount of money involved. Customer due diligence reporting obligations may provide some assistance in this regard. Specialist investigators and forensic accountants may reveal more, although they are expensive. Lawyers will have to be retained to work in the foreign jurisdiction in order to meet its procedural requirements for assistance. A decision will have to be made whether to proceed civilly or, if possible, criminally. It also takes time, particularly the recovery of assets stolen through corruption. For example, although the Philippines made its first request to Switzerland to freeze former President Ferdinand Marcos' bank accounts in 1986, it took more than ten years before the Swiss courts ordered that the money could be

---

[66] J McKeachie and J Simser, 'Civil Asset Forfeiture in Canada' in SNM Young (ed), *Civil Forfeiture of Criminal Property: Legal Measures for Targeting the Proceeds of Crime* (Cheltenham: Edward Elgar, 2009), 157, 165.

returned without a final conviction of Mr Marcos under article 74(a) of Switzerland's Federal International Mutual Assistance Act 1981.[67] There are no guarantees of success, although assistance is available for recovery of corruptly acquired assets from institutions such as the World Bank's Stolen Asset Recovery (StAR) initiative, which enhances the capacity of developing states to engage in asset recovery within the framework of the UNCAC.[68] Finally, the reluctance of states where the money is located will have to be overcome. UNCAC reviews reveal that developing states take the treaty obligations to cooperate in regard to asset recovery more seriously than developed states, which place a premium on discretion when responding to a mutual assistance request in this regard.[69]

19.6.9 Protecting human rights in transnational asset recovery

One of the issues largely neglected by transnational criminal law is the rights of property holders in the transnational asset recovery process. In some jurisdictions it is clear that the process of cooperation and in particular the legal position in the requesting state can be subject to a human rights assessment. *Saccoccia v Austria*[70] dealt with an Austrian court's authorization of the seizure of appellant's assets held in Vienna as a result of letters rogatory sent by the US District Court in Rhode Island. The appellant (later convicted in the US of laundering more than US$100 million) alleged the Austrian action in the European Court of Human Rights was a violation of article 6 of the European Convention's right to a fair trial, based on the Austrian court's failure to sufficiently consider deficiencies in the US criminal and confiscation proceedings. Among the deficiencies alleged was that the assets forfeited in Austria included substitute assets (ie not derived directly from criminal activity) and the fact that money laundering was not then a crime in Austria, failing double criminality. The Austrian Courts had dismissed these arguments finding inter alia there would good reasons to believe given he had transferred more than US$136 million from a sham company in the US to various foreign bank accounts for a ten per cent cut, that the money in Austria was received for or derived from the commission of a crime subject to withdrawal of enrichment. His challenge failed because the European Court found that the Austrian authorities had duly satisfied themselves that the decision at issue was not the result of a flagrant denial of justice and that he had had a fair trial in the US law. On the one hand, the European Court was willing to review the Austrian court's assessment the US process was not a flagrant denial of justice, thus opening the way to similar arguments. On the other, the case also shows that defendants' arguments that the process of cooperation does not provide protection of human rights are not likely

[67] See World Bank and UNODC, *Stolen Asset Recovery (StAR) Initiative: Challenges, Opportunities, and Action Plan* (Washington, DC: World Bank, 2007), 5, available at <https://www.unodc.org/pdf/Star_Report.pdf> last visited 2 April 2017.
[68] ibid.
[69] D Vlassis, 'International Economic Crime and Combating Corruption—Challenges and Responses', Conference of the International Society for the Reform of Criminal Law and the International Centre for Criminal Law Reform and Criminal Justice Policy, 'Globalization of Crime—Criminal Justice Responses', 7–11 August 2011, National Arts Centre, Ottawa, Canada.
[70] [2008] ECHR 1734, [2010] 50 EHRR 11. See also *Duboc v Austria* [2012] ECHR 1041 (5 June 2012).

to succeed due to the wide margin of appreciation granted to states in this process of cooperation.

One particular way in which a trial state seeking extradition of an individual can limit that individual's access to justice in a foreign state is to request the freezing and seizing of any funds which they might spend on legal defence. For example, it was argued on appeal in *United States v Batato*[71] that civil forfeiture orders made in the US under the Fugitive Disentitlement Act[72] would result if enforced in New Zealand in a breach of US obligations under international law, in particular the obligation under article 16 of the UNTOC, to which both states are party, to provide a 'guarantee of fair treatment at all stages of the proceedings including enjoyment of all the rights and guarantees provided by the domestic law of the State Party in the territory of which the person is present'. The claimants argued that it would do so because it would deny them the funds necessary to defend themselves from extradition in New Zealand. The Federal District Court's response[73] was implicitly approved by the Court of Appeal for the Fourth Circuit: 'That the exercise of their rights in New Zealand may cause disadvantages for the claimants with respect to litigation occurring in America does not mean they are being treated unfairly or that they are denied their enjoyment of rights in New Zealand.' The doctrine of 'fugitive disentitlement' prevents persons avoiding criminal prosecution in the US from being able to seek the assistance of US courts to pursue a claim in a civil forfeiture action. Moreover, US authorities will not provide foreign authorities who order the release of frozen funds for legal expenses with assurances that they will not pursue those funds or prosecute individuals such as lawyers in receipt of funds in the US.

19.7 Dispersal of Recovered Assets

Certain transnational crimes have an identifiable victim to whom confiscated proceeds should be restored.[74] In others, such as corruption, a victim may not be identifiable and there is a case for restoring confiscated proceeds to society as a whole. The suppression conventions usually do not dictate what parties should do with confiscated property. Article 14(1) of the UNTOC, for example, leaves disposal to the parties' domestic laws and administrative procedures. Once confiscated most assets are transferred to the general government account to be dispersed as the government sees fit.[75] In certain states recovered assets may be shared with the particular enforcement agency that engineered their confiscation.[76] The danger in doing so is that it may foster the progressively increasing dependence of government agencies on criminally generated funds, which may lead to pressure to increase confiscations with a potential

---

[71] 833 F 3d 413 (4th Circ 2016).   [72] 28 USC § 2.

[73] *All Assets Listed in Attachment A*, 89 F Supp 3d at 833.

[74] See, eg, the provisions under sections 462.41 and 490.4(3) of the Canadian Criminal Code to restore the property to 'lawful' owners or possessors.

[75] Section 460 of the UK's Proceeds of Crime Act, eg.

[76] See, eg, 21 USC § 881(e)(3), which mandates such sharing between federal, state, and local police forces in the US.

for executive abuse.[77] To counter this potential, in Australia, for example, confiscated funds are placed in the Confiscated Assets Account, a trust separate from either the judicial or executive branches, out of which funds are paid to benefit both law enforcement and to fund crime-related social projects.[78]

The situation is more difficult when other states have an interest in the property. A state that confiscates this property at its own initiative, will usually keep it. However, when property is confiscated at the behest of another, the requesting state may have a better claim in the sense that the criminal proceeds were generated in a way that harmed it or its inhabitants, while the requested state still has the concrete advantage of having the confiscated assets in its custody. Generally, the suppression conventions avoid imposing an obligation on requested parties to give up the recovered assets. Article 14(2) of the UNTOC, for example, only asks the requested party to consider giving priority to the requesting party so that it can compensate victims or return property to its legitimate owners. Article 14(3) of the UNTOC asks parties to give special consideration to (a) donating the assets to a special account for providing technical assistance to developing states and states in transition, and to intergovernmental bodies specializing in the fight against organized crime (the UNODC, Interpol, FATF); and (b) sharing with other parties on a regular or case-by-case basis. In the EU a more prescriptive scheme has been adopted, where states share on a 50–50 basis unless the amount is below €10,000 in which case the executing state takes the lot.[79]

The obligation to return assets to the requesting state is firmer at an international level in regard to returning a state's assets that have been embezzled by a corrupt former leader. Article 57(3)(a) of the UNCAC requires parties to return embezzled or laundered public property to the requesting party to which it belongs. Where, however, the property does not belong to the requesting party but was paid to the individual in acts of corruption, article 57(3)(b) of the UNCAC provides that the property must be returned to the requesting state if the latter can reasonably establish its prior ownership or where the requested party recognizes damages to the requesting party as a basis for returning the property. In all other cases, article 57(3)(c) provides that the requested party must prioritize the return of the property to the requesting party, or to its prior legal owners, or to compensate the victims of the crime.

Parties may still be reluctant to return such property out of a concern about where it will end up. Such concerns are not without foundation. Assets stolen by former Prime Minister Fujimori and returned to Peru were, for example, poorly used by Peruvian police interests to pay outstanding debts to police officers.[80] Article 57(5) of the UNCAC thus provides that parties may enter mutually acceptable arrangements for the disposal of confiscated property. Using such an approach Switzerland relied on the World Bank (which engaged Nigerian civil society) to monitor the agreed use of

---

[77] See E Blumenson and ES Nilsen, 'Policing for Profit: The Drug War's Hidden Economic Agenda' 65 *University of Chicago Law Review* (1998) 35, 51.

[78] Section 295 of the Proceeds of Crime Act 2002.

[79] Article 16(1)(a) of the Council Framework Decision 2006/783/JHA of 6 October 2006 on the application of the principle of mutual recognition to confiscation orders, OJ/L 328/59.

[80] StAR Report above n 67, 56.

funds stolen by former Nigerian President Sani Abacha released to Nigeria for development projects.[81] Under the UNCAC, parties that do release assets in full to requesting states are entitled to deduct costs.[82]

19.8 Legitimacy and Effectiveness

Asset recovery through conviction- or non-conviction-based confiscation or forfeiture has become an important tool in the arsenal of transnational law enforcement agencies, but its use endangers human rights. In his dissenting judgment in the *Air Canada Case* Martens J pointed to the risks to human rights of the inclination of governments to penalize without appearing to do so indicated by 'the wave of legislation for depriving criminals of the proceeds of their crimes'.[83] A significant amount of institutional development has, for example, accompanied the growth in asset recovery legislation. In the EU, the EU Council Directive on Asset Recovery Offices obliges member states to set up asset recovery offices.[84] Some of these offices, such as the Irish Criminal Assets Bureau, are considered successful; others, such as the English Assets Recovery Agency, have been disbanded for delivering too little at too much cost.[85] It is open to question whether effectiveness can be measured in terms of amounts confiscated. While huge amounts of money and property have been forfeited annually in the US, making the police richer because they tend to benefit directly, there is little evidence that the incidence of predicate offences such as drug supply has decreased as a result.[86] This may be because so little of the actual proceeds of these crimes are being recovered.[87] Research in the UK suggests that the courts do not routinely grant confiscation orders 'but when they do the orders tend to be of low value' and doing so tends to serve the goal of retribution rather than restoration.[88] Comparative global data is simply absent.

---

[81] ibid, 19.   [82] Article 57(4).   [83] *Air Canada v United Kingdom* (1995) 20 EHRR 150.
[84] Council Decision 2007/845/JHA of 6 December 2007 concerning cooperation between Asset Recovery Offices of the Member States in the field of tracing and identification of proceeds from, or other property related to, crime, OJ L 332/103.
[85] See respectively FJ McKenna and K Egan, 'Ireland: A Multi-Disciplinary Approach' in SNM Young (ed), *Civil Forfeiture of Criminal Property: Legal Measures for Targeting the Proceeds of Crime* (Cheltenham: Edward Elgar, 2009), 52, 85, and S Dayman, 'Is the Patient Expected to Live? UK Civil Forfeiture in Operation' in ibid, at 22.
[86] Levi and Reuter, above n 1, 325.   [87] Europol, above n 3, 5.
[88] K Bullock and S Lister, 'Post-Conviction Confiscation of Assets in England and Wales: Rhetoric and Reality' in C King and C Walker (eds), *Dirty Assets: Emerging Issues in the Regulation of Criminal and Terrorist Assets* (Farnham: Ashgate, 2014), 47, 65.

20

Extradition of Transnational Criminals

20.1 Introduction

Criminals have long fled across borders to escape justice, or used borders as shields for the commission of crime in other states. In a letter written in August 1876 by Canada's Minister of Justice, Edward Blake, to the British Colonial Secretary, the Earl of Carnarvon, Blake referred to the deplorable state of extradition relations between Canada and the US as the 'carnival of crime' on the border.[1] Extradition is key to stopping the carnival. In 2000 Australian Justice Michael Kirby commented that '[i]n a world of increased mobility, interactive technology and new forms of criminality, extradition represents an essential response to the characteristics of contemporary crime'.[2]

Extradition allows states lawfully to acquire custody of alleged criminals located in other states in order to exercise an already established criminal jurisdiction. An exception to the right to asylum, it is grounded in the alleged harm caused by the fugitive.[3] The modern reciprocal process appears to have evolved out of the restitution or *remittere* of nationals in ancient times, which rested on coercion, and applied to common and political offences.[4] The modern era of extradition was proclaimed by Villefort as dependent upon 'moral solidarity' among 'diverse modern nations'.[5] Grotius considered that all nations had a 'natural right and duty' to extradite or prosecute.[6] Today, however, the positivist conception that extradition is an imperfect obligation requiring agreement to perfect it, dominates.[7]

The extradition process is initiated by a request from law enforcement authorities in the requesting state directed to authorities in the requested state for the extradition of a specified individual for the purpose of prosecution or for enforcing a sentence.[8] While the procedure differs from state to state, the request can be made through the diplomatic channel, or more directly, depending on the strength of relations between states. A court in the requested state typically reviews the request, deciding whether it meets the conditions for extradition or not. Because recognition is based on comity

---

[1] The Sessional Papers, Volume 7, Fourth Session of the Third Parliament, Dominion of Canada, Session of 1877, 425.

[2] *Foster v Minister for Customs and Justice* (2000) 200 CLR 442, 474.

[3] I Stanbrook and C Stanbrook, *Extradition Law and Practice*, 2nd edn (Oxford: OUP, 2000), 4.

[4] C Blakesly, 'The Practice of Extradition from Antiquity to Modern France and the United States: A Brief History' 4 *Boston College International and Comparative Law Review* (1981) 39, 40.

[5] M Villefort, *Des Traités d'Extradition de la France avec les Pays Estrangers* (1851) 5, cited in Blakesly, above n 4, 44.

[6] H Grotius, *II De Jure Belli Ac Pacis Libri Tres* (F Kelsey trans) (1925), 526–29.

[7] S Pufendorf, *The Elements of Universal Jurisprudence* (1672; Oldfather trans 1931), c 3, paras 23–24, cited by Blakesly, above n 4, 53.

[8] See, eg, section 1 of the UN Model Law on Extradition (Vienna: UNODC, 2004).

(respect),[9] this judicial examination does not normally entail close scrutiny of the merits of the case. If the court accepts that extradition can take place, because the matter falls within inter-state relations, the executive then exercises a residual discretion as to whether to confirm or deny extradition, balancing the protection of the liberty of the individual subject to the process against the demands of international cooperation between states. It is common for states to check informally beforehand whether a request is likely to be positively received, so as to avoid making pointless formal requests.

Extradition is a difficult transnational process as it requires accommodation between different kinds of legal systems. Common law states, which do not extradite mere suspects, are, for example, often faced with extradition requests from civil law states where no decision has yet been made to try the individual because that decision awaits their appearance in the requesting state. English courts have adopted a cosmopolitan approach accepting that extradition can take place when trial is not inevitable, so long as the foreign authorities take a step in commencing procedures against the individual with the ultimate purpose of trial.[10] Nevertheless, for many civil law states this is too much if it forces the prosecution to show its hand. Canadian law is more accommodating. While it requires common law states to provide enough evidence to justify prosecution, civil law states need only provide evidence gathered pursuant to their laws.[11] On the other hand civil law states have struggled with the extradition of their nationals. Colombia, for example, was put under pressure in the 1970s to extradite its nationals implicated in drug trafficking (the so-called extraditables) to the US, but after a series of court decisions permitting then prohibiting extradition only amended its constitution in 1997 to permit the extradition of nationals.[12]

In the face of these legal conflicts, it might be thought that universal jurisdiction by the requested state would be the answer. However, key proponents of transnational criminal law such as the US, pursue a de facto policy of universal extradition. For practical reasons (the presence of witnesses and evidence) and on retributive and deterrent grounds, they believe that prosecution before a court where the offence occurred/impacted is preferable. Some international organizations have adopted the same position. The Financial Action Task Force, for example, recommends that countries act 'constructively' towards extradition.[13]

Sovereign interests in extradition must also be balanced with the liberty interests of the individuals concerned. Beccaria noted in 1764:

> But, whether international agreements for the reciprocal exchange of criminals be useful, I would not dare to decide until laws more in conformity with the needs of humanity, until milder punishments and an end to dependence on arbitrary power and opinion have provided security for oppressed innocence and hated virtue—until universal reason, which ever tends to unite the interests of throne and subjects, has confined tyranny to the vast plains of Asia, though, undoubtedly, the persuasion that

---

[9] *Kindler v Canada* [1991] 84 DLR (4th) 438, 488.   [10] *Re Ismail* [1998] UKHL 320, 327.
[11] Section 33(3)(a) of the Extradition Act 1999.
[12] Article 35 of the Political Constitution (as amended by Legislative Act no 1 of 1997).
[13] Recommendation 39.

there is not a foot of soil upon which real crimes are pardoned would be a most effi-
cacious means of preventing them.[14]

Requested states wary about enquiring into the quality of criminal justice applied in
the requesting state, developed mechanisms such as double criminality and speciality, to protect the substantive legality of the use of their systems on behalf of the
requested state. In insisting on these conditions the requested state was exercising its
own rights. More recently, human rights protections have been developed to ensure
procedural justice and to protect individual interests during punishment. Individuals
have been granted standing either to challenge violations of the extradition treaty or
to stop the extradition process through alleging prospective violations of their human
rights. But requested states are still reluctant to inquire into the criminal justice systems of requesting states. The US adheres to a rigid rule of non-inquiry which prevents
an extradition court from investigating the fairness of a requesting state's criminal
justice system.[15] The rule is based on the necessity of preserving international comity, and because of the institutional incompetency of an extradition court to engage
in a review of a foreign criminal justice system, the preserve of the executive branch.[16]
While not explicit, states from other traditions also show a deference to the other sovereign. In the *Yemeni Citizens Extradition Case*,[17] for example, the German Federal
Constitutional Court noted that in extradition 'the requesting state is, in principle, to
be shown trust as concerns its compliance with the principles of due process of law and
of the protection of human rights. This principle can claim validity as long as it is not
shaken by facts to the contrary'. The requested state's judicial authorities thus presume
that the extraditee will receive a fair trial and fair treatment in the requesting state.
Questions about the quality of justice are usually left to the executive when it decides
whether to enter extradition relations with the particular state in the first place. There
is a growing tendency, however, for states to engage in limited inquiry, because while
constitutional protections guaranteeing justice and reasonable treatment to individuals may not bind a requesting state in execution of its law, they do bind the requested
state when it joins the effort. Under Swiss law, for example, an extradition request
must be refused if the foreign proceedings do not meet the standards in the European
Convention on Human Rights or International Covenant on Civil and Political Rights
(ICCPR).[18] It is now more common for states to inquire into the likelihood of egregious treatment in the requesting state. Struggling at the same time to avoid what
Judge Bonello in *Al-Skeini and Others v UK*[19] referred to 'human rights imperialism',
these states insist on respect for a 'minimum content' of human rights.[20]

---

[14] C Beccaria, *Crimes and Punishment* (1764; Farrer trans 1880), 193–94.

[15] *Hoxha v Levi* 465 F3d 554 (3d Cir 2006). The only exception is if the treatment is 'so antipathetic to
a federal court's sense of decency' that it requires inquiry—*Gallina v Fraser* 278 F 2d 77 (2d Cir 1960).

[16] M Murchison, 'Note: Extradition's Paradox: Duty, Discretion, and Rights in the World of Non-
inquiry' 43 *Stanford Journal of International Law* (2007) 295, 302.

[17] Individual constitutional complaint, BVerfG, 2 BvR 1506/03; ILDC 10 (DE 2003), 5 November 2003.

[18] Article 2(a) of the Federal Act on International Mutual Assistance in Criminal Matters.

[19] ECtHR (2001) Series A n 1093.

[20] M Beltrán de Felipe and A Nieto Martín, 'Post 9/11 Trends in International Judicial
Cooperation: Human Rights as a Constraint on Extradition in Death Penalty Cases' 10 *Journal of
International Criminal Justice* (2012) 581, 592.

Civil law states tend to view extradition as a *sui generis* amalgam of international assistance with some very limited elements of criminal justice. Common law states have generally taken the view that the process is criminal. In 1943 Viscount Simon held in *Amand v Home Secretary and Minister of Defence of Royal Netherlands Government*: 'If the matter is one the direct outcome of which may be trial of the applicant or his possible punishment for an alleged offence by a court claiming jurisdiction to do so, the matter is criminal.'[21]

In 1995 Lord Hoffmann in *R v Governor of Brixton Prison: Ex Parte Levin*[22] had to explicitly reject the notion that extradition was *sui generis*: 'In our view proceedings before the committing magistrate are properly classed as criminal having their birth or origin in acts or conduct punishable under the criminal law. They are not in a separate class of their own.'[23]

However, the view that extradition proceedings are not criminal is becoming more common in common law jurisdictions.[24] In 2012 in *Pomiechowski v District Court of Legnica, Poland*[25] Lord Justice Mance held that what was at issue in an extradition hearing was the determination of the civil right to remain, which implies the process is an administrative one. Characterization of extradition as non-criminal significantly limits the human rights protections that may be available to the requested person from the full due process rights available in a criminal trial to a much more limited guarantee of fairness of the kind available to a party to an administrative process.

This chapter examines the function and development of extradition in the pursuit of a 'no-hiding place' strategy for alleged transnational criminals and fugitives. It begins by discussing the nature of the legal basis for extradition. The main focus is on the conditions for and bars to extradition including human rights bars. It then looks at future developments in the law of extradition. Finally, the chapter introduces those situations where the law fails and states engage in alternatives to extradition such as abduction, deportation, and extraordinary rendition.

20.2 The Legal Basis for Extradition

20.2.1 Extradition treaties, schemes, and national laws

There is no customary obligation to extradite; extradition is only obligatory if required by treaty. In the US, for example, bilateral treaties are essential for extradition;[26] there is neither an obligation to extradite apart from that imposed by treaty[27] nor a right to extradite apart from that granted by treaty.[28] The UN Model Treaty on Extradition[29] provides a template for bilateral extradition treaties. Some states are party to many,

---

[21] [1943] AC 147 at 156.   [22] [1996] 3 WLR 657.   [23] ibid, 666.
[24] *Canada v Schmidt* [1987] 1 SCR 500, *United States of America v Dynar* [1997] 2 SCR 462 (Canada); *Dotcom and others v United States* [2014] NZSC 24 (New Zealand).
[25] [2012] UKSC 20, para 32.
[26] See, eg, US–Mexico Extradition Treaty, 4 May 1978, 31 UST 5059, in force 25 January 1980.
[27] *Holmes v Jennison* 39 US 540 (1840).   [28] *Factor v Laubenheimer* 290 US 276 (1933).
[29] Annexed to GA Resolution 45/116 of 14 December 1990.

some to very few. The US, for example, has more than 100 bilateral extradition treaties, Nepal only one.[30] Bilateral treaties may be attractive to states executing a strong transnational interest in the suppression of crime on their own terms, because they exclude third party states that may be impacted such as the state of the individual's nationality or states with jurisdiction, from any legal interest in the extradition process.[31] It has been argued that reliance on bilateral treaties for extradition is appropriate because extradition is not a universal good requiring multilateral agreement; it is highly contingent on the aims of and differences between the extradition partners, something best resolved bilaterally.[32] States may also use the treaty negotiation process to vet human rights compliance in potential partners and may be reluctant to agree such treaties with states that do not respect human rights.[33]

Multilateral treaties provide a basis for extradition that is faster to negotiate and easier to adapt in a region or among states that enjoy a strong political or legal affinity or a shared conviction to basic human rights standards. Although other regional treaties, such as the 1981 Inter-American Convention on Extradition[34] have been influential, the Council of Europe's 1957 European Convention on Extradition[35] set the standard.

The Scheme for Extradition within the Commonwealth[36] is not a treaty because it does not insist on reciprocity but rather frames the use of reciprocating domestic legislation for extradition. Where no treaty or scheme exists, certain states are able, on a discretionary basis, to extradite relying on only their domestic law alone.

20.2.2 Extradition in the suppression conventions

While older suppression conventions were largely silent on extradition, more recent instruments such as the United Nations Convention against Corruption (UNCAC), establish obligations on parties to extradite individuals found within their territories for the particular offences in the convention.[37] They usually provide for three alternative approaches to extradition.

First, where there are extant extradition treaties between parties the suppression conventions rely entirely upon these treaties as the basis for extradition. Importantly, the suppression convention updates these treaties by expanding their scope to include

---

[30] Treaty of Extradition between the Government of India and the Government of Nepal, Kathmandu, 2 October 1953 (the two states have agreed to revise it).
[31] W Magnuson, 'The Domestic Politics of Extradition' 52 *Virginia Journal of International Law* (2011–12) 839, 874, gives the example of Russian anger at Thailand's extradition of the arms dealer Victor Bout to the US.
[32] G Blum, 'Bilateralism, Multilateralism, and the Architecture of International Law' 49 *Harvard International Law Journal* (2008) 323, 357.
[33] See, eg, B Zagaris, 'Proposed France-China Extradition Treaty Raises Human Rights Issues' 23(3) *International Law Enforcement Reporter* (2007) 96.
[34] 25 February 1981, 20 ILM 723 (1981), in force 28 March 1992.
[35] 12 December 1957, ETS 24, in force 18 April 1960. See also the Additional Protocol to the European Convention, 15 October 1975, ETS 86, in force 20 August 1979; Second Additional Protocol to the European Convention, 17 March 1978, ETS 98, in force 5 June 1983.
[36] The Scheme Relating to Fugitive Offenders within the Commonwealth, Cmnd 3008, May 1966; amended on several occasions, most recently in 2002.
[37] Article 44.

the crimes in that suppression convention. Thus, for example, article 8 of the 1949 Convention for the Suppression of Illicit Traffic in Persons[38] provides that convention offences shall be regarded as extraditable offences in any treaty which has been or may be concluded between the parties. This provision modifies the parties' existing extradition treaties by adding to the list of enumerated extraditable offences.[39] However, if the states concerned require but do not enjoy existing bilateral arrangements, a common situation, then the provision in the suppression convention is in effect a dead letter. In addition, provisions in the suppression conventions of this kind that add to the lists of extraditable offences in existing bilateral treaties must be assumed only to apply to offences the domestic criminalization of which is made obligatory by that suppression convention, and not to permissive offences such as 'illicit enrichment' in the UNCAC,[40] unless the requested state has taken the permissive option and criminalized that activity. The absence of double criminality would in any event defeat a request for extradition if the requested state had not criminalized.

Second, where the parties do not have extradition relations but one of the parties requires a treaty to enable extradition, the suppression convention itself may serve as a surrogate extradition convention. Thus, for example, article 36(2)(b)(ii) of the 1961 Single Convention on Narcotic Drugs (as amended by the 1972 Protocol) provides:

> If a Party which makes extradition conditional on the existence of a treaty receives a request for extradition from another Party with which it has no extradition treaty, it may at its option consider this Convention as the legal basis for extradition in respect of the offences enumerated in paragraphs 1 and 2 a) ii) of this article.

The United Nations Convention against Transnational Organized Crime (UNTOC) develops this approach by obliging parties to inform, at the time of ratification/accession, the UN Secretary-General of their willingness to rely on the UNTOC as a legal basis for extradition to the other parties.[41] Some states, such as India, have relied on article 16(5)(a) to declare that they will use the UNTOC as the legal basis for extradition with other parties.[42] Others, such as Botswana, have declared they will not do so (even in the absence of any other basis for extradition).[43] Although extraditions on the basis of the suppression conventions have occurred, states are wary of using suppression conventions as extradition treaties on their own mainly because of the lack of specific detail, and perhaps because of the dramatically increased scope of potential extradition parties.[44] They may, however, be willing to use them in combination with extant but aging bilateral treaties, and rely on the suppression convention to update

---

[38] Convention for the Suppression of the Traffic in Persons and of the Exploitation of the Prostitution of Others, 21 March 1950, 96 UNTS 271, in force 25 July 1951.

[39] RS Clark, 'Offenses of International Concern: Multilateral Practice in the Forty Years Since Nuremberg' 57 *Nordic Journal of International Law* (1988) 49, 65.

[40] Article 20.   [41] Article 16(5)(a).

[42] On signature, 12 December 2002, see UN Treaty Series, Status of the United Nations Convention against Transnational Organized Crime, as at 16 October 2016, 5.

[43] ibid, 10.

[44] Conference of the Parties to the UNTOC, Fifth Session, Catalogue of examples of cases of extradition, mutual legal assistance and other forms of international legal cooperation on the basis of the United Nations Convention against Transnational Organized Crime, CTOC/COP/2010/CR.P.5 (2010), para 22.

the crimes extraditable under those treaties. Where the parties are unwilling to rely on the suppression convention as the basis for extradition and do not have extant extradition treaties, more recent suppression conventions, such as the UNTOC in article 16(5)(b), oblige parties to seek to conclude such treaties in order to implement the extradition obligations in the suppression convention.

Third, those states that do not require a treaty basis for extradition, are obliged by the suppression conventions to recognize the specific convention offences as extraditable among themselves.[45]

20.3 The Conditions for and Exceptions to Extradition

20.3.1 Conditions, exceptions, and non-inquiry

Treaties and domestic law both enable extradition and limit it by imposing conditions for extradition and exceptions or grounds for refusal. Some of these conditions and exceptions enjoy customary status, although most are simply a matter for agreement between parties to a treaty. It follows that not every condition or exception will be found in every treaty or imposed in domestic legislation or practice. Many are, as we shall see below, included in the suppression conventions. Article 16(7) of the UNTOC, for example, subjects extradition to the conditions and exceptions in a state's domestic law and any applicable extradition treaty. If a suppression convention expressly removes a condition or exception then it follows from the *lex posteriori* and *lex specialis* rules that the parties' existing bilateral and regional extradition treaties will be impliedly amended to remove that condition or exception in regard to that specific transnational crime.

20.3.2 Double/dual criminality

The most significant condition for extradition is the principle of double (or dual) criminality. It requires that the offence for which extradition is requested is an offence in the domestic law of both the requested and requesting states. Claimed to be a rule of custom implied in all extradition relations,[46] the principle is designed to ensure reciprocal maintenance of the principle *nullum crimen sine lege* in the context of extradition (no one should be subject to a criminal process for something that is not a crime in the state they are in). Zeller notes:

> If the act did not constitute an offence under the law of the requested state, the latter will not be justified in interfering with the personal liberty and freedom of movement of the person alleged to have committed it by means of his arrest and delivery to the foreign power; no more than if, in the absence of a law of extradition, such person could have been so arrested and delivered even for an act which might have been an offence under the lex fori.[47]

---

[45] Article 16(6) of the UNTOC.
[46] I Shearer, *Extradition in International Law* (Manchester: University of Manchester Press, 1971), 138.
[47] SZ Zeller, 'The Significance of the Requirement of Double Criminality in Extradition' 10 *Israel Law Review* (1975) 51, 80.

In *MM v United States of America*[48] the Canadian Supreme Court emphasized that the principle of double criminality underlies all phases of the extradition process. Ensuring double criminality through obligations to criminalize is a goal of the suppression conventions, although they still condition extradition on double criminality and do not simply assume it will exist. Thus, for example, article 44(1) of the UNCAC obliges extradition for corruption offences 'provided that the offence for which extradition is sought is punishable under the domestic law of both the requesting State Party and the requested State Party'.

Double criminality has three aspects: double criminality of conduct, of place (jurisdiction), and of time (offence punishable at the time act was perpetrated).[49]

Conduct

Double criminality in regard to conduct has been marked by difficulty in settling on the degree of correspondence required between the crimes in the requested and requesting states. *In concreto* (objective) application of the rule insists on strict correlation of the title of the offence and its legal elements. *In abstracto* (subjective) application only compares the underlying conduct and whether it is criminal. There has been a general movement towards the latter broader approach because of the difficulty of assessing foreign law in an extradition court. In 1957 in *Re Gerber*[50] the German Federal Supreme Court held that the set of facts underlying the offence is decisive, not its legal title. In 1973 in *Shapiro v Ferrandina*[51] the US Court of Appeals for the Second Circuit held that 'when the laws of both the requesting and the requested party appear to be directed at the same basic evil, the statutes are analogous and can form the basis of dual criminality'. In 1979 in *Wilson v Sheehan*[52] the Irish Supreme Court explained how the requesting state's factual allegations set the scope for the enquiry in the requested state whether those allegations would hypothetically support a criminal offence:

> It is the essential factual ingredients that determine whether two offences have the necessary correspondence ... it is necessary for the specification of the offence in the warrant (or in the warrant and its attendant documentation) to go further and identify the offence by reference to the factual components relied on; it is only by looking at those components that a court in this State can decide whether the offence so specified (regardless of what name is attached to it) would constitute, if committed in this State, a corresponding offence of the required gravity.

In 2014, in *TGG, Final Appeal Judgment*,[53] the Italian Court of Cassation confirmed an extradition for organ trafficking to Brazil on the basis of the Italian offences of human trafficking and aggravated personal injury, holding that the conduct need not be described in exactly the same way by the requesting and requested states so long as there was an 'equivalence of the repressive elements' between them. It appears to follow that if the requesting state alleges an offence depending on acts A + B + C, while the requesting state only requires acts A + B for an offence under its law, there will be double criminality. However, in the reverse situation, there will be no double

[48] 2015 SCC 62, paras 16, 70.   [49] Zeller, above n 47, 69, 70.   [50] 24 ILR 493 (1957).
[51] 478 F2d 894 (1973).   [52] [1979] IR 423 at 428–29.
[53] No 30087/2014, ILDC 2215 (IT2014), 9 July 2014.

criminality. The 1990 UN Model Treaty on Extradition provides in article 2(2) that double criminality is met despite differences in denomination, categorization, and in the elements of the compared offences.[54] The suppression conventions have followed suit. Article 43(2) of the UNCAC, for example, provides that double criminality depends only on whether the underlying conduct of the offence has been criminalized in both states and 'shall be deemed fulfilled' irrespective of whether the laws of the requested state place the offence 'within the same category' of offence. Certain states have legislated for the conduct approach.

An even looser 'conduct approach' allows states latitude when dealing with a request based on an offence for which there is no specific analogue in the requested state's law. In *United States v Levy*,[55] for example, the appellant, after being extradited from Hong Kong, was convicted in the US of a Continuing Criminal Enterprise (CCE) violation for a number of drug offences committed in concert with others. He argued that as there was no similar offence in Hong Kong he should not have been extradited because of the absence of double criminality. The US Court of Appeals rejected the argument holding that he had misconstrued the nature of double criminality, which depends on the criminality of his conduct in both jurisdictions and not on how it is classed. How far the conduct approach can be stretched before double criminality becomes meaningless is uncertain. In 2009, for example, the South Jakarta District Court approved the extradition of an alleged people smuggler to Australia even though at that stage Indonesia had not enacted people smuggling offences, on the basis that his conduct would have constituted a violation of Indonesia's visa and immigration offences if it had occurred in Indonesia.[56] It has become a fairly common practice therefore to insist only that the alleged conduct is an offence, any offence, within the law of the requested state. Section 3(2) of the 1999 Canadian Extradition Act,[57] for example, provides: 'For greater certainty, it is not relevant whether the conduct referred to in subsection (1) is named, defined or characterized by the extradition partner in the same way as it is in Canada.' In 2009 in *US v Fischbacher* the Canadian Supreme Court rejected an argument that there should be some 'alignment' between the Canadian offence identified by the Minister of Justice and the criminal offence alleged by the requesting state.[58] Canadian practice does not require any investigation of the ingredients of the foreign offence at all, all that is required is evidence of some conduct that would be criminal in Canada. According to Botting, 'as long as the extradition judge has determined that some—*any*—aspect of the alleged conduct is criminal, the Minister routinely orders surrender for *all* the offences alleged by the requesting State'.[59] In contrast, in *Norris v United States of America*[60] a US request for extradition of a British national from the UK inter alia for price fixing failed in part because while US law had recognized price fixing as an offence in 1890, it was only criminalized in England after the events in question. The US prosecutors thus tried to rely on conspiracy to defraud to

---

[54] Annexed to GA Resolution 45/116 of 14 December 1990.
[55] 905 F 2d 326, 10th Circuit, 11 June 1990.   [56] *Daily Telegraph*, 22 April 2009.
[57] SC 1999, c18.   [58] [2009] 3 SCR 170, 2009 SCC 46 (SCC).
[59] G Botting, *Canadian Extradition Law and Practice*, 5th edn (Markham, Ontario: Lexis Nexis, 2015), 2.
[60] [2007] EWHC (Admin) 71.

establish double criminality, but the House of Lords quashed the decision ruling that mere price fixing was not a criminal offence at the time and could not be recharacterized as a conspiracy to make it extraditable. The principle of legality does appear to be under threat when an individual is extradited for a minor offence and the prohibition for which they are eventually punished is not clearly in their view. The application of the conduct test also opens up the domestic criminal laws in the requested state to a more flexible and purposive interpretation which tends to expand the scope of those offences to meet the requirements of double criminality. In the recent Jamaican Case of *Flowers v the Director of Public Prosecutions*,[61] for example, the conscious transmission of the HIV virus to uninformed sexual partners, a settled form of aggravated sexual assault contrary to section 273 of the Criminal Code in Canada,[62] was considered to involve conduct criminal within the definition of infliction of grievous bodily harm in terms of sections 20 and 22 of the Offences against the Persons Act 1864 in Jamaica, even though there was no precedent in Jamaican law for a charge or conviction under these sections for such conduct.

Place

The place in which the offence occurs is a troublesome aspect of the principle of double criminality. The Harvard Research Draft Convention on Jurisdiction provided that both parties must establish jurisdiction on the same basis over the same crime for double criminality to be satisfied.[63] Article 7(2) of the European Convention on Extradition provides:

> When the offence for which extradition is requested has been committed outside the territory of the requesting Party, extradition may only be refused if the law of the requested Party does not allow prosecution for the same category of offence, when committed outside the latter Party's territory or does not allow extradition for the offence concerned.

Absence of a hypothetically congruent jurisdiction is thus only an optional ground for refusal of extradition, a position also taken in the UN Model Treaty on Extradition.[64] The suppression conventions are silent on whether the inclusion of double criminality in their provisions includes this jurisdictional dimension. Some states continue to insist on it. In *United States of America v Wong*,[65] for example, the US sought the extradition of Wong from New Zealand to face trial for distributing drugs in Asia with the intent that they be imported into the US. The New Zealand court examined whether New Zealand law established extraterritorial jurisdiction in the same circumstances. It found that it would not have been an offence under New Zealand law to distribute drugs abroad with the intent to import them into New Zealand because New Zealand does not claim extraterritorial jurisdiction in such circumstances. Thus the action was not an extradition offence under section 4 of New Zealand's Extradition Act 1999, and the extradition request was denied. Jurisdictional double criminality appears, however, to be giving way to the

---

[61] [2016] JMFC FC3.
[62] A position clarified in the Canadian Decision of *R v Mabior* 2012 SCC 47 at para 104.
[63] Harvard Research in International Law, 'Draft Convention on Jurisdiction with Respect to Crimes' 29 *American Journal of International Law* (Supp 1935) 435, 445.
[64] Article 4(e).   [65] [2001] 2 NZLR 472.

aim of suppressing transnational crime in other states. In *R (Al-Fawwaz) v Governor of Brixton Prison*[66] three individuals facing extradition from the UK to the US appealed against the refusal of *habeas corpus* when they were incarcerated pending extradition to the US for allegedly conspiring with Osama Bin Laden and others to murder US citizens by bombing US embassies in East Africa. Conspiracy to murder had a limited territorial jurisdiction under English law, and they argued that the alleged conspiracy did not take place within the territory of the US, and therefore they were not 'fugitive criminals' for the purpose of the English Extradition Act 1989. Although the Court of Appeal required jurisdictional double criminality in order for extradition to be possible, the House of Lords reversed on this point, interpreting the requirement in the Act that a fugitive criminal be a person 'accused or . . . convicted of an extradition crime committed within the jurisdiction of a foreign state' to encompass a wider meaning than an extradition crime committed in the territory of the foreign state. The court reasoned that while the Act was passed when crime was territorial, crime was now global and trans-frontier, and the extradition process had to include the perpetrators of such crimes.

Time

Whether double criminality must exist at the time the offence was committed or only at the time the request was made depends on national law. In *Pinochet*[67] the House of Lords took the former view, and held that there was only double criminality in regard to a small number of torture offences enacted after the UK had become a party to the Torture Convention in the 1980s, omitting most of the allegations of torture made under General Pinochet's rule in Chile in the 1970s. In *US v Wathne*[68] it was argued on appeal in the US that there had been no double criminality as required for the requested individual's extradition from India to the US to face money laundering charges as India did not criminalize money laundering at the time the acts were committed (although it did at the time of the extradition). Relying on *Pinochet*, the Court found that under Indian law the time of commission was critical, and because extradition had already been granted by India, declined jurisdiction over Wathne as a remedy. German law, in contrast, takes the latter more comprehensive view that insists only on double criminality at the time of the request.[69]

Double criminality can present a formidable barrier to extradition in a limited number of cases. Article 44(2) of the UNCAC, which allows parties to waive the requirement of double criminality, appears to point to the future. Regional systems of surrender such as the Nordic Arrest Warrant[70] have completely abolished the double-criminality condition, requiring only that the crime for which extradition is sought carry a sentence of imprisonment or other form of detention.

---

[66] [2001] UKHL 69, [2002] 1 AC 556.

[67] *R v Bow Street Stipendiary Magistrate and others, ex parte Pinochet Ugarte (Amnesty International Intervening)* [1999] 2 WLR 827; [1999] 2 All ER 97 (HL).

[68] CR05-00594-VRW (US District Court for the Northern District of California, 22 September 2008).

[69] *Yemeni Citizens Extradition Case*, Individual constitutional complaint, BVerfG, 2 BvR 1506/03; ILDC 10 (DE 2003), 109, para 16.

[70] A Convention on a Nordic Arrest Warrant 2005, 15 December 2005, article 2(1).

20.3.3 Extraditability

Extradition is a significant infringement of liberty. Therefore the alleged transnational offender must only be extradited if the requested state agrees that the offence is sufficiently serious to warrant extradition. For it to occur, the particular offence must be recognized as extraditable by both states in their domestic law, thus also recognizing the reciprocity that underpins extradition. In Vietnam, for example, the Law on Legal Assistance 2007 prescribes that even if there is double criminality, if the crime does not fall into a list of extraditable offences, extradition must be refused.[71] States may mutually recognize offences as extraditable in the absence of a treaty, but recognition is usually a result of implementation of treaty obligations. By becoming party to a suppression convention, states recognize that they consider the convention offences extraditable.

The extraditability of an offence thus serves as a gravity bar to extradition. In the past common law states usually listed the crimes that they were under an obligation to extradite in both treaties and domestic extradition law. This enumerative approach has been retained in major suppression conventions such as the 1970 Hague Hijacking Convention[72] and the 1988 Drug Trafficking Convention[73] because they are directed at specific offences. However, listing encourages the matching of specific elements in double criminality. On the other hand, if a crime is listed in the treaty some states take the view that that listing is determinative of extraditability and does not require double criminality.[74] Lists require updating to keep pace with emerging transnational crimes.

The eliminative or evaluative approach developed by civil law states makes all sufficiently serious offences extraditable. The threshold is usually measured by whether the offence is subject to a penalty of one year or more in prison. This approach is more functional and now dominates state practice[75] and has been recognized in more recent suppression conventions such as the UNTOC.[76] The evaluative approach fosters a subjective approach to double criminality, automatically includes new crimes with the requisite penalty, and broadens the number of extraditable offences. However, it does have problems. An offender may commit a number of offences none of which individually carries a sufficient penalty to allow extradition. The requesting state may consider an offence serious and worthy of extradition but the requested state may not. In particular, it makes impossible the automatic updating of extradition treaties to include new suppression convention offences. Parties to a suppression convention may criminalize its offences but must attach a penalty sufficient to trigger extradition or breach the obligation to make the offence extraditable. The Council of Europe Human Trafficking Convention tries to avoid this by obliging parties in terms of article 23(1) to apply 'sanctions [that] shall include, for criminal offences established in accordance with Article 17 when committed by natural persons, penalties involving deprivation of liberty which can give rise to extradition'.

---

[71] Article 35(109d) and Article 33(1).   [72] Article 8(1).   [73] Article 6(1).
[74] See *Factor v Laubenheimer* 290 US 276 (1933) (US); *Riley v Commonwealth of Australia* (1985) 159 CLR 1 (HCA) (Australia); *United States v Cullinane* [2003] 2 NZLR 1 (CA) (New Zealand).
[75] See, eg, section 3(1) of the Fiji Extradition Act 2003.   [76] Article 16(7).

20.3.4 Sufficiency of evidence

Civil law states view extradition as assistance to another state. This means that the focus is on a formally valid process, concerned with verifying whether the formal conditions for extradition have been met. Article 23(1) of Portugal's Law No 144/99 on International Judicial Cooperation in Criminal Matters, for example, requires a request which must identify the requesting and requested authorities, the purpose of the request, the legal analysis of the facts and the grounds on which it is made, the identification of the person concerned, a description of the facts, and the text of laws relied upon. To make things even easier, article 23(2) explicitly does not require authentication of the request. Meeting domestic laws of evidence to a sufficient standard is not required because no such rules apply in normal criminal process in the preliminary/investigatory stages. They may, for example, consist of summaries of evidence made by a police officer and relayed back to the investigating magistrate. This formal approach is reflected in instruments like the 1957 European Convention on Extradition, which require a reservation from a party if it is going to impose more substantive evidence requirements.[77] Article 5 of the UN Model Treaty on Extradition also adopts a formal validity approach.

Civil law states generally do not extradite their nationals, making it politically less problematic to approach the process as an exercise in formal cooperation between states without evidence, where there is a strict division of roles between international assistance in one state and trial in another. In contrast, common law states do extradite their nationals and as a result provide for an extradition process that is comparable to the preliminary process for indictment, because they consider it unfair to send a person to trial in a distant place without the provision of 'evidence of the validity of a charge against them comparable to the evidence that would have been required that person being charged domestically'.[78] This threshold is justified in Canada, for example, in order to make the judicial element of the extradition process 'meaningful' and guarantee fairness to the fugitive.[79] In essence, common law states required (i) evidence meeting the domestic requirements for admissibility based on threshold reliability and (ii) that would be sufficient to justify committal to trial.

The greatest difficulty for civil law states is that common law states usually require that this evidence meet their evidential rules of admissibility (ie excluding hearsay and requiring evidence be given under oath), which poses problems for prosecutors from requesting states poorly tutored in these rules. Not all the common law rules of evidence are applied, however. Full disclosure of evidence sufficient for trial is not required. Generally extradition tribunals allow written evidence in the form of first person affidavits and do not require first person testimony, as they do not have to decide whether the evidence is sufficient for conviction by weighing it against defence evidence. This means witnesses do not have to appear, and there is no opportunity for cross-examination. But first person affidavits are required. *Re Reyat's Application for*

---

[77] Article 12.

[78] AW La Forest, 'The Balance between Liberty and Comity in the Evidentiary Requirements Applicable to Extradition Proceedings' 28 *Queens Law Journal* (2002–3) 95, 116.

[79] *United States of America v Ferras* 2006 SCC 33, paras 19 et seq.

a Writ of Habeas Corpus[80] illustrates the problems this rule may cause. It involved an extradition request by Canada to the UK. The offence had taken place in Japan where all the witnesses were located. Japanese law did not allow foreign officials to take evidence on commission so Canada was forced to fly seventy-eight witnesses to Hong Kong (at that point still under British rule) to depose as to what had happened in person in order to satisfy English rules of evidence. How difficult it is for civil law states to adhere to these rules is not easy to establish.[81]

When it comes to the assessment of the evidence, common law extradition tribunals do not generally weigh the evidence or test the credibility of the witnesses; the extradition judge assumes the admissible evidence is true and without assessing its weight tests it against the substantive requirements of double criminality and extraditability. The precise test applied to the resulting evidence varies from state to state. In some, the tribunal has to decide whether a prima facie case has been made out against the requested person; in others, whether there is evidence that would constitute reasonable and probable grounds to believe that the offence had been committed; and in others whether there is evidence sufficient to justify committal in the requested state's domestic criminal courts.[82] The Commonwealth Scheme retains a requirement of a sufficiency of evidence to a prima facie standard,[83] and the suppression conventions do not compel common law states to change this practice, while the UN Model Treaty recognizes in footnote 14 that sufficiency of proof, according to evidentiary standards of that state may be required at the party's election. However, more recent conventions do encourage parties to simplify their evidentiary requirements,[84] and under diplomatic pressure to abandon this position, certain common law states have been doing so, at least in regard to selected other states. Both the UK and Australia, for example, use a 'no-evidence' approach as their preferred approach to close partners. The UK abolished the prima facie test based on admissible evidence in respect of its European and certain other designated closer extradition partners (it requires only sufficient information to justify a reasonable suspicion that the person had committed the offence), but maintaining it with its other non-European partners.[85] Although Australia also took a no-evidence approach, it allowed for the retention of a sufficiency standard when altered by regulation where a statement of evidence similar to a record of case is required.[86] Canada has introduced a *via media* allowing requesting states to summarize the evidence in a Record of Case (ROC) that could include unsworn evidence and multiple hearsay, while still applying a prima facie test to that ROC, although prohibiting the weighing or assessing of the evidence's reliability.[87] It only requires certification either that the evidence is sufficient under the law of the requesting state to justify prosecution or that the evidence was gathered according

---

[80] Unreported, QBD, CO/1 1 577 88, MWC, 22 March 1989.
[81] La Forest, above n 79, 134, 141, notes that only *Reyat* and one other case was used as a motivation for change in Canada.
[82] See, eg, section 16(b)(ii) of the UN Model Law on Extradition 2004.   [83] Paragraph 5(4)(a).
[84] See, eg, article 6(7) of the 1988 UN Drug Trafficking Convention; article 16(18) of UNTOC; article 44(9) of the UNCAC.
[85] Sections 7 and 8 of the Extradition Act 1989.
[86] Sections 19(2)(3) and 11 of the Extradition Act 1988.
[87] Under section 33 of the 1999 Extradition Act; see La Forest, above n 79, 139.

to that law, and this establishes reliability.[88] Only evidence shown to be so manifestly unreliable that it would be dangerous or unsafe to convict can provide the basis for a defence challenge.[89] New Zealand has followed this approach to a degree, limiting the ROC approach to its close partners.[90] US law remains unchanged. It permits use of unsworn statements and hearsay evidence in the establishing of probable cause (sufficient evidence to furnish good reason to believe that the crime alleged has been committed by the person charged), even though such evidence is inadmissible in pre-trial proceedings.[91] However, US extradition magistrates retain a large discretion to weigh and assess the evidence.[92] Many other common law states have not relaxed their laws at all. Tanzanian law, for example, empowers a magistrate sitting in an extradition hearing to 'hear the case in the same manner and have the same jurisdiction and powers, as nearly as may be, as in a preliminary inquiry'.[93]

20.3.5 Specialty

First included in French treaties of the mid-nineteenth century, the principle of specialty is not a condition for extradition; it places a condition upon extradition. The US Supreme Court in the *United States v Rauscher*[94] explained the rule:

> [A] person who has been brought within the jurisdiction of the court by virtue of the proceedings under an extradition treaty, can only be tried for those offences described in that treaty, and for the offence with which he is charged in the proceedings of his extradition, unless a reasonable time has been given him, after his release or trial upon such charge, to return to the country from whose asylum he has been forcibly taken under those proceedings.

Specialty restricts what the extradited person can be charged with in the requesting state. It recognizes that extradition only takes place once the requested state is content that nothing bars extradition for that particular offence to that particular state. It can be raised as an objection to further charges not in the extradition order, based on the absence of jurisdiction.[95] Specialty can also be violated by re-extradition to a third state, and provisions in extradition treaties provide that re-extradition should not occur without the consent of the requested state.[96] The rule applies to extradition based on treaty and on domestic law. It has been claimed to be customary,[97] although in some legal systems if the particular treaty or national law does not specifically enforce specialty, it may not be applied.[98] Where a state relies on a suppression

---

[88] *Ferras*, above n 80, paras 52–54.   [89] *US v Thomlinson* 2007 ONCA 42, para 45.
[90] Section 25 of the Extradition Act 1999.
[91] 18 USC § 3190; *Elias v Ramirez* 215 US 398 (1910).   [92] La Forest, above n 79, 171.
[93] Section 7(1) of the Extradition Act, c368.   [94] 119 US 407 (1886), 430.
[95] See, eg, *NV ICLBLTR and NV S v JS*, Appeal judgment; ILDC 1503 (BE 2006) 25 October 2006, paras 9 and 10.
[96] See, eg, article 15 of the 1957 European Extradition Convention.
[97] MC Bassiouni, 'Extradition: Law and Practice of the United States' in MC Bassiouni (ed), 2 *International Criminal Law: Multilateral and Bilateral Enforcement Mechanisms*, 3rd edn (Leiden: Martinus Nijhoff, 2008), 319.
[98] See *United States v Valencia-Trujillo* 573 F3d 1171 (11th Cir 2009).

convention as the basis for extradition, the rule of specialty limits extradition to the offences in the particular convention and prevents re-extradition to non-parties.

Emphasizing the role of specialty as a corollary to double criminality, in *Daya Singh Lahoria v India and ors*[99] the Indian Supreme Court quashed terrorism charges laid against the appellant which had not been part of the extradition decree that had led to his extradition from the US for terrorism. Some national courts, however, have applied specialty flexibly. In *Truong v The Queen*,[100] for example, a majority of the Australian High Court ruled that specialty had not been breached when an accused extradited for conspiracy to kidnap and conspiracy to murder was actually tried and convicted of murder and kidnapping. They reasoned that if the conduct on which the conspiracy charge was based established a substantive offence, prosecution for that offence did not offend specialty. What determined the possible charge in Australia was the evidence disclosed in the statement by the Australian authorities, not the evidence relating to the particular offence for which extradition was requested. In dissent Kirby J held 'it is the offence in respect of which the person is surrendered that it important, not what was disclosed in evidence to the surrendering authorities. Were it otherwise, any country could call much evidence and then turn around and argue that the "other offence" was disclosed to the relevant authorities.'[101] Given specialty is based on reciprocal notice, one has to agree. Nevertheless, the UN Model Treaty on Extradition suggests that specialty not be applied to extraditable offences 'provable on the same facts, and carrying the same or a lesser penalty as the original offence for which extradition was requested'.[102]

The principal way of avoiding the rule is for the requesting state to request a waiver of specialty.[103] The individual may also consent to prosecution or open themselves to it by remaining in the requesting state's territory for an extended period after a failed prosecution.

20.3.6 Political offence exception

One of the few exceptions to extradition based on the character of offence, the political offence exception dates to the early part of the nineteenth century when states, in what amounted to a functional grant of asylum, refused to return individuals who had committed violent acts for political reasons to the states where those actions had been carried out, because of qualms about the political rights of individuals in non-democratic countries. The exception has remained popular. US courts, for example, consistently refused to hand over Irish Republican Army members to the UK to face terrorism charges.[104] The political offence exception does not appear to be a rule of

---

[99] Original Writ and Special Leave Petition, ILDC 170 (IN 2001), AIR 2001 SC 1716, 17 April 2001, para 8.

[100] (2004) 205 ALR 72.   [101] ibid, 103–04.

[102] UN Doc A/52/635 (1997) add to Article 14 of 1990 Model Treaty.

[103] Article 14(1)(b) of the UN Model Treaty.

[104] See, eg, *In re Mackin*, 668 F 2d 122, 125 (2d Cir 1981); *In re Doherty*, 599 F Supp 270 (SDNY 1984); *United States v Doherty* 506 US 1002 (1992).

custom, although many treaties and national laws do provide for it and in some states it is constitutional.[105]

There is, however, little agreement on its scope. Some states focus on the motive and purpose of the offence; others on the circumstances in which the offence was committed; others on whether the offence was connected to a political offence. English law softened and potentially broadened the exception by speaking of an offence of 'a political character'.[106] Its ambiguity has been key to its utility in allowing a requested state to refuse extradition without giving specific reasons. For example, the extradition request of the Medellín Cartel member Jorge Luis Ochoa on drug charges to the US from Spain was initially turned down by Spain's Audiencia Nacional because of its 'political context': the US's allegation was that Ochoa was connected to alleged cartel trafficking activity through Nicaragua with Sandinista involvement.[107]

Although article 3(a) of the UN Model Treaty provides that the political offence exception is a mandatory ground for refusal, there has long been pressure to exclude this exception. The 1985 UK–US Supplementary Extradition Convention deliberately omitted the political offence exception but was effectively blocked in the US Senate. Concerned about extradition of Irish republicans to the UK, the Senate added a provision authorizing a court to deny extradition where the accused faced prejudice because of his race, religion, nationality, or political opinions.[108] Attempts at eliminating the exception have also been made in the suppression conventions. The 1988 Drug Trafficking Convention appears to do so in article 3(10) but this is 'without prejudice to the constitutional limitations and the fundamental domestic law of the Parties'. Some anti-terrorism treaties take a more refined approach. Article 2(1) of the 1977 European Convention on Terrorism, for example, provides that a party 'may decide not to regard as a political offence . . . a serious offence involving an act of violence, other than one covered by Article 1, against the life, physical integrity or liberty of a person'. Belgium has relied on article 2's discretionary nature to turn down a Turkish extradition request for offences of violence which it considered to be of a political nature,[109] ignoring the fact that article 1(e) of the Convention expressly provides that 'an offence involving the use of a bomb, grenade, rocket, automatic firearm or letter or parcel bomb if this use endangers persons' shall not be regarded as a political offence. The Belgian Court of Cassation[110] subsequently recognized that the crimes allegedly committed involved the use of automatic firearms and thus fell within the list of offences, which in terms of article 1(e) could not be regarded as political offences. However, since article 2 of the

---

[105] Article 5(LII) of the Brazilian Constitution 1988.

[106] Section 3 of the Extradition Act 1870.

[107] See SY Otera, 'International Extradition and the Medellin Cocaine Cartel: Surgical Removal of Colombian Cocaine Traffickers for Trial in the United States' 13 *Loyola of Los Angeles International and Comparative Law Review* (1991) 955, 963.

[108] Article 3(a), Extradition Treaty Supplementary between the United States and the United Kingdom, 23 December 1986, TIAS no 12050.

[109] See *Erdal v Council of Ministers* Decision of Constitutional Court, no 73/2005; ILDC 9 (BE 2005), 20 April 2005.

[110] See *Sabanci v Erdal*, Cassation, No P.05.1491.N, 27 June 2006 (2006) *Journal des Tribunaux* 642; ILDC 592 (BE 2006).

Law of 2 September 1985 implementing the Convention reserved Belgian jurisdiction over these crimes, it held the individual in question could now be prosecuted in Belgium. These decisions serve to indicate how the political offence exception and the *aut dedere aut judicare* principle can serve as proxies for requesting state disquiet about the treatment that is likely to be meted out to the extraditee upon extradition. Article 20(1) of the 2005 European Prevention of Terrorism Convention[111] provides pointedly that none of the convention offences can be regarded as a political offence for the purposes of extradition, and thus 'a request for extradition or for mutual legal assistance based on such an offence may not be refused on the sole ground that it concerns a political offence or an offence connected with a political offence or an offence inspired by political motives'. Provisions in UN terrorism conventions, such as article 15 of the Nuclear Terrorism Convention, follow the same 'exception to the exception' approach.[112]

20.3.7 Non-discrimination

Article 3(2) of the 1957 European Convention on Extradition states that a person shall not be extradited if the requested state: 'has reasonable grounds for believing that a request for extradition for an ordinary criminal offence has been made for the purpose of prosecuting or punishing a person on account of his race, religion, nationality or political opinion, or that person's position may be prejudiced for any of these reasons'.

The inclusion in suppression conventions of non-discrimination clauses of this kind, modelled on that in the 1951 UN Refugee Convention, is a consequence of the slow demise of the political offence exception, but their reference to discrimination on the grounds of 'political opinion' as justifying a refusal to extradite partly resurrects that exception.[113] The range of bases for non-discrimination has been expanded in article 16(14) of the UNTOC to include sex and origin. While non-discrimination is only a discretionary ground for refusal in most suppression conventions,[114] the wording of the UNTOC which makes it clear that there is no obligation to extradite also clarifies that there is no right under the Convention to request extradition under the circumstances described.

20.3.8 Nationality exception

Many extradition conventions contain an optional exception to extradition based on the extraditee's nationality.[115] In practice, however, this status-based exception,

---

[111] CETS 196, 16 May 2005.
[112] See also article 11 of the Terrorist Bombings Convention; article 14 of the Terrorist Financing Convention.
[113] See, eg, also articles 15 and 16 of the Terrorism Financing Convention; article 16 of the Nuclear Terrorism Convention.
[114] See, eg, article 6(6) of the 1988 UN Drug Trafficking Convention.
[115] See, eg, article 4(a) of the UN Model Treaty; article 6(1)(a) of the European Convention on Extradition.

which preserves a national's right not to be subject to incomprehensible foreign legal orders, is foundational in most civil law states and is an absolute bar to extradition.[116] Article 5(LI) of the 1988 Constitution of Brazil, for example, provides that no Brazilian shall be extradited. Suppression conventions recognize this exception implicitly by obliging the extradition of 'any person' for the particular convention offences but always in conformity with their domestic law,[117] and by making nationality a discretionary exception, an approach pioneered in article 6 of the 1957 European Convention on Extradition. The exception has been held to be a rule of custom[118] but fails the generality of practice criterion as most common law states do not apply it.

The nationality exception presents an almost impermeable barrier to the effective suppression of transnational crime because it allows nationals of those states which retain the exception to commit crimes abroad with impunity if they either never leave their state of nationality or return to it before being apprehended. It also betrays a lack of confidence in the fairness of judicial proceedings in the requesting state. Moreover nationality is becoming an increasingly tenuous concept today, with nationalities available for sale in certain small countries.

A range of methods have been used to try to unlock nationality safe-havens, including tightening the rules for acquisition of nationality and revoking residency upon evidence of commission of a serious crime in another state. Civil law states such as Brazil will allow extradition of naturalized citizens and will also sometimes override this exception in serious cases where, for example, there is sufficient evidence of participation in illicit drug traffic. Some bilateral extradition treaties remove the exception for offences created by the suppression conventions.[119]

If the exception is used, civil law states may enforce jurisdiction on the basis of nationality. In terms of article 16(10) of the UNTOC, a requested party that declines on the basis of nationality to extradite, shall at the request of the requesting party, submit the case to their competent authorities for prosecution. Submission must be without undue delay, the decision to prosecute and the conduct of the prosecution must be taken seriously, and the parties must cooperate with each other to ensure efficiency of the prosecution. These obligations reveal the distrust of states that regularly request extradition of the willingness of states of nationality to engage in effective prosecution. Nevertheless, in the recent judgment of the Court of Justice of the EU in *Petruhhin*,[120] the Court held that Latvia would be entitled to reject an extradition request for a Lithuanian citizen from Russia, on the basis that citizens of other EU member states enjoyed the same level of protection as Latvian citizens (who enjoyed a nationality exception), and given that the refusal to extradite was counter-balanced by

---

[116] Z Deen-Racsmany, 'A New Passport to Impunity?' 2 *Journal of International Criminal Justice* (2004) 761, 766.
[117] See, eg, article 15(5) of the African Union Convention on Corruption.
[118] *Austrian Case* 38 ILR 133, 134.
[119] See, eg, article 3 of the Extradition Treaty between the Government of the United States of America and the Government of the Republic of Bolivia, 27 June 1995, US Treaty Doc No 104-22, 1995, in force 29 July 1995.
[120] Case 182/15, 2014, 6 September 2016.

the extradite or prosecute principle, a member state like Lithuania must first be given the option of prosecuting itself before surrender to a third state outside the EU's area of freedom and justice.[121] Aside from the fact that it appears to suggest the existence of an EU nationality exception even for those nationals of member states that don't apply the nationality exception if their national is arrested in a member state that does, it is based on an extradite or prosecute principle which in practice hardly ever results in actual prosecution (because of the absence of local prosecutorial enthusiasm for the case).

A more practical alternative is to urge states to allow the extradition of nationals on the basis that they will be returned to them for sentencing and punishment. It avoids the linguistic and adaptation problems of incarcerating foreign prisoners as well as the costs of doing so. Prisoner transfer treaties such as the Council of Europe's 1983 Convention on the Transfer of Sentenced Prisoners[122] enable this practice, and the Netherlands took the lead, providing in 1988 that it would extradite nationals on condition of their return for punishment.[123] Article 16(11) of the UNTOC anticipates the use of temporary surrender. It provides that when a party is permitted under its domestic law to extradite its nationals only on condition that they be returned to serve their sentence, such conditional extradition will discharge their obligation to extradite or prosecute UNTOC offences under article 16(10). In those cases where extradition is sought to enforce a sentence already passed (ie after conviction) a similar approach can be taken. Article 16(12) of the UNTOC, for example, provides for enforcement of the requesting party's sentence in such cases by the requested state, if its laws allow it to do so.

The usual conditions for a prisoner transfer are a final judgment convicting the individual concerned, a minimum period of time remaining to be served (usually six months), dual criminality, some kind of link (usually nationality) to the state to which they are to be transferred, the consent of the state, and the consent of the prisoner.[124] The latter condition was considered necessary in article 7(1) of the 1983 European Convention for the Transfer of Sentenced Prisoners, although it was excluded in the 1997 Additional Protocol if they had fled from the sentencing state to their nationality haven.[125] The EU Framework decision on mutual recognition of criminal matters imposing custodial sentences[126] goes even further providing that consent is not

[121] Paras 33, 39, 48.
[122] 21 March 1983, CETS No 112, in force 1 August 1985. See also the UN Model Agreement on the Transfer of Foreign Prisoners, 6 September 1985; the Scheme for the Transfer of Convicted Offenders within the Commonwealth, Harare, 1 August 1986 (as amended); and the Inter-American Convention on Serving Criminal Sanctions Abroad, 9 June 1993. See generally UNODC, *Handbook on the International Transfer of Sentenced Prisoners* (New York: UN, 2012).
[123] *Staatsblad* 1988 no S478 amending the *Uiteveringswet* of 9 March 1967 Staatsblad no S139.
[124] UNODC Handbook, above n 123, 25 et seq.
[125] Article 3 of the Additional Protocol to the Convention on the Transfer of Sentenced Persons, 18 December 1997, CETS No 167; in force 1 June 2000.
[126] Council Framework Decision 2008/909/JHA of 27 November 2008 on the application of the principle of mutual recognition to judgments in criminal matters imposing custodial sentences or measures involving deprivation of liberty for the purpose of their enforcement in the European Union OJ L 327, 27 November 2008, article 4(1), 6(1)–(2).

required when the individual is returned to a state party in which they live or of which they are a national. Prisoner transfer agreements signed by states have adopted this no-consent approach,[127] which absence highlights the necessity of a further condition—respect for human rights.[128]

Before such transfer to face trial is possible, however, the requested state will have to undertake to adhere to the penalties imposed by the requesting state's courts and the requesting state will have to have faith that the requested state will do so. The requested state may have to agree to penalties and conditions of confinement more onerous than those it usually applies, although these conditions may be subject to challenge as violating basic legal protections in the requested state once the prisoner has been transferred.[129]

20.3.9 Forum bar

The practice of requested state's taking jurisdiction rather than extraditing because they feel they have a better claim to jurisdiction, is relatively uncommon, although it has received a recent boost in the UK. Negative public reaction to extradition of the 'Natwest Three' to the US[130] led to the British Government introducing a 'forum bar' in England and Wales in 2013[131] barring extradition to another state if by reason of forum, the extradition would not be in the 'interests of Justice'. This depends on whether a substantial measure of the defendant's relevant activity was performed in the UK, relevant activity meaning activity material to the commission of the extradition offence. The judge's decision has to take account of specified matters which include the place where most of the loss or harm occurred was intended to occur, the availability of evidence and the interests of victims and witnesses, as well as the belief of the prosecutor that the UK is not the most appropriate jurisdiction in which to prosecute the defendant. This allows the prosecutor to 'trump' the process by making a formal decision that the defendant should not be prosecuted because of insufficient evidence because it would not be in the public interest or because it would involve the disclosure of sensitive material. Using a milder approach, the Canadian Courts apply a so-called *Cotroni* assessment in deciding whether the matter should be better prosecuted in Canada thus barring extradition, focusing on balancing the individual's rights against inter alia Canada's international obligations not to provide a safe haven, as well as the impact on the place where the offence occurred.[132]

---

[127] UK–Rwanda Agreement on the Transfer of Sentenced Prisoners, 11 February 2010, UKTS No 9 (2011), para 9.

[128] UNODC Handbook, above n 123, 37.

[129] *Re Baraldini*, Constitutional review, No 73; ILDC 292 (IT 2001), (2001) 84 *Rivista di diritto internazionale* 490 (in Italian), 22 March 2001.

[130] *R (on the application of Bermingham) v Director of the Serious Fraud Office* [2006] EWHC 2000 (Admin).

[131] Sections 19B–F and sections 83A–E of the Extradition Act 2003 as amended by the Crimes and Courts Act 2013.

[132] *United States v Cotroni* [1989] 1 SCR 1469.

20.3.10 *Nemo bis in idem*

The rule against double jeopardy, or *nemo bis in idem debet vexari*, provides that someone convicted or acquitted for the same offence cannot be charged with it again. Although recognized as a human right in article 14 of the ICCPR, many transnational crimes by definition involve the same conduct in different states, and a sovereign's right to suppress harms to its interests has in practice overridden the interests of the individual to not be punished for the same conduct twice.[133] Provisions in the early suppression conventions, such as article 36(2)(b)(iv) of the 1961 Single Convention, follow extradition treaties and recognize that this is a matter for domestic law.

State practice varies, but the tendency is to limit the transnational application of the principle. Brazil applies its Penal Code regardless of the fact that the individual has been acquitted or convicted outside Brazil.[134] In 1987 in *Canada v Schmidt*[135] the Canadian Supreme Court reasoned that as extradition was not a trial there was no jurisdiction in the court to hear defences such as double jeopardy. This was changed by section 47(a) of the Canadian Extradition Act 1999, which provides that surrender must be refused if the individual would be entitled, if tried in Canada, to a discharge under Canadian law because of a previous acquittal or conviction. Under English law, the principle is no longer applied to extradition of individuals acquitted of serious transnational crimes including drug trafficking and terrorism offences in other states.[136] US courts do not regard violation of article 14 of the ICCPR as so fundamental as to prevent extradition, and a double jeopardy violation does not occur if the requested state agrees that one has not occurred.[137]

There are exceptions, however. Article 9(2) of the European Extradition Convention as amended by the Protocol of 1975[138] does implement a qualified double jeopardy prohibition to extradition. Article 54 of the Schengen Implementing Agreement applies double jeopardy transnationally, although only if the sentence has actually been enforced,[139] but this principle was taken up in the EU.[140] When double jeopardy is applied to extradition, it will depend on the particular treaty or national law as to whether it prevents extradition only narrowly for the same or substantially similar offences, or more broadly for the same or substantially similar acts or facts. In US courts, if the treaty expressly uses the term 'offence', the individual must have been convicted or acquitted of exactly the same offence.[141] In *Gambino v United States*,[142] for

---

[133] See, eg, article 4(1) of Protocol 7 to the European Convention on Human Rights, ETS 117, 22 November 1984, which implicitly limits the double jeopardy prohibition to decisions within a state.

[134] Article 7(1) of the 1940 Criminal Code.   [135] [1987] 1 SCR 500 at 503.

[136] Section 74(4) of the Criminal Justice Act 2003.

[137] *United States v Salinas Doria*, District Court decision, No 01 Cr 21(GEL); ILDC 1245 (US 2008) 21 October 2008.

[138] Strasbourg, 15 October 1975.

[139] Article 54 of the Convention implementing the Schengen Agreement of 14 June 1985 between the Governments of the States of the Benelux Economic Union, the Federal Republic of Germany and the French Republic on the gradual abolition of checks at their common borders, OJ L 239, 22 September 2000, 19.

[140] Article 50 of the Charter of Fundamental Rights for the European Union, OJ 2000/C 264/1, 18 December 2000.

[141] *Elcock v United States* 80 F Supp 2d 70 (EDNY 2000).

[142] District court judgment, 421 F Supp 2d 283 (D Mass 2006); ILDC 1215 (US 2006) 13 March 2006.

example, the US District Court held that the extradition of Mafia Godfather Gambino to Italy to face various conspiracy and drugs charges under articles 75 and 71 of the Italian Penal Code relating to the trafficking of heroin out of Sicily to the US had not violated the *nemo bis in idem* clause in the Italy–US Extradition Treaty, even though he had already been convicted and punished in the US for RICO offences based in part on conspiracy to distribute heroin into the US. In contrast in *Van Esbroek*[143] the Court of Justice of the EU expanded the scope of the rule by confirming that the condition for the operation of the rule was not prosecution for the same offence, but on the same set of facts if they are inextricably linked together, irrespective of the legal classification given to them by either state. Whether facts are linked is for the particular court to decide, but the European Court has put limits on its test by holding in *Kraaijenbrink*,[144] for example, that holding drug proceeds in one state and attempting to launder proceeds from the same drug trafficking in another even if linked by the same criminal intention does not meet its test.

The failure to provide a universal conduct-based double jeopardy bar in extradition expresses the exclusive transnational interest that drives transnational criminal law. Nevertheless, it has been justifiably decried as fundamentally unfair.[145]

20.3.11 The military and fiscal offence exceptions

Extradition treaties often exclude military offences, which are not offences under the ordinary criminal law, from extradition.[146] The suppression conventions implicitly recognize existing military offence exceptions when they leave the conditions of extradition to domestic law. Some states will also refuse to extradite for breaches of another state's revenue laws because the power of taxation is considered a fundamental aspect of state sovereignty. While extradition treaties have usually allowed parties to agree to abandon the exception,[147] many transnational crimes have fiscal implications, and more recent provisions in the suppression conventions, such as article 16(15) of the UNTOC and article 44(16) of the UNCAC, obliges parties to remove it entirely.

20.3.12 Procedural and practical obstacles

Procedural obstacles such as statutes of limitations, delay, immunity, incapacity, *lis-pendens*, plea bargains,[148] amnesty, trials in absentia, lack of extraterritorial jurisdiction, and the prospect of trials by special tribunals in the requesting state may also

---

[143] C-436/04 (Judgment 9 March 2006).   [144] C-367/05 (Judgment 18 July 2007).

[145] S Gless, 'Birds-Eye View and Worm's Eye View: Towards a Defendant-Based Approach in Transnational Criminal Law' 6(1) *Transnational Legal Theory* (2015) 117, 130 et seq.

[146] See, eg, article 4 of the 1957 European Convention on Extradition; para 14(d) of the Commonwealth Scheme.

[147] Article 5 of the 1957 European Convention on Extradition.

[148] In *Natshvili and Togonidze v Georgia* (2014) ECHR 454, the European Court of Human Rights held that the practice did not breach the presumption of innocence or the right to a fair trial. In *Mckinnon v Government of the United States of America and another* [2008] UKHL 59, the House of Lords held that only in extreme cases would such a process be regarded as so unconscionable as to justify an abuse of process justifying refusal of extradition.

prevent extradition. The suppression conventions leave these hurdles intact in domestic law. Even extradition for serious crimes like terrorism can be hit by statutes of limitations. In *Office of the Public Prosecutor v LarizIriondo*,[149] which dealt with the attempt to extradite an alleged ETA terrorist from Argentina to Spain, the Argentinean Supreme Court held that the 1987 bilateral extradition treaty between Argentina and Spain,[150] which provided that expiry of the statute of limitations prevented extradition, had not been modified by the 1997 Terrorist Bombings Convention because there was nothing in the Convention about statutes of limitation. Practical matters such as hesitation to request provisional arrest pending an extradition request, or tardiness in making a provisional arrest, can also prevent extradition, as without speedy action the alleged criminal will usually leave the jurisdiction.

20.3.13 Penalty exceptions

Although the suppression conventions press states towards imposing severe punishments, the severity of the likely punishment may also serve as an obstacle to extradition, revealing the absence of a shared conception of appropriate penalties for transnational crimes. The most well-known of these grounds for refusal is the death penalty exception contained, for example, in article 11 of the 1957 European Convention on Extradition. It is now common in bilateral extradition treaties and national extradition laws. Potential imposition of the death penalty, a penalty imposed in a number of states for transnational crimes such as drug trafficking and corruption, presents an almost insurmountable barrier to extradition from states that have abolished it. Courts were traditionally wary of allowing themselves to be drawn into any deeper review of disproportionality between the likely penalty other than the death penalty to be faced in the requested state and those applied in similar cases domestically. Arguments of this kind have instead been framed on human rights grounds, which have largely subsumed penalty exceptions.

20.4 Human Rights in Extradition

20.4.1 The development of human rights bars

In orthodox extradition law fugitives benefited only incidentally from the conditions and exceptions examined above because they are rights held by states; individuals were an object of the acts of the states concerned, not a rights-asserting subject. In the US,[151] for example, individuals have no standing to challenge violations of extradition treaties; they may at most only make objections that the other state party might have raised and only if the state does not decline to make such objection. The recognition of human rights as a potential bar to extradition had been signalled by the Council

---

[149] Ordinary Appeal Judgment, L845XL, Vol 328; ILDC 125 (AR 2005), 10 May 2005.
[150] Treaty [between Spain and Argentina] on Extradition and Judicial Assistance in Criminal Matters, 3 March 1987, in force 15 July 1991.
[151] *United States v Amawi and ors*, Lower court decision, Case No 3:06CR719 (ND Ohio); ILDC 1153 (US 2008) 24 March 2008, paras 8 and 11.

of Europe in 1978.[152] However, it was the *Soering*[153] decision of the European Court of Human Rights and the *Ng*[154] decision of the UN Human Rights Committee that signalled a departure from existing practice because they allowed fugitives to assert rights on their own account (the burden of proof being on them to raise the breach[155]) during the extradition process and forced the courts to enquire into the potential breach of their rights in the requesting state by officials and by non-state actors.[156]

Post-*Soering* suppression conventions oblige parties to protect human rights both during the extradition procedure in the requested party, during physical transfer, and at trial in the requesting party.[157] While the suppression conventions can be relied on by the parties to uphold these guarantees, they omit any right of individual petition and do not spell out standards of treatment, leaving the decision as to whether individuals can raise violations of the relevant provisions in the suppression conventions and the content of these provisions to applicable human rights conventions and domestic law. Some states have incorporated human rights violation as a bar to extradition in their domestic extradition legislation,[158] but most rely explicitly on their constitutions.[159] Both the courts and the executive in these states scrutinize the substantive crimes, penalties, and procedures which are likely to be applied by the requested states for their adherence to the human rights norms.

Human rights thus strengthen the institutionalization of a system of transnational criminal justice. Indeed, for states that rely on multilateral treaties such as the 1957 European Convention, roughly congruent multilateral protection of human rights through the European Convention on Human Rights provides a base for cooperation. States relying only on their domestic constitutional protections have to decide whether and if so to what extent these have an extraterritorial aspect. Human rights are not, however, absolute bars to extradition,[160] and although critics might argue that the application of human rights undermines extradition by increasing hurdles and lengthening the process, tribunals give a wide margin of appreciation to what they consider to be a fair extradition process.[161] In the UK, for example, there is a presumption that a country with which it has extradition arrangements will not violate a requested person's human rights.[162]

---

[152] Such as article 3 of the Second Additional Protocol to the European Convention on Extradition of 1978.

[153] *Soering v UK* (1989) 11 EHRR 439.

[154] *Ng v Canada*, Communication No 469/1991/, 5 November 1993, UN Doc CCPR/C/49/D/469/1991; 98 ILR 479.

[155] *Saadi v Italy*, App No 37201/06, [2008] ECHR 179, (2009).

[156] *Scattergood v Attorney General*, Appeal decision, Civil appeal no 12/2005; ILDC 921 (CY 2005), (2005) CLR 142, 21 January 2005.

[157] See, eg, article 10(2) of the 1988 SUA Convention; article 14 of the Terrorist Bombings Convention.

[158] See, eg, section 21 of the UK Extradition Act 2003.

[159] See, eg, *Extradition Proceedings Case, Constitutional Complaint and Motion for a Temporary Injunction of the US Citizen M, alias B, alias K, Order of the Second Senate*, 2 BvR 2259/04; ILDC 432 (DE 2005); Entscheidungen des Bundesverfassungsgerichts, BVerfGE 113, 154, para 14.

[160] *Sami Memis v Germany*, ECtHR App No 10499/83, 15 March 1984.

[161] J Dugard and C van den Wyngaert, 'Reconciling Extradition with Human Rights' 92 *American Journal of International Law* (1998) 196, 203–04.

[162] House of Lords Select Committee on Extradition, *2nd Report, Extradition: UK Law and Practice*, 10 March 2016, HL Paper 126, 18, para 32.

20.4.2 Rights and prohibitions relevant to extradition

Restrictions on punishment conditions

The right to life is the most obvious human right appropriate to extradition. The ICCPR itself does not prohibit the death penalty, and although its Second Optional Protocol[163] does, the Protocol has a limited number of parties. The decision in *Soering* held that article 3 of the European Convention on Human Rights, an absolute prohibition against torture and 'inhuman or degrading treatment or punishment', was violated by the prospect of protracted periods on death row. For many states it will depend on whether the constitutional protections in the requested state accept that the right to life restricts extradition to death penalty states. The Canadian Supreme Court has, for example, held in *United States v Burns*[164] that extradition of an individual to a state where they may face the death penalty violated their rights to life, liberty, and security of the person under section 7 of the Canadian Charter. The breach was unjustified because the Canadian Government had not requested assurances from the US that the death penalty would not be asked for by the prosecutor. In *Mohamed v President of the Republic of South Africa*[165] the South African Constitutional Court similarly held that deportation to the US to face terrorism charges without a guarantee that the death penalty would not be asked for, violated the individual's constitutional right to life, to dignity, and not to be subjected to cruel, inhuman, or degrading punishment. Bilateral extradition treaties with the US now usually make it a condition for extradition that the requested party may insist on an unequivocal undertaking that the death penalty will not be sought by US prosecuting authorities.[166]

Life imprisonment is also considered inhuman or degrading treatment by civil law states (they impose maximum fixed-term penalties). Article 9 of the 1981 Inter-American Convention on Extradition[167] explicitly prohibits extradition where the offence is punishable by life imprisonment. In *Kafakaris v Cyprus*[168] the European Court of Human Rights decided that a life sentence would breach the absolute prohibition on article 3 of the European Convention on Human Rights, if it was irreducible both de jure (there were no legal remedies that would allow for the possibility of early release) and de facto (such sentences were never reduced by reason of these remedies). The Court glossed this test in *Vintner and Others v UK*[169] holding that there must be both a real prospect of release in the light of progress during detention as well as a review mechanism that is certain and clear and applies clear tests for release. Corporal punishment may also serve to bar extradition as it is prohibited by article 31 of the UN Standard Minimum Rules for the Treatment of Prisoners[170] and held to be in violation of the prohibition on inhuman and degrading treatment.[171]

---

[163] Second Optional Protocol to the International Covenant on Civil and Political Rights, Aiming at the Abolition of the Death Penalty, 15 December 1989, A/RES/44/128.

[164] [2001] 1 SCR 283.   [165] 2001 (3) SA 893 (CC).

[166] See, eg, article 6 of the US–Cyprus Extradition Treaty, 17 June 1996, US Treaty Doc 105-16, in force 14 September 1999.

[167] 20 ILM 723 (1981).   [168] (2009) 49 EHRR 35.   [169] [2013] ECHR 645.

[170] 30 August 1955 UN Standard Minimum Rules for the Treatment of Offenders, adopted at the First UN Congress on the Prevention of Crime and Treatment of Offenders, UN Doc E/3048 (1957), endorsed by ECOSOC Res 663C (XXIV), 31 July 1957.

[171] *Tyrer v United Kingdom*, 26 Eur Ct HR (ser A) (1978).

Potential for grossly disproportionate prison sentences in the other state does not appear to be a reason for refusal, however. While in *United States v Jamieson*[172] the Quebec Court of Appeals refused to extradite an alleged drug trafficker to the US to face a minimum sentence of twenty years' imprisonment with no option of parole (in Canada the offence was punishable by five years), considering this cruel and inhuman punishment, the Canadian Supreme Court[173] reversed the decision on appeal. Canadian courts have consistently upheld surrender orders where the person sought faced a lengthy sentence under harsh conditions.[174]

The conditions of incarceration engage various rights, particularly the provision in article 3(1) of the Torture Convention obliging parties to refuse extradition where there are 'substantial grounds for believing that [the requested person] would be in danger of being subjected to torture'.[175] Violations of article 3 of the European Convention on Human Rights are usually established by showing a 'real risk' of exposure to torture or inhuman or degrading treatment or punishment, established either through indirect evidence of the general conditions in a particular country (a difficult task) or through direct evidence of specific violations (an easier task). The prohibition is absolute, so if there is a risk, the courts do not engage in balancing that risk against reasons for expulsion.[176] Poor prison conditions, including gross overcrowding, qualify as inhuman and degrading punishment[177] and overcrowding has been held to be a breach of article 3 of the European Convention.[178] Evidence before the House of Lords recorded that British courts have refused extradition to Lithuania, Latvia, Poland, Italy, Romania, Moldova, Russia, Ukraine, Turkey, South Africa, Kenya, Greece, among others, on the basis of concerns about prison conditions.[179] The courts have only slowly become more critical of the prospect of solitary confinement. In *Babar Ahmad and Others v The United Kingdom*,[180] relying on what it considered a high level of in-cell stimulation through access to media, phone call, visits, exercise, and communication through ventilation systems and during exercise periods, the European Court of Human Rights had rejected the defendants' argument that incarceration in solitary confinement at an 'ADX Supermax' prison in Colorado would violate their article 3 rights under the European Convention. However, the English Court in *McKinnon* case grounded refusal to extradite on his exposure to more than brief periods of solitary confinement, which would exacerbate his Asperger's.[181] In *Attorney*

---

[172] 93 CCC 3d 265 (Que CA 1994).

[173] *United States of America v Jamieson* [1996] 1 SCR 465.

[174] *Gwynne v Canada (Minister of Justice)* (1998), 103 BCAC 1; *United States of America v Reumayr* 2003 BCCA 375; *United States of America v Johnstone* 2013 BCCA 2; and *United States of America v UAS* 2013 BCCA 483.

[175] 10 December 1984 Convention against Torture and Other Cruel, Inhuman or Degrading Treatment or Punishment 1465 UNTS 85; Article 3(f) of the UN Model Treaty on Extradition; section 6 of the UN Model Law on Extradition 2004.

[176] *Saadi v Italy* App No 37201/06, [2008] ECHR 179, (2009).

[177] See, eg, *Lareau v Manson*, 651 F2d 96, 106 (2nd Circ 1981), which referred to article 9 of the UN Standard Minimum Rules for the Treatment of Prisoners.

[178] *Carl Peter Vernon, Gregory Hamilton, Fraser Heesom v Republic of South Africa* (2014) EWHC 4417 (Admin).

[179] House of Lords Select Committee, above n 163, 91, para 373.   [180] (2013) 56 EHHR 1.

[181] *McKinnon v US* [2008] UKHL 59.

General v Damache[182] the Irish High Court refused extradition to the US for terrorism, Justice Donnelly finding:

> In all of the circumstances set out above, the institutionalisation of solitary confinement in the ADX with its routine isolation from meaningful contact and communication with staff and other inmates, for a prolonged pre-determined period of at least 18 months and continuing almost certainly for many years, amounts to a breach of the constitutional requirement to protect persons from inhuman and degrading treatment and to respect the dignity of the human being. Arbitrary deprivations of outdoor recreations for the actions of what may be mentally disturbed persons add further to the breaches. Even if those matters were insufficient on their own to amount to a violation, the lack of meaningful judicial review creates a risk of arbitrariness in the detention of the person in solitary confinement and therefore confirms that the prolonged detention in solitary confinement amounts to a breach of constitutional rights.[183]

Violation of article 8 of the European Convention on Human Rights, the right to respect for private and family life, home, and correspondence, also bears on post-extradition conditions of incarceration, although its use in extradition has been more difficult because of its relative nature. The test in UK law is, for example, whether the interference with the family life of the requested person, and other members of his family is outweighed by public interest in extradition, with acceptance that such an interest is weighty and constant, and that it will not be outweighed unless the interference with family life is exceptionally severe.[184]

The degree of specificity of the information necessary to show potential violation through conditions of treatment has been a problem for the courts. In 2016 in *Aranyosi* and *Căldăraru*[185] the Court of Justice of the EU laid down the test for assessing whether serious indications exist that the conditions of detention in a member state infringe the requested person's fundamental rights under the EU Charter of Fundamental Rights. In the first step the executing authority must initially rely on 'objective, reliable, specific and properly updated' information on the prevailing detention conditions that demonstrate the existence of either systemic or general deficiencies. In the second step, it must ascertain whether in the specific case the requested person would face a 'real risk' of inhuman or degrading treatment. It must ask for additional information and postpone surrender until it receives enough information to rule out the risk or in the absence thereof refuse surrender. It thus seems clear that general information is insufficient.

Process rights

Article 5 of the European Convention on Human Rights, the right to liberty and security of the person, and article 6, the right to a fair trial within a reasonable time, have not

---

[182] [2015] IEHC 339.   [183] ibid, para 11.11.19.
[184] *HH and others v Deputy Prosecutor of the Italian Republic, Genoa and others* (2012) 3 WLR 90.
[185] *Aranyosi* C-404/15, *Căldăraru* C-659/15, 5 April 2016.

been particularly useful in barring extradition because of the difficulties of prospective analysis of a pre-trial detention and criminal process in a foreign criminal justice system. Nor have allegations that torture will be used to gather evidence. In *France v Diab*,[186] the appellant complained that upon his extradition from Canada to France, his prosecution for terrorism would be based on evidence that was plausibly connected to the use of torture, in violation of Charter rights. The court held that the appellant had failed to establish (i) a plausible connection between the challenged evidence and the use of torture and (ii) that there was a real risk that torture-derived evidence would be used in the French process.[187] General allegations that France cooperated with Syria and Syria used torture, were not enough; he had to show a specific link between the impugned evidence and an act of torture.[188]

20.4.3 Assurances

States respond to potential human rights violation in the requesting state by seeking assurances from the requesting state that it will not engage in the particular treatment or ensure particular conditions. Paradoxically, simply by seeking assurances the requested state acknowledges that there is a potential risk of torture and ill treatment/death. Nonetheless a great weight is placed on them in the absence of much else. An obligation to give assurances can be made part of the bilateral extradition relations between the states, and the UN Model Treaty recognizes the use of assurances that the requested state will not impose capital punishment in the particular case.[189] In *Aleksnaya v Lithuania*,[190] despite many obvious faults with assurances given by Lithuania including the fact that local prosecutors had no knowledge of them, an English court still held that extradition could be based on them.

States have reformed their domestic law in order to make it possible to give assurances. The Indian Extradition Act 1962, for example, has a specific provision for non-imposition of the death penalty where a fugitive criminal accused of an offence punishable by death in India is extradited to India by a foreign country whose laws do not provide for the death penalty.[191] Giving such assurances comes at a cost to requesting states, however, because it distorts their justice system if the penalty a criminal faces and their treatment depends on where they are arrested.

The Council of Europe's Commissioner for Human Rights has commented that such convenient non-binding promises should not be allowed to undermine the principle of non-refoulement of refugees seeking asylum.[192] Assurances are regularly challenged by the person subject to extradition,[193] and states have begun to look deeper into the grounds for them. In *Suresh v Canada (Minister of Citizenship and Immigration)*[194]

---

[186] 2014 ONCA 374.   [187] ibid, para 272.   [188] ibid, para 268.   [189] Article 4(g)(d).
[190] [2014] EWHC 437 (Admin).   [191] Section 34-c.
[192] 'Viewpoint' of the Council of Europe Commissioner for Human Rights, Thomas Hammarberg, 27 June 2006.
[193] See, eg, *Ahmad and Aswat v United States, Appeal judgment* [2006] EWHC 2927 (Admin); ILDC 733 (UK 2006) 30 November 2006.
[194] 2002 SCC 1 at paras 124–25.

the Canadian Supreme Court accepted that the Minister could look at the requesting state's human rights record and its capacity to meet its assurances. In assessing the question whether assurances removed the real risk of ill-treatment in *Othman (Abu Qatada) v The United Kingdom*[195] the European Court of Human Rights spelled out the following test:

> 187. In any examination of whether an applicant faces a real risk of ill-treatment in the country to which he is to be removed, the Court will consider both the general human rights situation in that country and the particular characteristics of the applicant. In a case where assurances have been provided by the receiving State, those assurances constitute a further relevant factor which the Court will consider. However, assurances are not in themselves sufficient to ensure adequate protection against the risk of ill-treatment. There is an obligation to examine whether assurances provide, in their practical application, a sufficient guarantee that the applicant will be protected against the risk of ill-treatment. The weight to be given to assurances from the receiving State depends, in each case, on the circumstances prevailing at the material time.

The House of Lords Select Committee on Extradition[196] believes the arrangements in place in Britain for monitoring assurances are flawed. In *India v Badesha*,[197] the British Columbia Court of Appeal (BCCA) doubted India's capacity to carry out the assurances it had given. It did not accept the presumption that Canada's treaty party will keep its promises, and set aside the extradition order on review.[198] On appeal, the Canadian Supreme Court, emphasizing the seriousness of the crime and the importance of meeting the treaty obligations, but relying on the fact that the Minister had considered a range of contextual factors the BCCA had not fully taken into account, reversed the decision.[199]

20.5 Extradition Procedure

The suppression conventions give little guidance on the procedure for extradition; they rely on extradition treaties and domestic law. The initial request may have to be made through diplomatic channels and can thus be slowed by formality. The suppression conventions do make provision for parties to use provisional arrest to ensure presence.[200] Interpol assists by circulating Red Notices (wanted notices) passed on by the requesting state's National Central Bureau, which request the provisional arrest of a particular individual pending a formal request for extradition. The issuing of Red Notices surged from 2,343 in 2005 to 7,678 in 2011 to request provision arrest anticipating extradition, many issued by states without adequate protection of human rights.[201] Within the EU, the Schengen Information System II makes it possible for

---

[195] [2012] ECHR 56.
[196] *2nd Report, Extradition: UK Law and Practice*, 10 March 2016, HL Paper 126, paras 88–94.
[197] 2016 BCCA 88.   [198] ibid, para 61.   [199] 2017 SCC 44, at paras 6–7, para 66.
[200] See, eg, article 44(10) of the UNCAC.
[201] C Heard and A Tinsley, 'The Power of Interpol Red Notices' 28(8) *International Law Enforcement Reporter* (2012) 299.

almost instantaneous alerts to be sent requesting the arrest of individuals for extradition. When an arrest has been made the requesting state is informed and it formally requests extradition.

During the process representation for both sides is necessary. In most states national prosecutors will represent the requesting state, which helps to ensure compliance with domestic procedures. After arrest the individual may apply for bail, a sensitive issue for extradition because of the possibility of flight of the fugitive. Their right to be granted bail, and the conditions imposed if granted, is a matter of domestic law. As noted, the decision to extradite itself is usually a two-stage, part legal, part political procedure, although the scope of enquiry of the judiciary and executive varies from state to state. Both branches of governments play a role in balancing the liberty interests of the individual against international cooperation.

At the first stage, a tribunal gives an opinion on whether the various conditions for extradition have been met and whether extradition is precluded by one of the exceptions. The status of the court, and the exact procedure, and rights of review and appeal, depend on domestic law. The documents required for extradition usually include a copy of the warrant of arrest issued by a judge or other competent authority, a copy of the charging document, and documents, statements, or other types of information which described the identity and probable location of the person sought.[202] These documents must be in a form readily usable by the requested state's authorities. Poorly translated documents and copies rather than the originals, all cause problems. The authentic indication of documents can also be a problem, and states have taken steps to remedy the situation where documents do not meet domestic standards for authentication. In the US, for example, statute makes 'authentication' by a 'consular officer' the sole bar to admissibility.[203] Appeal rights from this hearing vary from state to state. In the US, for example, there is no direct right of appeal from the decision of the extradition court certifying extraditability.

The final decision is usually for the executive, the broad and indeterminate nature of which, inter alia, may permit an enquiry into the quality of criminal justice in the requesting state without appearing to do so. Certain discretionary and absolute human rights bars may be left to the executive, together with issues such as age and health of the accused.

There has been a lot of emphasis in recent years on the establishment of central authorities in states in order to enable extradition. The idea is to develop a coordinating role beyond simply being the official point of service of international documentation. The United States Department of Justice's Office of International Affairs (OIA), for example, is an organization of extradition experts who do not appear in court hearings, but coordinate US efforts in regard to extradition by, for example, assisting in the drafting of incoming and outgoing extradition requests and ensuring that time limits are met.

---

[202] See article 2(1), US–India Extradition Treaty, 25 June 1997, UST 105-30 (1997).
[203] 18 USC § 3190.

20.6 Simplified Extradition

'Simplified extradition' involves an invitation to the individual prior to or during an extradition hearing to waive their rights and consent to return to the requesting country without further judicial proceedings, and under some instruments to renounce their entitlement to the rule of specialty.[204] This is mainly to the advantage of the state because it speeds up the process significantly, although it can mean the defendant is better able to attend to their defence. The disadvantages to the individual are obvious: they lose the substantive protections available during the judicial leg of the extradition process—double criminality and in particular specialty.

20.7 Surrender under the European Arrest Warrant

Established in 2002 by a European Council Framework Decision,[205] the European Arrest Warrant (EAW) is 'an attempt to replace extradition in the traditional sense with a system of surrender without the involvement of the executive with a minimum of formality'.[206] According to article 1(1) of the Framework Decision, the EAW is 'a judicial decision issued by a Member State with a view to the arrest and surrender by another Member State of a requested person, for the purposes of conducting a criminal prosecution or executing a custodial sentence or detention order'. Mutual recognition is the founding principle of the EU and expressed through the EAW. It has been argued that to apply it properly, a state must abandon all but a vestige of sovereignty and admit a foreign decision as if it were its own, even when that decision does not fit with their legal system.[207]

Although it dramatically curtails the conditions for extradition, the Framework Decision does not abandon them entirely. Article 2(1) of the Framework Decision provides that an EAW may only be issued for offences that carry a penalty of at least twelve months or more. Article 2(2) lists thirty-two mostly generic transnational crimes such as 'laundering of the proceeds of crime', for which double criminality cannot be required so long as the particular offence carries a penalty of at least three years. Matching offences is considered unnecessary because the EAW is based on the notion that the offence is defined in the issuing state's law and does not require verification by the executing state. This argument was challenged in the Court of Justice of the EU in *Advocaten voor de Wereld*[208] on the basis that without double criminality, legality was not met. Advocate General Ruiz-Jarabo distinguished extradition involving two

---

[204] See, eg, articles 4 and 5 of the Third Additional Protocol to the European Convention on Extradition, Strasbourg, 10 November 2010, CETS 209.

[205] Council Framework Decision on the European Arrest Warrant and the Surrender Procedures between Member States of the European Union of 13 June 2002 OJ L 190/1, 18 July 2002, in force 1 January 2004.

[206] Sir Scott Baker, David Perry QC, and Anand Doobay, *A Review of the United Kingdom's Extradition Arrangements* (Home Office, 2011), 116.

[207] HG Nilsson, *Developments in Mutual Assistance and Extradition and the International Level*, HEUNI 125th International Training Course, Visiting Expert's Papers, 24.

[208] Case C-303/05, 12 September 2006.

states where issues of legality were protected by strict reciprocity and double criminality because the norms had their origins in different spheres, from the EU's supranational harmonized legal system where extradition did not involve a legal relationship between 'hermetically sealed spaces where a case by case assessment is required to determine that the assistance does not undermine the foundations of social organisation'.[209] The Grand Chamber held that the Framework Decision does not seek to harmonize the law of the member states; EU members were all part of the same human rights regime and it was their law which determined the specific definitions of offences and must meet legality.[210] Attempts to resurrect double criminality in member states' courts have been dismissed.[211]

The Framework Decision deals with the other elements of extradition in a piecemeal way. Article 4(7)(b) permits the executing state to refuse to execute the warrant if there is no jurisdictional double criminality for an extraterritorial offence. In terms of article 27(1) member states may notify the General Secretariat of the European Council that they consent to the abrogation of specialty unless the executing judicial authority in the particular case decides otherwise. Article 3 provides for mandatory exceptions while article 4 provides for discretionary exceptions. The exclusion of the political offence exception was not controversial, but the exclusion of the nationality exception was hard to swallow for some civil law states, even though article 5(3) allows the executing state to subject transfer of a national to the condition of return to serve their sentence, and article 4(2) makes nationality an optional exception if the executing state is itself prosecuting for the same matter. When Germany relaxed its constitutional prohibition on extradition of nationals within the EU,[212] the Federal Constitutional Court responded by declaring the statute implementing the EAW void.[213] Content to permit extradition of German nationals for transnational crimes with 'a significant connection to a foreign country', it considered the law a disproportionate restriction of a national's right against extradition because it did not provide for a discretion to refuse in situations where there was a significant domestic connection to the offence. The courts of Poland and Cyprus also struck down implementing legislation.[214] Legislative amendments have since been made to make possible the execution of the EAW against nationals.

The other major innovation of the EAW is that it eliminates the confirmatory role of the executive in the processing of the foreign warrant, in order to remove political considerations from the decision. In order to expedite the extradition process, a state issuing an EAW must follow a uniform format,[215] setting out the identity and

---

[209] ibid, Opinion of Advocate General Ruiz-Jarabo Colomer, paras 42–44.

[210] ibid, para 52 et seq.

[211] *Ektor v National Public Prosecutor of Holland* [2007] EWHC 3106 (UK).

[212] Article 16(2) of the Basic Law (*Grundgesetz*).

[213] *European Arrest Warrant Act Case*, Individual constitutional complaint, BVerfG, 2 BvR 2236/04; ILDC 433 (DE 2005), 113 BVerfGE 273–348; (2005) NJW 2289–2303, 18 July 2005.

[214] See, eg, the *Decision of 27 April 2005 of the Polish Constitutional Tribunal*, Orzecznictwie Trybunalu Konstytucyjnego. Zbiór urzendowy (Jurisdiction of the Constitutional Tribunal. Official Collection) No 4/A/2005, item 42; and the *Decision of the Supreme Court of Cyprus*, Judgment of 7.11.2005, Ap No 294/2005.

[215] Article 8 and annex.

nationality of the person sought, the details of the issuing judicial authority and the warrant it has issued for arrest, details of the offence and the circumstances of its commission. Execution must normally be within ten days of the requested person's consent to surrender, or in the absence of consent, within ninety days.[216]

Implementation of the Framework Decision across the EU has led to a steady increase in the number of EAWs issued. The UK, for example, receives thousands of EAW requests per year while conventional extradition requests number in the hundreds.[217] The EAW has also withstood attack on human rights grounds. The Court of Justice of the EU has consistently given priority to maintaining the effectiveness of the EAW.[218] In *Radu*[219] it ruled that the EU's Charter of Fundamental Rights does not allow refusal to execute a EAW on the basis that the person was not heard by the issuing authority. In *Melloni*[220] it upheld an EAW issued by the Italian authorities on the basis of an *in absentia* judgment, in spite of the fact that it conflicted with the individual's right to a fair trial under article 24(2) of the Spanish Constitution.

EU member states have been forced to adapt their practice to make execution of these warrants possible. In *Assange (Appellant) v The Swedish Prosecution Authority (Respondent)*,[221] for example, the UK Supreme Court held that the Swedish Prosecution Authority constituted a 'judicial authority' able to issue an EAW under section 2(2) of the Extradition Act 2003. Nevertheless, the complaints of EU member states that other member states required too much additional detailed information in support of extradition requests[222] were directed mainly at the British, who were exercised about the use of EAWs for less serious offending. The UK made a number of changes to its implementation of the EAW including applying a 'try or charge' requirement barring execution of an EAW unless the issuing state's authority has made a decision either to charge or try the person, which will cause difficulties for those states that do not make that decision unless the person concerned has made their first appearance.[223] The UK has also imposed a 'proportionality' requirement, barring extradition if inter alia the courts consider that execution of an incoming EAW would be disproportionate.[224] Three criteria are weighed by the judge: (a) the seriousness of the alleged conduct; (b) the likely penalty that would be imposed; and (c) the possibility that the foreign authorities might take less coercive measures than request extradition.[225] One such measure is implementation of a European supervision order, the possibility of transferring pre-trial non-custodial supervision

---

[216] Articles 17 and 23.   [217] House of Lords Select Committee, above n 163, 38.

[218] See generally V Mitsilegas, 'The Symbiotic Relationship between Mutual Trust and Fundamental Rights in Europe's Area of Criminal Justice' 6(4) *New Journal of European Criminal Law* (2015) 460.

[219] Case C-396/11, Judgment of 29 January 2013.

[220] Case C-399/11, Judgment of 26 February 2013.   [221] [2012] UKSC 22.

[222] See, eg, Evaluation Report On The Fourth Round Of Mutual Evaluations 'The Practical Application Of The European Arrest Warrant And Corresponding Surrender Procedures Between Member States' Report On Germany, 7058/1/09 REV 1, 31 March 2009, para 3.6, which records complaints from German officials about British requests for more information.

[223] Section 12A of the Extradition Act 2003.

[224] Section 21A of the Extradition Act 2003 (inserted by the Antisocial Behaviour, Crime and Policing Act 2014, section 157(2)).

[225] Section 21A(3).

measures such as release on bail from the state that requests arrest to the state where they are normally resident.[226]

Sovereignty concerns and distrust mean that a mechanism like the EAW for surrender based on the judicial orders of another state is unlikely to be included in a suppression convention in the near future. However, similar simplified systems exist in other parts of the world[227] and arrest warrants of this kind may serve as a model for future bilateral arrangements.

20.8 Alternatives to Extradition

The difficulties of extradition of alleged transnational criminals have led to the use of various forms of irregular rendition of dubious legality. Deportation is used as an alternative to extradition, even though it is a unilateral act to protect domestic order that offers none of the protections of an extradition treaty, and its use has been rejected by the courts of some states.[228] The US also resorts to luring someone out of a state where they cannot be extradited to one where they can, a practice it considers legal.[229] In the *Yemeni Citizens Extradition Case*, the German Federal Constitutional Court rejected a challenge by two Yemenis to their extradition to the US to face terrorism charges, who had been lured to Germany by an undercover US agent, on the basis that there was no rule of international law prohibiting extradition of persons who had been lured out of their home country and the sovereignty violation of the state from which they were lured was proportional to the serious nature of the offences involved.[230] The most notorious method of acquiring custody of alleged offenders located in other states is extraterritorial abduction. Abduction violates the sovereignty and territorial integrity of the asylum state. It may lead to reprisals[231] and to the discontinuance of international cooperation generally, and has been condemned by the UN Security Council.[232] The US has, however, taken the position since the 1990s in its wars on drugs and then terror that abduction is necessary because of the inadequacy of international law in prosecuting transnational criminals shielded from effective enforcement action by states that refuse extradition.[233] The argument relies on self-defence

---

[226] Council Framework Decision 2009/829/JHA of 23 October 2009 on the application, between Member States of the European Union, of the principle of mutual recognition to decisions on supervision measures as an alternative to provisional detention, OJ L 294/20, 11 November 2009.

[227] Eg, part 4 of the New Zealand Extradition Act 1999 which provides for the endorsement of arrest warrants issued by Australia and certain designated states. A backing of warrants system also operates between Singapore, Malaysia, and Brunei, in East Africa, between Ireland and the UK, between South Africa and associated states, and a Nordic Arrest Warrant is operative in the Nordic States.

[228] *Mohammed and Dalvie v The President of the Republic of South Africa and Others* 2001 (3) SA 893 (CC).

[229] *United States v Yunis* 681 F Supp 909 (DDC 1988).   [230] Above n 17, paras 53–62.

[231] In 2009 an Italian Court convicted twenty-three CIA agents *in absentia* for the kidnapping and abduction of Abu Omar, taken to Egypt in 2003 from Italy, where he was allegedly tortured. See *Public Prosecutor v Adler and ors*, First instance judgment, No 12428/09; ILDC 1492 (IT 2010), 1 February 2010.

[232] UN SC Res 579 (1985).

[233] See, eg, A Fletcher, 'Pirates and Smugglers: An Analysis of the use of Abductions to Bring Drug Traffickers to Trial' 32 *Virginia Journal of International Law* (1991) 233; D Kash, 'Abducting Terrorists under PDD 39: Much Ado about Nothing New' 13 *American University International Law Review* (1999) 139.

under article 51 of the UN Charter to override sovereignty, because the US considers itself specially affected by particular transnational crimes. The argument accepts that a state can simultaneously work both within multilateral international frameworks such as the drug conventions to achieve their aims, and unilaterally outside them if they are unable to achieve their aims. Abduction may also violate human rights such as the right to protection from arbitrary arrest[234] and individuals subject to rendition are vulnerable to abuse and maltreatment during the process itself.[235]

These issues play out in domestic courts when the accused is placed on trial and the prosecution attempts to rely on the doctrine of *mala captus bene dentus* (unlawfully captured, legally detained) to avoid defence challenges to jurisdiction. The granting of *in personam* jurisdiction following the Ker-Frisbie doctrine[236] to US courts over foreign defendants disregards the method used to bring the defendant before court. *US v Alvarez-Machain*[237] is perhaps the most well-known of the string of cases that have followed this precedent. A majority of the US Supreme Court held that Alvarez-Machain's abduction did not prohibit trial in the US for a violation of its criminal law, regardless of his Mexican nationality, the existence of an extradition treaty between the US and Mexico, and the strong protests of the Mexican government at the violation of international law. The basis of its decision was that unless the extradition treaty between Mexico and the US explicitly prohibited abduction or other means of gaining custody outside its terms then the Ker-Frisbie doctrine applied. Violation of Mexican territorial sovereignty was a matter for the executive. The minority held that the abduction was a flagrant violation of the territorial integrity of Mexico and of the extradition treaty. The only other limited restriction imposed on abduction is that the US government must not, in obtaining jurisdiction, have engaged in misconduct 'of the most shocking and outrageous kind'.[238] The US is not alone in using abduction. Brazil has also taken jurisdiction over abducted or irregularly rendered persons.[239] The European Court of Human Rights sanctioned Abdullah Öcalan's abduction from Kenya by finding that because it was legal in Turkey it was in accordance with a procedure prescribed by law and not in violation of article 5(1) of the European Convention on Human Rights.[240] In contrast, in *R v Horseferry Road Magistrates' Court, ex parte Bennett*[241] the House of Lords held that the Court had a role in the oversight of executive action. The process for Bennett's return to the UK was extradition; if that process was ignored, the Court would refuse jurisdiction. The European Court of Human Rights held in *El-Masri v The Former Yugoslav Republic of Macedonia*[242] that states responsible for aiding in such abductions breach the abductee's human rights, noting

---

[234] Article 9 of the UDHR; article 9(1) of the ICCPR.   [235] *Bozano v France* [1986] ECHR 16.

[236] *Ker v Illinois* 119 US 436; *Frisbie v Collins* 342 US 519.

[237] 112 USC 2188 (1992). The Ker-Frisbie doctrine has been followed consistently through the US war on terror—see, eg, *United States v Amawi and ors*, Lower court decision, Case No 3:06CR719 (ND Ohio); ILDC 1153 (US 2008) 24 March 2008, paras 13–15.

[238] *United States v Anderson* 472 F3d 662 (9th Cir 2006).

[239] *Re Louis Chedade Bachour, Habeas corpus proceeding, Appeal judgment*, No 54668–0 (1995); ILDC 1089 (BR 1996) 13 December 1995.

[240] *Öcalan v Turkey*, ECtHR Application no 46221/99, 12 March 2003.

[241] [1994] 1 AC 42. See also *S v Ebrahim* [1991] ZASCA 3 (South Africa).

[242] Application no 39630/09, Grand Chamber, Judgment of 13 December 2012, para 239.

that such a 'deliberate circumvention of due process, is anathema to the rule of law and the values protected by the Convention, and thus flagrantly denies the rights …'.

20.9 Conclusion

The society of states has slowly been moving away from the nineteenth-century model of extradition by reducing traditional state-based prerogatives that provide obstacles to extradition, and by harmonizing national laws and procedures. While human rights laws has added new bars, they too are being incorporated within a developing system of transnational criminal justice. Nonetheless, the pursuit of the fugitive transnational offender remains difficult, and given that extradition is a form of international relations, the key to resolving many of the problems with extradition is primarily political, and only secondarily legal. States are notoriously sceptical of extradition. Some are eager to request it but loath to grant it. Some want simultaneously to exploit both legal and extra-legal ways of gaining custody. Goal-directed behaviour of this kind weakens the international treaties, including the suppression conventions, directed at enabling extradition. The goal of an effective 'no-hiding-place strategy', universal extradition, is far from being realized.

PART IV

INSTITUTIONS, IMPLEMENTATION, AND DEVELOPMENT

21

Institutions

21.1 Introduction

The modern era of institutional development against crime probably began with the establishment of the International Penitentiary Commission in 1878. It has matured since then into a complex range of institutions that share a set of fairly inflexible beliefs about what transnational crime is, what causes it and how to respond to it, and this common sense of what is and is not valid assist them to generate a roughly common policy response.[1] This chapter provides a short guide to the institutions that currently play an important formal and practical role in the creation of new policies and new rules of transnational criminal law and in the administration of the resulting system.

The chapter is not comprehensive. A maze of rapidly evolving institutions (which soon dates any comprehensive survey) are involved in transnational criminal law in some way or another. In line with the general focus of the book on the global multilateral components of transnational criminal law, rather than regional or national elements, its main focus is on the UN criminal justice institutions, which are based mainly in Vienna. Within the UN different institutions play different roles: some make transnational criminal policy, some transform this into law, some provide oversight and some provide administrative and technical expertise. The following discussion follows this breakdown of functions, before looking at other significant intergovernmental institutions and the role of non-governmental organizations.

21.2 The UN's Drug Control and Criminal Justice Mandates

The UN's mandate in regard to drug control and criminal justice have evolved separately. Drug control has been the major preoccupation of the UN system since the Second World War. The much older (established in 1946[2]) Commission on Narcotic Drugs (CND), with fifty-three members, is more narrowly focused on the global drug situation. While the UN took over the League of Nation's drugs mandates under existing drug control conventions it did not on its founding take over mandates in regard to other forms of transnational crime.[3] The UN's criminal justice mandate emerged out of the UN's mandate under article 55 of the UN Charter to promote solutions to social problems and respect for human rights. In 1947 the United Nations Economic and Social Council (ECOSOC) signalled its intention to assume a leading

---

[1] Thus meeting the conditions for an epistemic community, see P Haas, 'Introduction: Epistemic Communities and International Policy Coordination' 46 *International Organization* (1992) 1, 3.

[2] ESC Res (I) of 16 February 1946.

[3] SM Redo, *Blue Criminology: The Power of United Nations Ideas to Counter Crime Globally* (Helsinki: HEUNI, 2012), 48.

role in responding to crime,[4] a role confirmed by the UN General Assembly in 1950.[5] ECOSOC convened the first United Nations Congress for the Prevention of Crime and Treatment of Offenders in 1955 (since renamed the UN Congress for Crime Prevention and Criminal Justice). The Congress is held every five years, and transnational organized crime and terrorism have preoccupied these meetings since the 1990 Congress in Cuba. Having relied on an ad hoc advisory committee of experts since 1950, ECOSOC also established an expert advisory group in 1971.[6] Its last incarnation, the Committee on Crime Prevention and Control,[7] was replaced in 1991 when the General Assembly established the UN Crime Prevention and Criminal Justice Programme.[8] Under this programme the inter-governmental UN Commission on Crime Prevention and Criminal Justice (CCPCJ) consisting of the representatives of forty member states,[9] took over from the expert committee in making policy on general crime prevention and criminal justice (other than drugs) primarily because in the highly politicized atmosphere of crime control states felt that it neither allowed adequate governmental participation and oversight nor had the required profile or resources to respond to global criminal justice issues.[10]

The CCPCJ and the CND meet annually in order to supervise implementation of the suppression conventions that fall within their mandates. Discussion ranges from the governance of the United Nations Office on Drugs and Crime (UNODC), to treaty implementation, crime trends, new crimes threats, and so forth. Although the administration of both organizations is run out of the UNODC and the crime and drug programmes were merged in 2003, the division between drugs and crime has never been entirely erased. The former has its own funding streams, and the UNODC reflects its special nature in the name.

21.3 Policy-making at the UN

The UN Crime Congress offers a forum for an exchange of views between states, inter-governmental organizations (IGOs), non-governmental organizations (NGOs) and individual experts representing various professions and disciplines, the presentation of research, and the provisions of advice and priorities to the CCPCJ. At the 13th Congress in Doha in 2015 over 4,000 individuals attended. Nonetheless, the extent of participation in these meetings is something of an illusion; they are substantially inter-governmental in nature, only governments may vote on the adoption of resolutions, and everyone else is there as Clark puts it, 'on sufferance'.[11] The UN Crime Congresses do function to develop policy ideas but are regarded as somewhat inconsequential as

---

[4] ESC Res 155C(VIII) of 13 August 1947; see Redo, above n 3, 109–14.
[5] GA Resolution 415 (V) of 1 December 1950.   [6] ESC Res 1584(L).
[7] See generally RS Clark, *The United Nations Crime Prevention and Criminal Justice Program: Formulation of Standards and Efforts at their Implementation* (Philadelphia: University of Pennsylvania Press, 1994), chs 1–3.
[8] GA Res 46/152, 18 December 1991.   [9] ESC Res 1992/1, 6 February 1992.
[10] See C Ram, 'The Commission on Crime Prevention and Criminal Justice: a Search for Complementarity between Politics and Criminology' in SM Redo, *Blue Criminology: The Power of United Nations Ideas to Counter Crime Globally* (Helsinki: HEUNI, 2012), 128–31.
[11] Clark, above n 7, 75.

a policy-making body and more as talking shops.[12] As a participant in the second UN Crime Congress in 1960, Williams noted: 'One cannot attend one of these vast international jamborees without wondering who is benefiting from the experience, and what contribution is being made in the debates (and outside) towards a deeper knowledge and understanding of the subject.'[13]

There were nearly 200 high level panels and side events at the Doha Congress in 2015; Bosetti 'couldn't help wonder about the value of these type of mega-gatherings'.[14]

ECOSOC's functional commissions drive criminal justice policy more directly. The CCPCJ, for example, functions as a forum for member states to set out their political priorities; expert opinion is gathered in subordinate bodies such as expert working groups administered by the UNODC and from think-tanks in the Programme Network of Institutes (PNI—see below). When the will of different states coheres to a consensus position, the CCPCJ itself makes a recommendation. Ram overstates the case when he claims that the outputs of the CCPCJ are 'seen by the Member States and their populations as valid and legitimate because they are the outputs of open and transparent deliberations, first in establishing criminological validity, and second in establishing political consensus'.[15] There may be political consensus at an international level among states but neither criminological validity nor political legitimacy are assured by its processes. The CCPCJ is largely controlled by diplomats with limited or no expertise, leading frequently to simplistic interventions reflective of parochial positions. The CCPCJ makes political recommendations which are then presented to political bodies—the ECOSOC and the General Assembly. While ECOSOC and then the General Assembly sanction their resolutions, these matters are largely a 'done deal' by the time it becomes seized of them.

The CCPCJ's work has traditionally been divided between criminal justice standards and its work on transnational crime control, although more recently member states of the CCPCJ have prioritized the suppression of transnational crimes in which they have a specific interest. This is revealed by the shift from expert to political opinion in the CCPCJ discussed above but also through direction of funding to special projects on the prevention of different forms of transnational crime and reduction of the amount going to the CCPCJ general budget.[16] In addition, the CCPCJ has lost influence over suppression of transnational organized crime and corruption to the conference of the parties (COPs) of the United Nations Convention against Transnational Organized Crime (UNTOC) and United Nations Convention against Corruption (UNCAC), leaving the CCPCJ to deal with other transnational crimes.[17]

---

[12] Redo, above n 3, 135.

[13] JE Hall Williams, 'Two International Congresses' 1 *British Journal of Criminology* (1961) 254, 260.

[14] L Bosetti, *The Post-2015 Development Agenda and its Rule of Law Dilemma: A Report from the 13th UN Crime Congress*, UNU Centre for Policy Research, 29 April 2015, at <http://cpr.unu.edu/the-post-2015-development-agenda-and-its-rule-of-law-dilemma-a-report-from-the-13th-un-crime-congress.html> last visited 15 September 2016.

[15] Ram, above n 10, 129.   [16] Ram, above n 10, 128.   [17] Redo, above n 3, 132.

21.4 Law-making at the UN

Usually the process of treaty-making under the auspices of the General Assembly begins in its Sixth (Legal) Committee. However, most suppression conventions are developed independently of this process. Negotiated in full diplomatic conferences, they, and the policies on which they are built, often originate in the policy-making activities of the ECOSOC's functional commissions. The CND, for example, adopts draft resolutions which it passes to the ECOSOC either to be rejected or adopted by ECOSOC as its resolutions. ECOSOC can then take the matter one step further by preparing draft suppression conventions for submission to the UN General Assembly.[18] These are adopted by the General Assembly in resolutions and then opened for signature. The General Assembly also sponsors political programmes of action to implement these treaties once they have been adopted. More recently, as we have seen in Chapter 7, the UN Security Council has begun to take Chapter VII action against transnational crimes considered to threaten international peace and security such as terrorism, bypassing the treaty-making process entirely.[19]

21.5 Oversight: The International Narcotics Control Board and Conferences of Parties

The International Narcotics Control Board (INCB), composed of eleven technical experts, is the only entirely independent quasi-judicial organ providing formal oversight within the UN drug control system. Created under the 1961 Single Convention to supervise the export and import of licit drugs, under successive drug conventions it has broadened its mandate to comment on the application of their penal provisions.[20] It usually only advises parties, but where the aims of the drug conventions are seriously endangered because of an implementation failure, it does ask for explanations and point out breach of treaty obligations (it also, as we shall see below, has embargo powers, but has never used them). In its Annual Report for 2009, for example, the INCB noted that the decriminalization of drugs in Mexico, Brazil, and Argentina means that these states were in breach of their obligations to prohibit personal use under article 3(2) of the 1988 Drug Trafficking Convention.[21] 'Advice' of this kind is not usually well received by states. At the 2010 meeting of the CND, the Argentinean delegation protested strongly, citing disrespect for Argentina's sovereignty. The incident illustrates why other than in drugs supervision, non-partisan specialist technical agencies have been eschewed in favour of supervision by politically representative institutions. Critics noted in 1975 that the INCB was not independent and pursued

---

[18] Article 92(3) of the UN Charter.
[19] M Koskenniemi, 'The Police in the Temple: Order, Justice and the UN: A Dialectical View' 6 *European Journal of International Law* (1995) 325, 336.
[20] In terms of articles 22 and 23 of the 1988 Drug Trafficking Convention.
[21] See the Report of the International Narcotics Control Board for 2009, UN Doc E/INCB/2009/I (New York: UN, 2009), para 408 (Mexico) and para 477 (Brazil).

the strict drug prohibition policies of key states in the drug control system.[22] More recently the INCB has responded negatively to the development of cannabis markets in some US states, pointing out that it 'was not in conformity with the international drug control treaties' and urging 'the Government of the United States to continue to ensure the full implementation of the international drug control treaties on its entire territory'.[23]

Mistrusting of expert oversight, states have turned for more politically representative supervision of implementation to the COPs of the UNTOC and UNCAC. Article 32(1) of the UNTOC, for example, establishes a 'conference of the parties' to 'improve the capacity of States Parties to combat transnational organized crime and to promote and review the implementation of this Convention'. Representative of all the parties, the COPs are empowered to gather information on implementation from parties and parties are obliged to provide that information.[24] Unlike the INCB, however, the COPs have no investigative or embargo powers. They work largely through recommendations, powerful soft-law instruments (and thus often the subject of intensive lobbying) in the implementation of convention obligations that put flesh on these obligations.

21.6 Administration: the UN Office on Drugs and Crime (UNODC)

The UNODC is the umbrella organ which administers all of the UN's efforts against transnational crime, which among many other things amounts to an interest in implementation of many hundreds of thousands of laws, both international and domestic.[25] It serves as the secretariat of the CND and CCPCJ and of the COPs of the main suppression conventions.[26] Under the control of a director, it operates globally through regional and liaison offices (it has fifty-two outposts globally). The UNODC is organized into different divisions, with the division for treaty affairs, for example, being divided up thematically into the 'Organized Crime and Anti-trafficking Branch', 'Corruption and Economic Crime Branch', the 'Terrorism Prevention Branch', and the Secretariat for the INCB.[27] The UNODC uses the suppression conventions as frameworks within which to provide technical support. Initially, it relied on official commentaries to the early conventions to clarify their meaning. It then began to develop model treaties to provide an adaptable basis for the drafting of bilateral treaties, and model laws to provide an adaptable guide to national legislators. Its newest innovations include guidelines and toolkits for legislative implementation that can be customized to particular legal traditions and used to develop different

---

[22] K Bruun, L Pan, and I Rexed, *The Gentlemen's Club: International Control of Drugs and Alcohol* (Chicago: University of Chicago Press, 1975), 280.
[23] Report of the International Narcotics Control Board for 2013 (New York: UN, 2014), 49, para 375 and 96, para 713.
[24] See, eg, article 63(5) and (6) of the UNCAC.   [25] Redo, above n 3, 197.
[26] See, eg, article 64(1) of the UNCAC.
[27] See Organizational Structure of the UNODC, at <https://www.unodc.org/unodc/en/evaluation/organizational-structure-of-unodc.html> last visited 15 June 2017.

forms of legislation (primary and secondary). With a budget of US$760.1 million in the biennium 2014–15,[28] a considerable increase since the budget of US$94.5 million in 2003–04,[29] its capacity to provide these services is growing. More than half of its funds have, however, usually been dedicated to drug control (56% in 2014–15).[30] Moreover, the vast bulk of funds are donated for special projects rather than for general purposes (98% in 2014–15[31]), allowing donor states to dictate the direction of UNODC activity. A reversal of the situation in 2003,[32] this dedicated funding model has had a fragmentary effect on its work, leaving the UNODC short of money for general expenditure while its budget has actually increased. This has led to greater pressure on the UNODC to be more efficient. As the Canadian delegate to the 2014 CCPCJ said, '[w]e do not want to spend money on special projects and have it spent on general non project costs'.[33] Since 2000 the UNODC has also been under pressure to catch up with the UN's general progress on human rights, the rule of law, and sustainable development, while achieving better geographic and gender representation on its staff.[34]

21.7 Networking: The Programme Network of Institutes (PNI)

The UNODC is able to rely for technical expertise on the seventeen specialized and regional affiliated research institutions that make up the PNI. The United Nations Interregional Crime and Justice Research Institute (UNICRI) based in Turin was established by the Secretary-General in 1967 to develop policy around criminality (it was renamed in 1998).[35] Founded in 1991 and based in Milan, the International Scientific and Professional Advisory Council of the United Nations Crime Prevention and Criminal Justice Program (ISPAC) plays a different role, serving to enhance expert and NGO contributions from developing states, and serving as the body for the coordination of NGO activities at UN crime congresses.[36] In theory, the various specialized institutes of the PNI should develop policy relative to their areas of expertise, while the regional institutes should ensure that policy reflecting regional concerns goes to the CCPCJ, but it has been pointed out that while coordination of their efforts does occur it is hampered by different mandates, priorities, capacities, orientation, and funding bases.[37]

---

[28] UNODC Budget, available at <https://www.unodc.org/unodc/en/donors/index.html?ref=menutop> last visited 15 June 2017.
[29] *UNODC Resources*, UNODC website, <http://www.unodc.org/unodc/en/donors/index.html?ref=menuside> last visited 12 May 2012. Ibid, see table entitled 'Funding Trend'.
[30] UNODC Budget, above n 28.   [31] ibid.   [32] Redo, above n 3, 160.
[33] Notes on file with author who attended.   [34] Redo, above n 3, 207.
[35] ESC Res 1989/56.
[36] It is a product of the foundation of the UN Crime and Criminal Justice Programme.
[37] M Joutsen, 'The United Nations Crime Prevention and Criminal Justice Programme Network of Institutes' in SM Redo, *Blue Criminology: The Power of United Nations Ideas to Counter Crime Globally* (Helsinki: HEUNI, 2012), 120–22.

21.8 Other Intergovernmental Institutions and Organizations

A large number of other intergovernmental organizations and international associations are also active against transnational crime, creating policy, engaging in oversight, and providing administrative support and technical expertise.

Various policing organizations play important roles in the system mostly at a technical level (although their policy influence is growing). Interpol plays a significant role as a way of sharing data and a conduit for requests between states, and this role is recognized expressly in many suppression conventions.[38] The World Customs Organization (WCO) plays a similar role in customs control. Professional organizations such as the International Association of Prosecutors and the World Summit of Prosecutors General, Attorneys General and Chief Prosecutors, serve to share best practice in regard to prosecution of transnational crime.

Other IGOs support law-making, make policy, and provide administrative backup (in different degrees) in regard to specific crimes within their mandates. The International Monetary Fund and World Bank play a significant role in protecting the integrity of the global financial system from abuse in regard to financial crimes such as money laundering, terrorist financing, and corruption. The Organisation for Economic Co-operation and Development works on specific projects such as bribery of foreign officials, piracy, and counterfeiting. The G8's increasing activity against transnational crime has found expression through its creation, the Financial Action Task Force, which both makes 'soft law' and engages in 'soft' oversight through the system of mutual evaluation in regard to money laundering control developed under its auspices and through allied regional organizations. In the Commonwealth Secretariat, the Legal and Constitutional Affairs Division has developed considerable expertise in the provision of technical support to common law states in the implementation of suppression conventions.

A number of regional bodies play a significant policy-making, law-making, and supervisory role. The Council of Europe is steward of more than thirty crime control treaties. It uses 'legislative approximation' to ensure implementation and provides oversight through the European Committee on Crime Problems. The EU is by comparison a relative latecomer to crime control, only establishing an interest in 'Justice and Home Affairs' in 1992. It is *sui generis*: it makes criminal laws for all the member states, but is itself party to many suppression conventions and has become active in the adoption of laws against transnational crime that member states are obliged to enact. It has built Europe-wide criminal justice institutions such as Europol, Eurojust (the European Prosecutor's Office), OLAF (the European Anti-Fraud Office), and Frontex (border security). The Organization of American States has also taken significant steps against transnational crime, sponsoring treaty and legislative development. At the institutional level, the Inter-American Drug Abuse Control Commission (CICAD) has been active in a range of drug-related areas as diverse as demand reduction and

---

[38] Eg, article 7(8) of the 1988 Drug Trafficking Convention.

money laundering. In Africa, the African Union is taking an increasingly prominent role in transnational crime control. Association of Southeast Asian Nations members have also agreed to prioritize transnational crime suppression and the association has pursued agreements on terrorism and mutual legal assistance. Sub-regional organizations like the Organization of Black Sea Economic Cooperation also function to develop regional integration of transnational criminal law.

21.9 Civil Society

A large number of NGOs now work in transnational criminal law. Some, such as Transparency International (TI) in regard to corruption, tend to be better informed and more able to guide policy development and assist implementation than many IGOs or states.[39] Suppression conventions increasingly recognize the important policy-making role of NGOs. The UNCAC, for example, permits (but does not oblige) the Conference of States Party (COSP) to consider inputs from relevant accredited NGOs.[40] Suppression conventions also recognize that NGOs may also have an operational role in regard particularly to protection of victims. The Human Trafficking Protocol, for example, implicitly recognizes that NGOs may be able to provide assistance to victims.[41] In practice, in states such as Cambodia, they provide the only assistance available. They are also able to raise funds, operate transnationally, be more open about problems, act independently of national politics, and may be in a position to expose incompetence and corruption. However, NGOs have tended to focus narrowly on specific crimes and ignore the broader criminal justice picture, and at a formal level they are invited into the inter-state system as guests and subject to exclusion at the insistence of parties. They are also vulnerable to criticism that they reflect Western moral concerns. Both concerns are well illustrated by the debacle over the ban on NGO representation at meetings of the UNCAC International Review Group (IRG), despite the fact that no specific rule prohibiting their attendance has been adopted and Rule 17 of the COSP rules of procedure permit NGOs to attend the plenary meetings of the COSP. The UN Legal Counsel's opinion when sought confirmed that as a subsidiary body of the COSP, the IRG should permit representation unless a rule was expressly adopted excluding their participation. Nonetheless, they remain excluded and no rule has been adopted.[42] The issue of NGO participation has spread to other aspects of the work of the UN crime prevention and criminal justice programme.

21.10 Conclusion

This brief review is incomplete. It does not, for example, take account of the privatization of the response to transnational crime through the 'deputization' of financial

---

[39] See M Naim, *Illicit: How Smugglers, Traffickers and Copycats are Hijacking the Global Economy* (London: Random House, 2005), 202–05.
[40] Article 63(6).   [41] Article 6(3).
[42] C Rose, *International Anti-Corruption Norms: Their Creation and Influence on Domestic Legal Systems* (Oxford: OUP, 2015), 53.

organizations in self-regulation in the anti-money laundering/counter-terrorist financing regime. It does reveal, however, that a fairly complex institutional structure exists for the management and supervision of transnational criminal law. Some elements of this structure (such as those in the anti-money laundering) are more functionally independent and enjoy a greater degree of delegated power than others. The structure appears successful at developing law and policy and at keeping channels of communication open between states and IGOs, although it is open to the criticism that it is too concerned with politics and not as enforcement-focused as it could be. It is, however, an interstate system; the UN manages rather than enforces the system of transnational criminal law. In the 'public' face of the system—the Commissions, COPs, and Crime Congresses—the players play carefully scripted parts and little is revealed about the uneven nature of the system's implementation. The really dynamic activity in regard to implementation takes place behind the scenes. These institutions are staffed by a community of transnational law enforcement professionals and advocates (many of whom are seconded national officials) who share specialist knowledge and form linkages that may counter the tendency at the national level to prioritize certain national interests, by focusing attention on shared goals.

22

Implementation and Compliance

22.1 Introduction

The goal of transnational criminal law is the suppression of crime. Achieving this goal requires effective implementation of the rules in the suppression conventions—both substantive and procedural—in national law, and effective compliance with these rules.[1] The Doha Declaration,[2] adopted in 2015 at the UN Crime Congress held in Doha, provides a convenient lens through which to introduce the implementation of and compliance with transnational criminal law. It seeks to integrate crime prevention into the wider UN agenda addressing social and economic challenges and promoting the rule of law, explicitly acknowledging that 'sustainable development and the rule of law are strongly interrelated and mutually reinforcing'.[3] Goal 16 of the UN's post-2015 sustainable development goals is the promotion of peaceful and inclusive societies for sustainable development, the provision of access to justice for all, and building of effective, accountable institutions at all levels. Among the targets spelled out in Goal 16 of direct relevance to the suppression of transnational organized crime are the ending of child trafficking, significant reduction of arms trafficking, significant reduction of illicit financial flows, strengthening of stolen asset recovery, combating organized crime, reducing corruption, and developing capacity to combat violence, terrorism, and crime.[4]

The Congress did not, however, serve as a platform for a debate as to how to respond to these crimes because the solution was already available. Opening the Congress, UN Secretary-General Ban Ki-moon encouraged 'every country to ratify and implement the conventions against drugs, crime and corruption, and the international instruments against terrorism, and to support the important and varied work of the United Nations Office on Drugs and Crime'.[5]

The Doha Declaration reiterated this encouragement.[6] These interstate legal obligations and their domestic implementation appear to be considered a crucial part of

---

[1] On the distinctions see K Raustiala and A Slaughter, 'International Law, International Relations and Compliance' in W Carlsnaes, T Risse, and BE Simmons (eds), *Handbook of International Relations* (London: Sage, 2002), 538, 538.

[2] Doha Declaration on Integrating Crime Prevention and Criminal Justice into the Wider United Nations Agenda to Address Social and Economic Challenges and to Promote the Rule of Law at the National and International Levels, and Public Participation (2015, UN), available on the UNODC Website at <https://www.unodc.org/documents/congress//Declaration/V1504151_English.pdf> last visited 5 May 2017.

[3] ibid, para 4.

[4] See UN website, <http://www.un.org/sustainabledevelopment/peace-justice/> last visited 5 May 2017.

[5] Press Release 'Rule of Law Central to Better Future, Secretary General Tells Crime Congress', 12 April 2015, <http://www.un.org/press/en/2015/sgsm16655.doc.htm> last visited 5 May 2017.

[6] Above n 2, para 8.

the maintenance and development of the rule of law, and they frame a cornucopia of forms of international cooperation, some general and some crime specific. Yet an overriding concern of many of the state representatives at Doha who spoke in plenary was the inadequate implementation of the suppression conventions.[7] The Romanian delegate noted, for example, that international adherence without concrete national follow through was insufficient. Calling for accountability at national, regional, and global levels, she noted: 'The functionality of a convention is not measured by the number of ratifications, but by the number of cases when it is actually used, and moreover the number of cases when such operations show to be successful.'

A month after the Doha Crime Congress, the US delegate said at the Commission on Crime Prevention and Criminal Justice (CCPCJ) that '[w]e do not have a shortage of conventions, what we have is a gap in their implementation'.[8]

The gap exists. As Dandurand and Chin put it, these conventions 'have not yielded the expected dividends in terms of effective international cooperation'.[9] Many states join these treaties, some reform their laws, but most never use them. The general support for them appears to be largely rhetorical. Neither implementation nor compliance is assured. Some states may (for any one of a range of reasons) not implement the law at all. Some may implement 'paper law' but not enforce it, permitting criminals to enjoy de facto impunity.

Various solutions are commonly offered to make up for these shortcomings. Further substantive law-making is generally unpopular. The emphasis is usually on compliance at an administrative level. A lot of emphasis is placed on increasing domestic criminal justice capacity. Another frequently touted option is the adoption of practical and flexible approaches such as relaxing administrative strictures on implementation of international cooperation. When it comes to procedural laws the main push is towards ever more simplification.

In a sense all of the efforts are trying to escape from the inadequacies of the indirect control system where a norm set in a treaty is 'completed' at the domestic level. It is seldom asked whether this indirect model which institutionalizes a highly legalized approach is a functional method of achieving suppression of a particular form of harmful conduct. The fact, however, that most effective cooperation today is either bilateral in nature, or occurs within relatively coherent regions such as the EU, or through heavily monitored soft law instruments like the Financial Action Task Force (FATF) recommendations with a broader global reach suggests that some states may be re-evaluating the commitment to multilateral treaty-making as an instrument against crime and as a foundation of the global rule of law.

This chapter reviews implementation and compliance very briefly and then turns to mechanisms for reviewing, supporting, and coercing action by parties to implement

---

[7] 'Debating Global Cooperation, UN Congress Speakers Call for Accountability, as "Paper Promises" Fail to Combat Cross-Border Criminal Activities', 16 April 2015, coverage of the 9th and 10th meetings, available at <http://www.un.org/press/en/2015/soccp364.doc.htm> last visited 5 May 2017.

[8] UNCCPCJ, 18 May 2015 (notes on file with the author).

[9] Y Dandurand and V Chin, 'Implementation of Transnational Criminal Law' in N Boister and R Currie (eds), *The Routledge Handbook of Transnational Criminal Law* (Abingdon: Routledge, 2014), 437, 440.

and comply. It then looks at the prospects of a transnational criminal court to further compliance, before concluding with some comments about whether the system is having the desired normative effect on states and individuals.

22.2 Implementation

The undertaking to implement the suppression conventions in national law is central to transnational criminal law. The suppression conventions usually contain a general obligation to implement the provisions of the treaty through legislative and administrative measures[10] and a range of specific obligations linked to specific measures. The quality of these specific legal obligations depends on the particular treaty. Some, such as the obligation to criminalize drug trafficking in article 3(1) of the Drug Trafficking Convention, are very clear with hardly any ambiguous terms and few escape clauses; others, such as the obligation to 'consider' criminalizing illicit enrichment under article 20 of the United Nations Convention against Corruption (UNCAC), are more ambiguous, use weaker language, and permit reservations. The basic principle of treaty law—*pacta sunt servanda* (agreements must be kept)—obliges parties to act in good faith and enact the substantive transnational crimes, and meet the necessary procedural obligations found in the conventions.[11] Sovereign delicacies are, however, an inherent feature of the context in which implementation occurs. They require that a careful balance be maintained between effective measures from a law enforcement point of view and preservation of sovereignty.

In practice, the assumption is that most parties do engage either in law reform or review of their existing legislation to satisfy themselves that they comply with their treaty obligations. Obviously, different conventions elicit different responses. Nevertheless, the implementation of the major suppression conventions has been criticized as 'slow, difficult and uneven', the regime as 'weak', and the results of implementation 'disappointing'.[12] The shortcomings identified range from the total absence of legislation, through only partially compatible crime and penalties, to the absence of enabling legislation for international cooperation and the retention of procedural barriers to international cooperation. There are three broad reasons for this implementation gap.

First, parties are not always willing to implement obligations undertaken at diplomatic conferences when the time comes. Many will have participated in the process of the development of the convention for reasons other than an authentic desire to suppress the particular conduct. They may have been pressured by other states, or promised aid, or have done so because they did not wish to be seen to be unwilling. They may not be facing the particular level of threat sufficient to convince domestic lawmakers to reform their laws. They may be subject to countervailing interests including

---

[10] See, eg, article 34(1) of the UNTOC.
[11] Article 27 of the Vienna Convention on the Law of Treaties.
[12] Y Dandurand and V Chin, 'Monitoring the Implementation of the International Cooperation Provisions of International Conventions' in ICCLR, *Promoting Criminal Justice Reform—A Collection of Papers from the Canada-China Cooperation Symposium* (Vancouver: International Centre for Criminal Law Reform and Criminal Justice Policy, 2007), 473, 474–75.

pressure from transnational criminals through force or corruption.[13] Sponsor states may lose interest/confidence in the particular convention. There may have been very little agreement to take concrete steps in the first place, something usually indicated by the fragmented nature of the legal obligations in a convention (eg take the Firearms Protocol).

Second, the suppression conventions are not designed with a coherent system of implementation in mind. Transnational criminal law has developed in a piecemeal, incremental fashion, as one then another crime has been added to specific regimes. In result, it is not a particularly well-integrated system. Every new convention presents states with an entirely separate law reform exercise.

Third, and most importantly, many states, particularly developing states, do not have the capacity to implement. Ratification exposes parties to a 'regulatory Tsunami'[14] of international obligations with which few states can keep up, never mind poorer states with moribund domestic criminal justice systems. States that join a treaty regime and come under pressure to adopt and implement it often see a rapid legislative change foreign to states more integrated into the diffusion of transnational criminal law. They are forced to adopt strategies for legislative change which may not be equally effective or legitimate. For example, in the very rapid process of adoption of transnational criminal laws in Poland after 2000 as it sought to join the EU, two methods of implementation were adopted—direct transposition of treaty obligations or decoding of the essence of these obligations, neither leading to a coherent implementation policy and leaving implementation in Poland open to criticism that the resulting laws were not clear enough to meet the requirements of the principle of legality.[15]

22.3 Compliance

It is not sufficient for a state simply to possess a legal system that is technically compliant with the formal obligations under the suppression conventions. Judgments in decisions like that of the European Court of Human Rights in *Rantsev v Cyprus and Russia*[16] clarify that states owe a human rights obligation to individual victims to act domestically and cooperate with other states in order to investigate alleged offences effectively.

The US, preoccupied domestically with criminal outcomes—convictions, fines, confiscation, and so forth—has tried to drive transnational criminal law towards greater measurement of these outcomes. Yet it remains very difficult to make even the most general judgement about compliance because there is little consensus on what is good compliance and data on compliance is patchy and very difficult to access.[17] Most

---

[13] It has been suggested, eg, that corruption prevents investigation and prosecution of human trafficking—see UNODC, *Corruption and Human Trafficking: The Grease That Facilitates the Crime* (Vienna: UNODC, 2008), 3.

[14] Nikos Passas, quoted in *The Economist*, 20 October 2005, available at <http://www.economist.com/node/5053373> last visited 12 June 2017.

[15] C Nowak, 'The Internationalization of Polish Criminal Law: How Polish Criminal Law Changed Under the Influence of Globalization' 59 *Crime, Law and Social Change* (2013) 139, 147.

[16] Application no 25965/04, ECtHR, 7 January 2010, para 281.

[17] See Dandurand and Chin, above n 12, 474.

reports measure effectiveness on the basis of the application of penalties, although these vary widely between states. Alternative measures such as resources dedicated to compliance vary widely between crimes. Measurement is complicated by the fact that law enforcement officials tend to use every tool at their disposal to pursue suspected transnational criminals, including ordinary domestic offences as well as transnational crimes, so the statistical picture of the incidence of arrests and prosecutions of transnational crimes does not reveal the actual level of suppression. Compliance is most accurately measured by state and by crime.

A comprehensive review of the data is impossible here (if the data were available), but prosecutions of certain crimes have historically been low. For example, between 2005 and 2006, only thirteen out of thirty-one states reported an increase in prosecution statistics for organized crime despite a rise in the incidence of the crime.[18] The effect of actual policing is very difficult to discern. Median rates for migrant smuggling in 2006, for example, were 1.4 police-recorded offences, 1 person prosecuted, and 0.7 people convicted per 100,000 persons.[19] That means either the crime does not occur that often or it is being poorly reported and policed. In regard to some crimes where there is clear evidence of heavy policing, policing appears effective. Maritime piracy statistics for 2016, for example, show the lowest number of incidences of piracy than in any of the previous ten years, something generally ascribed to major preventive and enforcement activity in the seas surrounding Somalia.[20] Compliance in regard to certain crimes in certain states is poor. Afghanistan and opium is an example. An interesting regional change in opium production observed by the *Afghanistan Opium Survey 2015* was that there were increases in all but one of the provinces in the region that abuts the Turkmenistan border.[21] For example, production in the Western province of Badghis rose from 5,721 to 12,391 hectares under production, an increase of 117 per cent. It can only be speculated whether the extensive enforcement action that has taken place in the South of Afghanistan along the supply route through Pakistan and Iran has resulted in a 'push down pop up' effect.

There are many reasons for poor compliance and they are highly contextual. Some states are in the fortunate position of having little opportunity to comply because for geographical, political, or social reasons they have a low incidence of particular transnational crimes. In some cases the mode of criminality is new. States also prioritize the enforcement of certain offences, such as terrorism, at the expense of others. De Bellaigue notes, for example:[22]

---

[18] S Harrendorf, M Heiskanen, and S Malby (eds), *International Statistics on Crime and Justice* (Helsinki: Heuni, 2010), 67. Figures are drawn from the Tenth UN Survey of Crime Trends and Operations of Criminal Justice Systems (UN-CTS) 2006.

[19] ibid, 68.

[20] International Commercial Crime Services, 'IMB Report: Sea kidnappings rise in 2016 despite Plummeting Global Piracy', available at <https://icc-ccs.org/index.php/news/1218-imb-report-sea-kidnappings-rise-in-2016-despite-plummeting-global-piracy> last visited 16 June 2017.

[21] UNODC and Islamic Republic of Afghanistan Ministry of Counter Narcotics, *Afghanistan Opium Survey 2015, Executive Summary*, 9–10, available at <https://www.unodc.org/documents/crop-monitoring/Afghanistan/Afg_Executive_summary_2015_final.pdf>.

[22] C de Bellaigue, 'Money as Weapon' 33 *London Review of Books* (2011) 13.

Kabul Bank, . . . [Afghanistan's] largest, has lost several hundred million dollars to dubious investments and unrecoverable loans, some of them made out to ministers and other government stalwarts. Not only that: the US Government was aware of what was going on and did nothing to stop it. American regulators were interested only in preventing the bank from being used to finance global terrorism.

In some cases the parties pursue criminal justice policies seemingly antagonistic to their treaty obligations and their own laws. They find the space to do so, in the principle, common in the suppression conventions, which insists that prosecution and punishment of crimes enacted under the conventions 'shall be prosecuted and punished in conformity with domestic law'. The Netherlands, for example, famously permits low-level supply and possession of cannabis in 'coffee shops' on the view that the drug conventions provide that enforcement is discretionary, thus permitting a blanket decision not to prosecute.[23] Perceptions of seriousness, the experience of law enforcers, the existence of specialist units, poor capacity, and corruption, all explain why some laws are enforced and others not. An important and often neglected reason, however, is that the effectiveness of national criminal laws varies extensively, and in many states adherence to the rule of law is flimsy. Sometimes poor compliance is the result of a lack of political will because of conflicts with parochial interests. For example, following the Panama Papers revelations that many foreign tax avoiders were the beneficiaries of trusts held in New Zealand, then Prime Minister John Key said in parliament that New Zealand was not a tax haven,[24] but when new disclosure rules were put in place fewer than 70 out of 11,645 New Zealand foreign trusts had re-registered three weeks before the final deadline.[25] Parties to the conventions sometimes engage in symbolic criminalization on paper in order to shield non-enforcement when enforcement is likely to hurt financial or political interests or simply to avoid international embarrassment. Cyprus, for example, has used implementation of money laundering conventions and FATF recommendations to deny that it is a hub for Eastern European sex trafficking and money laundering.[26] The Bulgarian creation of a specialized criminal court against organized crime, a radical reform driven by EU pre-accession demands, the political agenda of the government, and populist sentiment, has been criticized as amounting to a transparent attempt to appear to be doing something while ensuring nothing changed.[27] This is nothing new. *Só para o Inglês ver*, or 'just for the English to see', was the Portuguese name for the law enacted in Brazil in 1831 following its 1826

---

[23] The Netherlands made a reservation to article 3(6) of the Drug Trafficking Convention which obliges parties to endeavour to ensure that discretionary powers are used to maximize effectiveness of law enforcement.

[24] J Patterson, 'New Zealand's World Class Tax System Defended', *Radio New Zealand*, 4 April 2016, available at <http://www.radionz.co.nz/news/political/300644/nz's-'world-class'-tax-system-defended> last visited 15 June 2017.

[25] H Fletcher, 'More than 1800 Foreign Trusts Exit New Zealand', *New Zealand Herald* 9 June 2017, available at <http://www.nzherald.co.nz/business/news/article.cfm?c_id=3&objectid=11873317> last visited 17 June 2017.

[26] L Paoli, 'Implementation: Concepts and Actors' in HG Albrecht and C Fijnaut (eds), *The Containment of Transnational Organized Crime* (Freiburg: Iuscrim, 2002), 207, 220.

[27] Y Kuzmova, 'The Bulgarian Specialized Criminal Court After One Year: A Misplaced Transplant, a Tool of Justice or an Instrument of Executive Power' 32 *Boston University International Law Journal* (2014) 227, 231.

treaty with Britain abolishing the maritime slave-trade and providing for prosecution of slave-traders in Brazil,[28] a treaty seldom enforced before 1850 when it was supplemented by domestic legislation prohibiting the import of slaves.

22.4 Multilateral Review Mechanisms

An effective mechanism to review implementation and compliance is considered critical to the effectiveness of transnational criminal law.[29] When a state becomes a party to a suppression convention they undertake to inform the other parties about the steps they have taken to implement the convention. Gathering and reviewing this information is highly politicized because of the potential embarrassment to parties of publicity about poor performance. Various methods are used. Self-reporting in answer to a questionnaire is the most common method. Completed questionnaires must be submitted on a periodic basis and are used by convention secretariats to compile reports for the purpose of review. Reporting itself is encumbered by technical problems, lack of financial and human resources, language barriers, the complexity of the information required, and lack of clarity about its nature and relevance.[30] Reporting guidelines facilitate the uniform preparation and presentation of reports, thus enabling valid comparison. Under some regimes states also self-assess their compliance. Relying on the parties alone is, however, an invitation to abuse.

An alternative is to rely on expert review by an independent technical expert committee which gathers and assesses the relevant material. Under article 1(2) of the Council of Europe Convention on Human Trafficking, for example, a special monitoring mechanism, the Group of Experts on Action against Trafficking in Human Beings (GRETA), ensures implementation. It gathers information for evaluation from parties by questionnaire (which parties are obliged to answer) and from civil society. It may also use in-country visits and hearings before making a report.[31] Expert committees of this kind range from the independent to the relatively powerless. The Advisory Board set up under the auspices of the African Union (AU) Convention on Corruption has, for example, no role in monitoring and is in effect a toothless think tank.[32]

Peer review of a party's performance by other parties is a more potent review methodology because it involves peer pressure. While mutual evaluation of this kind is used in other regimes, it was pioneered in its treaty form under the Organisation for Economic Co-operation and Development (OECD) Convention on Combating Bribery of Foreign Public Officials. Article 12 of the Convention obliges parties to 'co-operate in carrying out a programme of systematic follow-up to monitor and

---

[28] Treaty Between Great Britain and Brazil for the Abolition of the Slave Trade, 23 November 1826, Martens, 6 Nouveau Recueil General des Traités 1087.

[29] Dandurand and Chin, above n 12, 476.   [30] ibid, 478.

[31] See the GRETA website, <http://www.coe.int/en/web/anti-human-trafficking/greta> last visited 19 June 2017.

[32] See J Wouters, C Ryngaert, and S Cloots, 'The International Legal Framework Against Corruption: Achievements and Challenges' 14 *Melbourne Journal of International Law* (2013) 205, 230–31.

promote the full implementation of this Convention'. In order to meet this obligation, a peer review system in which parties were invited to participate was set up by
the OECD Working Group on Bribery. It entails a three-phase process. In Phase 1
a group of examiners from parties in a similar position to the party under review
examine the laws used to implement the convention to assess conformity with the
convention. This is carried out on the basis of answers to a questionnaire provided
by the state under review. Phase 2 is designed to make possible an assessment of the
actual practice within the state, and relies on an intensive on-site visit by assessors
who interview government officials, academics, and members of civil society organizations on their views. Phase 3 involves a permanent cycle of regular visits to respond
to the dynamic nature of the crime. Unlike many systems where reports are confidential, the OECD reports are published, although the confidentiality of meetings is
maintained to facilitate an open exchange of information. The process, which is in
the hands of the parties, allows both reviewing and reviewed states an opportunity to
learn and hone best practice. Use of the system has revealed that peer review cannot
work without political will, sharing of ideas, and commitments to reform. Systems
like this are politically uncomfortable because they do make judgments about implementation and compliance. Consider for example the Committee's trenchant criticism of the UK's implementation of the OECD Convention (discussed in Chapter 9).
The OECD Working Group uses the label 'collective unilateralism' to describe how
its collective peer evaluation system, which is based on the unilateral commitment of
each state and grants a national margin of appreciation through the concept of functional equivalence, results in overall harmonization of practice, even of states not
party to the Convention.[33]

States parties to the UN crime suppression conventions have proved suspicious of peer
review. The UNCAC, for example, obliges the Conference of States Party (COSP) to agree
on a review mechanism.[34] Yet getting agreement on a peer review mechanism at a conference of the party (COP) has been extremely difficult, mainly because of political sensitivity. [35] The wariness of the COSP was revealed in Resolution 1/3 of the first COSP held in
2006 when it underlined that the review mechanism should

(a) be transparent, efficient, non-intrusive, inclusive and impartial;

(b) not produce any form of ranking;

(c) provide opportunities to share good practices and challenges;

(d) complement existing international and regional review mechanisms in order that
the Conference of the States Parties may, as appropriate, cooperate with them and
avoid duplication of effort.[36]

---

[33] M Delmas-Marty, *Ordering Pluralism: A Conceptual Framework for Understanding the Transnational
Legal World* (Oxford and Portland: Hart, 2009), 107.

[34] Article 64(3)(e).

[35] M Joutsen and A Graycar, 'When Experts and Diplomats Agree: Negotiating Peer Review of the UN
Convention against Corruption' 18 *Global Governance* (2012) 425, 427.

[36] Report of the Conference of the States Parties to the United Nations Convention against Corruption
on its First Session, held in Amman from 10 to 14 December 2006, UN Doc CAC/COSP/2006/12, 27
December 2006, 3.

It has taken until the third COSP in 2009 for the parties to agree on using a self-assessment checklist as a review mechanism.[37] Evaluation has three phases under the UNCAC process—beginning with self-assessment, then peer review, and then a country review report and executive summary drafted with the assistance of the United Nations Office on Drugs and Crime (UNODC). The UN Development Programme helps developing countries prepare for review. In theory the UNCAC peer review provides an opportunity for horizontal peer-to-peer development, rather a situation where change is driven by Western states in a top-down process. The regime is not really sanctions based; it is more educative in nature as one party teaches another about its obligations. It works through normative alignment. The underlying notion is that the system will not work if coercion is used. The UNCAC mechanism is a watered-down mechanism, however, mainly because the UNCAC review mechanism allows publication of reports to remain voluntary, ensuring in fact that this hardly ever happens. In spite of the fact that this system is much less exacting than that used by the OECD, the COP of the older United Nations Convention against Transnational Organized Crime (UNTOC), which is also obliged to agree on mechanisms for periodic review of implementation,[38] is still in the process of negotiating a review mechanism.[39]

22.5 Coordinated Unilateral Action: The FATF Evaluation and Sanctions Process

Although the use of the term 'recommendation' by the FATF contradicts any claim to a formal treaty obligation, in order implicitly to avoid the kind of symbolic support states engage in through ratification of a treaty, the FATF applies a *sui generis* review and sanctions mechanism for non-compliance that makes the 'soft' law of the FATF Recommendations 'harder' than much 'hard' law.

FATF members agree to be evaluated by other members in a mutual evaluation process in order to join the FATF and their overall evaluation has to be 'satisfactory'.[40] Currently the FATF model requires four rounds of mutual evaluations by interdisciplinary teams. The FATF has made three major changes to its approach to identification and sanction of defaulters since it was established in 1989.

The 1992 FATF Report set out a process of self-evaluation which allowed members to audit each other's implementation of anti-money laundering (AML) schemes. Peer pressure was used on members to bring them into line with the recommendations. Austria, for example, was put under pressure to scrap anonymous bank accounts.

From 2000 the FATF adopted a name and shame approach: the Non-Cooperating Countries and Territories (NCCT) process. FATF members and then controversially non-members were measured against twenty-five criteria based on the recommendations and those that fell short were identified and classified as non-cooperative, and subject to

---

[37] Res 3/1, in Report of the Conference of the States Parties to the United Nations Convention against Corruption on its Third Session, held in Doha from 9 to 13 November 2009, UN Doc CAC/COSP/ 2009/ 15, 1 December 2009, 3.

[38] Article 32(3)(d).   [39] In terms of COP Res 8/2 of 2016.

[40] C Rose, *International Anti-Corruption Norms: Their Creation and Influence on Domestic Legal Systems* (Oxford: OUP, 2015), 196.

'countermeasures'. In 2000 FATF identified fifteen states or territories with serious systemic problems and a further eight in 2001. Countermeasures were actually only applied to Nauru and Myanmar.[41] By the end of the NCCT process all had made progress sufficient for them to be removed from the list. The legal failures of the NCCT process were obvious. The 'countermeasures' were applied before Recommendation 19 was altered to permit them in 2003. Review criteria were published a few months before non-members were evaluated giving little notice to violators. Application to non-members of the OECD strongly echoed breach of the *pacta tertiis* rule[42] and clearly violated it in regard to calls for the application of suppression convention obligations to which the particular state was not party. Absence of notice and the fact that the blacklisted country had not engaged in an intentionally wrongful act directed at the injured state meant the NCCT measures were not countermeasures. They were acts of retorsion in response to similar act by the blacklisted state against the FATF member—evil for evil—acts that are not unlawful because of the absence of international legal obligations on states from imposing conditions on financial transactions emanating from other states.[43]

The NCCT was replaced by the International Cooperation and Review Group (ICRG) in 2006. It began operating in 2007. States revealed by the mutual evaluation process to have key deficiencies in implementation are referred for process of review by an ICRG regional review group and can be placed in one of two tiers either (i) calling for consideration of risks arising from strategic deficiencies (the 'grey' list) or (ii) application of countermeasures by FATF members (the 'black' list arising from absence of political commitment). Countermeasures include risk mitigation measures such as limiting dealings with the identified country or persons operating from that country.[44] Almost all states on the lists are non-Western.

The FATF's introduction of 'countermeasures' was criticized for violating the sovereignty guaranteed in the UN Charter and a host of suppression conventions.[45] Nonetheless, seventeen years later those countries that permit a higher risk of money laundering and terror financing in their financial sector expose themselves to the risk of adverse treatment by members of FATF.

22.6 The Carrots: Technical Assistance

In the negotiation of the suppression conventions it is understood, though never articulated, that many parties can (and some will) only change their laws and practices if granted technical assistance by parties with greater resources. Most of the suppression conventions acknowledge the necessity for technical assistance to aid parties with capacity problems. Article 32(2) of the UNTOC, for example, obliges parties to 'make concrete efforts to the extent possible', inter alia, to provide technical assistance to developing countries and countries in transition to assist them to implement the

---

[41] ibid, 204.   [42] ibid, 205.   [43] ibid, 208–09.

[44] L de Koker and M Turkington, 'Transnational Organised Crime and the Anti-Money Laundering Regime' in P Hauck and S Peterke (eds), *International Law and Transnational Organized Crime* (Oxford: OUP, 2016), 241, 248.

[45] T Doyle, 'Cleaning up Anti-Money Laundering Strategies: Current FATF Tactics Violate International Law' 24 *Houston Journal of International Law* (2001–2) 279, 298 et seq.

Convention. It is, however, only a best efforts obligation to provide technical assistance limited by capacity.

The UN organs and in particular the UNODC are often the conduit for this assistance, although all sorts of intergovernmental and non-governmental organizations (NGOs) provide a broad range of different kinds of support for states. In the past technical assistance tended to be donor-led and bilateral in nature.[46] Driven by the interests of rich and powerful states threatened by transnational crime, it tended to focus only on particular issues such as interdiction of drug supply, upgrading the response to the particular issue and ignoring local threats and the overall quality of the criminal justice system being assisted. For example, when the US provided assistance to Haiti in re-establishing its civilian police force with community-led policing it had an interest in ensuring that the new stations were located on Haiti's West Coast because this was a prime area for transit of Colombian drugs.[47]

More recently, there has been a clear shift to country-led, multilateral, coordinated, and participatory approaches to technical assistance. Qatar, for example, agreed in 2016 to provide US\$49 million to the UNODC for the financing of projects related to justice, prisoners, youth and justice education.[48] Today the UN framework for assistance is designed to try to ensure that the country seeking help has control of the assistance process and that local concerns, conditions, and the quality of criminal justice are taken into account.[49] Technical assistance programmes build capacity across a range of transnational crimes. A lot of this activity is delivered or managed by the UNODC, which has also become very active at a regional level. The emphasis has also shifted from law reform alone to teaching sufficient people how to use the legislation. Legislative toolkits, for example, provide a more informal guide to the comparative law landscape in which much international cooperation takes place. There is also a greater emphasis on legitimacy—on local ownership of projects—that takes into account human rights issues and fosters the participation of civil society groups. Tactics include providing incentives for reform, finding champions (South Africa, for example, is considered a champion of small arms control in Africa), and establishing achievable objectives.[50] More recent projects have placed a stronger emphasis on evaluation not just of enactment of laws but on impact on individuals. Technical

---

[46] See M Shaw, 'Solutions for the Future? Are there Key Components for Effective Assistance?' in M Shaw and Y Dandurand (eds), *Maximizing the Effectiveness of the Technical Assistance Provided in the Fields of Crime Prevention and Criminal Justice: Proceedings of the Workshop held by the Programme Network of Institutes during the 15th Session of the UN Commission on Crime Prevention and Criminal Justice* (Helsinki: HEUNI publication series no 49, 2006), 14.

[47] D Beer, MA Thesis, University of Windsor, 2001, 33, 52, conclusion, cited in ME Beare, 'Shifting Boundaries—between States, Enforcement Agencies, and Priorities' in HG Albrecht and C Fijnaut (eds), *The Containment of Transnational Organized Crime* (Freiburg: Iuscrim, 2002), 171, 173.

[48] See UNODC website, 'Unprecedented funding agreement between UNODC and Qatar leaves lasting legacy for Doha Declaration', 27 November 2015, available at <https://www.unodc.org/unodc/en/frontpage/2015/November/unprecedented-funding-agreement-between-unodc-and-qatar-leaves-lasting-legacy-for-doha-declaration.html?ref=fs1> last visited 16 November 2016.

[49] SM Redo, *Blue Criminology: The Power of United Nations Ideas to Counter Crime Globally* (Helsinki: HEUNI, 2012), 147.

[50] See M Shaw and Y Dandurand, 'Maximizing the Effectiveness of Technical Assistance by Member States in Crime Prevention and Criminal Justice: Background Note' in M Shaw and Y Dandurand (eds), *Maximizing the Effectiveness of the Technical Assistance Provided in the Fields of Crime Prevention and Criminal Justice: Proceedings of the Workshop held by the Programme Network of Institutes during the*

assistance to crime suppression programmes that violate the UN's own human rights standards are in particular open to criticism.[51]

22.7 The Sticks: Mechanisms for Enforcing Implementation and Compliance

Failure to enact laws or to enforce them can lead to breaches of treaty obligations under the suppression conventions. It is relatively simple to measure when parties to suppression conventions fail to enact laws they have undertaken to enact. Escape clauses and best efforts provisions make that determination difficult but not impossible. States parties are not in practice interested usually in pursuing other parties for these lapses. The failure to enforce them is more common but more difficult to ascertain. They may point, for example, to the exercise of a legitimate discretion by domestic prosecuting authorities in deciding not to prosecute an offence or to legally valid reasons for refusing a request for legal assistance. If, however, these decisions are palpably influenced by extra-legal considerations they will constitute a violation of treaty obligations and become the subject of dispute among parties.

The suppression conventions contain the standard compromissory clauses for the settlement of disputes about implementation: negotiation, arbitration, and finally submission for adjudication before the International Court of Justice (ICJ).[52] States wishing to resort to these measures may still, however, face a party that has rejected the jurisdiction of the Court, something permitted by the suppression conventions.[53] The dispute resolution mechanisms have not been used often because parties to suppression conventions only very occasionally hold each other to legal account for violation of suppression conventions, preferring to deal with these matters through diplomacy.

The most well-known example is the *Lockerbie* case, which involved the dispute settlement provisions of the Montreal Convention for the Suppression of Unlawful Acts against the Safety of Civil Aviation.[54] In January 1991 prosecution authorities in Scotland and the US charged two Libyans with the destruction of Pan Am Flight 103 and demanded Libya surrender them for trial. When Libya refused, the UN Security Council, at the behest of the US and UK, adopted Resolution 731,[55] which urged Libya to respond to the requests. Libya again refused. In Resolution 748[56] the Security Council demanded unsuccessfully that Libya cooperate by surrendering the suspects for trial on pain of sanction (sanctions supplemented by Resolution 883).[57] The Security Council construed Libya's failure to surrender the suspects as a threat to international peace and security. Libya challenged the resolutions in the ICJ on the basis that it was entitled to rely on the Montreal Convention and to try the Libyan suspects in Libya.

15th Session of the UN Commission on Crime Prevention and Criminal Justice (Helsinki: HEUNI publication series no 49, 2006), 19, at 24–25, 30–31.

[51] See, eg, P Gallahue, R Saucier, and D Barrett, *Partners in Crime: International Funding for Drug Control and Gross Violations of Human Rights* (London: Harm Reduction International, 2012).

[52] See, eg, article 35 of the UNTOC; article 66 of the UNCAC.

[53] See, eg, article 32(4) of the 1988 Drug Trafficking Convention.   [54] See Chapter 7.

[55] S/RES/731, 21 January 1992.   [56] S/RES/748, 31 March 1992.

[57] S/RES/883, 11 November 1993.

It alleged that the UK and US were in breach of the Convention for not, in terms of article 11, providing the 'greatest measure of assistance in connection with criminal proceedings'. The UK and US (reluctant to hand over information to individuals they regarded as the suspects) responded by arguing that the Security Council resolutions had superseded the provisions of the Montreal Convention, because they are binding on all member states and, under article 103 of the Charter, prevail over all conflicting treaty provisions. Although it refused Libya provisional measures of protection in April 1992,[58] in 1998 the ICJ rejected the UK and US's arguments that it did not have jurisdiction in the matter.[59] It based its decision on article 14(1) of the Montreal Convention, which concerns mandatory settlement procedures for any question involving the interpretation and application of the Convention. The ICJ also found the Libyan claims admissible. The compromise prosecution of the accused in the Netherlands before a Scottish court[60] (a single accused Al-Megrahi was eventually convicted of murder) saw the end to the need for the ICJ to rule on the merits of the Libyan case and to decide whether the prevailing law is contained in the Montreal Convention or in the Security Council resolutions. The Lockerbie case illustrates the practical difficulty of enforcing an obligation in a suppression convention, but also the use of a treaty obligation to try to prevent further action. In similar fashion, more recently, on 14 June 2016 Equatorial Guinea has relied on inter alia the compromissory clauses in the UNTOC to institute proceedings against France with regard to the immunity from criminal jurisdiction of its Second Vice-President in charge of State Defence and Security, and the legal status of the building which houses its Embassy in France.[61] The Guinean Vice-President is under investigation for corruption offences by French authorities, on the basis that he invested the proceeds of that corruption in France. French prosecutorial and judicial authorities have held that he has no claim to immunity. Somewhat more conventionally, the Ukraine has instituted proceedings against Russia[62] for failing to cooperate with Ukraine in preventing the financing of terrorism in terms of its general obligation to this effect in article 18 of the Terrorist Financing Convention because of its supply of weapons and other forms of assistance (article (1) defines 'funds' as 'assets of every kind') to separatists in Eastern Ukraine.[63] These suits suggest that the obligations in

---

[58] *Case Concerning Questions of Interpretation and Application of the Montreal Convention Arising out of the Aerial Incident at Lockerbie (Libyan Arab Jamahiriya v United Kingdom) (Provisional Measures)* 1992 ICJ Reports 15.

[59] *Questions of Interpretation and Application of the 1971 Montreal Convention Arising from the Aerial Incident at Lockerbie (Libyan Arab Jamahiriya v United States) (Preliminary Objections)* 1998 ICJ Reports 8.

[60] HM Advocate v Abdelbaset Ali Mohmed Al Megrahi and another, High Court of the Justiciary at Camp Zeist, case no 1475/99, available at <http://www.scotcourts.gov.uk/search-judgments/judgment?id=fd4c87a6-8980-69d2-b500-ff0000d74aa7> last visited 17 May 2017.

[61] *Immunities and Criminal Proceedings (Equatorial Guinea v France)* see ICJ Press Release, No 2016/18, 14 June 2016, available at <http://www.icj-cij.org/files/case-related/163/19028.pdf>.

[62] *Application of the International Convention for the Suppression of the Financing of Terrorism and of the International Convention on the Elimination of All Forms of Racial Discrimination (Ukraine v Russian Federation)*, available at ICJ, <http://www.icj-cij.org/docket/index.php?p1=3&p2=1&code=ur&case=166&k=f1> last visited 3 May 2017.

[63] It alleges violations of rights under Articles 8, 9, 10, 11, 12, and 18 of the Terrorism Financing Convention. An Application by Ukraine for provisional measures including stopping any further support to separatists in Eastern Ukraine failed because Ukraine did not give any evidence meeting the

the suppression conventions, customarily managed through diplomacy, are now being subject to formal dispute resolution measures.

The treaties themselves do not commonly grant powers of sanction to oversight bodies such as COPs. The 1961 Single Convention (as amended) and the 1971 Psychotropic Conventions[64] are exceptional in that they grant the International Narcotics Control Board (INCB) power to impose sanctions on parties. In terms of article 145 of the 1961 Single Convention, for example, the INCB can call the parties' attention to breaches and for special studies to be made. In the case of a serious endangerment of the Convention's aims or the development of a serious situation or where these measures are most appropriate to facilitate cooperative action, it can make a report to the United Nations Economic and Social Council (ECOSOC) and recommend an embargo on the import and export of drugs to the defaulting state. These powers have never been used and similar powers have not been included in other treaties. The UN criminal justice bodies prefer to use a mixture of public exposure of information given by states and diplomatic pressure to persuade states to comply.

The US has taken matters into its own hands by tying treaty implementation/compliance in regard to certain transnational crimes to provision of aid in what amounts to a 'large, if unofficial, enforcement stick'.[65] In 1986 through enactment of the Omnibus Anti-Drug Abuse Act the US amended the Foreign Assistance Act 1961[66] introducing section 490 which requires the US Administration to consider on an annual basis the extent to which major drug producing and transit countries have met the goals and objectives of the 1988 Drug Trafficking Convention. These states are classed as (a) cooperating with US counter narcotics goals and practices, (b) not cooperating, or (c) not cooperating but certified for reasons of US national interest. The Act requires the US Administration to de-certify not cooperating countries, which results in the suspension of most forms of assistance by the US together with the application of optional trade sanctions. De-certifications have occurred. The link to implementation/compliance obligations with the 1988 Drug Trafficking Convention means that in effect the US State Department has become the enforcement arm of international drug control law.[67] The US also uses this method in regard to terrorism.[68] It is not the only party to a suppression convention to link aid to crime control efforts. The UK and EU both use the tacit linkage of aid to cooperation in the suppression of drugs.[69] While states do make efforts to avoid de-certification, they publicly decry such measures. The suppression conventions do not make provision for these measures nor have the parties taking them complied with the procedures for conflict resolution in the

definition of the offence in article 2(1). See *Application of the International Convention for the Suppression of the Financing of Terrorism and of the International Convention on the Elimination of all Forms of Racial Discrimination (Ukraine v Russian Federation)* 19 April 2017, paras 72–77.

[64] Article 19.

[65] K Raustiala, 'Law, Liberalization and International Narcotics Trafficking' 32 *New York University Journal of International Law and Politics* (1999) 89, 111–12.

[66] Codified at 22 USC § 2291j.

[67] D Corva, 'Neoliberal Globalization and the War on Drugs: Transnationalizing Illiberal Governance in the Americas' in 27 *Political Geography* (2008) 176, 186–87.

[68] Export Administration Act 1979, 50 USC § 2405.

[69] P Green, *Drugs, Trafficking and Criminal Policy* (Winchester: Waterside Press, 1998), 33.

treaty. However, when a party blacklists and withholds aid it is not illegal under general international law because it is not withdrawing something it is obliged, under the suppression conventions, to provide; it is withdrawing a donation. It is not suspending its obligations under the conventions; it is engaging in retorsion, retaliatory measures of an unfriendly kind not involving the use of force. The legality of taking such steps will, however, become questionable if a compliance regime exists and has been agreed upon by the parties, because they have agreed to a procedure to resolve compliance issues and are resorting unilaterally to another method to enforce the convention.

A 'softer' stick that has become increasingly popular with the US is the production of national reports on compliance by other states. For example, the State Department's International Narcotics Control Strategy Report details perceived strengths and weakness of anti-money laundering/counter-terrorist financing in all states, and points out problematic jurisdictions and the reasons for problems.[70] The US produces similar reports ranking states according to their level of compliance with the Human Trafficking Protocol. The US practice of ranking states as non-compliant is something all parties are entitled to do. The ranked party can, however, legitimately complain and insist on arbitration/adjudication under the relevant convention to test the validity of the ranking and if they are considered compliant, may ask for an apology. It is not surprising that NGOs operating in the field have also adopted the approach. Transparency International's Corruption Perceptions Index (CPI)[71] is just one of many examples of systems for naming and shaming poor performers in the implementation of anti-corruption laws. It too occasions negative responses from poorly performing states. It is an open question whether this naming and shaming actually achieves greater suppression of transnational crime.

22.8 A Transnational Criminal Court?

In some cases of extradition, small states parties do not comply because they find themselves between 'the rock' of the large state seeking extradition and the 'hard place' of domestic popular disgruntlement at granting it. Transnational criminal law does not currently contain adjudicative mechanisms for the trial of transnational crimes at an international level which might provide a 'third way' in such situations. The development of the International Criminal Court (ICC) was initiated precisely by such a concern. Small island states wanted an international criminal tribunal to which they could delegate adjudicative jurisdiction over serious drug trafficking.[72] They feared the political consequences of extradition to the US (or invasion along the lines of Panama). Western states resisted international control over the system of transnational criminal law. At the Rome Conference the US demurred: 'Conferring such jurisdiction on the Court might hamper essential transnational efforts at effectively

---

[70] See the *International Narcotics Control Strategy Report 2016: Volume II Money Laundering and Financial Crimes* (2016), 28 et seq, available at <https://www.state.gov/documents/organization/253983.pdf> last visited 21 June 2017.

[71] Available at <https://www.transparency.org/research/cpi/overview> last visited 17 June 2017.

[72] See N Boister, 'Treaty Crimes, International Criminal Court?' 12(3) *New Criminal Law Review* (2009) 341.

fighting such crimes.'[73] The ICC's jurisdiction was limited to the core crimes in international law. The Rome Conference resolved to review the inclusion of treaty crimes such as drug trafficking in a review conference, but although a review conference has been held, they have not been included. The idea of an international tribunal to deal with transnational crimes still lingers, however. As part of the response to Somali piracy, the UN Security Council in Resolution 1918[74] called on the UN Secretary-General to examine the possibility of regional or international tribunals for piracy offences because of the failure of Somalia's criminal justice system to cope. This initiative ultimately did not bear fruit as aid was poured into the criminal justice systems of regional states in order to help them cope with piracy prosecutions.

Scholars have suggested that transnational crimes could be included within the jurisdiction of a stand-alone court developed to try those exceptional cases where the system of international cooperation does not work.[75] Any Transnational Criminal Court (TCC) would have to reflect the horizontal non-hierarchical nature of transnational criminal law rather than introduce a vertical element.[76] It would also have to preserve sovereign control of criminal law. The failed 1937 Convention for an International Criminal Court[77] provides a useful starting point for negotiation, because essentially it was to be an extraterritorial adjudicative venue for the trial of a transnational crime (terrorism) using the domestic criminal law and prosecutors of states with jurisdiction that declined to extradite, but relying on internationally appointed judges. A more conventional model is being pioneered by the AU in the Criminal Chamber of the African Court of Justice and Human Rights (African Court). Under Article 28(A) of its Amended Statute the Court[78] 'shall have power to try persons for the crimes provided hereunder' inter alia:

4) Unconstitutional change of Government
5) Piracy
6) Terrorism
7) Mercenarism
8) Corruption
9) Money Laundering
10) Trafficking in Persons
11) Trafficking in Drugs
12) Trafficking in Hazardous Wastes
13) Illicit Exploitation of Natural Resources

---

[73] UN Diplomatic Conference of Plenipotentiaries on the Establishment of an International Criminal Court, Rome, 15 June–17 July 1998, Official Records Vol II, Summary records of the plenary meetings and of the meetings of the Committee of the Whole, UN Doc A/CONF.183/13 (UN, New York, 2002), para 31.

[74] S/Res/1918, 27 April 2010.

[75] E Creegan, 'A Permanent Hybrid Court for Terrorism' 26 *American University International Law Review* (2011) 237.

[76] See RA Falk, 'International Jurisdiction: Horizontal and Vertical Conceptions of Legal Order' 32 *Temple Law Quarterly* (1959) 295.

[77] The Convention for the Creation of an International Criminal Court, Geneva, 16 November 1937, 7 Hudson 878, never in force.

[78] Protocol on the Statute of the African Court of Justice and Human Rights, 1 July 2008, amended by the Protocol on Amendments to the Protocol on the Statute of the African Court of Justice and Human Rights, 27 June 2014.

These crimes are either defined in existing AU instruments, or drawn from more general suppression conventions. Article 3 of the Amending Protocol vests the Court with original jurisdiction over these crimes while Article 46E bis (1) provides that states parties accept the jurisdiction of the court with respect to the crimes. Article 46B(1) provides that 'a person who commits an offence under this Statute shall be held individually responsible for this crime'. This suggests that (a) the amended Statute of the Court itself creates these crimes and (b) that given individual responsibility is being applied, the crime is by definition no longer just a transnational crime but is, at least within Africa, a regional international crime (ie a supra-national crime in the region, rather than just a crime in the domestic law of AU member states). The African Court is, to coin a phrase, a stand-alone regional transnational criminal court. This is a major step beyond other regional measures such as the EU's capacity to declare regional offences obliging member states to implement them or the quasi-criminal jurisdiction of the Inter-American Court of Human Rights. In regionalizing these crimes the AU is irreverently challenging the power balance that currently reflects the fact that international criminal law is a creature of the international community and transnational criminal law a creature of certain influential states and regions.

22.9 Conclusion

The enforcement provisions of the suppression conventions cannot explain why parties implement or comply, because states are seldom held legally accountable.[79] Some parties may do so because they are directly threatened by the targeted harm, some because they perceive that it is in their political or material interests to do so, and some because they are committed to the global rule of law.[80] Implementation and compliance is the product of a range of complex interactions between legal, political, social, and moral norms as well as the real advantages/disadvantages of compliance and the pressure that large powerful states and civil society exert in the promotion of compliance. Implementation and in particular compliance can be jeopardized by a range of circumstances. The low cost of commitment in systems where the rule of law is not entrenched, for example, encourages treaty ratification and jeopardizes compliance.[81] States 'with integrity deficits resist being scrutinized by others'.[82]

There are contending forces of pluralism and universalism in these systems that affect their practical impact. It has been argued that stronger states continue to support prohibition regimes even when there is clear evidence that they do not achieve their goals because these regimes function to extend the power of these stronger states

---

[79] See, among many others, A Chayes and AH Chayes, *The New Sovereignty: Compliance with International Regulatory Agreements* (1995); HJ Koh, 'Why do Nations Obey International Law' (1997) 106 *The Yale Law Journal* 2599.

[80] See P Lloyd, B Simmons, and B Stewart, 'Combating Transnational Crime: The Role of Learning and Norm Diffusion in the Current Rule of Law Wave' in M Zurn, A Nollkaemper, and R Peerenboom (eds), *Rule of Law Dynamics: In an Era of International and Transnational Governance* (Cambridge: CUP, 2012).

[81] See OA Hathaway, 'The Cost of Commitment', John M. Olin Center for Studies in Law, Economics, and Public Policy Working Papers No 273, available at <http://digitalcommons.law.yale.edu/lepp_papers/273/> last visited 20 June 2017.

[82] Redo, above n 49, 189.

into weaker states.[83] Stronger states, however, appear to be losing faith in multilateral treaty obligations and turning to soft power, something well illustrated in this chapter by the cross pollination of terms like 'not cooperating' from US domestic sanctions to the FATF's NCCT blacklisting process. There appears to be a growing perception among more powerful states that ever greater instrumentality will achieve results. In their view as Rose puts it 'inclusiveness may be inversely related to effective outcomes'.[84] But a linear explanation oversimplifies a complex situation. Each prohibition regime is a terrain of contest between multilateral control of the process where formal sovereign equality still has value and a more limited control of the system. Moreover, the more powerful states don't get it all their own way, as illustrated by the withdrawal of the FATF NCCT blacklisting.

This contest of interest cannot obscure the fact that there are serious doubts about whether the system is actually able to achieve suppression of transnational crimes, even if the actual goal is not complete suppression but holding criminal activities at acceptable levels. Garland's comment on failure of crime control policies within states[85] is apposite to the global implementation of transnational criminal law. Where poor compliance would once have been explained as a consequence of poor implementation, prompting demands for more resources both legal, human, and financial, there is cause to wonder whether poor compliance is a result of conceptual failure—of theory failure—because of the reliance on a model that is unfit for purpose. The relationship between implementation/compliance and suppression raises fundamental questions about the utility of a system that is still based on criminalization, no matter how far it spreads into other modes of control. The reasons for the existence of transnational crime are so complex, so bound up with global political, social, and economic questions that no matter how well implemented and complied with it may be, no system of transnational criminal laws could possibly provide the means for halting it. There is no single answer to the question of whether the effort of suppression is worth it, even as part of a much broader societal effort to confront the particular problem. Different parts of the system appear to be of different value. Thus it appears valuable to pursue efforts against corruption and to contribute further resources, no matter how poor existing performance may be, but the enforcement of drug prohibition may be more difficult to support because of the high cost to drug users and society as a whole and because the sustained effort that has been made so far has failed.

[83] J McCulloch, 'Transnational Crime as a Productive Fiction' 34(2) *Social Justice* (2007) 19, 26.
[84] Rose, above n 40, 58.
[85] D Garland, *The Culture of Control: Crime and Social Order in Contemporary Society* (Oxford and New York: OUP, 2002), 20.

23

The Future Development of Transnational Criminal Law

23.1 Development Thus Far

There is clear evidence of continuity of development within transnational criminal law. It has grown incrementally, newer suppression conventions in a particular prohibition regime drawing heavily on earlier treaties, and cross-pollination of policies and norms occurring between prohibition regimes. In particular, in regard to crimes that involve goods and services (rather than violence) there has been a perceptible pattern of development moving from treaty obligations in regard to regulation of licit production and supply, to criminalization of illicit production and supply, to ever more sophisticated procedural cooperation, to prevention strategies, to increased regulation of implementation and compliance. The development of transnational criminal law has not resulted in the complete harmonization of the domestic criminal laws of participating states. But domestic criminal laws and procedures (especially those for international cooperation) do look a lot more alike and, perhaps more importantly, they are able to work together without as much friction as they did a century ago. Cross pollination between functionally separate regimes results in a unified response to different forms of transnational crime. The goal is flexibility and compatibility. Describing the United Nations Convention against Transnational Organized Crime (UNTOC) and its protocols to a US Congressional Committee an official explained that:

> this growing array of cooperative initiatives was designed to create a platform for law enforcement, customs, and judicial cooperation that would function irrespective of the particular predicate criminal activity to which such initiatives would be applied. Although some of them had arisen in response to a particular problem, such as international drug trafficking, tax evasion, or computer crime, in general the initiatives were devised for general application regardless of the problem they would address.[1]

Yet commentators question why the choice of relying on treaty obligations was made, given the enormous cost to develop and maintain them, the length of time they take to bring into operation, and the weakness and inflexibility of their provisions.[2] They point out that hard law is credible only if its obligations are clear and precise, and

---

[1] JM Winer, 'Cops Across Borders: The Evolution of Transatlantic Enforcement and Judicial Cooperation', paper presented at the Council on Foreign Relations, Roundtable on Old Rules New Threats, 1 September 2004, cited in P Andreas and E Nadelmann, *Policing the Globe: Criminalization and Crime Control in International Relations* (Oxford: OUP, 2006), 174.

[2] C Jojarth, *Crime, War, and Global Trafficking: Designing International Cooperation* (Cambridge: CUP, 2009), 27.

substantive power is delegated to a third party to supervise the system.[3] The answer is that the architects of the suppression conventions—individuals with experience of different crimes—faced what they considered to be similar problems and they used familiar solutions: treaty obligations using a mixture of inflexible and flexible terms. The main barrier to be overcome was reform of national criminal law, something at the heart of the domain reserve, and once they settled on a particular way of overcoming this barrier that respected formal legitimacy by reflecting the sovereign interests of states while still making it possible to pursue suppression, they stuck to it. Doing so also had the benefit of reducing design costs and increasing interoperability. Ironically, however, while the suppression conventions' contractual nature makes possible the projection of parochial criminal justice policy through international law, it also serves to limit the effectiveness of that projection. Treaty obligations are frequently flouted and undermined by a lack of trust between states.

The perception that stronger measures are needed has over time led to a perceptible movement from fairly loose permissions to states to intervene against transnational criminals (such as the permissions to use universal jurisdiction against pirates) to more narrowly drawn obligations (such as the obligation to apply nationality jurisdiction in many newer conventions). Proponents of stronger measures have, however, begun, as noted, to engage in a highly instrumental shift to new kinds of instruments such as the Financial Action Task Force (FATF) Recommendations, non-contractual soft law easily changed and less costly to administer but less flexible and more repressive. This change suggests a shift from legality to substance.[4] In fact, however, these soft-law initiatives rely upon the core contractual obligations in the suppression conventions although they embroider heavily upon them. When this has failed to provide the level of compliance necessary in regard to the 'emergencies' caused by terrorism and piracy the Chapter VII powers of the Security Council has been resorted to as transnational criminal law legislator.

These changes have been made largely at the behest of major powers that have exercised de facto supervision over the system such as Great Britain in the nineteenth century and then the US in the twentieth century. When they have perceived the system is faltering they have tried to redesign it and press for greater effectiveness through more direct relationships. The motivation for their supervisory actions ranges from genuine concern about the incapacity of weaker states to protect themselves to pursuit of self-serving national interest. Poor legitimacy in the input process is, however, inevitably reflected in poor legitimacy in the output process.[5] However, the prospects seem likely that as US power wanes or it begins to lose interest in certain prohibition regimes like drugs, a range of regional policemen will step up to the plate, intent on taking over the supervision of transnational criminal law at a regional level.

---

[3] ibid, 29, drawing on KW Abbott and D Snidal, 'Hard and Soft Law in International Governance' 54 *International Organization* (2000) 421.

[4] See K Raustiala, 'Form and Substance in International Agreements' 99 *American Journal of International Law* (2005) 581, 581.

[5] See D Bodansky, 'The Concept of Legitimacy in International Law' in R Wolfrum and V Röben (eds), *Legitimacy in International Law* (Springer, 2008) 314–15.

23.2 Moving away from a System of Crime Control

Transnational criminal law is currently based on a crime control model, not a justice model. It stresses suppression of transnational crime through effective law enforcement and the application of deterrent punishment. Resort to criminalization carries with it the danger of over-criminalization in inexact terms in contravention of the principle of legality. Elements of transnational criminal law, claimed to be a logical response to globalization, may actually be the product of moral panics designed not to transcend boundaries but to create boundaries between insiders and outsiders/enemies/scapegoats.[6] Transnational criminal law compromises legality by providing for highly complex offences both in treaties and in domestic legislation, and pays little if any attention to the offender or to proportional responses.[7] It fosters instrumental procedural responses such as the resort to civil law (civil standards, reduced fair trial protections) to control crime in procedures like civil forfeiture.[8] It assumes a rule of law framework and largely ignores the rights of the perpetrator to consular assistance, to a fair trial, humane treatment, and so forth. Nor does it effectively protect the human rights of the victims of crime—protection by the state of life and bodily integrity from actions of criminals and through investigation, prosecution, and punishment,[9] the right to a legal remedy, adequate medical care, access to counselling, protection as witnesses, and so forth.

23.3 Using General Principles to Guide Development

Transnational criminal law requires a more coherent basis in a set of principles that can shape and direct the application of national rules so that the interests of individuals who find themselves caught in the web of national authority ultimately derived from transnational criminal law are fully respected. This suggestion, however, runs counter to foundational notions of transnational criminal law: state sovereignty over the *ius puniendi* and the incompatibility of different legal traditions. Currently few principles can be identified either by empirical examination of transnational criminal law or from its goals.

23.4 Principles for Criminalization

Crime suppression conventions, inter-governmental organization (IGO) recommendations, IGO resolutions, all have a substantive law-making role. Any system of transnational criminal justice must ensure first that criminalization is the result of a process that is open and transparent and permits input from all parties. While

---

[6] D Nelken, 'The Globalization of Crime and Justice' 50 *Current Legal Problems* (1997) 261–62.
[7] *Kokkinakis v Greece* (1993) 17 EHRR 397, para 52.
[8] *Secretary of State for the Home Department v AF and another* [2009] UKHL 28, para 59.
[9] UN Human Rights Committee, General Comment No 31 (The Nature of the General Legal Obligation Imposed on States Parties to the Covenant) (2004), CCPR/C/21/Rev.1/Add. 13, para 8.

policy norm diffusion may currently occur through voluntary embrace of these norms, it may also be deeply coercive and non-transparent both during negotiation (assuming there is much negotiation involved) of these international instruments and in the transfer of technical know-how during implementation.[10] It is basic to the global rule of law that the criminalization of conduct be undertaken by a valid legislative authority.[11] Second, criminalization must be regarded as a last resort. Third, when resorted to it must be with a clear realisable goal in mind, evidence based, drawing on exhaustive data, expertise and best practice, relevant to and beneficial to all parties. Fourth, proposed crimes must be trialled before being transnationalized, and their consequences measured, and they should be abandoned if they are not working.

23.5 Principles of Substantive Criminal Liability

It is debateable whether existing instruments for the suppression of transnational crime provide sufficient legal certainty to support transnational legality. They only provide broad guidance about the scope of criminalization in regard to the specific crime. Domestic criminalization gives that norm its penal nature and describes its elements. National general principles are used in the definition of the material and mental elements of the crimes, the rules regarding participation and inchoate offences, and defences, and so forth. The application of the international norms within the constraints of the general principles of a party's criminal law may in certain circumstances mean that what is criminal in one state is not criminal in another.

We have seen, for example, that the general principles on accessories of German law dictate that a perpetrator of a serious crime cannot be convicted of laundering the proceeds of their own crime, whereas this is common in other states. But when an individual from a state which only criminalizes intentional laundering falls into Germany's jurisdiction, they may find themselves open to prosecution for reckless laundering. The trends identified by Clark in the 1980s towards conceptual uniformity in the conduct and fault elements of crimes in the suppression conventions[12] once realized in domestic law may go some way to ameliorate any claim by such an individual that they are not being given fair warning, but an individual in this predicament may still have cause to complain given that parties are usually specifically entitled to enact broader offences in terms of the conventions. A more principled approach would not only set the base limit for criminalization, it would also set the upper limit, requiring states to undertake that they would not broaden the scope of criminalization beyond certain

---

[10] P Lloyd, B Simmons, and B Stewart, 'Combating Transnational Crime: The Role of Learning and Norm Diffusion in the Current Rule of Law Wave' in M Zürn, A Nollkaemper, and R Peerenboom (eds), *Rule of Law Dynamics: In an Era of International and Transnational Governance*, 1st edn (Cambridge: CUP, 2012), 164–70.

[11] MJJP Luchtman, 'Towards a Transnational Application of the Legality Principle in the EU's Area of Freedom, Security and Justice?' 9 *Utrecht Law Review* (2013) 11, 14.

[12] RS Clark, 'Offenses of International Concern: Multilateral State Treaty Practice in the Forty Years Since Nuremberg' 57 *Nordic Journal of International Law* (1988) 49, 72 et seq.

limits. Such variations of criminalization are in any event counterproductive from a practical point of view because they jeopardize international cooperation against crime, arguably the point of the whole exercise, when double criminality cannot be assured because one party's offence is so much broader than the others.

Principles of complicity like the joint enterprise/common purpose and inchoate offences like conspiracy introduced to reach the organizers of transnational crimes may present specific problems of legality for states thus the common opt out 'subject to the basic concepts of the parties' legal systems'. The undefined nature of these concepts is the problem here—it introduces a level of variability of criminalization where transnational criminal law is not simply acknowledging the existence of these general principles but driving their adoption. Again it is submitted that the outer limits of criminalization through these provisions should be settled and specified in order to guarantee transnational legality.

What is required more generally during the negotiation of the suppression convention is a much stronger scrutiny of the nature of the provisions being proposed. Particular attention should also be applied to the increased reliance on administrative sanctions, for example, because they avoid the *ne bis in idem* rule, impose a milder degree of censure less likely to draw public attention, and involve less formal processes and less rigorous standards of proof.

23.6 Principles of Punishment

Instruments for the suppression of transnational crime provide little in the way of principled guidance of punishment other than urging severity, although some more recent conventions do suggest proportionality, the emphasis remains on effective deterrence. While it is almost a premise of transnational criminal law that states agree that certain crimes are serious, states do not agree either on the stipulation of the quantum or method of punishment in suppression conventions.

General obligations in particular conventions to suppress a particular crime can be read to imply an obligation to punish effectively. In other words they set a base limit and preclude the imposition of sham punishments by parties as a breach of the treaty. The penalty imposed by a party to a convention can be evaluated relative to the particular standard for severity in that state. Thus, for example if State X applies a five-year maximum possible period of imprisonment to most severe crimes but then applies one year to a transnational crime where the suppression convention calls for severity, State X may be in breach of its obligations, because by its own standards it is not imposing a severe penalty. The Organisation for Economic Co-operation and Development Anti-Bribery Convention (discussed in Chapter 9) uses this internally relative test in article 3(1):

> The bribery of a foreign public official shall be punishable by effective, proportionate and dissuasive criminal penalties. The range of penalties shall be comparable to that applicable to the bribery of the Party's own public officials and shall, in the case of natural persons, include deprivation of liberty sufficient to enable effective mutual legal assistance and extradition.

The 2009 FATF methodology for evaluating penalties for money laundering used the same approach but more speculatively it also evaluated severity relative to the standards of other countries.[13]

What the suppression conventions do not do is set an upper limit for punishments. The same provisions which guarantee sovereignty over the definition of substantive crimes also guarantees sovereignty over punishment. States have not accepted the inclusion within a suppression convention of anything approaching either specific kinds of penalties (imprisonment, alternatives to imprisonment) or specific tariffs (maximum periods of imprisonment). Moreover, provisions that oblige severe punishment in the suppression conventions have been read as justifying extreme penalties by some parties. As we have seen in Chapter 6, for example, the call in the 1988 Drug Trafficking Convention for penalties to take into account the grave nature of the article 3(1) offences has been used to justify application of the death penalty to these offences. However, if as the FATF suggested what is severe punishment can be meaningfully evaluated by comparison to penalties available globally then certain upper limits on punishment—the non-application of the death penalty to drug trafficking for example—can, it is submitted, also be induced from the practice of parties. Moreover, these norms find significant support in human rights practice. Discretion as to tariffs and kinds of penalties is not absolute; restrictions arise out of the international human rights obligations of the specific parties.

In practice, there are manifestly divergent punishments for the same crimes across parties subject to the same international obligations. Substantial divergence of penalties potentially violates transnational fair warning to foreign nationals while it also undermines the effectiveness of international cooperation under the suppression conventions (eg, a state may refuse extradition because it considers the penalties in the requesting state to be too harsh). A more cautious approach is necessary during the negotiation of the conventions to the use of the adjectives such as severe, serious, etc, which suggest that deterrence and retribution are the major punishment principles. Greater exploration of the punitive goals of transnational crimes would expose the unintended consequences of the use of such adjectives.

23.7 Principles for Establishing Criminal Jurisdiction

Lex certa is essential to the rule of law. Transnational criminal law should be readily known and available, certain, and clear. The domestic establishment of very broad extraterritorial jurisdiction either obliged, encouraged by, or expressly permitted in the suppression conventions potentially presents a legal hazard to individuals unaware that they are straying into this jurisdiction and unable through a reasonable effort to find out. Ireland-Piper suggests that it is only reasonable to demand of a person that they

---

[13] Methodology for Assessing Compliance with the FATF 40 Recommendations and the FATF 9 Special Recommendations (2009, OECD/FATF), page 12, fn 6, available at <http://www.fatf-gafi.org/media/fatf/documents/reports/methodology.pdf> last visited 1 May 2017 (it appears to have been abandoned in subsequent FATF compliance methodology documents).

be familiar with the criminal laws of states into whose extraterritorial jurisdiction they venture, if it has been established 'for widely recognised crimes, such as those forming the subject of international agreements and treaties'.[14] However, the obscurity of many suppression conventions makes reliance on them to establish a reasonable presumption of consciousness of the wrongfulness of one's conduct under another state's law difficult. Alignment with local criminal jurisdiction is the only clear indicator of legality in this regard.

The suppression conventions also encourage the prescription of potentially overlapping jurisdiction without any principles to prevent the imposition of an unfair burden on alleged transnational criminals through the prospect of sequential prosecutions for the same crime. *Ne bis in idem* is not a global principle although it should be.[15] The parties to suppression conventions have never succeeded in establishing a theory of precedence in concurrent jurisdiction, they have only established duties to consult other interested states parties. What is necessary is provision for more principled guidance awarding exclusive priority to a state, because the centre of gravity of prosecution lies with it[16] unless there is credible evidence that establishing jurisdiction is being used to shield the accused from prosecution elsewhere.

23.8 Principles for Enforcing Criminal Jurisdiction

It is fundamental to the rule of law that the enforcement of criminal jurisdiction against alleged transnational criminals take place under legal authority. Much of the recent focus on transnational criminal law has explored the potential due process 'protection gaps' that open up in the space between national laws and outside the protection of international human rights law.[17] Although it is a principle of the rule of law that all individuals are entitled to a fair trial,[18] there is no basic transnational standard for a 'fair trial' beyond a state's domestic criminal jurisdiction.[19] Standards of fairness differ from state to state and within states depending on whether the process has some extraterritorial element or not. Specific mention of due process is rare in the suppression conventions. Article 13(1)(d) of the African Union Convention on Preventing and Combating Corruption, which reiterates the need for due process and makes mandatory provision for a fair trial in accordance with recognized principles of human rights including the right against double jeopardy, is very unusual. A system of transnational criminal justice requires a more principled approach to the rights of individuals during the process of legal assistance needs to be developed. For example, individuals should have the right to make use of these processes themselves, while states need to

---

[14] D Ireland-Piper, 'Prosecutions of Extraterritorial Conduct and the Abuse of Rights Doctrine' (2013) 9 *Utrecht Law Review* 68, 87.

[15] J Vervaele, 'Ne Bis in Idem: Towards a Transnational Constitutional Principle in the EU?' (2013) 9 *Utrecht Law Review* 211, 229.

[16] See the preliminary presumption in the Eurojust Guidelines, *Making the Decision—'Which Jurisdiction Should Prosecute?'* Eurojust Annual Report, 2003.

[17] S Gless and JAE Vervaele, 'Editorial: Law Should Govern: Aspiring General Principles for Transnational Criminal Justice' 9 *Utrecht Law Review* (2013) 1–2.

[18] Ireland-Piper, above n 14, 88.   [19] Gless and Vervaele, above n 17, 6.

preserve what remains of the substantive conditions for extradition while ensuring the protection of human rights in that process.

23.9 Restructuring the Transnational Legal Space

The international instruments directed at the suppression of transnational crime create a negative global citizenship in the sense that they impose obligations on individuals not to commit certain crimes, and then marshal a war chest of procedures to enable the investigation and prosecution of these individuals. This citizenship gives little in the way of positive protection against executive power in what might be called the transnational legal space.[20] Human rights officials are conscious of this gap. As the Council of Europe's Commissioner for Human Rights recommended in an Issues Paper relating to enforcement of the Cybercrime Convention in 2014:[21]

> 8. If any state party takes actions that affect individuals outside its territory, this does not exempt that party from its obligations under the Convention on Cybercrime or under international human rights treaties (in particular, the ECHR and the ICCPR); on the contrary, those obligations equally apply to such extraterritorial acts.

The comment is apposite to much of the substantive definition and enforcement of transnational criminal law. The proliferation of cross-border crime means that closure of this transnational legal space is impractical. However, a framework of general principles, many derived from domestic criminal law and policy-making, could go some way to structuring that space into a space of transnational criminal justice.

---

[20] See N Boister, 'The "Bad Global Citizen", "Naked", in the Transnational Penal Space' in MJ Christensen and N Boister (eds), *The Structure of Transnational Criminal Law: Special Issue of Brill Research Perspectives in Transnational Crime*, forthcoming, 2017.

[21] *The Rule of Law on the Internet and in the Wider Digital World* (Strasbourg: Council of Europe, 2014), 43.

Index

Abacha, Sani 144, 147
abduction 387–9
absolute prohibition systems 25, 378
absolute universality principle 268–70
abuse of power 9
accomplice liability
  aviation offences 108–9
  bribery and corruption 161
  criminalization 26, 82–3, 161, 194–5, 423–4
  cybercrime 194–5
  firearms offences 215
  illegal migration 81–3
  obstruction of justice 161
accountability, of transnational criminal
    law 39, 403
Achille Lauro hijacking 14, 49–50, 52
active personality principle 257–60
act of state doctrine 274
actus reus 25, 249
Afghanistan 406–7
African Court of Justice and Human
    Rights 417–18
African Union 154, 278, 400, 408, 417–18, 426
aggravating circumstances 83–4
aggression, crime of 29
Agreement on Cooperation in Combating
    Offences Related to Computer Information
    2001 (CIS) 197
Agreement on Cooperation in the field of
    International Information Security 2011
    (SCO) 197
aiding and abetting *see* accomplice liability
aircraft registration 252
air pollution 208
air transport *see* aviation offences
alcohol 93
Alldridge, Peter 171
Alliance against trafficking in Persons 74
Al-Megrahi, Abdelbaset Ali Mohmed 414
Al-Qaeda 116, 123
Al Yammah arms deal scandal 164–5
animals, illegal trade in 205–6
animus furandi 47
Anslinger, Harry 14–15, 37
anti-competitive conduct 232–3
Anti-Counterfeiting Trade Agreement 2011 235
Aoki, K. 235
AQ Khan Network 110
Arab Convention on Combating Information
    Technology Offences 2010 25, 197, 254, 263
Argentina 73, 101, 296, 376, 396–7
arms control *see* firearms
Arms Trade Treaty 2013 219–20
arrest
  arrest warrants and investigation
      orders 313–14
  European Arrest Warrants 384–7
  international cooperation 293, 363
ASEAN 72–3, 116, 313, 400

Assange, Julian 386–7
asset recovery
  assistance, challenges of 348–9
  assistance, grounds for refusal 347–8
  bank secrecy 303–4, 345
  challenges 344
  civil process mechanisms 341–2
  conviction-based confiscation 337–40, 346–7
  cooperation mechanisms 344–8
  corruption 335, 345, 348, 350–1
  cultural property trafficking 227, 345
  deterrence 333, 341–2
  dispersal of recovered assets 350–2
  double criminality 346–9
  drugs 337–8
  due process 342
  effectiveness 342
  Exequatur proceedings 346–7
  fair hearing, right to 349–50
  FATF recommendations 335
  forfeiture mechanisms 340–1, 346–8
  freezing 335–6
  fugitive disentitlement doctrine 350
  human rights, and 349–50
  innocence, presumption of 338
  innocent owner defence 342
  interim measures 335–7, 346
  international law, development 334–5
  investigation stage 335–6
  legitimacy 352
  money laundering 178, 333
  non-conviction based forfeiture 340–4
  organized crime 341–2, 346–7
  peaceful enjoyment of possessions 343
  powers, generally 333
  proceeds of crime 317
  proof, reverse burden 337–8
  property rights conflicts 342–3
  restitution 227, 333, 341–2
  Security Council sanctions 336–7
  seizure 173, 180–1, 302–3, 334
  terrorist financing 334, 336
  third-party confiscation 339–40
  third party rights 336–7
  tracing 335–6
  transnational recovery 344–5
  UN Model Law 334
  value confiscation 338–9
  value trends 333
  victims, compensation 336, 344
  World Bank StAR initiative 349
assistance, suspension 415
asylum-seekers 81, 85–7
Australia
  asset recovery 351
  cooperation 294
  counter terrorism 119–20
  double criminality 361
  extradition 361, 366, 368

piracy *(cont.)*
  law reform 55
  legal personality, and 29–30
  Malacca Straits 51
  maritime safety offences, and 52–3
  offence, purpose of 45–6
  penalties 44, 54
  private ends requirement 49–50
  sea-robbery, as 47
  shipriders 299–301
  Somalia 54–5, 300–1
  SUA Convention 14, 50, 52–4, 111, 261
  territorial waters, in 47, 51, 53–4
  trends 45–6
  two ship requirement 50, 53
  UNCLOS 47–8
  violence 48–9
  voluntary participation 49
plea bargaining 165, 232, 281, 375–6
plurality 32–3
Poland 190, 385
police
  European Arrest Warrant 384–7
  European Evidence Warrants 313
  Europol 282, 309, 399
  global policeman role 20
  Interpol 308–9, 382
  joint investigations 290–3
  police to police contact 283–4
policy-making
  international cooperation 14, 17–18
  NGO role in 22
  threat identification 13–16
political crime 7
pollution 200, 208
pornography 34, 62, 189, 193–4, 238–9
Port State Measures Agreement
    2009 (FAO) 203
Portugal
  anti-money laundering law 175
  cooperation 295–6
  drug possession, criminalization 101
  extradition 365
  financial controls 303
  international treaty obligations 24
possessions, peaceful enjoyment of 343
poverty 6
preparatory offences inchoate offences
Preventing and Combating Serious Crime
    (PCSC) agreements 287
price fixing 232–3
prisoners 371–2, 378
private and family life, right to respect
    for 296–7, 380
private crime 5
privateering 45
proceeds of crime
  conviction-based confiscation 337–40
  money laundering, and 178
  recovery, legal assistance 317
  in rem forfeiture 340–1
  seizure powers 173, 180–1, 302–3, 334
  UN Model Law on 334
  value confiscation 338–9
  value trends 335

Programme Network of Institutes
    (PNI) 395, 398
prohibition conventions 24–5
proportionality
  asset seizure 343
  extradition 382, 386–7
  extraterritorial jurisdiction, and 248–9
  suppression conventions 27
prostitution
  children, of 65, 193–4, 238–9, 258
  human trafficking for 61–2, 65, 358
  Islamic law treatment 71
protectionism 6–7
protective personality principle 27, 262–4
Protocol against the Illicit Manufacturing
    of and Trafficking in Firearms, their
    Parts and Components and Ammunition
    2001 136, 213–20
Protocol against the Smuggling of Migrants
    by Land, Sea and Air, Supplementing
    the United Nations Convention against
    Transnational Organized Crime 2000 78–
    88, 270, 285–6
Protocol Amending the International
    Convention for the High Seas Fisheries of
    the North Pacific Ocean 1978 202–3
Protocol for the Suppression of Unlawful Acts of
    Violence at Airports Serving International
    Civil Aviation 1988 109
Protocol of 2014 to the Forced Labour
    Convention 1930 72
Protocol on Substances that Deplete the Ozone
    Layer 1987 208
Protocol on the Illicit Trade in Tobacco Products
    2012 14, 25
Protocols for the Protection of Cultural
    Property in the Event of Armed Conflict
    1954 223
Protocol to Eliminate Illicit Trade in Tobacco
    Products 2012 240–1
Protocol to Prevent, Suppress and Punish
    Trafficking in Persons, Especially Women
    and Children 2000 62–4, 66, 69–70, 73
Protocol to the Convention for the Suppression
    of Unlawful Acts against the Safety of
    Maritime Navigation 2005 53
punishment *see* penalties and punishment
push and pull factors 6–7

Qatada, Abu 382
Qatar 412
questionnaires 408–9

racism 196
Racketeer Influenced Corrupt Organizations
    (RICO) Act 1970 (US) 129, 133, 340, 375
racketeering 129, 133, 138, 340
ratione loci 246
ratione materiae (functional immunity) 247
ratione personae (personal immunity) 273
reciprocity 33, 35, 137, 311–12, 357, 364
recklessness 26, 84
Recommended Principles and Guidelines on
    Human Rights and Human Trafficking
    2002 70

Made in the USA
Middletown, DE
13 January 2023

22029413R00285